PEARSON CUSTOM
BUSINESS RESOURCES

Compiled by

Financial Economics
Second Edition
Zvi Bodie/Robert C Merton/David Cleeton

Senior Vice President, Editorial: Patrick F. Boles
Sponsoring Editor: David J. Maltby
Development Editor: Megan Tully
Editorial Assistant: Hannah Coker
Operations Manager: Eric M. Kenney
Production Manager: Jennifer Berry
Art Director: Renée Sartell
Cover Designer: Renée Sartell

Cover Art: Courtesy of EyeWire/Getty Images and PhotoDisc/Getty Images. Photodisc, "Globe surrounded by business people on computer monitors," courtesy of Photodisc/Getty Images. Dave Cutler (Artist), "Man Dropping Coins Into Glass Jar," courtesy of David Cutler/Images.com. Dave Cutler (Artist), "Three Coins in Glass Jar," courtesy of David Cutler/Images.com. Dean Turner, "Stock Vector: Global Finance" Courtesy of Dean Turner/iStockphoto. Hal Bergman, "Refinery Silhouette" Courtesy of Hal Bergman/iStockphoto. Dan Barnes, "Cargo Container Ship Aerial View" Courtesy of Dan Barnes/iStockphoto. Franc Podgorsek, "Stock Numbers" Courtesy of Franc Podgorsek/iStockphoto. "Customer in Line at Grocery Store" Courtesy of Digital Vision Photography/Veer Inc. Owaki-Kulla, "Pumping Gas" Courtesy of Flirt Photography/Veer Inc. Lynn Johnson, "Yunnan Province, People's Republic of China" Courtesy of Lynn Johnson/Getty Images, Inc. Thomas Bendy, "Student Typing" Courtesy of Thomas Bendy/iStockphoto.

This special edition published in cooperation with Pearson Learning Solutions.

Printed in the United States of America.

Please visit our website at *www.pearsonlearningsolutions.com*.

Attention bookstores: For permission to return any unsold stock, contact us at *pe-uscustomreturns@pearson.com*.

Pearson Learning Solutions, 501 Boylston Street, Suite 900, Boston, MA 02116
A Pearson Education Company
www.pearsoned.com

ISBN 10: 0-558-78575-1
ISBN 13: 978-0-558-78575-8

267 2022

PEARSON

Contents

Financial Economics

OBJECTIVES

- Define finance.
- Explain why finance is worth studying.
- Introduce two of the main players in the world of finance—households and firms—and the kinds of financial decisions they make.

CONTENTS

- You have started to save for the future and all of your savings are in a bank account. Should you invest in mutual funds? What kind of mutual funds?
- You have decided to get a car. Should you buy it or lease it?
- You worked as a waiter during your college years and are thinking about starting your own restaurant when you graduate. Is it worth doing? How much money do you need to start? Where can you get the money?
- You are advising the chief financial officer (CFO) of a major computer manufacturer whether to expand into the telecommunications business. It is expected to cost $3 billion over the next few years to enter the business, and the expected benefits are increased profits of $1 billion per year thereafter. What do you recommend?
- You are part of a team working at the World Bank analyzing an application for a loan to a small country in Latin America to finance a major hydroelectric project. How do you decide what to recommend?

These are all examples of financial decisions. This book will provide you with a way of addressing these and similar questions by exploring the basic principles of finance. In this chapter we define finance and consider why it is worth studying; then we introduce the main players in the world of finance—households and firms—and the kinds of financial decisions they make.

1 Defining Finance

Finance is the study of how people allocate scarce resources *over time*. Two features that distinguish financial decisions from other resource allocation decisions are that the costs and benefits of financial decisions are (1) spread out over time and (2) usually not known with certainty in advance by either the decision makers or anybody else. In deciding whether to start your own restaurant, for example, you must weigh the *costs* (such as the investment in fixing up the place and buying the stoves, tables, chairs, little paper umbrellas for exotic drinks, and other equipment you need) against the uncertain *benefits* (your future profits) that you expect to reap over several years.

In implementing their decisions people make use of the **financial system,** defined as *the set of markets and other institutions used for financial contracting and the exchange of assets and risks.* The financial system includes the markets for stocks, bonds, and other financial instruments; financial intermediaries (such as banks and insurance companies); financial service firms (such as financial advisory firms); and the regulatory bodies that govern all of these institutions. The study of how the financial system evolves over time is an important part of the subject matter of finance.

Finance theory consists of a set of concepts that help you to organize your thinking about how to allocate resources over time and a set of quantitative models to help you evaluate alternatives, make decisions, and implement them. The same basic concepts and quantitative models apply at all levels of decision making, from your decision to lease a car or to start a business, to the decision of the CFO of a major corporation to enter the telecommunications business, to the decision of the World Bank about which development projects to finance.

A basic tenet of finance is that the ultimate function of the system is to satisfy people's *consumption preferences,* including all the basic necessities of life, such as food, clothing, and shelter. Economic organizations such as firms and governments exist in order to facilitate the achievement of that ultimate function.

2 Why Study Finance?

There are at least five good reasons to study finance:

- to manage your personal resources.
- to deal with the world of business.
- to pursue interesting and rewarding career opportunities.
- to make informed public choices as a citizen.
- to expand your mind.

Let us elaborate on each of these reasons one at a time.

First, knowing some finance helps you to manage your own resources. Can you get along without knowing anything about finance? Perhaps. But if you are completely ignorant, then you are at the mercy of others. Remember the old adage: "A fool and his money are soon parted."

In some cases you will seek the help of experts. There are many finance professionals and financial service firms that provide financial advice—bankers, stockbrokers, insurance brokers, and firms selling mutual funds and other financial products and services. Often the advice is "free" if you are a potential customer. But how do you evaluate the advice you are given? The study of finance provides a conceptual framework for doing so.

A second reason to study finance is that a basic understanding of finance is essential in the business world. Even if you do not intend to specialize in finance, you must have a sufficient understanding of the concepts, techniques, and terminology employed by finance specialists to communicate with them and to recognize the limits of what they can do for you.

Box 1	Job Opportunities in Financial Engineering

At the prestigious Ecole Polytechnique in Paris, mathematics professor Nicole El Karoui continues to lead the way in teaching the modeling of derivatives to future quantitative analysts. Professor El Karoui has been instrumental in providing knowledge on derivatives through classes in financial mathematics. Her students are highly sought after by the world's top investment banks for their understanding of these increasingly important financial instruments.

Derivatives—financial contracts that derive their values from the performance of an underlying asset—were once used primarily as a hedge for banks against market risk. In the past, investment banks made most of their profits from underwriting and trading stocks and bonds in addition to providing financial advice. Presently, around 30% of their stock-related revenue comes from derivatives. Professor El Karoui's classes teach the necessary skill for students to become competitive in working in the service-sector firms driven by much of the demand caused by this change in investment structure.

El Karoui first became interested in modeling derivatives during a six-month sabbatical she spent working at a consumer credit bank. She noticed that employees in the derivatives department experienced problems similar to those facing students of stochastic calculus—the study of the impact of random variation over time. When she returned to teaching she implemented a postgraduate mathematical finance program, meeting the growing demand for understanding of derivatives among banks. Professor El Karoui's students are eagerly sought after by recruiters for their technical skills, which enable them to understand the underlying behavior of derivatives. These core quantitative skills have come to constitute an integral part of the work of investment bankers.

Source: "Why Students of Prof. El Karoui Are in Demand," *Wall Street Journal*, March 9, 2006.

Third, you may be interested in a career in finance. There are varied and potentially rewarding career opportunities in the field of finance and many possible paths you can follow as a finance professional. Most finance professionals are employed in the financial services sector of the economy—such as banking, insurance, or investment management. However, many others work as financial managers in nonfinancial firms or in government. Some even pursue academic careers.

Households, businesses, and government agencies often seek the advice of financial consultants. Moreover, a background in finance provides a good foundation for a career in general management. Many of the chief executives of major corporations around the world started in finance.

Fourth, to make informed public choices as a citizen, you should have a basic understanding of how the financial system works. The financial system is an important part of the infrastructure of any market-oriented society. Indeed, a sound set of financial institutions is believed by many to be an essential element in economic growth and development. As citizens we sometimes must make political choices that affect the functioning of the financial system. For example, do you want to vote for a political candidate who favors abolishing government deposit insurance or one who would impose strict controls on stock-market trading?

Fifth, finance can be a fascinating field of study on purely intellectual grounds. It expands your understanding of how the real world works. The scientific study of finance has a long history. Adam Smith's *The Wealth of Nations,* published in 1776, is widely regarded as the beginning of the science of economics. Finance theorists today are generally economists specializing in financial economics. Indeed, in 1990 and again in 1997, the Nobel Prize in economics was awarded to scholars for their scientific contributions in the field of finance (see Box 3).

3 Financial Decisions of Households

Most households are families. Families come in many forms and sizes. At one extreme is the *extended family,* which consists of several generations living together under one roof and sharing their economic resources. At the other extreme is the single person living

Box 3 · Nobel Prize in Economics for Work in Finance

In 1990 the Nobel Prize in economics was awarded to three scholars—Harry Markowitz, Merton Miller, and William Sharpe—for scientific contributions that have had a powerful impact on both the theory and practice of finance. Let us briefly explain their contributions.

Harry Markowitz is the father of modern portfolio theory, the scientific study of how to trade off risk and reward in choosing among risky investments. In his seminal article, "Portfolio Selection," which appeared in the *Journal of Finance* in 1952, he developed a mathematical model showing how investors could achieve the lowest possible risk for any given target rate of return. The Markowitz model has been incorporated into basic finance theory and is widely used by practicing investment managers.

William Sharpe took Markowitz's results as his starting point and developed their implications for asset prices. By adding the assumption that at all times asset prices will adjust to equate demand and supply for each risky asset, he showed that a very specific structure must exist among the expected rates of return on risky assets ("Capital Asset Prices: A Theory of Market Equilibrium under Conditions of Risk," *Journal of Finance,* 1964). The structure suggested by Sharpe's theory is widely used today as the basis for making risk adjustments in many areas of finance theory and practice.

Merton Miller has contributed mainly to the theory of corporate finance. He and Franco Modigliani (an earlier recipient of the Nobel Prize in economics) addressed the dividend and borrowing policies of firms in a series of articles, starting with "The Cost of Capital, Corporation Finance, and the Theory of Investment," which appeared in the *American Economic Review* in 1958. Their fundamental contribution was to focus the attention of theorists and practitioners of finance on how corporate dividend and financing policies affect the total value of a firm. The M&M (Modigliani-Miller) propositions developed in their joint papers are among the basic building blocks of modern corporate finance.

Again in 1997 the Nobel Prize in economics was awarded to financial economists. The laureates were Robert C. Merton (one of the authors of this textbook) and Myron Scholes. The prize committee also mentioned a third scholar, Fischer Black, whose untimely death in 1995 at age 57 made him ineligible to share the prize. These three men discovered a mathematical formula for the pricing of options and other derivative securities that has had an enormous impact on both the theory and practice of finance. It is generally known as the Black-Scholes option pricing formula.

---

alone, whom most people wouldn't think of as a "family." In finance, however, all are classified as households.

Households face four basic types of financial decisions:

- *Consumption and saving decisions:* How much of their current wealth should they spend on consumption and how much of their current income should they save for the future?
- *Investment decisions:* How should they invest the money they have saved?
- *Financing decisions:* When and how should households use other people's money to implement their consumption and investment plans?
- *Risk-management decisions:* How and on what terms should households seek to reduce the financial uncertainties they face or when should they increase their risks?

As a result of saving part of their income for use in the future, people accumulate a pool of wealth, which can be held in any number of different forms. One form is bank accounts, another might be a piece of real estate or a share in a business venture. All of these are **assets.** *An asset is anything that has economic value.*

When people choose how to hold their pool of accumulated savings, it is called *personal investing* or **asset allocation.** In addition to investing in their own homes, people will often choose to invest in financial assets, such as stocks or bonds.

<table>
<tr><td>**Box 4**</td><td>## New Trends in the Market for College Loans</td></tr>
</table>

Private student loans have become a growing, lucrative segment of consumer finance. Their profitability is derived from the relatively high interest rates they carry and the continually increasing demand generated by a growing number of students financing college tuition. Unlike federal loans, private loans can earn revenue by charging market rates in addition to up-front fees. These fees, which make private loans so rewarding for investors, can constitute 6% to 7% of the total amount of the loan. Furthermore, tuition increases around the country, combining with a growing number of baby boomers' children attending colleges, are the main factors that underlie a strong demand for student loans. Not only do college costs continue to rise, but federal aid in the form of grants and loans has remaining stagnant—and in many cases actually declined. The gap between the higher price of an education and the ability of families to pay is widening; private student loans have come to fill this gap.

Private loans, packaged by lenders such as Sallie Mae, have recently exploded in popularity, currently capturing 22% of the volume of federal student loans, up from 5% in 1994–1995. They are being praised as the fastest-growing and most profitable segment of consumer finance, with a total of $13.8 billion in student loans in the 2004–2005 school year—with the expectation of a further doubling within the following three years. As the number of college students continues to increase along with their tuitions, the private student loan industry is expected to maintain its strong record of growth.

Source: "Thanks to the Banks," *The Economist,* February 16, 2006.

When people borrow, they incur a **liability,** which is just another word for debt. A household's wealth or **net worth** is measured by the value of its assets minus its liabilities. Say you own a house worth $100,000 and have a $20,000 bank account. You also owe $80,000 to the bank on your home mortgage loan (a liability) and have a $5,000 credit card debt outstanding. Your net worth is $35,000: your total assets ($120,000) minus your total liabilities ($85,000). Ultimately, all of society's resources belong to households because they own the firms (either directly or through their ownership of shares of stock, pension plans, or life insurance policies) and pay the taxes spent by governments.

Finance theory treats people's consumption preferences as given. Although preferences may change over time, how and why they change is not addressed by the theory.[1] People's behavior is explained as an attempt to satisfy those preferences. The behavior of firms and governments is viewed from the perspective of how it affects the welfare of people.

> **Quick Check 1**
>
> What are the four basic types of financial decisions households have to make? Give an example of each.

4 Financial Decisions of Firms

By definition, business firms—or simply firms—are entities whose primary function is to produce goods and services. Like households, firms come in many different shapes and sizes. At the one extreme are small workshops, retail outlets, and restaurants owned by a

---

[1]Elements of a theory that are not explained by the theory itself are called *exogenous.* In contrast, those elements that are explained by the theory are called *endogenous.* In finance, people's preferences are exogenous to the theory, but the objectives of firms are endogenous.

single individual or family. At the other extreme are giant corporations, such as Mitsubishi or General Motors, with a workforce of hundreds of thousands of people and an even greater number of owners. The branch of finance dealing with financial decisions of firms is called *business finance* or *corporate finance.*

In order to produce goods and services, all firms—small and large—need *capital.* The buildings, machinery, and other intermediate inputs used in the production process are called *physical capital.* The stocks, bonds, and loans used to finance the acquisition of the physical capital are called *financial capital.*

The first decision any firm must make is what businesses it wants to be in. This is called *strategic planning.* Because strategic planning involves the evaluation of costs and benefits spread out over time, it is largely a financial decision-making process.

Often a firm will have a core business defined by its main product line, and it may branch out into related lines of business. For example, a firm that produces computer hardware may also choose to produce the software. It may also choose to service computers.

A firm's strategic goals may change over time, sometimes quite dramatically. Some corporations enter into businesses that are seemingly unrelated to each other. They may even abandon their original core business altogether so that the company's name ceases to have any connection with its current business.

For example, ITT Corporation started out as a telephone company in 1920. Its name stood for International Telephone and Telegraph. In the 1970s ITT became a large multinational conglomerate, operating a diverse set of businesses including insurance, munitions, hotels, bakeries, automobile rentals, mining, forest products, and gardening products in addition to telecommunications. During the 1980s, ITT shed many of its businesses and focused on operating hotels and casinos. By 1996 it had abandoned its original core business of producing telephone equipment and telecommunication services.

Once a firm's managers have decided what businesses they are in, they must prepare a plan for acquiring factories, machinery, research laboratories, showrooms, warehouses, and other such long-lived assets and for training the personnel who will operate them all. This is the *capital budgeting process.*

The basic unit of analysis in capital budgeting is an *investment project.* The process of capital budgeting consists of identifying ideas for new investment projects, evaluating them, deciding which ones to undertake, and then implementing them.

Once a firm has decided what projects it wants to undertake, it must figure out how to finance them. Unlike capital budgeting decisions, the unit of analysis in *capital structure* decisions is *not* the individual investment project but the firm as a whole. The starting point in making capital structure decisions is determining a feasible financing plan for the firm. Once a feasible financing plan has been achieved, the issue of the optimal financing mix can be addressed.

Firms can issue a wide range of financial instruments and claims. Some are standardized securities that can be traded in organized markets, such as common stock, preferred stock, bonds, and convertible securities. Others are nonmarketable claims, such as bank loans, employee stock options, leases, and pension liabilities.

A corporation's capital structure determines who gets what share of its future cash flows. For example, bonds promise fixed cash payments, whereas stocks pay the residual value left over after all other claimants have been paid. Capital structure also partially determines who gets to control the company. In general, shareholders have control through their right to elect the board of directors. But often bonds and other loans include contractual provisions, called *covenants,* restricting the activities of management. These covenant restrictions give the creditors some control over the company's affairs.

Working capital management is extremely important to the success of a firm. The best long-term plans can go away if the firm's management does not attend to the day-to-day financial affairs of the business. Even in a growing, successful firm, cash flows in and out may not match up exactly in time. Managers must worry about collecting from customers, paying bills as they come due, and generally managing the firm's cash flow to ensure that operating cash-flow deficits are financed and that cash-flow surpluses are efficiently invested to earn a good return.

The choices that a firm makes in all areas of financial decision making—investment, financing, and working capital management—depend on its technology and on the specific regulatory, tax, and competitive environment in which it operates. The policy choices are also highly interdependent.

> **Quick Check 2**
>
> What are the basic types of financial decisions firms have to make? Give an example of each.

5 Forms of Business Organization

There are three basic types of organizational form for a firm: a sole proprietorship, a partnership, and a corporation. A **sole proprietorship** is a firm owned by an individual or a family, in which the assets and liabilities of the firm are the personal assets and liabilities of the proprietor. A sole proprietor has *unlimited liability* for the debts and other liabilities of the firm. This means that if the firm cannot pay its debts, the proprietor's other personal assets can be seized to satisfy the demands of the firm's creditors.

Many firms start out as sole proprietorships and then change their organizational form as they become established and expand. But frequently a business such as a restaurant, a real estate agency, or a small workshop will remain a sole proprietorship throughout its existence.

A **partnership** is a firm with two or more owners, called the partners, who share the equity in the business. A partnership agreement usually stipulates how decisions are to be made and how profits and losses are to be shared. Unless otherwise specified, all partners have unlimited liability as in the sole proprietorship.

However, it is possible to limit the liability for some partners called *limited partners*. At least one of the partners, called the general partner, has unlimited liability for the debts of the firm. Limited partners typically do not make the day-to-day business decisions of the partnership; the general partner does.

Unlike a sole proprietorship or a partnership, a **corporation** is a firm that is a legal entity distinct from its owners. Corporations can own property, borrow, and enter into contracts. They can sue and be sued. They are usually taxed according to rules that differ from the rules that apply to the other forms of business organization.

The charter of a corporation sets down the rules that govern it. Shareholders are entitled to a share of any distributions from the corporation (e.g., cash dividends) in proportion to the number of shares they own. The shareholders elect a *board of directors,* which in turn selects managers to run the business. Usually there is one vote per share, but sometimes there are different classes of stocks with different voting rights.

An advantage of the corporate form is that ownership shares can usually be transferred without disrupting the business. Another advantage is *limited liability,* which means that if the corporation fails to pay its debts, the creditors can seize the assets of the corporation but have no recourse to the personal assets of the shareholders. In that sense a corporation serves the same function as a general partner in a partnership, and its shareholders are like limited partners.

Box 5	How to Identify That a Firm Is a Corporation

In the United States, corporations are identified by the letters *Inc.* after their name. It stands for the English word *incorporated.* In France the letters are *SA* (Societé Anonime); in Italy *SpA* (Societa per Azioni); in the Netherlands *NV* (Naamloze Vennootschap); and in Sweden *AB* (Aktiebolag).

In Germany, public corporations are called Aktiengesellschaften, identifiable by the letters *AG* after the company name, whereas private corporations are Gesellschaften mit beschräkter Haftung, denoted by *GmbH*. The parallel designations in the United Kingdom are *PLC* for public limited company, and *LTD* for private corporations.

The earliest known corporations were formed in Amsterdam and in London in the 1600s and were called *joint stock companies* in English. That term has fallen into disuse.

Around the world, large firms are almost always organized as corporations, although ownership of the corporation may be restricted to a single person or family. In the United States, corporations with broadly dispersed ownership are called *public corporations;* those with concentrated ownership are called *private corporations.*

Laws governing the corporate form of organization differ in their details from country to country, and even within a country they may differ from one jurisdiction to another. In the United States, for example, laws governing corporations are created and administered at the state level (see Box 5).

Quick Check 3

A corporation owned by a single person is not a sole proprietorship. Why?

---

6 Separation of Ownership and Management

In sole proprietorships and even in many partnerships the owners and the active managers of the business are the same people. But in many firms, especially the large ones, the owners do not themselves manage the business. Instead they delegate that responsibility to professional managers, who may not own any shares in the business. There are at least five reasons for the owners of a firm to turn over the running of the business to others to manage.

First, professional managers may be found who have a superior ability to run the business. This may be because the professional managers have better technological knowledge, more experience, or a more suitable personality to run the business. In a structure in which the owner is also the manager, the owner must have both the talents of a manager and the financial resources necessary to carry out production. In the separated structure, no such coincidence is required.

For example, consider the entertainment industry. The people most qualified to manage a film studio or a television network may not have the financial resources to own the business, and the people with the wealth to own such a business may have no ability to manage it. Therefore, it makes sense for the managerially competent people to produce and distribute the movies and for the wealthy people to simply provide the capital.

Second, to achieve the efficient scale of a business the resources of many households may have to be pooled. For example, the cost of producing a single movie is in the millions of dollars for a low-budget film, and the average feature-length movie costs many millions of dollars to produce. The need to pool resources to achieve an efficient scale of production calls for a structure with many owners, not all of whom can be actively involved in managing the business.

Third, in an uncertain economic environment, owners will want to diversify their risks across many firms. To diversify optimally requires the investor to hold a portfolio of assets, in which each security is but a small part. Such efficient diversification is difficult to achieve without separation of ownership and management.

For example, suppose an investor thinks that firms in the entertainment industry will do well over the next few years and would like to buy a diversified stake in that industry. If the investor had to also manage the firms she invests in, there is no way she could diversify across many firms. The corporate form is especially well suited to facilitating diversification by investor-owners because it allows them to own a relatively small share of each firm.

Fourth, the separated structure allows for savings in the costs of information gathering. Managers can gather the most accurate information available about the firm's production technology, the costs of its inputs, and the demand for its products. The owners of the firm need to know relatively little about the technology of the firm, the intensity at which it is being operated, and the demand for the firm's products.

Again, consider the entertainment industry. The information needed to successfully manage the production and distribution of a movie is substantial. Although information about top actors and directors who might be hired to star in a movie is readily available at low cost, this is not so with respect to other resource inputs to movie production and distribution. Establishing information networks of agents and jobbers is costly and is most efficiently handled by having movie executives specialize in doing it.

Fifth, there is the "learning curve" or "going concern" effect, which favors the separated structure. Suppose the owner wants to sell all or part of his technology either now or at a later date. If the owner must also be the manager, the new owners have to learn the business from the former owner in order to manage it efficiently. However, if the owner does *not* have to be the manager, then when the business is sold, the manager continues in place and works for the new owners. When a company issues shares to the public for the first time, the original owner-managers often continue to manage the business even if they no longer own any shares in the business.

The corporate form is especially well suited to the separation of owners and managers because it allows relatively frequent changes in owners by share transfer without affecting the operations of the firm. Millions of shares in corporations around the world change hands and rarely is there any effect on the management or operations of the business.

Quick Check 4

What are the main reasons for having a separation of management and ownership of firms? How does the corporate form of organization facilitate this separation?

Offsetting all the reasons in favor of a separation of ownership and management, the separated structure creates the potential for a *conflict of interest* between the owners and the managers. Because the owners of a corporation have only incomplete information about whether the managers are serving their interests effectively, managers may neglect their obligations to the shareholders. In extreme cases, managers may even act *contrary* to the interests of their shareholders. Adam Smith, the father of classical economics, summed it up as follows:

The directors of such [joint-stock] companies, however, being the managers rather of other people's money than of their own, it cannot well be expected, that they should watch over it with the same anxious vigilance with which the partners in a private copartnery frequently watch over their own. Like the stewards of a rich man, they are apt to consider attention to small matters as not for their master's honour, and very easily give themselves a dispensation from having it. Negligence and profusion, therefore, must always prevail, more or less, in the management of the affairs of such a company.[2]

In those business environments in which the potential for conflicts of interest between owners and managers can be resolved at a reasonable cost, we would expect to find that the owners of business firms will not be the managers. And we would expect that the ownership of firms is dispersed among many individuals. Furthermore, we would expect to observe that, over time, the changes in the composition of the ownership would be far more common than the changes in the composition of the management.

7 The Goal of Management

Because the managers of corporations are hired by the shareholders (through the board of directors), the managers' primary commitment is to make decisions that are in the best interests of the shareholders. This is not the exclusive goal of management. Like everyone else in society, corporate managers must obey the law. They are also expected to respect ethical norms and to promote desirable social goals when it is possible to do so at a reasonable cost to shareholders.[3]

However, even if we restrict the goal of corporate management exclusively to serving the best interests of the shareholders, it is not obvious how managers can achieve this goal. In principle, managers could review each decision with the owners including the production choices, cost of obtaining capital, and so on and ask them which combination they prefer. But, in that case, the owners would have to have the same knowledge and spend essentially the same amount of time as they would if they were managing the business themselves. There would, therefore, be little point in hiring managers to run the business.

Moreover, although this procedure might be feasible when there are a few owners of the firm, it becomes completely impractical as the number of shareholders becomes large. Indeed, for a large multinational corporation, the number of shareholders can exceed a million, and they may reside in many different countries. Hence, it is essential to find a goal or rule to guide managers of the firm without having to "poll" the owners about most decisions.

To be effective, such a rule should not require the managers to know the risk preferences or opinions of the shareholders because such data are virtually impossible to obtain. And even if the data were available at one point in time, they change over time. Indeed, because shares of stock change hands every day, the owners of the corporation change every day. Thus, to be feasible, the right rule should be independent of who the owners are.

If a feasible rule for the managers to follow were found that would lead them to make the same investment and financing decisions that each of the individual owners would have made had they made the decisions themselves, then such a rule would clearly be the right one. To *maximize the wealth of current stockholders* is just such a rule.[4] Let us explain why.

For example, suppose you are the manager of a corporation trying to decide between two alternative investments. The choice is between a very risky investment project and

---

[2]Adam Smith, *The Wealth of Nations* (Chicago: University of Chicago Press, 1977).
[3]We assume that the goal of maximizing shareholder wealth does not necessarily conflict with other desirable social goals.
[4]This rule, like any all-encompassing dictum, is not always correct. It needs to be qualified in several respects. First, it assumes well-functioning and competitive capital markets. It also assumes that managers do not make decisions that are illegal or unethical.

a very safe one. Some shareholders might want to avoid taking these risks, and others might be pessimistic about the future of the investment. Still other shareholders might be risk lovers or might be optimistic about the outcome of the investment. How then can management make a decision in the best interests of all shareholders?

Suppose that undertaking the risky project would increase the market value of the firm's shares more than would the safe project. Even if some shareholders ultimately want to invest their money in safer assets, it would not be in their best interests for you as the firm's manager to choose the safer project.

This is because in well-functioning capital markets shareholders can adjust the riskiness of their personal portfolios by selling some of the shares in the firm you manage and investing the proceeds in safe assets. By your accepting the riskier project, even these risk-averse shareholders will wind up better off. They will have extra dollars today, which they can invest or consume as they see fit.

Thus, we see that individual owners would want managers to choose the investment project that maximizes the market value of their shares. The only risks relevant to the decision by managers are those of the project that affect the market value of the firm's shares.

The shareholder-wealth-maximization rule depends on the firm's production technology, market interest rates, market risk premiums, and security prices. It leads managers to make the same investment decisions that each of the individual owners would have made had they made the decisions themselves. At the same time, it does not depend upon the *risk aversion* or *wealth* of the owners, and so it can be made without any specific information about the owners. Thus, the shareholder-wealth-maximization rule is the "right" rule for managers to follow in running the firm. They can follow it without polling the owners each time a decision arises.

Scholars and other commentators on corporate behavior sometimes assert that the goal of managers is to maximize the firm's *profits.* Under certain specialized conditions, profit maximization and maximizing shareholder wealth lead to the same decisions. But in general there are two fundamental ambiguities with the profit-maximization criterion:

- If the production process requires many periods, then which period's profit is to be maximized?
- If either future revenues or expenses are uncertain, then what is the meaning of "maximize profits" when profits are described by a probability distribution?

Let us illustrate each of these problems with the profit-maximization criterion. First, the problem of many periods.

Suppose the firm faces a choice between two projects, both of which require an initial outlay of $1 million but last for a different number of years. Project A will return $1.05 million one year from now and then is over. Its profit is, therefore, $50,000 ($1.05 million–$1 million). Project B will last for two years, return nothing in the first year, and then $1.1 million two years from now. How do you apply a profit-maximization criterion in this case?

Now let us illustrate the difficulty of using a profit maximization criterion in an uncertain environment. Suppose you are the manager of a firm trying to choose between two investment projects, both of which require an initial outlay of $1 million and produce all of their returns one period from now. As in the previous example, project A will pay $1.05 million with certainty. We can, therefore, say unambiguously that the profit on project A is $50,000 ($1.05 million–$1 million).

Project C has an uncertain return. It will either pay $1.2 million or $0.9 million, each with probability 0.5. Thus, project C will either produce a profit of $200,000 or a loss of $100,000. What does it mean in this context to say "choose the project that maximizes the firm's profits"?

Unlike profits, it is clear that the current market value of the firm's shareholders' equity is still well defined (e.g., the future cash flows of the IBM corporation are uncertain, but there is a current price for its stock that is not uncertain). Hence, unlike the profit-maximization rule, the shareholder-wealth-maximization rule causes no ambiguities when future cash flows of the firm are uncertain.

Quick Check 5

Why is the shareholder-wealth-maximization rule a better one for corporate managers to follow than the profit-maximization rule?

Of course, management still has the difficult task of estimating the impact of its decision on the value of the firm's shares. Thus, in our preceding illustrations, in order to choose between projects A and B, or between A and C, management would have to determine which of them is likely to increase the value of the firm the most. This is not easy, but the criterion for making the decision is unambiguous.

Thus, the goal of management is to make decisions so as to maximize the firm's value to its shareholders. The main challenge in implementing this criterion is to obtain information about the likely impact of its decisions on the firm's value. Management's task is made much easier when it can observe market prices of its own and other firms' shares.

Indeed, in the absence of such market price information, it is difficult to see how they can implement this criterion at all. Although it is reasonable to assume that good managers will have as much information about their firm's production technology as anyone, such *internal* (to the firm) information is not sufficient to make effective decisions. In the absence of a stock market, managers would require *external* (to the firm) information that is costly if not impossible to obtain: namely, the wealth, preferences, and other investment opportunities of the owners.

Thus, the existence of a stock market allows the manager to substitute one set of external information that is relatively easy to obtain—namely, stock prices—for another set that is virtually impossible to obtain—information about the shareholders' wealth, preferences, and other investment opportunities. The existence of a well-functioning stock market, therefore, facilitates the efficient separation of the ownership and management of firms.

Note that in one respect the corporation's own senior managers and outside stock analysts who follow the corporation face a common task. Both groups are concerned with answering the question: How will the actions taken by management affect the market price of the firm's shares? The big difference is that the managers are the ones who actually make the decisions and have responsibility for implementing them.

One place to look for a statement of the goals of a corporation's top managers is the annual report to shareholders. Often the opening letter from the company's chief executive officer states what management's financial goals are and the general strategic plan for achieving them (see Box 6).

Quick Check 6

How does the existence of a well-functioning stock market facilitate the separation of ownership and management of firms?

Corporate Financial Goals and the Annual Report

Here is an excerpt from Honeywell Corporation's 1994 annual report to shareholders. Honeywell's chairman and chief executive officer, Michael R. Bonsignore, writes in his letter to the shareholders:

> Profitable growth. Delighted customers. Worldwide leadership in control. This is the vision for Honeywell that I and Honeywell people around the world have set for ourselves. It embodies what we want to be. It underpins how we set our goals. And it defines how we will fulfill the purpose of the company—which is to create value for our shareholders. . . .

> The company is now poised to achieve our primary financial objective: first-quartile total shareholder returns among our peers. We define total shareholder returns as share price appreciation plus dividends reinvested in the stock.

> Our management team is steadfast in achieving this objective. It is a key goal in our long-range incentive system. Our short-term executive compensation program rewards economic value added. We have constructed an integrated financial plan that sets aggressive targets in each driver of shareholder value: sales growth, operating margins, working capital, capital expenditures, and taxes.

8 Market Discipline: Takeovers

What forces are there to compel managers to act in the best interests of the shareholders? The shareholders could fire the managers by voting them out. But because a major benefit of the separated structure is that the owners can remain relatively uninformed about the operations of the firm, it is not apparent how these owners could know whether their firm is being mismanaged.

The value of voting rights as a means of enforcement is further cast into doubt if ownership of the firm is widely dispersed. If that is the situation, then the holdings of any single owner are likely to be so small that he or she would not incur the expense to become informed and to convey this information to other owners.[5] Thus, voting rights alone can do little to solve this dilemma.

The existence of a competitive stock market offers another important mechanism for aligning the incentives of managers with those of shareholders. It is called the *takeover*.

To see how the threat of a takeover can compel managers to act in the best interests of shareholders, suppose some entity, call it the takeover bidder, has identified a significantly mismanaged firm (i.e., one whose management has chosen an investment plan that leads to a market value that is significantly less than the maximum value that could be achieved from the firm's resources). If the bidder successfully buys enough shares of the undervalued firm to gain control, it replaces the managers with ones who will operate it optimally.

Having announced the change in the firm's investment plans, the bidder now sells the shares of the firm at the new market price for an immediate profit. Note that the bidder did not have to add any tangible resources to the firm to achieve this profit. Hence, the only expenses incurred are the cost of identifying a mismanaged firm and the cost of acquiring the firm's shares.

Although the cost of identifying a mismanaged firm will vary, it can be quite low if the takeover bidder happens to be a supplier, customer, or competitor of the firm because much of the information required may have been gathered for other purposes already. For this

---

[5]This is called the "paradox" of voting. The paradox is that when there are many voters, none of whose individual vote would appreciably affect the final outcome, it does not pay any individual voter to incur the costs of becoming informed and exercising the right to vote.

reason, the takeover mechanism can work even if resources are not spent for the explicit reason of identifying mismanaged firms.

However, if significant mismanagement of firms were widespread, then it would pay to spend resources in search of such firms in much the same way that resources are spent on research of new physical investment projects. There are indeed firms that specialize in making hostile (to the management) takeovers. Therefore, the threat of a takeover is credible and the subsequent replacement of management provides a strong incentive for current managers (acting in their self-interest) to act in the interests of the firm's current shareholders by maximizing market value.

Indeed, even in the absence of any explicit instructions from the shareholders or knowledge of the theory for good management, one might expect managers to move in the direction of value maximization as a matter of self-preservation. Moreover, it should be noted that it does not matter whether the source of the mismanagement is incompetence or the pursuit of different objectives, the takeover mechanism serves equally well to correct either one.

The effectiveness of the takeover mechanism can be reduced by government policies. For example, in an attempt to prevent the formation of monopolies in various product markets, the U.S. Department of Justice will take legal action under the antitrust laws to prevent mergers or acquisitions that might reduce competition. Because it is more likely that a supplier, customer, or competitor will be the takeover bidder who identifies the mismanaged firm, this public policy will tend to reduce the threat of takeover.

Quick Check 7

How does the threat of a takeover serve as a mechanism to deal with the conflict of interest between owners and managers of a corporation?

---

9 The Role of the Finance Specialist in a Corporation

Virtually all decisions made in a corporation are at least partially financial because they involve making trade-offs between costs and benefits that are spread over time. Therefore, in large corporations virtually all managers from the chief executive at the top down to managers of individual production units, marketing units, research labs, or other departments make use of the services of finance specialists.

The Financial Executives Institute, a voluntary organization of corporate executives who specialize in finance, offers a broad definition of a financial executive as anyone who has authority for one of the functions listed in Table 1.

The organization of the finance function and its relation to other departments vary from company to company, but Figure 1 shows a typical organization chart in a large corporation.

At the top is the firm's chief executive officer (CEO) who often is also the president. The chief financial officer (CFO) is a senior vice president with responsibility for all the financial functions in the firm and reports directly to the CEO. The firm also has senior vice presidents in charge of marketing and operations. In large firms, there is sometimes a chief operating officer (COO), who takes responsibility for implementing the CEO's strategy for the firm.

The CFO has three departments reporting to him or her: financial planning, treasury, and control, each headed by a vice president. The vice president for financial planning has responsibility for analyzing major capital expenditures such as proposals to enter new lines

TABLE 1 Financial Functions in a Corporation

1. PLANNING

Establishment, coordination, and administration, as an integral part of management, of an adequate plan for the control of operations. Such a plan, to the extent required in the business, would provide the following:

a. Long- and short-range financial and corporate planning

b. Budgeting for capital expenditures and/or operations

c. Sales forecasting

d. Performance evaluation

e. Pricing policies

f. Economic appraisal

g. Analysis of acquisitions and divestments

2. PROVISION OF CAPITAL

Establishment and execution of programs for the provision of the capital required by the business.

3. ADMINISTRATION OF FUNDS

a. Management of cash

b. Maintenance of banking arrangements

c. Receipt, custody, and disbursement of the company's monies and securities

d. Credit and collection management

e. Management of pension funds

f. Management of investments

g. Custodial responsibilities

4. ACCOUNTING AND CONTROL

a. Establishment of accounting policies

b. Development and reporting of accounting data

c. Cost standards

d. Internal auditing

e. Systems and procedures (accounting)

f. Government reporting

g. Report and interpretation of results of operations to management

h. Comparison of performance with operating plans and standards

5. PROTECTION OF ASSETS

a. Provision of insurance coverage as required

b. Assure protection of business assets and loss prevention through internal control and internal auditing

c. Real estate management

6. TAX ADMINISTRATION

a. Establishment and administration of tax policies and procedures

b. Relations with taxing agencies

c. Preparation of tax reports

d. Tax planning

TABLE 1 Continued

7. INVESTOR RELATIONS

a. Establishment and maintenance of liaison with the investment community

b. Establishment and maintenance of communications with company stockholders

c. Counseling with analysts—public financial information

8. EVALUATION AND CONSULTING

Consultation with and advice to other corporate executives on company policy, operations, objectives, and the effectiveness thereof

9. MANAGEMENT INFORMATION SYSTEMS

a. Development and use of electronic data processing facilities

b. Development and use of management information systems

c. Development and use of systems and procedures

Source: Financial Executives Institute.

FIGURE 1

Organization Chart for ZYX Corporation

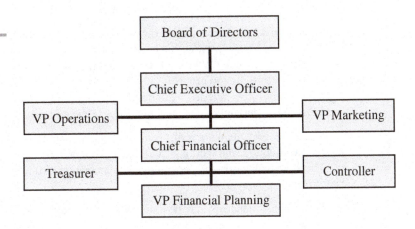

of business or to exit existing businesses. This includes analyzing proposed mergers, acquisitions, and spin-offs.

The treasurer has responsibility for managing the financing activities of the firm and for working capital management. The treasurer's job includes managing relations with the external investor community, managing the firm's exposure to currency and interest rate risks, and managing the tax department.

The controller oversees the accounting and auditing activities of the firm. This includes preparation of internal reports comparing planned and actual costs, revenues, and profits from the corporation's various business units. It also includes preparation of financial statements for use by shareholders, creditors, and regulatory authorities.

Summary

Finance is the study of how to allocate scarce resources over time. The two features that distinguish finance are that the costs and benefits of financial decisions are spread out over time and are usually not known with certainty in advance by either the decision maker or anybody else.

A basic tenet of finance is that the ultimate function of the system is to satisfy people's *consumption preferences.* Economic organizations such as firms and governments exist in order to facilitate the achievement of that ultimate function. Many financial decisions can be made strictly on the basis of improving the trade-offs available to people without knowledge of their consumption preferences.

There are at least five good reasons to study finance:

- To manage your personal resources.
- To deal with the world of business.
- To pursue interesting and rewarding career opportunities.
- To make informed public choices as a citizen.
- To expand your mind.

The players in finance theory are households, business firms, financial intermediaries, and governments. Households occupy a special place in the theory because the ultimate function of the system is to satisfy the preferences of people, and the theory treats those preferences as given. Finance theory explains household behavior as an attempt to satisfy those preferences. The behavior of firms is viewed from the perspective of how it affects the welfare of households.

Households face four basic types of financial decisions:

- *Saving decisions:* How much of their current income should they save for the future?
- *Investment decisions:* How should they invest the money they have saved?
- *Financing decisions:* When and how should they use other people's money to satisfy their wants and needs?
- *Risk-management decisions:* How and on what terms should they seek to reduce the economic uncertainties they face or to take calculated risks?

There are three main areas of financial decision making in a business: capital budgeting, capital structure, and working capital management.

There are five reasons for separating the management from the ownership of a business enterprise:

- Professional managers may be found who have a superior ability to run the business.
- To achieve the efficient scale of a business the resources of many households may have to be pooled.
- In an uncertain economic environment, owners will want to diversify their risks across many firms. Such efficient diversification is difficult to achieve without separation of ownership and management.
- To achieve savings in the costs of gathering information.
- The "learning curve" or "going concern" effect: When the owner is also the manager, the new owner has to learn the business from the former owner in order to manage it efficiently. If the owner is not the manager, then when the business is sold, the manager continues in place and works for the new owner.

The corporate form is especially well suited to the separation of ownership and management of firms because it allows relatively frequent changes in owners by share transfer without affecting the operations of the firm.

The primary goal of corporate management is to maximize shareholder wealth. It leads managers to make the same investment decisions that each of the individual owners would have made had they made the decisions themselves.

A competitive stock market imposes a strong discipline on managers to take actions to maximize the market value of the firm's shares.

Key Terms

- finance
- financial system
- assets
- asset allocation
- liability

- net worth
- sole proprietorship
- partnership
- corporation

Answers to Quick Check Questions

Quick Check 1   What are the four basic types of financial decisions households have to make? Give an example of each.

Answer:
- Consumption/saving decisions, such as how much to save for a child's education or for retirement.
- Investment decisions, such as how much to invest in stocks or bonds.
- Financing decisions, such as what type of loan to take to finance the purchase of a home or a car.
- Risk-management decisions, such as whether to buy disability insurance.

Quick Check 2   What are the basic types of financial decisions firms have to make? Give an example of each.

Answer:
- Capital budgeting decisions, such as whether to build a plant to produce a new product.
- Financing decisions, such as how much debt and how much equity it should have in its capital structure.
- Working capital decisions, such as whether it should extend credit to customers or demand cash on delivery.

Quick Check 3   A corporation owned by a single person is not a sole proprietorship. Why?

Answer: In a corporation the liability of the single shareholder would be limited to the assets of the corporation.

Quick Check 4   What are the main reasons for having a separation of management and ownership of firms? How does the corporate form of organization facilitate this separation?

Answer: Five reasons:
- Professional managers may be found who have a superior ability to run the business.
- To achieve the efficient scale of a business the resources of many households may have to be pooled.
- In an uncertain economic environment, owners will want to diversify their risks across many firms. Such efficient diversification is difficult to achieve without separation of ownership and management.
- To achieve savings in the costs of gathering information.
- The "learning curve" or "going concern" effect: When the owner is also the manager, the new owner has to learn the business from the former owner in order to manage it efficiently. If the owner is not the manager, then when the business is sold, the manager continues in place and works for the new owner.

The corporate form is especially well suited to the separation of ownership and management of firms because it allows relatively frequent changes in owners by share transfer without affecting the operations of the firm.

Quick Check 5   Why is the shareholder-wealth-maximization rule a better one for corporate managers to follow than the profit-maximization rule?

Answer: There are two fundamental ambiguities with the profit-maximization criterion:
- If the production process requires many periods, then which period's profit is to be maximized?
- If either future revenues or expenses are uncertain, then what is the meaning of "maximize profits" when profits are described by a probability distribution?

Quick Check 6   How does the existence of a well-functioning stock market facilitate the separation of ownership and management of firms?

Answer: In the absence of a stock market, managers would require information that is costly if not impossible to obtain: namely, the wealth, preferences, and other investment opportunities of the owners.

Quick Check 7   How does the threat of a takeover serve as a mechanism to deal with the conflict of interest between owners and managers of a corporation?

Answer: Managers know that if they fail to maximize the market value of the firm's shares, the firm will be vulnerable to a takeover in which managers might lose their jobs.

Sources of Information

On the Internet you can complement your understanding of the core structures of financial markets and corporations with the following links:

Survey on Corporate Social Responsibility, *The Economist,* January 20, 2005, http://www.economist.com/surveys/displayStory.cfm?Story_ID=3574392

Financial Market Trends, Organization for Economic Cooperation and Development http://www.oecd.org/document/36/0,2340,en_2649_201185_1962020_1_1_1_1,00.html

Quarterly Review, Bank for International Settlements http://www.bis.org/publ/quarterly.htm

EDGAR Database, U.S. Securities and Exchange Commission http://www.sec.gov/edaux/searches.htm

Questions and Problems

Defining Finance

1. What are your main goals in life? How does finance play a part in achieving those goals? What are the major tradeoffs you face?

Financial Decisions of Households

2. What is your net worth? What have you included among your assets and your liabilities? Would you list the value of your potential lifetime earning power as an asset or liability? How does it compare in value to other assets you have listed?

3. How are the financial decisions faced by a single person living alone different from those faced by the head of a household with responsibility for several children of school age? Are the tradeoffs they have to make different, or will they evaluate the tradeoffs differently?

4. Family A and Family B both consist of a father, mother, and two children of school age. In Family A both spouses have jobs outside the home and earn a combined income of $100,000 per year. In Family B, only one spouse works outside the home and earns $100,000 per year. How do the financial circumstances and decisions faced by the two families differ?

5. Suppose we define financial independence as the ability to engage in the four basic household financial decisions without resort to the use of relatives' resources when making financing decisions. At what age should children be expected to become financially independent?

6. You are thinking of buying a car. Analyze the decision by addressing the following issues:
   a. Are there other ways to satisfy your transportation requirements besides buying a car? Make a list of all the alternatives and write down the pros and cons.
   b. What are the different ways you can finance the purchase of a car?
   c. Obtain information from at least three different providers of automobile financing on the terms they offer.
   d. What criteria should you use in making your decision?

7. Match each of the following examples with one of the four categories of basic types of household financial decisions.
   • At the Safeway paying with your debit card rather than taking the time to write a check
   • Deciding to take the proceeds from your winning lottery ticket and use it to pay for an extended vacation on the Italian Riviera
   • Following Hillary's advice and selling your Microsoft shares to invest in pork belly futures
   • Helping your 15-years-old son learn to drive by putting him behind the wheel on the back road into town
   • Taking up the offer from the pool supply company to pay off your new hot tub with a 15-month loan with zero payments for the first three months

Forms of Business Organization

8. You are thinking of starting your own business, but have no money.
   a. Think of a business that you could start without having to borrow any money.
   b. Now think of a business that you would want to start if you could borrow any amount of money at the going market interest rate.
   c. What are the risks you would face in this business?
   d. Where can you get financing for your new business?

9. Choose an organization that is not a firm, such as a club or church group, and list the most important financial decisions it has to make. What are the key tradeoffs the organization faces? What role do preferences play in choosing among alternatives? Interview the financial manager of the organization and check to see whether he or she agrees with you.

Market Discipline: Takeovers

10. *Challenge Question:* While there are clear advantages to the separation of management from ownership of business enterprises, there is also a fundamental disadvantage in that it may be costly to align the goals of management with those of the owners. Suggest at

least two methods, other than the takeover market, by which the conflict can be reduced, albeit at some cost.

11. *Challenge Question:* Consider a poorly run local coffee shop with its prime location featuring a steady stream of potential clients passing by on their way to and from campus. How does the longtime disgruntled, sloppy, and inefficient owner-manager of Cup-a-Joe survive and avoid disciplining from the takeover market?

The Role of the Finance Specialist in a Corporation

12. Which of the following tasks undertaken within a corporate office are likely to fall under the supervision of the treasurer? The controller?
    - Arranging to extend a line of credit from a bank
    - Arranging with an investment bank for a foreign exchange transaction
    - Producing a detailed analysis of the cost structure of the company's alternative product lines
    - Taking cash payments for company sales and purchasing U.S. Treasury Bills
    - Filing quarterly statements with the Securities and Exchange Commission

Financial Markets and Institutions

OBJECTIVES

- To provide a conceptual framework for understanding how the financial system works and how it changes over time.
- To understand the meaning and determinants of rates of return on different classes of assets.

CONTENTS

From Chapter 2 of *Financial Economics*, 2/e. Zvi Bodie, Robert C. Merton, David L. Cleeton.
Copyright © 2008 by Pearson Prentice Hall. All rights reserved.

The main purpose of this book is to help you make better financial decisions. Such decisions are always made within the context of a financial system that both constrains and enables the decision maker. Effective financial decisions thus require an understanding of that system.

Suppose, for example, that you want to further your education, buy a house, or start a new business. Where can you get the funds to do it? The answers to these questions depend very much on where you are located. The roles played by families, governments, and private sector institutions (such as banks and securities markets) in financing economic activities vary considerably among countries. What's more, these roles change over time.

This chapter provides a conceptual framework for understanding how the financial system works and how it changes over time. It starts with an overview of the central role played by financial markets and intermediaries in facilitating the flow of funds, the transfer of risk, and several other basic financial functions. The chapter provides a broad overview of the current structure of financial markets and institutions around the world, and it shows that the way the basic financial functions are performed changes over time and differs across borders. Finally, the chapter provides a brief overview of how interest rates and rates of return on risky assets are determined and reviews the history of these rates.

1 What Is the Financial System?

The financial system encompasses the markets, intermediaries, service firms, and other institutions used to carry out the financial decisions of households, business firms, and governments. Sometimes a market for a particular financial instrument has a specific geographic location such as the New York Stock Exchange or the Osaka Options and Futures Exchange, which are institutions housed in buildings in New York City and in Osaka, Japan, respectively. Often, however, the market has no one specific location. Such is the case for the **over-the-counter markets**—or off-exchange markets—in stocks, bonds, and currencies, which are essentially global computer and telecommunications networks linking securities dealers and their customers.

Financial intermediaries are defined as firms whose primary business is to provide financial services and products. They include banks, investment companies, and insurance companies. Their products include checking accounts, commercial loans, mortgages, mutual funds, and a wide range of insurance contracts.

Today's financial system is global in scope. Financial markets and intermediaries are linked through a vast international telecommunications network, so that the transfer of payments and the trading of securities can go on virtually around the clock. If a large corporation based in Germany wants to finance a major new investment, for instance, it will consider a range of international possibilities, including issuing stock and selling it on the New York or London stock exchanges or borrowing from a Japanese pension fund. If it chooses to borrow from the Japanese pension fund, the loan might be denominated in German marks, in Japanese yen, or even in U.S. dollars.

2 The Flow of Funds

The interactions among the various players in the financial system are shown in Figure 1, a flow-of-funds diagram. Funds flow through the financial system from entities that have a surplus of funds (the box on the left) to those that have a deficit (the box on the right).

For example, a household that is saving a portion of its current income for retirement has a surplus of funds whereas another household seeking to buy a house has a deficit.

FIGURE 1

The Flow of Funds

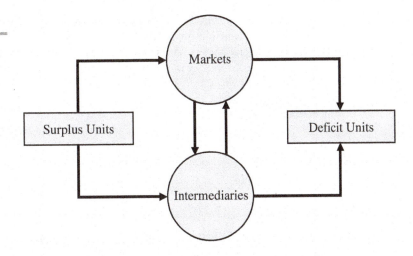

A firm with profits in excess of its need for new investment spending is a surplus unit, whereas another firm that needs to finance a major expansion is a deficit unit.[1]

Figure 1 shows that some funds flow from the surplus units to the deficit units through financial intermediaries such as banks (the lower route in Figure 1), whereas some funds flow through the financial markets without going through a financial intermediary (the upper route).

To illustrate the **flow of funds** along the upper route, a household (surplus unit) buys shares of stock from a firm (deficit unit) that issues them. In some cases—firms that have dividend reinvestment plans, for example—the household buys the shares directly from the firm issuing them without using a broker. In most cases, however, a broker or a dealer would likely be involved in this flow of funds, collecting the money from the household and transferring it to the issuing firm.

A large part of the funds flowing through the financial system, however, never flow through markets and, therefore, do not follow the upper route in Figure 1. Instead, as shown in the lower half of Figure 1, they go from the surplus units to the deficit units through financial intermediaries.

To illustrate the flow of funds through intermediaries, suppose you deposit your savings in an account at a bank, and the bank uses the funds to make a loan to a business firm. In this case, you do not own a direct claim on the borrowing firm; instead you have a deposit at the bank. The bank in turn has a claim on the borrowing firm. Your bank deposit has different risk and liquidity characteristics from the loan to the business firm, which is now an asset of the bank. Your deposit is safe and liquid (i.e., you can withdraw the full amount at any time), whereas the loan held as an asset by the bank has some default risk and may be illiquid. Thus, when funds flow from surplus units to deficit units through a bank, the risk and liquidity of the financial instruments created along the way can be substantially altered. Of course, someone has to absorb the risk of the loans—either the bank's owners or the government entity that insures the bank's deposits.

The arrow pointing from the circle labeled *intermediaries* up to the circle labeled *markets* indicates that intermediaries often channel funds into the financial markets. For example, a middle-aged couple saving for retirement (surplus unit) may invest its savings in an insurance company account (intermediary), which then invests its funds in stocks and bonds (markets). Through the insurance company, the couple indirectly provides funds to the firms (deficit units) issuing the stocks and bonds.

---

[1]Funds that flow among members of a family or among different units of the same firm are not usually considered part of the flows in the financial system.

The arrow pointing from the *markets* circle down to the *intermediaries* circle indicates that in addition to channeling funds *into* the financial markets, some intermediaries obtain funds *from* the financial markets. A finance company that makes loans to households might, for instance, raise those funds by issuing stocks and bonds in the markets for those securities.

> **Quick Check 1**
>
> A depositor puts $5,000 into a bank account and you take a $5,000 student loan from the bank. Trace this flow of funds in Figure 1.

3 The Functional Perspective

For a variety of reasons—including differences in size, complexity, and available technology, as well as differences in political, cultural, and historical backgrounds—financial institutions generally differ across borders. They also change over time. Even when the names of institutions are the same, the functions they perform often differ dramatically. For example, banks in the United States today are very different from what they were in 1928 or in 1958, and banks in the United States today are very different from the institutions called banks in Germany or the United Kingdom today.

In this section we try our hand at setting forth a unifying conceptual framework for understanding how and why financial institutions differ across borders and change over time. The key element in the framework is its focus on *functions* rather than on *institutions* as the conceptual "anchor." Hence, we call it the *functional perspective.* It rests on two basic premises:

- Financial functions are more stable than financial institutions—that is, functions change less over time and vary less across borders.
- Institutional form follows function—that is, innovation and competition among institutions ultimately result in greater efficiency in the performance of financial system functions.

From the most aggregated level of the single primary function of efficient resource allocation, we distinguish six basic or core functions performed by the financial system:

- To provide ways to *transfer economic resources* through time, across borders, and among industries.
- To provide ways of *managing risk.*
- To provide ways of *clearing and settling payments* to facilitate trade.
- To provide a mechanism for the *pooling of resources* and for the *subdividing* of ownership in various enterprises.
- To provide *price information* to help coordinate decentralized decision making in various sectors of the economy.
- To provide ways of *dealing with the incentive problems* created when one party to a transaction has information that the other party does not or when one party acts as an agent for another.

The rest of this chapter explains these functions of the financial system and illustrates how the performance of each has changed over time.

3.1 Function 1: Transferring Resources across Time and Space

A financial system provides ways to transfer economic resources through time, across geographic regions, and among industries.

Many of the funds flows shown in Figure 1 involve giving up something now in order to get something in the future, or vice versa. Student loans, borrowing to buy a house, saving for retirement, and investing in production facilities are all actions that shift resources from one point in time to another. The financial system facilitates such *intertemporal* (literally, "between time") transfers of resources.

Without the opportunity to take out a student loan, for example, many young people whose families do not have the means to send them to college might have to forgo a higher education. Similarly, without the ability to raise venture capital from investors, many businesses might never get started.

In addition to facilitating the shifting of resources through time, the financial system plays an important role in shifting resources from one place to another. At times the capital resources available to perform an activity are located far from where they are most efficiently employed. Households in Germany, for example, may be generating capital through saving that could be more efficiently employed in Russia. The financial system provides a variety of mechanisms for facilitating the transfer of capital resources from Germany to Russia. One way is for German citizens to invest in shares issued by firms located in Russia. Another is for German banks to make loans to those firms.

The more complex the economy, the more important is the role of the financial system in providing an efficient means for shifting resources across time and place. Thus, in today's global financial system, a complex network of markets and intermediaries makes it possible for the retirement savings of Japanese workers to be used to finance the house purchased by a young couple in the United States.

Innovation that allows scarce resources to be shifted over time or place from a use with a relatively low benefit to a use offering a higher benefit improves efficiency. For example, suppose that all families were constrained to invest their savings only within the family. In that case, Family A could earn a rate of return of 2% per year on its savings, at the same time that Family B has opportunities to earn a rate of return of 20%. Efficiency is increased by creating an investment company to collect Family A's savings and lend them to Family B.

Quick Check 2

Give an example of a transfer of resources over time that takes place through the financial system. Is there a more efficient way for this transfer of resources to be handled?

3.2 Function 2: Managing Risk

A financial system provides ways to manage risk.

Just as funds are transferred through the financial system, so are risks. For example, insurance companies are financial intermediaries that specialize in the activity of risk transfer. They collect premiums from customers who want to reduce their risks and transfer it to investors who are willing to pay the claims and bear the risk in return for some reward.

Often funds and risks are "bundled" together and transferred simultaneously through the financial system so that the flow of *funds* illustrated in Figure 1 can also characterize the flow of *risks*. Let us illustrate with the example of business finance and the transfer of business risk.

Suppose you want to start a business and need $100,000 to do so. You have no savings of your own, so you are a deficit unit. Let us assume that you convince a private investor (a surplus unit) to provide you with $70,000 in equity capital in return for a 75% share of the profits of the business, and you convince a bank (a financial intermediary) to lend you the other $30,000 at an interest rate of 6% per year. In Figure 1 this flow of $100,000 would appear as a flow of funds from others to you.

But what about the risk of business failure?

In general, it is the equity investors who absorb the risk of business failure. Thus, if your business venture goes sour, the private investor may get none of his or her $70,000 back. However, the bank may also face some risk that it will not get all of its principal and interest. For example, suppose that at the end of a year, the business has a value of only $20,000. Then the equity investors lose all of their investment of $70,000, and the bank loses $10,000 of the $30,000 it has lent to you. *Thus, lenders share some of the business risk of the firm along with the equity investors.*

Although funds and risks often come bundled together, they can be "unbundled." For example, consider the $30,000 loan from the bank to your business. Suppose the bank requires that you get other members of your family to guarantee the loan. The bank thereby transfers the risk of default from itself to your relatives. The bank is now providing you with $30,000 in funds at minimal risk to itself, and the risk of the loan has been transferred to your relatives.

As we will see, many of the financial contracts that we observe in the world of finance serve to transfer risks without transferring funds. This is the case with most insurance contracts and guarantees, and it is also the case with derivatives, such as futures, swaps, and options.

Quick Check 3

Give an example of a transfer of risk that takes place through the financial system.

Box 1 **The Return of the 30-Year Treasury**

There are many ways to be over $7 trillion in debt. In early 2006 that was the approximate size of the U.S. government debt, although in the second-half of the 1990's and into 2001 the debt was actually falling. During that period the federal government's budget surplus prompted the Treasury's decision to stop issuing 30-year Treasury bonds in October of 2001. The vacation didn't last long: as the government quickly returned to fiscal deficits the 30-year bond was called back into service less than 5 years later.

The maturity structure of the government's debt can have interesting implications. On the one hand, long-term bonds allow the government to lock in a particular interest rate and avoid the costs associated with reissuing debt. With interest rates at historically low levels, and long-term rates only slightly higher than short-term rates, long-term borrowing has been particularly appealing in recent years.

On the other hand, the government's motivations interact with the needs of the private sector. Government debt competes with private debt for available funds. At the same time, Treasury bonds act as a liquid, risk-free benchmark to the bond market, aiding in the pricing of private-sector issues.

Certain investors, especially pension funds, may have benefited the most from the return of the 30-year Treasury. Pension funds had been holding two-third of their assets in equities. Since their liabilities, corresponding to the benefits they are obliged to pay retirees, are more closely aligned with long-term debt, pension funds can reduce their risk exposure by reallocated their asset portfolios to the new long-term bonds. The government is expected to encourage pension funds to do exactly that. Pension plans nationwide are estimated to be insolvent by nearly half a trillion dollars, a burden that could fall on the Pension Benefit Guaranty Corporation, a federal entity that insures pensions.

The size of the public debt matters, but its structure also has important implications for bond markets and the private sector.

Source: "Long Ranger," *The Economist,* February 2, 2006.

3.3 Function 3: Clearing and Settling Payments

A financial system provides ways of clearing and settling payments to facilitate the exchange of goods, services, and assets.

An important function of the financial system is to provide an efficient way for people and businesses to make payments to each other when they wish to buy goods or services. Suppose you live in the United States and are planning a trip around the world. You believe that $5,000 should be enough money to cover your expenses while traveling. In what form should you take the funds? How will you pay for things?

Some hotels, youth hostels, and restaurants will accept U.S. dollars as payment, but others will not. You might be able to pay for everything with a credit card, but some places you're interested in visiting might not accept a credit card. Should you buy traveler's checks? In what currencies should they be denominated? Contemplation of your trip perhaps leads you to think how convenient it would be if every seller in every country were willing to accept the same means of payment.

Imagine instead that you are a wealthy person living in a country whose government limits your access to foreign currency and that you want to travel around the world. Inside your country you can buy whatever you want using the local currency, but outside your country, no one will accept that currency as a means of payment. A shortage of foreign exchange causes your government to prohibit its citizens from purchasing foreign currency or borrowing abroad. What can you do?

One possibility is to buy transportable goods (such as furs or jewelry) in your home country, pack them all in a suitcase, and try to use them to pay for your food and lodging abroad. In other words, you could engage in *barter,* the process of exchanging goods without using money. Needless to say, this would not be a convenient way to see the world. You would need to bring vast amounts of luggage, and instead of enjoying the sights much of your time and energy would be spent in finding a hotel or restaurant that accepts furs or jewelry in exchange for a room or a meal.

As these examples suggest, an important function of the financial system is to provide an efficient payments system, so that households and businesses do not have to waste time and resources in implementing their purchases. The replacement of gold with paper currency as a means of payment is an example of a change that increases efficiency of the payments system. Gold is a scarce resource that is used in medicine and in the production of jewelry. Paper money serves as a superior means of payment. Compared with gold, paper currency is easier to verify (harder to counterfeit) and more convenient to carry around in one's pocket. It doesn't cost as much to make and print currency as it does to mine, refine, and mint gold. The subsequent development of checks, credit cards, and electronic-funds-transfer as alternative means of payment to paper currency has further increased efficiency.

> **Quick Check 4**
>
> Would you accept an IOU from me in payment for a good or service that I buy from you? What factors will determine the answer?

3.4 Function 4: Pooling Resources and Subdividing Shares

A financial system provides a mechanism for the pooling of funds to undertake large-scale indivisible enterprise or for the subdividing of shares in large enterprises with many owners.

In modern economies, the minimum investment required to run a business is often beyond the means of an individual or even a large family. The financial system provides a variety of mechanisms (such as the stock market or banks) to *pool* or *aggregate* the wealth of households into larger masses of capital for use by business firms.

From the investor's perspective, the financial system provides opportunities for individual households to participate in investments that require large lump sums of money by pooling their funds and then subdividing shares in the investment. For example, suppose you want to invest in a racehorse that costs $100,000, but you only have $10,000 to invest. If there were a way of physically dividing the racehorse into ten pieces, then you could buy one piece. However, in this case the whole is surely worth more than the sum of its parts. A physical splitting of the horse will not do the trick. The financial system solves the problem of how to divide the horse without destroying it. By creating an investment pool and distributing shares to the investors, the $100,000 investment can be divided into $10,000 economic "pieces" without actually cutting up the horse. Any money the horse earns in race winnings or stud fees would, after training and upkeep expenses are taken out, be divided among all the shareholders.

As another example, consider money market funds. Suppose you want to invest in the most secure and liquid dollar-denominated asset, U.S. Treasury bills (T-bills). The minimum denomination is $10,000, and you have only $1,000 to invest. Therefore, the only way you can invest in T-bills is by pooling resources with other investors. In the 1970s, mutual funds that hold U.S. T-bills were developed to facilitate this process.

In a mutual fund, investors' money is pooled, and they are given accounts representing their proportional shares in the fund. The mutual fund frequently posts the price of a share and allows its customers to add or withdraw money at almost any time in almost any amount. Thus, if the price of a share is now $11 and you invest $1,000, the fund will credit your account with 1,000/11, or 90.91 shares. U.S. T-bill mutual funds, thus, improve the performance of Function 4 by transforming large-denomination Treasury bills into almost infinitely divisible securities.

> ### Quick Check 5
>
> Give an example of an investment that would not be undertaken if it were not possible to pool the savings of many different households.

3.5 Function 5: Providing Information

A financial system provides price information that helps coordinate decentralized decision making in various sectors of the economy.

Every day, newspapers, radio, and television announce stock prices and interest rates. Of the millions of people who receive these news reports, relatively few actually buy and sell securities. Many of those who do not trade securities nevertheless use the information generated from security prices to make other types of decisions. In deciding how much of their current income to save and how to invest it, households make use of information about interest rates and security prices.

An example may help to illustrate how even within families the intertemporal transfer of resources is often facilitated by knowledge of market interest rates. Suppose that you are 30 years old, just got married, and want to buy a house for $100,000. Your local bank will make you a mortgage loan for $80,000 or 80% of the purchase price of the house at an interest rate of 8% per year, but you need to pay 20% down (i.e., $20,000). Your 45-year-old sister has an account at a savings bank with $20,000 in it—just enough for your down payment. She is saving the money for her retirement, which is far in the future, and is currently earning 6% per year. If your sister is willing to lend you her retirement savings for your down payment, how do you decide what a "fair" rate of interest is? Clearly, it is useful to know current market interest rates. You already know that your sister is earning 6% per year on her savings account and that your local bank will charge you 8% per year on the mortgage loan.

Similarly, knowledge of market prices of assets can be helpful for decision making within families. For example, suppose you and your sister inherit a house or a family business, and it is to be divided equally between you. You don't want to sell it because one of you wants to live in it or continue to operate it. How much should the other sibling receive? Clearly, it would be useful to know the market prices of similar assets to settle on a reasonable price for the inheritance.

Asset prices and interest rates provide critical signals to managers of firms in their selection of investment projects and financing arrangements. Managers of firms with no anticipated need to transact in the financial markets routinely use those markets to provide information for decisions.

For example, a firm earns $10 million in profits in a good year and is faced with deciding whether to reinvest it in the business, pay it out in cash dividends to shareholders, or use it to buy back its own shares. Knowledge of its own and other firm's share prices as well as market interest rates will surely help in deciding what to do.

Whenever a new financial instrument is introduced, new possibilities for information extraction are created as a by-product. For example, the development of trading standardized option contracts on exchanges since 1973 has greatly increased the amount of quantitative information available about the riskiness of economic and financial variables. This information is particularly useful in making risk-management decisions.

> ### Quick Check 6
>
> Give an example of a financial transaction that provides important information to parties not involved in the transaction.

3.6 Function 6: Dealing with Incentive Problems

A financial system provides ways to deal with the incentive problems when one party to a financial transaction has information that the other party does not, or when one party is an agent that makes decisions for another.

As we discussed, financial markets and intermediaries serve several functions that facilitate the efficient allocation of resources and risks. There are, however, incentive problems that limit their ability to perform some of those functions. Incentive problems arise because parties to contracts often cannot easily monitor or control one another. Incentive problems take a variety of forms—among them, moral hazard, adverse selection, and principal-agent problems.

The **moral hazard** problem exists when having insurance against some risk causes the insured party to take greater risk or to take less care in preventing the event that gives rise to the loss. Moral hazard can lead to unwillingness on the part of insurance companies to insure against certain types of risk. For example, if a warehouse owner buys fire insurance, the existence of the insurance reduces his incentive to spend money to prevent a fire. Failure to take the same precautions makes a warehouse fire a more likely occurrence. In an extreme case, the owner may be tempted to actually start a fire in order to collect the insurance money if the coverage exceeds the market value of the warehouse. Because of this potential moral hazard, insurance companies may limit the amount they will insure or simply refuse to sell fire insurance under certain circumstances.

An example of moral hazard in the realm of contracting is what might happen if I pay you in advance for a job, and you get the same amount of money no matter how good or bad a job you do. There is less of an incentive for you to work hard than would be the case if I pay you after the job is done.

A more subtle example of the moral hazard problem arises in financing business ventures. Suppose you have an idea for a new business venture, and you need startup capital. Where can you get it? The first source you may look to is family and friends. Why? Because you trust them, and they know and trust you. You know your secret plans are safe with them. On the other side, your family believes that you will fully disclose the information you have about the business opportunity, including all of the pitfalls. Moreover, if the business does not immediately prosper and the going gets rough, they know that you will work hard to protect their interests.

What about a bank as a source for the loan? You are perhaps a little uncomfortable about discussing the details of your business plans with the bank loan officer, who is a complete stranger. She might disclose your plans to another customer, who could be a competitor. But even if you can resolve your concerns about the bank, there is the other side. The loan officer is reluctant to lend you the money you want because she knows that you have no incentive to disclose the pitfalls in your plans unless you have to. Thus, there is an imbalance or *asymmetry* in the exchange of information about the business opportunity: You know more about it than the loan officer.

Moreover, the loan officer knows that she is a stranger to you and that the bank is just an impersonal institution to you. Therefore, if the going gets rough, you will not necessarily work as hard to turn it around as you would for your family and friends. Instead, you may decide to walk away from the business and not repay your loan. The reduced incentive for you to work hard when part of the risk of the enterprise has been transferred to an entity whose welfare you do not care much about (such as a bank or an insurance company) is, thus, an example of the problem of moral hazard.

Quick Check 7

Give an example of how the problem of moral hazard might prevent you from getting financing for something you want to do. Can you think of a way of overcoming the problem?

Another class of problems caused by asymmetric information is **adverse selection**—those who purchase insurance against risk are more likely than the general population to be at risk. For example, consider **life annuities,** which are contracts that pay a fixed amount of money each month for as long as the purchaser lives. A firm selling such annuities cannot assume that the people who buy them will have the same expected length of life as the general population.

For example, suppose a firm sells life annuities to people retiring at age 65. There are equal numbers of three types of people in the general population: type A live for 10 years, type B for 15 years, and type C for 20 years. On average, people aged 65 live for 15 years. If the firm charges a price that reflects a 15-year life expectancy, however, it will find that the people who buy the annuities are disproportionately of types B and C. Type A people will find that your annuities are not a good deal for them and will not purchase them.

If the annuity firm knew the type of each potential customer, A, B, or C, and could charge a price that reflected the true life expectancy for that type, then there would be no adverse selection problem. But the annuity firm cannot get enough information about customers to know as much about their individual life expectancies as they themselves do. Unless the insurer can charge a price that accurately reflects each person's true life expectancy, a disproportionately large number of the annuities sold will be bought by healthy people who expect to live a long time. In our example, the average life expectancy of buyers of annuities might be 17.5 years, which is 2.5 years longer than in the general population.

Therefore, if annuity firms used life expectancies of the general population to price their annuities without adding an amount to adjust for the adverse selection problem, they would all lose money. As a result, firms in this market charge a price for annuities that is relatively unattractive to people with an average life expectancy, and the market is much smaller than it would be if there were no problem of adverse selection.

> ## Quick Check 8
> Suppose a bank offered to make loans to potential borrowers without checking their credit history. What would be true of the types of borrowers they would attract compared to banks that did checks of credit history? Would such a bank charge the same interest rate on loans as banks that check credit history?

Another type of incentive problem arises when critical tasks are delegated to others. For example, shareholders in a corporation delegate the running of the firm to its managers, and investors in a mutual fund delegate the authority to select the mix of their security holdings to a portfolio manager. In each case, the individual or organization responsible for the risks associated with a set of decisions gives up or delegates the decision-making authority to another individual or organization. Those who bear the risks associated with the decisions are called the *principals,* and those who assume the decision-making authority are called the *agents.*

The **principal-agent problem** is that agents may not make the same decisions that the principals would have made if the principals knew what the agents know and were making the decisions themselves. There can be a conflict of interest between agents and principals. In extreme cases, agents may even act contrary to the interests of their principals, as when a stockbroker "churns" a client's account only in order to generate commissions for himself.

A well-functioning financial system facilitates the resolution of the problems that arise from all of these incentive problems—moral hazard, adverse selection, and principal-agent—so that the other benefits of the financial system, such as pooling, risk sharing, and specialization, can be achieved. For example, **collateralization** of loans, which means giving the lender the right to seize specific business assets in the event of default, is a widely used device for reducing the incentive problems associated with lending. Collateralization reduces the costs to the lender of monitoring the behavior of the borrower. The lender need only be concerned that the market value of the assets serving as collateral is sufficient to repay the principal and interest due on the loan. Over time, advances in technology have lowered the costs of tracking and valuing certain types of business assets that can serve as collateral—such as goods in inventory—and thereby broadened the range of situations in which collateralized loan agreements are feasible to implement.

Principal-agent problems can be alleviated by using the financial system, too. If the compensation of management depends on the performance of the market value of the firm's shares, the interests of managers and shareholders can be more closely aligned. For example, consider the introduction of "equity-kickers" in loan contracts to help limit possible conflicts of interest between the shareholders and creditors of corporations. An equity-kicker is any provision of the loan contract that allows the lender to share in the benefits

---

Box 2	Does Investor Activism Improve Corporate Efficiency?

A company's managers and its shareholders don't always share the same objectives. As the owners of a company, shareholders usually hope for a high rate of growth in corporate earnings, which can translate into higher share prices and dividends. Managers, on the other hand, may seek things like a high salary, prestige, and a generous bonus. These goals can conflict: For example, money spent on executive compensation is not available to be distributed to shareholders.

Recently, influential shareholders at hedge funds and similar investment firms have taken a renewed interest in corporate management. Two of the most prominent are Kirk Kerkorian and Carl Icahn. In February of 2006, Kerkorian helped convince General Motors to cut its dividend, reduce executive compensation, and take on a new board member. Icahn, meanwhile, proposed splitting Time Warner into four separate companies.

Activist investors can play an important role in improving corporate efficiency by introducing new ideas and by forcing managers to act in shareholders' best interest. However, evidence is mixed over whether investor activism is actually effective, and some openly oppose it. Activist investors may distract a company's managers and divert resources away from better uses to address the concerns of a few powerful investors. A company's managers may, after all, be in the best position to determine how a company should be run.

Although managers often face incentives that cause them to pursue objectives other than shareholder value, it is not clear that interference by activist investors improves company performance.

Source: "Busy Bodies," *The Economist,* February 10, 2006.

---

accruing to shareholders. One common equity-kicker is a percentage sharing in profits while the loan is outstanding. Another is the right of the lender to convert the loan amount into a prespecified number of shares of stock.

Management is elected by the firm's shareholders. Thus, in cases in which there is a conflict of interest between shareholders and creditors, management has an incentive to take actions that benefit shareholders at the expense of the firm's creditors. The resulting moral hazard problem could prevent an otherwise mutually advantageous loan agreement from taking place. By including an equity-kicker in the loan contract, this problem can be reduced or even eliminated, leaving both the shareholders of the firm and the firm's creditors better off.

Quick Check 9

If you get financial planning advice from your insurance agent, how does this give rise to a principal-agent problem? Can you think of a way of overcoming the problem?

---

4 Financial Innovation and the "Invisible Hand"

Generally, financial innovations are not planned by any central authority but arise from the individual actions of entrepreneurs and firms. The fundamental economic forces behind financial innovation are essentially the same as for innovation in general. As Adam Smith observed:

> Every individual endeavors to employ his capital so that its produce may be of greatest value. He generally neither intends to promote the public interest, nor knows how much he is promoting it. He intends only his own security, only his own gain. And

he is in this led by an **invisible hand** to promote an end which was no part of his intention. By pursuing his own interest he frequently promotes that of society more effectually than when he really intends to promote it.[2]

To illustrate, compare the situation faced by a college graduate traveling around the world 40 years ago with the one faced by a college graduate undertaking such a journey today. Back then you had the constant worry that you would run out of money in some place where no one could speak your language. If you ran out, then you had to wire home and try to arrange a wire transfer of money from a bank back home to a local bank. The process was costly and time-consuming. Prearranged lines of credit were available only to the wealthiest travelers.

But now, you can pay for almost anything you buy almost anywhere with a credit card. VISA, MasterCard, American Express, and some others are accepted virtually everywhere on the globe. To pay your hotel bill, you simply give the clerk your card, and she slips it into a machine connected to the telephone. Within seconds, she has verified that your credit is good (i.e., that the bank that issued you the card will guarantee payment), and you need only sign the receipt and be on your way to your next destination.

Moreover, you need not worry about your money being lost or stolen. If you cannot find your credit card, you can go to any bank that is connected with your card's network. The bank will help you to cancel the missing card (so no one else can use it) and to get another. The bank will often lend you money in the meantime.

Clearly, world travel has become less costly and more convenient as a result of credit cards. Their invention and dissemination has made millions of people better off and contributed to the "democratization" of finance.

But how has this happened? Let us use the example of credit cards to trace the key factors in the development of a financial innovation.

Technology is an important factor. Credit cards depend on a complex network of telephones, computers, and other more sophisticated telecommunications and information processing hardware and software. But for credit cards to become an important part of the contemporary economic scene, financial service firms looking for profit opportunities had to employ the advanced technology in offering credit card services, and households and businesses had to buy them.

It is not uncommon in the history of innovations (financial or otherwise) that the firm that pioneers a commercially successful innovative idea is not the one to profit the most from it. And so it is here with the credit card. The first firm to offer credit cards to be used by global travelers was Diners Club, which was formed just after World War II. The initial success of Diners Club led two other firms, American Express and Carte Blanche, to offer similar credit card programs.

Firms in the credit card business earn their revenues from fees paid to them by retailers on credit card purchases (usually a percentage of the purchase price) and from interest paid on loans to credit card customers (on their unpaid balances). Major costs stem from transactions processing, stolen cards, and loan defaults by cardholders.

When commercial banks first tried to enter the credit card business in the 1950s, they found that they could not compete with the established firms because bank operating costs were too high. In the late 1960s, however, advances in computer technology lowered their costs to the point at which they could compete successfully. Today the two big bank networks, VISA and MasterCard, dominate the global credit card business. Diners Club and Carte Blanche account for only a modest share of the business.

---

[2]Adam Smith, *The Wealth of Nations* (Chicago: University of Chicago Press, 1977), p. 408.

Thus, competition among the major providers of credit cards keeps their cost comparatively low. For most people traveling today, it is not only more convenient but also less expensive to use a credit card when they travel than to use traveler's checks.

This last observation leads us to another basic point about financial innovation. Analysis of consumer preferences and the forces of competition among financial service providers helps one to make predictions about future changes in the financial system. For example, in light of the advantages of credit cards as a method of making payments, what prediction would you make about the future of traveler's checks? Are traveler's checks destined for the same fate as the slide rule after the invention of the handheld calculator?

Credit cards are only one of a wide array of new financial products developed over the past 40 years that have changed the way we carry on economic activities. Collectively, these innovations have greatly improved the opportunities for people to receive efficient risk-return trade-offs in their personal investments and more effective tailoring to their individual needs over the entire life cycle, including accumulation during the work years and distribution in retirement.

5 Financial Markets

The basic types of financial assets are *debt, equity,* and *derivatives.* Debt instruments are issued by anyone who borrows money—firms, governments, and households. The assets traded in debt markets, therefore, include corporate bonds, government bonds, residential and commercial mortgages, and consumer loans. Debt instruments are also called **fixed-income instruments** because they promise to pay fixed sums of cash in the future.

A different classification is by the *maturity* of the claims being traded. The market for short-term debt (less than one year) is called the **money market,** and the one for long-term debt and equity securities is called the **capital market.**

Money market instruments are mostly interest-earning securities issued by governments (such as U.S. Treasury bills) and secure private sector borrowers (such as commercial paper of large corporations). Money markets are today globally integrated and liquid in which **liquidity** is defined by the relative ease, cost, and speed with which an asset can be converted into cash.

Equity is the claim of the *owners* of a firm. Equity securities issued by corporations are called *common stocks* in the United States and *shares* in the United Kingdom. They are bought and sold in the *stock market.* Each share of common stock entitles its holder to an equal share in the ownership of the firm. In typical cases each share is entitled to the same amount of profits and is entitled to one vote on matters of corporate governance. However, some corporations issue two classes of common stock, one with voting rights and the other without.

Common stock represents a **residual claim** on the assets of a corporation. The owners of common stock are entitled to any assets of the firm left over after meeting all of the firm's other financial obligations. If, for example, the firm goes out of business and all of its assets are sold, then common stockholders receive what is left, if anything, after all of the various classes of creditors are paid what they are owed.

Common stock also has the feature of **limited liability.** This means that should the firm be liquidated and the proceeds from the sale of its assets not be sufficient to pay off all the firm's debts, the creditors cannot assess the common stockholders for more money to meet this shortfall. The claims of the creditors of the corporation are limited to the assets of the firm.

Derivatives are financial instruments that derive their value from the prices of one or more other assets such as equity securities, fixed-income securities, foreign currencies, or commodities. Their principal function is to serve as tools for managing exposures to the risks associated with the underlying assets.

Among the most common types of derivatives are *options* and *forward contracts.* A **call option** is an instrument that gives its holder the right to *buy* some asset at a specified price on or before some specified expiration date. A **put option** is an instrument that gives its holder the right to *sell* some asset at a specified price on or before some specified expiration date. When an owner of an asset buys a put option on that asset, he effectively is insuring it against a decline in its price below the price specified in the put-option contract.

Forward contracts are instruments that *oblige* one party to the contract to buy, and the other party to sell, some asset at a specified price on some specified date. They permit buyers and sellers of the asset to eliminate the uncertainty about the future price at which the asset will be exchanged.

Quick Check 10

What are the defining features of debt, equity, and derivative securities?

---

6 Financial Market Rates

Every day we are showered with newspaper, television, radio, and on-line computer reports of financial market indicators. These include interest rates, exchange rates, and indicators of stock market performance. In this section we explain the meaning of these rates.

6.1 Interest Rates

An interest rate is a *promised* rate of return, and there are as many different interest rates as there are distinct kinds of borrowing and lending. For example, the interest rate that home buyers pay on the loans they take to finance their homes is called the **mortgage rate,** whereas the rate charged by banks on loans made to businesses is called the **commercial loan rate.**

The interest rate on any type of loan or fixed-income instrument depends on a number of factors, but the three most important are its **unit of account,** its **maturity,** and its **default risk.** Let us define each of these factors.

- The *unit of account* is the medium in which payments are denominated. The unit of account is usually a currency, such as dollars, francs, pounds, euros, pesos, yen, and so on. Sometimes the unit of account is a commodity such as gold or silver or some standard "basket" of goods and services. The interest rate varies depending on the unit of account.
- The *maturity* of a fixed-income instrument is the length of time until repayment of the entire amount borrowed. The interest rate on short-term instruments can be higher, lower, or equal to the interest rate on long-term instruments.
- *Default risk* is the possibility that some portion of the interest or the principal on a fixed-income instrument will not be repaid in full. The greater the default risk, the higher the interest rate the issuer must promise to investors to get them to buy it.

Let us consider how each of these three factors affects interest rates in the real world.

EFFECT OF UNIT OF ACCOUNT

A fixed-income instrument is risk free only in terms of its own unit of account, and interest rates vary depending on the unit of account. To see this, consider bonds denominated in different currencies.

Suppose the interest rate on U.K. government bonds is much higher than on Japanese government bonds of comparable maturity. Because these bonds are all free of default risk, shouldn't all investors prefer the U.K. bonds?

The answer is no because the bonds are denominated in different currencies. The U.K. government bonds are denominated in pounds, and the Japanese government bonds are denominated in yen. *Although the bonds offer a risk-free rate of return in their own currency, the rate of return in any other currency is uncertain because it depends on the rate of exchange between the currencies when payments are received in the future.*

Let us illustrate with an example. Suppose you are investing for one year, and the interest rate on a one-year Japanese government bond is 3%, and at the same time it is 9% on a one-year U.K. government bond. The **exchange rate,** which is the price of one currency in terms of the other, is currently 150 yen to the pound.

Suppose you are a Japanese investor, who wants a safe investment in terms of yen. If you buy the Japanese bond, you will earn 3% for sure. If you buy the U.K. government bond, however, your rate of return in yen depends on the yen/pound exchange rate a year from now.

Suppose you invest £100 in a U.K. bond. To do so you will have to convert 15,000 yen into pounds, so your initial investment in yen is 15,000. Because the interest rate on the U.K. bond is 9%, you will receive £109 a year from now. The value of the £109 in yen is not known now because the future yen/pound exchange rate is unknown.

Your realized yen rate of return will be:

$$\text{Yen Rate of Return} = \frac{\left(£109 \times \text{Future Yen Price of the Pound}\left(¥/£\right)\right) - ¥15,000}{¥15,000}$$

Suppose the yen price of the pound falls during the year, so that the yen/pound exchange rate is 140 yen to the pound a year from now. What will the realized yen rate of return on the U.K. bond be?

Substituting into the preceding expression we get:

$$\text{Yen Rate of Return} = \frac{\left(£109 \times 140\left(¥/£\right)\right) - ¥15,000}{¥15,000} = 0.017333$$

Thus, your *realized* yen rate of return will be 1.73%, which is less than the 3% risk-free yen interest rate you could have earned on one-year Japanese bonds.

> **Quick Check 11**
>
> In the previous example, what does the change in the exchange rate have to be at year's end for the Japanese investor to earn exactly 3% per year on the investment in U.K. bonds?

EFFECT OF MATURITY

To illustrate the effect of maturity on interest rates consider Figure 2, which shows the U.S. Treasury **yield curve** on May 26, 2006. The yield curve depicts the relation between interest rates (yields) on fixed-income instruments issued by the U.S. Treasury and the maturity of the instrument at a given moment in time. In Figure 2 we see that the annualized yield on two-year Treasury obligations was about 4.95% per year and increased with maturity to about 5.15% per year on 30-year obligations. Although we do not see this in Figure 2, the shape and the level of the yield curve change significantly over time. At times in the past, short-term rates have been higher than long-term rates, so that the yield curve has been downward sloping.

Box 3 — An Anomaly in the Bond Market may Signal a Recession

Asset prices incorporate people's expectations about the future. That's why, when the bond market displays an unusual pattern called an inverted yield curve, market observers begin to worry about what future event this may foreshadow. Most of the time the yield on long-term debt securities (like 10-year Treasury bonds) is higher than the yield on short-term securities (like 3-month Treasuries). An inverted yield curve refers to a situation in which long-term bonds have a lower yield than their short-term cousins. All of the economic recessions of the past half-century have been preceded by an inverted yield curve. Only once in that time period has an inverted yield curve not been followed by a recession. In early 2006, with 10-year Treasuries yielding only 0.4 percentage points more than bonds maturing in three months, market analysts speculated that the yield curve could invert, with a recession likely to come next.

But what is the linkage between an inverted yield curve and an economic recession? The answer is expectations. Long-term rates are, to a large extent, just a combination of current and future short-term rates. Imagine that you needed a loan today that you would not be able to pay back for ten years. You could issue a single ten-year bond with an interest rate of 7.5%. At the end of ten years, you pay back the principal and interest on the loan. Alternatively, you could issue a 5-year bond with an interest rate of 5%, and in five years you could issue another 5-year bond at a 10% interest rate. In this example, you are indifferent between the two options;

your average interest rate is 7.5% either way. But what if you expected rates on 5-year bonds to be 15% five years from now? Then you (and any other borrower) should definitely issue a 10-year bond. Of course, if everyone is issuing 10-year bonds and avoiding series of 5-year bonds, the yield on 10-year bonds will rise, and the yield on 5-year bonds will fall, until all borrowers are indifferent between the two options. Looked at a different way, if long-term rates are not in line with reasonable expectations of future short-term rates, there is an opportunity for arbitrage. Money could be made by selling 10-year bonds and using the proceeds to invest in a series of 5-year bonds. This buying and selling will inevitably result in interest rates that are the same on average, regardless of the maturities of the bonds used.

The final piece of the puzzle? The Federal Reserve. In the United States, the Fed effectively decides short-term rates. An inverted yield curve therefore indicates that the market believes the Fed will lower rates in the future. If the Fed lowers rates, there's a good chance the U.S. economy is not growing very quickly. For the Fed to lower rates significantly (enough to overcome the usually upward-sloping yield curve), the United States is likely to be experiencing a recession. Ultimately it is people's expectations about the future that determine the shape of the yield curve.

Source: "The Long and the Short of It," *The Economist,* January 5, 2006.

FIGURE 2

U.S. Treasury Yield Curve

Source: Bloomberg.com, May 26, 2006.

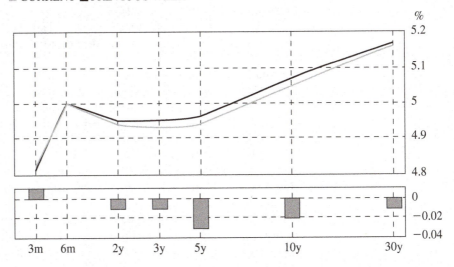

TABLE 1   Yield Comparisons

	Yields
Treasury 5-year	4.94
10-year	5.05
5-Year AAA Banking & Finance	5.58
10-Year AAA Banking & Finance	5.91

Source: Bloomberg.com, May 26, 2006.

Quick Check 12

Go on-line to Bloomberg.com and discover what the level and shape of the U.S. Treasury yield curve are. Do the same for the Japanese and German yield curves.

EFFECT OF DEFAULT RISK

The higher the default risk on fixed-income instruments, the higher the interest rate, holding all other features constant. Table 1 shows the interest rates on U.S.-dollar-denominated bonds for issuers with different degrees of default risk. U.S. Treasury bonds have the least default risk, followed by high-quality corporate bonds.

Consider the difference in yields—called the **yield spread**—between Treasury bonds with maturities of 10 years (10-yr)—5.05% per year and corporate bonds of high quality of the same maturity—5.91% per year. The yield spread is 0.86% per year.

Quick Check 13

Look on Bloomberg.com and discover what the yield spreads are between corporate bonds and U.S. Treasury bonds.

6.2 Rates of Return on Risky Assets

Interest rates are *promised* rates of return on fixed-income instruments that are a contractual obligation. However, many assets do not carry a promised rate of return. For example, if you invest in real estate, equity securities, or works of art, there is no promise of specified cash payments in the future. Let us now consider how to measure the rate of return on such risky assets.

When you invest in equity securities such as common stocks, the *return* comes from two sources. The first source is the cash dividends paid to the stockholder by the firm that issued the stocks. These dividend payments are not contractually required and, hence, are not called interest payments. Dividends are paid to stockholders at the discretion of the firm's board of directors.

The second source of return to the stockholder is any gain (or loss) in the market price of the stock over the period it is held. This second type of return is called a **capital gain** or **capital loss.** The length of the holding period for measuring returns on stock can be as short as a day or as long as several decades.

To illustrate how returns are measured, suppose you buy shares of stock at a price of $100 per share. One day later the price is $101 per share and you sell. Your *rate of return* for the day is 1%—a capital gain of $1 per share divided by the purchase price of $100.

Suppose you hold the stock for a year. At the end of the year, the stock pays a cash dividend of $5 per share and the price of a share is $105 just after the dividend is paid. The one-year rate of return, r, is:

$$r = \frac{\text{Ending Price of a Share} - \text{Beginning Price} + \text{Cash Dividend}}{\text{Beginning Price}}$$

In the example we have:

$$r = \frac{\$105 - \$100 + \$5}{\$100} = 0.10 \text{ or } 10\%$$

Note that we can present the *total* rate of return as the sum of the dividend income component and the price change component:

$$r = \frac{\text{Cash Dividend}}{\text{Beginning Price}} + \frac{\text{Ending Price of a Share} - \text{Beginning Price}}{\text{Beginning Price}}$$

$$r = \text{Dividend Income Component} + \text{Price Change Component}$$

$$r = 5\% + 5\% = 10\%$$

What if you decide *not* to sell your shares at the end of the year—how should we measure your rate of return?

The answer is that *you measure the rate of return exactly the same way whether or not you sell the stock.* The price appreciation of $5 per share is as much a part of your return as is the $5 dividend. That you choose to keep the stock rather than sell it does not alter the fact that you could convert it into $105 of cash at the end of the year. Thus, whether you decide to realize your capital gain by selling the stock or to reinvest it (by not selling), your rate of return is 10%.[3]

Quick Check 14

You invest in a stock costing $50. It pays a cash dividend during the year of $1, and you expect its price to be $60 at year's end. What is your expected rate of return? If the stock's price is actually $40 at year's end, what is your realized rate of return?

6.3 Market Indexes and Market Indexing

It is useful for many purposes to have a measure of the overall level of stock prices. For example, people holding stocks might want an indicator of the current value of their investment, or they might want a benchmark against which to measure the performance of their own investment in stocks. Table 2 is a list of the stock indexes generally reported in the financial press for the stocks traded on the other major national stock exchanges around the world.

Indexing is an investment strategy that seeks to match the investment returns of a specified stock market index. Indexing is based on a simple truth: It is impossible for all stock investors in the aggregate to outperform the overall stock market. When indexing, an investment manager attempts to replicate the investment results of the target index by holding all—or in the case of very large indexes, a representative sample—of the securities in the index. There is no attempt to use "active" money management or to make "bets" on individual stocks or narrow industry sectors in an attempt to outpace the index. Thus, indexing is a passive investment strategy emphasizing broad diversification and low portfolio trading activity.

---

[3]This is only true of your *before-tax* rate of return. Because selling the stock can affect the income taxes you pay, your *after-tax* rate of return may be affected.

| Box 4 | A Slowing Housing Market Threatens to Become a Drag on the Economy |

The housing boom that much of the world has experienced over the past several years may be coming to a close, and the consequences for GDP could be dire. Fueled by low interest rates, housing prices across the world have been increasing rapidly: between 1997 and 2005, average home prices in the United States increased 91%; in the United Kingdom, 167%; in Ireland, 212%; and in South Africa, an astounding 279%. As of early 2006, however, growth in prices had slowed considerably.

The housing boom has contributed significantly to GDP growth in the affected countries. Rising home prices can stimulate economic growth in at least two ways. First, homeowners are able to borrow against the value of their homes in the form of mortgages, home equity lines of credit, and so on. Second, increasing home prices make homeowners feel wealthier. Both of these cause consumers to spend more, and in the short run, spending can spur growth.

In the United States, diminished price growth, slowing sales of existing homes, and increasing housing inventories all point to a housing market that has peaked. Some analysts fear there may even be a housing "bubble," with prices that are up to 40% overvalued on average. If prices were to fall, the housing market's stimulating effect on GDP could be exactly reversed, leading to a period of slow growth or recession. Even if prices were to stagnate at current levels, the consequences for GDP could be severe. To prevent homeowners from losing money, housing prices have to increase to make up for transaction costs such as legal fees, real estate agents, and taxes, and foregone interest on the owner's down payment. Consumers losing money on their houses will have less to spend on other goods. A slowing housing market could seriously impede growth throughout the economy.

Source: "Soft Isn't Safe," *The Economist,* March 2, 2006.

Of course, there will always be actively managed funds that outperform index funds. It may just be luck—pure chance would say that some investment managers will provide exceptional returns and they may even have superior performance over lengthy "winning streaks." Or, it may be skill—there may be some investment managers with truly outstanding abilities who can earn superior returns over time. The problem in selecting actively managed funds is how to identify in advance those that will be consistently superior over time.

INDEXING'S COST ADVANTAGE

Since 1926, the U.S. stock market has provided investors with an average return of about 10% per year. That figure, however, is before costs. These costs come in the form of:

- The fund's expense ratio (including advisory fees, distribution charges, and operating expenses).
- Portfolio transaction costs (brokerage and other trading costs).

TABLE 2 Major Stock Indexes Around the World

Country	Indexes
United States	DJI, SP500
Japan	Nikkei, Topix
United Kingdom	FTSE-100, FTSE-ALL SHARE
Germany	DAX
France	CAC 40
Switzerland	SMI
Europe, Australia, Far East	MSCI, EAFE
China	Hang Seng

In 2005, the average general equity fund had an annual expense ratio of 1.54% (see Figure 3C on the following page) of investor assets. In addition, traditional mutual fund managers have high portfolio activity; the asset-weighted average fund's portfolio turnover rate was 47% (see Figure 3B below) in 2005. The trading costs of this portfolio turnover may be expected to subtract another 0.5% to 1% annually. Combined, fund expenses and transaction costs for the typical fund take a significant bite out of the investment-return pie. Funds charging sales commissions swallow even more of the returns.

By contrast, one of the key advantages of an index fund is its low cost. An index fund requires only minimal advisory fees, can keep operating expenses at the lowest level, and holds portfolio transaction costs to a minimum. Moreover, because index funds engage in much lower portfolio turnover than actively managed funds, there is a strong (but by no

FIGURE 3A

Stock Fund Operating Expense Ratios[1] (percent, 1990–2003)

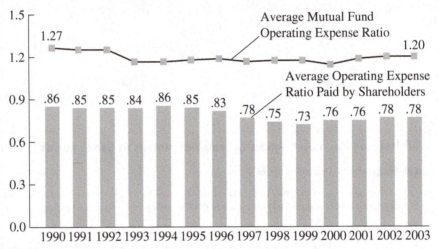

[1]Operating expense ratio is measured as the total expense ratio minus the 12b-1 fees. Download an Excel file of this data.

Sources: Investment Company Institute; Lipper; Value Line Publishing, Inc.; CDA/Wiesenberger Investment Companies Service; ©CRSP University of Chicago, used with permission, all rights reserved (773.702.7467/www.crsp.com); Primary datasource & ©Standard & Poor's Micropal, Inc. 1998 (617.451.1585/www.micropal.com); and Strategic Insight Mutual Fund Research and Consulting, LLC.

FIGURE 3B

Turnover Rate[1] Experienced by Stock Fund Investors Remains Low[2] (percent, 1971–2005)

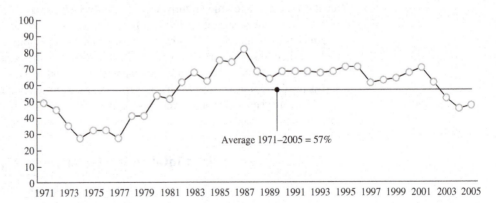

[1]asset-weighted average.
[2]excludes variable annuities.

Sources: Investment Company Institute; ©CRSP University of Chicago, used with permission, all rights reserved (312.263.6400/www.crsp.com); and Strategic Insight Simfund.

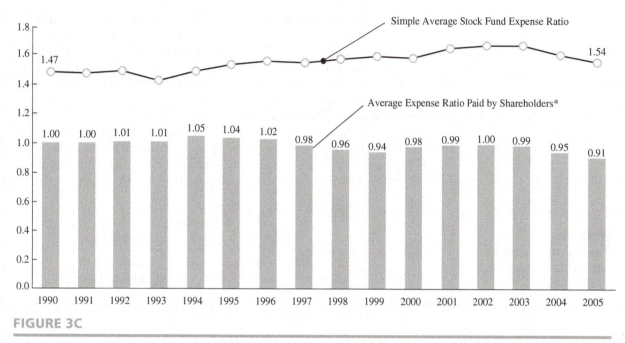

FIGURE 3C

Fund Shareholders Pay Lower-than-average-Expenses in Stock Funds (percent, 1990–2005)

*asset-weighted average of annual expense ratios for individual funds.

Sources: Investment Company Institute; Lipper; ValueLine Publishing, Inc.; CDA/Wiesenberger Investment Companies Service; ©CRSP University of Chicago, used with permission, all rights reserved (312.263.6400/www.crsp.com); and Strategic Insight Simfund.

means assured) tendency for index funds to realize and distribute only modest—if any—capital gains to shareholders. Because these distributions are taxable for all shareholders, it is an advantage to defer their realization as long as possible.

Over time, the broad stock market indexes have outperformed the average general equity fund. Table 3 shows the total return (capital change plus income) of the Wilshire 5000 (a measure of the total U.S. stock market) versus equity funds.

These returns would need to be adjusted for fund expenses and portfolio transaction costs. With low expense ratios and minimal transactions costs associated with portfolio rebalancing, the index fund returns would be reduced by around 0.3% per year.

Table 4 shows rates of return on different asset classes around the world. Each rate of return is initially measured in its own currency unit. For example, Table 4 shows that stocks in the United States rose 0.8% on the S&P 500 index over the period from the end of 2005 until May 26, 2006, and in Canada they increased by about 1.3%. To compare performance across the two countries, one must convert to the same currency unit.

The Canadian stock market over the same period rose by 5.2% in dollar terms. Ignoring any cash dividends earned on stocks, this must have been associated with an increase in the value of

TABLE 3   Annualized Total Return (ending May 26, 2006)

	1-year	3-year	5-year
DJ-Wilshire 5000 Index	11.06%	15.01%	3.36%
Average U.S. Stock Funds	13.45%	15.75%	3.48%

Source: Morningstar.

TABLE 4 Financial Market Indicators (May 27, 2006)

Stock Market		% Change Since End of 2005		Interest Rates (% per year)		Currency Units (per $)	
Country	Index	Local Currency	$ Terms	Short Term 3-month	Long Term 10-year	Latest	Year Ago
Australia	All ordinaries	6.10	8.70	5.87	5.68	1.33	1.31
Britain	FTSE-100	−0.60	8.10	4.64	4.57	0.54	0.55
Canada	Toronto Composite	1.30	5.20	4.08	4.34	1.12	1.27
Denmark	OMXCB	−4.90	2.90	2.95	3.88	5.84	5.91
Japan	Nikkei 225	−1.30	3.40	0.10	1.85	113.00	108.00
Sweden	Affarsvarlden Gen	−0.70	8.30	2.12	3.71	7.29	7.29
Switzerland	Swiss Market	−1.40	6.70	1.41	2.68	1.22	1.23
U.S.	S&P 500	0.80	0.80	5.06	5.05	–	−0.79
Euro area	FTSE Euro 100	0.90	9.20	2.91	3.83	0.78	0.79

Source: The Economist, May 27, 2006.

the Canadian (C$) compared to the U.S. (US$) dollar. In fact, the final two columns of Table 4 show that over a year-long period running up to May 26, 2006, the C$ strengthened in terms of the US$: Only C$1.12 was needed to convert to a US$ as opposed to C$1.27 per US$ one year earlier. The significant increase in the C$ in early 2006 turned a small positive gain in the Canadian stock market into a significantly larger gain in terms of a US$-based rate of return.

Box 5

Financing a College Education

Lending to college students makes sense. A college education can be very expensive, and college students are often relatively poor. College graduates, on the other hand, have extensive opportunities to earn a good living. The problem is, you have to be a college student first in order to be a college graduate later. A student loan helps you borrow against your future earnings to pay for college now.

One of the biggest providers of college loans in the United States is Sallie Mae, which was recently bought by a conglomeration of two private equity firms and two banks for $25 billion. The deal itself is what's called a leveraged buy-out—the banks and private equity firms borrowed two-thirds of the purchase price to complete the deal.

Sallie Mae is in an unusual business because of a high level of government involvement. Because the federal government wants to encourage young people to pursue college educations, it subsidizes many student loans. The government may pay the interest on a loan while a student is still in school, offer loans at low rates, or provide a loan guarantee. A guarantee on a loan is a kind of insurance whereby the government promises to pay back the lender if a student defaults.

Sallie Mae attracted its new buyers because of its healthy cash flow and profitability. It has also made money outside of its core business by providing unsubsidized private loans, debt collection services, and funds for saving for college. However, there are considerable risks in the market for student loans. The government can alter its subsidies at any time: cutting interest rates, limiting eligibility, or guaranteeing fewer loans. New York's attorney general recently took an interest in Sallie Mae because of its alleged use of deceptive sales techniques, and the company was forced to pay a $2 million settlement. Because interest rates on government-subsidized loans are regulated, margins can be very thin. Worst of all, students often turn out to be irresponsible borrowers, amassing large debts that they are later unable to pay off.

Despite the many risks, Sallie Mae's new owners seem to agree that, overall, lending to college students makes sense.

Source: "Pay-Back Time," *The Economist,* April 17, 2007.

6.4 Rates of Return in Historical Perspective

Figures 4A and 4B, along with Tables 5A and 5B, present information about returns on several broad asset classes on a worldwide basis and within the United States. The data covers the period 1926–2003. Figure 4A gives a graphic presentation of the data contained in Table 5A representing the total returns generated over time by investing in the asset categories. Note that the vertical axis is plotted using a log scale that has the property that a time series with a constant annual rate of growth will plot as a straight line. At any point in time we can think about the indices values as representing the cumulative value of $1 invested initially invested in 1926. For example, $1 initially invested at the beginning of 1926 in a diversified portfolio of large U.S. company equities would have grown to approximately $12.09 at the beginning of 1955. The same $1 in 1926 would have grown to $12.00 by the beginning of 1952 if the portfolio had been comprised of small U.S. company equities.

Table 5B and Figure 4B convert the total return indices into annual rates of returns and allow us to examine the relative volatilities of these annual returns across alternative asset classes. In the U.S. equity category we have divided equity portfolios between companies with large and small values of market capitalization. We have plotted the time series on the same set of axes. Clearly, small stocks have the most volatile series.

The next-to-last column of Table 5B shows the one-year rates of return on a policy of rolling over 30-day Treasury bills as they mature. As this rate changes from month to month, it is riskless only for a 30-day holding period. The column labeled Long-Term T-Bonds presents the annual rates of return an investor would have earned by investing in U.S. Treasury bonds with 20-year maturities. The last column gives the annual inflation rates as measured by the rate of change in the consumer price index.

On the final page of the table are several descriptive statistics. The arithmetic and geometric averages of the annual returns are calculated. For T-bills, the arithmetic average is 3.79%; for T-bonds, 5.64%; and for large common stock, 12.25%. These numbers imply an average risk premium (the average rate of return less the average risk-free rate of 3.79%) of 1.85% per year on T-bonds and 8.46% on large stocks.

Another statistic reported at the bottom of Table 5B is the standard deviation. The higher the standard deviation, the higher the volatility of the rate of return. The standard deviation of large stock returns has been 20.50%, compared to 8.19% for T-bonds, and 3.18% for T-bills.

The other summary measures in Table 5B are the highest and lowest annual rate of return (the range) for each asset over the 78-year period. The size of this range is another possible measure of the relative riskiness of each asset class. It too confirms the ranking of stocks as the riskiest and bills as the least risky of the three asset classes.

Table 5B reports on the annual returns on two global portfolios. The World Portfolio of stocks is a diversified portfolio of equities of companies with large capital market valuations coming from 16 developed economies including those of Japanese, European, and American companies. Up until 1986, index weights were proportional to countries' GDP, measured in U.S. dollars. Since 1987 the index weights have been shifted to be proportional to the U.S. dollar–based market valuations of the countries' aggregate equity markets.

The World Portfolio of bonds uses the same 16 countries as for the stock portfolio and includes the countries' long-term government bonds as instruments. We see in the summary statistics of Table 5B that the World Equity Index annual returns have a lower average and standard deviation than the U.S. large company equity index with corresponding values of 11.17% versus 12.25% for the average annual returns, and 18.38% versus 20.50% for the standard deviations of the returns. In the long-term bond comparisons the

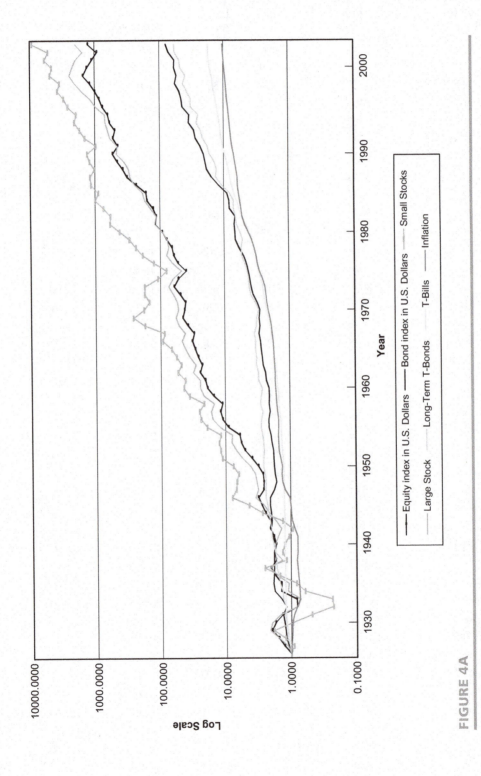

Total Return Indices (1926–2004)

TABLE 5A   Total Return Indices, 1926–2004 (beginning of the year)

Year	World Portfolio		U.S. Market				
	Equity index in U.S. Dollars	Bond index in U.S. Dollars	Small Stocks	Large Stock	Long-Term T-Bonds	T-Bills	Inflation
1926	1.0000	1.0000	1.0000	1.0000	1.0000	1.0000	1.0000
1927	1.2524	1.0776	0.9109	1.1221	1.0454	1.0319	0.9888
1928	1.5423	1.1819	1.2218	1.5259	1.1302	1.0641	0.9665
1929	1.9837	1.2100	1.8367	2.1255	1.1197	1.1047	0.9552
1930	1.7346	1.2513	0.9457	1.9627	1.1690	1.1571	0.9608
1931	1.3426	1.3271	0.4820	1.4543	1.2418	1.1843	0.8993
1932	0.8063	1.1650	0.2257	0.7917	1.1758	1.1964	0.8155
1933	0.8181	1.3794	0.2338	0.7194	1.3156	1.2061	0.7317
1934	1.3974	1.7833	0.6140	1.1119	1.3292	1.2096	0.7373
1935	1.3995	1.8536	0.8228	1.0861	1.4641	1.2114	0.7485
1936	1.7136	1.8250	1.4623	1.5821	1.5370	1.2134	0.7709
1937	2.0364	1.8166	2.5340	2.1129	1.6372	1.2155	0.7821
1938	1.6760	1.8036	1.1616	1.3516	1.6443	1.2194	0.8044
1939	1.7801	1.8093	1.3312	1.7493	1.7306	1.2199	0.7821
1940	1.6804	1.7176	1.2307	1.7307	1.8327	1.2200	0.7821
1941	1.8143	1.9081	1.0615	1.5637	1.9525	1.2193	0.7876
1942	2.0549	2.0128	0.9323	1.3886	1.9719	1.2198	0.8658
1943	2.0434	1.9376	1.3194	1.6774	2.0782	1.2229	0.9440
1944	2.4377	1.9947	2.7356	2.1226	2.1794	1.2271	0.9719
1945	2.7666	2.0532	4.3821	2.5674	2.2576	1.2310	0.9943
1946	3.1462	2.0558	7.9339	3.4946	2.4120	1.2350	1.0167
1947	2.6141	1.7826	6.8993	3.1710	2.4156	1.2393	1.2010
1948	2.5856	1.6354	6.7537	3.3257	2.3869	1.2450	1.3072
1949	2.6648	1.7198	6.3276	3.5016	2.4602	1.2572	1.3462
1950	3.1271	1.7574	7.6696	4.1403	2.6085	1.2711	1.3184
1951	3.8914	1.8006	11.2598	5.4934	2.5835	1.2865	1.3966
1952	5.0078	1.8104	11.9917	6.7827	2.5331	1.3056	1.4804
1953	5.7194	1.8976	12.5709	8.0653	2.5820	1.3270	1.4915
1954	6.0265	1.9671	11.8631	7.9250	2.6809	1.3506	1.5026
1955	8.9313	2.1205	19.4105	12.0895	2.8117	1.3622	1.4915
1956	10.9802	2.1254	24.0826	15.8905	2.7740	1.3835	1.4970
1957	11.9267	2.0338	25.3228	16.9154	2.6320	1.4169	1.5418
1958	11.1085	2.0954	21.6687	15.0310	2.8810	1.4613	1.5865
1959	15.1942	2.0860	35.8271	21.6116	2.7741	1.4820	1.6144
1960	18.9867	2.0952	43.4439	24.4103	2.6756	1.5238	1.6424
1961	20.4506	2.3149	41.2326	24.4567	3.0443	1.5631	1.6647
1962	24.5121	2.3608	53.1736	31.2141	3.0501	1.5969	1.6759
1963	22.7472	2.5879	47.1756	28.4703	3.2578	1.6403	1.6981
1964	26.0114	2.6593	55.7238	34.9132	3.2419	1.6920	1.7260
1965	28.8857	2.7441	66.4562	40.7332	3.3881	1.7516	1.7427

TABLE 5A **Continued**

Year	World Portfolio		U.S. Market				
	Equity index in U.S. Dollars	Bond index in U.S. Dollars	Small Stocks	Large Stock	Long-Term T-Bonds	T-Bills	Inflation
1966	31.9158	2.8224	92.4473	45.8249	3.3789	1.8211	1.7762
1967	29.8508	2.9739	86.0407	41.1278	3.5039	1.9069	1.8377
1968	36.9404	2.8752	174.9379	51.0437	3.2443	1.9860	1.8935
1969	44.2989	2.9356	262.8792	56.6585	3.2054	2.0911	1.9829
1970	41.5480	2.8672	180.6506	51.9389	2.9964	2.2289	2.1058
1971	40.3265	3.1479	149.1993	54.0684	3.3766	2.3711	2.2231
1972	48.0772	3.6207	175.9060	61.7299	3.9665	2.4735	2.2958
1973	60.2071	3.9067	176.2930	73.5449	4.1867	2.5697	2.3741
1974	51.5614	4.0747	109.1606	62.6971	4.2453	2.7512	2.5809
1975	39.1815	4.2813	79.5017	46.1450	4.4800	2.9734	2.8994
1976	51.6568	4.6024	126.2646	63.3387	4.8608	3.1465	3.1006
1977	60.3145	5.1192	187.8059	78.5273	5.3989	3.3089	3.2513
1978	64.1928	5.9470	239.3399	72.8262	5.4475	3.4793	3.4691
1979	77.7631	6.7540	298.0978	77.5599	5.2209	3.7336	3.7820
1980	91.7760	6.7837	419.8707	92.1179	5.6918	4.1327	4.2847
1981	119.7035	6.9764	588.1549	122.0378	6.4414	4.6088	4.8211
1982	114.6999	6.7189	579.2738	115.9603	6.6740	5.2937	5.2512
1983	127.6151	8.2079	740.6015	141.5760	7.1091	5.8580	5.4523
1984	158.0640	8.3474	993.2948	173.2465	7.0714	6.3764	5.6589
1985	163.3592	8.9768	891.8794	184.4382	8.1527	7.0115	5.8824
1986	229.3073	12.0477	1151.1487	243.4585	10.8169	7.5500	6.1060
1987	317.7740	15.7416	1195.8133	288.2549	13.4087	8.0075	6.1731
1988	369.2216	18.6931	1029.1169	303.6477	13.0534	8.4383	6.4466
1989	449.8965	19.6558	1220.6356	354.8427	14.1498	8.9716	6.7316
1990	535.1519	20.9177	1331.1031	466.0503	16.9076	9.7091	7.0446
1991	440.6441	23.4237	968.9100	451.1367	18.1132	10.4548	7.4750
1992	524.0580	27.7828	1441.3504	589.4553	21.4442	11.0308	7.7037
1993	491.2520	29.0914	1745.4754	634.9023	23.1147	11.4059	7.9271
1994	592.0078	34.9736	2078.5121	697.5671	26.6928	11.7366	8.1451
1995	631.4947	34.3861	1967.1038	706.5657	24.7763	12.1920	8.3626
1996	761.3300	43.5362	2630.8047	973.0117	32.6229	12.8723	8.5750
1997	854.2123	45.1297	3067.7813	1197.4855	32.3587	13.5340	8.8597
1998	990.6300	48.2301	3799.7540	1594.6914	37.2384	14.2215	9.0103
1999	1194.2045	56.5835	3524.6518	2050.4542	42.2730	14.9013	9.1554
2000	1517.8339	53.4148	4939.7995	2481.8697	38.5783	15.5808	9.4008
2001	1318.9976	57.8483	4651.8092	2256.0196	46.3982	16.4829	9.7194
2002	1110.3322	57.6400	5993.8561	1987.7789	48.3515	17.0961	9.8701
2003	921.3537	70.6897	5297.9694	1548.4797	56.4698	17.3799	10.1050
2004	1269.2568	78.7695	9248.6652	1992.7386	57.8137	17.5554	10.2950

TABLE 5B **Annual Rates of Return, 1926–2003 (over the year)**

	World Portfolio		U.S. Market				
Year	Equity Return in U.S. Dollars	Bond Return in U.S. Dollars	Small Stocks	Large Stock	Long-Term T-Bonds	T-Bills	Inflation
1926	25.24	7.76	−8.91	12.21	4.54	3.19	−1.12
1927	23.15	9.68	34.13	35.99	8.11	3.12	−2.26
1928	28.62	2.38	50.33	39.29	−0.93	3.82	−1.16
1929	−12.56	3.41	−48.51	−7.66	4.41	4.74	0.58
1930	−22.6	6.06	−49.03	−25.90	6.22	2.35	−6.40
1931	39.94	−12.22	−53.18	−45.56	−5.31	1.02	−9.32
1932	1.46	18.41	3.58	−9.14	11.89	0.81	−10.27
1933	70.81	29.28	162.67	54.56	1.03	0.29	0.76
1934	0.15	3.94	34.00	−2.32	10.15	0.15	1.52
1935	22.44	−1.54	77.72	45.67	4.98	0.17	2.99
1936	18.84	−0.46	73.29	33.55	6.52	0.17	1.45
1937	−17.7	−0.72	−54.16	−36.03	0.43	0.32	2.86
1938	6.21	0.32	14.60	29.42	5.25	0.04	−2.78
1939	−5.6	−5.07	−7.55	−1.06	5.90	0.01	0.00
1940	7.97	11.09	−13.75	−9.65	6.54	−0.06	0.71
1941	13.26	5.49	−12.17	−11.20	0.99	0.04	9.93
1942	−0.56	−3.74	41.52	20.80	5.39	0.26	9.03
1943	19.3	2.95	107.34	26.54	4.87	0.34	2.96
1944	13.49	2.93	60.19	20.96	3.59	0.32	2.30
1945	13.72	0.13	81.05	36.11	6.84	0.32	2.25
1946	−16.91	−13.29	−13.04	−9.26	0.15	0.35	18.13
1947	−1.09	−8.26	−2.11	4.88	−1.19	0.46	8.84
1948	3.06	5.16	−6.31	5.29	3.07	0.98	2.99
1949	17.35	2.19	21.21	18.24	6.03	1.11	−2.07
1950	24.44	2.46	46.81	32.68	−0.96	1.21	5.93
1951	28.69	0.54	6.50	23.47	−1.95	1.48	6.00
1952	14.21	4.82	4.83	18.91	1.93	1.64	0.75
1953	5.37	3.66	−5.63	−1.74	3.83	1.78	0.75
1954	48.2	7.8	63.62	52.55	4.88	0.86	−0.74
1955	22.94	0.23	24.07	31.44	−1.34	1.56	0.37
1956	8.62	−4.31	5.15	6.45	−5.12	2.42	2.99
1957	−6.86	3.03	−14.43	−11.14	9.46	3.13	2.90
1958	36.78	−0.45	65.34	43.78	−3.71	1.42	1.76
1959	24.96	0.44	21.26	12.95	−3.55	2.82	1.73
1960	7.71	10.49	−5.09	0.19	13.78	2.58	1.36
1961	19.86	1.98	28.96	27.63	0.19	2.16	0.67
1962	−7.2	9.62	−11.28	−8.79	6.81	2.72	1.33
1963	14.35	2.76	18.12	22.63	−0.49	3.15	1.64
1964	11.05	3.19	19.26	16.67	4.51	3.52	0.97
1965	10.49	2.85	39.11	12.50	−0.27	3.97	1.92

TABLE 5B **Continued**

| Year | World Portfolio | | U.S. Market | | | | |
	Equity Return in U.S. Dollars	Bond Return in U.S. Dollars	Small Stocks	Large Stock	Long-Term T-Bonds	T-Bills	Inflation
1966	−6.47	5.37	−6.93	−10.25	3.70	4.71	3.46
1967	23.75	−3.32	103.32	24.11	−7.41	4.15	3.04
1968	19.92	2.1	50.27	11.00	−1.20	5.29	4.72
1969	−6.21	−2.33	−31.28	−8.33	−6.52	6.59	6.20
1970	−2.94	9.79	−17.41	4.10	12.69	6.38	5.57
1971	19.22	15.02	17.90	14.17	17.47	4.32	3.27
1972	25.23	7.9	0.22	19.14	5.55	3.89	3.41
1973	−14.36	4.3	−38.08	−14.75	1.40	7.06	8.71
1974	−24.01	5.07	−27.17	−26.40	5.53	8.08	12.34
1975	31.84	7.5	58.82	37.26	8.50	5.82	6.94
1976	16.76	11.23	48.74	23.98	11.07	5.16	4.86
1977	6.43	16.17	27.44	−7.26	0.90	5.15	6.70
1978	21.14	13.57	24.55	6.50	−4.16	7.31	9.02
1979	18.02	0.44	40.85	18.77	9.02	10.69	13.29
1980	30.43	2.84	40.08	32.48	13.17	11.52	12.52
1981	−4.18	−3.69	−1.51	−4.98	3.61	14.86	8.92
1982	11.26	22.16	27.85	22.09	6.52	10.66	3.83
1983	23.86	1.7	34.12	22.37	−0.53	8.85	3.79
1984	3.35	7.54	−10.21	6.46	15.29	9.96	3.95
1985	40.37	34.21	29.07	32.00	32.68	7.68	3.80
1986	38.58	30.66	3.88	18.40	23.96	6.06	1.10
1987	16.19	18.75	−13.94	5.34	−2.65	5.38	4.43
1988	21.85	5.15	18.61	16.86	8.40	6.32	4.42
1989	18.95	6.42	9.05	31.34	19.49	8.22	4.65
1990	−17.66	11.98	−27.21	−3.20	7.13	7.68	6.11
1991	18.93	18.61	48.76	30.66	18.39	5.51	3.06
1992	−6.26	4.71	21.10	7.71	7.79	3.40	2.90
1993	20.51	20.22	19.08	9.87	15.48	2.90	2.75
1994	6.67	−1.68	−5.36	1.29	−7.18	3.88	2.67
1995	20.56	26.61	33.74	37.71	31.67	5.58	2.54
1996	12.2	3.66	16.61	23.07	−0.81	5.14	3.32
1997	15.97	6.87	23.86	33.17	15.08	5.08	1.70
1998	20.55	17.32	−7.24	28.58	13.52	4.78	1.61
1999	27.1	−5.6	40.15	21.04	−8.74	4.56	2.68
2000	−13.1	8.3	−5.83	−9.10	20.27	5.79	3.39
2001	−15.82	−0.36	28.85	−11.89	4.21	3.72	1.55
2002	−17.02	22.64	−11.61	−22.10	16.79	1.66	2.38
2003	37.76	11.43	74.57	28.69	2.38	1.01	1.88

(Continued)

TABLE 5B **Continued**

| Year | World Portfolio | | U.S. Market | | | | |
	Equity Return in U.S. Dollars	Bond Return in U.S. Dollars	Small Stocks	Large Stock	Long-Term T-Bonds	T-Bills	Inflation
Rate of Return Statistics							
Geometric Average	9.41	5.34	11.80	10.23	5.10	3.71	2.98
Arithmetic Average	11.17	6.13	18.43	12.25	5.64	3.79	3.12
Standard Deviation	18.38	9.14	38.11	20.50	8.19	3.18	4.35
Minimum	−39.94	−13.29	−54.16	−45.56	−8.74	−0.06	−10.27
Maximum	70.81	34.21	162.67	54.56	32.68	14.86	18.13
Excess Return Statistics							
Average	7.37	2.34	14.64	8.46	1.85		
Standard Deviation	18.69	8.98	38.72	20.80	8.00		
Minimum	−41.02	−18.40	−54.48	−46.58	−13.30		
Maximum	70.51	28.99	162.38	54.27	26.09		

Sources:
Inflation data: Bureau of Labor Statistics.
Security return data for 1926–1995: Center for Research in Security Prices.
Security return data since 1996: Returns on appropriate index portfolios:
  Large stocks: S&P 500
  Small stocks: Fama & French 1st quantile
LT Government bonds: Lehman Bros. LT Treasury index.
ST Government bonds: Lehman Bros. Intermediate term Treasury index.
T-bills: Salomon Smith Barney 3-month U.S. T-bill index.

World Portfolio of bonds has both a higher average annual return, at 6.13% versus 5.64% for U.S. T-bonds, and a higher standard deviation of returns, at 9.14% versus 8.19% for U.S. T-bonds.

6.5 Inflation and Real Interest Rates

People have long recognized that the prices of goods, services, and assets must be corrected for the effects of inflation in order to make meaningful economic comparisons over time. To correct for the effects of inflation, economists distinguish between what they call **nominal prices,** or prices in terms of some currency, and **real prices,** or prices in terms of purchasing power over goods and services.

Just as we distinguish between nominal and real prices, so too we distinguish between *nominal* and *real* interest rates. The **nominal interest rate** on a bond is the promised amount of money you receive per unit you lend. The **real rate of return** is defined as the nominal interest rate you earn corrected for the change in the purchasing power of money. For

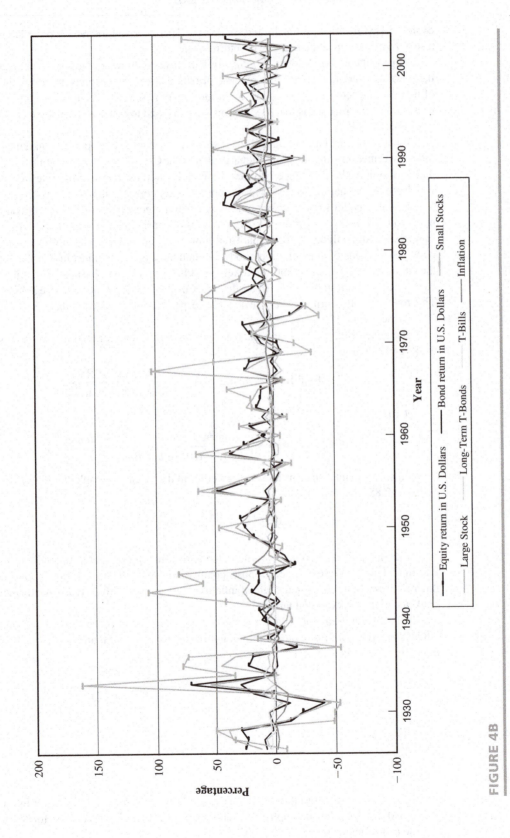

Annual Returns (1926–2003)

example, if you earn a nominal interest rate of 8% per year and the rate of price inflation is also 8% per year, then the real rate of return is zero.

What is the unit of account for computing the real rate of return? It is some standardized basket of consumption goods. The real rate of return, therefore, depends on the composition of the basket of consumption goods. In discussions of real rates of return in different countries, the general practice is to take whatever basket is used to compute the national consumer price index (CPI).

What is the real rate of return if the nominal interest rate is 8% per year, and the rate of inflation as measured by the proportional change in the CPI is 5% per year? Intuition suggests that it is simply the difference between the nominal interest rate and the rate of inflation, which is 3% per year in this case. That is approximately correct, but not exactly so.

To see why, let's compute the real rate of return precisely. For every $100 you invest now, you will receive $108 a year from now. But a basket of consumption goods, which now costs $100, will cost $105 a year from now. How much will your future value of $108 be worth in terms of consumption goods? To find the answer we must divide the $108 by the future price of a consumption basket: $108/$105 = 1.02857 baskets. Thus, for every basket you give up now, you will get the equivalent of 1.02857 baskets a year from now. The real rate of return (baskets in the future per basket invested today) is, therefore, 2.857% per year.

The general formula relating the real rate of return to the nominal rate of interest and the rate of inflation is:

$$1 + \text{Real Rate of Return} = \frac{1 + \text{Nominal Interest Rate}}{1 + \text{Rate of Inflation}}$$

or equivalently,

$$\text{Real Rate} = \frac{\text{Nominal Interest Rate} - \text{Rate of Inflation}}{1 + \text{Rate of Inflation}}$$

Substituting into this formula, we can confirm that in our example the real rate works out to be 2.857% per year:

$$\text{Real Rate} = \frac{0.08 - 0.05}{1.05} = 0.02857 = 2.857\%$$

Note that a fixed-income instrument that is risk free in nominal terms will not be risk free in real terms. For example, suppose a bank offers depositors a risk-free dollar interest rate of 8% per year. Because the rate of inflation is not known with certainty in advance, the bank account is risky in real terms.

If the expected rate of inflation is 5% per year, then the expected real rate of return is 2.857% per year. But if the rate of inflation turns out to be higher than 5%, the realized real rate will be less than 2.857%.

Quick Check 15

Suppose the risk-free nominal interest rate on a one-year U.S. Treasury bill is 6% per year and the expected rate of inflation is 3% per year. What is the expected real rate of return on the T-bill? Why is the T-bill risky in real terms?

To protect against inflation risk, one can denominate interest rates in terms of real goods and services. For example, one can specify that the unit of account for the fixed-income instrument is some commodity.

Some bonds have their interest and principal denominated in terms of the basket of goods and services used to compute the cost of living in a particular country. For example, the government of the United Kingdom has been issuing such **index-linked bonds** since 1981. The U.S. Treasury started issuing such bonds in January 1997. They are called Treasury Inflation Protected Securities (TIPS). The interest rate on these bonds is a risk-free real rate. In September 1998, the U.S. Treasury added inflation-protected savings bonds.

To illustrate how TIPS work, consider one that matures in one year. Assume that it offers a risk-free real rate of interest of 3% per year. The rate of return in dollars is not known with certainty in advance because it depends on the rate of inflation. If the inflation rate turns out to be only 2%, then the realized dollar rate of return will be approximately 5%; if, however, the rate of inflation turns out to be 10%, then the realized dollar rate of return will be approximately 13%.

To summarize, an interest rate is a promised rate of return. Because most bonds offer an interest rate that is denominated in terms of some currency, their real rate of return in terms of consumption goods is uncertain. In the case of inflation-indexed bonds the interest

---

Box 6 — Germany's Inflation-Linked Bonds

Inflation can be a bondholder's worst enemy, unless she happens to own a bond that is inflation-protected. Most bonds work in nominal terms: They entitle the holder to a specific amount of money paid some time in the future. If inflation is stable, it can be incorporated into the bond's nominal interest rate and the bondholder can be assured of the real value of her bond when it comes due. However, if inflation increases significantly and unexpectedly, the money received when the bond is redeemed can have a purchasing power that is much less than was anticipated.

Imagine that Jane lends Mark $900 today. Mark promises to pay Jane back $1,000 in one year. Jane anticipates inflation of 1% during the year, so she expects that the real return on her loan to Mark will be about 10%. As the year goes by, something unexpected happens—the inflation rate turns out to be 50%: All prices increase by 50%. Now when Mark pays Jane back, the $1,000 she receives is only worth $500 in purchasing power: Jane has lost $400 on the loan! She is only able to buy five-ninths of what she could have purchased last year had she spent her money instead of lending it to Mark.

Nowadays, many national governments offer bonds that are "inflation-protected." The yield on these bonds is linked to a price index so that if inflation is higher (or lower) than anticipated, the interest rate can adjust accordingly. The real return on these bonds is therefore much less uncertain. Britain introduced inflation-linked bonds in 1981 and the United States followed in 1997. Several other developed countries, like France, Italy, and most recently Germany now also issue inflation-linked bonds.

Germany's situation is particularly interesting. In the 1920s, the Reichsbank—Germany's central bank at the time—got into the habit of printing too much money. Inflation soon followed: it was 1,024% in 1922 and by 1923 it had increased to 105,700,000,000%! By late 1923, one U.S. dollar was worth about 4.2 billion Reichsmarks (the German currency unit), and paper money was the most inexpensive form of heating fuel available. German bonds issued during the First World War became nearly worthless.

To a large extent this inflationary spiral was self-reinforcing: People expected inflation to be high and so prices continued to rise. The Germans blamed inflation-linked financial contracts for feeding expectations, and in 1948 all such contracts were banned. In the 50 years that followed, the Bundesbank—Germany's new Central Bank—developed a reputation as one of the toughest inflation-fighters in the world.

Germany reintroduced inflation-linked bonds in early 2006. As long as inflation remains low, this is one of the cheapest ways for a government to borrow. The bonds can also be attractive to investors who wish to mitigate inflation risk. Pension funds, for example, may have liabilities that are indexed to inflation. Holding inflation-linked bonds eliminates the possibility that inflation will erode away the value of assets.

Source: "Laying the Ghost of 1923," The Economist, March 14, 2006.

rate is denominated in terms of some basket of consumer goods and it is a risk-free real rate for that basket.

6.6 Interest Rate Equalization

Competition in financial markets ensures that *interest rates* on equivalent assets are the same. Suppose, for instance, that the interest rate the U.S. Treasury currently pays on its one-year T-bills is 4% per year. What interest rate would you expect a major institution such as the World Bank to pay on its one-year dollar-denominated debt securities (assuming they are virtually free of default risk)?

Your answer should be approximately 4% per year.

To see why, suppose that the World Bank offered significantly *less* than 4% per year. Well-informed investors would not buy the bonds issued by the World Bank; instead they would invest in one-year T-bills. Thus, if the World Bank expects to sell its bonds, it must offer at least as high a rate as the U.S. Treasury.

Would the World Bank offer significantly *more* than 4% per year? Assuming that it wants to minimize its borrowing costs, it would offer no more than is necessary to attract investors. Thus, interest rates on any default-free borrowing and lending denominated in dollars with a maturity of one year will tend to be around the same as the 4% per year interest rate on one-year U.S. T-bills.

If there are entities that have the ability to borrow and lend on the *same* terms (e.g., maturity, default risk) at *different* interest rates, then they can carry out **interest-rate arbitrage:** borrowing at the lower rate and lending at the higher rate. Their attempts to expand their activity will bring about an equalization of interest rates.

6.7 The Fundamental Determinants of Rates of Return

There are four main factors that determine rates of return in a market economy:

- *productivity of capital goods*—expected rates of return on mines, dams, roads, bridges, factories, machinery, and inventories;
- *degree of uncertainty regarding the productivity of capital goods;*
- *time preferences of people*—the preference of people for consumption now versus consumption in the future; and
- *risk aversion*—the amount people are willing to give up in order to reduce their exposure to risk.

Let us briefly discuss each of the four factors.

THE EXPECTED PRODUCTIVITY OF CAPITAL GOODS

The first determinant of expected rates of return is the **productivity of capital goods.** Recall that *capital goods* are goods produced in the economy that can be used in the production of other goods. Typical examples of capital goods are mines, roads, canals, dams, power stations, factories, machinery, and inventories. In addition to such physical goods (tangible capital), capital also includes patents, contracts, formulas, brand-name recognition, and production and distribution system designs that contribute to output. Such nonphysical goods (*intangible capital*) are often the result of expenditures on research and development and advertising.

Capital's productivity can be expressed as a percentage per year, called the **rate of return on capital.** This return on capital is the source of the dividends and interest paid to the holders of the stocks, bonds, and other financial instruments issued by firms. These instruments represent claims to the return on capital. The expected rate of return on capital varies over time and place according to the state of technology, the availability of other factors of production such as natural resources and labor, and the demand for the goods and services the capital can produce. *The higher the expected rate of return on capital, the higher the level of interest rates in the economy.*

THE DEGREE OF UNCERTAINTY ABOUT THE PRODUCTIVITY
OF CAPITAL GOODS

The rate of return on capital is always uncertain for a host of reasons. The uncertainties of the weather affect agricultural output; mines and wells often turn out to be "dry"; machines break down from time to time; the demand for a product may change unpredictably due to changing tastes or the development of substitutes; and above all, technological progress that comes from the development of new knowledge is by its nature unpredictable. Even the simple production process of storing goods in inventory for use at a future date is not risk free because an unknown quantity could go bad or become obsolete.

Equity securities represent claims to the profits earned on capital goods. *The greater the degree of uncertainty about the productivity of capital goods, the higher the risk premium on equity securities.*

TIME PREFERENCES OF PEOPLE

Another factor determining the level of rates of return is the preferences of people for consumption now versus consumption in the future. Economists generally assume that the rate of interest would still be positive even if there were no capital goods to invest in and the only reason for borrowing and lending was that people wanted to alter their patterns of consumption over time. In general, the greater the preference of people for current consumption over future consumption, the higher the rate of interest in the economy.

One reason people may prefer greater consumption in the present than in the future is uncertainty about their time of death. They know they are alive now to enjoy their consumption spending, but there is some uncertainty about whether they will be around to enjoy it in the future.

RISK AVERSION

As discussed, the rate of return on capital is always risky. How then is it possible for people to earn a risk-free rate of interest, and what determines the risk-free rate?

The answer is that the financial system provides contractual mechanisms for people who want to invest in risk-free assets to do so by giving up some of their expected return. People who are more tolerant of risk offer to those who are more averse to risk the opportunity to earn a risk-free rate of interest in return for accepting a rate that is lower than the average expected rate of return on risky assets. The greater the degree of risk aversion of the population, the higher the risk premium required, and the lower will be the risk-free rate of interest.

Quick Check 18

What are the fundamental determinants of the rate of interest?

7 Financial Intermediaries

Financial intermediaries are firms whose primary business is to provide customers with financial products and services that cannot be obtained more efficiently by transacting directly in securities markets. Among the main types of intermediaries are banks, investment companies, and insurance companies. Their products include checking accounts, loans, mortgages, mutual funds, and a wide range of insurance contracts.

Perhaps the simplest example of a financial intermediary is a mutual fund, which pools the financial resources of many small savers and invests their money in securities. The mutual fund has substantial economies of scale in record keeping and in executing purchases and sales of securities and, therefore, offers its customers a more efficient way of investing in securities than the direct purchase and sale of securities in the markets.

7.1 Banks

Banks are today the largest (in terms of assets) and oldest of all financial intermediaries. The earliest banks appeared hundreds of years ago in the towns of Renaissance Italy. Their main function was to serve as a mechanism for clearing and settling payments, thereby facilitating the trade in goods and services that had started to flourish in Italy at that time. The early banks evolved from money changers.[5] Indeed, the word *bank* comes from *banca,* the Italian word for "bench" because money changers worked at benches in converting currencies.

Most firms called banks today, however, perform at least two functions: They take deposits and make loans. In the United States they are called **commercial banks.**

In some countries banks are virtually all-purpose financial intermediaries, offering customers not just transaction services and loans, but also mutual funds and insurance of every kind. In Germany, for example, *universal banks* fulfill virtually all of the functions performed by the more specialized intermediaries to be discussed in the remaining sections of this chapter.

Indeed, it is becoming increasingly difficult to differentiate among the various financial firms doing business around the world on the basis of what type of intermediary or financial service provider they are. Thus, although Deutsche Bank is classified as a universal bank, it performs pretty much the same set of functions around the world as does Merrill Lynch, which is usually classified as a broker/dealer.

7.2 Other Depository Savings Institutions

Depository savings institutions, thrift institutions, or simply *thrifts* are the terms used to refer collectively to savings banks, savings and loan associations (S&Ls), and credit unions. In the United States, they compete with commercial banks in both their deposit and lending activities. U.S. thrifts specialize in making home mortgage and consumer loans. In other countries there is a variety of special-purpose savings institutions that are similar to the thrifts and credit unions in the United States.

---

[5]An excellent survey of what historians have discovered about the origins of banking can be found in Raymond de Roover, "New Interpretations of the History of Banking," *Business, Banking, and Economic Thought in Late Medieval and Early Modern Europe* (Chicago: The University of Chicago Press, 1974).

7.3 Insurance Companies

Insurance companies are intermediaries whose primary function is to allow households and businesses to shed specific risks by buying contracts called insurance policies that pay cash compensation if certain specified events occur. Policies that cover accidents, theft, or fire are called *property and casualty* insurance. Policies that cover sickness or the inability to work are called *health and disability* insurance, and policies that cover death are called *life insurance.*

Insurance policies are assets of the households and businesses that buy them, and they are liabilities of the insurance companies that sell them. Payments made to insurance companies for the insurance they provide are called *premiums.* Because customers pay insurance premiums before benefits are received, insurance companies have the use of the funds for periods of time ranging from less than a year to several decades. Insurance companies invest the premiums they collect in assets such as stocks, bonds, and real estate.

7.4 Pension and Retirement Funds

The function of a pension plan is to replace a person's preretirement earnings when combined with Social Security retirement benefits and private savings. A pension plan can be sponsored by an employer, a labor union, or an individual.

Pension plans are classified into two types: defined contribution and defined benefit. In a **defined-contribution pension plan,** each employee has an account into which the employer and usually the employee make regular contributions. At retirement, the employee receives a benefit whose size depends on the accumulated value of the funds in the retirement account.

In a **defined-benefit pension plan,** the employee's pension benefit is determined by a formula that takes into account years of service to the employer and, in most cases, wages or salary. A typical benefit formula would be 1% of average retirement salary for each year of service.

The sponsor of a defined-benefit plan or an insurance company hired by the sponsor guarantees the benefits and, thus, absorbs the investment risk. In some countries, such as Germany, Japan, and the United States, a government or quasi-governmental agency backs the sponsor's guarantee of pension benefits up to specified limits.

7.5 Mutual Funds

A **mutual fund** is a portfolio of stocks, bonds, or other assets purchased in the name of a group of investors and managed by a professional investment company or other financial institution. Each customer is entitled to a pro rata share of any distributions and can redeem his or her share of the fund at any time at its then current market value.

The company that manages the fund keeps track of how much each investor has and reinvests all distributions received according to the rules of the fund. In addition to divisibility, record keeping, and reinvestment of receipts, mutual funds provide an efficient means of diversification.

There are two types of mutual funds: *open end* and *closed end.* Open-end mutual funds stand ready to redeem or issue shares at their net asset value (NAV), which is the market value of all securities held divided by the number of shares outstanding. The number of shares outstanding of an open-end fund changes daily as investors buy new or redeem old shares.

Closed-end mutual funds do not redeem or issue shares at NAV. Shares of closed-end funds are traded through brokers just like other common stocks, and their prices can, therefore, differ from NAV.

7.6 Investment Banks

Investment banks are firms whose primary function is to help businesses, governments, and other entities raise funds to finance their activities by issuing securities. Investment banks also facilitate and sometimes initiate mergers of firms or acquisitions of one firm by another.

Investment banks often *underwrite* the securities they distribute. Underwriting means insuring. In the case of securities, underwriting means committing to buy them at a guaranteed future price.

In many countries, universal banks perform the functions of U.S. investment banks, but in the United States the Glass Steagall Act of 1933 prohibited commercial banks from engaging in most underwriting activities. In recent years, however, commercial banks in the United States have again been permitted to engage in some of these activities.

7.7 Venture Capital Firms

Venture capital firms are similar to investment banks, except their clients are startup firms rather than large corporations. Young firms with inexperienced managers often need considerable advice in running their business in addition to financing. Venture capital firms provide both.

Venture capitalists invest their funds in new businesses and help the management team get the firm to the point at which it is ready to "go public"—that is, sell shares of stock to the investing public. Once that point is reached, the venture capital firm will typically sell its stake in the corporation and move on to the next new venture.

7.8 Asset Management Firms

Asset management firms are also called *investment management firms.* They advise and often administer mutual funds, pension funds, and other asset pools for individuals, firms, and governments. They may be separate firms or they may be a division within a firm, such as a trust company that is part of a bank, insurance company, or brokerage firm.

7.9 Information Services

Many financial service firms provide information as a by-product of their main activities, but there are firms that specialize in providing information. The oldest information service firms are rating agencies, such as Moody's and Standard & Poor's for the securities business and Best's for the insurance industry. A more recent growth sector is the firms or divisions within firms offering analysis of financial data (such as Bloomberg and Reuters) or performance statistics on mutual funds (such as Lipper, Morningstar, and SEI).

8 Financial Infrastructure and Regulation

All social activity is conducted within the bounds of certain rules of behavior. Some rules are codified in the law and constrain the financial system as they constrain all other realms of economic activity. Prime among these are laws outlawing fraud and enforcing contracts. Moreover, these laws may differ from country to country and change over time. They are part of the legal infrastructure of a society, and we generally treat them as outside the financial system, although changes in the law are sometimes a response to changing needs for the operation of the financial system.

The financial infrastructure consists of the legal and accounting procedures, the organization of trading and clearing facilities, and the regulatory structures that govern the relations among the users of the financial system. Those who take a historical perspective of several centuries have identified the evolution of the infrastructure of the financial system as a key factor in understanding the economic development of nations.

Some regulatory tasks are performed by private sector organizations and some are performed by governmental organizations. The performance of some regulatory tasks that are legally assigned to government are delegated to private sector organizations. This is true in the United States as well as in other countries. Some of these private sector organizations are professional associations with special expertise such as the Financial Accounting Standards

Board in the United States, some are securities exchanges, and some are trade associations such as the International Swap Dealers Association (ISDA).

As in other areas of the economic system, so too in the financial system, government can play a useful role in promoting economic efficiency. However, successful public policy depends importantly on recognizing the limits of what government can do to improve efficiency and on recognizing when government *inaction* is the best choice.

8.1 Rules for Trading

Rules for trading securities are usually established by organized exchanges and then sometimes given the sanction of law. These rules serve the function of standardizing procedures so that the costs of transacting are kept to a minimum. Ideally, the rules are well thought out to promote low-cost trading, but sometimes they are seemingly arbitrary. Even arbitrary rules, however, are usually preferable to no rules at all.

8.2 Accounting Systems

To be useful, financial information must be presented in a standard format. The discipline that studies the reporting of financial information is called *accounting*. Accounting systems are perhaps the most important part of the infrastructure of the financial system.

Not surprisingly, the earliest accounting systems developed in parallel with the development of financial contracting. Archaeologists have found elaborate and detailed accounts of financial transactions dating back to ancient Babylon (around 2000 B.C.). The development of *double-entry bookkeeping*—a major leap forward in accounting systems—occurred in Renaissance Italy in response to the need to keep track of the complex financial transactions arising from trade and banking.

9 Governmental and Quasi-Governmental Organizations

As the maker and enforcer of a society's laws, government is ultimately responsible to regulate the financial system. As demonstrated in the previous section, there are some regulatory tasks that are delegated to private sector organizations such as trade or industry associations or the securities exchanges. This is true in the United States as well as in other countries.

For example, in the United States, the *Securities Exchange Commission* (SEC) establishes the precise disclosure requirements that must be satisfied for a public offering of securities. Other countries have similar regulatory bodies.

However, in addition to their role as regulators of the financial system, governments use the financial system to achieve other public policy goals. An example is the use of monetary policy to achieve national targets for economic growth or employment. In the following sections we describe some of the main governmental organizations that either seek to regulate the operation of some part of the financial system or use the financial system as the principal means of achieving other economic goals.

9.1 Central Banks

Central banks are intermediaries whose primary function is to promote public policy objectives by influencing certain financial market parameters such as the supply of the local currency. In some countries the central bank is subject to the direct control of the executive body of government; in others it is semiautonomous.[6]

---

[6]In the United States, the central bank has a great deal of autonomy from the government. It consists of 12 regional banks and a seven-member board of governors in Washington, DC. All seven members of the board of governors are, however, appointed by the president of the United States and confirmed by the Senate.

In many countries the central bank is identifiable through its title: the Bank of England, the Bank of Japan, and so on. But in the United States the central bank is called the *Federal Reserve System* (or the "Fed" for short), and in Sweden the *Riksbank*.

A central bank is usually at the heart of a country's payments system. It provides the supply of local currency and operates the clearing system for the banks. An efficient payments system requires at least a moderate degree of price stability. Central banks, therefore, usually view this as their primary goal. But central banks in many countries are also expected to promote the goals of full employment and economic growth. In these countries, central banks must balance the sometimes conflicting goals of price stability and full employment.

9.2 Special-Purpose Intermediaries

This group of organizations includes entities that are set up to encourage specific economic activities by making financing more readily available or by guaranteeing debt instruments of various sorts. Examples are government agencies that make loans or guarantee loans to farmers, students, small businesses, new home buyers, and so on.

A different class of governmental organization is the agencies that are designed to insure bank deposits. Their main function is to promote economic stability by preventing a breakdown in part or all of the financial system.

The worst-case scenario is a banking panic. Depositors are content to leave their deposits in banks as long as they are confident that their money is safe and accessible. However, depositors know that the bank is holding illiquid and risky assets as collateral for its obligation to depositors. If they believe that they will not be able to get back the full value of their deposits, then depositors will race to be first in line to withdraw their money.

This forces the bank into liquidating some of its risky assets. If the collateral assets are illiquid, then being forced to liquidate them quickly means that the bank will have to accept less than full value for them. If one bank does not have sufficient funds to pay off its depositors, then contagion can set in, and other banks are then faced with a run. However, such a contagion problem occurs for the banking system as a whole only if there is a "flight to currency," in which people refuse to hold deposits of *any* bank and insist on having currency.

9.3 Regional and World Organizations

Several international bodies currently exist for the purpose of coordinating the financial policies of national governments. Perhaps the most important is the Bank for International Settlements (BIS) in Basel, Switzerland, whose objective is to promote uniformity of banking regulations.

In addition, two official international agencies operate in the international financial markets to promote growth in trade and finance: the International Monetary Fund (IMF) and the International Bank for Reconstruction and Development (World Bank). The IMF monitors economic and financial conditions in member countries, provides technical assistance, establishes rules for international trade and finance, provides a forum for international consultation, and most important, provides resources that permit lengthening the time necessary for individual members to correct imbalances in their payments to other countries.

The World Bank finances investment projects in developing countries. It raises funds primarily by selling bonds in developed countries and then makes loans for projects that must meet certain criteria designed to encourage economic development.

Summary

The financial system is the set of markets and intermediaries used by households, firms, and governments to implement their financial decisions. It includes the markets for stocks, bonds, and other securities, as well as financial intermediaries such as banks and insurance companies.

Funds flow through the financial system from entities that have a surplus of funds to those that have a deficit. Often these fund flows take place through a financial intermediary.

There are six core functions performed by the financial system:

- To provide ways to *transfer economic resources* through time, across borders, and among industries.
- To provide ways of *managing risk.*
- To provide ways of *clearing and settling payments* to facilitate trade.
- To provide a mechanism for the *pooling of resources* and for the *subdividing* of shares in various enterprises.
- To provide *price information* to help coordinate decentralized decision making in various sectors of the economy.
- To provide ways of *dealing with the incentive problems* created when one party to a transaction has information that the other party does not or when one party acts as agent for another.

The fundamental economic force behind financial innovation is competition, which generally leads to improvements in the way financial functions are performed.

The basic types of financial assets traded in markets are *debt, equity,* and *derivatives:*

- Debt instruments are issued by anyone who borrows money—firms, governments, and households.
- Equity is the claim of the owners of a firm. Equity securities issued by corporations are called common stocks.
- Derivatives are financial instruments such as options and futures contracts that derive their value from the prices of one or more other assets.

An interest rate is a promised rate of return, and there are as many different interest rates as there are distinct kinds of borrowing and lending. Interest rates vary depending on the unit of account, the maturity, and the default risk of the credit instrument. A *nominal* interest rate is denominated in units of some currency; a *real* interest rate is denominated in units of some commodity or basket of goods and services. Bonds that offer a fixed nominal interest rate have an uncertain real rate of return; and inflation-indexed bonds offering a fixed real interest rate have an uncertain nominal rate of return.

There are four main factors that determine rates of return in a market economy:

- *productivity of capital goods*—expected rates of return on mines, dams, roads, bridges, factories, machinery, and inventories;
- *degree of uncertainty regarding the productivity of capital goods;*
- *time preferences of people*—the preference of people for consumption now versus consumption in the future; and
- *risk aversion*—the amount people are willing to give up in order to reduce their exposure to risk.

Indexing is an investment strategy that seeks to match the returns of a specified stock market index.

Financial intermediaries are firms whose primary business is to provide customers with financial products that cannot be obtained more efficiently by transacting directly in securities markets. Among the main types of intermediaries are banks, investment companies, and insurance companies. Their products include checking accounts, loans, mortgages, mutual funds, and a wide range of insurance contracts.

Key Terms

- over-the-counter markets
- flow of funds
- moral hazard
- adverse selection
- life annuities
- principal-agent problem
- collateralization
- fixed-income instruments
- money market
- capital market
- liquidity
- residual claim
- limited liability
- derivatives
- call option
- put option
- forward contracts
- mortgage rate
- commercial loan rate
- unit of account
- maturity

- default risk
- exchange rate
- yield curve
- yield spread
- capital gain
- capital loss
- nominal prices
- real prices
- nominal interest rate
- real rate of return
- index-linked bonds
- interest-rate arbitrage
- productivity of capital goods
- rate of return on capital
- commercial banks
- defined-contribution pension plan
- defined-benefit pension plan
- mutual fund
- investment banks
- market-weighted stock indexes

Answers to Quick Check Questions

Quick Check 1   A depositor puts $5,000 into a bank account and you take a $5,000 student loan from the bank. Trace this flow of funds in Figure 1.

Answer: The funds flow from the depositor (a surplus unit) to a financial intermediary, and then from the intermediary to you (a deficit unit).

Quick Check 2   Give an example of a transfer of resources over time that takes place through the financial system. Is there a more efficient way for this transfer of resources to be handled?

Answer: An example would be a young person saving for his or her own retirement by saving money in a bank account. A more efficient way might be for the individual to save for retirement through an insurance company or mutual fund retirement account whose sole function is to provide retirement income.

Quick Check 3   Give an example of a transfer of risk that takes place through the financial system.

Answer: Whenever anyone buys an insurance policy, risk is being transferred.

Quick Check 4   Would you accept an IOU from me in payment for a good or service that I buy from you? What factors will determine the answer?

Answer: The answer depends upon the size of the transaction and the nature of the IOU. If our transaction is very small in size, I will be less concerned with the riskiness of the IOU, as my exposure is small. However, for larger transactions, I would want a guarantee of your IOU from a financial institution. I would accept payment by credit card because I am sure to receive payment from the bank issuing the credit card, but I might not be willing to accept a personal check unless you are a long-standing customer with whom I have done a lot of business.

Quick Check 5   Give an example of an investment that would not be undertaken if it were not possible to pool the savings of many different households.

Answer: Any investment that requires a large minimum investment to complete. One example would be a bridge or a dam.

Quick Check 6   Give an example of a financial transaction that provides important information to parties not involved in the transaction.

Answer: Whenever shares of stock are traded on a competitive stock market, information is being conveyed to everyone who can observe the price about how much investors think the stock is worth.

Quick Check 7   Give an example of how the problem of moral hazard might prevent you from getting financing for something you want to do. Can you think of a way of overcoming the problem?

Answer: If you ask a bank to lend you 100% of the funds you need to enter a certain business venture, the bank may refuse for fear that you will take large risks with its money. One way of overcoming the problem is to offer the bank additional collateral—your own personal assets—or a third-party guarantee of the loan.

Quick Check 8   Suppose a bank offered to make loans to potential borrowers without checking their credit history. What would be true of the types of borrowers they would attract compared with banks that did check credit history? Would such a bank charge the same interest rate on loans as banks that check credit history?

Answer: The bank that did no credit checks would attract borrowers with a higher probability of defaulting on their loans. To survive as a viable business such a bank would have to charge higher interest rates.

Quick Check 9   If you get financial planning advice from your insurance agent, how does this give rise to a principal-agent problem? Can you think of a way of overcoming the problem?

Answer: Insurance agents want you to buy insurance products on which they earn commissions, even if those products are not necessarily in your best interest. To avoid this conflict of interest you should seek financial advice from a qualified adviser who does not profit from selling you a particular financial product other than good advice.

Quick Check 10   What are the defining features of debt, equity, and derivative securities?

Answer: Debt instruments are issued by anyone who borrows money. Equity is the claim of the owners of a firm. Derivatives are financial instruments that derive their value from the prices of one or more other assets such as equity securities, fixed-income securities, foreign currencies, or commodities.

Quick Check 11   In the previous example, what does the change in the exchange rate have to be at year's end for the Japanese investor to earn exactly 3% per year on the investment in U.K. bonds?

Answer:

$$\frac{\left(£109 \times \text{Future Yen Price of Pound}\left(\frac{¥}{£}\right)\right) - ¥15{,}000}{¥15{,}000} = 0.03$$

Solving for the future yen price of the pound we obtain:

$$\text{Future Yen Price of Pound} = 141.74\left(\frac{¥}{£}\right)$$

Quick Check 12 Go on-line to Bloomberg.com and discover what the level and shape of the U.S. Treasury yield curve are. Do the same for the Japanese and German Treasury yield curves.

Answer: Answers will vary.

Quick Check 13 Look on Bloomberg.com and discover what the yield spreads are between corporate bonds and U.S. treasury bonds.

Answer: Answers will vary.

Quick Check 14 You invest a stock costing $50. It pays a cash dividend during the year of $1, and you expect its price to be $60 at year's end. What is your expected rate of return? If the stock's price is actually $40 at year's end, what is your realized rate of return?

Answer:

$$\text{Expected Rate of Return} = \frac{\$1 + \$60 - \$50}{\$50} = 0.22 \text{ or } 22\%$$

$$\text{Realized Rate of Return} = \frac{\$1 + \$40 - \$50}{\$50} = -0.18 \text{ or } -18\%$$

Quick Check 15 Suppose the risk-free nominal interest rate on a one-year U.S. Treasury bill is 6% per year and the expected rate of inflation is 3% per year. What is the expected real rate of return on the T-bill? Why is the T-bill risky in real terms?

Answer:

$$\text{Real Rate} = \frac{\text{Nominal Interest Rate} - \text{Rate of Inflation}}{1 + \text{Rate of Inflation}} = 0.02913 = 2.913\%$$

Because the actual inflation rate is not known when the nominal interest rate is set, investors can never know for certain what their real return will be (it will depend on what inflation actually turns out to be).

Quick Check 16 Suppose that the real rate of interest on TIPS is 3.5% per year and the expected rate of inflation in the United States is 4% per year. What is the expected nominal rate of return on these bonds?

Answer: 1 + Nominal Interest Rate = (1 + Real Interest Rate) × (1 + Rate of Inflation) hence, Nominal Interest Rate = (1.035 × 1.04) − 1 = 0.0764 = 7.64%

Quick Check 17 Suppose you have $10,000 in a bank account earning an interest rate of 3% per year. At the same time you have an unpaid balance on your credit card of $5,000 on which you are paying an interest rate of 17% per year. What is the arbitrage opportunity you face?

Answer: You could take $5,000 out of your bank account and pay down your credit-card balance. You would give up 3% per year in interest earnings ($150 per year), but you would

save 17% per year in interest expenses ($850 per year). So the arbitrage opportunity is worth $700 per year.

Quick Check 18   What are the fundamental determinants of the rate of interest?

Answer:

- The *productivity of capital goods*—expected rates of return on mines, dams, roads, bridges, factories, machinery, and inventories;
- the *degree of uncertainty regarding the productivity of capital goods;*
- *time preferences of people*—the preference of people for consumption now versus consumption in the future; and
- *risk aversion*—the amount people are willing to give up in order to reduce their exposure to risk.

Sources of Financial Data

Thanks to the Internet, there is a vast amount of free information about the financial system that is accessible at the click of a computer mouse. Here is a list of some of them:

Flow of Funds Accounts of the United States
http://www.federalreserve.gov/releases/z1/

Investment Company Fact Book
http://www.icifactbook.org/

U.S. and International Government Yield Curves
http://www.bloomberg.com/markets/rates/

U.S. and International Markets and Funds Data
http://markets.ft.com/markets/overview.asp

Questions and Problems

What Is the Financial System?

1. How does the financial system contribute to economic security and prosperity in a capitalist society?

The Flow of Funds

2. Suppose your great uncle decides to take this month's savings and purchase a bond issued by the Gateway Computer Company to finance an increase in computer components in their new factory. Describe how this exchange can be analyzed in the flow-of-funds framework.

The Functional Perspective

3. Would you be able to get a student loan without someone else offering to guarantee it?
4. Give an example of a new business that would not be able to get financing if insurance against risk were not available.
5. Suppose you invest in a real-estate development deal. The total investment is $100,000. You invest $20,000 of your own money and borrow the other $80,000 from the bank. Who bears the risk of this venture and why?
6. Give an example of how the problem of moral hazard might prevent you from getting financing for something you want to do. Can you think of a way of overcoming this problem?

7. Give an example of how the problem of adverse selection might prevent you from getting financing for something you want to do. Can you think of a way of overcoming this problem?

8. Give an example of how the principal-agent problem might prevent you from getting financing for something you want to do. Can you think of a way of overcoming this problem?

9. Give an example of how each of the six functions of the financial system are performed more efficiently today than they were in the time of Adam Smith (1776).

10. You are living in the United States and are thinking of traveling to Germany 6 months from now. You can purchase an option to buy euros now at a fixed rate of $1.50 per euro 6 months from now. How is the option like an insurance policy?

Financial Innovation and the "Invisible Hand"

11. Do you agree with Adam Smith's view that society can rely more on the "invisible hand" than on government to promote economic prosperity?

12. Why is it that a country's postage stamps are not as good a medium of exchange as its paper currency?

13. Who is hurt if I issue counterfeit U.S. dollars and use them to purchase valuable goods and services?

14. Some say the only criterion to use in predicting what will serve as money in the future is the real resource cost of producing it, including the transaction costs of verifying its authenticity. According to this criterion what do you think will be the money of the future?

Financial Markets

15. *Challenge Question:* Suppose Delta Airlines signs a contract to purchase 50 new Boeing 787 planes at fixed negotiated prices and with fixed delivery dates over the next five years. In addition the contract has a special clause stating that an additional 20 planes may be purchased at the buyer's discretion. The clause gives Delta the ability to buy four more planes each year for a 5 percent premium to the prices set for the original 50 planes. What sort of derivative security does this special clause represent? What is the primary factor that will determine the value of this clause over the life of the contract? What value does this clause have in terms of Delta's risk management?

Financial Market Rates

16. Should all governments issue debt that is indexed to their domestic price level? Is there a moral hazard problem that citizens face with regard to their public officials when government debt is fixed in units of the domestic currency?

17. Use the Internet to answer the following question by navigating to the URL: (http://markets.ft.com/ft/markets/researchArchive.asp?report=Gov&cat=BR). From the data on *bid yields* plot the German, Japanese, and American yield curves and summarize the major differences in the term structure.

Financial Intermediaries

18. Describe your country's system for financing higher education. What are the roles played by households, voluntary nonprofit organizations, businesses, and government?

19. Describe your country's system for financing residential housing. What are the roles played by households, businesses, and government?

20. Describe your country's system for financing new enterprises. What are the roles played by households, businesses, and government?

Financial Infrastructure and Regulation

21. How does a competitive stock market accomplish the result that Adam Smith describes? Should the stock market be regulated? How and why?

Governmental and Quasi-Governmental Organizations

22. The structure of central banking in Europe has undergone a major transformation over the past few years as twelve countries have joined together to operate under the European Union's (EU) Economic and Monetary Union (EMU) and now conduct transactions in a new single currency, the euro. Navigate the Internet to the official Web site of the European Central Bank at the URL: (http://www.ecb.int). Find the background material on the organization of the ECB and describe briefly the makeup and role of it's Governing Council. Name the two EU member states to become the most recent members of the euro area.

APPENDIX

Alternative Stock Market Indexes

In the United States, perhaps the stock index most often cited in the news is the Dow Jones Industrial Index (DJI). It is an index of the prices of 30 stocks of major industrial U.S. corporations. The DJI has two major defects that limit its usefulness as a benchmark for measuring stock performance. One is that it is not broadly diversified enough to accurately reflect the wide spectrum of stocks in the United States. The other is that it corresponds to a portfolio strategy that is unsuitable as a performance benchmark.

Most investment professionals, therefore, prefer to use other indexes such as the Standard and Poor's 500 (S&P 500) as a performance benchmark. The S&P 500 index corresponds to a portfolio of 500 stocks selected from among the largest public corporations in the United States, with dollar amounts invested in each in proportion to their shares of the total market value.

To illustrate the construction of these two types of indexes and to compare them, let us simplify matters by analyzing a hypothetical two-stock index. The two stocks in the index are IBM (International Business Machines) and HPQ (Hewlett-Packard Company). The relevant data on the two stocks are presented in Table A.1.

The DJI-type index is computed by taking the average current price of a share, dividing by the average price in the base year, and multiplying the result by 100.

$$\text{DJI-Type Index} = \frac{\text{Average of Current Stock Prices}}{\text{Average of Stock Prices in Base Year}} \times 100$$

Let us say that in the base year the prices were $100 per share for IBM and $50 for HPQ. The average price per share, computed by adding the two prices and dividing by 2, is, therefore, $75. A year later, the prices are $50 per share for IBM and $110 per share for HPQ, and the average is $80. The DJI-type index would, therefore, show a value of 106.67, indicating an increase of 6.67%.

$$\text{DJI-Type Index} = \frac{(50 + 110)/2}{(100 + 50)/2} \times 100 = \frac{80}{75} \times 100 = 106.67$$

The DJI-type index assumes that the benchmark portfolio consists of one share of each stock. Had investors bought one share of IBM stock and one share of HPQ in the base year, then their portfolio would have increased in value by 6.67%. Such a portfolio is not

TABLE A.1   Data for Constructing Stock Price Indexes

Company	Stock Price		Number of Shares	Market Value	
	Base Year	Now		Base Year	Now
IBM	$100	$50	200 million	$20 billion	$10 billion
HPQ	$50	$110	100 million	$5 billion	$11 billion
			Total	$25 billion	$21 billion

a natural benchmark for measuring performance, because the total value of all stocks declined from $25 billion to $21 billion in our example, which is a 16% decline.

Investment professionals typically use a market-weighted index as a benchmark for measuring the performance of common stock mutual funds. **Market-weighted stock indexes** represent the price performance of a portfolio that holds each stock in proportion to its total market value. In the preceding example, IBM accounted for 80% of the total value of the stock market and HPQ for 20%. A market-weighted index gives each stock these weights:

$$\text{S\&P-Type Index} = \left(\text{Weight of IBM} \times \frac{\text{Current Price of IBM}}{\text{IBM's Price in Base Year}} \right.$$

$$\left. + \text{Weight of HPQ} \times \frac{\text{Current Price of HPQ}}{\text{HPQ's Price in Base Year}} \right) \times 100$$

$$= (0.8 \times 0.5 + 0.2 \times 2.2) \times 100 = 84$$

Thus, this index shows a 16% decline, which accurately reflects what has happened to the total market value of all stocks.

Alternative Stock Market Indexes

23. Assume there are only two stocks traded in the stock market, and you are trying to construct an index to show what has happened to stock prices. Let us say that in the base year the prices were $20 per share for stock 1 with 100 million shares outstanding and $10 for stock 2 with 50 million shares outstanding. A year later, the prices are $30 per share for stock 1 and $2 per share for stock 2. Using the two different methods explained in the chapter, compute stock indexes showing what has happened to the overall stock market. Which of the two methods do you prefer and why?

Suggested Readings

Crane, D., K. Froot, S. Mason, R. C. Merton, A. Perold, Z. Bodie, E. Sirri, and P. Tufano. *The Global Financial System: A Functional Perspective.* Boston: Harvard Business School Press, 1995.

Kohn, M. *Financial Institutions and Markets.* 2nd Ed. Oxford University Press, 2004.

Merton, R. C., and Z. Bodie. "Design of Financial Systems: Toward a Synthesis of Function and Structure." *Journal of Investment Management* 3, 1st Quarter 2005.

Miller, M. *Financial Innovations & Market Volatility.* Cambridge: Blackwell, 1991.

Managing Financial Health and Performance

OBJECTIVES

- To contrast the economic and accounting models of the firm.
- To show how accounting information can be useful to the financial decision maker when used with care.
- To understand the purpose and process of financial planning.
- To understand why firms need working capital and how to manage it to maximize shareholder value.

CONTENTS

From Chapter 3 of *Financial Economics*, 2/e. Zvi Bodie, Robert C. Merton, David L. Cleeton.
Copyright © 2008 by Pearson Prentice Hall. All rights reserved.

Much of the information about businesses and other organizations available to financial decision makers comes in the form of standard financial statements published in annual and quarterly reports to shareholders. These financial statements—balance sheets, income statements, and statements of cash flow—are prepared according to rules established by the accounting profession, and it is, therefore, important to understand what those rules are. But financial analysts sometimes disagree with how the accounting profession has decided to measure certain key financial variables. The most fundamental disagreement is about how to measure the values of assets and liabilities.

In this chapter we review basic financial statements and show how to use them as templates for financial planning. We begin by reviewing current accounting rules. We then examine how accounting measures of value and income can differ from the underlying economic concepts needed to make good financial decisions. We then construct a financial planning model for a typical manufacturing firm starting from the firm's financial statements for the last few years. Finally, we discuss short-term planning and the management of working capital.

1 Functions of Financial Statements

Financial statements serve three important economic functions:

- *They provide information to the owners and creditors of the firm about the company's current status and past financial performance.*

Although published financial statements rarely provide enough information to enable one to form conclusive judgments about a company's performance, they can provide important clues about aspects of a firm's operations that should be examined more carefully. Sometimes through a careful audit of financial statements it is possible to detect mismanagement and even fraud. For example, by analyzing financial statements an accounting professor uncovered fraud in one of his university's investments.

- *Financial statements provide a convenient way for owners and creditors to set performance targets and to impose restrictions on the managers of the firm.*

Financial statements are used by boards of directors to specify performance targets for management. For example, the board might set targets in terms of a growth rate of accounting earnings or return on equity (*ROE*). Creditors often specify restrictions on management's actions in terms of measures like the ratio of current assets to current liabilities.

- *Financial statements provide convenient templates for financial planning.*

By preparing projections of income statements, balance sheets, and statements of cash flow for the company as a whole, managers can check the overall consistency of separate plans made on a project-by-project basis and estimate the firm's total financing requirements. Although other templates can be substituted for standard financial statements in the planning process, a major advantage of using standard income statements and balance sheets is that the people involved are probably familiar with them from their professional education and training.

Quick Check 1

What are the three basic economic functions served by financial statements?

Box 1 — Backdated Options

Corporate executives' enormous payoffs often result from holding a large amount of stock options in a company, and behaving unethically and—unfortunately in today's world—as a combination of both. Supplying executives with a large share of stock options is usually justified as an incentive for the CEOs to make sure their company performs well in the equity market. After all, if the company's stock price increases, so do the returns of the executive. Yet if these options are manipulated so that they are coincidentally awarded to the executive right before a company's stock price increases, this justification seems moot.

Recent investigations have revealed that it is very likely that companies have falsely report when stock options were assigned to top executives. In particular, firms frequently report that shares are dated as of an opportune low moment right before the price of the firms' stock prices jumped. This process of backdating shares may or may not be illegal in certain circumstances, but it certainly calls into question whether stock option compensation provides the best incentive for a corporate executive to do his or her job. An executive can do a number of things to increase the price of a stock, such as supplying fewer dividends to shareholders. This, in combination with backdating, could significantly alter the real motives behind an executive's actions, and cause firms more trouble in the future.

In the end, giving CEOs stock options in lieu of higher salaries may motivate the executives to better serve the firms, but if the executives can determine precisely when these options are dated with the benefit of twenty-twenty hindsight, what's the point?

Source: Adapted from "Time and Money," *The Economist,* May 30, 2006.

2 Review of Financial Statements

To explain the three basic financial statements, we will use the hypothetical example of Generic Products Corporation (GPC). GPC is a company that was founded 10 years ago to manufacture and sell generic products for the consumer market.

Tables 1, 2, and 3 show GPC's balance sheet, income statement, and statement of cash flows. They are fairly typical of a U.S. manufacturing firm. Let us consider each in turn.

2.1 The Balance Sheet

A firm's balance sheet shows its assets (what it owns) and its liabilities (what it owes) at a point in time. The difference between assets and liabilities is the firm's net worth, also called owners' equity. For a corporation, net worth is called stockholder's equity.

The values of assets, liabilities, and net worth carried on a company's published balance sheet are measured at historical acquisition costs in accordance with generally accepted accounting principles, otherwise known as GAAP. These rules (GAAP) are determined and modified periodically by the Financial Accounting Standards Board. Any U.S. or non-U.S. corporation that wishes to list its shares on an exchange in the United States must conform with the accounting standards and report regularly on its activities by filing financial statements with the Securities and Exchange Commission.

Table 1 presents GPC's balance sheet at two different points in time that bracket the year 20x1. Let us first examine the balance sheet on December 31, 20x0, just before the start of 20x1.

The first section of the balance sheet lists the assets of the firm, beginning with its current assets, defined as cash and other items that will be converted into cash within one year. In GPC's case, cash and marketable securities are valued at $100 million. The other current assets consist of $50 million in receivables, which is the amount owed to GPC by customers,

TABLE 1   GPC Balance Sheet on December 31

Assets	20x0	20x1	Change
Current assets			
Cash and marketable securities	100.0	120.0	20.0
Receivables	50.0	60.0	10.0
Inventories	150.0	180.0	30.0
Total current assets	300.0	360.0	60.0
Property, plant, and equipment (PP&E)	400.0	490.0	90.0
less Accumulated depreciation	100.0	130.0	30.0
Net PP&E	300.0	360.0	60.0
Total assets	600.0	720.0	120.0
Liabilities and Stockholders' Equity			
Current liabilities			
Accounts payable	60.0	72.0	12.0
Short-term debt	90.0	184.6	94.6
Total current liabilities	150.0	256.6	106.6
Long-term debt (8% interest bonds maturing in 20x7)	150.0	150.0	0.0
Stockholders' equity (1 million shares outstanding)	300.0	313.4	13.4
Paid-in capital	200.0	200.0	0.0
Retained earnings	100.0	113.4	13.4
Total liabilities and equity	600.0	720.0	120.0
Other data: Market price per common share	$200.0	$187.2	−$12.8

All figures, except in the final row, are in millions of U.S. dollars.

and $150 million in inventories. Inventories consist of raw materials, goods in process of production, and finished goods.

Next come GPC's noncurrent assets. These consist of property, plant, and equipment. The reported value of these assets net of depreciation is listed as $300 million. Total assets are $600 million.

Next come GPC's liabilities. Liabilities that must be paid off within a year are called current liabilities. For GPC these consist of $60 million in accounts payable, which is the amount owed to its suppliers, and $90 million in short-term debt.

The difference between a firm's current assets and its current liabilities is called net working capital. It does not explicitly appear as an item on the balance sheet. GPC's net working capital at the end of 20x0 was $150 million: current assets of $300 million less current liabilities of $150 million.

The next liability item on GPC's balance sheet is long-term debt, which consists of bonds with a face value of $150 million maturing in 20x7. The interest rate on these bonds is fixed at 8% per year, which means that each year the interest expense associated with them is $12 million. This interest expense shows up on GPC's income statement.

The final category on GPC's balance sheet is shareholders' equity. The paid-in capital, which is the amount that GPC raised in the past by issuing common stock, is $200 million, and the retained earnings, which is the cumulative amount of past earnings that have been retained in the business, is $100 million.

Let us now consider the changes in GPC's balance sheet between December 31, 20x0, and December 31, 20x1. During the year assets grew by 20%, as did accounts payable. GPC's short-term debt increased by $94.6 million, and its long-term debt remained fixed at $150 million. Shareholders' equity increased by $13.4 million, which was the net income retained in the business. No new shares were issued, so paid-in capital stayed the same.

Quick Check 2

What difference would it have made to the end-of-year balance sheet if GPC had issued an additional $50 million in long-term debt during the year and added that amount to its holdings in cash and marketable securities?

2.2 The Income Statement

The income statement summarizes the profitability of the firm over a period of time, in this case a year. Income, profit, and earnings all mean the same thing—the difference between revenues and expenses. The income statement is also known as the statement of earnings or the statement of profit and loss. Table 2 shows that in 20x1 GPC had sales revenue of $200 million, and its net income was $23.4 million.

GPC's expenses are broken down into four major categories. The first is cost of goods sold, which was $110 million. This is the expense GPC incurred in producing the products it sold during the year, and includes the materials and labor used to manufacture them. The difference between revenues and cost of goods sold is called gross margin. GPC's gross margin in 20x1 was $90 million.

The second expense category is general, administrative, and selling (GS&A) expense. This represents the expenses incurred in managing the firm (such as the salaries of the managers) and in marketing and distributing the products produced during the year. The difference between gross margin and GS&A expenses is called operating income. GPC's GS&A expenses in 20x1 were $30 million, and its operating income was, therefore, $60 million.

TABLE 2   GPC Income Statement for 20x1

Sales revenue	$200.0
Cost of goods sold	(110.0)
Gross margin	90.0
General, selling, and administrative expenses	(30.0)
Operating income	60.0
Interest expense	(21.0)
Taxable income	39.0
Income tax	(15.6)
Net income	23.4
Allocation of net income:	
Dividends	10.0
Change in retained earnings	13.4
Earnings per share (1 million shares outstanding)	$23.4

All figures, except those in the final row, are in millions of U.S. dollars.

The third category of expense is the interest expense on GPC's debt, and in 20x1 it was $21 million. After deducting interest expense, GPC's taxable income (i.e., its income subject to corporate income tax) was $39 million.

The fourth and last category of expense is corporate income taxes. GPC paid taxes at an average rate of 40% on its taxable income in 20x1 and, therefore, its corporate income tax was $15.6 million. GPC's net income after taxes was, therefore, $23.4 million. Because there were 1 million shares of GPC stock outstanding, the earnings per share were $23.40.

The income statement also shows that GPC paid cash dividends of $10 million in 20x1. This means that $13.4 million of the net income is retained in the business and shows up as an increase in shareholders' equity in the balance sheet at the end of 20x1. It is important to note that this latter figure ($13.4 million) is not an addition to the cash balance of the firm because net income is not the same as cash flow.

Quick Check 3

What difference would it have made to the income statement and the end-of-year balance sheet if GPC had retained all of its net income instead of paying out cash dividends of $10 million?

2.3 The Cash Flow Statement

The statement of cash flows shows all of the cash that flowed into and out of the firm during a period of time. It differs from the income statement, which shows the firm's revenues and expenses.

The cash flow statement is a useful supplement to the income statement for two reasons. First, it focuses attention on what is happening to the firm's cash position over time. Even very profitable firms can experience financial distress if they run out of cash. Paying attention to the cash flow statement allows the firm's managers and outsiders to see whether the firm is building up or drawing down its cash and to understand why. Often, for example, rapidly growing, profitable firms run short of cash and have difficulty meeting their financial obligations.

The cash flow statement is also useful because it avoids the judgments about revenue and expense recognition that go into the income statement. The income statement is based on accrual accounting methods according to which not every revenue is an inflow of cash and not every expense is an outflow. A firm's reported net income is affected by many judgments on the part of management about issues such as how to value its inventory and how quickly to depreciate its tangible assets and amortize its intangible assets.

The statement of cash flows is not influenced by these accrual accounting decisions. Therefore, by examining the differences between the firm's cash flow statement and its income statement an analyst is able to determine the impact of these accounting decisions.

Let us illustrate by examining Table 3, which presents GPC's cash flow statement for 20x1. It organizes cash flows into three sections: operating activities, investing activities, and financing activities. Let us look at each section in turn.

Cash flow from operating activities (or cash flow from operations) consists of the cash inflows from selling the firm's products less the cash outflows for expenses such as materials and labor. GPC's cash flow from operations in 20xl is $25.4 million, whereas its net income is $23.4 million. Why are these two numbers different?

There are four items that explain the difference between a firm's net income and its cash flow from operations: depreciation charges, the change in accounts receivable, the change in inventories, and the change in accounts payable. Let us consider each of these items for the case of GPC in 20x1.

TABLE 3 GPC Cash Flow Statement for 20x1

Cash Flow from Operating Activities	
Net income	$23.4
+ Depreciation	+30.0
− Increase in accounts receivable	−10.0
− Increase in inventories	−30.0
+ Increase in accounts payable	+12.0
Total cash flow from Operations	25.4
Cash Flow from Investing Activities	
− Investment in plant and equipment	−90.0
Cash Flow from Financing Activities	
− Dividends paid	−10.0
+ Increase in short-term debt	+94.6
Total change in cash and marketable securities	20.0

First, depreciation charges for 20x1 were $30 million. This was a noncash expense deducted from revenues in computing net income. The cash outlays for the plant and equipment that gave rise to the depreciation charges occurred when they were originally purchased, but the depreciation charges are recognized as an expense in each period over their assumed useful life. Therefore, to get from net income to cash flow from operations, we have to add back the depreciation charges.

The second item is an increase in accounts receivable of $10 million. This is the difference between the revenue recognized during the year and the actual cash collected from customers. The revenue figure of $200 million on the income statement means that $200 million worth of goods and services were shipped and billed to customers in 20x1, but only $190 million in cash was collected. Therefore, to get from net income to cash flow from operations, we have to subtract the $10 million increase in accounts receivable.

The third item is an increase in inventories of $30 million. This means the value of inventories at the end of the year was $30 million more than at the beginning. Thus, $30 million in cash was used to purchase or to produce goods that went into inventory. This cash outlay was not accounted for in computing net income. Therefore, to get from net income to cash flow from operations, we have to subtract the $30 million increase in inventories.

The fourth item is an increase in accounts payable of $12 million. This is the difference between GPC's cost of goods sold during the year ($110 million) and the amount of cash it paid to its suppliers and employees. In computing net income, the full $110 million was deducted, but in computing cash flow from operations only the $98 million in cash that it paid out should be deducted. Therefore, to go from net income to cash flow from operations, $12 million must be added back.

Thus, we can see that there is no reason to expect equality between cash flow from operations and net income. To reconcile the two measures, we must adjust net income for the four items detailed previously. Cash flow statements can be particularly important in making comparisons of companies reporting their net income in different countries that have different accrual accounting standards.

The second section of Table 3—cash flows from investing activities—shows GPC's $90 million cash outlay on new plant and equipment in 20x1. The third section—cash

TABLE 4 Summary of Financial Statements

Balance Sheet

Assets = Liabilities + Stockholders' Equity

- A snapshot at a point in time of the value of the firm's assets and liabilities.
- Long-term assets given at historic cost, depreciated over time.

Income Statement

Net Income = Revenues − Expenses

- A record of the flow of revenues and related expenses over the period.
- Use of accrual principles implies that net income usually does not equal net cash flow.

Statement of Cash Flows

Total Cash Flow = Cash from Operating Activities + Cash from Financing Activities + Cash from Investing Activities

- A flow statement showing how much cash has flowed into and out of the firm over the period.
- Each source and use of cash is placed in one of three categories.

flows from financing activities—shows that GPC paid out $10 million in cash dividends to shareholders and raised $94.6 million in cash by increasing its short-term debt.

To summarize, the net impact on GPC's cash balances of its operating, investing, and financing activities was to increase cash by $20 million. GPC's operating activities produced $25.4 million in cash, and GPC increased its borrowing by $94.6 million, so a total of $120 million in cash flowed in. Of that amount, $90 million in cash was used to purchase new plant and equipment and $10 million was used to pay dividends.

> **Quick Check 4**
>
> What difference would it have made to the cash flow statement if GPC had retained all of its net income instead of paying out cash dividends of $10 million?

Table 4 presents a summary of the features of each of the three main financial statements.

2.4 Notes to Financial Statements

When a corporation publishes its financial statements, it includes notes providing greater detail about the accounting methods it has used and the financial condition of the company. Frequently there is more information relevant to understanding the true financial condition of the company in the notes to the financial statements than in the statements themselves.

Some of the specific items commonly found in the notes are the following:

- *An explanation of accounting methods used.* Because firms are allowed some latitude in how to report certain costs (e.g., straight-line versus accelerated depreciation charges or LIFO versus FIFO inventory costing methods), the notes must explain which specific methods the company has actually employed. Moreover, accounting standards often change, and companies restate prior year results in the notes using the new standards.
- *Greater detail regarding certain assets or liabilities.* Notes provide details regarding the conditions and expiration dates for long- and short-term debt, leases, and the like.

Box 2	Pensions Crunch

Actuaries in the world of corporate finance are frequently called on to assess the liabilities associated with a pension fund, and determine what sort of asset portfolio will be required to meet the demands of those liabilities. This process is complex, has had a variable success rate, and has altered the way in which firms provide pensions.

Actuaries make predictions about the many things that could affect the welfare of a pension fund, or at least this is what they are supposed to do. Yet across the world, corporate pension funds have fared terribly in the market. These funds have encountered unforeseen liabilities that have had to be paid, resulting in fewer net gains for the overall fund.

Are all the actuaries in the world incompetent? Well, no. The variables that an actuary must consider are staggering—interest rates, life expectancies, rates of return on alternative investments. All these things and more are considered when making a prediction as to what assets a firm will need in the future to cover a given pension fund's set of liabilities.

Actuaries in the past have tended to recommend that pension funds invest in assets that generated high returns in the short run, but proved risky in the long term. Actuaries' predictions about the assets needed to cover future liabilities therefore proved more variable. The losses associated with some of the funds' performance have led firms to restructure who qualifies for pension benefits. These past results and the resulting worker, and executive, dissatisfaction have produced a new set of ideas among actuaries about how to provide more consistent returns for a pension fund.

These ideas include some basic observations: The amount you make out of a particular fund will not alter the amount that you will owe in the future. For example, if a firm borrows to invest in an asset, the fact that an asset generates a return doesn't affect the fact that the initial liability must be paid off. More generally, many policies that actuaries are now considering involve ways to control and reduce risk. Actuaries now consider liability-driven investing, or investment techniques that reduce the risk associated with large liabilities—if large liabilities have less risk, the predictions about what future assets are required of a firm will be more accurate.

If these policies are properly prudent, the returns from pension funds should be less variable, the predictions actuaries make will be more accurate, and future policies regarding pension fund distribution will be more consistent for workers.

Source: Adapted from "When the Spinning Stops," *The Economist*, January 26, 2006.

- *Information regarding the equity structure of the firm.* Notes explain conditions attached to the ownership of shares, and these can be particularly useful for assessing the vulnerability of the firm to takeovers.
- *Documentation of changes in operations.* Two main activities that can have a great impact on financial statements are acquisitions and divestitures, and the notes explain the impact of these.
- *Off-balance-sheet items.* Financial contracts entered into by the firm that do not appear on the balance sheet, but that can profoundly affect its financial condition, are often disclosed in the notes. Among these are derivative contracts such as forward contracts, swaps, and options, which are typically used to reduce certain risk exposures.

Quick Check 5

What potentially important information about a firm can be found in the footnotes to its financial statements?

Box 3	What Is Fair Value?

Accountants are expected to make fair and accurate reports about a firm's finances, and these reports are supposed to be in a standardized form so that they can be easily compared to the financial statements of other firms. One way that financial statements can be standardized is if all the assets and liabilities a firm owns are reported at a fair value. That is, if the firm's assets and liabilities are reported at existing market prices, individuals can make reasonable comparisons across the assets and liabilities numerous firms hold.

This can become complicated and controversial when firms are asked to assign market prices to particular types of financial instruments and pension liabilities. For example, structured derivative transactions may be assigned market prices, even though complex derivative arrangements are often not traded on secondary markets. The models that firms use to assign market prices to these types of transactions can vary widely from firm to firm—which makes it almost impossible to argue that standardization has taken place.

This modeling-based problem also exists for pension accountants. Some investors are applying pressure on firms to more fully detail the assumptions behind the valuation models, in an effort to make more reasonable comparisons across companies. In the end, standardizing these reporting methods may have to be done in a way that combines fair market prices, as well as some other method of calculating these prices, so investors can increase the confidence in comparisons across firms' assets and liabilities mixes.

Source: Adapted from "Complexity Dogs the Benefits of Fair Value," *Financial Times*, January 12, 2006.

3 Market Values versus Book Values

The official accounting values of assets and shareholders' equity are called **book values**. A company's book value per share is the number we get if we divide the total dollar amount in the shareholders' equity account of the firm's official balance sheet by the number of shares of common stock outstanding.[1]

Thus, in Table 1 we see that the book value per share of GPC stock at the end of 20x1 was $313.40. But the market price of a share of GPC stock at the end of 20x1 was only $187.50. This was the price that investors were willing to pay for a share of GPC common stock. The market value of the stock does not appear on the official balance sheet.

Why doesn't the market price of a company's stock equal its book value? And which of the two values is more relevant to the financial decision maker? We now turn our attention to these important questions.

There are essentially two reasons why the market price of a company's stock does not necessarily equal its book value:

- The book value does not include all of a firm's assets and liabilities.
- The assets and liabilities included on a firm's official balance sheet are (for the most part) valued at original acquisition cost less depreciation, rather than at current market values.

Let us consider each of these reasons separately.

First, the accounting balance sheet often omits some economically significant assets. For example, if a firm builds up a good reputation for the quality and reliability of its products, this will not appear as an asset on the balance sheet. Similarly, if a firm builds up

---

[1]Note that shares outstanding do not include Treasury stock, which are shares of stock that the firm has repurchased.

a knowledge base as the result of past research and development spending or as the result of training its workforce, these too will not appear as assets. These kinds of assets are called **intangible assets,** and clearly they add to the firm's market value and are relevant in decision making.

Accountants do report some intangible assets on the balance sheet, but not at their market values. For example, if a firm buys a patent from another firm, the value of that patent is recorded as an asset and amortized over time. Also, when one firm acquires another firm for a price that exceeds its book value, accountants will record an intangible asset called **goodwill** on the balance sheet of the acquiring firm. The value of goodwill is the difference between the market price of the acquisition and its book value. Despite these cases of intangible assets that are recorded on the accounting balance sheet, many others are not.

The accounting balance sheet also omits some economically significant liabilities. For example, if the firm has lawsuits pending against it, these will not appear on the balance sheet. The existence and amount of such contingent liabilities will at best only be disclosed in the footnotes to the financial statements.

Now let us consider whether it is market value or book value that is relevant for financial decision making. In almost all cases, book values are irrelevant. For example, say three years ago IBM purchased equipment needed for molding computer shells for $3.9 million and today the equipment is carried on its books at $2.6 million, after three years of depreciation. But today, owing to technological change in the manufacture of computer shells, the market value of the machine has fallen to $1.2 million.

Now suppose you are considering replacing the equipment with more modern equipment. What is the relevant value to use to compare the alternatives? If we ignore tax considerations for the moment, we know from first principles in economics that the relevant value is the asset's opportunity cost, which is the asset's value in the best alternative use. Clearly, this value is best approximated by the market value of the equipment of $1.2 million, whereas the book value is essentially irrelevant.

As another example, let us consider your inventory of copper to be used in the manufacturing process of heating furnaces. You paid $29,000 at the beginning of the year for the copper, but today its market value has risen to $60,000. What is the relevant cost to include for the copper in your production decisions? Again, the original cost of $29,000 is not meaningful because the copper could be sold and to replace the inventory will cost $60,000. If you use the copper in production, you are actually using up $60,000 worth of resources.

The difference in value between the two measures can vary drastically depending on the situation. For example, in the case of cash there is literally no difference between book value and market value. In the case of fixed assets, such as specialized plant and equipment, the difference can be, and often is, huge. Thus, the difference between the market and book values of an asset depends on the type of asset. Again, for decision-making purposes, the correct value to use is the market value, whenever available.

It is worth noting that the accounting profession has moved slowly toward market-value–based accounting in an effort to be more relevant to decision makers. For example, assets held by corporations in their pension funds are now reported at current market values rather than acquisition cost. Revaluing and reporting a firm's assets and liabilities at their current market prices is called **marking to market.**

Quick Check 6

Why does the market price of a firm's stock usually differ from its book value?

4 Accounting versus Economic Measures of Income

The distinctions made about market values and book values carry over to our notions of income. A commonsense definition of income is the amount that you could spend during the period while maintaining the wealth with which you started the period. That is, what you could spend from incoming cash and still have the amount you started with remaining at the end of the period. Loosely speaking, this is the definition that the English Nobel Prize–winning economist John R. Hicks used in his classic treatise on the subject and the one that is generally used today by economists.[2] The accounting definition of income or earnings or profits (which all mean the same thing) ignores unrealized gains or losses in the market values of assets and liabilities, such as the increase or decrease in value of your shares of stock or the value of your property over the period.

As an example, suppose your net wages over the year were $100,000, which you spent on your family consumption, but your assets overall declined in value by $60,000. Generally speaking, accountants would ignore the decline in the market value of your assets because it is unrealized. The economist, on the other hand, would say that the decline in value must be counted in the income calculation because it affects your consumption possibilities, which are currently $60,000 less than at the beginning of the year. Thus, your income is only $40,000.

One other feature, often overlooked, is that accounting income allows as an income deduction the interest expense for the cost of borrowed funds, but not a comparable deduction for the equity funds employed. For example, if a company earned $2 million but used $50 million in shareholders' equity to finance the firm's assets at an approximate cost of 10% then from an economic perspective the firm incurred a loss of about $3 million (i.e., $2 m − $50 m × 0.10 = −$3 m). Here is a case in which the accounting profit is positive but the firm is not covering its basic costs, including its costs of capital.

Box 4	Measuring EVA

Economic Value Added (EVA) is a method of measuring the economic performance of a firm. EVA can be thought of as the earnings a company has after accounting for required capital costs. The idea behind this measurement is that a company increases in value only if the return on its capital is greater than the opportunity cost of the capital investment. EVA is one of many measures that firms are using to diagnose their financial health. This measure is very clear, and is easily generated: It is either positive or negative, and is clearly based on standard measurements and not hidden assumptions. That is, the opportunity costs and returns on capital are known statistics that are little disputed.

EVA also makes the full costs a firm faces much more transparent, as well as the additional opportunities a firm has for investment. The problem with EVA is that it is a measure that bases its calculations on the historical record of past expenditures. Thus the calculation provides little information as to how a firm's current investments will likely impact on the future returns a firm will receive. Some argue that such a basis of measurement has a tendency to reward shortsighted decision making.

If the earnings of a firm are currently high, the EVA of the firm will also be high and this doesn't provide an additional incentive to make prudent long-run investments. Thus while EVA is an alternative method of examining economic performance, it isn't a method that, if adopted, will necessarily transform how a firm operates for the better.

Source: Adapted from "A Star to Sail By?," *The Economist*, July 31, 1997.

---

[2]J. R. Hicks, *Value and Capital*, 2nd ed. (New York: Oxford University Press, 1946), p. 172.

5 Returns to Shareholders versus Return on Book Equity

When shareholders of a corporation ask how well their company performed in a particular period (a quarter, a year, or several years), they mean by how much did the company add to their personal wealth in that period. A direct way to measure this is to compute the rate of return on an investment in the company's stock over the period. Recall that we defined the rate of return from investing in a firm's stock as:

$$r = \frac{\text{Ending Price of a Share} - \text{Beginning Price} + \text{Cash Dividend}}{\text{Beginning Price}}$$

This is called **total shareholder returns**.

For example, consider the case of GPC Corp. From observed market data, we know that at the beginning of 20x1 GPC had a market price of $200 per share and at the end of the year after paying dividends the market price was $187.20 per share. Cash dividends for the year were $10; the rate of return on an investment in GPC's stock in 20x1 was, therefore, −1.4% computed as follows:

$$\text{Total Shareholder Returns} = \frac{\$187.20 - \$200 + \$10}{\$200} = -0.014 \text{ or } -1.4\%$$

Traditionally, however, corporate performance has also been measured by looking at a ratio called the *return on equity* (*ROE*). *ROE* is defined as net profit (the bottom line from the company's income statement) divided by the book value of shareholders' equity (the bottom line from the firm's balance sheet).

For GPC's *ROE* we get:

$$ROE = \frac{\text{Net Income}}{\text{Shareholders' Equity}} = \frac{\$23.4 \text{ million}}{\$300 \text{ million}} = 0.078 \text{ or } 7.8\%$$

Thus, we see that there need be no correspondence between a firm's *ROE* in any year and the total rate of return earned by shareholders on their investment in the company's stock.

Quick Check 7

In 20x7 VGI corporation reported earnings per share of $5 and paid a cash dividend to shareholders of $3.00 per share. Its beginning-of-year book value per share was $30, and its market price was $40. At the end of the year, the book value per share was $32 and the market price was $35. Compare VGI's *ROE* and total shareholder returns.

---

6 Analysis Using Financial Ratios

Despite the differences between accounting and finance principles and practices listed previously, a firm's published financial statements can often offer some clues about its financial condition and insights into its past performance that may be relevant for the future.

Box 5	Sarbanes-Oxley

After Enron and other well-known corporate scandals, Congress responded to public outcry for reform by passing the Sarbanes-Oxley statute. The effectiveness and overall worth of this action remains up for debate. The law created the Public Company Accounting Oversight Board, an institution that monitors the work of auditors, largely as a result of Arthur Anderson LLP's actions with regard to the Enron scandal.

The statute also instituted provisions meant to reduce corporate corruption: Corporations can't make loans to executives; executives must certify the account records of their respective firms; and, if someone believes any corruption is occurring and blows the whistle, these individuals can't be persecuted. The law also holds managers and auditors more accountable for their routine actions. In order to comply with the law, however, firms have had to spend tremendous amounts of money. Some estimate the aggregate costs of compliance in the trillions of dollars.

These costs have become a significant problem as today four firms—Ernst & Young, Deloitte, PricewaterhouseCoopers, and KPMG—are responsible for auditing 97% of all large companies in America. The higher prices these auditing firms are now charging, to meet the demand to be in compliance with the law have caused a spillover, increasing the auditing costs for small firms as well. Of course these small firms have fewer additional options outside of using any of the "final four." Some analysts have claimed that the costs associated with adhering to the law will discourage foreign companies from listing on the New York exchange and that the law overly penalizes regular types of business errors.

Many of the costs associated with these legal compliance issues may be expected to decrease once auditors are accustomed to the new regulations. Only time will tell, however, when it comes to seeing how effective Sarbanes-Oxley will be in preventing corporate malfeasance, and whether the costs associated with the law are worthwhile.

Source: Adapted from "A Price Worth Paying?" *The Economist*, May 19, 2005.

In analyzing a firm's performance using its financial statements, it is helpful to define a set of ratios to facilitate comparisons over time and across companies.

We can analyze five main aspects of the firm's performance through ratios: profitability, asset turnover, financial leverage, liquidity, and market value. In Table 5 we present these ratios, and calculate them for GPC.

First are *profitability* ratios. Profitability can be measured with respect to sales (return on sales), assets (return on assets), or its equity base (return on equity). Income here is taken as earnings before interest and taxes (*EBIT*) in the case of return on sales and return on assets, but as net income in the case of return on equity. Also, whenever a financial ratio contains one item from the income statement, which covers a period of time, and another from the balance sheet, which is a "snapshot" at a point in time, the practice is to take the average of the beginning and end-of-year balance sheet figures, and use this average as the denominator.

Second are *asset turnover* ratios, which assess the firm's ability to use its assets productively in generating revenue. Asset turnover is a broad measure, whereas receivable turnover and inventory turnover are specific measures for these particular asset categories.

Third, *financial leverage* ratios highlight the capital structure of the firm, and the extent to which it is burdened with debt. The debt ratio measures the capital structure, and the times interest earned measure indicates the ability of the firm to cover its interest payments.

Fourth, *liquidity* ratios measure the ability of the firm to meet its short-term obligations, or to pay its bills and remain solvent. The main ratios for measuring liquidity are the current ratio and the more stringent quick ratio or acid test, which considers only the most liquid of current assets: cash and marketable securities.

TABLE 5 Classification of Financial Ratios

Ratio	Formula	Calculation	
Profitability			
Return on sales (*ROS*)	$\dfrac{EBIT}{\text{Sales}}$	$\dfrac{\$60}{\$200}$	= 30%
Return on assets (*ROA*)	$\dfrac{EBIT}{\text{Average Total Assets}}$	$\dfrac{\$60}{(\$600 + \$720)\,/\,2}$	= 9.1%
Return on equity (*ROE*)	$\dfrac{\text{Net Income}}{\text{Stockholders' Equity}}$	$\dfrac{\$23.4}{(\$300 + \$313.4)\,/\,2}$	= 7.6%
Asset Turnover			
Receivables turnover	$\dfrac{\text{Sales}}{\text{Average Receivables}}$	$\dfrac{\$200}{(\$50 + \$60)\,/\,2}$	= 3.6 times
Inventory turnover	$\dfrac{\text{Cost of Goods Sold}}{\text{Average Inventory}}$	$\dfrac{\$110}{(\$150 + \$180)\,/\,2}$	= 0.7 times
Asset turnover	$\dfrac{\text{Sales}}{\text{Average Total Assets}}$	$\dfrac{\$200}{(\$600 + \$720)\,/\,2}$	= 0.3 times
Financial Leverage			
Debt	$\dfrac{\text{Total Debt}}{\text{Total Assets}}$	$\dfrac{\$406.6}{\$720}$	= 57%
Times interest earned	$\dfrac{EBIT}{\text{Interest Expense}}$	$\dfrac{\$60}{\$21}$	= 2.9 times
Liquidity			
Current	$\dfrac{\text{Current Assets}}{\text{Current Liabilities}}$	$\dfrac{\$360}{\$256.6}$	= 1.4 times
Quick, or acid test	$\dfrac{\text{Cash} + \text{Receivables}}{\text{Current Liabilities}}$	$\dfrac{\$180}{\$256.6}$	= 0.7 times
Market Value			
Price to earnings	$\dfrac{\text{Price per Share}}{\text{Earnings per Share}}$	$\dfrac{\$187.2}{\$23.4}$	= 8.0
Market to book	$\dfrac{\text{Price per Share}}{\text{Book Value per Share}}$	$\dfrac{\$187.2}{\$313.4}$	= 0.6

Fifth are *market value* ratios, which measure the relation between the accounting representation of the firm and the market value of the firm. The two most common ratios are price to earnings (*P/E*) and market to book (*M/B*).[3]

When analyzing a firm's financial ratios, we need first to establish two things:

- whose perspective to adopt—shareholders, creditors, or some other group of stakeholders.
- what standard of comparison to use as a benchmark.

---

[3]A measure similar to the market to book (M/B) ratio is Tobin's Q ratio, which is named for the American Nobel Prize–winning economist, James Tobin. The ratio is defined as:

$$Q = \text{Market Value of Assets/Replacement Cost}$$

The denominator includes an adjustment to the original cost of assets for inflation.

Benchmarks can be of three types:

- financial ratios of other companies for the same period of time.
- financial ratios of the company itself in previous time periods.
- information extracted from financial markets such as asset prices or interest rates.

A variety of sources are available that produce ratios for a number of industries, including (1) Dun & Bradstreet, (2) *Annual Statement Studies* by Robert Morris Associates, (3) the Commerce Department's *Quarterly Financial Report,* and (4) trade associations. Additionally, these data have become available on-line via the Internet.

Quick Check 8

What are the five types of financial ratios used to analyze a company's performance?

6.1 The Relations among Ratios

It is useful to decompose a firm's *ROA* into the product of two ratios as follows:

$$ROA = \frac{EBIT}{Sales} \times \frac{Sales}{Assets}$$

$$= \text{Return on Sales} \times \text{Asset Turnover}$$

$$= ROS \times ATO$$

The decomposition of *ROA* into *ROS* and *ATO* highlights the fact that firms in different industries can have vastly different *ROS* and turnover ratios yet the same return on assets. Thus, a supermarket typically has a low profit margin on sales and a high asset turnover, whereas a high-priced jewelry store typically has a high profit margin and a low turnover. Both may have the same *ROA*.

To illustrate, let us take two firms with the same *ROA* of 10% per year. The first is a supermarket chain, the second a public utility company. As Table 6 shows, the supermarket chain has a "low" *ROS* of 2% and achieves a 10% *ROA* by "turning over" its assets five times per year. The capital-intensive utility, on the other hand, has a "low" *ATO* of only 0.5 times per year and achieves its 10% *ROA* by having an *ROS* of 20%.

The point here is that a "low" *ROS* or *ATO* ratio need not be a sign of a troubled firm. Each of these ratios must be interpreted in light of industry norms. Even in the same industry systematic differences may exist. For example, a Rolls Royce dealership will almost certainly have a higher margin and lower turnover than a Chevrolet dealership, even though both may have the same *ROA*.

Quick Check 9

If firm A has a higher *ROA* than firm B but the same *ATO,* what must be true of its *ROS?*

TABLE 6 **Difference Between *ROS* and *ATO* Across Industries**

	ROS	×	ATO	=	ROA
Supermarket chain	0.02		5.0		0.10
Public utility	0.20		0.5		0.10

6.2 The Effect of Financial Leverage

Financial leverage simply means the use of borrowed money. The shareholders of a firm use financial leverage in order to boost their *ROE,* but in so doing they increase the sensitivity of *ROE* to fluctuations in the firm's underlying operating profitability as measured by its *ROA.* In other words, by making use of financial leverage, the firm's shareholders are subjected to financial risk as well as to the operating risk of the firm.

An increase in a firm's financial leverage will increase its *ROE* if and only if its *ROA* exceeds the interest rate on the borrowed funds. This makes intuitive sense. If *ROA* exceeds the borrowing rate, then the firm earns more on the capital it employs than it pays to its creditors. The surplus is thus available to the firm's shareholders, and so raises *ROE.* If, on the other hand, *ROA* is less than the interest rate, the shareholders would have been better off not borrowing at all.

For example, Halfdebt Co. uses financial leverage, whereas Nodebt Co. does not. Let us compare their *ROE* under two different assumptions about the interest rate: (1) 10% per year, and (2) 15% per year. The results are given in Table 7.

Increased financial leverage magnifies the variability that firms experience in their *ROE* over the business cycle and increases the likelihood of bankruptcy. Table 8 illustrates the behavior of *ROA* and *ROE* under three scenarios, representing phases of the business cycle. We assume that the interest rate on Halfdebt's debt is 10% per year.

TABLE 7   Effect of Interest Rate on *ROE*

	Nodebt	Halfdebt
Total Assets	$1,000,000	$1,000,000
Equity	1,000,000	500,000
Debt	0	500,000
EBIT	120,000	120,000
ROA (EBIT/ASSETS)	12.0%	12.0%
Case (1): Borrowing at an interest rate of 10% per year		
EBIT	120,000	120,000
Interest Expense	0	50,000
Taxable Income	120,000	70,000
Taxes (@ 40%)	48,000	28,000
Net Income	72,000	42,000
Equity	1,000,000	500,000
ROE	7.2%	8.4%
Case (2): Borrowing at an interest rate of 15% per year		
EBIT	120,000	120,000
Interest Expense	0	75,000
Taxable Income	120,000	45,000
Taxes (@ 40%)	48,000	18,000
Net Income	72,000	27,000
Equity	1,000,000	500,000
ROE	7.2%	5.4%

TABLE 8   **Effect of Business Cycle on *ROE***

Economic Conditions	*ROA*	ROE Nodebt	ROE Halfdebt
Bad year	1.0%	0.6%	−4.8%
Normal year	12.0	7.2	8.4
Good year	30.0	18.0	30.0

The exact relationship between *ROE, ROA,* and leverage can be summarized in the following equation:

$$ROE = (1 - \text{Tax Rate}) \times \left[ROA + \left(\left(\frac{\text{Debt}}{\text{Equity}} \right) \times (ROA - \text{Interest Rate}) \right) \right]$$

This equation has the following implications. If a firm's *ROA* exceeds the interest rate that it pays to its creditors, then its *ROE* will exceed (1 − tax rate) times *ROA* by an amount that will be greater the higher the debt/equity ratio.

From the perspective of a creditor, an increase in a firm's debt ratio is generally a negative sign. Bond-rating agencies, such as Moody's and Standard and Poors Corporation, will often downgrade a firm's securities if its debt ratio goes up. But from the shareholder's perspective, it might be positive for the firm to increase its debt ratio.

> **Quick Check 10**
>
> What is the effect of increased leverage on a firm's *ROE* if the interest rate on its debt is equal to its *ROA*?

6.3 Limitations of Ratio Analysis

Finally, the user of ratios must be aware of their limitations. The basic problem is there is no absolute standard by which to judge whether the ratios are too high or too low. Moreover, ratios are comprised of accounting numbers, often calculated in arbitrary ways. Furthermore, it is difficult to define a set of comparable firms because firms, even within the same industry, are often quite different. For example, firms vary in their level of diversification, in their size, in their age, in the extent to which they are international, and in the accounting methods used (e.g., their inventory and depreciation methods may differ). The punch line of financial ratio analysis, then, is that it may provide a rough guide that should not be relied upon exclusively for decisions.

7 The Financial Planning Process

Financial planning is a dynamic process that follows a cycle of making plans, implementing them, and revising them in the light of actual results. The starting point in developing a financial plan is the firm's strategic plan. Strategy guides the financial planning process by establishing overall business development guidelines and growth targets. Which lines of business does the firm want to expand, which to contract, and how quickly?

For example, ITT Corporation decided in 1995 to quit the insurance business and to concentrate on expanding its gaming and resort businesses. This decision meant that its financial plans starting in that year would be based on redeploying its assets. For several years there would not be any growth in total sales at the corporate level. Indeed, there would be significant "downsizing."[4]

The length of the *planning horizon* is another important element in financial planning. In general, the longer the horizon, the less detailed the financial plan. A five-year financial plan will typically consist of a set of forecasted income statements and balance sheets showing only general categories with few details. On the other hand, a financial plan for next month will show detailed forecasts of revenues and expenses for specific product lines and detailed projections of cash inflows and outflows. Multiyear plans are usually revised on an annual basis, and annual plans on a quarterly basis.

The financial planning cycle can be broken down into several steps:

1. Managers forecast the key external factors that determine the demand for the firm's products and its production costs. These factors include the level of economic activity in the markets in which the firm sells its products, inflation, exchange rates, interest rates, and the output and prices charged by the firm's competitors.

2. Based on these external factors and their own tentative decisions regarding investment outlays, production levels, research and marketing expenditures, and dividend payments, managers forecast the firm's revenues, expenses, and cash flows, and estimate the implied need for external financing. They check that the firm's likely future financial results are consistent with their strategic plan for creating value for shareholders and that financing is available to implement the plan. If there are any inconsistencies, then managers revise their decisions until they come up with a workable plan, which becomes a blueprint for the firm's operating decisions during the year. It is good practice to make contingency plans in case some of the forecasts turn out to be wrong.

3. Based on the plan, senior managers establish specific performance targets for themselves and their subordinates.

4. Actual performance is measured at regular intervals (either monthly or quarterly), compared to the targets set in the plan, and corrective actions are taken as needed. Management may adjust targets during the year to take into account large deviations from forecast values.

5. At the end of each year, rewards (e.g., bonuses or raises) are distributed and the planning cycle starts again.

8 Constructing a Financial Planning Model

Financial plans are usually embodied in quantitative models derived in whole or in part from a firm's financial statements. For example, let us construct a one-year financial plan for Generic Products Corporation (GPC), the same hypothetical firm whose financial statements we analyzed earlier in this chapter. GPC is a company that was founded 10 years ago to manufacture and sell generic products for the consumer market. Table 9 shows GPC's income statements and balance sheets for the last three years.

Let us assume that these financial statements are the only information about the company available. How could one formulate a plan for the coming year? The simplest approach is to make a forecast of sales for the next year and assume that most of the items on the income statement and balance sheet will maintain the same ratio to sales as in the previous year. This is called the **percent-of-sales method**. Let us illustrate the method with GPC.

The first step is an examination of past financial data to determine which items on the income statement and balance sheet have maintained a fixed ratio to sales. This enables us to

---

[4]The stock market reacted quite favorably to this shift in strategy. ITT's stock price rose dramatically compared to the change in the S&P 500 index. ITT's stock price tripled over the period from 1991 to 1995, during which its new strategy was formulated and ultimately implemented.

TABLE 3.9   GPC Financial Statements: 20x1–20x3

Income Statement	20x1	20x2	20x3
Sales	$200.00	$240.00	$288.00
Cost of goods sold	110.00	132.00	158.40
Gross margin	90.00	108.00	129.60
Selling, general, and administrative expenses	30.00	36.00	43.20
EBIT	60.00	72.00	86.40
Interest expense	30.00	45.21	64.04
Taxes	12.00	10.72	8.94
Net income	18.00	16.07	13.41
Dividends	5.40	4.82	4.02
Change in shareholders' equity	12.60	11.25	9.39

Balance Sheet	20x0	20x1	20x2
Assets	600.00	720.00	864.00
Cash and equivalents	10.00	12.00	14.40
Receivables	40.00	48.00	57.60
Inventories	50.00	60.00	72.00
Property, plant, and equipment	500.00	600.00	720.00
Liabilities	300.00	407.40	540.15
Payables	30.00	36.00	43.20
Short-term debt	120.00	221.40	346.95
Long-term debt	150.00	150.00	150.00
Shareholders' equity	$300.00	$312.60	$323.85

In millions of U.S. dollars.

decide which items can be forecast strictly on the basis of our projected sales and which have to be forecast on some other basis. In the case of GPC, it is clear from the record that costs, *EBIT*, and assets have maintained fixed ratios to sales. However, interest expense, taxes, net income, and most liabilities (with the exception of payables) have not. This is shown in Table 10.

The second step is to forecast sales. Because so many items are linked to sales, it is important to have an accurate sales forecast and later to test the sensitivity of the plan to variations in sales. For GPC we will assume that sales will continue to grow by 20% next year, so that sales for 20x4 are forecast to be $345.6 million.

The third step is to forecast those items on the income statement and balance sheet that are assumed to maintain a constant ratio to sales. Thus, because cost of goods sold has historically been 55% of sales, the 20x4 forecast is 0.55 × $345.6 million, which is $190.08 million. Because total assets at the end of the year have been 3.6 times annual sales, the total asset figure forecast for the end of 20x4 is $1,244.16 million.

The final step is to fill in the missing items in the income statement and balance sheet (i.e., the items that do not maintain a fixed ratio to sales). Let us assume that the interest rate on the long-term debt is 8% per year and on the short-term debt 15% per year. Then our forecast for interest expense is 8% times the amount of long-term debt plus 15% times the amount of short-term debt outstanding at the beginning of the year (i.e., at the end of 20x3). Thus, total interest expense for 20x4 will be $87.26 million. Taxes are assumed to be 40% of

TABLE 10   GPC Common-Size Financial Statements: 20x1–20x3

Income Statement	20x1	20x2	20x3
Sales	100.0%	100.0%	100.0%
Cost of goods sold	55.0	55.0	55.0
Gross margin	45.0	45.0	45.0
Selling, general, and administrative expenses	15.0	15.0	15.0
EBIT	30.0	30.0	30.0
Interest expense	15.0	18.8	22.2
Taxes	6.0	4.5	3.1
Net income	9.0	6.7	4.7
Dividends	2.7	2.0	1.4
Change in shareholders' equity	6.3	4.7	3.3
Balance Sheet	**20x1**	**20x2**	**20x3**
Assets	360.0%	360.0%	360.0%
Cash and equivalents	6.0	6.0	6.0
Receivables	24.0	24.0	24.0
Inventories	30.0	30.0	30.0
Property, plant, and equipment	300.0	300.0	300.0
Liabilities	203.7	225.1	244.3
Payables	18.0	18.0	18.0
Short-term debt	110.7	144.6	174.2
Long-term debt	75.0	62.5	52.1
Shareholders' equity	156.3	134.9	115.7

All figures are percentages of sales for the respective years.

income after interest expense, or $6.57 million. Net income after taxes is, therefore, $9.85 million. The income statement for 20x4 will be as shown in the last column of Table 11.

Now let us consider the balance sheet at the end of 20x4. Because GPC will pay out 30% of net income as dividends, shareholders' equity will increase by $6.9 million (from $333.24 million to $340.14 million). Total assets will increase by $207.36 million, and payables will increase by $10.37 million. To find the total need for additional funds to be raised either by issuing new stock or by increased borrowing, we subtract the increase in retained earnings and the increase in payables from the change in assets as follows:

$$\text{Additional Financing Needed} = \text{Change in Assets}$$
$$- \text{Increase in Retained Earnings} - \text{Increase in Payables} = \$207.36 \text{ million}$$
$$- \$6.9 \text{ million} - \$10.37 \text{ million} = 190.09 \text{ million}$$

Thus, there will be a need for an additional $190.09 million in external financing. In the balance sheet data of Table 11, we have assumed that all of this financing will be in the form of an increase in short-term debt, which therefore increases from $501.72 million to $691.81 million.

Quick Check 11

If the sales revenue forecast for 20x4 is $360 million instead of $345.60, what will be the need for additional external financing?

TABLE 11 GPC Forecast Income Statement and Balance Sheet for 20x4

Income Statement		20x1	20x2	20x3	20x4e
Sales		$200.00	$240.00	$288.00	$345.60
Cost of goods sold		110.00	132.00	158.40	190.08
Gross margin		90.00	108.00	129.60	155.52
Selling, general, and administrative expenses		30.00	36.00	43.20	51.84
EBIT		60.00	72.00	86.40	103.68
Interest expense		30.00	45.21	64.04	87.26
Taxes		12.00	10.72	8.94	6.57
Net income		18.00	16.07	13.41	9.85
Dividends		5.40	4.82	4.02	2.96
Change in equity		12.60	11.25	9.39	6.90
Balance Sheet	20x0	20x1	20x2	20x3	20x4e
Assets	$600.00	$720.00	$864.00	$1,036.80	$1,244.16
Cash and equivalents	10.00	12.00	14.40	17.28	20.74
Receivables	40.00	48.00	57.60	69.12	82.94
Inventories	50.00	60.00	72.00	86.40	103.68
Property, plant, and equipment	500.00	600.00	720.00	864.00	1,036.80
Liabilities	300.00	407.40	540.15	703.56	904.02
Payables	30.00	36.00	43.20	51.84	62.21
Short-term debt	120.00	221.40	346.95	501.72	691.81
Long-term debt	150.00	150.00	150.00	150.00	150.00
Equity	300.00	312.60	323.85	333.24	340.14

In millions of U.S. dollars.

9 Growth and the Need for External Financing

We now know that if GPC's sales grow by 20% during 20x4, it will need to raise an additional $190.09 million in funds from external sources. Management may decide to raise this money either by increasing its short-term borrowing (as assumed in Table 11), by increasing its long-term debt, or by issuing new stock. Let us now see how sensitive this external financing need is to the assumed growth rate of sales.

One way to carry out such a sensitivity analysis is to repeat the procedure we just did in the previous section using different growth rates of sales. This can easily be done by creating an automated spreadsheet model with a computer program such as the one at this textbook's companion Web site.[5] The result is shown in Figure 1.

9.1 The Firm's Sustainable Growth Rate

Figure 1 tells us the amount of external financing the firm needs in order to achieve a certain targeted growth rate of sales. But we can ask the reverse question: How fast can a firm grow if it is constrained in the amount of external financing available to it?

---

[5]See www.prenhall.com/bodie.

FIGURE 1

External Funds Needed as a Function of the Growth Rate

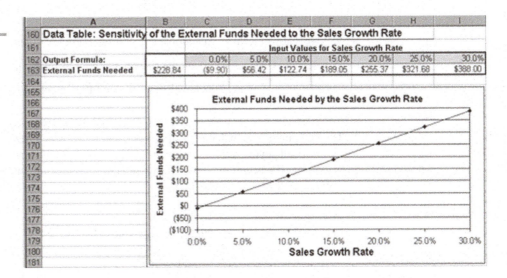

	A	B	C	D	E	F	G	H	I
160	Data Table: Sensitivity of the External Funds Needed to the Sales Growth Rate								
161				Input Values for Sales Growth Rate					
162	Output Formula:		0.0%	5.0%	10.0%	15.0%	20.0%	25.0%	30.0%
163	External Funds Needed	$228.84	($9.90)	$56.42	$122.74	$189.05	$255.37	$321.68	$388.00

To address this question we assume that the financing constraint takes the following form:

- The firm will not issue any new equity shares, so that growth in equity capital occurs only through the retention of earnings.
- The firm will not increase its ratio of debt to equity, so that external debt financing will grow at the same rate as equity grows through retained earnings.

Under these circumstances, the firm cannot grow any faster than the growth rate in owners' equity, which is called the firm's **sustainable growth rate.** The formula for the sustainable growth rate is:

$$\text{Sustainable Growth Rate} = \text{Earnings Retention Rate} \times ROE$$

DERIVATION OF THE SUSTAINABLE GROWTH EQUATION

$$\text{Sustainable Growth Rate} = \text{Growth Rate of Shareholders' Equity}$$

Without the issuance of new shares, the rate of growth in shareholders' equity is just the increase in retained earnings divided by the beginning-of-year shareholders' equity:

$$\text{Growth Rate of Shareholders' Equity}$$
$$= \text{Increase in Retained Earnings} \div \text{Shareholders' Equity at Beginning of Year}$$

But:

$$\text{Increase in Retained Earnings}$$
$$= \text{Earnings Retention Rate} \times \text{Net Income}$$

The earnings retention rate is the proportion of net income not paid out in dividends or used to repurchase outstanding shares of stock. By definition it is equal to:

$$\text{Earnings Retention Rate}$$
$$= 1 - \text{Dividend Payout Ratio} - \text{Share Repurchase Rate}$$

Therefore, by substitution:

$$\text{Growth Rate of Shareholders' Equity}$$
$$= \text{Earnings Retention Rate} \times \text{Net Income} \div \text{Shareholders' Equity}$$

93

or in other words:

Growth Rate of Shareholders' Equity = Earnings Retention Rate $\times$ *ROE*

And, thus, we have derived the sustainable growth equation:

Sustainable Growth Rate = Earnings Retention Rate $\times$ *ROE*

IMPLICATIONS OF THE SUSTAINABLE GROWTH EQUATION

The maximum sustainable growth rate is equal to the firm's *ROE,* and it is achieved when the dividend payout ratio is zero, that is, when all of net income is retained and reinvested in the firm. If a firm tries to grow faster than this rate, then it will have to issue new shares and/or increase its debt ratio.

EXAMPLE OF SUSTAINABLE GROWTH

Rapid Industries (RI) has the following fixed ratios:

Asset Turnover = 0.5 Times per Year

Debt/Equity Ratio = 1.0

Dividend Payout Ratio = 0.4

ROE = 20% per Year

Last year sales were $1 million. That means that assets were $2 million, and debt and shareholders' equity were $1 million each. Because *ROE* was 20%, net income must have been $200,000, of which $80,000 was paid out in dividends and $120,000 retained as new equity capital. With a debt/equity ratio of 1, RI could increase its assets by $240,000 and its sales by as much as $120,000.

The sustainable growth rate of sales is, therefore:

$$g = \frac{\$120,000}{\$1 \text{ million}} = 0.12 \text{ or } 12\%$$

We get the same answer by applying the formula:

$$g = ROE \times (1 - \text{Dividend Payout Ratio})$$
$$= 20\% \times (1 - 0.4)$$
$$= 12\%$$

The financial statements of Rapid Industries for three years of sustainable growth are shown in Table 12.

> ### Quick Check 12
>
> What are the implications for financing if a firm grew at a rate less than its sustainable rate?

10 Working Capital Management

In most businesses cash must be paid out to cover expenses before any cash is collected from the sale of the firm's products. As a result, a typical firm's investment in assets such as inventories and accounts receivable exceeds its liabilities such as accrued expenses and accounts payable. The difference between these current assets and current liabilities is called **working capital.** If a firm's need for working capital is permanent rather than seasonal,

TABLE 12   Rapid Industries Financial Statements for 20x1–20x3

Income Statements	20x1	20x2	20x3
Sales	$1,000,000	$1,120,000	$1,254,400
Net income	200,000	224,000	250,880
Dividends	80,000	89,600	100,352
Increase in retained earnings	120,000	134,400	150,528
Balance Sheets	**20x0**	**20x1**	**20x2**
Assets	$2,000,000	$2,240,000	$2,508,800
Debt	1,000,000	1,120,000	1,254,400
Equity	1,000,000	1,120,000	1,254,400

it usually seeks long-term financing for it. Seasonal financing needs are met through short-term financing arrangements, such as a loan from a bank.

The main principle behind the efficient management of a firm's working capital is to minimize the amount of the firm's investment in nonearning assets such as receivables and inventories and maximize the use of "free" credit such as prepayments by customers, accrued wages, and accounts payable. These three sources of funds are free to the firm in the sense that they usually bear no explicit interest charge.[6]

Policies and procedures that shorten the lag between the time that the firm sells a product and the time that it collects cash from its customers reduce the need for working capital. Ideally, the firm would like its customers to pay in advance. The firm can also reduce its need for working capital by extending the time between when it purchases its inputs and when it pays cash for them.

To gain a clearer understanding of the relation between these time lags and the firm's investment in working capital, consider Figure 2.

The **cash cycle time** is the number of days between the date the firm must start to pay cash to its suppliers and the date it begins to receive cash from its customers. From Figure 2, we see that the cash cycle time is the difference between the sum of the inventory and receivables periods on the one hand and the payables period on the other.

Cash Cycle Time = Inventory Period + Receivables Period − Payables Period

The firm's required investment in working capital is directly related to the length of its cash cycle time. If the payables period is long enough to cover the sum of the inventory and receivables periods, then the firm needs no working capital at all.

FIGURE 2

The Cash Flow Cycle

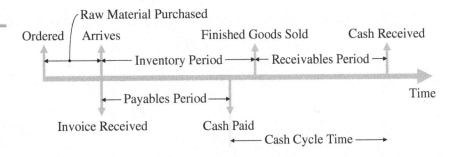

[6]If, however, the firm gives price discounts on its products to customers who pay in advance, then the size of this discount represents an implicit interest charge. Similarly, if the firm forgoes a discount from its suppliers by delaying payment to them, this forgone discount represents an implicit interest charge.

What kinds of actions can a firm take to reduce its need for working capital? From the equation for cash cycle time, we can see that a firm can reduce its need for working capital by:

- *reducing the amount of time that goods are held in inventory.* This can be accomplished by improving the inventory control process or by having suppliers deliver raw materials exactly when they are needed in the production process.
- *collecting accounts receivable more quickly.* Among the methods available to speed up the collection process are improving the efficiency of the collection process, offering discounts to customers who pay faster, and charging interest on accounts that are overdue.
- *paying its own bills more slowly.*

Quick Check 13

How can a firm reduce its need for working capital?

11 Liquidity and Cash Budgeting

There is an apocryphal story about how the billionaire Howard Hughes found himself without any cash or credit cards in a place where no one recognized him. Without any means to pay for food, drink, shelter, or transportation, the billionaire nearly died of starvation and exposure. The same point applies to corporations: A firm that is profitable in the long run can experience serious difficulties and even fail if it runs out of cash or credit in the short run. Rarely does a firm become spectacularly successful simply by managing well the short-term flows of cash into and out of the business, but failure to manage them properly can lead to ruin.

Howard Hughes's problem was that he became temporarily illiquid. **Liquidity** means that one has the means to make *immediate* payment for some purchase or to settle a debt that has come due. *Illiquidity* is a situation in which one has sufficient wealth to afford the purchase or to settle the debt, but one does not have the means to pay immediately.[7]

To avoid the difficulties caused by illiquidity, firms need to forecast their cash outflows and inflows carefully. A plan that shows these forecasts is called a **cash budget**.

Quick Check 14

Why is liquidity important to a firm?

Summary

Financial statements serve three important economic functions:

- They provide information to the owners and creditors of the firm about the company's current status and past financial performance.
- They provide a convenient way for owners and creditors to set performance targets and impose restrictions on the managers of the firm.
- They provide convenient templates for financial planning.

---

[7]The liquidity of an asset can be defined as one's ability to immediately convert it into cash at full value. A good measure of an asset's liquidity is the cost of buying it and then immediately reselling it. Thus, the liquidity of a new car that you buy is the gap between the price you paid for it and the price you could get for it if you sold it to someone else the next instant. For an asset that is traded in a dealer market this cost is its bid-asked spread. Cash is defined as the asset with a zero bid-asked spread.

The basic accounting statements reviewed are the income statement, the balance sheet, and the statement of cash flows. The *income statement* reports the results of operations over the period and is based on the model of revenues minus costs (including depreciation and taxes) equals net income or earnings. The *balance sheet* shows the assets (both current and long-term or fixed assets) on the one hand, and the claims against them (i.e., the liabilities and equity) on the other. The *statement of cash flows* gives a summary of cash flows from operating, investing, and financing activities for the period.

A firm's accounting balance sheet differs from an economic balance sheet because:

- it omits some economically significant assets and liabilities, and
- it does not report all assets and liabilities at their current market values.

Analysts use financial ratios as one mode of analysis to better understand the company's strengths and weaknesses, whether its fortunes are improving, and what its prospects are. These ratios are often compared with the ratios of a comparable set of companies and to ratios of recent past periods. The five types of ratios are profitability, turnover, financial leverage, liquidity, and market value ratios. Finally, it is helpful to organize the analysis of these ratios in a way that reveals the logical connections among them and their relation to the underlying operations of the firm.

The purpose of financial planning is to assemble the firm's separate divisional plans into a consistent whole, to establish concrete targets for measuring success, and to create incentives for achieving the firm's goals. The tangible outcome of the financial planning process is a set of "blueprints" in the form of projected financial statements and budgets. The longer the time horizon, the less detailed the financial plan.

In the short run, financial planning is concerned primarily with the management of working capital. The need for working capital arises because for many firms cash needed to conduct production and selling activities starts to flow out before cash flows in. The longer this time lag, which is called the length of the cash flow cycle, the more the amount of working capital the firm needs.

A firm's need for working capital is measured as the sum of cash equivalents, prepaid expenses, receivables, and inventories minus the sum of customer advances, payables, and accrued expenses. The main principle behind the efficient management of a firm's working capital is to minimize the amount of the firm's investment in low-earning current assets such as receivables and inventories and maximize the use of low-cost financing through current liabilities such as customer advances and accounts payable.

Cash management is important because even a profitable firm can get into financial distress or even go bankrupt if it becomes illiquid.

Key Terms

- book values
- intangible assets
- goodwill
- marking to market
- total shareholder returns
- percent-of-sales method

- sustainable growth rate
- working capital
- cash cycle time
- liquidity
- cash budget

Answers to Quick Check Questions

Quick Check 1 What are the three basic economic functions served by financial statements?

Answer:

- They provide information to the owners and creditors of the firm about the company's current status and past financial performance.
- They provide a convenient way for owners and creditors to set performance targets and to impose restrictions on the managers of the firm.
- Financial statements provide convenient templates for financial planning.

Quick Check 2   What difference would it have made to the end-of-year balance sheet if GPC had issued an additional $50 million of long-term debt during the year and added that amount to its holdings of cash and marketable securities?

Answer: The liability, long-term debt, and the asset, cash and marketable securities, would both have increased by $50 million, and shareholder's equity would have remained unchanged.

Quick Check 3   What difference would it have made to the income statement and the end-of-year balance sheet if GPC had retained all of its net income instead of paying out cash dividends of $10 million?

Answer: Net income would have been the same. The end-of-year balance sheet, however, would have shown an increase of $10 million in cash and in shareholders' equity.

Quick Check 4   What difference would it have made to the cash flow statement if GPC had retained all of its net income instead of paying out cash dividends of $10 million?

Answer: If GPC had not paid a cash dividend of $10 million, it could have borrowed $10 million less. Therefore, the cash flow statement would have showed no dividend and an increase in debt of only $84.6 million.

Quick Check 5   What potentially important information about a firm can be found in the footnotes to its financial statements?

Answer:

- An explanation of accounting methods used.
- Greater detail regarding certain assets or liabilities.
- Information regarding the equity structure of the firm.
- Documentation of changes in operations.
- Off-balance-sheet items.

Quick Check 6   Why does the market price of a firm's stock usually differ from its book value?

Answer: The book value does not include all of a firm's assets and liabilities. The assets and liabilities included on a firm's official balance sheet are not marked to market.

Quick Check 7   In 20x7 VGI corporation reported earnings per share of $5 and paid a cash dividend to shareholders of $3.00 per share. Its beginning-of-year book value per share was $30, and its market price was $40. At the end of the year, the book value per share was $32 and the market price was $35. Compare VGI's *ROE* and total shareholder returns (*TSR*).

Answer:

$$ROE = 5/30 = 16.67\%$$

$$TSR = (3 + 35 - 40)/40 = -5\%$$

Quick Check 8   What are the five types of financial ratios used to analyze a company?

Answer: The five ratios are profitability, activity, financial leverage, liquidity, and market price ratios.

Quick Check 9   If firm A has a higher *ROA* than firm B but the same *ATO,* what must be true of its *ROS*?

Answer: Firm A's *ROS* must be higher than B's.

Quick Check 10   What is the effect of increased leverage on a firm's *ROE* if the interest rate on its debt is equal to its *ROA*?

Answer: The firm's *ROE* will not change.

Quick Check 11   If the sales revenue forecast for 20x4 is $360 million instead of $345.60, what will be the need for additional external financing?

Answer: The total asset figure forecast for the end of 20x4 is now 3.6 × $360 million, which is $1,296 million. So the change in assets for the year is $1,296 − $1,036.8, which is $259.20. This growth in assets will be partially financed from the increase in retained earnings and the growth in payables, but the rest of the financing needed will have to come from external sources. Payables will increase by 18% (the ratio of payables to sales) times the increase in sales, which is 0.18 × $72 million or $12.96 million. Now let us forecast the firm's net income. *EBIT* is 0.3 × $360 million, which is $108 million. Total interest expense is unchanged at $87.26 million. Taxes are 40% of income after interest expense: Taxes = 0.4 × (108 − 87.26) = $8.296 million. Net income after taxes is, therefore, 0.6 × (108 − 87.26) = $12.444 million. Because GPC will pay out 30% of net income as dividends, the increase in retained earnings will be 0.7 × $12.444 = $8.711 million.

Additional Financing Needed =
Change in Assets − Increase in Retained Earnings − Increase in Payables =
$259.2 million − $8.711 million − $12.96 million = $237.529 million

Quick Check 12   What are the implications for financing if a firm grows at a rate less than its sustainable rate?

Answer: The firm will be able to lower its debt ratio or repurchase its own shares.

Quick Check 13   How can a firm reduce its need for working capital?

Answer: By either reducing inventories, speeding up collections, or slowing down the payment of its own bills.

Quick Check 14   Why is liquidity important to a firm?

Answer: A firm that is profitable in the long run can experience serious difficulties and even fail if it runs out of cash or credit in the short run.

Questions and Problems

Review of Financial Statements

1. Suggest if and how the following assets and liabilities would be recorded on their owner's balance sheets.
   a. a lottery ticket
   b. a successful song
   c. an unsuccessful movie
2. Show how the following events and transactions should appear on your personal income statement, balance sheet, and cash flow statement.
   a. On July 1, 200X, you receive $20,000 in gifts upon graduation from school and pay off a $10,000 student loan.

b. On August 1, 200X, you get a job as a finance intern at General Financial Services Inc. You are promised a salary of $4,000 per month, payable on the last day of each month.

c. On August 31, you receive your first statement of GFS salary and benefits showing the following items:

Gross salary	$4,000
Income tax withholding	1,400
Social Security and Medicare tax	500
Health care premium	150
Contribution to pension plan	200
Employer Social Security tax	300
Employer contribution to pension plan	200
Employer contribution to health care	150
Amount credited to employee checking account at GFS Bank	1,750
Total employer benefit	650

d. On September 1, you purchase a new car for $20,000. You make a down payment of $5,000 and borrow the remaining $15,000 from GFS bank at a monthly interest rate of 1%. Your monthly payment is $498.21 for 36 months.

e. As an individual or a household, why might you want to maintain a balance sheet? How often would you update it? Should you mark-to-market or leave your assets and liabilities at their historical values?

Problems 3 through 10 are based on the following information:
The Ruffy Stuffed Toy Company's balance sheet at the end of 20x1 is given below.

Assets		Liabilities and Shareholders' Equity	
Cash	$27,300	Payable	
Accounts Receivable	35,000	Accounts payable	$65,000
Inventory	57,000	Salary Payable	3,000
Total current assets	119,300	Utilities Payable	1,500
Property, Plant, and Equipment		Loans (Long-term debt)	25,000
Equipment	25,000	*Total Liabilities*	94,500
Less Accumulated Depreciation	(2,500)	Common Stock	45,000
Net Equipment	22,500	Retained Earnings	16,300
Furniture	16,000	*Total Shareholders' Equity*	61,300
Less Accumulated Depreciation	(2,000)	**Total Liabilities & Equity**	**155,800**
Net Furniture	14,000		
Total Prop, Plant, and Equipment	36,500		
Total Assets	**155,800**		

During 20x2, the Ruffy Stuffed Toy Company recorded the following transactions:
- Early in the year, purchased a new toy stuffing machine for $9,000 cash and signed a 3-year note for the balance of $12,000.
- Had cash sales of $115,000 and sales on credit of $316,000.
- Purchased raw materials from suppliers for $207,000.

- Made payments of $225,000 to its raw materials suppliers.
- Paid rent expenses totaling $43,000.
- Paid insurance expenses totaling $23,000.
- Paid utility bills totaling $7,500; $1,500 of this amount reversed the existing payable from 20x1.
- Paid wages and salaries totaling $79,000; $3,000 of this amount reversed the payable from 20x1.
- Paid other miscellaneous operating expenses totaling $4,000.
- Collected $270,000 from its customers who made purchases on credit.
- The interest rate on the loan payable is 10% per year. Interest was paid on 12/31/20x2.

Other information:
- The equipment has been estimated to have a useful life of 20 years, with no salvage value. Two years have been depreciated through 20x1.
- The existing furniture has been estimated to have a useful life of 8 years (no salvage value), of which one year has been depreciated through 20x1.
- The new stuffing machine has been estimated to have a useful life of 7 years, and will probably have no salvage value.
- The corporate income tax rate is 35% and taxes are paid on 12/31/20x2.
- Dividend payout, if possible, will be 10% of net income.
- Cost of Goods Sold for the year's sales were $250,000.
- Accounts Receivable Ending Balance = Beginning Balance − cash received from credit customers + sales on credit.
- Accounts Payable Ending Balance = Beginning Balance + purchases − cash payments to suppliers
- Inventory Ending Balance = Beginning Balance + purchases of raw material − cost of goods sold
- The company's stock price at market close on 12/31/20x2 was 4.625. It has 20,000 shares outstanding.

3. Construct the balance sheet for the Ruffy Stuffed Toy Company as of 12/31/20x2.
4. Construct the income statement for operations during the year 20x2.
5. Construct a cash flow statement for the year 20x2.

Analysis Using Financial Ratios

6. Calculate the following Profitability Ratios: Return on Sales, Return on Assets, Return on Equity.
7. Calculate the following Asset Turnover Ratios: Receivables turnover, Inventory turnover, Asset turnover.
8. Calculate the following Financial Leverage and Liquidity Ratios: debt, times interest earned, current ratio, quick (acid) test.
9. What is the Ruffy's book value per share at the end of 20x2?

Market Values versus Book Values

10. Calculate the firm's price-to-earnings ratio and the ratio of its market share price to its book value per share.

Analysis Using Financial Ratios

11. You have the following information taken from the 2001 financial statements of Computronixs Corporation and Digitek Corporation: (*All figures are in $ millions except for the second and final three rows.*)

	Computronix	Digitek
Net income	153.7	239.0
Dividend payout ratio	40%	20%
EBIT	317.6	403.1
Interest expense	54.7	4.8
Average assets	2,457.9	3,459.7
Sales	3,379.3	4,537.0
Average shareholders' equity	1,113.3	2,347.3
Market price of the common stock:		
beginning of year	$15	$38
end of year	$12	$40
Shares of common stock outstanding	200 million	100 million

Compare and contrast the financial performance of the two companies using the financial ratios discussed in this chapter.

Review of Financial Statements

12. You are thinking of taking a trip to Florida for your spring vacation, which begins two months from now. You use Excite's free preview Travel service on the Internet to find the cheapest round trip fare from Boston to Fort Lauderdale. It tells you that the cheapest airline is AirTran. You have never heard of this airline before and are concerned that it may go out of business before you can use your ticket two months from now. How can you use financial data available on the Internet (e.g., at http://www.quicken.com) to investigate the risk to you of buying an AirTran ticket? Which firms are in the relevant "benchmark" group for your purposes?

13. Using the income statements and balance sheets (see below):
   a. Determine which items varied in constant proportion to sales between 20x6 and 20x7.
   b. Determine the rate of growth in sales that was achieved from 20x6 to 20x7.
   c. What was the firm's return on equity for 20x7? Can you calculate it for 20x6?
   d. What was the firm's external (additional) funding requirement determined to be for 20x7? How was the funding obtained?

14. *Challenge Problem:* Prepare financial statements for 20x8 with the following assumptions:
   - Rate of growth in sales = 15%.
   - The firm intends to pay down $100,000 of its short-term debt on Jan. 1, 20x8.
   - Interest rates on debt are as stated in the balance sheet, and are applied to the start-of-year (20x8) balances for short-term and long-term debt. Remember that the firm intends to pay down part of the short-term loan on 1/1/20x8.
   - The firm's dividend payout in 20x8 will be reduced to 30%.
   What would be the firm's forecasted return on equity for 20x8? How much additional funding will the firm need for 20x8? The firm will close 40% of any additional funding gap by issuing new stock. It will then use up to $100,000 of long-term debt, with the remainder coming from 9% short-term borrowing. Complete the balance sheet for 20x8. Suppose the firm anticipates an increase in the corporate tax rate to 38%. Determine the amount of additional funding that would be required.

15. *Challenge Problem:* Take the financial statements (with tax rate = 35%) developed in the previous problem, and: Revise them assuming a growth rate in sales from 20x7 to 20x8 of 10%. What is the additional funding required for 20x8 under this scenario?

Refer to the following financial statements for Problems 13, 14, and 15:

INCOME STATEMENT	20x6	20x7	20x8
Sales	$1,200,000	$1,500,000	
Cost of Goods Sold	$750,000	$937,500	
Gross Margin	$450,000	$562,500	
Operating Expenses			
Advertising Expense	$50,000	$62,500	
Rent Expense	$72,000	$90,000	
Salesperson Commission Expense	$48,000	$60,000	
Utilities Expense	$15,000	$18,750	
EBIT	$265,000	$331,250	
Interest Expense	$106,000	$113,000	
Taxable Income	$159,000	$218,250	
Taxes (35%)	$55,650	$76,388	
Net Income	$103,350	$141,863	
Dividends (40% payout)	$41,340	$56,745	
Change in Retained Earnings	$62,010	$85,118	
BALANCE SHEET	20x6	20x7	20x8
Assets			
Cash	$300,000	$375,000	
Receivables	$200,000	$250,000	
Inventory	$700,000	$875,000	
Property, Plant, Equipment	$1,800,000	$2,250,000	
Total Assets	$3,000,000	$3,750,000	
Liabilities and Shareholders' Equity			
Liabilities			
Payables	$300,000	$375,000	
Short-term debt (10% interest)	$500,000	$989,882	
Long-term debt (7% interest)	$800,000	$900,000	
Shareholders' Equity			
Common Stock	$1,100,000	$1,100,000	
Retained Earnings	$300,000	$385,118	
Total Liabilities and Equity	$3,000,000	$3,750,000	

Now, develop financial statements for 20x9 assuming a growth rate in sales of 20% from 20x8 to 20x9. What is the additional funding needed for 20x9? The firm plans to use 9% short-term debt to cover this entire amount.

Growth and the Need for External Financing

16. Suppose that after analyzing the results of 20x8 and forecasting the financial statements for 20x9, the Give Me Debt Company anticipates an increase in total assets of $50, an increase in retained earnings of $25, and an increase in payables

of $40. Assume that other than the payables, the firm's liabilities include short-term and long-term debt, and that its equity includes common stock and retained earnings. The Chief Financial Officer of the company asks you to determine the required amount of external funding in 20x9. What do you tell the CFO?

What actions can Give Me Debt Co. undertake to address the situation you have found?

The Financial Planning Process

17. Place the following planning events in their likely order of occurrence within the planning cycle:
—Funding needs for implementation of tactical plans are estimated.
—The final firm-wide plan and budgets are completed
—CEO and top management team establish strategic objectives for the firm (ex: increase market share from 10% to 12%)
—Line managers devise action plans to support strategic objectives
—Revisions are made to the strategic plan and divisional budgets based on feedback from divisional managers with regard to resource (money, people) requirements
—Decisions are made as to which sources of external financing to tap
—Integration of divisional budgets into a preliminary firm-wide budget by CEO and top management team
—The firm determines the amount of required external financing
—Tactical plans and budgets are reviewed with division management; priorities are assigned to planned activities
—Division managers review the strategic objectives with their line (or tactical) management

Constructing a Financial Planning Model

18. Suppose that the sharply abbreviated actual 20x8 and forecasted 20x9 income statement and balance sheet for Cones 'R' Us, an ice-cream retailer, appear as follows:

INCOME STATEMENT	20x8	20x9
EBIT		$100
Interest Expense		25
Taxable Income		75
Net Income (33% tax rate)		50
Dividends		20
Change in Retained Earnings		30
BALANCE SHEET		
Assets	$800	$1,000
Liabilities		
Payables	80	100
Debt	300	450
Shareholders' Equity	420	450

The $25 interest expense projected for 20x9 is based on a rate of 8.33% applied to the outstanding debt balance of $300 at the end of 20x8. Debt increases from $300 to $450 because of external financing that is obtained to close the gap exhibited in the relationship:

Additional Financing Needed = Change in Assets − Increase in Retained Earnings − Increase in Payables

    a. What problems are created in using the forecasted statements to determine the required amount of additional (external) financing if the debt that will be used to satisfy the funding need is acquired in total at the beginning of 20x9, rather than at the end of 20x9 as is implied in these statements?

    b. Is this problem likely to be significant? Why?

Growth and the Need for External Financing

19. The sustainable growth rate is given by the expression: $g = \text{ROE}(1 - \text{Dividend Payout Ratio})$ Substitution of the definitions of ROE and the Dividend Payout Ratio allows the growth rate to be expressed as:

g = (Net Income/Shareholders' Equity) (Retention Ratio)

   = (Net Income)(Retention Ratio)/(Shareholder's Equity)

How then can a firm ensure its sustainable growth rate will be zero?

20. Assume a firm has net income in 20x9 of $20 and its end-of-year 20x8 total assets were $450. Further assume that the firm has a standing requirement to maintain a debt/equity ratio of 0.8, and that its managers are prohibited from further borrowing or stock issuance.

    a. What is this firm's maximum sustainable growth rate?

    b. If the firm pays $6 of the $20 net income as a dividend, and plans to maintain this payout ratio into the future, now what is its maximum sustainable growth rate?

    c. If the firm uses $12 of the $20 net income to repurchase some of its outstanding shares, and plans to maintain the use of this ratio of net income for future repurchases, now what is its maximum sustainable growth rate?

    d. If the firm takes action as described in parts (b) and (c), what would its maximum sustainable growth rate be?

Working Capital Management

21. Suppose it is 3/13/x2, and you just received your monthly credit card statement with a new balance of $2,000. The payment is due on 4/5/x2, but your spouse panics at the sight (and size) of the balance and wants to pay it immediately. If you practice the principles of cash cycle time management in your personal finances, when would you make the payment? Why? What danger exists in adopting this strategy?

22. Suppose you own a firm that manufactures pool tables. Thirty days ago, you hired a consultant to examine your business and suggest improvements. The consultant's proposal, if implemented, would allow your firm to shorten the time between each sale and the subsequent cash collection by 20 days, slightly lengthen the time between inventory purchase and sale by only 5 days, but shorten the time between inventory purchase and your firm's payment of the bill by 15 days. Would you implement the consultant's proposal? Why?

23. In general, the principles of cash cycle time management call for a firm to shorten (minimize) the time it takes to collect receivables, and lengthen (maximize) the time it takes to pay amounts it owes to suppliers. Explain what tradeoffs need to be managed if the firm offers discounts to customers who pay early, and the firm also foregoes discounts offered by its suppliers by extending the time until it pays invoices.

24. Some furniture companies conduct highly advertised annual sale events in which customers can either take an up-front discount for a cash (or credit card) purchase, or defer finance charges for up to one year on their purchases by charging it to the company's credit account. Assume that the two options do not present a time value of money advantage for the company. In terms of cash cycle management: (1) Why does the company offer the discount? (2) Why might the company be willing to forego cash collection for one year if a customer chooses to defer? What risk does the company assume in the deferment case that it does not assume in the discount case?

Liquidity and Cash Budgeting

25. Compare the frequency with which you think a firm may monitor its working capital situation, and move to correct a problem, with the frequency of the firm's planning exercise in forecasting future sales and determining the need for additional financing. If a firm were to monitor its working capital situation closely, what problem might it be looking to avoid?

Suggested Readings

Fraser, L., and A. Ormiston. *Understanding Financial Statements,* 8th ed. Upper Saddle River, NJ: Pearson Prentice Hall, 2007.

Hutton, A., "Beyond Financial Reporting: An Integrated Approach to Corporate Disclosure." *Journal of Applied Corporate Finance* 16, Fall 2004.

Penman. S. *Financial Statement Analysis and Security Valuation,* 3rd ed. New York, NY: McGraw-Hill Irwin, 2007.

Wild, J., K. R. Subramanyam, and R. Halsey. *Financial Statement Analysis,* 9th ed. New York: McGraw-Hill Irwin, 2007.

Allocating Resources Over Time

OBJECTIVES

- To explain the concepts of compounding and discounting, and future value and present value.
- To show how these concepts are applied in making financial decisions.

CONTENTS

From Chapter 4 of *Financial Economics*, 2/e. Zvi Bodie, Robert C. Merton, David L. Cleeton.
Copyright © 2008 by Pearson Prentice Hall. All rights reserved.

Financial decisions involve costs and benefits that are spread over time. Financial decision makers in households and firms all have to evaluate whether investing money today is justified by the expected benefits in the future. They must, therefore, compare the values of sums of money at different dates. To do so requires a thorough understanding of the **time value of money** concepts and **discounted cash flow** techniques presented in this chapter.

The time value of money (*TVM*) refers to the fact that money (a dollar, a euro, or a yen) in hand today is worth more than the expectation of the same amount to be received in the future. There are at least three reasons why this is true. The first is that you can invest it, earn interest, and end up with more in the future. The second is that the purchasing power of money can change over time because of inflation. The third is that the receipt of money expected in the future is, in general, uncertain.

In this chapter we study how to take account of the first of these: interest. We leave the study of how to deal with inflation and uncertainty to later chapters.

1 Compounding

We begin our study of the time value of money and discounted cash flow analysis with the concept of **compounding**—the process of going from today's value, or **present value** (*PV*), to **future value** (*FV*). Future value is the amount of money an investment will grow to at some date in the future by earning interest at some compound rate. For example, suppose you put $1,000 (the *PV*) into an account earning an interest rate of 10% per year. The amount you will have in five years, assuming you take nothing out of the account before then, is called the future value of $1,000 at an interest rate of 10% per year for five years.

Let us define our terms more precisely:

PV = present value or beginning amount in your account. Here, it is $1,000.

i = interest rate, usually expressed in percent per year. Here, it is 10% (or 0.10 as a decimal).

n = number of years the account will earn interest.

FV = future value at the end of *n* years.

Now let's calculate the future value in this example one step at a time. First, how much will you have after the first year? You will have your original $1,000 plus interest of $100 (10% of $1,000 or $0.1 \times \$1,000$). Your future value at the end of year 1 will, therefore, be $1,100:

$$FV = \$1,000 \times 1.10 = \$1,100$$

If you redeposit this entire sum of $1,100 for another year, how much will you have at the end of year 2? During year 2 you will earn 10% interest on the entire $1,100. The interest earned is, thus, $0.10 \times \$1,100$ or $110. You will, therefore, have $1,210 at the end of year 2.

To gain a good understanding of the nature of compound interest, we can break this future value of $1,210 into its three components. First, there is the original principal of $1,000. Next, there is the interest on this principal—$100 in the first year and another $100 in the second year. The interest on the original principal is called **simple interest** ($200 in our example). Finally, there is $10 of interest earned in the second year on the $100 of interest earned in the first year. Interest earned on interest already paid is called **compound interest.** The total interest earned ($210) is the sum of the simple interest ($200) plus the compound interest ($10).

Practically speaking, you do not care how much of your total interest of $210 is simple interest and how much is compound interest. All you really care about is how much you will have in your account in the future, that is, the future value. The most direct way to calculate the future value at the end of year 2 is to recognize that it is the original principal multiplied by 1.1 (here we drop the zero from 1.10 to shorten our equations) and then multiplied by 1.1 again:

$$FV = \$1,000 \times 1.1 \times 1.1 = \$1,000 \times 1.1^2 = \$1,210$$

After three years you will have:

$$FV = \$1,000 \times 1.1 \times 1.1 \times 1.1 = \$1,000 \times 1.1^3 = \$1,331$$

By this chain of reasoning, we can find future value after five years by repeated multiplication:

$$\$1,000 \times 1.1 \times 1.1 \times 1.1 \times 1.1 \times 1.1 = \$1,100 \times 1.1^5 = \$1,610.51$$

Thus, we have our answer to the original question. The future value of $1,000 at an interest rate of 10% per year for five years is $1,610.51. The total interest earned over the five years is $610.51, of which $500 is simple interest and $110.51 is compound interest.

Quick Check 1

If the interest rate is only 5% per year in the previous example, what is the future value? What are the simple interest and the compound interest?

To help in understanding the effect of compounding, look at Table 1, which shows the growth of the amount in your account over the five-year period. The table shows clearly that the total interest earned each year is equal to the beginning amount multiplied by the interest rate of 10%. When the information in the table is graphed in Figure 1, it shows the part of the growth in the account that is due to simple interest and the part that is due to compound interest. Although the cumulative total of simple interest grows each year by the same $100, the cumulative total of compound interest grows by larger and larger amounts each year. This is because the compound interest is 10% of the sum of all previous interest earned.

More generally, if i is the interest rate and n is the number of years, the future value of the $1,000 is given by the formula:

$$FV = \$1,000(1 + i)^n \tag{1}$$

TABLE 1   **Future Value and Compound Interest**

Year	Beginning Amount	Interest Earned	Ending Amount
1	$1,000.00	$100.00	$1,100.00
2	$1,100.00	$110.00	$1,210.00
3	$1,210.00	$121.00	$1,331.00
4	$1,331.00	$133.10	$1,464.10
5	$1,464.10	$146.41	$1,610.51
	Total Interest Earned	$610.51	

Note: Table 1 and Figure 1 show the future value of $1,000 at 10% per year. Simple interest in the graph is the cumulative total of $100 per year. Compound interest in the graph is the cumulative total of all compound interest earned up to that point.

FIGURE 1

**Future Value and
Compound Interest**

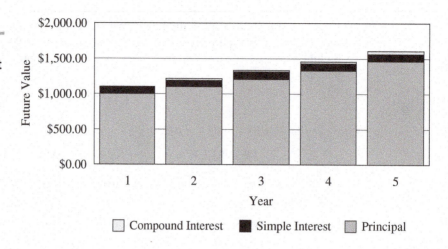

In general, for any present value invested, the **future value factor** is given by:

$$FV = (1+i)^n$$

The future value factor is greater the higher the interest rate and the longer the time the investment is held. Table 2 and the graph in Figure 2 illustrate this relationship for various interest rates and holding periods.

1.1 Calculating Future Values

There are also special-purpose financial calculators available designed to make doing the calculations even easier. By pressing the appropriately labeled keys, you enter (in any order you please) the values for the number of periods (n), the interest rate (i), and the amount of the investment (PV), and then compute future value (FV). Like magic, the answer appears in the calculator's display. Similarly, spreadsheet programs have a simple and convenient way to compute future values. In an Excel spreadsheet the future value is calculated using the built-in *FV function: FV(i, n, 0, −PV)*. In Excel cash inflows and outflows are represented with positive and negative signs respectively. This requires that the entry for the

TABLE 2   Future Value of $1 for Different Periods and Interest Rates

Number of Periods, n	Interest Rate, i					
	2%	4%	6%	8%	10%	12%
1	1.0200	1.0400	1.0600	1.0800	1.1000	1.1200
2	1.0404	1.0816	1.1236	1.1664	1.2100	1.2544
3	1.0612	1.1249	1.1910	1.2597	1.3310	1.4049
4	1.0824	1.1699	1.2625	1.3605	1.4641	1.5735
5	1.1041	1.2167	1.3382	1.4693	1.6105	1.7623
10	1.2190	1.4802	1.7908	2.1589	2.5937	3.1058
15	1.3459	1.8009	2.3966	3.1722	4.1772	5.4736
20	1.4859	2.1911	3.2071	4.6610	6.7275	9.6463

Note: Table 2 and Figure 2 show the future value of $1 for different holding periods at various interest rates. The higher the interest rate, the faster the future value grows.

FIGURE 2

**Future Value of $1
at Interest Rates
from 2% to 12%**

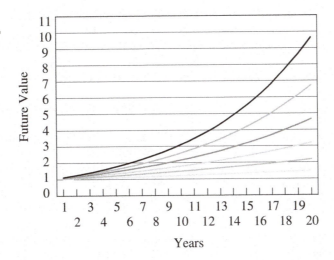

present value be negative. The built-in Excel function can be used directly in a single spreadsheet cell by entering $= FV(10\%, 5, 0, -\$1,000)$ and $1,610.51 would be displayed or in a tabled format to allow for sensitivity analysis and quick recalculations. For example, changing the interest rate in Cell A1 from 10% to 15% would return a new FV in Cell A4 equal to $2,011.36

	A	B
1	10%	i
2	5	n
3	($1,000.00)	PV
4	$=FV$(A1, A2, 0, A3) RETURNS $1,610.51	FV

1. We can use tables of future value factors, such as those in Table 2, to compute future values. In our example, we would look for the factor corresponding to n of 5 and an interest rate of 10%. The table shows 1.6105 as the appropriate future value factor. We then multiply our $1,000 by this factor.

2. Finally, there is a handy rule of thumb that can help you estimate future values when you do not have your calculator or a table available. It is called the **Rule of 72.** This rule says that the number of years it takes for a sum of money to double in value (the "doubling time") is approximately equal to the number 72 divided by the interest rate expressed in percent per year:

$$\text{Doubling Time} = \frac{72}{\textit{Interest Rate}}$$

So at an interest rate of 10% per year, it should take approximately 7.2 years to double your money. If you start with $1,000, you will have $2,000 after 7.2 years, $4,000 after 14.4 years, $8,000 after 21.6 years, and so on.

From this point on we shall use a straightforward notation to aid our time value of money computations. To compute the future value of a present amount we will use the **compound amount factor** defined as:

$$FV_{PV}(PV, i, n) = PV(1+i)^n$$

The notation indicates that we are calculating a future value from a present value (FV_{PV}) knowing the magnitude of the present value (PV), the periodic interest rate (i), and the number of compounding periods (n). The compound amount factor is the simple product of the present value and the future value factor and represents the total future value. For example, $FV_{PV}(\$1,000, 10\%, 5) = \$1,610.51$ and $FV_{PV}(\$1,000, 12\%, 5) = \$1,762,34$.

1.2 Saving for Old Age

You are 20 years old and are considering putting $100 into an account paying 8% per year for 45 years. How much will you have in the account at age 65? How much of it will be simple interest, and how much compound interest? If you could find an account paying 9% per year, how much more would you have at age 65?

Using the compound amount factor, we find:

$$FV_{PV}(\$100, 8\%, 45) = \$100 \times 1.08^{45} = \$3,192.04$$

Because the original principal is $100, total interest earned is $3,092.04. The simple interest is $45 \times 0.08 \times \$100$ or $360, whereas the compound interest is $2,732.04.

At an interest rate of 9% per year, we find:

$$FV_{PV}(\$100, 9\%, 45) = \$100 \times 1.09^{45} = \$4,832.73$$

Thus, a seemingly small increase of 1% in the interest rate results in an extra $1,640.69 ($4,832.73 − $3,192.04) at age 65. This is more than a 50% increase $\left(\dfrac{\$1,640.69}{\$3,192.04} = 0.514 \right)$.

The general point of this example is that a small difference in interest rates can make a big difference in future values over long periods of time.

Note that the Rule of 72 can help us to find a pretty good approximate answer to our questions. At an interest rate of 8% per year, your $100 would double about every nine years. Thus, after 45 years, it would double five times, giving an approximate future value of $3,200:

$$\$100 \times 2 \times 2 \times 2 \times 2 \times 2 = \$100 \times 2^5 = \$100 \times 32 = \$3,200$$

which is not too far from the exact answer of $3,192.04.

At an interest rate of 9% per year, your money would double about every eight years. In 45 years it would double about 5.5 times. Therefore, the future value should be about 50% greater than when the interest rate is 8% per year: Again, this is not too far from the exact answer of $4,832.73.

1.3 Reinvesting at a Different Rate

You are faced with the following investment decision. You have $10,000 to invest for two years. You have decided to invest your money in bank certificates of deposit (CDs). Two-year CDs are paying 7% per year and one-year CDs are paying 6%. What should you do?

To make this decision you must first decide what you think the interest rate on one-year CDs will be next year. This is called the **reinvestment rate,** that is, the interest rate at which money received before the end of your planning horizon can be reinvested. Suppose you are sure that it will be 8% per year.

Now you can use the concept of future value to make this investment decision. You compute the future value under each investment alternative and choose the one giving the most money at the end of two years. With the two-year CD, the future value will be:

$$FV_{PV}(\$10,000, 7\%, 2) = \$10,000 \times 1.07^2 = \$11,449$$

With the sequence of two 1-year CDs, the future value will be:

$$FV = \$10,000 \times 1.06 \times 1.08 = \$11,448$$

Thus, you are slightly better off if you invest in the two-year CD.

1.4 Paying Back a Loan

Fifty years after graduation, you get a letter from your college notifying you that they have just discovered that you failed to pay your last student activities fee of \$100. Because it was your college's oversight, it has decided to charge you an interest rate of only 6% per year. Your college would like you to pay it back at the coming fiftieth reunion of your graduating class. As a loyal alumnus, you feel obliged to pay. How much do you owe them?

Using any of the methods discussed earlier, we find:

$$FV_{PV}(\$100, 6\%, 50) = \$100 \times 1.06^{50} = \$1,842.02$$

Quick Check 2

In 1626, Peter Minuit purchased Manhattan Island from the Native Americans for about \$24 worth of trinkets. If the tribe had taken cash instead and invested it to earn 6% per year compounded annually, how much would they have had in 2006, 380 years later?

---

2 The Frequency of Compounding

Interest rates on loans and saving accounts are usually stated in the form of an **annual percentage rate** (*APR*), (e.g., 6% per year) with a certain frequency of compounding (e.g., monthly). Because the frequency of compounding can differ, it is important to have a way of making interest rates comparable. This is done by computing an **effective annual rate** (*EFF*), defined as the equivalent interest rate, *if compounding were only once per year.*

For example, suppose your money earns interest at a stated annual percentage rate (*APR*) of 6% per year compounded monthly. This means that interest is credited to your account every month at 1/12th the stated *APR*. Thus, the true interest rate is actually 1/2% per month (or 0.005 per month as a decimal).

We find the *EFF* by computing the future value at the end of the year per dollar invested at the beginning of the year. In this example we get:

$$FV = 1.005^{12} = 1.0616778$$

The effective annual rate is just this number minus one.

$$EFF = 1.0616778 - 1 = 0.0616778 \text{ or } 6.16778\% \text{ per year}$$

The general formula for the effective annual rate is:

$$EFF(APR, m) = \left(1 + \frac{APR}{m}\right)^m - 1 \tag{2}$$

where *APR* is the annual percentage rate, and *m* the number of compounding periods per year. Table 3 presents the effective annual rates corresponding to an annual percentage rate of 6% per year for different compounding frequencies.

TABLE 3 **Effective Annual Rates for an *APR* of 6%**

Compounding	*m*	*EFF*
Annually	1	6.00000%
Semiannually	2	6.09000%
Quarterly	4	6.13636%
Monthly	12	6.16778%
Weekly	52	6.17998%
Daily	365	6.18313%
Continuously	∞	6.18365%

If compounding is done once per year, then the effective annual rate is the same as the annual percentage rate. As the compounding frequency increases, the effective annual rate gets larger and larger but approaches a limit. With this modification the compound amount factor becomes $FV_m\left(PV, APR, m, n\right) = PV \cdot \left(1 + \frac{APR}{m}\right)^{mn}$ where $\frac{APR}{m}$ is the interest rate per compounding period and mn the total number of compounding periods over the n years. As m grows without limit, $\left(1 + \frac{i}{m}\right)^{mn}$ approaches e^{in} where e is the constant 2.71828 (rounded off to the fifth decimal place). So with continuous compounding the future value is calculated as: $FV_{con}(PV, i, n) = PV \cdot e^{i \cdot n}$. In the above example, $e^{0.06} = 1.0618365$. Therefore, if interest is continuously compounded at 6%, the $EFF = 0.0618365$ or 6.18365% per year.

In Excel the effective annual rate can be calculated using the built-in EFFECT function. The arguments for the function are EFFECT(*APR*, *m*). In an Excel cell, entering =EFFECT(10%, 4) would return 0.1038129, which says that a 10% annual percentage rate with quarterly compounding corresponds to an effective annual rate of 10.38129%. The symmetric Excel built-in NOMINAL function calculates the annual percentage rate corresponding to a given effective annual rate and number of compounding periods per year. The functional structure is NOMINAL(*EFF*, *m*). Thus entering = NOMINAL(12%, 12) in an Excel cell will return 0.1138655. This is interpreted to say that to produce an effective annual rate of 12% under monthly compounding, the *APR* must be 11.38655%.

Quick Check 3

You take out a loan at an *APR* of 12% with monthly compounding. What is the effective annual rate on your loan?

3 Present Value and Discounting

When we compute future values, we are asking questions like "How much will we have in 10 years if we invest $1,000 today at an interest rate of 8% per year?" (The answer is: $FV = \$2,158.92$. Check it!)

But suppose we want to know how much to invest today in order to reach some target amount at a date in the future. For example, if we need to have $15,000 for a child's college education eight years from now, how much do we have to invest now? To find the answer to this kind of question, we need to calculate the present value of a given future amount.

Calculating present values is the reverse of calculating future values. That is, it tells us the amount you would have to invest today to have a certain amount in the future. Let's take a look at calculating *PV* step by step.

Suppose we want to have $1,000 one year from now and can earn 10% interest per year. The amount we must invest now is the present value of $1,000. Because the interest rate is 10%, we know that for every dollar we invest now we will have a future value of $1.1. Therefore, we can write:

$$PV \times 1.1 = \$1,000$$

Then the present value is given by:

$$PV = \frac{\$1,000}{1.1} = \$909.09$$

So if the interest rate is 10% per year, we need to invest $909.09 in order to have $1,000 a year from now.

Now suppose the $1,000 is not needed until two years from now. Clearly, the amount we need to invest today at an interest rate of 10% is less than $909.09, because it will earn interest at the rate of 10% per year for two years. To find the present value, we use our knowledge of how to find future values:

$$\$1,000 = PV \times 1.1^2 = PV \times 1.21$$

In our example the present value is:

$$PV = \frac{\$1,000}{1.1^2} = \$826.45$$

Thus, $826.45 invested now at an interest rate of 10% per year will grow to $1,000 in two years.

Calculating present values is called *discounting,* and the interest rate used in the calculation is often referred to as the *discount rate.* Thus, discounting in finance is very different from discounting in retailing. In retailing it means reducing the price in order to sell more goods; in finance it means computing the present value of a future sum of money. To distinguish the two kinds of discounting in the world of business, the calculation of present values is called *discounted cash flow (DCF)* analysis.

The general formula for the present value of $1 to be received *n* periods from now at a discount rate of *i* (per period) is:

$$PV = \frac{1}{(1+i)^n} \qquad \textbf{(3)}$$

This is called the **present value of $1** at an interest rate of *i* for *n* periods.

The present value of $1 to be received five years from now at an interest rate of 10% per year is:

$$PV = \frac{1}{1.1^5} = 0.62092$$

To find the present value of $1,000 to be received in five years at 10%, we simply multiply this factor by $1,000 to get $620.92.

TABLE 4 **Present Value of $1 for Different Periods and Interest Rates**

Number of Periods, n	Interest Rate, i					
	2%	4%	6%	8%	10%	12%
1	0.9804	0.9615	0.9434	0.9259	0.9091	0.8929
2	0.9612	0.9246	0.8900	0.8573	0.8264	0.7972
3	0.9423	0.8890	0.8396	0.7938	0.7513	0.7118
4	0.9238	0.8548	0.7921	0.7350	0.6830	0.6355
5	0.9057	0.8219	0.7473	0.6806	0.6209	0.5674
10	0.8203	0.6756	0.5584	0.4632	0.3855	0.3220
15	0.7430	0.5553	0.4173	0.3152	0.2394	0.1827
20	0.6730	0.4564	0.3118	0.2145	0.1486	0.1037

Because discounting is just the reverse of compounding, we could use the same table (see Table 2) that we used before for future value factors to find present values of $1. Instead of multiplying by the factor, however, we would divide by it. Thus, we can find the present value of $1,000 to be received in five years at 10% by looking up the future value factor of 1.6105 in Table 2 and dividing $1,000 by it:

$$\frac{\$1,000}{1.6105} = \$620.92$$

For convenience, there are tables of present values of $1 such as the one shown as Table 4 containing the reciprocals of the factors in Table 2. Look in Table 4 for the present value of $1 for an interest rate of 10% and five periods, and verify that it is 0.62092.

The general formula for the present value of $1 is:

$$PV = \frac{1}{(1+i)^n}$$

where i is the interest rate expressed as a decimal fraction and n is the number of periods.

By going down any column in Table 4, note how present values decline the further in the future the $1 is to be taken out of the account. At an interest rate of 10%, for example, the present value of $1 to be received in one year is $0.9091, but the present value of $1 to be received in 20 years is only $0.1486.

Consistent with our previous notation for time value of money computations, we can calculate the present value of a future amount using the **present value factor** defined as:

$$PV_{FV}(FV, i, n) = \frac{FV}{(1+i)^n}$$

The notation indicates that we are calculating a present value from a future value (PV_{FV}) knowing the magnitude of the future value (FV), the periodic interest rate (i), and the number of compounding periods (n). The present factor is the simple product of the future value and the present value of $1 and represents the total present value. For example, $PV_{FV}(\$1,000, 10\%, 5) = \$620.92$ and $PV_{FV}(\$1,000, 12\%, 5) = \$567.43$.

3.1 When a $100 Gift Is Not Really $100

It is your brother's tenth birthday, and he receives a $100 savings bond maturing in five years. This type of bond pays nothing until its maturity date. In adding up the value of his birthday "loot," he mistakenly writes down $100 for this bond. How much is it really worth if the discount rate is 8% per year and the bond does not mature for another five years? How could you explain your brother's mistake to him, so that he would understand?

We are looking for the present value of $100 to be received in five years at a discount rate of 8% per year. There are several ways we could compute it. The formula is:

$$PV = \frac{\$100}{1.08^5} = \$68.06$$

On an ordinary calculator, we could find this present value by dividing 100 by 1.08 five times to find that it is 68. On a financial calculator, we would enter the values for n, i, and FV, and then compute the present value by pressing the key labeled PV. Or we could use the present value factor of $1 in Table 4. The table entry corresponding to an interest rate of 8% and five periods is 0.6806. Multiply this factor by $100 to find the present value of $68.

Explaining the answer to your brother is a tough assignment. Probably the best way to do it is to use the idea of future value rather than present value. You could explain to him that his $100 savings bond is worth only $68 because all he has to do to get $100 five years from now is to put $68 into a savings account paying interest of 8% per year.

> ### Quick Check 4
>
> What is the present value of $100 to be received in four years at an interest rate of 6% per year?

3.2 Discounting with Compounding More Frequently Than Annually

When interest is compound more frequently than on an annual basis we need to make the appropriate adjustments in the method for discounting. Here the formula for present value would be modified to $PV_m\left(FV, APR, n, m\right) = \dfrac{FV}{\left(1 + \frac{APR}{m}\right)^{mn}}$ where APR is the annual percentage rate and m is the number of compounding periods per year. For example, the present value of $500 in 5 years with semiannual compounding at a 10% annual rate would be:

$PV_m(\$500,\ 10\%,\ 5,\ 2) = \dfrac{\$500}{\left(1 + \frac{10\%}{2}\right)^{10}} = \$306.96$. Note that, using Excel, we could perform

the compounding adjustment directly and convert the 10% annual rate into a 5% semiannual rate over 10 six-month periods into the built-in present value function and enter $=PV(5\%, 10, 0, -\$500)$.[1] This would return an entry equal to $306.96.

In the continuous discounting case, the present value formula is $PV_{con} = FV \cdot e^{-APR \cdot n}$. Suppose a T-bill matures in six months with a face value of $10,000 and a competitive continuously compounding rate of return is 5%. What is the present value of the T-bill? Discounting the $10,000 on a continuous basis we would have: $PV = \$10,000 \cdot e^{-0.10 \cdot \frac{1}{2}} = \$9,512.29$.

---

[1]The Excel PV function has the form: $PV(i, n, PMT, FV)$.

4 Alternative Discounted Cash Flow Decision Rules

The discounted cash flow concepts that we have studied so far in this chapter provide a powerful set of tools for making investment decisions. The essential ideas are captured in the equation relating future value, present value, the interest rate, and the number of periods:

$$FV = PV(1+i)^n \qquad (4)$$

Given any three of the variables in this equation, we can find the fourth and formulate an investment decision rule based on it. The most common decision rule is the **net present value** (*NPV*) rule. This rule is not only widely used and universally applicable (i.e., correctly used it never leads to the wrong decision), but it is also very intuitive. Simply put, the *NPV* rule sounds almost obvious: *Accept any project with a present value of future cash flows that exceed the initial investment.* The only trick is to make sure that one does not compare apples to oranges. Thus, when calculating the future cash flows (which happens some time from now), we must use their present value in order to make them comparable.

Formally, the *NPV* rule says the following:

The *NPV* is the difference between the present value of all future cash inflows minus the present value of all current and future cash outflows. Accept a project if its *NPV* is positive. Reject a project if its *NPV* is negative.

For example, suppose that a $100 savings bond maturing in 5 years is selling for a price of $75. Your next best alternative for investing is an 8% bank account. Is the savings bond a good investment? Let's show how to use the *NPV* decision rule in evaluating this investment. The initial investment for the savings bond is $75 (this happens today, no discounting necessary). What is the present value of the cash inflows that the bond generates? It is simply the present value of $100 to be received in five years from now. The relevant interest rate is the rate that the money could earn if it were not invested in the bond.

In general, for the *NPV* calculation of any investment, we use the **opportunity cost of capital** (also called the *market capitalization rate*) as the interest rate. The opportunity cost of capital is simply the rate that we could earn somewhere else if we did not invest it in the project under evaluation. In this example, the opportunity cost of capital of investing in the savings bond is the rate that we could earn if we put our money in a bank instead—8% per year in this case.

For convenience in keeping track of the calculations (especially if they are being done in a spread sheet or on a financial calculator), we organize our information in the following table:

Time Value of Money (*TVM*) Calculation Table	
10%	*i*
5	*n*
?	*PV*
100	*FV*
PV = $68.06	**Result**

A question mark indicates the variable that has to be computed.

In this case we use three of the variables, FV, n, and i, to compute the fourth, PV. We then compare this computed present value to the known initial investment of the savings bond. Using the formula, we find:

$$PV = \frac{\$100}{1.08^5} = \$68.06$$

Comparing the $68.06 to the $75 necessary to obtain the bond, we conclude that investing in the bond is not worthwhile. In other words, the *NPV* of the investment is negative.

The *NPV* is a measure of how much your *current* wealth changes as a result of your choice. Clearly, if the *NPV* is negative, it does not pay to undertake the investment. In this case, if you choose to invest in the bond, your current wealth decreases by approximately $7.

Another way to arrive at the same conclusion is to use a slightly different rule known as the *future value rule*. Simply stated, it says to *invest in the project if its future value is greater than the future value that will obtain in the next best alternative*. This rule is actually slightly more intuitive (and leads to the same decision as the *NPV* rule). The reason it is not used as often in practice is that in many circumstances (as will be shown later in the book) the future value of an investment cannot be computed whereas the *NPV* rule can still be used. Let us illustrate how the future value rule would have worked in the same example just used to illustrate the *NPV* rule.

Investing in a savings bond (initial investment $75, future value of cash flows $100 in five years) clearly leads to a future value of $100. Putting the money into a bank at 8% is the next best thing we can do with the money. Does the savings bond have a higher future value than we could get from the bank? Again, we organize our information in the table:

Time Value of Money (*TVM*) Calculation Table	
8%	i
5	n
$75.00	PV
?	FV
$FV = \$110.20$	**Result**

Using the formula, we get that the future value from the bank account is given by

$$FV = \$75 \times 1.08^5 = \$110.20$$

This is clearly better than the $100 future value of the savings bond. Again, we find that the savings bond is an inferior investment.

There are other decision rules that are also used in practice. Each has its own intuition and each is useful for certain problems. It should be noted, however, that none of the rules are as universally applicable as the *NPV* rule. Here is another widely used rule, which in many circumstances is also equivalent to the *NPV* rule:

Accept an investment if its return is greater than the opportunity cost of capital.

This rule is (clearly) based on the concept of rate of return. Recall that in our example the opportunity cost of capital from putting the money into the bank is 8% per year.

By investing $75 in the savings bond today, you can get $100 five years from now. What interest rate would you be earning? In other words, we want to find i that solves the equation:

$$\$75 = \frac{\$100}{(1+i)^5}$$

This is called the bond's **yield to maturity** or **internal rate of return** (*IRR*). The internal rate of return is the discount rate that makes the present value of the future cash inflows equal to the present value of cash outflows. In other words, the *IRR* is exactly that interest rate at which the *NPV* is equal to zero. Thus, if the rate at which the *NPV* is zero (the *IRR*) is higher than the opportunity cost of capital, then we know that the *NPV* at the opportunity cost of capital itself must be positive. In other words, if the *IRR* is (say) 10% (i.e., the *NPV* at 10% is zero), then the *NPV* at the opportunity cost of capital (say) 8% must be positive. Why? We know that the *NPV* calculation discounts future cash flows. We also know that the present value of future cash flows is greater when the discount rate is small. Thus, if the *NPV* is zero at 10%, it will be positive at 8%. Hence, having a 10% *IRR* and an 8% opportunity cost of capital is equivalent to saying that the *NPV* must be positive.[2]

To find i (the *IRR*) on a financial calculator, enter *PV*, *FV*, and *n* and compute i:

Time Value of Money (*TVM*) Calculation Table	
?	*i*
5	*n*
($75.00)	*PV*
$100.00	*FV*
$i = 5.92\%$	**Result**

We have put brackets (representing a negative sign) around the $75 in the table column labeled *PV* because it signifies an investment (i.e., a cash outflow). Most financial calculators and spreadsheets require you to enter the initial investment or cash outflow as negative. It should not be surprising that the model assumes that an investment (negative cash flow) is needed in order to earn a positive cash flow in the future. If all cash flows were positive, we would have created a money machine and that, sadly, is an impossibility.

If you don't have a spreadsheet, you can solve for i using some algebra:

$$\$100 = 75 \times (1+i)^5$$

$$(1+i)^5 = \frac{\$100}{\$75}$$

$$i = \left(\frac{\$100}{\$75}\right)^{\frac{1}{5}} - 1 = 0.0592 = 5.92\%$$

Thus, the yield to maturity (*IRR*) on the bond is 5.92% per year. This should be compared to the 8% per year you could earn by putting your money in the bank. Clearly, you are better off putting your money in the bank.

The rate of return decision rule is equivalent to the *NPV* rule in evaluating a single investment for which there are no negative future cash flows. Even with that condition, it

---

[2]This conclusion applies only if all future cash flows are positive.

will not in general produce the same rankings from best to worst among several investment opportunities.

When you have to choose among several alternative investments, choose the one with the highest *NPV*.

There is one more variable in this example for which we can solve with our calculator in order to arrive at a decision: *n* (the number of years). Let us do this for the savings bond. We know that the *FV* is $100, the *PV* is $75, and the opportunity cost of capital is 8%; what is *n*?

$$\$75 = \frac{\$100}{1.08^n}$$

On the financial calculator we input *PV*, *FV*, and *i* and compute *n*:

n	i	PV	FV	Result
?	8	−$75	$100	n = 3.74

We find that *n* is 3.74 years. Now, what does this mean? It means that if we put the money into the bank (at 8%), it would take 3.74 years for $75 to grow to $100. With the savings bond, it takes five years for the $75 to grow to $100. This observation has suggested to some the following rule:

Choose the investment alternative with the shortest payback period.

In other words, choose the investment in which you can "get your money back", or meet your growth goal, (i.e., turn the $75 investment into $100) in the shortest period of time.

This rule, however, applies only in special cases. As with the *IRR* rule, the "payback" rule is not a reliable one for general investment choice purposes. Although these alternative rules are sometimes used in practice, stick with the *NPV* rule as the safe and universal rule of choice.

4.1 Investing in Land

You have the opportunity to buy a piece of land for $10,000. You are sure that five years from now it will be worth $20,000. If you can earn 8% per year by investing your money in the bank, is this investment in the land worthwhile?

Invest in a project if its net present value (*NPV*) is positive. Do not invest if the *NPV* is negative.

What is the present value of having $20,000 (the future cash flow) in five years from now? In this case we input *FV*, *n*, and *i*, and compute *PV*. We then compare this computed present value to the $10,000 initial outlay, and make our decision based on which one is greater.

n	i	PV	FV	Result
5	8	?	$20,000	PV = $13,612

Thus, the investment in the land has a present value of $13,612. Comparing this to the $10,000 cost of the land, it clearly seems like a bargain. Its *NPV* is $3,612.

Quick Check 6

Show that the alternative decision criteria presented previously lead to the same result—that the investment is worthwhile.

4.2 Other's People Money

In the preceding example, we considered an investment in which you are required to lay out money in the present and receive cash at some future date. But often financial decisions involve just the reverse. For example, suppose that you need to borrow $5,000 to buy a car. You go to a bank and they offer you a loan at an interest rate of 12% per year. You then go to a friend who says he will lend you the $5,000 if you pay him $9,000 in four years. What should you do?

First, let's identify the project that you need to evaluate. The cash flow that you want to evaluate is the $5,000 (today) you can borrow from your friend (a cash inflow). The investment you must make is the present value of the $9,000 repayment (a cash outflow) after four years.

The way to proceed is to calculate the *NPV* of the project. The opportunity cost of capital is 12% (the bank's rate, your next best alternative). The cash flows are given. What is the *NPV*?

n	i	PV	FV	Result
4	12	?	−$9,000	PV = $5,719.66

We find that the present value of the cash outflow is $5,719.66. Thus, the *NPV* of the project is −$719.66. Hence, the project of borrowing from your friend is not worthwhile. You are better off borrowing from the bank.

What is the implied interest rate that your friend is charging you? The answer is to solve the present value equation for *i:*

$$\$5,000 = \frac{\$9,000}{(1+i)^4}$$

Using a financial calculator:

n	i	PV	FV	Result
4	?	$5,000	−$9,000	i = 15.83%

We find that the interest rate is 15.83% per year. You are better off borrowing from the bank.

Note that the rate you have just computed is the *IRR* of borrowing from your friend. It is 15.83%. Now, in the previous examples we stated that the *IRR* rule works as follows: *Invest* in a project if the *IRR* is *greater* than the opportunity cost of capital. This rule works for projects that have the feature of a one-time investment (i.e., the initial cash flow is negative and the future cash flows are positive).

However, it should be clear that for projects that have the feature of borrowing (i.e., the initial cash flow is positive and the future repayment cash flow is negative) the rule must be turned on its head: *Borrow* from a source if the *IRR* of the loan is *less* than the opportunity cost of capital.

As noted previously, a major potential problem with the *IRR* rule rears its head whenever there are multiple cash inflows. In such cases the *IRR* may not be unique (e.g., there are many) or the *IRR* may not exist at all. More on this problem later.

5 Multiple Cash Flows

So far we have considered situations in which there is a single cash flow in the future. What happens if there is more than one? For example, suppose you want to save for a child's college education or for your own retirement by putting a certain amount each year into an interest-bearing account; or you are evaluating an investment such as a bond that offers a stream of future payments; or you are considering taking a loan that requires you to make periodic installment payments. To deal with all of these more complicated situations we need only extend the concepts already presented.

5.1 Time Lines

A useful tool in analyzing the timing of cash flows is a diagram known as a **time line.** It is illustrated in Figure 3.

A negative sign in front of a cash flow means that you put in that amount of money (a cash *outflow* from you), whereas no sign means that you take out that amount (cash *inflow* to you). In our example, you put in 100 at time 0 and take out 20 at the end of the first period, 50 at the end of the second, and 60 at the end of the third.

5.2 Future Value of a Stream of Cash Flows

We begin with a savings decision and the concept of future value. Each year you deposit $1,000 into an account paying an interest rate of 10% per year starting immediately. How much will you have after two years if you do not withdraw any money before then?

The original $1,000 grows to $1,100 at the end of the first year. Then you add another $1,000, so there is $2,100 in the account at the beginning of the second year. By the end of the second year there is $2,100 × (1.1) or $2,310 in the account.

An alternative way to find this future value of $2,310 is to calculate the future values of each of the two $1,000 deposits separately and then add them together. The future value of the first deposit is:

$$\$1,000 \times 1.1^2 = \$1,210$$

The future value of the second deposit will be:

$$\$1,000 \times 1.1 = \$1,100$$

Adding the two together, we get the same $2,310 that we found by multiplying each year's accumulation by 1.1.

> **Quick Check 7**
>
> Suppose you deposit $1,000 now and then $2,000 a year from now. How much will you have two years from now, if the interest rate is 10% per year?

FIGURE 3

Time Line

Time	0	1	2	3
Cash Flow	−100	20	50	60

5.3 Present Value of a Stream of Cash Flows

Often we need to compute the present value rather than the future value of a series of cash flows. For example, suppose you want to have $1,000 one year from now and then $2,000 in two years. If the interest rate is 10% per year, how much would you have to put into an account today in order to satisfy your requirement?

In this case we have to compute the present value of the two cash flows depicted in Figure 4. Just as the future value of a stream of cash flows is the sum of the future values of each, so too with the present value.

5.4 Investing with Multiple Cash Flows

Suppose you are offered an opportunity to invest in a project that will pay you $1,000 a year from now and another $2,000 two years from now. The project requires you to invest $2,500 now. You are convinced that the project is completely free of risk. Is it a worthwhile investment if you can earn 10% per year on your money by leaving it in the bank?

Note that this problem bears a striking resemblance to the previous one. The cash flows that this project will generate are the same as depicted in Figure 4—$1,000 a year from now and $2,000 two years from now. We already know that if you put your money in the bank, it would take $2,562 to generate the same future cash flows. Because the outlay required on the project is only $2,500, it has a net present value of $62. As we saw earlier in this chapter, an investment with a positive *NPV* should be undertaken.

6 Annuities

Often the future cash flows in a savings plan, an investment project, or a loan repayment schedule are the same each year. We call such a level stream of cash flows or payments an **annuity.** The term comes from the life insurance business, in which an annuity contract is one that promises a stream of payments to the purchaser for some period of time. In finance it is applied more generally and applies to any level stream of cash flows. Thus, the stream of payments on an installment loan or a mortgage is called an annuity, too.

If the cash flows start immediately, as in a savings plan or a lease, it is called an **immediate annuity.** If the cash flows start at the end of the current period rather than immediately, it is called an **ordinary annuity.** A mortgage is an example of an ordinary annuity. There are some convenient formulas, tables, and calculator functions for computing the present and future values of annuities, which come in handy when the stream of cash flows lasts for many periods.

6.1 Future Value of Annuities

For example, suppose that you intend to save $100 each year for the next three years. How much will you have accumulated at the end of that time if the interest rate is 10% per year? If you start saving immediately, you will have:

$$FV = \$100 \times 1.1^3 + \$100 \times 1.1^2 + \$100 \times 1.1$$

FIGURE 4

Present Value of Multiple Cash Flows

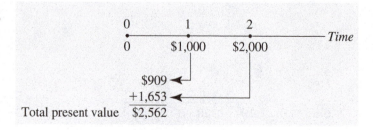

Factoring out the constant annual cash flow of $100, we get:

$$FV = \$100 \times (1.1 + 1.1^2 + 1.1^3)$$

The result is a future value of $364.10. The factor multiplying the $100 is the future value of a $1 payment per year for three years. Although tables containing such future value factors for various interest rates and numbers of periods are available, most people today use financial calculators. The calculator key used to input the periodic contribution is labeled *PMT* (short for *payment*) on most models.

In our example, we know *i*, *n*, and *PMT*, and want to compute *FV*. We enter the givens in the appropriate cells of the table and insert a ? (question mark) for the entry that we want to compute.

n	i	PV	FV	PMT	Result
3	10	0	?	$100	FV = $364.10

In computing the future value of an annuity it matters, of course, whether it is an immediate annuity, as in our current example, or whether it is an ordinary annuity. In the case of an ordinary annuity, the first $100 contribution is made at the end of the first period. Figure 5 shows a time line that contrasts the two situations.

Although in both cases there are the same number of payments, under the immediate annuity pattern the entire amount earns interest for an additional year. Thus, an immediate annuity would have an *FV* equal to that of the ordinary annuity multiplied by $1 + i$. For an ordinary annuity of $1 per year the formula for future value is:

$$FV = \frac{(1+i)^n - 1}{i}$$

We find that the future value of our savings plan of $100 per year for three years is $364.10 if the first deposit is made immediately (an immediate annuity), and $331 if delayed until the end of the first year (an ordinary annuity).

Some financial calculators have a special key to press to let the calculator know whether the annuity payments start at the beginning or end of the first period.

6.2 Present Value of Annuities

Often we want to compute the present value rather than the future value of an annuity stream. For example, how much would you have to put into a fund earning an interest rate of 10% per year to be able to take out $100 per year for the next three years? The answer is the present value of the three cash flows.

The present value of the annuity is the sum of the present values of each of the three payments of $100:

$$PV = \frac{\$100}{1.1} + \frac{\$100}{1.1^2} + \frac{\$100}{1.1^3}$$

FIGURE 5

Cash Flow Diagram of Annuities

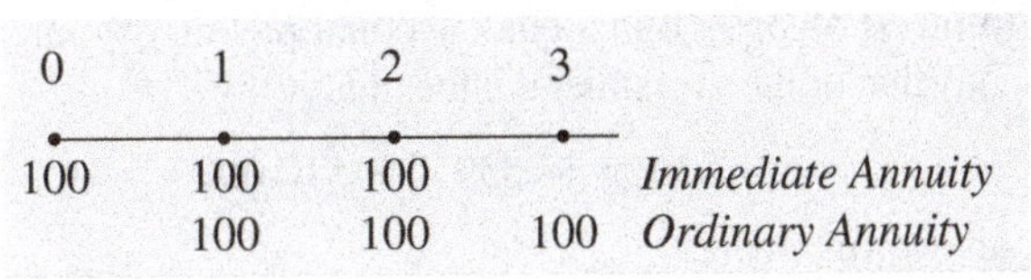

0	1	2	3	
100	100	100		*Immediate Annuity*
	100	100	100	*Ordinary Annuity*

TABLE 5 Proof That Putting in $248.69 Allows You to Take Out $100 per Year for 3 Years

Year	Amount at Beginning of Year	Multiply by	Amount at End of Year	Subtract $100
1	$248.69	1.1	$273.56	$173.56
2	$173.56	1.1	$190.91	$90.91
3	$90.91	1.1	$100.00	$0.00

Factoring out the constant payment of $100 per year, we get:

$$PV = \$100 \times \left(\frac{1}{1.1} + \frac{1}{1.1^2} + \frac{1}{1.1^3} \right)$$

The result is a present value of $248.69. The factor multiplying the $100 payment is the present value of an ordinary annuity of $1 for three years at an interest rate of 10%.

Table 5 verifies that indeed $248.69 is all you would have to put in the account to be able to take out $100 each year for the next three years.

The formula for the present value of an ordinary annuity of $1 per period for n periods at an interest rate of i is:

$$PV = \frac{1 - (1+i)^{-n}}{i}$$

On a financial calculator, we would enter the values for n, i, and PMT, and compute the PV.

n	i	PV	FV	PMT	Result
3	10	?	0	$100	$PV = \$248.69$

6.3 Buying an Annuity

You are 65 years old and are considering whether it pays to buy an annuity from an insurance company. For a cost of $10,000 the insurance company will pay you $1,000 per year for the rest of your life. If you can earn 8% per year on your money in a bank account and expect to live until age 80, is it worth buying the annuity? What implied interest rate is the insurance company paying you? How long must you live for the annuity to be worthwhile?

The most direct way to make this investment decision is to compute the present value of the payments from the annuity and compare it to the annuity's $10,000 cost. Assuming it is an ordinary annuity, then it is expected to make 15 payments of $1,000 each starting at age 66 and ending at age 80. The present value of these 15 payments at a discount rate of 8% per year is $8,559.48.

n	i	PV	FV	PMT	Result
15	8	?	0	$1,000	$PV = \$8,559.48$

In other words, to generate the same 15 annual payments of $1,000 each, it would be enough to invest $8,559.48 in a bank account paying 8% interest per year. Therefore, the net present value of the investment in the annuity is:

$$NPV = \$8,559.48 - \$10,000 = -\$1,440.52$$

and it is not worth buying.

To compute the implied interest rate on the annuity, we need to find the discount rate that makes the *NPV* of the investment zero. The correct answer is 5.56% per year. On a financial calculator we find it by entering the values for *n*, *PMT*, and *PV*, and computing *i*.

n	i	PV	FV	PMT	Result
15	?	−$10,000	0	$1,000	i = 5.56%

In other words, if a bank were offering you an interest rate of 5.56% per year, you could deposit $10,000 now and be able to withdraw $1,000 per year for the next 15 years.

To find the number of years one would have to live to make this annuity worthwhile, we must ask what value of *n* would make the *NPV* of the investment zero. The correct answer is 21 years. On a financial calculator we find it by entering the values for *i*, *PMT*, and *PV*, and computing *n*.

n	i	PV	FV	PMT	Result
?	8	−$10,000	0	$1,000	n = 20.91

Looking at it differently, if you live for 21 years rather than 15, the insurance company would wind up paying you an implied interest rate of 8% per year.

6.4 Taking a Mortgage Loan

Now let's look at an example of a financing decision. You have just decided to buy a house and need to borrow $100,000. One bank offers you a mortgage loan to be repaid over 30 years in 360 monthly payments. If the interest rate is 12% per year, what is the amount of the monthly payment? (Although the interest rate is quoted as an annual percentage rate, the rate is actually 1% per month.) Another bank offers you a 15-year mortgage loan with a monthly payment of $1,100. Which loan is the better deal?

The monthly payment on the 30-year mortgage is computed by using a monthly period (*n* = 360 months) and a monthly interest rate of 1%. The payment is $1,028.61 per month. It is calculated as follows:

n	i	PV	FV	PMT	Result
360	1	−$100,000	0	?	PMT = $1,028.61

At first glance, it might seem as if the 30-year mortgage is a better deal because the $1,028.61 monthly payment is less than the $1,100 for the 15-year mortgage. But the 15-year mortgage is finished after only 180 payments. The monthly interest rate is 0.8677%, or an annual percentage rate of 10.4%. To find this rate:

n	i	PV	FV	PMT	Result
180	?	−$100,000	0	$1,100	i = 10.41%

The 15-year mortgage is, therefore, the better deal in this case.

7 Perpetual Annuities

An important, special type of annuity is a perpetual annuity or **perpetuity.** A perpetuity is a stream of cash flows that lasts forever. The classic example is the "consol" bonds issued by the British government in the nineteenth century, which pay interest each year on the stated face value of the bonds but have no maturity date. Another example, and perhaps a more relevant one, is a share of preferred stock that pays a fixed cash dividend each period (usually every quarter year) and never matures.

A disturbing feature of any perpetual annuity is that you cannot compute the future value of its cash flows because it is infinite. Nevertheless, it has a perfectly well-defined and determinable present value. It might at first seem paradoxical that a series of cash flows that lasts forever can have a finite value today. But consider a perpetual stream of $100 per year. If the interest rate is 10% per year, how much is this perpetuity worth today?

The answer is $1,000. To see why, consider how much money you would have to put into a bank account offering interest of 10% per year in order to be able to take out $100 every year forever. If you put in $1,000, then at the end of the first year you would have $1,100 in the account. You would take out $100, leaving $1,000 for the second year. Clearly, if the interest rate stayed at 10% per year, and you had a fountain of youth nearby, you could go on doing this forever.

More generally, the formula for the present value of a level perpetuity is:

$$PV \text{ of a Level Perpetuity} = \frac{C}{i}$$

where C is the periodic payment and i is the interest rate expressed as a decimal fraction. This is the present value of an ordinary annuity with $n = \infty$.

7.1 Investing in Preferred Stock

Suppose you are currently earning a nominal interest rate of 8% per year on your money. The preferred stock of Boston Gas and Electric Co. offers a cash dividend of $10 per year, and it is selling at a price of $100 per share. Should you invest some of your money in BG&E preferred stock?

The first step is to compute the yield on the preferred stock. To do so, we need only divide the cash dividend of $10 per share by the price of $100:

$$\text{Yield on Preferred Stock} = \frac{Annual\ Dividend}{Price}$$

In this case the yield is 10% per year (i.e., the 10% yield on the preferred stock exceeds the 8% interest rate you are currently earning). To make your investment decision, however, you must also consider risk, a subject we will consider in detail later in the text.

Often one encounters situations in which the cash flows from an investment grow at a constant rate. For example, suppose that you are considering investing in a property for which you expect the first year's cash flow to be $1,000, and you expect it to grow by 4% each year in perpetuity. To evaluate such an investment you need a formula for computing the present value of a **growth perpetuity.** That formula is:

$$PV = \frac{C_1}{i - g}$$

where C_1 is the first year's cash flow and g is the growth rate.

In the example at hand suppose that the discount rate is 9%. Then the present value of the property would be:

$$PV = \frac{\$1,000}{0.09 - 0.04} = \frac{\$1,000}{0.056} = \$20,000$$

If you can purchase the property for less than $20,000, it would be a worthwhile investment.

7.2 Investing in Common Stock

You have the opportunity to buy stock in a company that is known to pay a cash dividend that grows by 3% every year. The next dividend will be $1 per share, and is to be paid a year from now. If you require a 10% per year rate of return, how much should you be willing to pay for the stock?

The answer is that you should be willing to pay the PV of the expected future cash flows discounted at 10% per year. The stream of expected future cash dividends is a growth perpetuity. Using the formula for a growth perpetuity:

$$PV = \frac{\$1}{0.10 - 0.03} = \frac{\$1}{0.07} = \$14.29$$

8 Loan Amortization

Many loans, such as home mortgage loans and car loans, are repaid in equal periodic installments. Part of each payment is interest on the outstanding balance of the loan and part is repayment of principal. After each payment, the outstanding balance is reduced by the amount of principal repaid. Therefore, the portion of the payment that goes toward the payment of interest is lower than the previous period's interest and the portion going toward repayment of principal is greater than the previous period's principal payment.

For example, let us assume you take a $100,000 home mortgage loan at an interest rate of 9% per year to be repaid with interest in three annual installments. First, we calculate the annual payment by finding the PMT that has a PV of $100,000 when discounted at 9% for three years:

n	i	PV	FV	PMT	Result
3	9	−$100,000	0	?	$PMT = \$39,505.48$

So the annual payment is $39,505.48. In the first year, how much of the $39,505.48 is interest and how much is repayment of principal? Because the interest rate is 9% per year, the interest portion of the first payment must be or $9,000. The remainder of the $39,505.48, or $30,505.48, is repayment of the original $100,000 principal. The remaining balance after the first payment is, therefore, $100,000 − $30,505.48 or $69,494.52. The process of paying off a loan's principal gradually over its term is called loan **amortization.**

In the second year, how much of the $39,505.48 is interest and how much is repayment of principal? Because the interest rate is 9% per year, the interest portion of the second payment must be ($69,494.52(0.09)) or $6,254.51. The remainder of the $39,505.48, or $33,250.97, goes toward the repayment of the outstanding $69,494.52 balance remaining after the first payment. The remaining balance after the second payment is, therefore ($69,494.52 − $33,250.97), or $36,243.55.

The third and final payment covers both interest and principal on this remaining $36,243.55 (i.e., Table 6 contains all of this information in what is called an

TABLE 6 **Amortization Schedule for 3-Year Loan at 9%**

Year	Beginning Balance	Total Payment	Interest Paid	Principal Paid	Remaining Balance
1	$100,000	$39,505	$9,000	$30,505	$69,495
2	$69,495	$39,505	$6,255	$33,251	$36,244
3	$36,244	$39,505	$3,262	$36,244	($0)
	Totals	$118,516	$18,516	$100,000	

amortization schedule for the mortgage loan. Its breakdown shows how with each successive payment of $39,505.48, the portion that pays interest declines and the portion that repays principal increases.

8.1 A Bargain Car Loan?

You are buying a car and thinking of taking a one-year installment loan of $1,000 at an *APR* of 12% per year (1% per month) to be repaid in 12 equal monthly payments. The monthly payment is $88.85.

The salesperson trying to sell you the car makes the following pitch:

Although the *APR* on this loan is 12% per year, in fact it really works out to be a much lower rate. Because the total interest payments over the year are only $66.19, and the loan is for $1,000, you will only be paying a "true" interest rate of 6.62%.

What is the fallacy in the salesperson's reasoning?

The fallacy is that with your first monthly payment (and each subsequent payment), you are paying not only interest on the outstanding balance, you are also repaying part of the principal. The interest payment due at the end of the first month is 1% of $1,000, or $10. Because your monthly payment is $88.85, the other $78.85 is repayment of principal. The full amortization schedule is presented in Table 7.

TABLE 7 **Amortization Schedule for a 12-Month Loan at 1% per Month**

Month	Beginning Balance	Total Payment	Interest Paid	Principal Paid	Remaining Balance
1	$1,000.00	$88.85	$10.00	$78.85	$921.15
2	$921.15	$88.85	$9.21	$79.64	$841.51
3	$841.51	$88.85	$8.42	$80.43	$761.08
4	$761.08	$88.85	$7.61	$81.24	$679.84
5	$679.84	$88.85	$6.80	$82.05	$597.79
6	$597.79	$88.85	$5.98	$82.87	$514.91
7	$514.91	$88.85	$5.15	$83.70	$431.21
8	$431.21	$88.85	$4.31	$84.54	$346.67
9	$346.67	$88.85	$3.47	$85.38	$261.29
10	$261.29	$88.85	$2.61	$86.24	$175.05
11	$175.05	$88.85	$1.75	$87.10	$87.96
12	$87.96	$88.85	$0.88	$87.97	$0.00
	Totals	$1,066.20	$66.20	$1,000.00	

9 Exchange Rates and Time Value of Money

Suppose you are considering investing $10,000 either in dollar-denominated bonds offering an interest rate of 10% per year or in yen-denominated bonds offering 3% per year. Which is the better investment for the next year and why?

The answer depends on how much the dollar/yen exchange rate will change during the year. Suppose that the exchange rate is now 100 yen per dollar and, therefore, your $10,000 is now worth 1 million yen. If you invest in yen-bonds, you will have 1,030,000 yen a year from now. If you invest in dollar-bonds, you will have $11,000 which will be worth more?

If the dollar falls in yen value by 8% per year, then the exchange rate a year from now will be 92 yen per dollar. The yen-bond will have a dollar value of $11,196 (i.e., 1,030,000/92), which is $196 more than the $11,000 you would have from the dollar-bond. If, on the other hand, the dollar falls in yen value by only 6% per year, then the exchange rate a year from now will be 94 yen per dollar. The yen-bond will have a dollar value of $10,957 (i.e., 1,030,000/94) which is $43 less than the $11,000 you would have from the dollar-bond.

At what future exchange rate would you be indifferent between the two bonds? To find the break-even exchange rate, divide 1,030,000 yen by $11,000. The result is 93.636 yen/dollar. Thus, we conclude that if the yen value of the dollar falls by more than 6.364% during the year, the yen-bond would be a better investment.[3]

Quick Check 8

If the exchange rate between the U.S. dollar and the British pound is $2 per pound, the dollar interest rate is 6% per year, and the pound interest rate is 4% per year, what is the "break-even" value of the future dollar/pound exchange rate one year from now?

9.1 Computing *NPV* in Different Currencies

To avoid confusion when making financial decisions with different currencies there is a simple rule that one must observe:

> In any time value of money calculation, the cash flows and the interest rate must be denominated in the same currency.

Thus, to compute the present value of cash flows denominated in *yen* you must discount using the *yen* interest rate, and to compute the present value of cash flows denominated in *dollars* you must discount using the *dollar* interest rate. If you compute the present value of payments denominated in yen using the dollar interest rate, you will get a misleading number.

For example, suppose that you are trying to decide whether you should invest in a Japanese project or an American project, both of which require an initial outlay of $10,000. The Japanese project will pay you ¥575,000 per year for five years, whereas the American one will pay $6,000 per year for five years. The dollar interest rate is 6% per year, the yen interest rate is 4% per year, and the current dollar price of a yen is $0.01 per yen. Which project has the higher *NPV*?

First, we compute the *NPV* of the American project using the dollar interest rate of 6%:

n	i	PV	FV	PMT	Result
5	6	?	0	$6,000	PV = $25,274

---

[3]Of course, you do not know in advance how much the exchange rate will change, so there is uncertainty in this investment. We deal with this uncertainty explicitly in later chapters.

Subtracting the $10,000 initial outlay, we find that $NPV = $15,274$.

Next we compute the NPV of the Japanese project using the yen interest rate to find:

n	i	PV	FV	PMT	Result
5	4	?	0	¥575,000	$PV = $¥2,559,798

Next we convert the PV of the Japanese project from yen into dollars at the current exchange rate of $0.01 per yen to get a PV of $25,598. Subtracting the $10,000 initial outlay, we find that the NPV is $15,598. Thus, the Japanese project has a higher NPV and is the one that you should choose.

Note, however, that if you mistakenly computed the PV of the Japanese project using the dollar interest rate of 6% per year, you would get an NPV of only $14,221. You would, therefore, be led to choose the American project.

10 Inflation and Discounted Cash Flow Analysis

Dealing with inflation leads to a similar set of rules as dealing with different currencies. Let us consider the issue of saving for retirement. At age 20 you save $100 and invest it at a dollar interest rate of 8% per year. The good news is that at age 65 your $100 investment will have grown to $3,192. The bad news is that it will cost a lot more to buy the same things you buy today. For example, if the prices of all the goods and services you want to buy go up at 8% per year for the next 45 years, then your $3,192 will buy no more than your $100 will buy today. In a "real" sense, you will not have earned any interest at all. Thus, to make truly meaningful long-run savings decisions, you must take account of inflation as well as interest.

To take account of both interest and inflation we distinguish between nominal and real interest rates. The *nominal interest rate* is the rate denominated in dollars or in some other currency, and the *real interest rate* is denominated in units of consumer goods.

The general formula relating the real rate of interest to the nominal rate of interest and the rate of inflation is:

$$1 + \text{Real Rate} = \frac{1 + \textit{Nominal Interest Rate}}{1 + \textit{Rate of Inflation}}$$

or equivalently,

$$\text{Real Rate of Interest} = \frac{\textit{Nominal Interest Rate} - \textit{Rate of Inflation}}{1 + \textit{Rate of Inflation}}$$

Using *APR*s with continuous compounding simplifies the algebraic relationship between real and nominal rates of return. With continuous compounding, the relation between *APR*s becomes:

$$\text{Real Rate of Interest} = \text{Nominal Rate} - \text{Inflation Rate}$$

So if we assume a nominal *APR* of 6% per year compounded continuously and an inflation rate of 4% per year compounded continuously, the real rate is exactly 2% per year compounded continuously.

10.1 Inflation and Future Values

From a financial planning perspective, there is a great advantage to knowing the real interest rate. This is because ultimately it is what you can buy with your accumulated savings in the future that you care about. Returning to our specific example of saving $100 at age 20, not to be taken out until age 65, what we really want to know is how much you will have accumulated in the account when you reach age 65 in terms of real purchasing power. There are two alternative ways of calculating it—a short way and a long way. The short way is to compute the future value of the $100 using the real interest rate of 2.857% per year for 45 years. We define this as the **real future value.**

$$\text{Real Future Value} = \$100 \times 1.02857^{45} = \$355$$

Alternatively, we can arrive at the same number in stages. First, we compute the **nominal future value** by using the nominal interest rate of 8% per year:

$$\text{Nominal } FV \text{ in 45 Years} = \$100 \times 1.08^{45} = \$3,192$$

Next, we figure out what the price level will be 45 years from now if the inflation rate is 5% per year:

$$\text{Price Level in 45 Years} = 1.05^{45} = 8.985$$

Finally, divide the nominal future value by the future price level to find the real future value:

$$\text{Real } FV = \frac{\textit{Nominal Future Value}}{\textit{Future Price Value}} = \frac{\$3,192}{8.985} = \$355$$

The end result is the same. We find that by saving $100 today (age 20) and investing it for 45 years, we expect to have enough at age 65 to buy what would cost $355 at today's prices.

Thus, we see that there are two equivalent ways of computing the real future value of $355:

1. Compute the future value using the real rate of interest.
2. Compute the nominal future value using the nominal rate, and then deflate it to find the real future value.

Which of the two equivalent approaches one adopts depends on the particular context.

10.2 Saving for College: 1

Your daughter is 10 years old, and you are planning to open an account to provide for her college education. Tuition for a year of college is now $15,000 and is expected to increase at the rate of 5% per year. If you put $8,000 into an account paying an interest rate of 8% per year, will you have enough to pay for her first year's tuition eight years from now? If you compute the future value of the $8,000 at an interest rate of 8% per year for eight years, you find:

$$FV = \$8,000 \times 1.08^{8} = \$14,807$$

Because $14,807 is very close to $15,000, it might appear that saving $8,000 now is enough to provide for the first year of college tuition. But tuition level is a moving target. College tuition in the past increased at least at the general rate of inflation. For example, if inflation turns out to be 5% per year, the cost of the first year's college tuition will be $15,000 × 1.05^{8} or $22,162. So your $14,807 will be short by about one-third.

10.3 Investing in Inflation-Proof CDs

You are investing $10,000 for the next year. You face a choice between a conventional, one-year CD paying an interest rate of 8% or a CD that will pay you an interest rate of 3% per year plus the rate of inflation. We will call the former a *nominal CD* and the latter a *real CD*. Which will you choose?

Your choice depends on your forecast for inflation over the next year. If you are sure that the rate of inflation will be greater than 5%, you will prefer the real CD. Suppose, for example, that you think the rate of inflation will be 6%. Then your nominal rate of interest on the real CD will be 9%. If, however, you are sure that inflation will be 4% per year, then the nominal rate of interest on the real CD will be only 7%, so you are better off investing in the nominal CD.

Of course, because you do not know with certainty what the inflation rate will be, the decision is more complicated. We will return to this problem later when we discuss how to take account of uncertainty in investment decisions.

10.4 Why Debtors Gain from Unanticipated Inflation

Suppose you borrow $1,000 at an interest rate of 8% per year and have to pay back principal and interest one year later. If the rate of inflation turns out to be 8% during the year, the real interest rate on the loan is zero. Although you must pay back $1,080, its *real* value will be only $1,000. The $80 in interest just offsets the decline in the purchasing power of the $1,000 principal. Another way to state this is that you are paying back the loan with "cheaper" dollars than the ones you borrowed. No wonder that when the interest rate on a loan is fixed in advance, debtors like unanticipated inflation and creditors do not.

10.5 Inflation and Present Values

In many financial problems in which present values are calculated, the future amount is not fixed in dollars. For example, suppose you plan to buy a car four years from now and want to invest enough money now to pay for it. Say the kind of car you have in mind now costs $10,000, and the interest rate you can earn on your money is 8% per year.

In attempting to figure out the amount to invest now, it is natural to compute the present value of $10,000 to be received in four years at 8%:

$$PV = \frac{\$10,000}{1.08^4} = \$7,350$$

So you might conclude that investing $7,350 now is adequate to pay for the car four years from now.

But that would be a mistake. Almost surely, if the car you want costs $10,000 today, a similar car will cost more four years from now. How much more? That depends on the rate of inflation. If inflation in car prices is 5% per year, then the car will cost $10,000 \times 1.05^4$ or $12,155 in four years.

There are two equivalent ways to take account of inflation in problems such as this. The first is to compute the present value of the $10,000 real future amount using the real discount rate. As we saw earlier in this chapter the real discount rate is:

$$\text{Real Rate of Interest} = \frac{\text{Nominal Interest Rate} - \text{Rate of Inflation}}{1 + \text{Rate of Inflation}}$$

$$\text{Real Rate of Interest} = \frac{0.08 - 0.05}{1.05} = 0.02857 = 2.857\%$$

Using this real rate to compute the present value of the $10,000, we find:

$$PV = \frac{\$10,000}{1.02857^4} = \$8,934$$

The second way is to compute the present value of the $12,155 nominal future amount using the nominal discount rate of 8% per year:

$$PV = \frac{\$12,155}{1.08^4} = \$8,934$$

Either way, we get the same result: You must invest $8,934 now in order to pay the car's inflated price in four years. The reason we at first mistakenly computed the amount we needed to invest as only $7,350, was that we discounted a real future amount of $10,000 at a nominal discount rate of 8% per year.

10.6 Saving for College: 2

Recall that your daughter is 10 years old, and you are planning to open an account to provide for her college education. Tuition for a year of college is now $15,000. How much must you invest now in order to have enough to pay for her first year's tuition eight years from now, if you think you can earn a rate of interest that is 3% more than the inflation rate?

In this case you do not have an explicit estimate of the rate of inflation. But do you need one to answer the practical question before you? The answer is that you do not, provided you think that college tuition will rise at whatever the general inflation rate is. Under that assumption the real cost of college tuition eight years from now will be the same $15,000 it is today. By assuming that you can earn 3% per year more than the rate of inflation, you are, in effect, saying that the real discount rate is 3% per year. So you should calculate present value by discounting the $15,000 at 3% for eight years:

$$PV = \frac{\$15,000}{1.03^8} = \$11,841$$

If, by mistake, you were to discount the $15,000 using a nominal rate such as 8% per year, you would get a very different answer:

$$PV = \frac{\$15,000}{1.08^8} = \$8,104$$

The result is that you would not have enough to pay for tuition in eight years.

Beware: Never use a nominal interest rate when discounting real cash flows or a real interest rate when discounting nominal cash flows.

10.7 Inflation and Savings Plans

When considering a plan for long-run savings, it is essential to take account of inflation. The amount of money you can afford to save each year is likely to rise with the general cost of living because your income will probably also be going up. One easy way to take account of this without having to make an explicit forecast of the rate of inflation is to make your plans in terms of constant *real* payments and a *real* rate of interest.

10.8 Saving for College: 3

Recall that your daughter is 10 years old, and you are planning to open an account to provide for her college education. Tuition for a year of college is now $15,000. You want to save in equal real annual installments over the next eight years to have enough to pay for her first year's tuition eight years from now. If you think you can earn a real rate of interest of 3% per year, how much must you save each year? How much will you actually put into the account each year (in nominal terms) if the rate of inflation turns out to be 5% per year?

To find the annual real amount to save we first solve for *PMT*:

n	i	PV	FV	PMT	Result
8	3	0	$15,000	?	*PMT* = $1,686.85

So the amount to save each year must be the equivalent of $1,686.85 of today's purchasing power. At an inflation rate of 5% per year, the actual amount of dollars that will have to be contributed to the plan each year are as shown in Table 8.

With this plan the nominal amount saved each year has to be adjusted upward in accordance with the actual rate of inflation. The result will be that the amount accumulated in the account in eight years will be enough to pay for tuition. Thus, if the rate of inflation turns out to be 5% per year, then the nominal amount in the account eight years from now will turn out to be $22,162. The tuition required eight years from now is $15,000 in real terms and $22,162 in nominal terms.

To verify that the nominal future value of this saving plan will be $22,162 if the inflation rate is 5% per year, we can compute the future value of the nominal cash flows in the last column of Table 9. First, note that if the real rate of interest is 3% per year, then the nominal rate of interest must be 8.15%:

$$1 + \text{Real Rate of Interest} = \frac{1 + Nominal\ Rate\ of\ Interest}{1 + Rate\ of\ Inflation}$$

$$1 + \text{Nominal Rate} = (1 + \text{Real Rate}) \times (1 + \text{Inflation})$$

$$\text{Nominal Rate} = \text{Real Rate} + \text{Inflation} + \text{Real Rate} \times \text{Inflation}$$

$$\text{Nominal Rate} = 0.03 + 0.05 + 0.03 \times 0.05 = 0.0815$$

Compounding each year's nominal payment forward at the nominal interest rate of 8.15%, as shown in Table 9, we find that the total nominal future value is indeed $22,162.

Note that if your income goes up at 5% per year, then the nominal payment will remain a constant fraction of your income.

If the rate of inflation turns out to be 10% per year, and you increase your nominal payments into the plan at that rate, then the nominal amount in the account eight years from

TABLE 8 Nominal Dollar Amounts of a Real Annuity

Payment Number	Real Payment	Inflation Factor	Nominal Payment
1	$1,686.85	1.05000	$1,771.19
2	$1,686.85	1.10250	$1,859.75
3	$1,686.85	1.15763	$1,952.74
4	$1,686.85	1.21551	$2,050.38
5	$1,686.85	1.27628	$2,152.90
6	$1,686.85	1.34010	$2,260.54
7	$1,686.85	1.40710	$2,373.57
8	$1,686.85	1.47746	$2,492.25

TABLE 9 Computing Nominal Future Value of a Real Annuity

Payment Number	Real Payment	Inflation Factor	Nominal Payment	Future Value Factor	Nominal Future Value
1	$1,686.85	1.05000	$1,771.19	1.73056	$3,065.15
2	$1,686.85	1.10250	$1,859.75	1.60014	$2,975.87
3	$1,686.85	1.15763	$1,952.74	1.47956	$2,889.20
4	$1,686.85	1.21551	$2,050.38	1.36806	$2,805.04
5	$1,686.85	1.27628	$2,152.90	1.26497	$2,723.34
6	$1,686.85	1.34010	$2,260.54	1.16964	$2,644.02
7	$1,686.85	1.40710	$2,373.57	1.08150	$2,567.01
8	$1,686.85	1.47746	$2,492.25	1.00000	$2,492.25
			Total nominal future value		$22,161.89

now will turn out to be $15,000 \times 1.1^8$ or $32,154. This will have a real value in today's dollars of $15,000—just enough to pay the tuition.

10.9 Inflation and Investment Decisions

It is just as essential to take account of inflation in investment decisions as it is in saving decisions. When investing money in real assets such as real estate or plant and equipment, the future cash flows from the investment are likely to rise in nominal value because of inflation. If you fail to make the appropriate adjustments, you will tend to pass up worthwhile investment opportunities.

To see how important it is to take proper account of inflation, consider the following example. You currently heat your house with oil and your annual heating bill is $2,000. By converting to gas heat you estimate that this year you could cut your heating bill by $500, and you think that the cost differential between gas and oil is likely to remain the same for many years. The cost of installing a gas heating system is $10,000. If your alternative use of the money is to leave it in a bank account earning an interest rate of 8% per year, is the conversion worthwhile?

Note that there is no natural time horizon for this decision. We will, therefore, assume that the $500 cost differential will remain forever. We will also assume that the future outlays on replacement of heating equipment will be the same under both the oil and gas alternatives, so that we can ignore them for purposes of making this decision. Therefore, the investment is a perpetuity—you pay $10,000 now and get $500 per year forever. The internal rate of return on the investment in gas heat is 5% per year $\left(\text{i.e.,} \frac{\$500}{\$10,000} \right)$.

Comparing this 5% per year rate of return to the 8% per year alternative, you might be inclined to reject the gas investment opportunity. But wait a minute. The 8% per year rate on the bank account is a nominal rate of interest. What about the 5% per year rate of return on the investment in gas heat?

If you think that the $500 cost differential between gas and oil will increase over time with the general rate of inflation, then the 5% rate of return on the investment is a *real* rate of return. You should, therefore, compare it to the expected *real* rate of interest on the bank account. If you expect the rate of inflation to be 5% per year, then the expected real interest rate on the bank account is 2.857% $\left(\text{i.e.,} \frac{(0.08 - 0.05)}{1.05} \right)$. The 5% per year real yield on the investment in gas heat exceeds this, so perhaps the investment is worthwhile after all.

This example leads us to the following rule:

When comparing investment alternatives, never compare a real rate of return to a nominal opportunity cost of money.

This rule is just a slightly different version of the caution we issued earlier in this chapter:

Never use a nominal interest rate when discounting real cash flows or a real interest rate when discounting nominal cash flows.

11 Taxes and Investment Decisions

Up to this point our discussion has ignored income taxes. But what you have to spend in the future will be what is left after paying income taxes to the government. For example, suppose that you must pay 30% in taxes on any interest that you earn. You put $1,000 into a bank account offering an interest rate of 8% per year. This is the **before-tax interest rate.** Your **after-tax interest rate** is defined as what you earn after paying your income taxes.

Let us compute what it is. The interest income you will have to report on your income tax return is $0.08 \times \$1,000$ or $80.[4] The tax on this interest income is $0.3 \times \$80$ or $24. Thus, you will be left with $56 in interest income after taxes. Your after-tax interest rate is this $56 divided by your original investment of $1,000, or 5.6%. A shortcut way of computing your after-tax interest rate is to multiply the before-tax interest rate by 1 minus your tax rate:

$$\text{After-Tax Interest Rate} = (1 - \text{Tax Rate}) \times \text{Before-Tax Interest Rate}$$

In our example we get:

$$\text{After-Tax Interest Rate} = (1 - 0.3) \times 8\% = 0.7 \times 8\% = 5.6\%$$

The rule for investing is:

Invest so as to maximize the net present value of your after-tax cash flows.

Note that this is not necessarily the same as investing so as to minimize the taxes you pay. To see this, consider the following example.

11.1 Invest in Tax-Exempt Bonds?

In the United States, municipal bonds are exempt from income taxes. If you are in a high enough tax bracket, you might prefer to invest your money in municipal bonds. For example, if the interest rate on municipal bonds is 6% per year, and they are just as safe as the bank account paying an after-tax interest rate of 5.6% per year, then you would prefer to invest in the municipal bonds. The higher your tax bracket the bigger the advantage to you of investing in tax-exempt securities.

Suppose you are in a 20% tax bracket. Would it make sense for you to invest in municipal bonds paying 6% per year, if you can earn 8% per year from the bank? The answer is no, because even after paying income taxes on the interest from the bank, you would still have an after-tax interest rate that is higher than the tax-exempt rate on municipals:

$$\text{After-Tax Interest Rate on Bank Account} = (1 - 0.2) \times 8\% = 6.4\%$$

---

[4]You had better report it, too! In the United States, your bank directly informs the Internal Revenue Service how much it pays you in interest.

Therefore, if you followed the rule of minimizing your taxes, you would be led to make the wrong investment!

What is the personal tax bracket at which an individual would be exactly indifferent between investing in taxable and tax-exempt securities? The answer in our example is 25%. At a tax rate of 25%, the after-tax interest rate on the bank account is 6% (i.e., $0.75 \times 8\%$), the same as the rate on tax-exempt municipal bonds.

Summary

- Compounding is the process of going from present value (PV) to future value (FV). The future value of $1 earning interest at rate i per period for n periods is $(1 + i)^n$.
- Discounting is finding the present value of some future amount. The present value of $1 discounted at rate i per period for n periods is $\dfrac{1}{(1+i)^n}$.
- One can make financial decisions by comparing the present values of streams of expected future cash flows resulting from alternative courses of action. The present value of cash inflows less the present value of cash outflows is called net present value (NPV). If a course of action has a positive NPV, it is worth undertaking.
- In any time value of money calculation, the cash flows and the interest rate must be denominated in the same currency.
- Never use a nominal interest rate when discounting real cash flows or a real interest rate when discounting nominal cash flows.
- Always compare investment alternatives in terms of their returns net of income taxes.

Key Terms

- time value of money
- discounted cash flow
- compounding
- present value
- future value
- simple interest
- compound interest
- future value factor
- Rule of 72
- compound amount factor
- reinvestment rate
- annual percentage rate
- effective annual rate
- present value of $1
- present value factor
- net present value
- opportunity cost of capital
- yield to maturity
- internal rate of return
- time line
- annuity
- immediate annuity
- ordinary annuity
- perpetuity
- growth perpetuity
- amortization
- amortization schedule
- real future value
- nominal future value
- before-tax interest rate
- after-tax interest rate

Answers to Quick Check Questions

Quick Check 1 If the interest rate is only 5% per year in the previous example, what is the future value? What are the simple interest and the compound interest?

Answer: $\$1{,}000 \times 1.05^5 = \$1{,}276.28$

Simple interest: $\$1{,}000 \times 0.05 \times 5 = \$250$

Compound interest: $\$276.28 - \$250 = \$26.28$

Quick Check 2 In 1626, Peter Minuit purchased Manhattan Island from the Native Americans for about $24 worth of trinkets. If the tribe had taken cash instead and invested it to earn 6% per year compounded annually, how much would they have had in 2006, 380 years later?

Answer: To answer this question, students can use the following formula (the answer is too large for most calculator displays):

$$\$24 \times 1.06^{380} = \$99{,}183{,}639{,}918 \text{ (99 billion, 183 million, 639 thousand and 918 dollars)}$$

Quick Check 3 You take out a loan at an *APR* of 12% with monthly compounding. What is the effective annual rate on your loan?

Answer:

$$EFF = \left(1 + \frac{0.12}{12}\right)^{12} - 1, \text{ hence, } EFF = 12.68\%$$

Quick Check 4 What is the present value of $100 to be received in four years at an interest rate of 6% per year?

Answer:

$$PV = \frac{\$100}{1.06^4} = \$79.21.$$

Quick Check 5 Suppose a $10,000 T-bill which will mature in 3 months is currently selling for $9,800. If you purchase and hold the T-bill to maturity what rate of return would you earn on this investment computed as a continuously compounding annual rate (over the 3-month period)?

Answer: Using $10,000 as the future value and the $9,800 selling price as the present value we have the following relationship: $PV = \$9{,}800 = \$10{,}000 \cdot e^{-i \cdot \frac{1}{4}}$. Solving for the unknown i we find

$$\frac{\ell n\left(\dfrac{PV}{FV}\right)}{-\dfrac{1}{4}} = \frac{\ell n\left(\dfrac{\$9{,}800}{\$10{,}000}\right)}{-0.25} = 0.0808108 = 8.081\% = i.$$

Quick Check 6 Show that the alternative decision criteria presented previously lead to the same result—that the investment is worthwhile.

Answer:

1. Invest if the future value of the investment is larger than the future value that can be obtained from the next best alternative.

   First, we compute the future value of the $10,000 if invested in the bank.

$$FV = \$10{,}000 \times 1.08^5 = \$14{,}693$$

   Comparing the $14,693 computed future value to the $20,000 from the land, we conclude that investing in the land is worthwhile.

2. Invest if the *IRR* is greater than the opportunity cost of capital. Now we are ready to consider the investment's internal rate of return (*IRR*). By investing $10,000 in the land today, you can get $20,000 five years from now. What interest rate are you earning? In other words, we want to find *i* that solves the equation:

$$\$10,000 = \frac{\$20,000}{(1+i)^5}$$

$$i = 14.87\%$$

Thus, the internal rate of return on the investment in land is 14.87% per year. This should be compared to the 8% per year you could earn by putting your money in the bank. Clearly, you can earn a higher rate of return by investing in the land.

Note that because in this problem the $10,000 investment in land is expected to double over the next five years, the Rule of 72 could be applied to get a "quick and dirty" approximation for the *IRR*. By manipulating the Rule of 72 we find that the *IRR* on an investment that doubles in *n* years is approximately equal to the number 72 divided by *n*:

$$Doubling\ Time = \frac{72}{Interest\ Rate}$$

hence

$$IRR = \frac{72}{Doubling\ Time}$$

In our example, the approximate *IRR* would be:

$$IRR = \frac{72}{5} = 14.4\% \text{ per year}$$

This is close to the *IRR* of 14.87%. Even though the payback period rule is subject to many potential pitfalls, in this simple example it does work.

3. Choose the investment alternative with the fastest payback. We could ask how long it would take for our $10,000 investment to grow to $20,000 if we invested in the bank at 8% per year. To answer this question we are solving the equation for the number of periods, *n*:

$$\$10,000 = \frac{\$20,000}{1.08^n}$$

On the financial calculator we input *PV*, *FV*, and *i* and compute *n*. We find that *n* is 9.01 years. Because it takes only five years to double your money with the investment in land, clearly the land investment is better than putting your money in the bank. Note that using the Rule of 72 to find *n* we get:

$$Doubling\ Time = \frac{72}{8} = 9 \text{ Years}$$

Quick Check 7 Suppose you deposit $1,000 now and then $2,000 a year from now. How much will you have two years from now, if the interest rate is 10% per year?

Answer: Future Value of the Initial $1,000 = $1,000 $\times$ 1.1^2 = $1,210
Future Value of the $2,000 = $2,000 $\times$ 1.1 = $2,200
Total Future Value $3,410

Quick Check 8   If the exchange rate between the U.S. dollar and the British pound is $2 per pound, the dollar interest rate is 6% per year, and the pound interest rate is 4% per year, what is the "break-even" value of the future dollar/pound exchange rate one year from now?

Answer: You could invest $1 today in dollar-denominated bonds and have $1.06 one year from now. Or you could convert the dollar today into ½ pound and invest in pound-denominated bonds to have 0.52 pounds one year from now. For you to break even, the 0.52 pounds would have to be worth $1.06 one year from now, so the break-even exchange rate is: $\dfrac{\$1.06}{£0.52}$, or $2.03846 per pound.

Questions and Problems

1. If you invest $1,000 today at an interest rate of 10% per year, how much will you have 20 years from now, assuming no withdrawals in the interim?
2. **a.** If you invest $100 every year for the next 20 years starting one year from today and you earn interest of 10% per year, how much will you have at the end of the 20 years?
   b. How much must you invest each year if you want to have $50,000 at the end of the 20 years?
3. What is the present value of the following cash flows at an interest rate of 10% per year?
   a. $100 received five years from now.
   b. $100 received 60 years from now.
   c. $100 received each year beginning one year from now and ending 10 years from now.
   d. $100 received each year for 10 years beginning now.
   e. $100 each year beginning one year from now and continuing forever. (Hint: You do not need to use the financial keys of your calculator for this, just some common sense.)
4. You want to establish a "wasting" fund, which will provide you with $1,000 per year for four years, at which time the fund will be exhausted. How much must you put in the fund now if you can earn 10% interest per year?
5. You take a one-year installment loan of $1,000 at an interest rate of 12% per year (1% per month) to be repaid in 12 equal monthly payments.
   a. What is the monthly payment?
   b. What is the total amount of interest paid over the 12-month term of the loan?
6. You are taking out a $100,000 mortgage loan to be repaid over 25 years in 300 monthly payments.
   a. If the interest rate is 16% per year, what is the amount of the monthly payment?
   b. If you can only afford to pay $1,000 per month, how large a loan could you take?
   c. If you can afford to pay $1,500 per month and need to borrow $100,000, how many months would it take to pay off the mortgage?
   d. If you can pay $1,500 per month, need to borrow $100,000, and want a 25-year mortgage, what is the highest interest rate you can pay?
7. In 1626 Peter Minuit purchased Manhattan Island from the Native Americans for about $24 worth of trinkets. If the tribe had taken cash instead and invested it to earn 8% per year compounded annually, how much would the Indians have had in 1986, 360 years later?
8. You win a $1 million lottery, which pays you $50,000 per year for 20 years. How much is your prize really worth, assuming an interest rate of 8% per year?
9. Your great-aunt left you $20,000 when she died. You can invest the money to earn 12% per year. If you spend $3,540 per year out of this inheritance, how long will the money last?

10. You borrow $100,000 from a bank for 30 years at an *APR* of 10.5%. What is the monthly payment? If you must pay two points up front, meaning that you only get $98,000 from the bank, what is the true *APR* on the mortgage loan?

11. Suppose that the mortgage loan described in question 10 is a one-year adjustable rate mortgage (ARM), which means that the 10.5% interest applies for only the first year. If the interest rate goes up to 12% in the second year of the loan, what will your new monthly payment be?

12. You just received a gift of $500 from your grandmother and you are thinking about saving this money for graduation, which is four years away. You have your choice between Bank A, which is paying 7% for one-year deposits, and Bank B, which is paying 6% on one-year deposits. Each bank compounds interest annually.
    a. What is the future value of your savings one year from today if you save your money in Bank A? Bank B? Which is the better decision?
    b. What savings decision will most individuals make? What likely reaction will Bank B have?

13. Sue Consultant has just been given a bonus of $2,500 by her employer. She is thinking about using the money to start saving for the future. She can invest to earn an annual rate of interest of 10%.
    a. According to the Rule of 72, approximately how long will it take for Sue to increase her wealth to $5,000?
    b. Exactly how long does it actually take?

14. Larry's bank account has a "floating" interest rate on certain deposits. Every year the interest rate is adjusted. Larry deposited $20,000 three years ago, when interest rates were 7% (annual compounding). Last year the rate was only 6%, and this year the rate fell again to 5%. How much will be in his account at the end of this year?

15. You have your choice between investing in a bank savings account, which pays 8% compounded annually (BankAnnual), and one that pays 7.5% compounded daily (BankDaily).
    a. Based on effective annual rates, which bank would you prefer?
    b. Suppose BankAnnual is only offering one-year certificates of deposit and if you withdraw your money early you lose all interest. How would you evaluate this additional piece of information when making your decision?

16. What are the effective annual rates of the following:
    a. 12% *APR* compounded monthly?
    b. 10% *APR* compounded annually?
    c. 6% *APR* compounded daily?

17. Harry promises that an investment in his firm will double in six years. Interest is assumed to be paid quarterly and reinvested. What effective annual yield does this represent?

18. Suppose you know that you will need $2,500 two years from now in order to make a down payment on a car.
    a. BankOne is offering 4% interest (compounded annually) for two-year accounts and BankTwo is offering 4.5% (compounded annually) for two-year accounts. If you know you need $2,500 two years from today, how much will you need to invest in BankOne to reach your goal? Alternatively, how much will you need to invest in BankTwo? Which bank account do you prefer?
    b. Now suppose you do not need the money for three years. How much will you need to deposit today in BankOne? BankTwo?

19. Lucky Lynn has a choice between receiving $1,000 from her great-uncle one year from today or $900 from her great-aunt today. She believes she could invest the $900 at a one-year return of 12%.

a. What is the future value of the gift from her great-uncle upon receipt? From her great-aunt?

b. Which gift should she choose?

c. How does your answer change if you believed she could invest the $900 from her great-aunt at only 10%? At what rate is she indifferent?

20. As manager of short-term projects, you are trying to decide whether or not to invest in a short-term project that pays one cash flow of $1,000 one year from today. The total cost of the project is $950. Your alternative investment is to deposit the money in a one-year bank certificate of deposit, which will pay 4% compounded annually.

    a. Assuming the cash flow of $1,000 is guaranteed (there is no risk you will not receive it), what would be a logical discount rate to use to determine the present value of the cash flows of the project?

    b. What is the present value of the project if you discount the cash flow at 4% per year? What is the net present value of that investment? Should you invest in the project?

    c. What would you do if the bank increases its quoted rate on one-year CDs to 5.5%?

    d. At what bank one-year CD rate would you be indifferent between the two investments?

21. Calculate the net present value of the following cash flows: You invest $2,000 today and receive $200 one year from now, $800 two years from now, and $1,000 a year for 10 years starting four years from now. Assume that the interest rate is 8%.

22. Your cousin has asked for your advice on whether or not to buy a bond for $995, which will make one payment of $1,200 five years from today, or invest in a local bank account.

    a. What is the internal rate of return on the bond's cash flows? What additional information do you need to make a choice?

    b. What advice would you give her if you learned the bank is paying 3.5% per year for five years (compounded annually)?

    c. How would your advice change if the bank were paying 5% annually for five years? If the price of the bond were $900 and the bank pays 5% annually?

23. You and your sister have just inherited $300 and a savings bond from your great-grandfather who had left them in a safe deposit box. Because you are the oldest, you get to choose whether you want the cash or the bond. The bond has only four years left to maturity at which time it will pay the holder $500.

    a. If you took the $300 today and invested it at an interest rate 6% per year, how long (in years) would it take for your $300 to grow to $500? (Hint: You want to solve for n or number of periods.) Given these circumstances, which are you going to choose?

    b. Would your answer change if you could invest the $300 at 10% per year? At 15% per year? What other decision rules could you use to analyze this decision?

24. Suppose you have three personal loans outstanding to your friend Elizabeth. A payment of $1,000 is due today, a $500 payment is due one year from now, and a $250 payment is due two years from now. You would like to consolidate the three loans into one, with 36 equal monthly payments, beginning one month from today. Assume the agreed interest rate is 8% (effective annual rate) per year.

    a. What is the annual percentage rate you will be paying?

    b. How large will the new monthly payment be?

25. As CEO of ToysRFun, you are offered the chance to participate, without initial charge, in a project that produces cash flows of $5,000 at the end of the first period, $4,000 at the end of the next period, and a loss of $11,000 at the end of the third and final year.

a. What is the net present value if the relevant discount rate (the company's cost of capital) is 10%?

b. Would you accept the offer?

c. What is the internal rate of return? Can you explain why you would reject a project that has an internal rate of return greater than its cost of capital?

26. You must pay a creditor $6,000 one year from now, $5,000 two years from now, $4,000 three years from now, $2,000 four years from now, and a final $1,000 five years from now. You would like to restructure the loan into five equal annual payments due at the end of each year. If the agreed interest rate is 6% compounded annually, what is the payment?

27. Find the future value of the following ordinary annuities (payments begin one year from today and all interest rates compound annually):

    a. $100 per year for 10 years at 9%.

    b. $500 per year for 8 years at 15%.

    c. $800 per year for 20 years at 7%.

    d. $1,000 per year for 5 years at 0%.

    e. Now find the present values of the annuities in a–d.

    f. What is the relationship between present values and future values?

28. Suppose you will need $50,000 ten years from now. You plan to make seven equal annual deposits beginning three years from today in an account that yields 11% compounded annually. How large should the annual deposit be?

29. Suppose an investment offers $100 per year for five years at 5% beginning one year from today.

    a. What is the present value? How does the present value calculation change if one additional payment is added today?

    b. What is the future value of this ordinary annuity? How does the future value change if one additional payment is added today?

30. You are trying to decide whether to buy a car for 4.0% APR for the full $20,000 purchase price over three years or receive $1,500 cash back and finance the rest at a bank rate of 9.5%. Both loans have monthly payments over three years. Which should you choose?

31. You are looking to buy a sports car costing $23,000. One dealer is offering a special reduced financing rate of 2.9% APR on new car purchases for three-year loans, with monthly payments. A second dealer is offering a cash rebate. Any customer taking the cash rebate would, of course, be ineligible for the special loan rate and would have to borrow the balance of the purchase price from the local bank at the 9% annual rate. How large must the cash rebate be on this $23,000 car to entice a customer away from the dealer who is offering the special 2.9% financing?

32. Show proof that investing $475.48 today at 10% allows you to withdraw $150 at the end of each of the next four years and have nothing remaining.

33. As pension manager, you are considering investing in a preferred stock, which pays $5,000,000 per year *forever* beginning one year from now. If your alternative investment choice is yielding 10% per year, what is the present value of this investment? What is the highest price you would be willing to pay for this investment? If you paid this price, what would be the dividend yield on this investment?

34. A new lottery game offers a choice for the grand prize winner. You can either receive a lump sum of $1,000,000 immediately or an annuity of $100,000 per year forever, with the first payment *today*. (If you die, your estate will still continue to receive payments.) If the relevant interest rate is 9.5% compounded annually, what is the difference in value between the two prizes?

35. Find the future value of a $1,000 lump-sum investment under the following compounding periods: (Hint: Either figure out effective annual rate or change number of periods and interest rate as compounding period shortens.)
    a. 7% compounded annually for 10 years.
    b. 7% compounded semiannually for 10 years.
    c. 7% compounded monthly for 10 years.
    d. 7% compounded daily for 10 years.
    e. 7% compounded continuously for 10 years.

36. Sammy Jo charged $1,000 worth of merchandise one year ago on her MasterCard, which has a stated interest rate of 18% *APR* compounded monthly. She made 12 regular monthly payments of $50, at the end of each month, and refrained from using the card for the past year. How much does she still owe?

37. Suppose you are considering borrowing $120,000 to finance your dream house. The annual percentage rate is 9% and payments are made monthly.
    a. If the mortgage has a 30-year amortization schedule, what are the monthly payments?
    b. What effective annual rate would you be paying?
    c. How do your answers to parts a and b change if the loan amortizes over 15 years rather than 30?

38. Suppose last year you took out the loan described in problem 37a. Now interest rates have declined to 8% per year. Assume there will be no refinancing fees.
    a. What is the remaining balance of your current mortgage after 12 payments? (Hint: Look for future value.)
    b. What would be your payment if you refinanced your mortgage at the lower rate for 29 years?

Exchange Rates and the Time Value of Money

39. The exchange rate between the pound sterling and the dollar is currently $1.50 per pound, the dollar interest rate is 7% per year, and the pound interest rate is 9% per year. You have $100,000 in a one-year account that allows you to choose between either currency, and it pays the corresponding interest rate.
    a. If you expect the dollar/pound exchange rate to be $1.40 per pound a year from now and are indifferent to risk, which currency should you choose?
    b. What is the break-even value of the dollar/pound exchange rate one year from now?

Real versus Nominal Interest Rates

40. The interest rate on conventional 10-year Treasury bonds is 7% per year and the interest rate on 10-year TIPS (Treasury inflation-protected securities) is 3.5% per year. You have $10,000 to invest in one of them.
    a. If you expect the average inflation rate to be 4% per year, which bond offers the higher expected rate of return?
    b. Which would you prefer to invest in?

41. You are 20 years from retirement, and expect to live another 20 years after retirement. If you start saving now, how much will you be able to withdraw *each year* for every dollar *per year* that you save, assuming an effective annual interest rate of:
    a. 0, 1%, 2%, 3%, 3.5%, 4%, 6%, 8%, and 10%?
    b. How would your answer change if you expect the rate of inflation to be 4% per year?

APPENDIX

Adjusting a Mortgage for Points

Many banks offer mortgages that include *points*. Points are essentially an extra fee paid to the bank up front. Thus, if you take out a three-year $10,000 mortgage with two points, you have to pay 2% of the mortgage amount to the bank at inception. In other words, instead of getting $10,000 at the beginning from the bank, you really only get $9,800. Let us see what points do to the actual interest rate on a mortgage. Suppose you take out the three-year, $10,000 (two points) mortgage from the bank at a stated *APR* of 12% with monthly payments. This corresponds to a monthly interest rate of 1%.

The first step is to compute the actual payment that the bank requires each month. This is done based on the total amount of the mortgage, $10,000.

n	i	PV	FV	PMT	Result
36	1	$10,000	0	?	*PMT* = $332.14

The *PV* of the mortgage is not really $10,000, but only $9,800. Thus, together with the monthly payments of $332.14, we can compute the monthly interest rate:

n	i	PV	FV	PMT	Result
36	?	$9,800	0	−$332.14	*i* = 1.11757%

This monthly interest rate corresponds to an *APR* of $12 \times 1.11757\% = 13.41\%$

Thus, when one bank offers you an *APR* of 13% on the preceding three-year mortgage and charges no points and a second bank offers you an *APR* of 12% with two points, you now know which bank offers the better deal. (Hint: It is not the second bank.)

Suggested Readings

Fisher, I. *The Theory of Interest: As Determined by Impatience to Spend Income and Opportunity to Invest It.* 1930. New York: Augustus M. Kelley, 1965.

Household Saving
and Investment Decisions

From Chapter 5 of *Financial Economics*, 2/e. Zvi Bodie, Robert C. Merton, David L. Cleeton.

Household Saving and Investment Decisions

OBJECTIVES

- Analyze how much to save for retirement.
- Determine whether to defer taxes or pay them now.
- Determine whether to get a professional degree.
- Determine whether to buy or rent a house?

CONTENTS

Recall how discounted cash flow analysis can be used in making financial decisions. In this chapter we apply those discounted cash flow concepts to the major financial decisions we all must make at different stages of our lives. Starting with the decision about how much to save for retirement, we develop a life-cycle model for comprehensive financial planning. We then analyze whether you should defer taxes or pay them immediately, whether you should invest in a professional education, and whether you should buy or rent a house.

1 A Life-Cycle Model of Saving

Consider the following example. You are currently 35 years old, expect to retire in 30 years at age 65, and then to live for 15 more years until age 80. Your current labor income is $30,000 per year, and you have not yet accumulated any assets.

We simplify the example by ignoring taxes. Also let us assume that your *real* labor income adjusted for inflation remains at $30,000 per year until age 65. In other words, we assume that your income will keep pace with inflation, but not beat it.

How much should you spend for consumption now and how much should you save for retirement?

Every dollar you save will earn interest until you take it out. Of course, the cost of living will be going up, too. We will assume that the interest rate you earn will exceed the rate of inflation by 3% per year. In other words, the real rate of interest is 3% per year.

There are two approaches that you could take to computing how much you should save for your retirement: (1) Aim for a target replacement rate of preretirement income, and (2) aim for maintaining the same level of consumption spending before and after retirement. We will examine both approaches next.

1.1 Approach 1: Target Replacement Rate of Preretirement Income

Many experts recommend that in making a savings plan, you should aim for a replacement rate equal to 75% of your preretirement income. Let us apply this rule to our situation. With a real income before retirement of $30,000, the target level of retirement income is 0.75 × 30,000 or $22,500 per year.

The method for computing how much saving is needed to reach the desired target consists of two steps:

- First compute the amount you need to have accumulated in your personal retirement account when you reach retirement age.
- Then compute the annual amount of saving needed to reach that future value.

So, first we compute the amount that you have to have in your retirement fund at age 65 to be able to withdraw $22,500 per year for 15 years:

Using the *Annuity Present Value Factor:*

$$PV_{PMT}(PMT, i, n) = PMT \cdot \frac{1 - (1 + i)^{-n}}{i} \quad PV_{PMT}(\$22,500, 3\%, 15) = \$268,603.54$$

n	15
i	3%
PMT	$22,500.00
PV	$268,603.54

Next we compute how much you need to save each year to have $268,603.54 accumulated 30 years from now. Using the *Sinking Fund Factor:*

$$PMT_{FV}(FV, i, n) = FV \cdot \frac{i}{(1+i)^n - 1} \qquad PMT_{FV}(\$268,603.54, 3\%, 30) = \$5,645.85$$

n	30
i	3%
FV	$268,603.54
PMT	$5,645.85

So the conclusion from this procedure is that in order to be able to take out a retirement benefit of $22,500 per year for 15 years, you would need to save $5,645.85 per year in each of the next 30 years.

Now, let us consider a problem that arises when you use this approach. The solution does not necessarily result in your having the same consumption level after retirement as you did during your working years. In the preceding example, your consumption spending during the working years when you are saving $5,645.85 of your $30,000 annual income will be $24,354.15 per year, but then in retirement you will have only $22,500 to spend each year.

One way to deal with this problem is to redo the calculations using a higher replacement rate than 75%. If that replacement rate turns out to be too high, then try a lower one. You could continue applying this trial-and-error procedure until you find a replacement rate that results in the same consumption spending before and after retirement. Approach 2 addresses the problem directly without resorting to a trial-and-error search.

Box 1 — Demographic Pressures on European Pension Systems

A growing number of state pension systems in Europe have become unsustainable because of early retirement, increased life expectancy, and low birth rates. European pension systems operate in a pay-as-you-go fashion, in which current workers finance the pensions of retirees. This system operates on the assumption that current workers greatly outnumber retired workers, but their ratio has been steadily shrinking. Many current European governments have acknowledged this problem but have not done much besides postponing the problem for future administrations to address. The failure to address the fundamental underlying issues and potential solutions is primarily due to resistance from many workers, who are generally unhappy about the proposed changes to public pension schemes. However, European governments must greatly reduce the scope of the pay-as-you-go system in order to ensure that today's workers will be able to count on a secure retirement system.

Employees can be encouraged to put more savings in private retirement accounts, either through their employers or with fund-management firms. Such actions would force workers to take more responsibility for their own retirement. State retirement ages are expected to be restructured or eliminated, and people are expected to be encouraged to retire later as life expectancies continue to increase. An increase in immigration, although controversial, would also ease the burden of younger workers. Finally, birth rates, which have been in rapid decline throughout Europe, could increase—ensuring that Europe's current workers would continue to greatly outnumber retirees. This can be accomplished by removing structural obstacles that make it difficult for women in Europe to simultaneously have a career and a family, possibly through revisions in the tax system and employment law. Unless governments take action, the pay-as-you-go state pensions in Europe could fail as a growing number of workers live longer and retire earlier.

Source: Adapted from "Work Longer, Have More Babies," *The Economist,* September 25, 2003.

1.2 Approach 2: Maintain the Same Level of Consumption Spending

Let us now consider how much you need to save if your goal is to spend the same amount on consumption before and after retirement. This implies a constant stream of the same amount in each of the next 45 years, denoted by C. The amount saved each year from age 35 to 65 is $30,000 minus C. At age 65, the total accumulation will be $47.58(\$30,000 - C)$.[1] The amount withdrawn from the retirement account each year after age 65 will be C. Its present value at age 65 is $11.94C$.[2]

To find C we set the two amounts equal to each other:

$$\$47.58(\$30,000 - C) = \$11.94C$$

$$C = \$23,982$$

So consumption spending is $23,982 per year. Annual savings during the working years must, therefore, be $6,018 per year (i.e., $30,000 – $23,982). The total accumulation at age 65 will be $286,298.

Columns 1 through 4 in Table 1 and Figure 1 show the time profiles of income, consumption, and saving derived in this example. They demonstrate that income is $30,000 until age 65, and then it drops off to zero. Consumption stays level at $23,982 per year from age 35 until age 80.

TABLE 1 Salary, Consumption, and Saving over the Life Cycle

Age	Salary	Consumption	Saving	Human Capital	Retirement Fund
(1)	(2)	(3)	(4)	(5)	(6)
35	$30,000	$23,982	$6,018	$588,013	0
45	30,000	23,982	6,018	446,324	$68,987
55	30,000	23,982	6,018	255,906	161,700
65	30,000	23,982	(23,982)	0	286,298
66	0	23,982	(23,982)	0	270,905
70	0	23,982	(23,982)	0	204,573
75	0	23,982	(23,982)	0	109,832
80	0	23,982	(23,982)	0	0

---

[1]The computation uses the *Annuity Compound Amount Factor:* $FV_{PMT}(PMT, i, n) = PMT \cdot \frac{(1+i)^n - 1}{i}$ or $FV_{PMT}(\$1, 3\%, 30) = \$47.58$.

[2]The computation is based on the *Annuity Present Value Factor:* $PV_{PMT}(PMT, i, n) = PMT \cdot \frac{1 - (1+i)^{-n}}{i}$ or $PV_{PMT}(\$1, 3\%, 15) = \$11.94$.

FIGURE 1

Salary, Consumption, and Saving over the Life Cycle

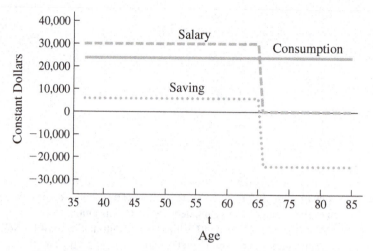

The equation that we have solved in order to find C can be written in a slightly different and more general way:

$$\sum_{t=1}^{45} \frac{C}{(1+i)^t} = \sum_{t=1}^{30} \frac{Y_t}{(1+i)^t} \tag{1}$$

where i is the interest rate and Y_t is labor income in year t.

Equation 1 says that the present value of consumption spending over the next 45 years equals the present value of labor income over the next 30 years. Economists call the present value of one's future labor income **human capital,** and they call the constant level of consumption spending that has a present value equal to one's human capital **permanent income.** (See Box 2 about the economists who were awarded Nobel Prizes for their contributions to the theory of human capital and consumption spending.)

In our example, with labor income of $30,000 per year for 30 years, your human capital is $588,013 at age 35, and your permanent income is $23,982 per year.[3] As you get older, the *PV* of your remaining labor income declines, so your human capital falls steadily until it reaches zero at age 65.

Figure 2 and columns 5 and 6 in Table 1 show the time profiles of human capital and the accumulated amount in the retirement fund implied by the pattern of income and saving in Figure 1 and columns 2 and 4 of Table 1. The retirement fund starts out at zero at age 35,

FIGURE 2

Human Capital, Retirement Assets, and Total Wealth over the Life Cycle

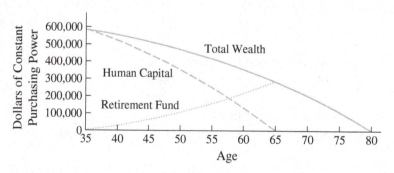

---

[3]Using the *Annuity Present Value Factor* we solve for the value of human capital at age 35: $PV_{PMT}(PMT, i, n) = PMT \cdot \dfrac{1-(1+i)^{-n}}{i}$ or $PV_{PMT}(\$30,000, 3\%, 30) = \$588,013$. Then using the *Capital Recovery Factor* we can compute the value of permanent income: $PMT_{PV}(PV, i, n) = PV \cdot \dfrac{i}{1-(1+i)^{-n}}$ or $PMT_{PV}(\$588,013, 3\%, 45) = \$23,982$.

Box 2	Nobel Prizes for the Theory of Permanent Income, Life-Cycle Savings and Human Capital

Milton Friedman was awarded the Nobel Prize in economic science in 1976. A contribution cited by the prize committee as being of primary importance was his theory that permanent income and not year-to-year income is the determining factor when assessing total consumption outlays. Friedman demonstrated that a much greater proportion of the former type of income is saved than the latter. (Adapted from http://nobelprize.org/nobel-prizes/economics/laureates/1976/press.html.)

Franco Modigliani received the Nobel Prize in 1985 in part for the construction and development of the life-cycle hypothesis of household saving. The underlying idea of the life-cycle hypothesis—that people save for their old age—is, of course, not new; nor is it Modigliani's own. His achievement lies primarily in the rationalization of the idea into a formal model, which he developed in different directions and integrated within a well-defined and established economic theory. The life-cycle model is today the basis of most dynamic models used for the study of consumption and saving. (Adapted from http://nobelprize.org/nobel-prizes/economics/laureates/1985/press.html.)

Gary Becker received the Nobel Prize in 1992 for having extended the domain of microeconomic analysis to a wide range of human behavior. His most noteworthy contribution is in the area of human capital. The theory of human capital is considerably older than Becker's work, but his achievement was to have formulated and formalized the microeconomic foundations of the theory. The theory of human capital has created a uniform analytical framework for studying the return on education and on-the-job training. The human capital approach also helps explain trade patterns across countries; in fact, differences in the supply of human capital among countries have been shown to have more explanatory power than differences in the supply of real capital. (Adapted from http://nobelprize.org/nobel-prizes/economics/laureates/1992/press.html.)

and it gradually grows to a high of $285,298 at age 65. It then declines to zero at age 80. The individual's total wealth, defined as human capital plus retirement assets, declines continuously between ages 35 and 80.

Quick Check 2

Georgette is currently 30 years old, plans to retire at age 65, and expects to live to age 85. Her salary is $25,000 per year, and she intends to maintain a constant level of real consumption spending over the next 55 years. Assume no taxes, no growth in real labor income, and a real interest rate of 3% per year.

A. What is the value of Georgette's human capital?
B. What is her permanent income?

Let us consider what effect a different interest rate would have on both permanent income and human capital. Table 2 shows that the higher the interest rate, the lower the value of human capital, but the higher the level of permanent income. Because you save throughout your work years, you are better off with a higher real interest rate, even though the value of your human capital is lower.

Quick Check 3

In Table 2, what would human capital and permanent income be at a real interest rate of 3.5% per year?

TABLE 2 **Human Capital and Permanent Income as Functions of the Real Interest Rate (*i*%)**

i =	Human Capital (*i*) =	Permanent Income (*i*) =	Saving (*i*) =
0	900000	20000	10000
1	774231	21450	8550
2	671894	22784	7216
3	588013	23982	6018
4	518761	25037	4963
5	461174	25946	4054
6	412945	26718	3282
7	372271	27362	2638
8	337734	27892	2108
9	308210	28325	1675
10	282807	28674	1326

Assumptions: You are currently 35 years old, expect to retire in 30 years at age 65, and then live for 15 more years until age 80. Your real salary is $30,000 per year, and you have not yet accumulated any assets.

Now suppose that instead of starting out at age 35 with no accumulated assets, you have $10,000 in a savings account. How does that affect the amount you can consume over your lifetime? The answer is that it enables you to increase consumption spending in each of the next 45 years by $407.85, assuming the interest rate is 3% per year.

On the other hand, suppose you wanted to leave a bequest of $10,000 to your children after you die at age 80. With unchanged lifetime income, how does the intended bequest affect your lifetime consumption stream? Answer: It would reduce your consumption by $107.85 in each of the next 45 years.

The general formula that expresses the lifetime consumption possibilities open to you as a function of your income, initial wealth, and bequests is:

$$\sum_{t=1}^{T}\left[\frac{C_t}{(1+i)^t}+\frac{B_t}{(1+i)^t}\right]=W_0+\sum_{t=1}^{R}\frac{Y_t}{(1+i)^t} \tag{2}$$

Where:

C_t = consumption spending in year t

Y_t = labor income in year t

i = interest rate

R = number of year until retirement

T = number of year of life

W_0 = value of initial wealth

B_t = bequest made in year t

Equation 2 says that the present value of your lifetime consumption spending and bequests equals the present value of your lifetime resources—initial wealth and future labor income. This is the **intertemporal budget constraint** that you face in deciding on a lifetime consumption spending plan.

Note that any lifetime consumption spending plan that satisfies your budget constraint (i.e., equation 2) is a **feasible plan.** There are many possible feasible plans. To choose among them you must specify a criterion for quantitatively assessing the welfare or satisfaction (economists use the term *utility*) that you receive from each feasible plan. A quantitative model that enables you to choose the best among all feasible plans is called an **optimization model.** Developing optimization models for lifetime financial planning is beyond the scope of this text.[4]

Now let us consider the effect of changes in real income over the life cycle. For example, Dr. Omar Ben Holim has just graduated from medical school at age 30 and has started training to be a surgeon at Mount Heaven Hospital. Omar's real salary for the next five years will be $25,000 per year. After completing his residency, however, Omar expects to earn $300,000 per year in real terms until he retires at age 65. Given his future expectations, he decides to start enjoying a high standard of living immediately. If he wants to maintain the same level of real consumption spending for the rest of his life and his life expectancy is 85 years, how much should he plan to save now and in the future? Assume that the real interest rate is 3% per year, and that Omar can either borrow or lend at that same rate.

TABLE 3   Omar's Life-Cycle Saving Plan

Age	Salary	Consumption	Saving	Human Capital	Other Assets or Liabilities
30	0	0	0	5,186,747	0
31	25,000	193,720	(168,720)	5,317,349	(168,720)
32	25,000	193,720	(168,720)	5,451,869	(342,502)
33	25,000	193,720	(168,720)	5,590,425	(521,497)
34	25,000	193,720	(168,720)	5,733,138	(705,862)
35	25,000	193,720	(168,720)	5,880,132	(895,758)
36	300,000	193,720	106,280	5,756,536	(816,351)
37	300,000	193,720	106,280	5,629,232	(734,562)
38	300,000	193,720	106,280	5,498,109	(650,319)
39	300,000	193,720	106,280	5,363,053	(563,549)
40	300,000	193,720	106,280	5,223,944	(474,175)
44	300,000	193,720	106,280	4,624,507	(89,053)
45	300,000	193,720	106,280	4,463,242	14,555
65	300,000	193,720	106,280	0	2,882,067
66	0	193,720	(193,720)	0	2,774,809
84	0	193,720	(193,720)	0	188,078
85	0	193,720	(193,720)	0	0

[4]For a review of life-cycle optimization models see R. C. Merton, *Continuous-Time Finance,* chapters 4–6.

FIGURE 3

Omar's Life-Cycle Savings Plan

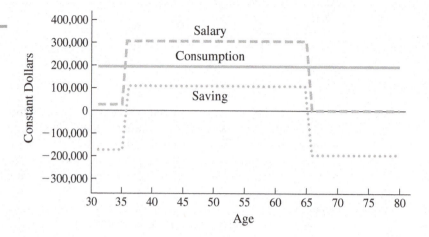

FIGURE 3

Omar's Life-Cycle Savings Plan

Table 3 and Figure 3 show Omar's expected pattern of salary and planned consumption spending and saving on the assumption that he wants to have the same real consumption every year. His human capital initially is $5,186,747, and his permanent income is $193,720. In order to spend $193,720 per year during the five years of his residency, he will have to borrow ("dissave") $168,720 each year to supplement his $25,000 salary. His total indebtedness will grow to a maximum of $895,758 at age 35, and then decline thereafter as a result of his saving $106,280 every year from age 36 until he retires at age 65. Note that he will not have paid off his debt until age 45. One is never too young to start learning finance (see Box 3).

Quick Check 5

Suppose that Omar is credit constrained and cannot borrow during the next five years. How does that affect his lifetime saving and consumption plan?

Box 3 — **Financial Literacy and Retirement Savings**

There is a rising trend in the United States and Europe for people to take on more responsibility for their investments, specifically their retirement funds. However, many people face obstacles in their own lack of financial understanding.

Most of us tend to think that we know more than we actually do about basic financial concepts, such as inflation, risk diversification, and compound interest. The low personal savings rates and frequent bankruptcy in the United States and Great Britain attest to the lack of financial literacy among many citizens. Governments can suffer by taking responsibility for citizens who have not saved enough for their retirement, and therefore many private firms and government agencies have put programs in place to teach younger workers about basic financial concepts—such as saving and keeping track of their investments.

However, it is important to distinguish between financial education and financial advice—which can be offered by firms and fund managers, and can be less objective. Nevertheless, people with a greater understanding of financial concepts have been shown to save more and make higher returns on their long-term investments.

Source: Adapted from "Caveat Investor," *The Economist*, January 12, 2006.

2 Taking Account of Social Security

In many countries the government obliges citizens to participate in a mandatory retirement income system called social security.[5] Under such systems, people pay a tax during their working years and in return qualify for a lifetime annuity in their old age. Such a system of mandatory saving should influence the amount of voluntary saving that we do for retirement. Let us use our life-cycle planning model to examine the right way to take account of social security.

To address this question in the context of our life-cycle discounted cash flow planning model, we first recognize that social security alters the profile of our lifetime net cash inflows. We return to our first example in which you are 35 years old, and your salary will be $30,000 per year for the next 30 years. Your human capital is $588,013—the *PV* of labor income at an interest rate of 3% per year. Suppose the optimal level of consumption spending is a constant $23,982 per year (equal to your permanent income). Annual savings in the preretirement years, must, therefore be $6,018 per year. The total accumulation at age 65 will be $286,309, which is enough to support a retirement income of $23,982 per year for 15 years.

Suppose that social security benefits are equal to what you would have if you had saved each year an amount equal to the amount you pay in social security taxes and earned a real interest rate of 3% per year. Thus, if you pay $2,000 per year in social security taxes for 30 years, you will receive in benefits $7,970 per year for 15 years starting at age 66.[6] What impact will social security have on your savings and your welfare under these circumstances?

The answer is that you will simply reduce your personal voluntary savings by the amount of social security taxes. So your savings will fall from $6,018 per year to $4,018. The difference of $2,000 is the amount you will pay in social security taxes. Thus, you reduce your private saving by an amount equal to the "savings" imposed on you by the social security system. Your pool of private savings will suffice to provide a life annuity of $16,012, which when added to your social security benefit of $7,970 will give you a total retirement income of $23,982 per year.

Thus, if social security pays you the same rate of return you could earn on your private saving, your lifetime consumption plan will not be affected by the existence of social security. There will only be a substitution of forced saving for voluntary private saving.

But what happens if social security pays an implied real interest rate that differs from 3%? If it pays a rate higher than 3%, you will be able to afford a higher lifetime consumption stream than $23,982; if it pays less than 3% per year, your consumption stream will be lower.

In many countries, the social security system offers a higher rate of return to people in the lower end of the income distribution than to those in the upper end. But the fact that benefits are paid in the form of a lifetime annuity implies that no matter how rich or poor you are, the longer you live, the higher your actual rate of return. The effective rate of return earned in the social security system is an important issue (see Box 4).

Quick Check 6

Suppose that social security offers a 3% real rate of return to someone who pays a 10% tax on a salary of $30,000 per year for 40 years. How large must the annual benefit payment be if it is calculated to last for 20 years?

---

[5]In the United States, the social security system is called OASDI, which stands for old age, survivors, and disability insurance. As the name implies, it provides not only old age benefits, but also benefits for dependent family members of workers who die during their working years, and benefits to those who can no longer work due to disability.

[6]Using the *Annuity Compound Amount Factor* we find the retirement fund in 30 years to be: $FV_{PMT}(PMT, i, n) =$

$PMT \cdot \dfrac{(1+i)^n - 1}{i}$ or $FV_{PMT}(\$2,000, 3\%, 30) = \$95,151$. Then taking the *Capital Recovery Factor* we can calculate

the yearly retirement benefit as: $PMT_{PV}(PV, i, n) = PV \cdot \dfrac{i}{1-(1+i)^{-n}}$ or $PMT_{PV}(\$95,151, 3\%, 15) = \$7,970$.

Box 4	Financial Innovation to Combat Longevity Risks

As life expectancies around the world continue to rise, insurance companies and corporate pension schemes must find a way to accommodate the consequences of this significant demographic trend. Many annuity providers and pension schemes have few or no risk management tools to deal with increased life expectancy. This can pose a serious problem for organizations that must pay individuals an income from retirement until death.

Several institutions have posed solutions for this dilemma, for instance, the longevity bonds issued by the European Investment Bank. This bond issue is tied to an index of the survivorship of Welsh and English men who were 65 years old at the time of the placement. The bonds are structured so that the payments decline over the bond's life depending on the realization of this longevity index.

Insurance companies in the United Kingdom have expressed interest in buying pension promises from firms that don't want to assume such risks. Hedging these risks would minimize the impact of the rising demographic trend of early retirees living longer and collecting more pension money. Such longevity trading has emerged, and will continue to expand as more people live longer and enjoy lengthier retirements.

Source: Adapted from "When Old Age Becomes a Risk Factor," *Financial Times,* December 12, 2005.

3 Deferring Taxes Through Voluntary Retirement Plans

In many countries governments encourage voluntary saving for retirement through provisions of the tax code. In the United States, people are permitted to establish tax-advantaged accounts, known as individual retirement accounts (IRAs), to which contributions are deductible from current income for tax purposes, and interest on these contributions is not taxed until the money is withdrawn. These plans are called *tax deferred* rather than *tax exempt* because any amounts withdrawn from the plan are taxed at the time of withdrawal.

Some people believe that there is an advantage to such tax deferral only if you will be in a lower tax bracket when you withdraw the money. But that is not correct. Tax deferral is quite advantageous even for people who remain in the same tax bracket after retirement.

To see why, consider the following example, summarized in Figure 4. Suppose that you face a tax rate of 20% both before and after retirement. The interest rate is 8% per year. You are 30 years before your retirement date and contribute $1,000 to the plan. Your total before-tax amount accumulated at retirement will be $1,000 \cdot 1.08^{30} = \$10,062.65$. You will have to pay taxes at the rate of 20% on the entire amount, if you choose to withdraw it at that time. Thus, your taxes will be $0.20 \cdot \$10,062.65 = \$2,012.53$ and you will be left with $8,050.12 after taxes.

If, instead, you choose not to participate in the retirement plan and invest in an ordinary savings plan, you have to pay 20% of the $1,000 or $200 immediately in additional taxes. The remaining $800 will go into the ordinary savings plan, and interest earnings on the $800 will be taxed each year. The after-tax interest rate earned is, therefore, $(1 - 0.20) \cdot 8\%$ or 6.4%. The amount accumulated at retirement from this ordinary savings plan is $800 \cdot 1.064^{30} = \$5,144.45$. Because you have paid the taxes on the original contribution and on the interest along the way, the amount accumulated is not subject to further tax.

Clearly, the tax-deferred savings plan provides a larger after-tax benefit because $8,050.12 is greater than $5,144.45. Thus, even though you remain in the same 20% tax bracket both before and after retirement, the amount you have to spend in the future is almost twice as much under the tax-deferred savings plan.

FIGURE 4

The Advantage of Tax-Deferred Saving

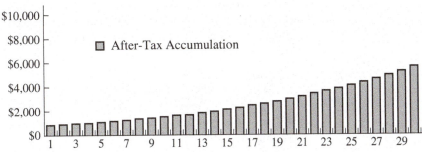

Advantage of Tax Deferral

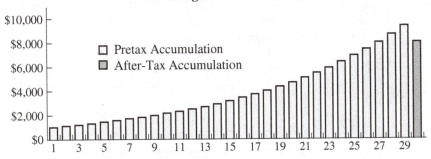

Advantage of Tax Deferral: IRA

When your tax rate remains unchanged, the benefit of deferral can be summarized in the rule: *Deferral earns you the pretax rate of return after tax.* That is, if you paid the initial tax and invested $800 at the pretax rate of 8%, you would have $800 \cdot 1.08^{30} = \$8,050.12$.

Quick Check 7

Suppose that the investor's tax rate is 30% instead of 20%. How large would be the advantage of tax deferral compared to our example with a 20% tax rate?

---

4 Should You Invest in a Professional Degree?

Education and training can be viewed as an investment in human capital. Although there may be many reasons for acquiring additional schooling, one purpose is to increase people's earning power, that is, increase their human capital.

Let us consider the costs and benefits of additional education. The economic costs consist of *explicit* costs such as tuition and the *implicit* costs of forgone earnings during the time spent in school. The economic benefits consist of the value of the increased stream of earnings attributable to the additional years of education. Like other investment decisions, the investment is worthwhile if the present value of the expected incremental benefits exceeds the present value of the expected incremental costs.

For example, consider Joe Grad who has just graduated from college and is deciding whether to go on for his master's degree. Joe figures that if he takes a job immediately, he can earn $30,000 per year in real terms for the remainder of his working years. If he goes on for two more years of graduate study, however, he can increase his earnings to $35,000 per year. The cost of tuition is $15,000 per year in real terms. Is this a worthwhile investment if the real interest rate is 3% per year?

Ignoring uncertainty, Joe must give up $45,000 (tuition plus forgone earnings) in each of the next two years in order to increase his earnings by $5,000 per year over his remaining career.

Suppose Joe is now 20 years old and expects to retire at age 65. The relevant cash flows for this investment are incremental outflows of $45,000 in each of the next two years and then incremental inflows of $5,000 in each of the succeeding 43 years. The present value of the outflows is $86,106; the present value of the inflows is $113,026. The net present value of the investment in human capital is, therefore, $26,920, and it is worthwhile.[7]

> **Quick Check 8**
>
> Suppose that Joe is 30 years old instead of 20. If all the other assumptions remain the same, does the investment in the graduate degree still have a positive *NPV*?

5 Should You Buy or Rent?

You are currently renting a house for $10,000 per year and have an option to buy it for $200,000. Property taxes are deductible for income tax purposes, and your tax rate is 30%. The maintenance and property taxes are estimated to be:

Maintenance	$1,200
Property Taxes	$2,400
Total	$3,600

These costs are currently included in the rent.

Let us assume that your objective is to provide yourself with housing at the lowest present value of cost. Should you buy or continue to rent?

The present value of cost equals the discounted value of the after-tax outflows discounted at the after-tax rate of interest. Because property taxes can be deducted from income for federal income tax purposes, the after-tax outflow for property taxes each year is $0.7 \cdot \$2,400$, or $1,680. Because no date for eventually selling the house has been specified, we will assume for simplicity an infinite horizon.

If you buy the house, then you will have to pay $200,000 immediately, and the expected after-tax cash outflow will consist of the maintenance expenses and property taxes net of the income tax savings from deductibility of the property taxes:

$$\text{Cash Outflow in Year } t = \$1,200 + \$1,680 = \$2,880$$

Letting i be the before-tax discount rate, the present value cost of owning the house is:

$$PV \text{ Cost of Owning} = \$200,000 + \frac{\$2,880}{0.7i}$$

where we have assumed that the properly maintained house continues in perpetuity and have applied the annuity formula. Similarly, the present value cost of renting the house can be written as:

$$PV \text{ Cost of Renting} = \frac{\$10,000}{0.7i}$$

If *PV* Cost of Renting > *PV* Cost of Owning, then it is better to own rather than rent.

---

[7]We first compute the present value of the outflows using the *Annuity Present Value Factor*:

$PV_{PMT}(PMT, i, n) = PMT \cdot \dfrac{1-(1+i)^{-n}}{i}$ or in this case $PV_{PMT}(\$45,000, 3\%, 2) = \$86,106$. Next we compute the present value of the inflow using both the *Annuity Present Value Factor* and the *Present Value Factors*: $PV_{PMT}(\$5,000, 3\%, 43) = \$119,910$ and $PV_{FV}(\$119,910, 3\%, 2) = \$113,026$.

Because we are assuming that the maintenance costs and property taxes are fixed in *real* terms, i should be a *real* interest rate. Let us assume no inflation so that the real and nominal before-tax discount rate is 3% per year. Then the real after-tax rate is 2.1% per year.[8] Computing the present value costs under each alternative, we find:

$$PV \text{ Cost of Owning} = \$200,000 + \frac{\$2,880}{0.021} = \$337,143$$

and

$$PV \text{ Cost of Renting} = \frac{\$10,000}{0.021} = \$476,190$$

Therefore, you would be better off buying the house.

The buy-or-rent decision is really an investment decision. In effect you are laying out $200,000 today in order to receive future cash benefits equal to the after-tax savings in rental costs. In present value terms, you save $139,047 (i.e., $476,190 − $337,143). This is the *NPV* of the investment in the house.

Of course, the relation between *PV* Cost of Renting and *PV* Cost of Owning depends on the rent charged. At what rent would you be indifferent between buying and renting?

This break-even rent (i.e., the annual rental costs at which you would be indifferent between owning or renting) is found by setting *PV* Cost of Owning equal to *PV* Cost of Renting and solving for *X*:

$$\frac{X}{0.021} = \$200,000 + \frac{\$2,880}{0.021}$$

$$X = 0.021 \cdot \$200,000 + \$2,880$$

$$X = \$4,200 + \$2,880 = \$7,080$$

Thus, if the rent is less than $7,080 per year, you would prefer to keep on renting rather than to buy.

> **Quick Check 9**
>
> Suppose that the real interest rate before taxes was 4% instead of 3%. What would be the break-even rent?

Summary

- In making lifetime saving/consumption decisions: (1) Do the analysis in real terms (constant dollars) to simplify the calculations and to avoid having to forecast inflation. (2) Start by computing the present value of your lifetime resources. The present value of your lifetime spending cannot exceed this amount.
- Social security or any other forced saving program will offset voluntary saving. It may have a positive or a negative effect on the present value of your total lifetime resources.
- Tax-deferred retirement accounts are advantageous because they allow you to earn a before-tax rate of return until money is withdrawn from the account. They are advantageous if you are in the same tax bracket before and after you retire, and even more so if your tax bracket is lower after you retire.

---

[8]With no inflation the real after-tax rate equal $(1 - \text{tax rate})$ times the before-tax rate. In this case: $(1 - 0.3) \cdot 3\% = 0.7 \cdot 3\% = 2.1\%$.

- Getting a professional degree or other training can be evaluated as an investment in human capital. As such, it should be undertaken if the present value of the benefits (such as increase in your earnings) exceeds the present value of the costs (such as tuition and forgone salary.)
- In deciding whether to buy or rent an apartment or a consumer durable, choose the alternative with the lower present value of costs.

Key Terms

- human capital
- permanent income
- intertemporal budget constraint

- feasible plan
- optimization model

Internet Reference Materials

Insurance and Pensions, Organization for Economic Co-operation and Development (OECD):
http://www.oecd.org/about/0,2337.en_2649_37411_1_1_1_1_37411,00.html
Savings Calculator, MSN Money: http://moneycentral.msn.com/Investor/calcs/n_savapp/main.asp

Answers to Quick Check Questions

Quick Check 1 Recompute the saving needed in the example if the target replacement rate is 80%. What does the new saving level imply about consumption spending before and after retirement?

Answer: The target level of spending in retirement is $0.8 \cdot \$30,000$, or $24,000 per year. First, we compute the amount that you have to have in your retirement fund at age 65 to be able to withdraw $24,000 per year for 15 years:

Using the *Annuity Present Value Factor* we have:

n	15
i	3%
PMT	$24,000.00
PV	$286,510.44

$$PV_{PMT}(PMT, i, n) = PMT \cdot \frac{1 - (1+i)^{-n}}{i} \text{ or}$$

$$PV_{PMT}(\$24,000, 3\%, 15) = \$286,510.44.$$

Next we compute how much we need to save each year to have $286,510.44 accumulated 30 years from now using the *Sinking Fund Factor*:

n	30
i	3%
FV	$286,510.44
PMT	$6,022.24

$$PMT_{FV}(FV, i, n) = FV \cdot \frac{i}{(1+i)^n - 1} \text{ or}$$

$$PMT_{FV}(\$286,510, 3\%, 30) = \$6,022.24.$$

Your consumption spending before retirement will be $23,977.76 per year, which is very close to the level of $24,000 you will have after retirement. So in this case, aiming for a replacement rate of 80% results in almost the same consumption spending before and after retirement.

Quick Check 2 Georgette is currently 30 years old, plans to retire at age 65 and to live to age 85. Her labor income is $25,000 per year, and she intends to maintain a constant level of real consumption spending over the next 55 years. Assume no taxes, no growth in real salary, and a real interest rate of 3% per year.

- What is the value of Georgette's human capital?
- What is her permanent income?

Answer:

n	35
i	3%
PMT	$25,000.00
PV	$537,180.50

Using the *Annuity Present Value Factor* we solve for the current level of human capital as:
$PV_{PMT}(\$25,000, 3\%, 35) = \$537,180.50$.

n	55
i	3%
PV	$537,180.50
PMT	$20,063.19

Using the *Capital Recovery Factor* we can calculate permanent income as:
$$PMT_{PV}(PV, i, n) = PV \cdot \frac{i}{1 - (1+i)^{-n}} \text{ or}$$
$PMT_{PV}(\$537,180.50, 3\%, 55) = \$20,063.19$.

Quick Check 3 In Table 2, what would be human capital and permanent income at a real interest rate of 3.5% per year?

Answer:

n	30
i	3.5%
PMT	$30,000.00
PV	$551,761.36

Using the *Annuity Present Value Factor* we solve for the current level of human capital as:
$PV_{PMT}(\$30,000, 3.5\%, 30) = \$551,761.36$.

n	45
i	3.5%
PV	$551,761.36
PMT	$24,527.69

Using the *Capital Recovery Factor* we can calculate permanent income as:
$PMT_{PV}(\$551,761.36, 3.5\%, 45) = \$24,527.69$.

Quick Check 4 What effect would a $1 million inheritance that you expect to receive 30 years from now have on your permanent income?

Answer: The present value of your lifetime resources would increase by the *PV* of the expected inheritance and permanent income would increase by the annuitized value of that increase in lifetime resource. Assuming a real interest rate of 3% per year and assuming that the $1 million inheritance is in constant dollars:

n	30
i	3%
FV	$1,000,000.00
PV	$411,986.76

Using the *Present Value Factor* we compute the increase in the present value of your lifetime resources: $PV_{FV}(FV, i, n) = FV \cdot \dfrac{1}{(1+i)^n}$ or
$PV_{FV}(\$1,000,000, 3\%, 30) = \$411,986.76$.

n	45
i	3%
PV	$411,986.76
PMT	$16,802.95

Then compute the increase in permanent income using the *Capital Recovery Factor:*
$PMT_{PV}(\$411{,}986.76, 3\%, 45) = \$16{,}802.95.$

Quick Check 5   Suppose that Omar cannot borrow during the next five years. How does that affect his lifetime saving and consumption plan?

Answer: If he cannot borrow, he will only be able to consume what he earns, namely $25,000 per year for five years. At the end of that time he will increase his consumption to equal his permanent income. Let us figure out what his human capital and permanent income will be in another five years.

n	30
i	3%
PMT	$300,000.00
PV	$5,880,132.40

Using the *Annuity Present Value Factor* we can solve for the level of Omar's human capital after five years as: $PV_{PMT}(\$300{,}000, 3\%, 30) = \$5{,}880{,}132.40.$

n	50
i	3%
PV	$5,880,132.40
PMT	$228,534.25

Using the *Capital Recovery Factor* we can recalculate permanent income as:
$PMT_{PV}(\$5{,}880{,}132.40, 3\%, 50) = \$228{,}534.25.$ So starting at age 35, Omar can consume $228,534.25 per year for the remainder of his life.

Quick Check 6   Suppose that social security offers a 3% real rate of return to someone who pays a 10% tax on a salary of $30,000 per year for 40 years. How large must the annual benefit payment be if it is calculated to last for 20 years?

Answer: The future value of the taxes paid over 40 years should equal the present value of the benefits received over the following 20 years when both streams are discounted at 3% per year.

n	40
i	3%
PMT	$3,000.00
FV	$226,203.78

First calculate the future value of the taxes using the *Annuity Compound Amount Factor:*
$$FV_{PMT}(PMT, i, n) = PMT \cdot \frac{(1 + i)^n - 1}{i} \text{ or}$$
$FV_{PMT}(\$3{,}000, 3\%, 20) = \$226{,}203.78.$

n	20
i	3%
PV	$226,203.78
PMT	$15,204.45

Then compute the annual retirement benefit using the *Capital Recovery Factor:*
$PMT_{PV}(\$226{,}203.78, 3\%, 20) = \$15{,}204.45.$

So the annual benefit payment should be $15,204.45 in real terms, which is a replacement rate of preretirement income of about 50%.

Quick Check 7   Suppose that the investor's tax rate is 30% instead of 20%. How large would be the advantage of tax deferral compared to our example with a 20% tax rate?

Answer: As in the example in the text, your total before-tax amount accumulated at retirement will still be $\$1{,}000 \cdot 1.08^{30} = \$10{,}062.65$. You will have to pay taxes at the rate of 30% on the entire amount so your taxes will be $0.3 \cdot \$10,062.65 = \$3,018.80$, and you will be left with \$7,043.85 after taxes. If, instead, you choose not to participate in the retirement plan and invest in an ordinary savings plan, you have to pay 30% of the \$1,000 or \$300 immediately in additional taxes. The remaining \$700 will go into the ordinary savings plan, and interest earnings on the \$700 will be taxed each year. The after-tax interest rate earned is, therefore, $(1 - 0.3) \cdot 8\%$, or 5.6%. The amount accumulated at retirement from this ordinary savings plan is $\$700 \cdot 1.056^{30} = \$3,589.35$.

Quick Check 8   Suppose that Joe is 30 years old instead of 20. If all the other assumptions remain the same, does the investment in the graduate degree still have a positive *NPV?*

Answer: As in the example in the text, Joe must give up \$45,000 (tuition plus forgone earnings) in each of the next two years in order to increase his earnings by \$5,000 per year over his remaining career. Joe is now 30 years old and expects to retire at age 65. The relevant cash flows for this investment are incremental outflows of \$45,000 in each of the next two years and then incremental inflows of \$5,000 in each of the succeeding 33 years. The present value of the outflows is \$86,106; the present value of the inflows is \$97,869. The net present value of the investment in human capital is, therefore, \$11,763, and it is still worthwhile.

Quick Check 9   Suppose that the real interest rate before taxes was 4% instead of 3%. What would be the break-even rent?

Answer: The after-tax real discount rate is now $0.7 \cdot 4\% = 2.8\%$ per year. The annual rental costs at which you would be indifferent between owning or renting, is found by setting *PV* Cost of Owning equal to *PV* Cost of Renting and solving for *X:*

$$\frac{X}{0.028} = \$200,000 + \frac{\$2,880}{0.028}$$

$$X = 0.028 \cdot \$200,000 + \$2,880 = \$5,600 + \$2,880 = \$8,480$$

Questions and Problems

1. Fred's company has a defined-benefit pension plan. Suppose the plan pays a benefit equal to 1% of final salary per year of service. Fred is 40 years old and has worked for the company for 15 years. His last year's salary was \$50,000 and is expected to remain so in real terms until retirement. The expected rate of inflation is 4%.

   a. If normal retirement age is 65, the interest rate is 8%, and Fred's life expectancy is 80, what is the present value of his accrued pension benefit?

   b. What effect should his pension benefit have on Fred's planned saving, assuming he has a 75% target replacement rate?

2. Analyze the "expert's" responses to the following questions:

   Question: How early do you recommend people begin saving for retirement? Would it be too early for my 14-year-old to start saving?

   Expert: It's never too early.

   Question: For a college student, what would you suggest for a savings plan?

   Expert: I'd suggest deciding on a specific amount to set aside each month, then making sure you do it, no matter the temptations not to.

3. Analyze the following newspaper column:

   Many of us who started families late share a nightmare image: having to pay huge college bills just as we're giving up paychecks and shouldering the steep costs of retirement. In fact, the double whammy might not be so bad, assuming the parents have prepared properly. On the plus side, older parents are likely to have enjoyed their best earnings years before the college costs begin, allowing them to put aside more than younger parents can. They've also had more years for investments to compound. In the ideal situation, older parents can avoid borrowing to meet college costs, taking the preferred route of earning interest on investments rather than paying it on student loans.

(Excerpted from Jeff Brown's Personal Finance column in the *Philadelphia Inquirer*, May 11, 1998.)

4. Assume that you are 40 years old and wish to retire at age 65. You expect to be able to average a 6% annual rate of interest on your savings over your lifetime (both prior to retirement and after retirement). You would like to save enough money to provide $8,000 per year beginning at age 66 in retirement income to supplement other sources (social security, pension plans, etc.). Suppose you decide that the extra income needs to be provided for only 15 years (up to age 80). Assume that your first contribution to the savings plan will take place one year from now.

   a. How much must you save each year between now and retirement to achieve your goal?

   b. If the rate of inflation turns out to be 6% per year between now and retirement, how much will your first $8,000 withdrawal be worth in terms of today's purchasing power?

5. You are saving for retirement and you come across the following table. It shows the percentage of your current salary that you should save for your retirement in order to retire with an annuity equal to 70% of your salary if you have not yet saved anything. It assumes that your annual salary will remain constant in real terms until retirement, and that you will live for 25 years after retiring. For instance, if you have 35 years left before you retire and earn 3.5% per year on your investments, then you should save 17.3% of your current salary.

TABLE A   **Saving Rate Needed to Achieve 70% Replacement Rate**

Real Interest Rate	Years to Retirement		
	15	25	35
3.5% per annum	?	?	17.30%
4.5% per annum	?	?	?

Fill in the missing numbers in Table A.

6. Continuing the previous problem, now fill in Table B. It assumes that instead of targeting a 70% replacement rate of preretirement income, your goal is to maintain the same level of consumption spending both before and after retirement.

TABLE B   **Saving to Maintain Lifetime Consumption Spending**

Real Interest Rate	Years to Retirement		
	15	25	35
3.5% per annum	?	?	19.82%
4.5% per annum	?	?	?

7. Willie is 35 years old, plans to retire at 50, and to live to the ripe old age of 100. His labor income as a plumber is $150,000 per year, and he expects to maintain a constant level of real consumption spending for the remainder of his life. Assuming a steady real salary, the complete absence of taxes, and a real interest rate of 2% per annum:
   a. What is the value of Willie's human capital?
   b. What is the level of his permanent income?

8. You are saving for retirement and you come across the following table. It shows the increase in the annual benefit you can receive in retirement per dollar that you increase your annual retirement saving in the years before retirement. It assumes that you will live for 20 years after retiring. For instance, if you have 30 years left before you retire and earn an interest rate of 3% per year, then you will obtain an increase of $3.20 in your annual retirement benefit for every $1 per year increase in annual saving. Fill in the missing table values.

Interest Rate	Years to Retirement		
	20	25	30
0.0%	$1.00	$1.25	$1.50
0.5%	$1.10	$1.40	$1.70
1.0%	$1.22	$1.57	?
1.5%	$1.35	$1.75	$2.19
2.0%	$1.49	$1.96	$2.48
3.0%	$1.81	?	$3.20
3.5%	?	$2.74	$3.63
4.0%	$2.19	$3.06	$4.13
4.5%	$2.41	$3.43	$4.69
5.0%	$2.65	$3.83	?

9. Analyze the following newspaper column:

   What's the best age for a person to start collecting Social Security benefits? According to conventional wisdom, retirement starts at age 65. It's true that full benefits don't start until age 65, but 62-year-olds can retire and collect 80% of their benefits.

   Take the hypothetical cases of John and Mary, who have the same birthday and who are both slated to start drawing $1,000 a month in Social Security benefits at age 65. On his 62nd birthday, John decides to go ahead and start claiming his benefits of $800 a month (80% of $1,000). Mary decides to wait until she's 65, when she can claim the full $1,000. Three years later, Mary turns 65 and begins receiving $1,000 a month from the Social Security Administration. John continues to receive $800 a month. But he has already been paid $28,800 whereas Mary received nothing.

   Five years go by, with Mary drawing $1,000 a month and John $800 a month. At 70, John has received $76,800, compared to Mary's $60,000. When they reach 77, Mary will pull ahead. So, it seems if a person doesn't live past 76, it would better to start collecting Social Security benefits at 62. For those who reach their upper 70's, it pays to wait until they are 65 to collect Social Security.

   (Adapted from ©1998, *Atlanta Business Chronicle*, Gary Summer, contributing writer, June 29, 1998.)

10. *Challenge Question:* George Thriftless is 45 years old, earns $50,000 per year, and expects that his future earnings will keep pace with inflation, but will not exceed inflation. He has not yet saved anything toward his retirement. His company does not offer any pension plan. George pays Social Security taxes equal to 7.5% of his salary, and he assumes that when he retires at age 65, he will receive $12,000 per year in inflation-adjusted Social Security benefits for the rest of his life. His life expectancy is age 85.

    George buys a book on retirement planning that recommends saving enough so that when private savings and Social Security are combined, he can replace 80% of his preretirement salary. George buys a financial calculator and goes through the following calculations:

    First, he computes the amount he will need to receive in each year of retirement to replace 80% of his salary: 0.8 × $50,000 = $40,000.

    Since he expects to receive $12,000 per year in Social Security benefits, he calculates that he will have to provide the other $28,000 per year from his own retirement fund.

    Using the 8% interest rate on long-term default-free bonds, George computes the amount he will need to have at age 65 as $274,908 (the present value of $28,000 for 20 years at 8% per year). Then he computes the amount he will have to save in each of the next 20 years to reach that future accumulation as $6,007 (the annual payment that will produce a future value of $274,908 at an interest rate of 8% per year). George feels pretty confident that he can save 12% of his salary (i.e., $6,007/$50,000) in order to ensure a comfortable retirement.

    a. If the expected long-term *real* interest rate is 3% per year, approximately what is the long-term expected rate of inflation?

    b. Has George correctly taken account of inflation in his calculations? If not, how would you correct him?

    c. How much should George save in each of the next 20 years (until age 65) if he wants to maintain a constant level of consumption over the remaining 40 years of his life (from age 45 to age 85)? Ignore income taxes.

11. You are 30 years old and are considering full-time study for an MBA degree. Tuition and other direct costs will be $15,000 per year for two years. In addition you will have to give up a job with a salary of $30,000 per year. Assume tuition is paid and salary received at the *end* of the year. By how much does your salary have to increase (in real terms) as a result of getting your MBA degree to justify the investment? Assume a real interest rate of 3% per year and ignore taxes. Also assume that the salary increase is a constant real amount that starts after you complete your degree (at the end of the year following graduation) and lasts until retirement at age 65.

12. Suppose you currently rent an apartment and have an option to buy it for $200,000. Property taxes are $2,000 per year and are deductible for income tax purposes. Annual maintenance costs on the property are $1,500 per year and are *not* tax deductible. You expect property taxes and maintenance costs to increase at the rate of inflation. Your income tax rate is 40%, you can earn an *after-tax* real interest rate of 2% per year, and you plan to keep the apartment forever. What is the "break-even" annual rent such that you would buy it if the rent exceeds this amount?

13. You have decided to acquire a new car that costs $30,000. You are considering whether to lease it for 3 years or to purchase it and finance the purchase with a 3-year installment loan. The lease requires no down payment and lasts for 3 years. Lease payments are $400 monthly starting *immediately,* whereas the installment loan will require monthly payments starting a month from now at an annual percentage rate (*APR*) of 8%.

    a. If you expect the resale value of the car to be $20,000 3 years from now, should you buy or lease it?

    b. What is the break-even resale price of the car 3 years from now, such that you would be indifferent between buying leasing it?

14. Using the finance concepts presented in this chapter, construct a personal balance sheet showing your assets, liabilities, and net worth.

    a. Did you value your assets at cost or at current market value? Why?

    b. Did you include your human capital as an asset? Why?

    c. Did you include deferred taxes as a liability? Why?

15. *Challenge Question:* Suppose you buy a house for $200,000 when you are 35 years old. You make a 20% down payment and borrow the other 80% from a mortgage lender. The mortgage loan is at a fixed interest rate of 8% per year for 30 years and requires level annual payments. At age 65, you plan to take out a "reverse mortgage" loan that will allow you to borrow a constant annual amount for the rest of your life to be paid off by the sale of your house when you die. Your life expectancy is age 85. The interest rate on both the original mortgage loan and the reverse mortgage will be 8% per year.

    a. Suppose that you expect the inflation rate to be 3% per year and you can rent an equivalent house for $10,000 per year. Is it worth buying the house?

    b. Show how buying the house will affect your assets, liabilities, and cash flow over the next 50 years.

    c. In *Making the Most of Your Money,* J. B. Quinn has written:

Over the long run, the value of homes should follow the inflation rate. But over the time that you own your particular house, its value might rise or fall or stall. You can't predict. But there are reasons other than profit for owning a house.

- Mortgage payments force to save, while rental payments don't.
- You get tax deductions, and can tax-shelter your capital gains.
- You're landlord free.
- You know the deep contentment of holding a spot of ground that others can enter by invitation only.
- You won't lose your lease.
- You can renovate to suit.
- A house is collateral for a loan.

Please comment on Ms. Quinn's analysis.

Suggested Readings

Bodie, Z. "Thoughts on the Future: Life-Cycle Investing in Theory and Practice." *Financial Analysts Journal* 59, January–February 2003.

———. D. McLeavey, and L. Siegel, ed. *The Future of Life-Cycle Saving and Investing.* Charlottesville, VA: Research Foundation of CFA Institute, 2007.

Merton, R. C. "Thoughts on the Future: Theory and Practice in Investment Management." *Financial Analysts Journal* 59, January–February 2003.

Modigliani, F., and R. Brumberg. "Utility Analysis and the Consumption Function: An Interpretation of Cross-Section Data." *Post Keynesian Economics.* Ed. K. Kurihara. New Brunswick, N. J.: Rutgers University Press, 1954.

The Analysis of Investment Projects

From Chapter 6 of *Financial Economics*, 2/e. Zvi Bodie, Robert C. Merton, David L. Cleeton.

The Analysis of Investment Projects

OBJECTIVES

- To show how to use discounted cash flow analysis to make investment decisions such as whether to enter a new line of business.
- Analyze how to decide whether to invest in equipment to reduce operating costs.

CONTENTS

Previously, we discussed how to apply discounted cash flow analysis to some of the major financial decisions that people face in their personal lives. In this chapter we apply those same techniques to the analysis of investment decisions by business firms, such as whether to launch a new product or to invest in research laboratories, factories, machinery, warehouses, showrooms, marketing campaigns, and training of employees. The process of analyzing such decisions is called *capital budgeting*.

This chapter discusses how businesses handle the capital budgeting process. Although the details vary from firm to firm, any capital budgeting process consists of three elements:

- coming up with proposals for investment projects
- evaluating them
- deciding which ones to accept and which to reject

What criteria should management use in deciding which investment projects to undertake? Earlier, we showed that in order to maximize the welfare of its shareholders, the objective of a firm's management is to only undertake those projects that increase— or at least do not decrease—the market value of shareholders' equity. For this, management needs a theory of how the decisions it makes affect the market value of the firm's equity shares: Management should compute the discounted present value of the future expected cash flows from a project and undertake only those projects with positive net present value (*NPV*).

1 The Nature of Project Analysis

The basic unit of analysis in the capital budgeting process is the individual investment project. Investment projects start with an idea for increasing shareholder wealth by producing a new product or improving the way an existing product is produced. Investment projects are analyzed as a sequence of decisions and possible events over time starting with the original concept, gathering information relevant to assessing the costs and benefits of implementing it, and devising an optimal strategy for implementing the project over time.

To illustrate the sequence of stages involved in investment project analysis, suppose you are a film industry executive whose job is to come up with proposals for new movies and to analyze their potential value to your company's shareholders. Typically, producing a movie for the mass market involves major outlays of cash over several years before there are any cash inflows from customers who pay to see it. Roughly speaking, the movie will increase shareholder wealth only if the present value of the cash inflows exceeds the present value of the outlays.

Forecasting the likely cash outlays and inflows from the movie is a complicated task. The cash flows will depend on a sequence of decisions and actions that are under your control and on a sequence of events that are not entirely under your control. At each stage in the project's life, from conceiving the idea for the movie's theme to the distribution of the final product to movie theaters and video stores, unpredictable events will occur that affect the stream of cash flows. At each stage you will have to decide whether to continue the project, to discontinue it, to delay it, or to accelerate it. You will also have to decide whether to reduce the level of spending (e.g., by eliminating some costly scenes) or to increase it (e.g., by launching a television advertising campaign).

It is not simply forecasting a project's cash flows that is difficult. Evaluating their likely effect on the market value of shareholders' equity is also complicated. To simplify our exposition of the complicated nature of project analysis in this chapter, we will proceed in stages. In this chapter we will analyze projects as if the future cash flows are known with certainty, using a discounted cash flow valuation. Then, later, we will consider ways to take account of uncertainty and of the value of managerial options.

2 Where Do Investment Ideas Come From?

Most investment projects requiring capital expenditures fall into three categories: new products, cost reduction, and replacement of existing assets. Here are some examples:

- Should the firm start a new-product line that requires investment in plant, equipment, and inventories?
- Should the firm invest in automated equipment that will allow it to reduce its labor costs?
- Should the firm replace an existing plant in order to expand capacity or lower operating costs?

A common source of ideas for investment projects is the firm's existing customers. Surveys of customers, both formal and informal, can suggest new demands that can be met by producing new products and services or by improving existing ones. A firm that manufactures computer equipment, for example, may discover from surveying its customers that providing a repair service for computers might be a profitable new line of business.

Many firms establish a research and development (R&D) department to identify potential new products that are technologically feasible to produce and that seem to satisfy a perceived customer demand. In the pharmaceutical industry, for example, the R&D activity is the source of virtually all new-product ideas.

Another source of project ideas is the competition. For example, if the XYZ software company, which produces a financial planning package for personal computers, knows that a competitor, ABC software company, is working on a new upgrade in its competing product, XYZ may want to consider upgrading its own product. XYZ may want to consider acquiring ABC. Acquisitions of one company by another are capital budgeting projects.

Ideas for capital projects to improve products or reduce costs often come from the production divisions of corporations. For example, engineers, production managers, or other employees who are in close contact with the production process may spot ways to cut costs by reorganizing an assembly line or by replacing labor-intensive operations with automated equipment requiring a capital outlay.

In corporations with incentive systems that encourage managers and other employees to think about opportunities for profitable growth and operating improvements, there is generally a regular flow of proposals for investment projects. The rest of this chapter discusses techniques for evaluating projects and deciding which ones are likely to enhance shareholder value.

> **Quick Check 1**
>
> Where do you think new project ideas come from in the movie business?

3 The Net Present Value Investment Rule

Recall the investment criterion that is most obviously related to the goal of maximizing shareholder wealth—the *net present value rule*. A project's **net present value** (*NPV*) is the amount by which it is expected to increase the wealth of the firm's current shareholders. Stated as an investment criterion for the firm's managers, the *NPV* rule is: *Invest if the proposed project's NPV is positive.*

FIGURE 1

Cash Flow Forecasts for the Protojean Project

Year (t)	Cash Flows (CF_t) (in thousands of dollars)
0	−$100
1	$50
2	$40
3	$30

Year	0	1	2	3
Net cash flow	−100	50	40	30

To illustrate how to calculate a project's *NPV* we present the following example. Generic Jeans Company, a manufacturer of casual clothing, is considering whether to produce a new line of jeans called Protojeans. It requires an initial outlay of $100,000 for new specialized equipment, and the firm's marketing department forecasts that given the nature of consumer preferences for jeans the product will have an economic life of three years. The cash flow forecasts for the Protojean project are shown in Figure 1.

A negative sign in front of a cash flow forecast for a particular year means a cash out-flow. In the case of the Protojean project, there is only one negative cash flow, and that is at the start of the project (time zero). Subsequent cash flows are all positive: $50,000 at the end of the first year, $40,000 at the end of year 2, and $30,000 at the end of year 3.

To calculate the project's *NPV* we need to specify the capitalization rate (k) to use to discount the cash flows. This is called the project's **cost of capital.**

$$NPV(k) = \sum_{t=0}^{n} \frac{CF_t}{(1+k)^t}$$

Table 1 shows the calculation of the net present value of the Protojean project. Each year's cash flow is discounted at a rate of 8% per year, and the resulting present value is shown in column 3. Thus, the present value of the $50,000 to be received at the end of the first year is $46,296.30, and so on. Column 4 shows the cumulative sum of the present values of all of the cash flows.

The project's *NPV* is the last entry in column 4 of Table 1. To the nearest penny it is $4,404.82. This means that by going forward with the Protojean project, management expects to increase the wealth of the shareholders of the Generic Jeans Company by $4,404.82.

TABLE 1 Calculation of *NPV* of the Protojean Project

Year (1)	Cash Flows (thousands of dollars) (2)	Present Value of Cash Flow at 8% per Year (3)	Cumulative Present Value (4)
0	−100	−100.00000	−100.00000
1	50	46.29630	−53.70370
2	40	34.29355	−19.41015
3	30	23.81497	4.40482

$$NPV(k = 8\%) = \sum_{t=0}^{3} \frac{CF_t}{(1+8\%)^t}$$

Quick Check 2

Suppose that the Protojean project is expected to have a third-year cash flow of only $10,000 instead of $30,000. If all other cash flows are the same and the discount rate is still 8% per year, what is its *NPV*?

4 Estimating a Project's Cash Flows

Calculating a project's *NPV* once one has the cash flow forecasts is the easy part of capital budgeting. Much more difficult is estimating a project's expected cash flows. Project cash flow forecasts are built up from estimates of the incremental revenues and costs associated with the project. Let us illustrate how cash flow estimates can be derived from estimates of a project's sales volume, selling price, and fixed and variable costs.

Suppose you are a manager in the personal computer division of Compusell Corporation, a large firm that manufactures many different types of computers. You come up with an idea for a new type of personal computer, which you call the PC1000. You may be able to develop a prototype of the PC1000 and even test market it for relatively little money and, therefore, you do not bother doing a full-fledged discounted cash flow analysis in the early phases of the project.

If your project idea gets to the point at which a large sum of cash must be expended, then you must prepare a capital appropriation request that details the amount of capital required and the projected benefits to the corporation from undertaking the project. Table 2 shows the estimated annual sales revenue, operating costs, and profit for the PC1000. It also shows the estimated capital outlay required.

Your estimates assume that sales will be 4,000 units per year at a price of $5,000 per unit. A new production facility will be leased for $1.5 million per year and production equipment will have to be purchased at a cost of about $2.8 million. The equipment will be depreciated over seven years using the straight-line method. In addition, you estimate a need for $2.2 million for working capital—primarily to finance inventories—thus bringing the total initial outlay required to $5 million.

Now consider the project's expected cash flows in the future. First, over how long a period will the project generate cash flows? The natural planning horizon to use in the analysis is the seven-year life of the equipment because at that time presumably a new decision would have to be made about whether to renew the investment.

In years 1 through 7 the net cash inflow from operations can be computed in two equivalent ways:

(1)   Cash Flow = Revenue − Cash Expenses − Taxes

(2)   Cash Flow = Revenue − Total Expenses − Taxes + Noncash Expenses

$$= \text{Net Income} + \text{Noncash Expenses}$$

The two approaches (if done properly) will always result in precisely the same estimates of net cash flow from operations.

The only noncash operating expense in the case of the PC1000 is depreciation, and the relevant numbers are (in $ millions):

Revenue	Cash Expenses	Depreciation	Total Expenses	Taxes	Net Income	Cash Flow
$20	$18.1	$0.4	$18.5	$0.6	$0.9	$1.3

TABLE 2   Forecasting Cash Flows for the PC1000 Project

Sales:	
4,000 units at a price of $5,000	$20,000,000 per year
Fixed Costs:	
Lease payments	$1,500,000 per year
Property taxes	200,000
Administration	600,000
Advertising	500,000
Depreciation	400,000
Other	300,000
Total Fixed Costs	$3,500,000 per year
Variable Costs:	
Direct labor	$2,000 per unit
Materials	1,000
Selling expenses	500
Other	250
Variable Cost Per Unit	$3,750 per unit
Total Variable Costs for 4,000 Units	$15,000,000 per year
Total Annual Operating Costs	$18,500,000 per year
Annual Operating Profit	$1,500,000 per year
Corporate Income Taxes at 40%	$600,000 per year
After-Tax Operating Profit	$900,000 per year
Forecast of Initial Capital Outlay for PC1000	
Purchase of Equipment	$2,800,000
Working Capital	$2,200,000
Total Capital Outlay	$5,000,000

Using approach 1, we get:

$$(1) \qquad \text{Cash Flow} = \$20 - \$18.1 - \$0.6 = \$1.3 \text{ million}$$

Using approach 2, we get:

$$(2) \qquad \text{Cash Flow} = \$0.9 + \$0.4 = \$1.3 \text{ million}$$

To complete the estimation of project cash flows we need to estimate the cash flow in the final year (year 7) of the planning horizon. The natural assumption to make in this case is that the equipment will have no residual value at the end of the seven years, but that the working capital will still be intact and, therefore, be worth $2.2 million. This does not mean that the project will be liquidated at the end of seven years. It only means that were Compusell to liquidate it, it could probably get back the full $2.2 million in working capital it had to invest initially.

To summarize the project's cash flows, there is an initial outlay of $5 million, cash inflows of $1.3 million at the end of years 1 through 7, and an additional $2.2 million cash inflow at the end of the project's life in year 7. The cash flow diagram for the investment, therefore, looks as follows:

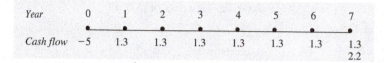

Notice that the cash flow pattern from this project looks like a seven-year coupon bond with an annual coupon payment of $1.3 million, a face value of $2.2 million, and a price of $5 million. This similarity makes the calculation of the project's *NPV* and *IRR* very simple using the standard time-value-of-money keys on a financial calculator.

The next step is to figure out what rate (k) to use to discount these cash flows and compute the project's net present value (*NPV*). Suppose that k is 15%. Then using the financial calculator to compute *NPV* we find:

$$NPV(k = 15\%) = \sum_{t=0}^{7} \frac{CF_t}{(1 + 15\%)^t}$$

$$= -\$5 \text{ million} + PV_{PMT}(\$1.3 \text{ million}, 15\%, 7)$$
$$+ PV_{FV}(\$2.2 \text{ million}, 15\%, 7)$$
$$= -\$5 \text{ million} + \$5.409 \text{ million} + \$0.827 \text{ million}$$
$$= \$1.236 \text{ million}.$$

> **Quick Check 3**
>
> What would be the *NPV* of the PC1000 project if the variable costs are $4,000 per unit instead of $3,750?

5 Cost of Capital

Cost of capital is the risk-adjusted discount rate (k) to use in computing a project's net present value. The standard way of dealing with uncertainty about future cash flows is to use a larger discount rate. There are, however, three important points to keep in mind when figuring out a project's cost of capital:

- The risk of a particular project may be different from the risk of the firm's existing assets.
- The cost of capital should reflect only the market-related risk of the project.
- The risk that is relevant in computing a project's cost of capital is the risk of the project's cash flows and not the risk of the financing instruments (stocks, bonds, etc.) the firm issues to finance the project.

Let us explain each of these three points.

The first point to keep in mind is that the discount rate relevant to a particular project may be different from the rate that is relevant to the firm's existing assets. Consider a firm whose *average* cost of capital for its existing assets is 16% per year. In evaluating a project, does this mean that the firm should use a 16% discount rate? If the project happens to be a "mini-replica" of the assets currently held by the firm, then the answer is yes.

However, in general, using the firm's average cost of capital to evaluate specific new projects will not be correct.

To see why, take an extreme example. Assume the project under consideration is nothing more than the purchase of riskless U.S. government securities in which the firm has the opportunity to buy these securities at below-market prices. That is, suppose that 25-year U.S. Treasury bonds paying $100 per year are selling in the market at $1,000, but the firm has the opportunity to buy $1 million worth of these bonds for $950 each. If these cash flows are discounted at the firm's cost of capital (16% per year), the present value of each bond is $634 and, hence, the *NPV* of the project appears to be $-$315,830!*

Common sense tells us if the firm can buy for $950 something that can be immediately sold for $1,000, then the firm should do so. The problem is not the *NPV* method itself, but its improper use. The risk class of this project is not the same as that of the overall firm. The proper discount rate for this project is 10% not 16%, and when the *NPV* is computed using this proper rate, we find that the *NPV* = $50,000.

Having made the point in the extreme, consider a more practical example of an all-equity-financed firm with three divisions: (1) an electronics division, which is 30% of the market value of the firm's assets and has a cost of capital of 22%; (2) a chemical division, which is 40% of the market value of the firm with a cost of capital of 17%; and (3) a natural gas transmission division, which is 30% of the firm's value and has a cost of capital of 14%. The cost of capital for the firm is the weighted average of the costs of capital of each of its divisions or $0.3 \times 22\% + 0.4 \times 17\% + 0.3 \times 14\% = 17.6\%$.

If the firm adopts the capital budgeting rule of using 17.6% as the cost of capital for all projects, then it is likely to accept projects in the electronics division that have significantly negative *NPV* and to pass up profitable natural gas transmission projects with positive *NPV*. The fact that 17.6% is close to the correct discount rate for chemical projects is simply lucky. In this case, the firm should adopt a policy of using different costs of capital, at least at the divisional level.

Sometimes it may be necessary to use a cost of capital that is totally unrelated to the cost of capital of the firm's current operations. For example, imagine an all-equity-financed steel company that is considering the acquisition of an integrated oil company that is 60% crude oil reserves and 40% refining. Suppose that the market capitalization rate on crude oil investments is 18.6% and on refining projects is 17.6%. The market capitalization rate on the oil company shares is, therefore, $0.6 \times 18.6\% + 0.4 \times 17.6\% = 18.2\%$.

Suppose further that the market price of the oil company's shares is "fair" in the sense that at the current price of $100 per share, the expected return on the shares is 18.2%. Suppose that the market capitalization rate for steel projects is 15.3%. An analysis of the expected cash flows of the oil company shows that the present value computed using the *steel company's cost of capital* of 15.3% is $119.

An investment banker further reports that all the shares could be acquired for a tender offer bid of $110 per share. It would appear, therefore, that to undertake this acquisition will provide a positive *NPV* of $-110 + \$119 = \$9$ per share. In fact, the correct *NPV* is $-110 + \$100 = -\$10$ per share! If undertaken, we would expect to observe the oil company's shares rise and the steel company's shares fall in value to reflect this negative *NPV* decision.

To return to the PC1000 project, it should now be clear that the relevant discount rate to use in calculating the project's *NPV* must reflect the risk of the PC business and not Compusell's existing mix of businesses.

The second point to keep in mind is that *the risk that is relevant in computing a project's cost of capital is the risk of the project's cash flows and not the risk of the financing instruments used to fund the project.*

---

*Per bond $PV = PV_{PMT}(\$100, 16\%, 25) + PV_{FV}(\$1,000, 16\%, 25) = \$634.17$
On a per bond basis, the *NPV* is: $NPV = PV - \$950 = -\$315.83$

For example, suppose that Compusell Corporation is planning to finance the $5 million outlay required to undertake the PC1000 project by issuing bonds. Suppose Compusell has a high credit rating because it has almost no debt outstanding and, therefore, can issue $5 million worth of bonds at an interest rate of 6% per year.

It would be a mistake to use 6% per year as the cost of capital in computing the *NPV* of the PC1000 project. The way a project is financed can have an effect on its *NPV*, but that effect is not measured correctly by discounting the project's expected future cash flows using the interest rate on the debt that is issued to finance the project.

The third point to make about the project's cost of capital is that it should reflect only the systematic or market-related risk of the project, not the project's unsystematic risk.

Quick Check 4

Suppose that the average cost of capital for Compusell's existing mix of businesses is 12% per year. Why might this not be the right discount rate to use in computing the *NPV* of the PC1000 project?

---

6 Sensitivity Analysis Using Spreadsheets

Sensitivity analysis in capital budgeting consists of testing whether the project will still be worthwhile even if some of the underlying variables turn out to be different from our assumptions. A convenient and ubiquitous tool for doing sensitivity analysis is a computerized spreadsheet program such as Excel, which is illustrated in Table 3.

Table 3 lays out the estimation of the net cash flows for the PC1000 project in a spreadsheet format. Rows 1 through 5 state the input assumptions behind the forecast values in the spreadsheet. The formulas in each of the cells are written in terms of the variables in cells B2 through B5, so that when these inputs are changed, the entire table is recalculated. Thus, the input in cell B3 is unit sales. Initially this is set at 4,000 units.

Rows 8 through 15 are forecasts of the project's income statements over the next seven years. Row 16 contains the forecasts of operating cash flows in each year, calculated by adding together the contents of row 15 (net profit) and row 12 (depreciation). Rows 17 through 20 show the calculation of the investment cash flows—investment in working capital and plant and equipment. Row 17 contains the forecast of the working capital required each year, and row 18 calculates the change in this amount from year to year (i.e., the additional cash invested in working capital during that year). Note that the only nonzero entries in row 18 are a cash inflow of $2,200,000 in cell B18 and a cash outflow of $2,200,000 in year 7. Row 19 contains the forecasts of new investment in plant and equipment in each year. Row 20 is the total investment cash flow in each year, the sum of rows 18 and 19. Finally, row 21 shows the net cash flow in each year, which is the sum of the operating cash flow (row 16) and the investment cash flow (row 20). The *NPV* is computed in cell B22.

Table 4 and Figure 2 show the sensitivity of the project's *NPV* to this assumed value for unit sales. It was produced by changing the entry in cell B3 of Table 3 and tracing the corresponding changes in net cash flow from operations and in *NPV*.

6.1 Break-Even Point

A particularly interesting question to ask is at what sales volume the *NPV* of the project would be zero. This is the project's **break-even point,** which means the point of indifference between accepting and rejecting the project.

TABLE 3 Spreadsheet Analysis of the PC1000 Project

	A	B	C	D	E	F	G	H	I
						YEAR			
			0	1	2	3	4	5	6	7
1	*Assumptions:*								
2	*Cost of capital*	15%							
3	*Unit sales in year 1*	4,000							
4	*Sales growth rate*	0%							
5	*Price*	$5,000							
6	*Cash Flow Forecasts*								
7			0	1	2	3	4	5	6	7
8	Sales revenue		$20,000,000	$20,000,000	$20,000,000	$20,000,000	$20,000,000	$20,000,000	$20,000,000
9	Expenses								
10	Cash fixed costs		$3,100,000	$3,100,000	$3,100,000	$3,100,000	$3,100,000	$3,100,000	$3,100,000
11	Variable costs		$15,000,000	$15,000,000	$15,000,000	$15,000,000	$15,000,000	$15,000,000	$15,000,000
12	Depreciation		$400,000	$400,000	$400,000	$400,000	$400,000	$400,000	$400,000
13	Operating profit		$1,500,000	$1,500,000	$1,500,000	$1,500,000	$1,500,000	$1,500,000	$1,500,000
14	Taxes		$600,000	$600,000	$600,000	$600,000	$600,000	$600,000	$600,000
15	Net profit		$900,000	$900,000	$900,000	$900,000	$900,000	$900,000	$900,000
16	**Operating Cash Flow**		$1,300,000	$1,300,000	$1,300,000	$1,300,000	$1,300,000	$1,300,000	$1,300,000
17	Working capital	$2,200,000	$2,200,000	$2,200,000	$2,200,000	$2,200,000	$2,200,000	$2,200,000	–
18	Change in working capital	$2,200,000	–	–	–	–	–	–	$(2,200,000)
19	Investment in plant and equipment	$2,800,000	–	–	–	–	–	–	–
20	**Investment Cash Flows**	$(5,000,000.00)							$2,200,000
21	**Net cash flow**	$(5,000,000.00)	$1,300,000	$1,300,000	$1,300,000	$1,300,000	$1,300,000	$1,300,000	$3,500,000
22	*NPV*	$1,235,607							

11

TABLE 4   Sensitivity of the PC1000's NPV to Sales Volume

Sales Volume (units per year)	Net Cash Flow from Operations	Net Present Value of Project
2,000	−$200,000	−$5,005,022
3,000	$550,000	−$1,884,708
3,604*	$1,003,009	0
4,000	$1,300,000	$1,235,607
5,000	$2,050,000	$4,355,922
6,000	$2,800,000	$7,476,237

*NPV break-even point.

Assumptions: The investment in working capital is fixed at $2,200,000 for all levels of sales and is received back as a cash inflow in year 7.

From Figure 2 we can see that the break-even point is approximately 3,600 units per year. A little algebra shows that its exact value is 3,604 units per year. Thus, as long as the sales volume exceeds 3,604 units per year over the seven-year life of the equipment, the project shows a positive *NPV*.

The algebraic solution for the break-even volume is as follows. In order for the *NPV* to be 0, cash flow from operations must be $1,003,009. To find this break-even value for the cash flow from operations we do the following calculation:

Find the *PMT* that satisfies:

$$PV_{PMT}(PMT, 15\%, 7) + PV_{FV}(\$2.2 \text{ million}, 15\%, 7) - \$5 \text{ million} = 0$$

or:

$$PV_{PMT}(PMT, 15\%, 7) = \$5 \text{ million} - PV_{FV}(\$2.2 \text{ million}, 15\%, 7) = \$4,172,939$$

$$PMT_{PV}(\$4,172,939, 15\%, 7) = \$1,003,009$$

Now we must find the number of units per year (*Q*) that corresponds to an operating cash flow of this amount. A little algebra reveals that the break-even level of *Q* is 3,604 units per year:

$$\text{Cash Flow} = \text{Net Profit} + \text{Depreciation}$$
$$= 0.6(1,250Q - 3,500,000) + 400,000 = 1,003,009$$
$$Q = \frac{4,505,015}{1,250} = 3,604 \text{ units per year}$$

FIGURE 2

Sensitivity of the PC1000's *NPV* to Sales Volume

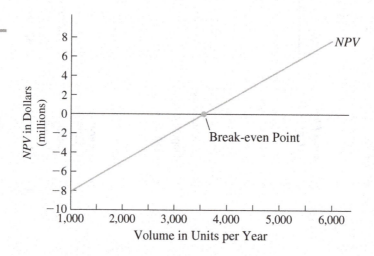

6.2 Sensitivity of *NPV* to Sales Growth

What happens if we change the assumed sales growth rate from zero to 5% per year? The answer is found in Table 5. Operating cash flow (row 16) grows by more than 5% per year because many of the production costs are fixed. Working capital (row 17), which is a fixed proportion of sales, grows at 5% per year. The increase in working capital (row 18) is a cash outflow each year and is recouped as a cash inflow in year 7. The net result is that the *NPV* of the project increases from $1,235,607 to $2,703,489.

7 Analyzing Cost-Reducing Projects

Our analysis of the PC1000 project was an example of a decision about whether to launch a new product. Another major category of capital budgeting projects is cost saving.

For example, suppose a firm is considering an investment proposal to automate its production process to save on labor costs. It can invest $2 million now in equipment and thereby save $700,000 per year in pretax labor costs. If the equipment has an expected life of five years and if the firm pays income tax at the rate of $33\frac{1}{3}\%$, is this a worthwhile investment?

To answer this question we must compute the *incremental* cash flows due to the investment. Table 6 shows the cash inflows and outflows associated with this project. Column 1 shows the firm's revenues, costs, and cash flow *without* the investment; column 2 shows them *with* the investment. Column 3, the difference between columns 1 and 2, is the increment due to the investment.

There is an initial cash outflow of $2 million to purchase the equipment. In each of the five subsequent years, there is a cash inflow of $600,000, which is the increased net profit of $200,000 plus the $400,000 in annual depreciation charges. The depreciation charges, although an expense for accounting purposes, are not a cash outflow. The cash flow diagram for this project is:

Year	0	1	2	3	4	5
Cash flow *(in $ millions)*	−2	.6	.6	.6	.6	.6

Now let us consider the impact of the project on the firm's value. How much will the firm be worth if it undertakes the project as compared to not undertaking it?

The firm must give up $2 million now, but in return it will receive an incremental after-tax cash flow of $600,000 at the end of each of the next five years. To compute the *NPV* of the project, we need to know the project's cost of capital, k. Let us assume that it is 10% per year.

Discounting the $600,000 per year for five years at 10% per year, we find that the present value of the after-tax cash flows is $2,274,472:

$$NPV = PV_{PMT}(\$0.6\,\text{million}, 10\%, 5) - \$2\text{ million} = \$2,274,472 - \$2,000,000 = \$274,472$$

Thus, the labor cost savings are worth $274,472 more than the $2 million cost of acquiring them by undertaking the project. The wealth of current shareholders of the firm is expected to increase by this amount if the project is undertaken.

TABLE 5 PC1000 Project with 5% Growth

		0	1	2	3	4	5	6	7
Assumptions:									
Cost of capital	15%								
Unit sales in year 1	4,000								
Sales growth rate	5%								
Price	$5,000								
Cash Flow Forecasts									
Sales			$20,000,000	$21,000,000	$22,050,000	$23,152,500	$24,310,125	$25,525,631	$26,801,913
Expenses									
Cash fixed costs			$ 3,100,000	$ 3,100,000	$ 3,100,000	$ 3,100,000	$ 3,100,000	$ 3,100,000	$ 3,100,000
Variable costs			$15,000,000	$15,750,000	$16,537,500	$17,364,375	$18,232,594	$19,144,223	$20,101,435
Depreciation			$ 400,000	$ 400,000	$ 400,000	$ 400,000	$ 400,000	$ 400,000	$ 400,000
Operating profit			$ 1,500,000	$ 1,750,000	$ 2,012,500	$ 2,288,125	$ 2,577,531	$ 2,881,408	$ 3,200,478
Taxes			$ 600,000	$ 700,000	$ 805,000	$ 915,250	$ 1,031,013	$ 1,152,563	$ 1,280,191
Net profit			$ 900,000	$ 1,050,000	$ 1,207,500	$ 1,372,875	$ 1,546,519	$ 1,728,845	$ 1,920,287
Operating Cash Flow			$ 1,300,000	$ 1,450,000	$ 1,607,500	$ 1,772,875	$ 1,946,519	$ 2,128,845	$ 2,320,287
Working capital		$ 2,200,000	$ 2,310,000	$ 2,425,500	$ 2,546,775	$ 2,674,114	$ 2,807,819	$ 2,948,210	—
Change in working capital		$ 2,200,000	$ 110,000	$ 115,500	$ 121,275	$ 127,339	$ 133,706	$ 140,391	$(2,948,210)
Investment in plant and equipment		$ 2,800,000	—	—	—	—	—	—	—
Investment Cash Flow		$ (5,000,000)	$ (110,000)	$ (115,500)	$ (121,275)	$ (127,339)	$ (133,706)	$ (140,391)	$ —
Net Cash Flow		$ (5,000,000)	$ 1,190,000	$ 1,334,500	$ 1,486,225	$ 1,645,536	$ 1,812,813	$ 1,988,454	$ 2,948,210
NPV		$ 2,703,489							$ 5,268,497

TABLE 6 Cash Flows With and Without Investment in Labor Saving Equipment

	Without Investment (1)	With Investment (2)	Difference Due to Investment (3)
Revenue	$5,000,000	$5,000,000	0
Labor costs	1,000,000	300,000	−700,000
Other cash expenses	2,000,000	2,000,000	0
Depreciation	1,000,000	1,400,000	400,000
Pretax profit	1,000,000	1,300,000	300,000
Income taxes (at $33\frac{1}{3}\%$)	333,333	433,333	100,000
After-tax profit	666,667	866,667	200,000
Net cash flow (after-tax profit + depreciation)	1,666,667	2,266,667	600,000

Quick Check 6

Suppose that investing in the equipment would reduce labor costs by $650,000 per year instead of $700,000. Would the investment still be worthwhile?

8 Projects with Different Lives

Suppose in the previous example of labor-saving equipment that there are two different types of equipment with different economic lives. The longer-lived equipment requires twice the initial outlay but lasts twice as long. A difficulty that arises in this situation is how to make the two investments comparable given that they last for different periods of time.

One approach is to assume that the shorter-lived equipment will be replaced at the end of five years with the same type of equipment that will last for another five years. Both alternatives will then have the same expected life of 10 years, and their *NPV*s can be computed and compared.

An easier approach is to employ a concept called **annualized capital cost.** It is defined as the annual cash payment that has a present value equal to the initial outlay. The alternative with the lowest annualized capital cost is the preferred alternative.

In our example, when we convert the $2 million initial capital outlay into an equivalent five-year annuity at a discount rate of 10% per year, we find that the *PMT* is $527,595.

Or we solve for the *PMT*

$$PMT_{PV}(\$2 \text{ million}, 10\%, 5) = \$527,595$$

The longer-lived machine will last for 10 years but costs $4 million. What is its annualized capital cost?

We solve for the *PMT* such that

$$PMT_{PV}(\$4 \text{ million}, 10\%, 10) = \$650,982$$

So the machine that lasts for only five years and costs $2 million is the preferred alternative because it has the lower annualized capital cost.

9 Ranking Mutually Exclusive Projects

Sometimes two or more projects are mutually exclusive, meaning that the firm will take at most only one of them. An example is a project that requires exclusive use of the same unique resource such as a particular parcel of land. In all such cases, a firm should choose the project with the highest *NPV.* Some firms, however, rank projects according to their *IRR,* and this ranking system may be inconsistent with the objective of maximizing shareholder value.

For example, suppose that you own a parcel of land and have two alternatives for developing it. You can construct an office building on it, requiring an initial outlay of $20 million, or you can make a parking lot out of it, requiring an initial outlay of $10,000. If you build an office building, you estimate that you will be able to sell it in one year for $24 million and your *IRR* is, therefore, 20% ($24 million minus $20 million divided by $20 million). If you make it into a parking lot, you estimate that you will have a cash inflow of $10,000 per year forever. Your *IRR* on the parking lot is, therefore, 100% per year. Which project should you choose?

The parking lot has the higher *IRR,* but you would not necessarily want to choose it because at any cost of capital below 20% per year, the *NPV* of the office building is greater. For example, at a cost of capital of 15%, the *NPV* of the office building is $869,565 whereas the *NPV* of the parking lot is $56,667. Therefore, at a cost of capital of 15%, the shareholders of the corporation are better off if the office building project is taken.

Figure 3 shows the *NPV* profiles of both projects, *NPV* plotted as a function of the cost of capital. The discount rate used to compute the project's *NPV* (the project's cost of capital) is measured along the horizontal axis and the *NPV* is measured along the vertical axis. The figure shows clearly that a discount rate of 20% per year is the critical "switch-over point" for the two mutually exclusive projects. At any discount rate above 20% per year the parking lot has a higher *NPV,* and at rates below 20% the office building has a higher *NPV.*

To understand better why *IRR* is not a good measure for ranking mutually exclusive projects, note that a project's *IRR* is independent of its *scale.* In our example, the parking lot has a very high *IRR,* but its scale is small compared to the office building. If the parking lot were on a larger scale, it might offer a higher *NPV* than the office building.

Thus, suppose that the parking lot project requires an initial outlay of $200,000 to build a multistory facility and that the annual net cash flow will then be $200,000 per year forever. The *NPV* of the parking lot project would now be 20 times greater than before.

10 Inflation and Capital Budgeting

Now let us consider how to take account of inflation in evaluating capital projects. Consider an investment that requires an initial outlay of $2 million. In the absence of inflation it is expected to produce an annual after-tax cash flow of $600,000 for five years and the cost of capital is 10% per year. Under these assumptions we found that the project has an *NPV* of $274,472.

FIGURE 3

NPV as a Function
of the Discount
Rate

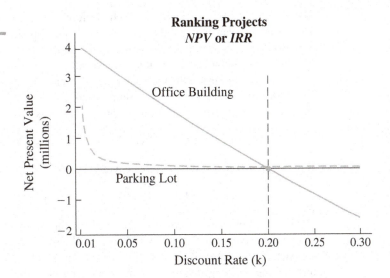

Now let us assume an inflation rate of 6% per year. The expected cash flows are presented in Table 7.

The *nominal* cash flow projections are inflated at the rate of 6% per year to reflect our expectations in terms of "then-year dollars." The *real* cash flow projections are in terms of "today's dollars."

Just as we distinguish between real and nominal cash flow projections, so too we distinguish between the real and nominal cost of capital. The real rate is the rate that would prevail in a zero-inflation scenario. The nominal rate is the rate that we actually observe.

Even if a firm does not explicitly set its cost of capital in real terms, setting one in nominal terms implies a certain real rate. For example, if the nominal cost of capital is 14% per year, and the expected rate of inflation is 6% per year, then the implied real cost of capital is approximately 8% per year.

RULE: There are two correct ways of computing *NPV:*
 1. Use the nominal cost of capital to discount nominal cash flows.
 2. Use the real cost of capital to discount real cash flows.

Let us illustrate the correct way of adjusting for inflation in our numerical example. We have already computed the *NPV* and *IRR* using the second approach that uses real cash flow estimates and a real cost of capital of 10% per year:

$$NPV = \$274,472$$

Because the *NPV* is positive, this project is worthwhile.

TABLE 7   **Investment under 6% Inflation**

Year	Real Cash Flow	Nominal Cash Flow (6% inflation)
1	$600,000	$636,000
2	600,000	674,160
3	600,000	714,610
4	600,000	757,486
5	600,000	802,935

Now let us take the nominal approach. Before doing so, we must make a slight modification in the way we calculate the nominal rate. For most purposes it would be perfectly adequate to approximate the nominal rate as 16%—the real rate of 10% plus the 6% expected rate of inflation. But in this case we want to be exact in order to demonstrate the exact equivalence of using the real and nominal approaches to capital budgeting, so we must present the exact relation between nominal and real rates.

The exact relation between the nominal and real rates is:

$$\text{Nominal Rate} = (1 + \text{Real Rate})(1 + \text{Expected Inflation}) - 1$$

Therefore, in our example the nominal rate would be 16.6% rather than 16% per year:

$$\text{Nominal Rate} = 1.1 \times 1.06 - 1 = 0.166 \text{ or } 16.6\%$$

Using this 16.6% rate to compute the *NPV* of the nominal cash flow estimates in Table 7 will produce an *NPV* of \$274,472, exactly the same result as we obtain using the real approach. This is logical because the increase in the current wealth of shareholders from undertaking the project should not be affected by the unit of account chosen to compute the project's *NPV* (i.e., whether we use inflated dollars or dollars of constant purchasing power).

$$NPV(k = 16.6\%) = \sum_{t=1}^{5} \frac{\$600,000(1 + 6\%)^t}{(1 + 16.6\%)^t} - \$2,000,000 = \$274,472$$

Beware: Never compare the *IRR* computed using real cash flow estimates to a nominal cost of capital.

Quick Check 9

Analyze the same project assuming an expected rate of inflation of 8% per year instead of 6%.

Summary

- The unit of analysis in capital budgeting is the investment project. From a finance perspective, investment projects are best thought of as consisting of a series of contingent cash flows over time, whose amount and timing are partially under the control of management.
- The objective of capital budgeting procedures is to assure that only projects that increase shareholder value (or at least do not reduce it) are undertaken.
- Most investment projects requiring capital expenditures fall into three categories: new products, cost reduction, and replacement. Ideas for investment projects can come from customers and competitors, or from within the firm's own R&D or production departments.
- Projects are often evaluated using a discounted cash flow procedure wherein the incremental cash flows associated with the project are estimated and their *NPV* is calculated using a risk-adjusted discount rate, which should reflect the risk of the project.
- If the project happens to be a "mini-replica" of the assets currently held by the firm, then management should use the firm's cost of capital in computing the project's net

present value. However, sometimes it may be necessary to use a discount rate that is totally unrelated to the cost of capital of the firm's current operations. The correct cost of capital is the one applicable to firms in the same industry as the new project.

- It is always important to check whether cash flow forecasts have been properly adjusted to take account of inflation over a project's life. There are two correct ways to make the adjustment: (1) Use the nominal cost of capital to discount nominal cash flows, and (2) use the real cost of capital to discount real cash flows.

Key Terms

- net present value
- cost of capital
- sensitivity analysis

- break-even point
- annualized capital cost

Answers to Quick Check Questions

Quick Check 1   Where do you think new project ideas come from in the movie business?

Answer: Sources of new project ideas in the movie business are:
- sequels to successful movies (e.g., *The Godfather II, III, IV,* etc.).
- best-selling novels.

Quick Check 2   Suppose that the Protojean project is expected to have a third-year cash flow of only $10,000 instead of $30,000. If all other cash flows are the same and the discount rate is still 8% per year, what is its *NPV*?

Answer: The new cash flow diagram for the Protojean project is:

Year	0	1	2	3
Net cash flow	-100	50	40	10

$$NPV@8\% \text{ per year} = -\$11,471.83$$

Quick Check 3   What would be the *NPV* of the PC1000 project if the variable costs are $4,000 per unit instead of $3,750?

Answer: If the variable costs for the PC1000 were $4,000 per unit instead of $3,750 we would have the following profit and cash flow projections:

Sales Revenue (4,000 units at a price of $5,000)	$20,000,000 per year
Total Fixed Costs	$3,500,000 per year
Total Variable Costs (4,000 units at $4,000 per unit)	$16,000,000 per year
Total Annual Operating Costs	$19,500,000 per year
Annual Operating Profit	$500,000 per year
Corporate Income Taxes at 40%	$200,000 per year
After-Tax Operating Profit	$300,000 per year
Net Cash Flow from Operations	$700,000 per year

In other words, the net cash flow from operations in years 1 through 7 would fall by $600,000. This is because before-tax costs are higher by $1 million per year (4,000 units $\times$ $250 per unit). Because the tax rate is 0.4, after-tax profits and cash flow are lower by 0.6 $\times$ $1 million or $600,000.

Using a financial calculator to find the new NPV, we find:

$$PV_{PMT}(\$0.7 \text{ million}, 15\%, 7) + PV_{FV}(\$2.2 \text{ million}, 15\%, 7) - \$5 \text{ million}$$
$$= \$2,912,294 + \$827,061 - \$5,000,000 = -\$1,260,645$$

So the project would not be worthwhile if the variable costs were $4,000 per unit.

Quick Check 4 Suppose that the average cost of capital for Compusell's existing mix of businesses is 12% per year. Why might this not be the right discount rate to use in computing the NPV of the PC1000 project?

Answer: Compusell's existing lines of business may have a different risk than the risk of the PC business.

Quick Check 5 What would be the break-even volume for the PC1000 project if the cost of capital is 25% per year instead of 15% per year?

Answer: In order for the NPV to be 0 when the cost of capital is 25% per year, cash flow from operations must be $1,435,757. To find this break-even value for the cash flow from operations we do the following calculation: Solve for PMT that makes $NPV = 0$

$PV_{PMT}(PMT, 25\%, 7) + PV_{FV}(\$2.2 \text{ million}, 25\%, 7) - \$5 \text{ million} = 0$ or $PV_{PMT}(PMT, 25\%, 7) = \$4,538,627$. Solving for the payment:
$PMT_{PV}(\$4,538,627, 25\%, 7) = \$1,435,757$

Now we must find the number of units per year (Q) that corresponds to an operating cash flow of this amount. A little algebra reveals that the break-even level of Q is 4,181 units per year:

$$\text{Cash Flow} = \text{Net Profit} + \text{Depreciation}$$
$$= 0.6(1,250Q - 3,500,000) + 400,000 = 1,435,757$$
$$Q = \frac{5,226,262}{1,250} = 4,181 \text{ units per year}$$

Quick Check 6 Suppose that investing in the equipment would reduce labor costs by $650,000 per year instead of $700,000. Would the investment still be worthwhile?

Answer: Let us first show what the incremental after-tax cash flow is:

	Without Investment	With Investment	Difference Due to Investment
Revenue	$5,000,000	$5,000,000	0
Labor costs	1,000,000	350,000	−650,000
Other cash expenses	2,000,000	2,000,000	0
Depreciation	1,000,000	1,400,000	400,000
Pretax profit	1,000,000	1,250,000	250,000
Income taxes (at $33\frac{1}{3}\%$)	333,333	416,667	83,334
After-tax profit	666,667	833,333	166,666
Net cash flow (after-tax profit + depreciation)	1,666,667	2,233,333	566,666

Thus, if the labor cost saving is only $650,000 per year, the incremental net cash flow in years 1–5 is only $566,666 instead of $600,000. In other words, the incremental net cash flow falls by $33,333, which is $(1 - \text{tax rate}) \times$ the change in before-tax labor cost savings. The project's *NPV* falls but still remains positive.

$$PV_{PMT}(\$566,666, 10\%, 5) = \$2,148,110$$

$$NPV = \$2,148,110 - \$2,000,000 = \$148,110$$

Quick Check 7   What would have to be the economic life of the machine that costs $4 million for it to be preferred over the machine that costs $2 million?

Answer: To match the annualized capital cost of $527,595 per year for the first machine, the second machine would have to last 14.89 years. We find this number using a financial calculator as follows:

n	i	PV	FV	PMT	Result
?	10	−4,000,000	0	527,595	$n = 14.89$ years

Or n which solves

$$PV_{PMT}(\$527,595, 10\%, n) = \$4,000,000$$

Therefore, to be preferred to the first machine, the second machine would have to have an economic life longer than 14.89 years. Rounding to the nearest year, we get 15 years.

Quick Check 8   At what scale would the *NPV* of the parking lot project be equal to that of the office building project?

Answer: The parking facility project has an *NPV* of $56,667 for an investment of $10,000, and the office building project has an *NPV* of $869,565. To find the scale at which the parking facility has an *NPV* of $869,565 we solve:

$$\text{Scale} = \$869,565/\$56,667 = 15.345$$

Thus, at a cost of capital of 15% per year, the scale of the parking facility project has to increase by a factor exceeding 15 to make its *NPV* greater than that of the office building project.

Quick Check 9   Analyze the same project assuming an expected rate of inflation of 8% per year instead of 6%.

Answer:

Year	Real Cash Flow	Nominal Cash Flow (8% inflation)
1	$600,000	$648,000
2	600,000	699,840
3	600,000	755,827
4	600,000	816,293
5	600,000	881,597

$$NPV(k = 18.8\%) = \sum_{t=1}^{5} \frac{\$600,000(1.08)^t}{(1.188)^t} - \$2,000,000 = \$274,472$$

Nominal cost of capital $= 1.1 \times 1.08 - 1 = 0.188$ or 18.8%

Questions and Problems

The Net Present Value Investment Rule

1. Your firm is considering two investment projects with the following patterns of expected future net after-tax cash flows:

Year	Project A	Project B
1	$1 million	$5 million
2	2 million	4 million
3	3 million	3 million
4	4 million	2 million
5	5 million	1 million

The appropriate cost of capital for both projects is 10%.
If both projects require an initial outlay of $10 million, which is the better project?

2. Consider the previous problem. Given the patterns of the two cash flow series is the ranking of the projects dependent on the cost of capital? Explain.

3. You have taken a product management position within a major consumer goods firm after graduation. The contract is for four years and your compensation package is as follows:

- $5,000 relocation expense
- $55,000 annual salary
- $10,000 bonus if annual goals are met
- $15,000 additional bonus at the end of four years if your team achieves a given market share

You are confident in your abilities and assume there is a 65% chance in receiving each annual bonus and a 75% chance in receiving the fourth year additional bonus. The effective annual interest rate is 8.5%. What is the net present value of your compensation package?

4. A. Fung Fashion, Inc. anticipates real net cash flows to be $100,000 this year. The real discount rate is 15% per year.

   a. What is the present value of these cash flows if they are expected to continue forever?
   b. What is the present value of these cash flows if the real net cash flows are expected to grow at 5% per year forever?
   c. What is the present value of these cash flows if the expected growth rate is −5% per year?

Estimating a Project's Cash Flows

5. A firm is considering investing $10 million in equipment which is expected to have a useful life of four years and is expected to reduce the firm's labor costs by $4 million per year. Assume the firm pays a 40% tax rate on accounting profits and uses the straight-line depreciation method. What is the after-tax cash flow from the investment in years 1 through 4? If the firm's discount rate for this investment is 15% per year, is it worthwhile? What are the investment's *IRR* and *NPV*?

6. Hu's Software Design, Inc. is considering the purchase of a computer that has an economic life of 4 years and it is expected to have no salvage value. It will cost $80,000 and it will be depreciated using the straight-line depreciation method. It will save the company $35,000 the first year and it is assumed that the savings after that

will have a growth rate of -5%. It will also reduce net working capital requirements by $7,000. The corporate tax rate is 35% and the appropriate discount rate is 14%. What is the value that the purchase will add to the firm?

7. Leather Goods Inc. wants to expand its product line into wallets. It is considering producing 50,000 units per year. The price will be $15 per wallet the first year and the price will increase 3% per year. The variable cost is expected to be $10 per wallet and will increase by 5% per year. The machine will cost $400,000, and will have an economic life of 5 years. It will be fully depreciated using the straight line method. The discount rate is 15% and the corporate tax is 34%. What is the *NPV* of the investment?

8. Steiness Danish Ham, Inc. is contemplating buying a new machine that has an economic life of 5 years. The cost of the machine is 1,242,000 krone and will be fully depreciated using the straight-line depreciation method over the 5 years. At the end of 5 years, it will have a market value of 138,000 krone. It is estimated that the new machine will save the company 345,000 krone per year due to reduced labor costs. Moreover, it will lead to a reduction in net working capital of 172,500 krone because of the higher yield from raw materials inventory. The net working capital will be recovered by the end of the 5 years. If the corporate tax rate is 34% and the discount rate is 12% what is the *NPV* of the project?

Cost of Capital

9. Capital budgeting is the formalized analytical approach to deciding what new investment projects a firm should be engaged in undertaking. As such the appropriate cost of capital must consider:

. . . the risk of the project's cash flows and not the risk of the financing instruments, e.g., stocks, bonds, etc., the firm issues to finance the project.

Discuss this statement in terms of the firm's balance sheet.

Sensitivity Analysis

10. Tax-Less Software Corporation is considering an investment of $400,000 in equipment for producing a new tax preparation software package. The equipment has an expected life of 4 years. Sales are expected to be 60,000 units per year at a price of $20 per unit. Fixed costs excluding depreciation of the equipment are $200,000 per year, and variable costs are $12 per unit. The equipment will be depreciated over 4 years using the straight-line method with a zero salvage value. Working capital requirements are assumed to be 1/12 of annual sales. The market capitalization rate for the project is 15% per year, and the corporation pays income tax at the rate of 34%. What is the project's *NPV*? What is the break-even volume?

11. Pepe's Ski Shop is contemplating replacing its ski boot foam injection equipment with a new machine. The old machine has been completely depreciated but has a current market value of $2,000. The new machine will cost $25,000 and have a life of ten years and have no value after this time. The new machine will be depreciated on a straight-line basis assuming no salvage value. The new machine will increase annual revenues by $10,000 and increase annual nondepreciation expenses by $3,000.

   a. What is the additional after-tax net cash flow realized by replacing the old machine with the new machine? (Assume a 50% tax rate for all income, i.e., the capital gains tax rate on the sale of the old machine is also 50%. Draw a time line.)
   b. What is the *IRR* of this project?
   c. At a cost of capital of 12%, what is the net present value of this cash flow stream?
   d. At a cost of capital of 12%, is this project worthwhile?

12. Saunders' Sportswear, Inc. is planning on expanding its line of sweatshirts. This will require an initial investment of $8 million. This investment will be depreciated on a straight-line method over 4 years and will have no salvage value. The firm is in the 35% tax bracket. The price of the sweatshirts will be $30 the first year and will increase in price by 4% per year in nominal terms thereafter. The unit cost of production will be $5 the first year and will increase by 3% per year in nominal terms thereafter. Labor costs will be $10 per hour the first year and will increase by 3.5% in nominal terms each subsequent year. Revenues and costs are paid at year-end. The nominal discount rate is 12%. Calculate the *NPV* of the project using the following additional data.

	Year 1	Year 2	Year 3	Year 4
Unit sales	50,000	100,000	125,000	100,000
Labor hours	20,800	20,800	20,800	20,800

13. PCs Forever is a company that produces personal computers. It has been in operation for two years and is at capacity. It is considering an investment project to expand its production capacity. The project requires an initial outlay of $1,000,000: $800,000 for new equipment with an expected life of four years and $200,000 for additional working capital. The selling price of its PCs is $1,800 per unit, and annual sales are expected to increase by 1,000 units as a result of the proposed expansion. Annual fixed costs (excluding depreciation of the new equipment) will increase by $100,000, and variable costs are $1,400 per unit. The new equipment will be depreciated over four years using the straight-line method with a zero salvage value. The hurdle rate for the project is 12% per year, and the company pays income tax at the rate of 40%.
    a. What is the accounting break-even point for this project?
    b. What is the project's *NPV*?
    c. At what volume of sales would the *NPV* be zero?

14. Healthy Hopes Hospital Supply Corporation is considering an investment of $500,000 in a new plant for producing disposable diapers. The plant has an expected life of 4 years. Sales are expected to be 600,000 units per year at a price of $2 per unit. Fixed costs excluding depreciation of the plant are $200,000 per year, and variable costs are $1.20 per unit. The plant will be depreciated over 4 years using the straight-line method with a zero salvage value. The discount rate for the project is 15% per year, and the corporation pays income tax at the rate of 34%.
    Find:
    a. The level of sales that would give a zero accounting profit.
    b. The level of sales that would give a 15% after-tax accounting rate of return on the $500,000 investment.
    c. The *IRR, NPV,* and payback period (both conventional and discounted) if expected sales are 600,000 units per year.
    d. The level of sales that would give an *NPV* of zero.

Analyzing Cost-Reducing Projects

15. Determine which of the following cash flows are incremental cash flows that should be incorporated into a *NPV* calculation.
    a. The sale of an old machine, when a company is replacing property, plant, and equipment for a new product launch.
    b. The cost of research and development for a new product concept that was conducted over the past year that is now being put into production.

    c. A dividend payment partially funded by a given project's contribution to the net income for that year.

    d. New equipment purchased for a project.

    e. The annual depreciation expense on new equipment purchased for a project.

    f. Net working capital expenditures of $10 million in year 0, $12 million in year 1, and $5 million in year 2.

    g. Potential rental income that was forgone from a previously unused warehouse owned by the company, which is now being used as part of a new product launch.

16. Real Estate, Inc. has purchased a building for $1 million dollars. The economic life of the building is thirty years and it will be fully depreciated over the thirty years using the straight-line depreciation method. The discount rate is 14% and the corporate tax rate is 35%. Assume there is no inflation. What is the minimum lease payment the company should ask for? Assume that the lease payment is due immediately.

17. You are in the finance department of a firm and you are evaluating a project proposal. You have developed the following financial projections and you are calculating:

    a. The incremental cash flows of the project.

    b. The net present value of the project given a discount rate of 15%.

The corporate tax rate is 34% and the financial projections are in thousands.

	Year 0	Year 1	Year 2	Year 3	Year 4	Year 5
Sales revenue		10,000	10,000	10,000	10,000	10,000
Operating costs		3,000	3,000	3,000	3,000	3,000
Investment	17,500					
Depreciation		3,500	3,500	3,500	3,500	3,500
Net working capital	300	350	400	300	200	0

Projects with Different Lives

18. Suppose you are considering replacing the pin setters in your bowling alley. The manufacturer offers you the regular model costing $12,000 or the heavy-duty model costing $15,000. The regular model has an economic life of 10 years. Assuming the models have identical operating characteristics and maintenance costs what does the economic life of the deluxe model have to be for it to be preferred? Assume a 10% cost of capital.

19. Suppose Hu's Software Design, Inc. from problem 6 has a choice between two computer systems. The first one will cost $80,000 and will have an economic life of 4 years. Annual maintenance costs would be $10,000. The other alternative would cost $135,000 and would have an economic life of 6 years. The annual maintenance would cost $13,000. Both alternatives would be fully depreciated using the straight-line method. Neither computer system will have a salvage value. The cost savings generated on an annual basis are assumed to be the same and the company expects to generate sufficient profits to realize the depreciation tax shield. The discount rate is 11% and the corporate tax rate is 35%. Which computer should be chosen?

20. Electricity, Inc. is choosing between two pieces of equipment. The first choice costs $500,000 and will last five years. It will be depreciated using the straight-line depreciation method and will have no salvage value. It will have an annual maintenance cost of $50,000. The second choice will cost $600,000 and will last eight years. It will also be depreciated using the straight-line depreciation method and will have no salvage value. It will have an annual maintenance cost of $55,000. The discount rate is 11% and the tax rate is 35%. Which machine should be chosen and what assumptions underlie that choice?

21. Refer to the previous problem. Electricity, Inc. is faced with the same choices; however, it now expects that a new technology will be introduced into the industry in year nine. This will force the company to replace the choice made today at the end of year nine, because the new technology will be so cost effective. All the other necessary information is the same as explained in problem 20. Which choice should be made?

22. Kitchen Supplies, Inc. must replace a machine in its manufacturing plant that will have no salvage value. It has a choice between two models. The first machine will last 5 years and will cost $300,000. It will generate an annual cost savings of $50,000. Annual maintenance costs will be $20,000. The machine will be fully depreciated using the straight-line depreciation method and will have no salvage value. The second machine will last 7 years and will cost $600,000. It will generate an annual cost savings of $70,000. This machine will also be fully depreciated using the straight-line depreciation method, but is expected to have a salvage value of $60,000 at the end of the seventh year. The annual maintenance cost is $15,000. Revenues in each case are expected to be the same. The annual tax rate is 35% and the cost of capital is 10%. Which machine should the company purchase?

Ranking Mutually Exclusive Projects

23. Assume the following three mutually exclusive projects, each requiring an initial outlay of $10,000, have the following after-tax cash flow streams:

Year	Project 1	Project 2	Project 3
1	$0	$2,000	$4,000
2	$2,500	$2,000	$4,000
3	$10,000	$8,000	$4,000

Which project should be undertaken if the cost of capital is 8%? What if the cost of capital is 10%?

24. *Challenge Question:* Your firm is considering two investment projects with the following patterns of expected future net after-tax cash flows:

Year	Project A	Project B
1	$0	$2,000
2	$2,500	$200

Suppose both projects require an initial outlay of $2,000 and have identical costs of capital. Determine a complete decision rule conditional on the cost of capital for undertaking the projects if they are independent projects. Repeat the decision rule if they are mutually exclusive. Hint: Calculate the project *IRR*s and *NPV*s of the two projects at alternative costs of capital equal to 0%, 5%, 10%, and 15%.

Inflation and Capital Budgeting

25. Finnerty's Brew Pub is considering buying more machinery that will allow the pub to increase its portfolio of beers on tap. The new machinery will cost $65,000 and will be

depreciated on a 10-year basis. It is expected to have no value after 10 years. The improved selection is anticipated to increase sales by $30,000 for the first year and increase at the rate of inflation of 3% for each year after that. Production costs are expected to be $15,000 for the first year and are also expected to increase at the rate of inflation. The real discount rate is 12% and the nominal risk-free interest rate is 6%. The corporate tax rate is 34%. Should Mr. Finnerty buy the machinery?

26. You are a financial analyst at Wigit, Inc. and you are considering two mutually exclusive projects. Unfortunately, the figures for project 1 are in nominal terms and the figures for project 2 are in real terms. The nominal discount rate for both projects is 17%, and inflation is projected to be 3%.

    a. Determine which project to choose.
    b. You are troubled about the cash flows in real terms. You are concerned that there may be a problem in determining the total cash flow in real terms and the depreciation tax shield. What is it that has you concerned?

	Project 1	Project 2
0	−$100,000	−$90,000
1	30,000	25,000
2	60,000	55,000
3	75,000	80,000

27. *Challenge Problem:* Your next assignment at Wigit, Inc. also entails determining the *NPV* of a project that is expected to last four years. There is an initial investment of $400,000, which will be depreciated at the straight-line method over four years. At the end of four years, it is assumed that you will be able to sell some of the equipment that is part of the initial investment for $35,000 (a nominal figure). Revenues for the first year are expected to be $225,000 in real terms. The costs involved in the project for the first year are as follows: (1) parts will be $25,000 in real terms the first year; (2) labor will be $60,000 in real terms for the first year and (3) other costs will be $30,000 in real terms for the first year. The growth rates of revenues and costs are as follows: (1) revenue will have a real growth rate of 5%; (2) the cost of parts will have a 0% real growth rate; (3) cost of labor will have a 2% real growth rate; and (4) other costs will have a 1% real growth rate from year 2 to year 3 and a −1% growth rate the last two years. The real changes in net working capital for the year 0 to year 4 are as follows: (1) −$20,000; (2) −$30,000; (3) −$10,000; (4) $20,000; (5) $40,000. The real discount rate is 9.5% and the inflation rate is 3%. The tax rate is 35%.

28. Patriots Foundry (PF) is considering getting into a new line of business: producing souvenir statues of Paul Revere. This will require purchasing a machine for $40,000. The new machine will have a life of two years (both actual and for tax purposes) and will have no value after two years. PF will depreciate the machine on a straight-line basis. The firm thinks it will sell 3,000 statues per year at a price of $10 each, variable costs will be $1 per statue and fixed expenses (not including depreciation) will be $2,000 per year. PF's cost of capital is 10%. All of the foregoing figures assume that there will be no inflation. The tax rate is 40%.

    a. What is the series of expected future cash flows?
    b. What is the expected net present value of this project? Is the project worth undertaking?
    c. What is the *NPV* break-even quantity?

Now assume instead that there will be inflation of 6% per year during each of the next two years and that both revenues and nondepreciation expenses increase at that rate. Assume that the real cost of capital remains at 10%.

    d. What is the series of expected nominal cash flows?

    e. What is the net present value of this project, and is this project worth undertaking now?

    f. Why does the *NPV* of the investment project go down when the inflation rate goes up?

29. Mr. Salles is considering a business venture that would offer guided tours of the romantic Greek isles and the Italian countryside. After four years, Mr. Salles intends to retire. The initial investment would be $50,000 in a computer and phone system. This investment would be depreciated on the straight-line method, and is expected to have no salvage value. The corporate tax rate is 35%. The price of each tour will be $5,000 per customer and the price will remain constant in real terms. Mr. Salles will pay himself $50 per hour and anticipates an annual increase in salary of 5% in real terms. The cost of each customer during the tours is $3,500, and this cost is expected to increase by 3% in real terms. Assume that all revenues and costs occur at year end. The inflation rate is 3.5%. The risk-free nominal rate is 6% and the real discount rate for costs and revenues is 9%. Using the additional following data, calculate the *NPV* of the project.

	Year 1	Year 2	Year 3	Year 4
Number of customers	100	115	130	140
Hours worked	2,080	2,080	2,080	2,080

30. Camile, the owner of the Germanos Tree farm has contracted with the government of his native land to provide cedar tree saplings to aid in that government's efforts to reforest part of the country and return the cedar tree to its past glory. The project is expected to continue in perpetuity. At the end of the first year, the following nominal and incremental cash flows are expected:

Revenues	$125,000
Labor Costs	$65,000
Other Costs	$45,000

Camille has contracted with an air freight shipping company to transport the saplings. The contract is for a fixed payment of $35,000 in nominal terms per year. The first payment is due at the end of the first year. Revenues are expected to grow at 4% in real terms. Labor costs are expected to grow at 3% per year. Other costs are expected to decrease at 0.5% per year. The real discount rate for revenues and costs is 8% and inflation is expected to be 3.5%. There are no taxes and all cash flows occur at year-end. What is the *NPV* of the contract?

Suggested Readings

Berk, J., and P. DeMarzo. *Corporate Finance*. Boston, MA: Pearson Addison Wesley, 2007.

Brealey, R., S. Myers, and F. Allen. *Principles of Corporate Finance,* 8th ed. New York: McGraw-Hill Irwin, 2006.

Hishleifer, J. "On the Theory of Optimal Investment Decision." *Journal of Political Economy* 66, August 1958.

Ross, S., R. Westerfield, and J. Jaffe. *Corporate Finance,* 8th ed. New York: McGraw-Hill Irwin, 2008.

Principles of Market Valuation

OBJECTIVES

- Understand why market valuation of assets is important in financial economics.
- Explain the *Law of One Price* as the principle underlying all asset-valuation procedures.
- Explain the meaning and role of valuation models.
- Explain how information gets reflected in security prices.

CONTENTS

From Chapter 7 of *Financial Economics*, 2/e. Zvi Bodie, Robert C. Merton, David L. Cleeton.
Copyright © 2008 by Pearson Prentice Hall. All rights reserved.

Many financial decisions boil down to figuring out how much assets are worth. For example, in deciding whether to invest in a security such as a stock or a bond or in a business opportunity, you have to determine whether the price being asked is high or low relative to other investment opportunities. In addition to investment decisions, there are many other situations in which one needs to determine the value of an asset. For example, suppose that the tax assessor in your town has assessed your house at $500,000 for property tax purposes. Is this value too high or too low? Or suppose you and your siblings inherit some property, and you decide to share it equally among yourselves. How do you decide how much it is worth?

Asset valuation is the process of estimating how much an asset is worth, and it is the second of the three analytical pillars of finance (the other two being time value of money and risk management). Asset valuation is at the heart of much of financial decision making. For firms, value maximization (maximizing the wealth of shareholders) is assumed to be the main objective of management. For households, too, many financial decisions can be made by selecting the alternative that maximizes value. This chapter explains the principles of asset valuation.

The key idea underlying all valuation procedures is that to estimate how much an asset is worth, you must use information about one or more comparable assets whose market prices you know. By the Law of One Price, the prices of all equivalent assets must be the same.

1. The Relation between an Asset's Value and Its Price

In this chapter, we define an asset's **fundamental value** as the price well-informed investors must pay for it in a free and competitive market.

There can be a temporary difference between the market price of an asset and its fundamental value. Security analysts make their living by researching the prospects of various firms and recommending which stocks to buy because their price appears low relative to fundamental value and which to sell because their price seems high relative to fundamental value.

However, in making most financial decisions, it is good practice to start by assuming that for assets that are bought and sold in competitive markets, price is an accurate reflection of value. As we will see, this assumption is generally warranted precisely because there are many well-informed professionals looking for mispriced assets who profit by eliminating discrepancies between the market prices and the fundamental values of assets.

2 Value Maximization and Financial Decisions

In many instances personal financial decisions can be made by selecting the alternative that maximizes value without even considering the individual's consumption or risk preferences. To give a simple example, consider the choice between alternative A—you get $100 today—and alternative B—you get $95 today.

Suppose you had to guess how a stranger, about whose preferences and future expectations you knew nothing at all, would choose. If the two alternatives are equivalent in every other respect, surely you would guess A on the grounds that more wealth is better than less.

Few financial decisions are this simple and straightforward. Suppose, now, that the choice is between a share of very risky stock and a completely safe bond. The stranger hates taking risks and is pessimistic about the price of the stock in the future. However, the current market price of the stock is $100, and the market price of the bond is $95.

Because the stranger hates taking risks and is pessimistic about the price of the stock in the future, you might predict that he would choose the bond. However, even if he ultimately wants to invest his money in safe bonds, the stranger should choose the stock.

Why?

The answer is that the stranger can sell the stock for $100 and buy the bond for $95. As long as the broker fees and other transaction costs of buying and selling the securities are less than the $5 difference in price, the stranger will come out ahead by choosing the stock. This simple example makes two important points:

1. The financial decision can rationally be made purely on the basis of value maximization, regardless of the stranger's risk preferences or expectations about the future.
2. The markets for financial assets provide the information needed to value the alternatives.

Just as households make financial decisions based on the criterion of value maximization, so too do firms. Managers of publicly held corporations are faced with the question of how to make capital budgeting, financing, and risk-management decisions. Because they are hired by the shareholders, their job is to make decisions that are in the best interests of shareholders. But a large corporation's managers do not even know the identities of many of their shareholders.[1]

Managers of corporations, therefore, look for a rule that will lead to the same decisions that each of the individual shareholders would have made had they made the decisions themselves. Both economic theory and common sense suggest the following rule for corporate financial decision-making: *Choose investment to maximize current shareholders' wealth.* Virtually every shareholder would agree with it, and so it can be made without any other information about shareholder preferences.

How can decision makers estimate the values of the assets and investment opportunities that are available to them? In some cases, they can look up the market price of the asset in the newspaper or on a computer screen. But some assets are not traded in any market and, therefore, we do not know their prices. To compare alternatives in such a case, we need to figure out what their market value would be if they were traded.

The essence of asset valuation in these cases is to estimate how much an asset is worth using information about one or more comparable assets whose current market prices we know. The method used to accomplish this estimation depends on the richness of the information set available. If we know the prices of assets that are virtually identical to the asset whose value we want to estimate, then we can apply the Law of One Price.

Quick Check 1

You win a contest, and the prize is a choice between a ticket to the opera and a ticket to the ball game. The opera ticket has a price of $100 and the ticket to the ball game has a price of $25. Assuming you prefer ball games to opera, which ticket should you choose?

---

[1]Because the shares of many firms change hands every day, even if CEOs tried, it is virtually impossible for them to know the identities of all their shareholders.

3 The Law of One Price and Arbitrage

The **Law of One Price** states that *in a competitive market, if two assets are equivalent, they will tend to have the same market price.* The Law of One Price is enforced by a process called **arbitrage,** the purchase and immediate sale of equivalent assets in order to earn a sure profit from a difference in their prices.

We illustrate how arbitrage works using gold. For thousands of years, gold has been widely used as a store of value and as a means of settling payments. It is a well-defined commodity whose quality can be precisely determined. When we talk about the price of gold, we mean the price of an ounce of gold of standard quality.

Consider the following question: If the price of gold in New York City is $800 per ounce, what is its price in Los Angeles?

The answer should be approximately $800 per ounce. To see why, let us consider what the economic consequences would be if the L.A. price were very different from $800 per ounce.

Suppose, for example, that the price of gold in Los Angeles was only $750. Consider how much it would cost to buy gold in Los Angeles and sell it in New York. There are the costs of shipping, handling, insuring, and broker fees. We call the totality of such costs **transaction costs.** If total transaction costs were less than $50 per ounce, it would pay for you to buy gold in Los Angeles and sell it in New York for $800 per ounce.

Say the transaction costs are $2 per ounce, and it takes a day to ship the gold by air. Then your profit would be $48 per ounce, and you would buy gold where it is cheap and sell it where it is dear. To eliminate the risk that the price in New York might fall while the gold was on its way from Los Angeles to New York, you would try to lock in the selling price of $800 at the same time that you buy the gold for $750. Moreover, if you can delay paying for the gold you purchase until you receive payment from selling it, then you will not have to use any of your own money in the transaction. If you can achieve both of these goals, then you will have engaged in a "pure," riskless arbitrage transaction.

If such a price discrepancy in the price of gold between New York and Los Angeles ever developed, it is unlikely that you would be the first or only person to find out about it. It is much more likely that gold dealers, who are in the business of buying and selling gold on a daily basis, would discover the discrepancy first. The first dealer to discover it would seek to buy as large a quantity as possible in Los Angeles at that price.

In addition to gold dealers, there is another group of market participants, called **arbitrageurs,** who watch the price of gold in different regions looking for large enough price discrepancies. Arbitrageurs engage in arbitrage for a living. (Arbitrageurs are active participants in many asset markets, not just the one for gold.)

Regardless of who or what group is doing the buying and selling, the acts of buying a lot of gold in Los Angeles and simultaneously selling it in New York would drive the price up in Los Angeles and down in New York. The arbitrage would stop only when the price in Los Angeles was within $2 per ounce of the price in New York. If the price in Los Angeles were *higher* than in New York (say the price of gold in New York is again $800 per ounce, but in Los Angeles it is $850), the force of arbitrage would work in the opposite direction. Gold dealers and arbitrageurs would buy gold in New York and ship it to Los Angeles until the price differential fell to $2 per ounce.

Thus, the force of arbitrage maintains a relatively narrow band around the price difference between the gold market in Los Angeles and the one in New York. The lower the transaction costs, the narrower the band.

Quick Check 2

Quick Check 2

If the price of silver is $20 per ounce in Chicago and the total transaction costs of shipping silver to New York is $1 per ounce, what can we say about the price of silver in New York?

4 Arbitrage and the Prices of Financial Assets

Now let us consider how the Law of One Price operates in the market for financial assets such as shares of stock, in which the transaction costs are much lower than those for gold. Shares of General Motors (GM) are traded on both the New York Stock Exchange (NYSE) and on the London Stock Exchange. If shares of General Motors stock were selling for $54 a share on the New York Stock Exchange at the same time they were selling for $56 on the London Stock Exchange, what would happen?

If the transaction costs were negligible, investors would sell their shares in London and would buy in New York. This activity would tend to drive down the price in London and drive up the price in New York.

Arbitrageurs could earn sure profits without investing a penny of their own money by buying 100,000 shares of GM on the NYSE for a total of $5,400,000 and then immediately (with a few strokes on the computer keyboard) selling them on the London Stock Exchange for a total of $5,600,000. Because they pay only $5,400,000 for the shares bought in New York but receive $5,600,000 for the shares sold in London, they are left with $200,000 in profits.

Notice that even though this set of transactions requires no cash outlays by the arbitrageurs at any time,[2] the arbitrageurs immediately increase their wealth by $200,000 as a result of these transactions. Indeed, as long as the prices for GM stock on the two exchanges are different, arbitrageurs can continue to increase their wealth by making these transactions and can continue to get something for nothing.

This process would be like the mythical goose that laid golden eggs except for an important fact: Such arbitrage opportunities do not persist for very long. The large profits earned by the arbitrageurs will attract attention to the price discrepancy. Other arbitrageurs will compete for the same arbitrage profits, and as a result, the stock prices in the two locations will converge.

As this simple example illustrates, the Law of One Price is a statement about the price of one asset *relative* to the price of another; it tells us that if we want to know the current price of GM stock, it is enough to know its price on the NYSE. If that price is $54, we can be reasonably sure that its price in London is the same.

The Law of One Price is the most fundamental valuation principle in finance. Indeed, if observed prices appeared to violate the law, so that seemingly identical assets were selling at different prices, our first suspicion would not be an exception to the Law of One Price but instead we would suspect that (1) something was interfering with the normal operation of the competitive market or (2) there was some (perhaps undetected) economic difference between the two assets.

---

[2]However, it does require that their credit standing be good enough to enable them to purchase the shares in New York without paying for them in advance.

To see this point, consider the following example. Normally a dollar bill is worth four quarters. We know that because we could take a dollar and exchange it costlessly for four quarters at a bank, a retail store, or with a person we meet on the street.

Yet we can describe a situation in which a dollar bill will be worth *less* than four quarters. Suppose you are desperate to do your laundry now. You need two quarters for the washer and one quarter for the dryer. You have no change, but you do have a dollar bill. If you are in a big hurry and the only other person at the laundromat has three quarters, you would likely agree to part with your dollar for three quarters.

When would a dollar be worth *more* than four quarters? Perhaps you are at a bus stop and are very thirsty. You find a beverage vending machine that will only accept dollar bills and not change. Under those circumstances you may be willing to pay someone more than four quarters in exchange for a dollar.

These situations do not violate the Law of One Price because in each instance the dollar bill is not really equivalent to the four quarters in all respects that have a bearing on their value. At the laundromat, a dollar bill is useless because it will not start the washer or dryer. At the bus stop, quarters are useless because they will not operate the vending machine. And in both situations you do not have costless access to a party who will exchange the two in the normal ratio.

Tautologically, no two distinct assets are identical in *all* respects. For example, even two different shares of stock in the same company differ in their serial numbers. Nevertheless, we would expect the shares to have the same price because they are the same in all respects that have a bearing on their value to investors (e.g., expected return, risk, voting rights, marketability, and so on).

Quick Check 3

Under what circumstances might two 25-cent coins have different values?

---

5 Interest Rates and the Law of One Price

Competition in financial markets ensures that not only the *prices* of equivalent assets are the same but also that *interest rates* on equivalent assets are the same. Suppose, for instance, that the interest rate the U.S. Treasury currently pays on its one-year T-bills is 4% per year. What interest rate would you expect a major institution such as the World Bank to pay on its one-year, dollar-denominated debt securities (assuming them to be virtually free of default risk)?

Your answer should be approximately 4% per year.

To see why, suppose that the World Bank offered significantly *less* than 4% per year. Well-informed investors would not buy the bonds issued by the World Bank; instead they would invest in one-year T-bills. Thus, if the World Bank expects to sell its bonds, it must offer at least as high a rate as the U.S. Treasury.

Would the World Bank offer significantly *more* than 4% per year? Assuming that it wants to minimize its borrowing costs, it would offer no more than is necessary to attract investors. Thus, interest rates on *any* default-free borrowing and lending denominated in dollars with a maturity of one year will tend to be the same as the 4% per year interest rate on one-year U.S. T-bills.

If there are entities that have the ability to borrow and lend on the same terms (e.g., maturity, default risk) at different interest rates, then they can carry out *interest-rate arbitrage:* borrowing at the lower rate and lending at the higher rate. Their attempts to expand their activity will bring about an equalization of interest rates.

Quick Check 4

Suppose you have $10,000 in a bank account earning an interest rate of 3% per year. At the same time you have an unpaid balance on your credit card of $5,000 on which you are paying an interest rate of 17% per year. What is the arbitrage opportunity you face?

6 Exchange Rates and Triangular Arbitrage

The Law of One Price applies to the foreign exchange market as well as to other financial markets. Arbitrage ensures that for any three currencies that are freely convertible in competitive markets, it is enough to know the exchange rates between any two in order to determine the third. Thus, as we show, if you know that the yen price of the U.S. dollar is ¥100 and the yen price of the U.K. pound is ¥200, it follows by the Law of One Price that the dollar price of the pound is $2.

To understand how arbitrage works in the foreign exchange market, it is helpful to start by considering the price of gold in different currencies. Suppose you know that the current dollar price of gold is $1,000 per ounce and its price in yen is ¥100,000 per ounce. What would you expect the exchange rate to be between the dollar and the yen?

The Law of One Price implies that it should not matter which currency you use to pay for gold. Thus, the ¥100,000 price should be equivalent to $1,000, which implies that the dollar price of the yen must be $0.01 or 1 cent per yen.

Suppose that the Law of One Price is violated, and the dollar price of the yen is $0.009 rather than $0.01. Suppose you currently have $10,000 in cash sitting in the bank. Because, by assumption, you can buy or sell gold either for ¥100,000 per ounce or for $1,000 per ounce, you would convert your $10,000 into $10,000/$0.009 = ¥1,111,111.11. You would use the yen to buy 11.1111 ounces of gold (¥1,111,111.11/¥100,000 per ounce) and sell the gold for dollars to receive $11,111.11 (11.1111 ounces × $1,000 per ounce). You would now have $11,111.11 less the transaction costs of buying and selling the gold and the yen. As long as these transaction costs are less than $1,111.11, it would pay you to engage in the arbitrage.

> Note that to carry out this risk-free arbitrage transaction, you did not require any special knowledge, did not have to make any forecasts of future prices, and did not have to bear any risk.

This type of transaction is called **triangular arbitrage** because it involves three assets: gold, dollars, and yen.

Quick Check 5

Suppose that the exchange rate is $0.011 to the yen. How could you make arbitrage profits with your $10,000 if the dollar price of gold is $1,000 per ounce and the yen price is ¥100,000 per ounce?

Now let's look at the relations among the prices of three different currencies: yen, dollars, and pounds. Suppose the U.S. dollar price of the yen is $0.01 per yen (or equivalently ¥100 to the dollar), and the price of the yen in terms of British pounds is a half pence (£0.005) to the yen (or equivalently, ¥200 to the pound). From these two exchange rates, we can determine that the U.S. dollar price of the pound is $2.

Although it may not be immediately obvious, there are two ways to buy pounds for dollars. One way is *indirectly* through the yen market—by first buying yen for dollars and then using the yen to buy pounds. Because, by assumption, one pound costs ¥200, and ¥200 costs $2.00, this indirect way costs $2.00 per pound. Another way to buy pounds for dollars is to just do it *directly*.

The direct purchase of pounds for dollars must cost the same as the indirect purchase of pounds for dollars because of the Law of One Price. If it is violated, there will be an arbitrage opportunity that cannot persist for very long.

To see how the force of arbitrage works to uphold the Law of One Price in this example, let's look at what would happen if the price of the pound were $2.10 rather than $2. Suppose you walk into a bank in New York City, and you observe the following three exchange rates—$0.01 per yen, ¥200 per pound, and $2.10 per pound. Suppose that there is one window for exchanging dollars and yen, another for exchanging yen and pounds, and a third window for exchanging dollars and pounds.

Here is how you can make an instantaneous $10 profit without leaving the bank:

1. At the dollar/yen window, convert $200 into ¥20,000;
2. At the yen/pound window, convert the ¥20,000 into £100; and then
3. At the dollar/pound window, convert the £100 into $210.

Congratulations, you have just converted $200 into $210!

But why limit the scale of this arbitrage to a mere $200? If you did it with $2,000, your profit would be $100; and if you did it with $20 million, your arbitrage profit would be $1 million. If you could find an arbitrage opportunity like this, it would be the equivalent of alchemy—changing base metals into gold!

In the real world, you or I would not be able to find such an arbitrage opportunity. Not only would we not be able to make a profit through such transactions, but we would probably lose money because banks charge fees for exchanging foreign currencies.[3] As retail customers, therefore, the transactions costs we would face would eliminate any arbitrage profits.

Although retail customers like us would not be able to find or exploit arbitrage opportunities in foreign currencies, banks and other dealers in foreign exchange might be able to. Some banks and other financial service firms employ professional arbitrageurs who carry out purchases and sales of currencies from their trading desks using desktop computers. Rather than walking from one bank window to the next, they can execute arbitrage transactions at "windows" on their computer screens via an electronic hookup to other banks located almost anywhere in the world.

If professional arbitrageurs were faced with the three exchange rates in our example—$0.01 per yen, ¥200 per pound, and $2.10 per pound, they might seek to make an instantaneous profit of $1 billion by converting $20 billion into £10 billion via the yen market while selling the £10 billion for $21 billion in the market for pounds. The attempt to carry out such large transactions would immediately attract attention, and subsequent transactions would eliminate the price discrepancies. Thus, given the prices of the yen in dollars ($0.01 per yen) and in pounds (£0.005 per yen), arbitrage ensures that the dollar price of the pound will obey the Law of One Price and equal $2.00 per pound.

The general principle at work here is:

For any three currencies that are freely convertible in competitive markets, it is enough to know the exchange rates between any two in order to know the third.

---

[3]There are two types of charges: explicit fees and the difference between the prices at which the bank buys and sells various currencies.

In our example, the dollar/yen rate was $0.01 per yen, and the pound/yen rate was £0.005 per yen. The dollar/pound exchange rate is the ratio of the two:

$$\$0.01 \text{ per Yen}/£0.005 \text{ per Yen} = \$2.00 \text{ per Pound}$$

The Law of One Price is a great convenience for anyone who needs to keep track of many different exchange rates. For example, suppose that as part of your job, you always need to know the exchange rates between four different currencies: the dollar, the yen, the pound, and the euro. There is a total of six possible exchange rates: dollar/yen, dollar/pound, dollar/euro, yen/pound, yen/euro, and pound/euro.

To know all six, however, you only need to know the three dollar-denominated exchange rates. Each of the other three can easily be computed as the ratio of two dollar-denominated exchange rates. The activities of professional, "high-technology" arbitrageurs, who carry out their trades quickly at very low cost, ensure that the direct exchange rates will conform closely with the computed indirect or "cross" rates.

Quick Check 6

You observe that the dollar prices of the peso and the shekel are $0.20 per peso and $0.30 per shekel. What must be the exchange rate between pesos and shekels?

---

7 Valuation Using Comparables

As stated previously, no two distinct assets are identical in all respects. The process of valuation requires that we find assets comparable to the one whose value we want to estimate and make judgments about which differences have a bearing on their value to investors.

For example, consider valuing a house using the observed prices of comparable houses. Suppose that you own a house and that each year you pay real estate taxes on it to the local town government that are computed as a proportion of the house's estimated market value. You have just received a notice from the town's real estate assessor notifying you that the estimated market value of your house this year is $500,000.

Suppose that your next-door neighbors just sold a house identical to yours for $300,000. You could justifiably appeal the town's assessment of $500,000 for the value of your house as being too high on the grounds that a house virtually identical to yours just sold for a price $200,000 less than your assessed value.

You are applying the Law of One Price in your valuation of your house. You are implying that if you were to put the house up for sale, your expectation is that it would fetch a price of $300,000 because a comparable house just sold for that amount.

Of course, the house next door is not *exactly* identical to yours because it is not located on your lot but on the one next to it. And you probably cannot *prove* that if you actually put your house up for sale it would fetch only $300,000 rather than the $500,000 that the town's assessor says it is worth. Nonetheless, unless the town's assessor can point to some economically relevant feature of your house that would make it worth $200,000 more than your neighbor's house (such as more land or floor space), you would have a strong logical case (and probably a strong legal case, too) for appealing the town's assessment.

The point is that even when the force of arbitrage cannot be relied on to enforce the Law of One Price, we still rely on its logic to value assets.

8 Valuation Models

Valuation is fairly simple when you can apply the Law of One Price directly. However, because you almost never know the prices of assets that are exactly equivalent to the one being evaluated, you must employ some other method for estimating value from the known prices of other assets that are comparable but not quite the same. The quantitative method used to infer an asset's value from information about the prices of other comparable assets and market interest rates is called a **valuation model.**

The type of model that is best to use depends on its specific purpose. If you want to estimate the value of an asset over which you have no control, you might use a different model than if you can influence the asset's value through your actions. Thus, if you are an individual estimating a firm's stock as a personal investment, you will probably use a different model from the one used by a corporation contemplating taking over the firm and reorganizing it.

8.1 Valuing Real Estate

For example, consider the valuation problem faced by the town assessor discussed previously. He has to estimate the values of all houses in the town once a year. Because homeowners will have to pay taxes based on his assessments, the assessor must choose a valuation method that is perceived as fair and accurate. Valuation models used in real estate assessment vary significantly in their level of complexity and mathematical sophistication. Because the town's taxpayers will have to pay for the cost of the annual assessment, they will want the method chosen to be implementable at low cost.

Consider one simple model the assessor might use. He can collect all available data on prices of houses in the town that were sold during the past year (since the last revaluation of houses), average them, and use that average as his assessed value for all houses. This model is certainly inexpensive to construct and implement, but it almost surely would not be perceived as fair by those homeowners with houses that are worth less than the average.

Another simple method would be to take the original purchase price of each house and adjust it by a factor reflecting the general change in house prices in the town from the date of purchase to the current date. Thus, suppose that house prices in the town have increased at an average rate of 4% per year for the past 50 years. A house bought 50 years ago for a price of $30,000 would then have a current assessed value of $30,000 \times 1.04^{50}$ or $213,200.

But some homeowners are sure to object that this method ignores changes that have occurred over time in the house itself. Some houses will have undergone major improvements and others will have deteriorated. Moreover, the relative desirability of various locations in the town will have changed.

The assessor faces a difficult problem in choosing among valuation methods and may wind up using more than one.

8.2 Valuing Shares of Stock

A relatively simple model widely used in estimating the value of a share of a firm's stock is to take its most recent earnings per share (*EPS*) and multiply it by a price/earnings multiple derived from comparable firms. A firm's **price/earnings multiple** is the ratio of its stock price to its earnings per share.

Thus, suppose that you want to estimate the value of a share of XYZ stock and XYZ's earnings per share are $2. Suppose further comparable firms in the same line of business have an average price/earnings multiple of 10. Using this model, we would estimate the value of a share of XYZ stock to be $20:

$$\text{Estimated Value of a Share of XYZ Stock} = \text{XYZ Earnings per Share}$$
$$\times \text{Industry Average Price/Earnings Multiple} = \$2 \times 10 = \$20$$

In applying the price/earnings-multiple model, one must use great care to make sure that what is being measured is truly comparable. For example, shares of stock issued by two firms with identical assets but different debt/equity ratios are not really comparable. Moreover, firms classified as being in the same industry may have very different opportunities for profitable growth in the future and, therefore, differ in their price/earnings multiples.

> **Quick Check 9**
>
> A firm's earnings per share are $5, and the industry average price/earnings multiple is 10. What would be an estimate of the value of a share of the firm's stock?

Now, we'll digress to say a few words about *book values,* which are measures of value as they appear on accounting statements.

9 Accounting Measures of Value

The value of an asset or a liability as reported on a balance sheet or other financial statement often differs from the asset's current market value because accountants usually measure assets by their original cost and then depreciate or "write them down" over time according to rules that ignore market values. The value of the asset as it appears on the balance sheet is called the asset's **book value.**

An example will help to clarify. You buy a house for $100,000 on January 1, 20x0, and rent it out to make a profit. You finance the purchase with $20,000 of your own money (equity financing) and an $80,000 mortgage loan from the bank (debt financing). You set up a small real estate company to operate this rental business. Table 1 shows your company's starting balance sheet.

The $100,000 you paid for the property is allocated between the value of the land and the value of the building. Initially, all assets and liabilities are recorded at market prices. However, from that point on, book and market values will probably diverge. Accountants depreciate (i.e., mark down) the value of the building even if its market value goes up. The book value of the land remains fixed.

For example, suppose that on January 2 someone makes you a bona fide offer of $150,000 for the property. On the company's balance sheet it is still $100,000 (less one day's depreciation). This is its *book* value. What you could get for it if you sold it, however, is $150,000. This is its *market* value.

TABLE 1 ABC Realty Balance Sheet

January 1, 20x0	
Assets	
Land	$25,000
Building	75,000
Liabilities	
Mortgage Loan	80,000
Owner's Equity (Net Worth)	20,000

TABLE 2 ABC Realty Market Value Balance Sheet

January 2, 20x0	
Assets	
Land and Building	$150,000
Liabilities	
Mortgage Loan	80,000
Owner's Equity (Net Worth)	70,000

Table 2 shows ABC Realty's market-value balance sheet on January 2 assuming that the market value of the property is $150,000 and the value of the mortgage loan has remained unchanged from the previous day.

If someone asks you on January 2 how wealthy you are, which measure of the business's value do you use to compute your net worth?[4] If you use the book value of owner's equity, the answer is $20,000, the amount that you invested in the business on January 1. But if you use the market value, your net worth is $70,000.

The point is that the user of financial statements must be careful not to interpret the values of assets that appear there as estimates of market values *unless they are specifically revalued to reflect their current market values.*

Quick Check 10

Suppose that on January 3 the market value of ABC Realty's property falls to $80,000. What is the market value of your net worth? What is its book value?

---

10 How Information Is Reflected in Security Prices

At the outset of this chapter we stated that the market price of an asset is a good measure of its fundamental value. In this section we develop more fully the reasoning behind this statement.

Sometimes a corporation's stock price "jumps" in response to a public announcement conveying news about the company's future prospects. For example, suppose that QRS

---

[4]Earlier that the net worth (or owner's equity) is the difference between the assets and the liabilities.

Pharmaceuticals Corporation announces that its research scientists have just discovered a drug that will cure the common cold. The stock price will probably rise dramatically on this news. On the other hand, if it is announced that a judge has just ruled against QRS Pharmaceuticals in a lawsuit involving the payment of millions of dollars in compensation to customers who bought one of its products, QRS's stock price will probably fall.

In such situations, people say that the stock market is "reacting" to the information contained in these announcements. Implicit in this statement is the view that at least some of the investors who buy or sell QRS stock (or the stock analysts advising them) are paying attention to the fundamental factors that determine the stock's value. When those fundamentals change, so does the stock price. Indeed, if the stock price does not move when an important news item is officially made public, many observers of the stock market would say that the news was already reflected in the stock price. It is this idea that is behind the **efficient markets hypothesis.**

11 The Efficient Markets Hypothesis

The *efficient markets hypothesis* (*EMH*) is the proposition that an asset's current price fully reflects all publicly available information about future economic fundamentals affecting the asset's value.[5]

The reasoning behind the EMH can be explained by considering the following somewhat simplified description of a typical analyst-investor's actions in making a decision about a particular company's stock.

First, the analyst collects the information or "facts" about the company and related matters that may affect the company. Second, she analyzes this information in such a way so as to determine her best estimate (as of today, time 0) of the stock price at a future date (time 1). This best estimate is the expected stock price at time 1, which we denote by $\overline{P}(1)$.

From looking at the current stock price, $P(0)$, she can estimate an *expected* return on the stock, $\overline{r}$, which is

$$\overline{r} = \frac{\overline{P}(1)}{P(0)} - 1$$

However, the analyst's job is not finished. Because she recognizes that her information is not perfect (e.g., subject to error or unforeseen events that may occur), she must also give consideration to the range of possible future prices.

In particular, she must estimate how disperse this range is about her best estimate and how likely is a deviation of a certain size from this estimate. This analysis then gives her an estimate of the deviations of the rate of return from the expected rate and the likelihood of such deviations. Obviously, the more accurate her information, the smaller will be the dispersion around her estimate and the less risky the investment.

Third, armed with her estimates of the expected rate of return and the dispersion, she makes an investment decision or recommendation of how much of the stock to buy or sell. How much will depend on how good the risk-return trade-off on this stock is in comparison with alternative investments available and on how much money she has to invest (either personally or as an agent for others). The higher the expected return and the more money

---

[5]Stock market prices often reflect private information as well. See L. K. Meulbroek, "An Empirical Analysis of Illegal Insider Trading," *Journal of Finance,* December 1992, and L. K. Meulbroek and C. Hart, "The Effect of Illegal Insider Trading on Takeover Premia," *European Finance Review,* 1, 1997.

Box 1 — Instantaneous Trading on the News

One common critique of the Efficient Markets Hypothesis (EMH) takes aim at the notion that new information can immediately be reflected in the market price of a stock. Humans, after all, take some finite amount of time to read new information, process it and decide how to act, and then to execute any trades in response. But recent developments in the use of computers to automatically execute trades after interpreting news reports has undermined the saliency of this critique of the EMH.

For some time now, investors have used computer programs that scan news reports and corporate announcements for specific terms that could have an impact on the investor's decision to buy, hold, or sell a stock. A spate of reports with the term "heat wave" could, for instance, suggest the purchase of shares of firms that manufacture cooling appliances. As impressive as this may be, recent developments have allowed computers to move well beyond this level of interpretation.

Today there are computer programs that can evaluate many years' worth of news issued by or about a given firm to determine how announcements of a certain kind have tended to affect the share price. From this analysis, such computers can immediately determine upon receiving a new announcement whether to trade (buy or sell) shares of the stock in question. One direct result of this technology has been a sharp increase in demand for so-called machine readable news, that is, news stories that contain words and numbers in strings easily interpreted by the relevant software programs, rather than in normal English sentences.

In this new framework, it could potentially be the case that information will, quite literally, travel instantaneously from machine to machine in a cycle beginning with computer-generated news and ending with computer-executed trading.

How might such a scenario bear on the EMH? First, we have to remember that the EMH supposes that the moment new information about a firm comes to light, that information is incorporated in the firm's stock price. When human investors must interpret news reports and analyze their content before executive trades, this hypothesis seems unrealistic. But in a world in which information travels, can be interpreted, and can lead to trades, all in less than a second, the EMH does not strike us as unreasonable. Indeed, the advent of this technology only serves to bolster the significance of the EMH.

Source: Adapted from "Automatic News Makes Headlines and Money," *Financial Times,* April 15, 2007.

she has (or controls), the more of the stock she will want to buy or sell. The larger the dispersion (i.e., the less accurate the information that she has), the smaller the position she will take in the stock.

To see how the current market price of the stock is determined, we look at the aggregation of all analysts' estimates, and assume that on the average the market is in equilibrium (i.e., on average, the price will be such that total (desired) demand equals total supply). Analysts' estimates may differ for two reasons:

1. They could have access to different amounts of information (although presumably public information is available to all); or
2. They could analyze the information differently with regard to its impact on future stock prices.

Nonetheless, each analyst comes to a decision as to how much to buy or sell at a given market price, $P(0)$. The aggregation of these decisions gives us the total demand for shares of the company at the price, $P(0)$.

Suppose that the price were such that there were more shares demanded than supplied (i.e., it is too low); then one would expect the price to rise, and vice versa, if there were more shares available at a given price than were demanded. Hence, the market price of the stock will reflect a *weighted average* of the opinions of all analysts.

The key question is what is the nature of this weighting? Because "votes" in the marketplace are cast with dollars, the analysts with the biggest impact will be the ones who control the larger amounts of money, and among these, the ones who have the strongest opinions about the stock will be the most important.

Note that the analysts with the strongest opinions have them because they believe that they have better information (resulting in a smaller dispersion around their best estimate). Furthermore, because an analyst who consistently overestimates the accuracy of his estimates will eventually lose his customers, one would expect that among the analysts who control large sums, the ones that believe that they have better information, on average, probably do.

From all this, we conclude that the market price of the stock will reflect the weighted average of analysts' opinions with heavier weights on the opinions of those analysts with control of more than the average amount of money and with better than average amounts of information. Hence, the estimate of "fair" or "intrinsic" value provided by the market price will be more accurate than the estimate obtained from an average analyst.

Now, suppose that you are an analyst and you find a stock whose market price is low enough that you consider it a "bargain" (if you never find this situation, then there is no point to being in the analyst business). From the previous discussion, there are two possibilities:

1. You *do* have a bargain—your estimate is more accurate than the market's (i.e., you have either better than average information about future events that may affect stock price and/or you do a better than average job of analyzing information); or
2. Others have better information than you do or process available information better, and your "bargain" is not a true bargain.

One's assessment of which it is depends on how good the other analysts are relative to oneself. There are important reasons why one would expect the quality of analysts to be high:

- The enormous rewards to anyone who can consistently beat the average attract large numbers of intelligent and hardworking people to the business;
- The relative ease of entry into the (analyst) business implies that competition will force the analysts to find better information and develop better techniques for processing this information just to survive; and
- The stock market has been around long enough for these competitive forces to take effect.

Precisely because professional analysts compete with each other, the market price becomes a better and better estimate of "fair value," and it becomes more difficult to find profit opportunities.

Quick Check 11

The DEF Corporation announces that over the next few years it will spend several billion dollars on developing a new product. The firm's stock price falls dramatically after the announcement. According to the efficient markets hypothesis, what is the reason for the drop in price? If you were the president of DEF Corporation, what conclusions would you draw from the decline in your firm's stock price?

Box 2	The Efficient Markets Hypothesis in the Law

The Efficient Markets Hypothesis (EMH) has come to influence not only financial markets and economic theory, but also legal interpretation of market happenings. The EMH, as discussed in this chapter, essentially holds that the market price of a share of stock completely and correctly incorporates all public information pertinent to its worth. In this view, stock prices only ever rise or fall because new information becomes available. Such information, the EMH holds, is promptly reflected in the market price of a share.

The EMH has a special role in the legal world because it has been accepted by the U.S. Supreme Court. That tribunal, in the 1988 case *Basic Inc. v. Levinson,* accepted as a legal standard a concept known as "fraud on the market," which presupposes the EMH. This standard is concerned with deceptive news releases by firms. Such statements, the Court ruled, defraud traders who buy the firm's shares, whether their purchases were directly founded on the deceptive statements or not. After this ruling, civil cases invoking the "fraud on the market" standard multiplied rapidly. Recently the EMH seems to have found its way into criminal prosecutions, too.

Consider the case of Mr. Jamie Olis, a tax accountant involved in a scandal at the energy company Dynegy. Mr. Olis was sentenced to a stiff 24-year prison term in 2004 for his role in a set of fraudulent accounting activities at Dynegy known as Project Alpha. The judge presiding over the case sentenced Mr. Olis to a prison term based on the calculated loss to Dynegy shareholders when the stock tanked upon news that Project Alpha was a scam. Though the sentence was expected to be reduced on appeal, it is clear that the EMH has meant some serious time for at least one businessman.

The focus of Mr. Olis's appeal was the degree to which the stock's decline resulted specifically from news of Project Alpha's fraudulence. Economists working for both the prosecution and the defense were expected to estimate the loss due to the news of that scandal. The EMH was the foundation on which the case was built.

For years, however, the EMH—originally developed in the 1950s and 1960s—has come under fire by academics. Recently a pair of scholars argued that even the world's most advanced financial markets are not, in practice, as efficient as the EMH would have them. Certainly, these scholars claimed, such markets are not efficient enough to warrant the use of stock price falls to determine the magnitude of financial losses in a legal case.

Still, the standard in law has remained unchanged in the United States. In both civil and criminal cases, the EMH can play an important role. And so we see that the influence of this hypothesis expands well beyond the halls of the world's universities.

Source: Adapted from "Dismal Science, Dismal Sentence," *The Economist,* September 7, 2006.

Summary

In finance, the measure of an asset's value is the price it would fetch if it were sold in a competitive market. The ability to value assets accurately is at the heart of the discipline of finance because many personal and corporate financial decisions can be made by selecting the alternative that maximizes value.

The Law of One Price states that in a competitive market, if two assets are equivalent they will tend to have the same price. The law is enforced by a process called *arbitrage,* the purchase and immediate sale of equivalent assets in order to earn a sure profit from a difference in their prices.

Even if arbitrage cannot be carried out in practice to enforce the Law of One Price, unknown asset values can still be inferred from the prices of comparable assets whose prices are known.

The quantitative method used to infer an asset's value from information about the prices of comparable assets is called a *valuation model.* The best valuation model to employ varies with the information available and the intended use of the estimated value.

The *book value* of an asset or a liability as reported in a firm's financial statements often differs from its current market value.

In making most financial decisions, it is a good idea to start by assuming that for assets that are bought and sold in competitive markets, price is a pretty accurate reflection of fundamental value. This assumption is generally warranted precisely because there are many well-informed professionals looking for mispriced assets who profit by eliminating discrepancies between the market prices and the fundamental values of assets. The proposition that an asset's current price fully reflects all publicly available (and some private) information about future economic fundamentals affecting the asset's value is known as the *efficient markets hypothesis.*

The prices of traded assets reflect information about the fundamental economic determinants of their value. Analysts are constantly searching for assets whose prices are different from their fundamental value in order to buy/sell these "bargains." In deciding the best strategy for the purchase/sale of a "bargain," the analyst has to evaluate the accuracy of her information. The market price of an asset reflects the weighted average of all analysts' opinions with heavier weights on analysts who control large amounts of money and on those analysts who have better than average information.

Key Terms

- fundamental value
- Law of One Price
- arbitrage
- transaction costs
- arbitrageurs
- triangular arbitrage

- valuation model
- price/earnings multiple
- book value
- efficient markets hypothesis
- purchasing power parity
- real interest-rate parity

Answers to Quick Check Questions

Quick Check 1   You win a contest, and the prize is a choice between a ticket to the opera and a ticket to the ball game. The opera ticket has a price of $100 and the ticket to the ball game has a price of $25. Assuming you prefer ball games to opera, which ticket should you choose?

Answer: Provided the cost to you of taking the time and trouble to exchange the tickets does not exceed the $75 difference in the price of the tickets, you should take the opera ticket. Even if you prefer the ball game to the opera, you can exchange it for $100, buy a ticket to the ball game for $25, and pocket the $75 difference.

Quick Check 2   If the price of silver is $20 per ounce in Chicago and the total transaction costs of shipping silver to New York is $1 per ounce, what can we say about the price of silver in New York?

Answer: The price of silver in New York must be within $1 per ounce of its price in Chicago. Thus, the price of silver in New York must be between $19 and $21 per ounce.

Quick Check 3   Under what circumstances might two 25-cent coins have different values?

Answer: One of them might be a rare coin that is especially valuable to collectors. Alternatively, one of them might be slightly worn, so that a soda machine will reject it. To a thirsty person, the nonworn coin is more valuable.

Quick Check 4   Suppose you have $10,000 in a bank account earning an interest rate of 3% per year. At the same time you have an unpaid balance on your credit card of $5,000 on which you are paying an interest rate of 17% per year. What is the arbitrage opportunity you face?

Answer: You could take $5,000 out of your bank account and pay down your credit card balance. You would give up 3% per year in interest earnings ($150 per year) but you would save 17% per year in interest expenses ($850 per year). So the arbitrage opportunity is worth $700 per year.

Quick Check 5   Suppose that the exchange rate is $0.011 to the yen. How could you make arbitrage profits with your $10,000 if the dollar price of gold is $1,000 per ounce and the yen price is ¥100,000 per ounce?

Answer:
   a. Take $10,000, buy 10 ounces of gold for $1,000 per ounce.
   b. Sell 10 ounces of gold in Japan for 1,000,000 yen (¥100,000 per ounce).
   c. Take 1,000,000 yen and exchange it into dollars worth $11,000.

   You make an arbitrage profit of $1,000.

Quick Check 6   You observe that the dollar prices of the peso and the shekel are $0.20 per peso and $0.30 per shekel. What must be the exchange rate between pesos and shekels?

Answer: Divide $0.20 per peso into $0.30 per shekel to get 1.5 pesos per shekel.

Quick Check 7   Suppose the town's assessor says that he arrived at his assessment of $500,000 for the value of your house by computing how much it would cost to rebuild your house from scratch using the current cost of building materials. What would be your response?

Answer: The cost to rebuild your house is not a measure of its market value. To estimate market value one should look at the actual prices of comparable houses—such as the one your neighbor just sold for $300,000.

Quick Check 8   Can you offer the assessor a way to alter his valuation model so as to take account of the specific neighborhood the house is located in?

Answer: One way to take account of the neighborhood effect in the valuation model would be to calculate average price changes *by neighborhood.* Then the assessor could apply a neighborhood price index in estimating price changes for individual houses.

Quick Check 9   A firm's earnings per share are $5, and the industry average price/earnings multiple is 10. What would be an estimate of the value of a share of the firm's stock?

Answer: An estimate of the value is $50 (*EPS* of $5 × *P/E* ratio of 10).

Quick Check 10   Suppose that on January 3 the market value of ABC Realty's property falls to $80,000. What is the market value of your net worth? What is its book value?

Answer: If the property value falls to $80,000, your net worth is 0. Its book value, however, is $20,000.

Quick Check 11   The DEF Corporation announces that over the next few years it will spend several billion dollars on developing a new product. The firm's stock price falls dramatically after the announcement. According to the efficient markets hypothesis, what is the reason for the drop in price? If you were the president of DEF Corporation, what conclusions would you draw from the decline in your firm's stock price?

Answer: According to the EMH, the price drop reflects a predominant view in the marketplace that DEF Corporation's proposed new product is not worth developing. If you were CEO and believed that the market analysts had as much information as you did, you might reconsider the desirability of developing the new product. However, if you had superior information about the new product that the market analysts were not aware of, then you might go ahead with the product development despite market opinion. Alternatively, you might make the information you have public in order to gauge the reaction of the market to this new piece of information.

Quick Check 12 (See appendix at the end of this chapter.) *Suppose the expected rate of inflation in the Swiss franc is 10% per year. What should be the nominal interest rate in francs according to real interest rate parity?*

Answer: Swiss Franc Interest Rate $= 1.03 \times 1.1 - 1 = 13.3\%$ per Year

---

Questions and Problems

The Relation between an Asset's Value and Its Price

1. Discuss whether the New Economy boom and bust in equity prices for telecommunications and Internet businesses over the past several years is compatible with the notion that market prices for assets can temporarily differ from fundamental values.

Value Maximization and Financial Decisions

2. Discuss whether the value maximization principle in financial decision making is independent of expectations about future asset prices.

The Law of One Price and Arbitrage

3. IBX stock is trading for $35 on the NYSE and $33 on the Tokyo Stock Exchange. Assume that the costs of buying and selling the stock are negligible.
   a. How could you make an arbitrage profit?
   b. Over time what would you expect to happen to the stock prices in New York and Tokyo?
   c. Now assume that the cost of buying or selling shares of IBX is 1% per transaction. How does this affect your answer?

4. Suppose you live in the state of Taxachusetts, which has a 16% sales tax on liquor. A neighboring state called Taxfree has no tax on liquor. The price of a case of beer is $25 in Taxfree and it is $29 in Taxachusetts.
   a. Is this a violation of the Law of One Price?
   b. Are liquor stores in Taxachusetts near the border with Taxfree going to prosper?

5. Suppose the price of white truffles is 400 euros per kilo in Paris and price of a euro is 1.453 Swiss francs. With transportation and transactions costs, such as insurance, of 1% in moving truffles from Paris to Geneva, within what range do you expect to observe the price of white truffles in Geneva?

6. Comment on the following statement: Applying the Law of One Price to bond markets implies that all bond investors have identical information about the term structure of interest rates.

7. Discuss the validity of the following statement: Since a pure riskless arbitrage transaction requires no investment of funds it cannot be of any significant duration since borrowing funds to finance the holding of an asset is ruled out.

Interest Rates and the Law of One Price

8. *Challenge Question:* During the week of April 29, 2002, several new dollar-denominated international bond issues came to market. Among those rated by

Moodys and Standard and Poor in the Aaa/AAA categories, the spread over Treasury bonds ranged from 39 to 44 basis points. (A basis point is 1/100th of one percent.) This means that the new corporate bonds were paying effective returns around 4/10th of one percent above the returns on Treasury bonds with similar characteristics. What should you expect the relationship to be between current market spreads and bond rating categories? Should spreads lead, lag, or move in step with changes in ratings? Does it matter that one measure is continuous, that is, spreads can take on a continuous range of values, and the other measure is discrete, meaning there are a small number of distinct rating categories?

Exchange Rates and Triangular Arbitrage

9. You observe that the dollar price of the euro is $1.20 and the dollar price of the yen is $0.01. What must be the exchange rate between euro and yen if there is no arbitrage opportunity?

10. Suppose the price of gold is $755 per ounce.
    a. If the pound sterling price of gold is £500 per ounce, what should you expect the pound price of a dollar to be?
    b. If it actually only costs £0.60 to purchase a dollar, how could one make arbitrage profits?

11. In Argentina these days many forms of cash are circulating. In addition to the national currency, the peso, and the U.S. dollar there are a variety of small debt instruments or IOUs issued by regional and local governments that are accepted for transactions. Suppose you go to a private beach in Buenos Aires and find a sign with the following prices for an adult admission and use of a lounge chair:

Currency	Price
Hasta Pesos	3
Lecop	5
Patacones	2
Dollars & Quebrachos also accepted!!	

Suppose you know that on the black market a U.S. dollar buys 4 patacones or 6 hasta pesos. And a lecop can be traded for 5 quebrachos. Digging around in your pockets you find only dollars and a few quebrachos. Assuming no arbitrage opportunities, what should you expect to pay to gain admission to the beach?

12. Fill in the missing exchange rates in the following table:

	US dollar	British pound	Euro	Japanese yen
US dollar	$1	$1.75	$1.25	$0.01
British pound	£0.5714			
Euro	€0.80			
Japanese yen	¥100			

13. Suppose you purchase a house and some time later discover a collection of vintage Barbie dolls in a box in the attic. How would you go about finding the current market value of the collection? What characteristics will determine the market value?

14. Suppose you own a home that you purchased four years ago for $475,000. The tax assessor's office has just informed you that they are increasing the taxable value of your home to $525,000.

    a. How might you gather information to help you appeal the new assessment?

    b. Suppose the house next door is comparable to yours except that it has one fewer bedroom. It just sold for $490,000. How might you use that information to argue your case? What inference must you make about the value of an additional bedroom?

Valuation Models

15. The P/E ratio of ITT Corporation is currently 6 while the P/E ratio of the S&P 500 is 10. What might account for the difference?

16. Suppose you are chief financial officer of a private toy company. The chief executive officer has asked you to come up with an estimate for the company's price per share. Your company's earnings per share were $2.00 in the year just ended. You know that you should look at public company comparables; however, they seem to fall into two camps: those with P/E ratios of 8x earnings and those with P/E ratios of 14x earnings. You are perplexed at the difference until you notice that on average, the lower P/E companies have higher leverage than the higher P/E group. The 8x P/E group has a debt/equity ratio of 2:1. The 14x P/E group has a debt/equity ratio of 1:1. If your toy company has a debt/equity ratio of 1.5:1, what might you tell the CEO about your company's equity value per share?

Accounting Measures of Value

17. The table below represents the current balance sheet of the soccer team Brugge Bears K.V. (in euros).

Assets		Liabilities	
Stadium and Equipment	25,000,000	Bonds	35,000,000
Broadcasting Rights	20,000,000	*Owner's Equity*	10,000,000

   Suppose the collapse of the European pay-t.v. market drops the market value of the club's broadcasting rights to 10,000,000 euros. Flemish real estate and equipment appraisals produce a market value of 30,000,000 euros and the current market price of the outstanding bond issues are 25,000,000 euros. What is the current ratio of the firm's market to book to value?

18. Assume that you have operated your business for 15 years. Sales for the most recent fiscal year were $12,000,000. Net income for the most recent fiscal year was $1,000,000. Your book value is $10,500,000. A similar company recently sold for the following statistics:

Multiple of Sales:	0.8x
Multiple of Net Income	12x
Multiple of Book Value	0.9x

    a. What is an appropriate range of value for your company?

    b. If you know that your company has future investment opportunities that are far more profitable than the company above, what does that say about your company's likely valuation?

How Information Is Reflected in Security Prices

19. Suppose the Federal Reserve is holding a meeting to address the question of whether to undertake actions to raise interest rates. The level and term structure of interest rates determine the fundamental discount rates used to value securities, for example, stocks and bonds. If market participants are convinced that the Fed will raise interest rates how will this be reflected in security prices?

The Efficient Markets Hypothesis

20. The price of Fuddy Co. stock recently jumped when the sudden unexpected death of its CEO was announced. What might account for such a market reaction?

21. Suppose we study the returns earned by corporate officers trading on the basis of inside information, that is, information which is known to corporate insiders but not publicly available. If these types of trades produce above average returns what does this tell us about market efficiency?

22. Your analysis leads you to believe that the price of Outel's stock should be $25 per share. Its current market price is $30.

    a. If you do not believe that you have access to special information about the company, what do you do?

    b. If you are an analyst with much better than average information, what do you do?

23. *Challenge Question:* Suppose managers trading on the basis of inside information do earn above average returns. What does this tell us about the incentives of management to release information and the timing of the release compared to the timing of the trades?

Integrative Problem

24. Suppose an aunt has passed away and bequeathed to you and your siblings (one brother, one sister) a variety of assets. The original cost of these assets follows:

Item	Cost	When Purchased
Jewelry	$500	by Grandmother 75 years ago
House	$1,200,000	10 years ago
Stocks and Bonds	$1,000,000	3 years ago
Vintage (used) Car	$200,000	2 months ago
Furniture	$15,000	various dates during last 40 years

Because you are taking a course in finance, your siblings put you in charge of dividing the assets fairly among the three of you. Before you start, your brother approaches you and says: "I'd really like the car for myself, so when you divide up the assets, just give me the car and deduct the $200,000 from my share."

Hearing that, your sister says: "That sounds fair, because I really like the jewelry and you can assign that to me and deduct the $500 from my share."

You have always loved your aunt's house and its furnishings, so you would like to keep the house and the furniture.

    a. How do you respond to your brother and sister's requests? Justify your responses.

    b. How would you go about determining appropriate values for each asset?

Purchasing Power and Real Interest Rate Parity

The Law of One Price is the basis for a theory of exchange rate determination known as **purchasing power parity** (PPP). The essence of the theory is that exchange rates adjust so as to maintain the same "real" price of a "representative" basket of goods and services around the world. In other words, the theory says that although some goods may cost different amounts in different countries, the general cost of living should be about the same.

To illustrate the reasoning behind PPP, assume that there are only two different countries—Japan and the United States—with their own currencies—the dollar and the yen. There is, therefore, only one exchange rate to be determined—the dollar price of the yen. There is a single good produced and consumed in both countries—wheat.

Suppose that the price of wheat is $1 per bushel in the United States and ¥100 per bushel in Japan. The equilibrium exchange rate is $0.01 per yen.

Consider what would happen at an exchange rate of $0.009 per yen. There would be an arbitrage opportunity. An arbitrageur could buy wheat in Japan and sell it to consumers in the United States. A bushel of imported Japanese wheat would cost $0.90 ($0.009 per yen × ¥100 per bushel) and sell for $1.00 in the United States market. To do this, arbitrageurs need to convert more dollars into yen than they would at the equilibrium exchange rate of $0.01 per yen. Japan would experience a trade surplus (i.e., it would be an exporter of wheat to the United States), and there would be excess demand for yen. This excess demand for yen would drive up the dollar price of the yen.

At an exchange rate that is higher than the equilibrium rate, the situation is reversed. The "undervalued" dollar makes United States wheat cheaper to Japanese consumers than Japanese wheat. Japan imports wheat from the U.S. instead of exporting it to the United States. There is an excess supply of yen, which drives its dollar price down toward the equilibrium level.

In reality, our simple example illustrating PPP has to be modified for several reasons. We assume that the same good is consumed in both countries and that it is transportable at low cost. In reality, although some are the same, many of the goods produced and consumed in each country are different. Moreover, many of them are too costly to transport across national borders. In many cases, governments restrict the flow of imports and exports through tariffs and quotas.

For all of these reasons, PPP, if it holds at all, holds only approximately and only in the long run.

Just as we have the theory of PPP to explain the relations among exchange rates, there is an analogous theory to explain the relations among interest rates denominated in different currencies. We call it the theory of **real interest-rate parity.** This theory states that the expected real interest rate on risk-free loans is the same all over the world. Given a value for this real interest rate, *the nominal interest rate for a loan denominated in any currency is determined by the expected rate of inflation in that currency.*

Recall that we distinguish between real interest rates and nominal interest rates. We show that the realized real rate of interest on a loan is related to the nominal interest rate as follows:

$$1 + \text{Nominal Interest Rate} = (1 + \text{Real Interest Rate}) \times (1 + \text{Rate of Inflation})$$

Quick Check 12

Suppose the expected rate of inflation in the Swiss franc is 10% per year. What should be the nominal interest rate in francs according to real interest rate parity?

Box 3	Predicting the Currency Market (Or Not)

Standard economic modeling and empirical testing has failed to systematically discern any rhyme or reason to the fluctuations of the currency market. Recent work, however, suggests that information in such markets is by no means instantaneously absorbed. This finding calls into question a fundamental axiom of the Efficient Markets Hypothesis (EMH) as it applies to the currency market.

Economists studying currency markets have tended to keep their distance from practitioners—the actual traders who execute foreign exchange transactions. This separation has not proved to be fruitful. In 1983 an oft-cited study was published that held that macroeconomic modeling simply could not account for the ebb and flow of the currency market. Scholars have been puzzled, and are generally just as successful predicting the direction of a currency's value with the flip of a fair coin as they are with received economic models.

At least one pair of scholars recently decided it was time for a new approach. When UC Berkeley economist Richard Lyons recently spent time in the pit with real traders, he gained some insight into how economists should model currency markets. He decided that the trader himself should be the focus of the model. Teaming up with Georgetown University economist Martin Evans, Lyons suggested a novel idea.

Consider, these two scholars said, that a currency dealer acts as a market intermediary who accepts orders from all sorts of currency traders. Each order is based on the beliefs of the trader who placed it—beliefs held with enough confidence to be backed by real money. The insight of Lyons and Evans, then, was that such dealers are endowed with access to a large set of beliefs held by market actors, whereas each individual trader has access only to his own beliefs. What could this mean for the prospect of predicting the movements of the currency market?

Note that in any given period of time, the currency dealer may have more orders to buy U.S. dollars, for instance, than to sell them. Such a situation is dubbed a positive "order flow," and Lyons and Evans found that it has some predictive power. Using data from a large currency dealer, Citibank, the economists suggest that 16% of the dollar's fluctuations four weeks down the road can be explained by current order flow.

This result may surprise us. The EMH, after all, suggests that information is incorporated into markets instantaneously. How, then, could it be that it takes all of four weeks for order flow information to be reflected in exchange rates? In practice, it seems that there is simply too much to process immediately: It takes time for the aggregates of demand for and supply of dollars in the market to reach all traders. The currency markets simmer as always, but the saliency of the EMH has been challenged.

Source: Adapted from "Marking the Dealer's Cards," *The Economist,* November 24, 2005.

Under the real interest-rate parity theory, this relation holds with respect to expected inflation.

To illustrate the implications of the theory of real interest-rate parity, let us assume that the worldwide risk-free real interest rate is currently 3% per year. Let us assume that the expected rate of inflation in Japan is 1% per year and in the United States it is 4% per year. The nominal interest rates in yen and dollars implied by real interest rate parity are

$$\text{Yen Interest Rate} = 1.03 \times 1.01 - 1 = 4.03\% \text{ per Year}$$

$$\text{Dollar Interest Rate} = 1.03 \times 1.04 - 1 = 7.12\% \text{ per Year}$$

Appendix: Purchasing Power and Real Interest Rate Parity

25. *Challenge Problem:* Suppose a new Buick Regal costs $27,000 in Detroit and the identical car costs C$32,000 a few miles away in Windsor, Ontario. Ignoring any transaction costs or taxation differentials, what exchange rate between the U.S. and Canadian dollars is consistent with an absence of an arbitrage opportunity? Suppose the domestic price of the Regal is expected to rise by 2% (all rates are considered to

be *APR*s with continuous compounding) over the next year whereas the Canadian price is expected to rise by 4%. What exchange rate between the U.S. and Canadian dollars realized in one year would be consistent with an absence of an arbitrage opportunity? What change in the exchange rate over the year is consistent with the maintenance of no arbitrage opportunities? How is this exchange rate change related to the two rates of Regal price inflation?

Suggested Readings

Campbell, J., M. Lettau, B. Malkiel, and Y. Xu. "Have Individual Stocks Become More Volatile? An Empirical Exploration of Idiosyncratic Risk." *Journal of Finance* 56, February 2001.

Fama, E. F. "Efficient Capital Markets: A Review of Theory and Empirical Work." *Journal of Finance* 25, May 1970.

———. "Efficient Capital Markets II." *Journal of Finance* 46, December 1991.

Samuelson, P. A. "Proof That Properly Anticipated Prices Fluctuate Randomly." *Industrial Management Review* 6, Spring 1965.

Valuation of Known Cash Flows: Bonds

From Chapter 8 of *Financial Economics*, 2/e. Zvi Bodie, Robert C. Merton, David L. Cleeton.
Copyright © 2008 by Pearson Prentice Hall. All rights reserved.

Valuation of Known Cash Flows: Bonds

OBJECTIVES

- To show how to value contracts and securities that promise a stream of cash flows that is known with certainty.
- To understand how bond prices and yields change over time.

CONTENTS

The essence of the valuation process is to estimate an asset's market value using information about the prices of comparable assets, making adjustments for differences. A *valuation model* is a quantitative method used to infer an asset's value (the output of the model) from market information about the prices of other assets and market interest rates (the inputs to the model).

In this chapter, we examine the valuation of fixed-income securities and other contracts promising a stream of known future cash payments. Examples are fixed-income securities such as bonds and contracts such as mortgages and pension annuities. These securities and contracts are important to households because they represent major sources of income and sources of financing for housing and other consumer durables. They are also important to firms and governments, primarily as sources of financing.

Having a method to value such contracts is important for at least two reasons. First, the parties to the contracts need to have an agreed-upon valuation procedure in setting the terms of the contracts at the outset. Second, fixed-income securities are often sold before they mature. Because the market factors determining their value—namely, interest rates—change over time, both buyers and sellers have to reevaluate them each time they are traded.

Section 1 presents a basic valuation model that uses a discounted cash flow formula with a single discount rate to estimate the value of a stream of promised future cash flows. Section 2 shows how to modify such a model to take account of the fact that generally the yield curve is not flat (i.e., that interest rates vary with maturity). Sections 3–5 explain the main features of bonds in the real world and discuss how these features affect the prices and yields of bonds. Section 6 explores how changes in interest rates over time affect the market prices of bonds.

1 Using Present Value Factors to Value Known Cash Flows

In a world with a single risk-free interest rate, computing the present value of any stream of future cash flows is relatively uncomplicated. It involves applying a discounted cash flow formula using the risk-free interest rate as the discount rate.

For example, suppose you buy a fixed-income security that promises to pay $100 each year for the next three years. How much is this three-year annuity worth if you know that the appropriate discount rate is 6% per year? The answer—$267.30—can be found easily using a financial calculator, a table of present value factors, or by applying the algebraic formula for the present value of an annuity.

Recall that the formula for the present value of an ordinary annuity of PMT per period for n periods at an interest rate of i is:

$$PV_{PMT}(PMT, i, n) = PMT \frac{1 - (1 + i)^{-n}}{i}$$

On a financial calculator, we would enter the values for n, i, and PMT, and compute the PV_{PMT}:

n	i	PV	FV	PMT	Result
3	6	?	0	100	$PV = 267.30$

Now suppose that an hour after you buy the security, the risk-free interest rate rises from 6% to 7% per year, and you want to sell. How much can you get for it?

The level of market interest rates has changed, but the promised future cash flows from your security have not. In order for an investor to earn 7% per year on your security, its price has to drop. How much? The answer is that it must fall to the point at which its price equals the present value of the promised cash flows discounted at 7% per year:

n	i	PV	FV	PMT	Result
3	7	?	0	100	PV = 262.43

At a price of $262.43, a fixed-income security that promises to pay $100 each year for the next three years offers its purchaser a rate of return of 7% per year. Thus, the price of any existing fixed-income security falls when market interest rates rise because investors will only be willing to buy them if they offer a competitive yield.

Thus, a *rise* of 1% in the interest rate causes a *drop* of $4.87 in the market value of your security. Similarly, a fall in interest rates causes a rise in its market value.

This illustrates a basic principle in valuing known cash flows:

A change in market interest rates causes a change in the *opposite direction* in the market values of all existing contracts promising fixed payments in the future.

Because interest rate changes are not predictable, it follows that the prices of fixed-income securities are uncertain up to the time they mature.

Quick Check 1

What happens to the value of a three-year fixed-income security promising $100 per year if the market interest rate falls from 6% to 5% per year?

In practice, valuation of known cash flows is not as simple as we just described because in practice *you do not usually know which discount rate to use in the present value formula.* Market interest rates are not the same for all maturities. We reproduce as Figure 1 the graph showing the yield curve for U.S. Treasury bonds.

It is tempting to think that the interest rate corresponding to a three-year maturity can be applied as the correct discount rate to use in valuing the three-year annuity in our example. But that would not be correct. The correct procedure for using the information

FIGURE 1

U.S. Treasury Yield Curve

Source: http://www. bloomberg.com/markets/rates/ index.html (May 22, 2006). Reprinted with permission from Bloomberg LP, 731 Lexington Avenue, New York, NY 10022.

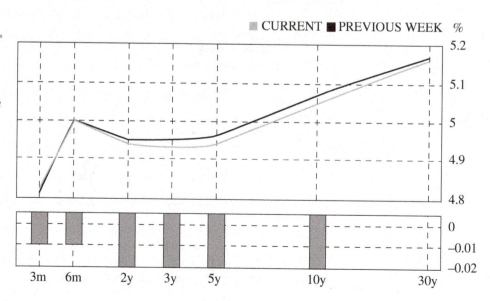

contained in the yield curve to value other streams of known cash payments is more complicated; that is the subject of the next few sections.

2 The Basic Building Blocks: Pure Discount Bonds

In valuing contracts promising a stream of known cash flows, the place to start is a listing of the market prices of **pure discount bonds** (also called *zero-coupon bonds*). These are bonds that promise a single payment of cash at some date in the future, called the maturity date.

Pure discount bonds are the basic building blocks for valuing all contracts promising streams of known cash flows. This is because we can always decompose any contract—no matter how complicated its pattern of certain future cash flows—into its component cash flows, value each one separately, and then add them up.

The promised cash payment on a pure discount bond is called its **face value** or *par value*. The interest earned by investors on pure discount bonds is the difference between the price paid for the bond and the face value received at the maturity date. Thus, for a pure discount bond with a face value of $1,000 maturing in one year and a purchase price of $950, the interest earned is the $50 difference between the $1,000 face value and the $950 purchase price.

The *yield* (interest rate) on a pure discount bond is the annualized rate of return to investors who buy it and hold it until it matures. For a pure discount bond with a one-year maturity such as the one in our example, we get

$$\text{Yield on 1-Year Pure Discount Bond} = \frac{\text{Face Value} - \text{Price}}{\text{Price}}$$

$$= \frac{\$1,000 - \$950}{\$950} = 0.0526 \text{ or } 5.26\%$$

If, however, the bond has a maturity different from one year, we would use the present value formula to find its annualized yield. Thus, suppose that we observe a two-year pure discount bond with a face value of $1,000 and a price of $880. We would compute the annualized yield on this bond as the discount rate that makes its face value equal to its price. On a financial calculator, we would enter the values for *n*, *PV*, *FV*, and compute *i*.

$$PV_{FV}(FV, i, n) = \frac{FV}{(1+i)^n}$$

n	i	PV	FV	PMT	Result
2	?	−880	1,000	0	$i = 6.60\%$

Return to the valuation of the security of section 1 that promises to pay $100 each year for the next three years. Suppose that we observe the set of pure discount bond prices in Table 1. Following standard practice, the bond prices are quoted as a fraction of their face value.

TABLE 1 Prices of Pure Discount Bonds and Yields

Maturity	Price per $1 of Face Value	Yield (per year)
1 year	0.95	5.26%
2 years	0.88	6.60%
3 years	0.80	7.72%

There are two alternative procedures that we can use to arrive at a correct value for the security. The first procedure uses the prices in the second column of Table 1, and the second procedure uses the yields in the last column. Procedure 1 multiplies each of the three promised cash payments by its corresponding per-dollar price and then adds them up:

Present Value of First Year's Cash Flow = $100 × 0.95 = $95.00

Present Value of Second Year's Cash Flow = $100 × 0.88 = $88.00

Present Value of Third Year's Cash Flow = $100 × 0.80 = $80.00

Total Present Value = $263

The resulting estimate of the security's value is $263.

Procedure 2 gets the same result by discounting each year's promised cash payment at the yield corresponding to that maturity:

Present Value of First Year's Cash Flow = $100/1.0526 = $95.00

Present Value of Second Year's Cash Flow = $100/1.0660^2 = $88.00

Present Value of Third Year's Cash Flow = $100/1.0772^3 = $80.00

Total Present Value = $263

Note, however, that it would be a mistake to discount all three cash flows using the same three-year yield of 7.72% per year listed in the last row of Table 1. If we do so, we get a value of $259, which is $4 too low:

$$PV_{PMT}(100, 7.72\%, 3) = 259.02$$

n	i	PV	FV	PMT	Result
3	7.72%	?	0	100	PV = $259

Is there a single discount rate that we can use to discount all three of the payments the way we did in Section 1 to get a value of $263 for the security? The answer is yes: That single discount rate is 6.88% per year. To verify this, substitute 6.88% for i in the formula for the present value of an annuity or in the calculator:

$$PV_{PMT}(100, 6.88\%, 3) = 263.01$$

n	i	PV	FV	PMT	Result
3	6.88%	?	0	100	PV = $263

The problem is that the 6.88% per-year discount rate appropriate for valuing the three-year annuity is not one of the rates listed anywhere in Table 1. We derived it from our knowledge that the value of the security has to be $263. In other words, we solved the present value equation to find i:

$$PV_{PMT}(100, i, 3) = \sum_{t=1}^{3} \frac{100}{(1+i)^t} = 263 \text{ implies } i = 6.88\%$$

n	i	PV	FV	PMT	Result
3	?	−263	0	100	i = 6.88%

But it was that value (i.e., $263) that we were trying to estimate in the first place. Therefore, we have no direct way to find the value of the three-year annuity using a single discount rate with the bond price information available to us in Table 1.

We can summarize the main conclusion from this section as follows: When the yield curve is not flat (i.e., when observed yields are not the same for all maturities), the correct procedure for valuing a contract or a security promising a stream of known cash payments is to discount each of the payments at the rate corresponding to a pure discount bond of its maturity and then add the resulting individual payment values.

Quick Check 2

Suppose the observed yield on two-year pure discount bonds falls to 6% per year, but the other rates reported in Table 1 remain unchanged. What is your estimate of the value of the three-year annuity paying $100 per year? What single discount rate applied to the present value formula for annuities would give this same value?

3 Coupon Bonds, Current Yield, and Yield to Maturity

A **coupon bond** obligates the issuer to make periodic payments of interest—called *coupon payments*—to the bondholder for the life of the bond, and then to pay the face value of the bond when the bond matures (i.e., when the last payment comes due). The periodic payments of interest are called *coupons* because at one time most bonds had coupons attached to them that investors would tear off and present to the bond issuer for payment.

The **coupon rate** of the bond is the interest rate applied to the face value to compute the coupon payment. Thus, a bond with a face value of $1,000 that makes annual coupon payments at a coupon rate of 10% obligates the issuer to pay $0.10 \times \$1,000 = \$100$ every year. If the bond's maturity is six years, then at the end of six years, the issuer pays the last coupon of $100 *and* the face value of $1,000.[1]

The cash flows from this coupon bond are displayed in Figure 2. We see that the stream of promised cash flows has an annuity component (a fixed per period amount) of $100 per year and a "balloon" or "bullet" payment of $1,000 at maturity.

The $100 annual coupon payment is fixed at the time the bond is issued and remains constant until the bond's maturity date. On the date the bond is issued, it usually has a price (equal to its face value) of $1,000.

The relation between prices and yields on coupon bonds is more complicated than for pure discount bonds. As we will see, when the prices of coupon bonds are different from their face value, the meaning of the term *yield* is itself ambiguous.

Coupon bonds with a market price equal to their face value are called **par bonds.** When a coupon bond's market price equals its face value, its yield is the same as its coupon rate. For example, consider a bond maturing in one year that pays an annual coupon at a rate of 10% of its $1,000 face value. This bond will pay its holder $1,100 a year from

FIGURE 2

Cash Flows for 10% $1,000 Coupon Bond

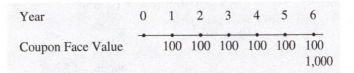

Year	0	1	2	3	4	5	6
Coupon Face Value		100	100	100	100	100	100 1,000

---

[1]In the United States, coupon payments on bonds are usually made semiannually. Thus, a bond with a coupon rate of 10% per year actually pays a coupon of $50 every six months. To keep the calculations in the chapter simple, we will ignore this fact.

now—a coupon payment of $100 and the face value of $1,000. Thus, if the current price of our 10% coupon bond is $1,000, its yield is 10%.

Bond Pricing Principle I: Par Bonds

If a bond's price equals its face value, then its yield equals its coupon rate.

Often the price of a coupon bond and its face value are not the same. This situation would occur, for instance, if the level of interest rates in the economy changes after the bond is issued. So, for example, suppose that our one-year 10% coupon bond was originally issued as a 20-year-maturity bond 19 years ago. At that time, the yield curve was flat at 10% per year. Now the bond has one year remaining before it matures, and the interest rate on one-year bonds is 5% per year.

Although the 10% coupon bond was issued at par ($1,000), its market price will now be $1,047.62. Because the bond's price is now higher than its face value, it is called a **premium bond.**

What is its yield?

There are two different yields that we can compute. The first is called the **current yield,** the annual coupon divided by the bond's price:

$$\text{Current Yield} = \frac{\text{Coupon}}{\text{Price}} = \frac{\$100}{\$1,047.62} = 9.55\%$$

The current yield overstates the true yield on the premium bond because it ignores the fact that at maturity you will receive only $1,000—$47.62 less than you paid for the bond.

To take account of the fact that a bond's face value and its price may differ, we compute a different yield called the **yield to maturity.** The yield to maturity is defined as the discount rate that makes the present value of the bond's stream of promised cash payments equal to its price.

The yield to maturity takes account of all of the cash payments you will receive from purchasing the bond, including the face value of $1,000 at maturity. In our example, because the bond is maturing in one year, it is easy to compute the yield to maturity.

$$\text{Yield to Maturity} = \frac{\text{Coupon} + \text{Face value} - \text{Price}}{\text{Price}}$$

$$\text{Yield to Maturity} = \frac{\$100 + \$1,000 - \$1,047.62}{\$1,047.62} = 5\%$$

Thus, we see that if you used the current yield of 9.55% as a guide to what you would be earning if you bought the bond, you would be seriously misled.

When the maturity of a coupon bond is greater than a year, the calculation of its yield to maturity is more complicated than just shown. For example, suppose that you are considering buying a two-year 10% coupon bond with a face value of $1,000 and a current price of $1,100. What is its yield?

Its current yield is 9.09%:

$$\text{Current Yield} = \frac{\text{Coupon}}{\text{Price}} = \frac{\$100}{\$1,100} = 9.09\%$$

But as in the case of the one-year premium bond, the current yield ignores the fact that at maturity, you will receive less than the $1,100 that you paid. The yield to maturity when bond maturity is greater than one year is the discount rate that makes the present value of the stream of cash payments equal to the bond's price:

$$PV_{Bond}(PMT, FV, YTM, n) := PV_{PMT}(PMT, YTM, n) + PV_{FV}(FV, YTM, n)$$

$$= \sum_{t=1}^{n} \frac{PMT}{(1 + YTM)^n} + \frac{FV}{(1 + YTM)^n} \qquad (1)$$

where n is the number of annual payment periods until the bond's maturity, YTM is the annual yield to maturity, PMT is the coupon payment, and FV is the face value of the bond received at maturity.

The yield to maturity on a multiperiod coupon bond can be computed easily on most financial calculators by entering the bond's maturity as n, its price as PV (with a negative sign), its face value as FV, its coupon as PMT, and computing i.

n	i	PV	FV	PMT	Result
2	?	−1,100	1,000	100	$i = 4.65\% = YTM$

YTM satisfies the equation $\$1,100 = PV_{PMT}(100, YTM, 2) + PV_{FV}(1,000, YTM, 2)$, which implies $YTM = 4.65\%$.

Thus, the yield to maturity on this two-year premium bond is considerably less than its current yield.

These examples illustrate a general principle about the relation between bond prices and yields:

Bond Pricing Principle 2: Premium Bonds

If a coupon bond has a price higher than its face value, its yield to maturity is less than its current yield, which is in turn less than its coupon rate.

For a Premium Bond:

Yield to Maturity < Current Yield < Coupon Rate

Now let us consider a bond with a 4% coupon rate maturing in two years. Suppose that its price is $950. Because the price is below the face value of the bond, we call it a *discount bond*. (Note it is not a *pure* discount bond because it does pay a coupon.)

What is its yield? As in the previous case of a premium bond, we can compute two different yields—the current yield and the yield to maturity.

$$\text{Current Yield} = \frac{\text{Coupon}}{\text{Price}} = \frac{\$40}{\$950} = 4.21\%$$

The current yield understates the true yield in the case of the discount bond because it ignores the fact that at maturity you will receive more than you paid for the bond. When the discount bond matures, you receive the $1,000 face value, not the $950 price that you paid for it.

The yield to maturity takes account of all of the cash payments you will receive from purchasing the bond, including the face value of $1,000 at maturity. Using the financial calculator to compute the bond's yield to maturity, we find:

n	i	PV	FV	PMT	Result
2	?	−950	1,000	40	$i = 6.76\% = YTM$

YTM satisfies the equation $\$950 = PV_{PMT}(40, YTM, 2) + PV_{FV}(1000, YTM, 2)$, which implies $YTM = 6.76\%$.

Thus, the yield to maturity on this discount bond is greater than its current yield.

Bond Pricing Principle 3: Discount Bonds

If a coupon bond has a price lower than its face value, its yield to maturity is greater than its current yield, which is in turn greater than its coupon rate.

For Discount Bonds:

Yield to Maturity > Current Yield > Coupon Rate

3.1 Beware of "High-Yield" U.S. Treasury Bond Funds

In the past, some investment companies that invest exclusively in U.S. Treasury bonds have advertised yields that appear much higher than the interest rates on other known investments of the same maturity. The yields that they are advertising are *current* yields, and the bonds that they are investing in are premium bonds that have relatively high coupon rates. Thus, according to Bond Pricing Principle 2, the actual return you will earn is expected to be considerably less than the advertised current yield.

Suppose that you have $10,000 to invest for one year. You are deciding between putting your money in a one-year, government-insured, bank CD offering an interest rate of 5% and investing in the shares of a U.S. Treasury bond fund that holds one-year bonds with a coupon rate of 8%. The bonds held by the fund are selling at a premium over their face value: For every $10,000 of face value that you will receive at maturity a year from now, you must pay $10,285.71 now. The current yield on the fund is $800/$10,285.71 or 7.78%, and this is the yield that the fund is advertising. If the fund charges a 1% annual fee for its services, what rate of return will you actually earn?

If there were no fees at all for investing in the fund, your rate of return for the year would be 5%, precisely the same rate of return as on the bank CD. This is because investing your $10,000 in the fund will achieve the same return as buying an 8% coupon bond with a face value of $10,000 for a price of $10,285.71:

$$\text{Rate of Return} = \frac{\text{Coupon} + \text{Face Value} - \text{Price}}{\text{Price}}$$

$$= \frac{\$800 + \$10,000 - \$10,285.71}{\$10,285.71} = 5\%$$

Because you have to pay the fund a fee equal to 1% of your $10,000, your rate of return will be only 4% rather than the 5% you can earn on the bank CD.

> **Quick Check 3**
>
> What are the current yield and yield to maturity on a three-year bond with a coupon rate of 6% per year and a price of $900?

4 Reading Bond Listings

The prices of bonds are published in a variety of places. For investors and analysts who need the most up-to-the-minute price data, the best sources are on-line information services

TABLE 2   Listing of Prices of U.S. Treasury Strips

Maturity	Type	Bid	Asked	Change	Ask Yld.
Aug 08	bp	89:25	89:26	1	4.87
Aug 12	np	73:22	73:22	3	4.96
Aug 16	ci	59:08	59:08	4	5.18

Notes: U.S. Treasury strips as of 3 P.M. Eastern time, also based on transactions of $1 million or more. Net changes in 32nds. Yields calculated on the asked quotation.
Source: Bear, Stearns & Co. via Street Software Technology Inc.

that feed the information electronically to computer terminals. For those who do not need data that are quite so up-to-date, the daily financial press provides bond listings.

Table 2 is a partial listing of the prices of U.S. Treasury strips on May 22, 2006, taken from the *Wall Street Journal.* U.S. Treasury strips are pure discount bonds that are created from U.S. Treasury coupon bonds by firms that buy the coupon bonds and then resell each of the coupon payments and the repayment of the principal as separate securities. (This activity is called stripping the coupon bonds.)

To interpret the prices, we must understand several conventions:

1. *Type* in the second column tells the original source of the strip: *ci* is coupon interest, *bp* is principal from a Treasury bond, and *np* is principal from a Treasury note. Bonds have original maturities of more than 10 years; notes have original maturities of 10 years or less.
2. The ask price is the price at which dealers in Treasury bonds are willing to sell, and the bid price is the price at which they are willing to buy. Therefore, the asked price always exceeds the bid price. The difference is, in effect, the dealer's commission. *Ask Yld.* in the last column is the yield to maturity computed using the asked price. It assumes semiannual compounding.
3. The price quotations are cents per $1 of face value.
4. The numbers after the colon mean 32nds and not 100ths of a cent. Thus, 97:11 means 97 and (or $0.9734375) not $0.9711.

   Table 2 shows that the ask price for a Treasury strip maturing in August 2008 was 89 and 26/32 (89.8125) cents per dollar of face value and for one maturing in August 2012, 73 and 22/32 (or 73.6875 cents per dollar of face value).

Table 3 is a partial listing of the prices of U.S. Treasury Bonds taken from Bloomberg.com on May 22, 2006. It differs from the previous listing in that it displays information on bills, bonds, and notes. For example, in the notes and bonds section each bond's coupon rate is given in the second column. Here the yields are based on asked quotations.

5 Why Yields for the Same Maturity May Differ

Often we observe that two U.S. Treasury bonds with the same maturity have different yields to maturity. Is this a violation of the Law of One Price? The answer is no. In fact, for bonds with different coupon rates, the Law of One Price implies that, unless the yield curve is flat, bonds of the same maturity *will* have different yields to maturity.

TABLE 3   Listing of Prices of U.S. Treasury Bills and Bonds

U.S. TREASURIES (May 22, 2006)

Bills

	Maturity Date	Discount/Yield	Discount/Yield Change
3-Month	08/17/2006	4.68/4.80	0.02/−.016
6-Month	11/16/2006	4.80/4.98	0.02/−.011

Notes/Bonds

	Coupon	Maturity Date	Current Price/Yield	Price/Yield Change
2-Year	4.875	04/30/2008	99-28/4.94	0-01+/−.021
3-Year	4.875	05/15/2009	99-26+/4.94	0-01¾/−.020
5-Year	4.875	04/30/2011	99-22¾/4.94	0-03+/−.023
10-Year	5.125	05/15/2016	100-20+/5.04	0-04+/−.018
30-Year	4.500	02/15/2036	90-12½/5.13	0-01¾/−.004

Source: http://www.bloomberg.com/markets/rates/index.html. Reprinted with permission from Bloomberg LP, 731 Lexington Avenue, New York, NY 10022.

5.1 The Effect of the Coupon Rate

For example, consider two different two-year coupon bonds—one with a coupon rate of 5% and the other with a coupon rate of 10%. Suppose the current market prices and yields of one- and two-year pure discount bonds are as follows:

Maturity	Price per $1 of Face Value	Yield (per year)
1 year	$0.961538	4%
2 years	$0.889996	6%

According to the Law of One Price, the first-year cash flows from each coupon bond must have a per-dollar price of $0.961538, and the second-year cash flows must have a per-dollar price of $0.889996. Therefore, the market prices of the two different coupon bonds should be:

For the 5% coupon bond:

$$0.961538 \times \$50 + 0.889996 \times \$1,050 = \$982.57$$

For the 10% coupon bond:

$$0.961538 \times \$100 + 0.889996 \times \$1,100 = \$1,075.15$$

Now let us compute the yields to maturity on each of the coupon bonds that correspond to these market prices. Using the financial calculator we find:

For the 5% coupon bond:

YTM satisfies the equation $\$982.57 = PV_{PMT}(50, YTM, 2) + PV_{FV}(1000, YTM, 2)$, which implies $YTM = 5.95\%$.

n	i	PV	FV	PMT	Result
2	?	−982.57	1,000	50	$i = 5.95\% = YTM$

For the 10% coupon bond:
YTM satisfies the equation $\$1,075.15 = PV_{PMT}(100, YTM, 2) + PV_{FV}(1,000, YTM, 2)$, which implies $YTM = 5.91\%$.

n	i	PV	FV	PMT	Result
2	?	−1,075.15	1,000	100	$i = 5.91\% = YTM$

Thus, we see that in order to obey the Law of One Price, the two bonds must have different yields to maturity. As a general principle:

When the yield curve is not flat, bonds of the same maturity with different coupon rates have different yields to maturity.

Quick Check 4

Using the same prices for pure discount bonds as in the previous example, what would be the price and yield to maturity on a two-year coupon bond with a coupon rate of 4% per year?

5.2 The Effect of Default Risk and Taxes

At times, one will encounter examples of bonds with the same coupon rate and maturity selling at different prices. These differences occur because of the other ways *seemingly* identical securities differ.

Bonds offering the same future stream of promised payments can differ in a number of ways, but the two most important are default risk and taxability. To illustrate, consider a bond promising to pay $1,000 a year from now. Suppose that the one-year U.S. Treasury rate is 6% per year. If the bond is completely free of default risk, its price would, therefore, be $1,000/1.06 = $943.40. But if it is subject to some default risk (i.e., that what is promised may not be paid), no matter how slight, its price will be less than $943.40, and its yield will be higher than 6% per year.

The taxability of bonds can vary according to the issuer or type of bond, and this fact will certainly influence their price. For example, interest earned on bonds issued by state and local governments in the United States is exempt from federal income taxes. Other things equal, this feature makes them more attractive to tax-paying investors and will cause their prices to be higher (and their yields lower) than otherwise comparable bonds.

5.3 Other Effects on Bond Yields

There are many other features that may differentiate seemingly identical fixed-income securities and, therefore, cause their prices to differ. Check your intuition about the effect of the following two bond features. In each case consider whether the inclusion of the feature should increase or decrease the price of an otherwise identical bond (i.e., one which offers the same stream of promised cash flows) that does not have the feature:

1. *Callability.* This feature gives the issuer of the bond the right to redeem it before the final maturity date. A bond that has this feature is a **callable bond.**
2. *Convertibility.* This feature gives the holder of a bond issued by a corporation the right to convert the bond into a prespecified number of shares of common stock. A bond that has this feature is a **convertible bond.**

Your intuition should tell you that any feature that makes the bond more attractive to the issuer will lower its price, and any feature that makes it more attractive to the bond-holders will raise its price. Thus, callability will cause a bond to have a lower price (and a higher yield to maturity). On the other hand, convertibility will cause a bond to have a higher price and a lower yield to maturity.

6 The Behavior of Bond Prices over Time

In this section we examine how bond prices change over time as a result of the passage of time and changes in interest rates.

6.1 The Effect of the Passage of Time

If the yield curve were flat and interest rates did not change, any default-free discount bond's price would rise with the passage of time, and any premium bond's price would fall. This is because eventually bonds mature, and their price must equal their face value at maturity. We should, therefore, expect the prices of discount bonds and premium bonds to move toward their face value as they approach maturity. This implied price pattern is illustrated for the case of 20-year pure discount bonds in Figure 3.

Let us illustrate the calculation assuming the face value of the bond is $1,000 and the yield remains constant at 6% per year. Initially the bond has a maturity of 20 years and its price is given by PV_{FV} ($1,000, 6\%, 20$) = $311.80.

n	$i = YTM$	PV	FV	PMT	Result
20	6%	?	1,000	0	$PV = \$311.80$

Movement of a Pure Discount Bond's Price over Time

Note: In the absence of changes in interest rates and with a flat term structure, the price of a zero-coupon bond might be expected to rise over time at a rate equal to its yield to maturity. In the figure, we assume a face value of $1,000 and a yield of 6% per year.

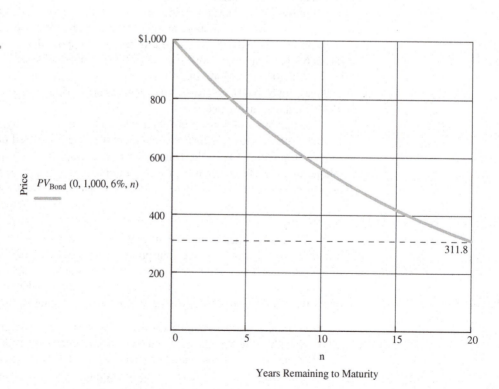

Years Remaining to Maturity

TABLE 4 Price of Zero-Coupon Bond

Years Remaining to Maturity	Price of Zero-Coupon Bond
$n =$	$PV_{\text{Bond}}(0, 1{,}000, 6\%, n) =$
0	$1,000.00
1	943.40
2	890.00
3	839.62
4	792.09
5	747.26
6	704.96
7	665.06
8	627.41
9	591.90
10	558.39
11	526.79
12	496.97
13	468.84
14	442.30
15	417.27
16	393.65
17	371.36
18	350.34
19	330.51
20	311.80

After one year goes by, the bond has a remaining maturity of 19 years and its price is:

n	$i = YTM$	PV	FV	PMT	Result
19	6%	?	1,000	0	$PV = \$330.51$

The proportional change in price is, therefore, exactly equal to the 6% per year yield on the bond:

$$\text{Proportional Change in Price} = \frac{\$330.51 - \$311.80}{\$311.80} = 6\%$$

Quick Check 5

What will the pure discount bond's price be after two years, assuming the yield stays at 6% per year? Verify that the proportional change in price during the second year is 6%.

6.2 Interest-Rate Risk

Normally, we think of buying U.S. Treasury bonds as a conservative investment policy because there is no risk of default involved. However, an economic environment of changing interest rates can produce big gains or losses for investors in long-term bonds.

Figure 4A illustrates how long-term bond prices change with interest rates. It shows the alternative prices of 30-year pure discount bonds and 30-year and 10-year 8% coupon bonds if the level of interest rates ranged from 2% to 12%. For example, at a yield to maturity of 8%, the 30-year 8% coupon bond would be priced at the par value of $1,000, while at a yield to maturity of 6%, the same 8% coupon bond would sell for a premium at $1,275.30, and at a yield to maturity of 10%, the bond would become a discount bond and sell for $811.46. The 30-year zero-coupon bond will be a deep discount bond selling far below its $1,000 face value. If priced to yield 6% it would sell for $174.11, if priced to yield 8% it would sell for $99.38, and if priced to yield 10% it would sell for only $57.31.

Figure 4B considers the price sensitivity of the bonds to changes in the yield to maturity. Along the ordinate we measure the ratio of the bond's price computed using the indicated yield to maturity to its price computed at a reference discount rate, in this case of 8%.

For example, at the 8% yield, the price of a 30-year 8% coupon bond with a face value of $1,000 would be $1,000, whereas at a yield of 10% per year its price is $811.46. The ratio of its price at a 10% interest rate to its price at an 8% interest rate is, therefore, 0.8115. We can, therefore, say that if the level of interest rates were to rise from 8% to 10%, an increase of 25%, the price of the par bond would fall by 18.85%. The ratio of these percentage changes gives us an elasticity, $\eta = \dfrac{\%\Delta\text{Price}}{\%\Delta\text{YTM}}$, which measures the sensitivity of the bond price to a change in the yield to maturity. In this example, for a 30-year 8% coupon bond priced at par a 25% increase in the interest rate, from the 8% yield to a 10% yield, would decrease the bond's price by 18.85%. The ratio of the percentage change in the bond's price to the percentage change in the bond's yield would be approximately −0.75, an inelastic response.

FIGURE 4A

Bond Prices at Alternative Yields

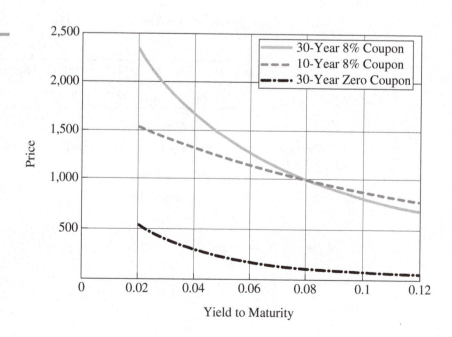

FIGURE 4B

Bond Price Sensitivity to Yield Changes

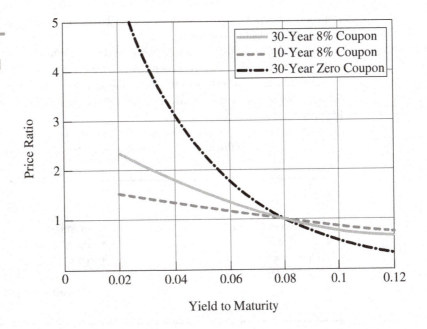

On the other hand, the price sensitivity of a 30-year pure discount bond is greater than for the 8% coupon bond. If the yield to maturity increased by 25%, from 8% to 10%, the bond's price would fall from $99.38 to $57.31, a 42.33% drop in the price. The corresponding elasticity would be -1.69, a much more elastic response for the 30-year zero-coupon bond versus the 30-year 8% coupon bond.

Note in Figure 4B that the curve corresponding to the pure discount bond is steeper than the bond's curve. This greater steepness reflects its greater interest-rate sensitivity.

Holding the coupon rate constant we can also investigate how the maturity of the bonds affect price sensitivity by comparing the 10-year and 30-year 8% coupon bonds. With a movement from 8% to 10%, both bonds would fall from the $1,000 par price to prices of $877.11 and $811.46 respectively for the 10-year and 30-year bonds. Holding the coupon rate constant the price of the longer bond changes more. This translates in Figure 4B to a steeper price-ratio curve for the longer-term bond. In fact the elasticity coefficient for the 10-year bond would be only -0.49 versus -0.75 for the 30-year bond.

Quick Check 6

Suppose you buy a 30-year pure discount bond with a face value of $1,000 and a yield of 6% per year. A day later market interest rates rise to 7% and so does the yield on your bond. What is the proportional change in the price of your bond? What is the elasticity of the bond price to the change in the yield?

Summary

A change in market interest rates causes a change in the opposite direction in the market values of all existing contracts promising fixed payments in the future.

The market prices of $1 to be received at every possible date in the future are the basic building blocks for valuing all other streams of known cash flows. These prices are inferred from the observed market prices of traded bonds and then applied to other streams of known cash flows to value them.

An equivalent valuation can be carried out by applying a discounted cash flow formula with a different discount rate for each future time period.

Differences in the prices of fixed-income securities of a given maturity arise from differences in coupon rates, default risk, tax treatment, callability, convertibility, and other features.

Over time the prices of bonds converge toward their face value. Before maturity, however, bond prices can fluctuate a great deal as a result of changes in market interest rates.

Key Terms

- pure discount bonds
- face value
- coupon bond
- coupon rate
- par bonds

- premium bond
- current yield
- yield to maturity
- callable bond
- convertible bond

Internet Reference Materials

Bloomberg.com: Market Data—Rates & Bonds http://www.bloomberg.com/markets/rates/
Financial Times: Market Data—Bonds & Rates http://markets.ft.com/ft/markets/
    researchArchive.asp?cat=BR

Answers to Quick Check Questions

Quick Check 1   What happens to the value of the three-year fixed-income security promising $100 per year if the market interest rate falls from 6% to 5% per year?

Answer: If the interest rate falls to 5% per year, the value of the fixed-income security rises to $272.32.

Quick Check 2   Suppose the observed yield on two-year pure discount bonds falls to 6% per year, but the other rates reported in Table 1 remain unchanged. What is your estimate of the value of the three-year annuity paying $100 per year? What single discount rate applied to the present value formula for annuities would give this same value?

Answer: The value of the three-year annuity would be:
Present Value of First Year's Cash Flow = $100/1.0526 = $95.00
Present Value of Second Year's Cash Flow = $100/1.06^2 = $89.00
Present Value of Third Year's Cash Flow = $100/1.0772^3 = $80.00
Total Present Value = $264

So the value of the annuity increases by $1.
To find the single discount rate that makes the present value of the three promised payments equal to $264, we solve:

n	i	PV	FV	PMT	Result
3	?	−264	0	100	$i = 6.6745\% = YTM$

Quick Check 3   What are the current yield and yield to maturity on a three-year bond with a coupon rate of 6% per year and a price of $900?

Answer: The current yield is $\dfrac{60}{900} = 0.0667 = 6.67\%$

We find the yield-to-maturity as follows:

n	i	PV	FV	PMT	Result
3	?	−900	1,000	60	$i = 10.02\% = YTM$

Quick Check 4   Using the same prices for pure discount bonds as in the previous example, what would be the price and yield to maturity on a two-year coupon bond with a coupon rate of 4% per year?

Answer: For the 4% coupon bond the price would be:

$$0.961538 \times \$40 + 0.889996 \times \$1,040 = \$964.05736$$

and the yield to maturity:

n	i	PV	FV	PMT	Result
2	?	−964.057	1,000	40	$i = 5.9593\% = YTM$

Quick Check 5   What will the pure discount bond's price be after two years, assuming the yield stays at 6% per year? Verify that the proportional change in price during the second year is 6%.

Answer: After two years the bond has a remaining maturity of 18 years and its price is:

n	i = YTM	PV	FV	PMT	Result
18	6%	?	1,000	0	$PV = \$350.34$

The proportional change in price is, therefore, exactly equal to the 6% per year yield on the bond:

$$\text{Proportional Change in Price} = \frac{\$330.51 - \$311.80}{\$311.80} = 6\%$$

Quick Check 6   Suppose you buy a 30-year pure discount bond with a face value of $1,000 and a yield of 6% per year. A day later market interest rates rise to 7% and so does the yield on your bond. What is the proportional change in the price of your bond?

Answer: The 30-year pure discount bond's initial price is:

n	i = YTM	PV	FV	PMT	Result
30	6%	?	1,000	0	$PV = \$174.11$

A day later its price is:

n	i = YTM	PV	FV	PMT	Result
30	7%	?	1,000	0	$PV = \$131.37$

The proportional decline in price is 24.55%.

The elasticity is $\eta = \dfrac{\%\Delta \text{Price}}{\%\Delta \text{YTM}} = \dfrac{-24.55\%}{16.67\%} = -1.47$.

Questions and Problems

Using Present Value Formulas to Value Known Cash Flows

1. Suppose you purchase a Treasury bill that matures in three months. The bill is a pure discount instrument paying its face value of $100,000 at maturity. If the bill is priced to yield 1% over the three months, or an *APR* of 4% with quarterly compounding, what is its current selling price? Convert the bill's yield into an effective annual rate.

2. Suppose you decide to sell the Treasury bill from the previous problem one month after you purchased it. At the time of the sale suppose the bill is priced to yield 3/4 of 1% over the remaining 2 months. What was your rate of return on the one-month investment quoted as an effective annual rate?

3. Suppose you observe the following prices for zero-coupon bonds (pure discount bonds) that have no risk of default:

Maturity	Price per $1 of Face Value	Yield to Maturity
1 year	0.97	3.093%
2 years	0.90	

   a. What should be the price of a 2-year coupon bond that pays a 6% coupon rate, assuming coupon payments are made once a year starting one year from now?
   b. Find the missing entry in the table.
   c. What should be the yield to maturity of the 2-year coupon bond in Part a?
   d. Why are your answers to parts b and c of this question different?

The Basic Building Blocks: Pure Discount Bonds

4. Suppose you can purchase for a price of $99,128.817 a Treasury bill which matures with a face value of $100,000 in three months, or a quarter of a year. As a pure discount instrument calculate the yield on the bill quoted as an *APR* with continuous compounding. Recall the relationship between a present and future value with continuous compounding is: $FV = PV \cdot e^{rt}$, where r is the *APR*, t is the number of years, and e is the base of the natural logarithms, 2.71828.

5. Consider a pure discount bond with 10 years remaining to maturity selling for $61.39133 per $100 of face value. If the bond's yield remains constant over the next three years what price will the bond be selling for with 9, 8, and 7 years remaining to maturity? How high would the yield have to rise in order that, with 6 years remaining to maturity, the bond's price would be the same as two years' prior, when it had 8 years remaining to maturity?

6. Comment on the following statement: Ruling out negative interest rates, an upward-sloping term structure for zero-coupon Treasury notes and bonds implies the relationship between prices and time remaining to maturity is inverse for such pure discount instruments.

7. Assume a fifty-year zero-coupon bond with $1,000 face value is priced to yield 10%. If the yield were to instantly drop to 5% what would be the new price for the bond? How does the change in yield compare in a relative manner to the change in the price?

Coupon Bonds, Current Yield, and Yield to Maturity

8. What is the current yield on a five-year 5% coupon bond priced to yield 7%? Assume annual compounding.

9. State the relationships among the current yield, the coupon rate, and the yield to maturity based on the bond's price relative to its par, or face value.

10. A coupon bond's price can be broken down into two components. The bond's price is the sum of the present value of the coupon interest payments and the present value of the repayment of the face value. Under a flatterm structure that remains constant over time, how do these two components change?

11. Suppose you want to know the price of a 10-year 7% coupon Treasury bond that pays interest annually.
    a. You have been told that the yield to maturity is 8%. What is the price (per $100 of face value)?
    b. What is the price if coupons are paid semiannually, and the yield to maturity is 8% per year?
    c. Now you have been told that the yield to maturity is 7% per year. What is the price? Could you have guessed the answer without calculating it? What if coupons are paid semiannually?

12. Assume a year ago the U.S. Treasury yield curve was flat at a rate of 4% per year (with annual compounding) and you bought a 30-year U.S. Treasury bond. Today it is flat at a rate of 5% per year (with annual compounding). What rate of return did you earn on your initial investment:
    a. If the bond was a 4% coupon bond?
    b. If the bond was a zero-coupon bond?

13. *Challenge Problem:* Repeat the previous problem with semiannual compounding. Now the yields and rates of return will be given as APRs with semiannual compounding. The initial flat term structure was at 4% per year with annual compounding. What rate per year with semiannual compounding produces the same effective annual rate? Make a similar adjustment for the current rate.

14. Assume that all of the bonds listed in the following table are the same except for their pattern of promised cash flows over time. Prices are quoted per $1 of face value. Use the information in the table and the Law of One Price to infer the values of the missing entries. Assume that coupon payments are annual.

Coupon Rate	Maturity	Price	Yield to Maturity
6%	2 years		5.5%
0	2 years		
7%	2 years		
0	1 year	$0.95	

Reading Bond Listings

15. Based on the following listing for 5-year Treasury note calculate the yield to maturity (with semiannual compounding) if you purchase the T-note.

Rate	Bid	Asked
6	99:15	99:17

16. You would like to create a 2-year synthetic zero-coupon bond. Assume you are aware of the following information: 1-year zero-coupon bonds are trading for $0.93 per dollar of face value and 2-year 7% coupon bonds (annual payments) are selling at $985.30 (face value = $1,000).
    a. What are the two cash flows from the 2-year coupon bond?
    b. Assume you can purchase the 2-year coupon bond and unbundle the two cash flows and sell them.
       i. How much will you receive from the sale of the first payment?
       ii. How much do you need to receive from the sale of the 2-year Treasury strip to break even?

Why Yields for the Same Maturity May Differ

17. Suppose you have the following information from the market for zero-coupon bonds.

Maturity	Price per $100 Face Value	Yield (APR with Semiannual Compounding)
1 year	$95.18144	5.0%
2 years	$95.62377	4.5%

What would be the price of a 2-year 5% coupon bond paying interest semiannually? What would be its yield to maturity?

18. Referring to the previous problem, what would be the price of a 2-year 4.5% coupon bond paying interest semiannually? What would be its yield to maturity? Why is this bond a discount bond?

19. What effect would adding the following features have on the market price of a similar bond which does not have this feature?
    a. 10-year bond is *callable* by the company after 5 years (compare to a 10-year *noncallable* bond);
    b. bond is *convertible* into 10 shares of common stock at any time (compare to a *nonconvertible* bond);
    c. 10-year bond can be "put back" to the company after 3 years at par (*puttable* bond) (compare to a 10-year *nonputtable* bond);
    d. 25-year bond has tax-exempt coupon payments.

20. *Challenge Problem:* Suppose that the yield curve on dollar bonds that are free of the risk of default is flat at 6% per year. A 2-year 10% coupon bond (with annual coupons and $1,000 face value) issued by Dafolto Corporation is rated B, and it is currently trading at a market price of $918. Aside from its risk of default, the Dafolto bond has no other financially significant features. How much should an investor be willing to pay for a guarantee against Dafolto's defaulting on this bond?

21. *Challenge Problem:* Suppose that the yield curve on bonds that are free of the risk of default is flat at 5% per year. A 20-year default-free coupon bond (with annual coupons and $1,000 face value) that becomes callable after 10 years is trading at par and has a coupon rate of 5.5%.
    a. What is the implied value of the call provision?

VALUATION OF KNOWN CASH FLOWS: BONDS

b. A Safeco Corporation bond that is otherwise identical to the callable 5.5% coupon bond described above, is also convertible into 10 shares of Safeco stock at any time up to the bond's maturity. If its yield to maturity is currently 3.5% per year, what is the implied value of the conversion feature?

The Behavior of Bond Prices over Time

22. All else being equal, if interest rates rise along the entire yield curve, you should expect that:
  i. Bond prices will fall.
  ii. Bond prices will rise.
  iii. Prices on long-term bonds will fall more than prices on short-term bonds.
  iv. Prices on long-term bonds will rise more than prices on short-term bonds.

  a. ii and iv are correct.
  b. We can't be certain that prices will change.
  c. Only i is correct.
  d. Only ii is correct.
  e. i and iii are correct.
  Explain your answer!

23. Consider two 10-year bonds; one with a 5% coupon rate and the other with a 10% coupon rate, both paying semiannual interest. Assuming the term structure remains flat, price these bonds at three alternative yields: 5, 10, and 15% (*APRs* compounded semiannually). Draw a diagram showing how the prices vary with the YTM.

24. Now consider two 10% coupon bonds; one with 5 years to maturity and the other with 10 years to maturity, both paying semiannual interest. Assuming the term structure remains flat, price these bonds at three alternative yields: 5, 10, and 15% (*APRs* compounded semiannually). Draw a diagram showing how the prices vary with the YTM. If the yield is currently 10% for both bonds, which bond's price will be more sensitive to a given change in the yield?

25. *Challenge Problem:* The price of a coupon bond has two parts: the present value of the coupon interest stream and the present value of the face value repayment. Consider a 5-year, 8% coupon bond paying semiannual interest. What would be the pattern of the bond's price and the breakdown into the two component parts over time if the term structure is flat at 10% (*APR* with semiannual compounding) and remains so over the next five years? Make these calculations for the bond today and each subsequent year until it matures. Draw a diagram showing the bond prices and components as a function of years *remaining to maturity.*

Suggested Readings

Bodie, Z., A. Kane, and A. Marcus. *Investments.* 7th Ed. Boston: Irwin/McGraw-Hill, 2008.
Fabozzi, F. J., and T. D. Fabozzi, eds. *The Handbook of Fixed Income Securities.* 4th Ed. Burr Ridge, Ill.: Irwin, 1995.

Valuation of Common Stocks

From Chapter 9 of *Financial Economics*, 2/e. Zvi Bodie, Robert C. Merton, David L. Cleeton.

Valuation of Common Stocks

O B J E C T I V E S

- To explain the theory and application of the discounted cash flow valuation method as applied to the equity of a firm.
- To explain how a firm's dividend policy can affect shareholder wealth.

C O N T E N T S

The Law of One Price can be used to deduce the value of known cash flows from the observed market prices of bonds. In this chapter we consider the valuation of uncertain cash flows using a *discounted cash flow* (*DCF*) approach. The method is applied to the valuation of common stock.

1 Reading Stock Listings

Table 1 shows the Bloomberg.com listing for IBM stock, which is traded on the New York Stock Exchange. The quote was obtained by entering the stock symbol, IBM, into the "Enter Symbol" box on the main page of the Bloomberg.com Web site.

The quote provided the current price along with the change, and percentage change in the price since the close of the market on the previous day. In addition the price at the opening of the day's trading and the volume of shares traded are given. Along with the day's high and low prices, the past year's high and low prices are also presented. The **dividend yield** is defined as the annualized dollar dividend divided by the stock's price, expressed as a percentage. The **price/earnings ratio** is the ratio of the stock price to the annualized earnings per share. In the detailed quote for IBM, information on actual and forecasted dividends and earnings per share are used to give both backward- and forward-looking calculations for the dividend yield and price-earnings ratio.

2 The Discounted Dividend Model

The *DCF* approach to determining the value of a stock discounts the expected cash flows—either dividends paid to shareholders or net cash flows from operations of the firm. A **discounted-dividend model** (*DDM*) is defined as any model that computes the value of a share of stock as the present value of its expected future cash dividends.

Any *DDM* starts from the observation that an investor in common stock expects a return consisting of cash dividends and the change in price. For example, assume a one-year holding period, and suppose that ABC stock has an expected dividend per share, D_1, of \$5, and the expected *ex-dividend* price at the end of the year, P_1 is \$110.[1]

The **risk-adjusted discount rate** or **market capitalization rate** is the expected rate of return that investors require in order to be willing to invest in the stock. In this chapter

TABLE 1 New York Stock Exchange Listing

IBM: US International Business Machines Corp More on IBM:US

06/02 13:16 New York Currency: USD Industry Computers

Price	Change	% Change	Bid	Ask	Open	Volume
79.360	−1.330	−1.648	N.A.	N.A.	80.500	4,499,600

High	Low	52-Week High (11/29/05)	52-Week Low (06/28/05)	1-Year Return
80.560	79.150	89.94	73.45	3.682%

Source: Bloomberg.com, http://www.bloomberg.com/apps/quote?ticker=IBM:US. Reprinted with permission from Bloomberg LP, 731 Lexington Avenue, New York, NY 10022.

---

[1] The *ex-dividend* price is the price of the stock without the right to receive a recently declared dividend.

we take it as given and denote it by k. In the current example, suppose that it is 15% per year.

The rate of return that investors *expect*, $E(r_1)$, is D_1 plus the expected price appreciation, $P_1 - P_0$, all divided by the current price P_0. Setting this expected rate of return equal to the 15% required rate of return, we get

$$E(r_1) = \frac{D_1 + P_1 - P_0}{P_0} = k$$

$$0.15 = \frac{5 + 110 - P_0}{P_0} \tag{1}$$

Equation 1 embodies the most important feature of the *DDM:* that the expected rate of return during *any* period equals the market capitalization rate, k. From this equation, we can derive the formula for the current stock price in terms of the expected end-of-year price:

$$P_0 = \frac{D_1 + P_1}{1 + k} \tag{2}$$

In other words, the price is the present value of the expected end-of-year dividend plus the expected ex-dividend price discounted at the required rate of return. In the case of ABC, we find:

$$P_0 = \frac{\$5 + \$110}{1.15} = \$100$$

The model to this point relies on an estimate of the end-of-year price, P_1. But how can investors forecast this price? Using the same logic employed to derive P_0, the expected price of ABC stock at the beginning of the second year is:

$$P_1 = \frac{D_2 + P_2}{1 + k} \tag{3}$$

By substitution, we can express P_0 in terms of D_1, D_2, and P_2:

$$P_0 = \frac{D_1 + P_1}{1 + k} = \frac{D_1 + \dfrac{D_2 + P_2}{(1 + k)}}{1 + k}$$

$$P_0 = \frac{D_1}{1 + k} + \frac{D_2 + P_2}{(1 + k)^2} \tag{4}$$

By repeating this chain of substitutions, we get the general formula of the *DDM:*

$$P_0 = \frac{D_1}{(1 + k)} + \frac{D_2}{(1 + k)^2} + \cdots = \sum_{t=1}^{\infty} \frac{D_t}{(1 + k)^t} \tag{5}$$

In other words, the price of a share of stock is the present value of all expected future dividends per share, discounted at the market capitalization rate.

Note that despite what seems like its exclusive focus on dividends, the discounted dividend model is not in conflict with the notion that investors look at both dividends and expected future prices when they evaluate a stock. On the contrary, we have just seen that the *DDM* is derived from that assumption.

2.1 The Constant-Growth-Rate, Discounted Dividend Model

Because in the general form expressed by equation 5 the *DDM* requires forecasts of an *infinite* number of future dividends, it is not very practical. But by making some simplifying assumptions about future dividends, the *DDM* can be made into a practical tool.

A simplified assumption would be that dividends will grow at a constant rate, *g*. For example, suppose that Steadygrowth Corporation's dividends per share are expected to grow at a constant rate of 10% per year.

The expected stream of future dividends is:

D_1	D_2	D_3	etc.
$5	$5.50	$6.05	etc.

Substituting the dividend growth forecasts, $D_t = D_1(1 + g)^{t-1}$, into equation 5 and simplifying, we find that the present value of a perpetual stream of dividends growing at a constant rate, *g*, is

$$P_0 = \frac{D_1}{k - g} \tag{5}$$

With Steadygrowth's data, this formula implies that the price of the stock is:

$$P_0 = \frac{5}{0.15 - 0.10} = \frac{5}{0.05} = \$100$$

Let us explore some implications of the constant-growth-rate *DDM*. First, note that if the expected growth rate is zero, then the valuation formula reduces to the formula for the present value of a level perpetuity: $P_0 = D_1/k$.

Holding constant D_1 and *k*, the higher the value of *g*, the higher the price of the stock. But as *g* approaches *k* in value, the model starts to "explode," that is, the price of the stock tends to infinity. Thus, the model is valid only if the expected growth rate of dividends is less than the market capitalization rate, *k*. In section 3 we consider how analysts adjust the discounted-dividend valuation model to deal with firms that have growth rates that are greater than *k*.

Note that another implication of the constant growth rate *DDM* is that the stock price is expected to grow at the same rate as dividends. For example, consider Table 2, which shows the expected dividends and expected future prices for Steadygrowth over the next three years.

To see why this is so, let us write down the formula for next year's price:

$$P_1 = \frac{D_2 + P}{1 + k}$$

TABLE 2   Steadygrowth's Future Dividends and Price

Year	Price at Beginning of Year	Expected Dividend	Expected Dividend Yield	Expected Rate of Price Increase
1	$100	$5.00	5%	10%
2	$110	$5.50	5%	10%
3	$121	$6.05	5%	10%

Because $D_2 = D_1(1 + g)$, we get by substitution:

$$P_1 = \frac{D_1(1 + g)}{k - g} = P_0(1 + g)$$

and the expected proportional change in price is:

$$\frac{P_1 - P_0}{P_0} = \frac{P_0(1 + g) - P_0}{P_0} = g$$

Therefore, *the DDM implies that in the case of constant growth of dividends, the rate of price appreciation in any year will equal the constant growth rate, g.* In the case of Steadygrowth, the expected rate of return of 15% per year, therefore, consists of an expected dividend yield of 5% per year and a rate of price appreciation of 10% per year.

In the Constant-Growth Dividend Discount Model the stream of earnings, dividends, and stock prices all grow at exactly the same constant growth rate, g.

Quick Check 1

XYZ stock is expected to pay a dividend of $2 per share a year from now, and its dividends are expected to grow by 6% per year thereafter. If its price is now $20 per share, what must be the market capitalization rate?

3 Earnings and Investment Opportunities

A second approach to *DCF* valuation focuses on future earnings and investment opportunities. Focusing on earnings and investment opportunities rather than dividends helps to concentrate the analyst's attention on the core business determinants of value. A firm's dividend policy is not such a core determinant. To see this, consider an investor planning to take over the firm. Takeover investors are not concerned with the pattern of future dividends because they can choose any pattern they wish.

Assuming that no new shares of stock are issued, the relation between earnings and dividends in any period is:[2]

$$\text{Dividends}_t = \text{Earnings}_t - \text{Net New Investment}_t$$

Therefore, we get as a formula for the value of the stock:

$$P_0 = \sum_{t=1}^{\infty} \frac{D_t}{(1 + k)^t} = \sum_{t=1}^{\infty} \frac{E_t}{(1 + k)^t} - \sum_{t=1}^{\infty} \frac{I_t}{(1 + k)^t}$$

where E_t is earnings in year t and I_t is net investment in year t.

An important point to recognize from this equation is that the value of a firm is not equal to the present value of its expected future earnings. Instead, the firm's value equals the present value of expected future earnings *less* the present value of the earnings reinvested in the firm. Note that computing the value of the firm as the present value of expected future earnings may either overstate or understate the correct market value because net new investment can be either negative or positive.

---

[2]The issuance of new shares complicates the analysis but does not change the basic result.

In a *declining* industry, one might expect to find that gross investment may not be as large as required for full replacement of current capital: Net investment is negative and, hence, capacity would decline over time. In a *stable* or stagnant industry, gross investment typically just matches replacement requirements: Net investment is zero, and capacity remains about constant over time. In an *expanding* industry, gross investment would probably exceed replacement requirements, net investment is positive, and capacity increases over time.

A useful way to estimate a firm's value based on earnings and investment opportunities is to partition the firm's value into two parts: (1) the present value of the current level of earnings projected into the future as a perpetuity, and (2) the net present value of any future investment opportunities (i.e., new earnings generated less the new investments necessary to generate them). We can express this as:

$$P_0 = \frac{E_1}{k} + NPV \text{ of Future Investments}$$

For example, consider a firm called Nogrowth Corporation, whose earnings per share are $15. The firm invests an amount each year that is just sufficient to replace the production capacity that is wearing out, and so its net investment each year is zero. Thus, it pays all of its earnings out as dividends, and there is no growth.

Assuming that the capitalization rate is 15% per year, Nogrowth's stock price would be $100:

$$P_0 = \$15/0.15 = \$100$$

Now consider Growthstock Corporation. Growthstock initially has the same earnings as Nogrowth, but it reinvests 60% of its earnings each year into new investments that yield a rate of return of 20% per year (i.e., 5% per year higher than the market capitalization rate of 15% per year). As a consequence, Growthstock's dividends per share are initially lower than Nogrowth's. Instead of paying out $15 per share in dividends like Nogrowth, Growthstock will pay out only 40% of $15, or *$6 per share* beginning next period. The other $9 per share are reinvested in the firm to earn a rate of return of 20% per year.

Although Growthstock's dividend per share is initially lower than Nogrowth's, Growthstock's dividends will grow over time. Growthstock's share price is higher than Nogrowth's. To see why, let us compute what its growth rate of dividends will be and then apply the discounted dividend model.

The formula for the growth rate of dividends and earnings per share is:[3]

$$g = \text{Earnings Retention Rate} \times \text{Rate of Return on New Investments} = r \cdot r_i$$

---

[3]Proof: By definition, the expected growth rate of earnings is equal to the change in earnings divided by current earnings:

$$g = \frac{\Delta E}{E}$$

By multiplying both numerator and denominator by net investment (I), we find:

$$g = \frac{I}{E} \times \frac{\Delta E}{I}$$

Now note that the first term on the right-hand side is the earnings retention rate and that the second is the rate of return on net new investment.

In this case it is also true that the price-earnings ratio (P/E) will be a fixed constant directly related to the constant growth rate, for example, with a higher growth rate the stock price will be a larger fixed multiple of periodic earnings. This can be seen by simplfying the definition of a forward-looking price-earnings ratio:

$$\frac{P_t}{E_{t+1}} = \frac{\dfrac{(1-r)E_{t+1}}{k-g}}{E_{t+1}} = \frac{1-r}{k-g}$$

The dividend yield (D/P) will also be a fixed constant inversely related to the constant growth rate. Working with a definition of a forward-looking dividend yield:

$$\frac{D_{t+1}}{P_t} = \frac{D_t(1+g)}{\dfrac{D_t(1+g)}{k-g}} = k-g$$

For Growthstock we get:

$r = 60\%$ and $r_i = 20\%$ so $g = r \cdot r_i = 0.6 \times 0.2 = 0.12$ or 12% per year.

Using the constant growth formula to estimate Growthstock's stock price, we have:

$$P_0 = \frac{6}{0.15 - 0.12} = \frac{6}{0.03} = \$200$$

The net present value of Growthstock's future investments is the $100 difference in price between its shares and Nogrowth's shares:

$$NPV \text{ of Future Investments} = \$200 - \$100 = \$100$$

It is important to realize that the reason that Growthstock has a higher share price than Nogrowth is not growth per se, but rather the fact that its reinvested earnings yield a rate of return in excess of the market capitalization rate—20% per year versus 15% per year. To emphasize this point, let us consider what would happen if the rate of return on future investments were only 15% per year instead of 20% per year. To distinguish this case from the case of Growthstock, we will call the firm with the lower rate of return Normalprofit.

Normalprofit's rate of return on future investments is 15% per year and it reinvests 60% of its earnings each year beginning next year. Its growth rate of earnings and dividends is, therefore, 9% per year:

$$g = r \cdot r_i$$
$$g = 0.6 \times 0.15 = 0.09, \text{ or } 9\% \text{ per year}$$

Applying the constant-growth *DDM* formula, we find Normalprofit's share price to be:

$$P_0 = \frac{6}{0.15 - 0.09} = \frac{6}{0.06} = \$100$$

Normalprofit has the same current share price as Nogrowth, even though Normalprofit's dividend per share is expected to grow at 9% per year. This is because Normalprofit's higher growth rate exactly offsets its lower initial dividend. Table 3 and Figure 1 compare the expected earnings and dividends for Nogrowth and Normalprofit for the next few years.

TABLE 3 **Comparison of Nogrowth and Normalprofit**

			NOGROWTH Price/		Growth	Dividend
Year	Stock Price	Earnings	Earnings*	Dividends	Rate	Yield**
0	$100.00					
1	$100.00	$15.00	6.67	$15.00	0%	15%
2	$100.00	$15.00	6.67	$15.00	0%	15%
3	$100.00	$15.00	6.67	$15.00	0%	15%
4	$100.00	$15.00	6.67	$15.00	0%	15%
5	$100.00	$15.00	6.67	$15.00	0%	15%

*Forward-looking Price/Earnings ratio with current stock price divided by next period's earnings. The general formula is $(1 - r)/(k - g)$. Here with $g = r = 0$ we have $1/k = 1/0.15 = 6.67$.
**Forward-looking dividend yield is the ratio of next period's dividend to the current stock price. The general formula is $k - g$. Here with $g = 0$ we have $k = 0.15$.

			NORMALPROFIT Price/		Growth	Dividend
Year	Stock Price	Earnings	Earnings~	Dividends	Rate	Yield~~
0	$100.00					
1	$109.00	$15.00	6.67	$6.00	9%	6%
2	$118.81	$16.35	6.67	$6.54	9%	6%
3	$129.50	$17.82	6.67	$7.13	9%	6%
4	$141.16	$19.43	6.67	$7.77	9%	6%
5	$153.86	$21.17	6.67	$8.47	9%	6%

~Forward-looking Price/Earnings ratio with current stock price divided by next period's earnings. The general formula is $(1 - r)/(k - g)$. Here we have $= (1 - 0.60)/(0.15 - 0.09) = 0.4/0.06 = 6.67$.
~~Forward-looking dividend yield is the ratio of next period's dividend to the current stock price. The general formula is $k - g$. Here we have $0.15 - 0.09 = 0.06$.

Nogrowth and Normalprofit have the same current stock price, which is equal to the present value of a perpetual annuity of next year's earning per share:

$$P_0 = E_1/k = \$15/0.15 = \$100$$

Thus, even though the earnings per share, dividends per share, and the price of Normalprofit stock are expected to grow at 9% per year, this growth does not add any value to the firm's current stock price beyond what it would be if all of its earnings are paid as dividends. The reason is that the rate of return on Normalprofit's reinvested earnings is equal to the market capitalization rate.

To summarize the main point of this section: Growth per se does not add value. What adds value is the opportunity to invest in projects that can earn rates of return in excess of the required rate, k. When a firm's future investment opportunities yield a rate of return equal to k, the stock's value can be estimated using the formula $P_0 = E_1/k$.

Quick Check 2

An analyst uses the constant growth *DDM* to evaluate QRS stock. She assumes expected earnings of $10 per share, an earnings retention rate of 75%, an expected rate of return on future investments of 18% per year, and a market capitalization rate of 15% per year. What is her estimate of QRS's price? What is the implied net present value of future investments?

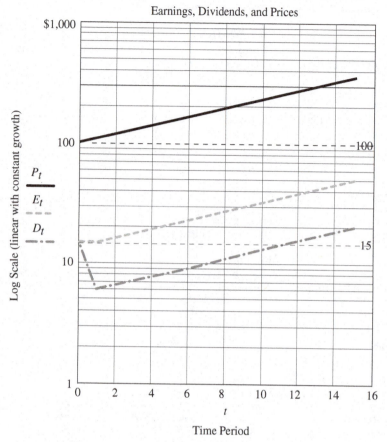

FIGURE 1

Nogrowth and Normalprofit

4 A Reconsideration of the Price/ Earnings Multiple Approach

Earlier, we briefly discussed the price/earnings multiple approach to valuing a firm's stock. We said that a widely used approach for quickly estimating the value of a share of a firm's stock is to take its projected earnings per share and to multiply it by an appropriate price/earnings (*P/E*) multiple derived from other comparable firms. We can now gain some further insight into that approach by using the discounted cash flow model discussed in the previous section.

As we have seen, one can write the formula for a firm's stock price as:

$$P_0 = E_1/k + NPV \text{ of Future Investments}$$

Firms with consistently high *P/E* multiples are, therefore, interpreted to have either relatively low market capitalization rates or relatively high present value of value-added investments, that is, opportunities to earn rates of return on future investments that exceed their market capitalization rates.

Stocks that have relatively high *P/E* ratios because their future investments are expected to earn rates of return in excess of the market capitalization rate are called **growth stocks.**

Some observers of the stock market say that the reason growth stocks have high *P/E* ratios is that their earnings per share are expected to grow. But that is a misleading statement. As we saw in section 3, Normalprofit had an expected growth rate of 9% per year, yet it is priced with the same *P/E* ratio as Nogrowth, which was not expected to grow at all. It is not growth per se that produces a high *P/E* ratio, but rather the presence of future investment opportunities that are expected to yield a rate of return greater than the market's required risk-adjusted rate, *k*.

For example, suppose that you are trying to value the common stock of Digital Biomed Corporation, a hypothetical firm in the pharmaceutical industry that applies biotechnology to the discovery of new drugs. The average price/earnings multiple in the pharmaceutical industry is 15. Digital Biomed's expected earnings per share are $2. If you apply the industry average multiple, the resultant value for Digital Biomed stock is $30. However, suppose that the actual price at which Digital Biomed stock is trading in the stock market is $100 per share. How can you account for the difference?

The $70 difference ($100 − $30) may reflect the beliefs of investors that Digital Biomed will have much better future investment opportunities than the average for the pharmaceutical industry.

P/E ratios tend to vary over time. As new information arrives in the market, investor expectations of earnings change. Relatively small changes in expected growth rates of earnings or capitalization rates can result in large changes in *P/E* ratios. This is true for individual stocks and for the stock market as a whole.

5 Does Dividend Policy Affect Shareholder Wealth?

Dividend policy means a corporation's policy regarding paying out cash to its shareholders *holding constant its investment and borrowing decisions.* In a "frictionless" financial environment, in which there are no taxes and no transaction costs, the wealth of shareholders is the same no matter what dividend policy the firm adopts. In the real world, there are a number of frictions that can cause dividend policy to have an effect on the wealth of shareholders. These include taxes, regulations, the costs of external finance, and the informational or "signaling" content of dividends.

5.1 Cash Dividends and Share Repurchases

There are two ways a corporation can distribute cash to its shareholders: by paying a **cash dividend** or by repurchasing the company's shares in the stock market. When a company pays a cash dividend, all shareholders receive cash in amounts proportional to the number of shares they own. Let us assume that when cash is distributed through a cash dividend, all else the same, the share price declines immediately after payment by the amount of the dividend.

In a **share repurchase,** the company pays cash to buy shares of its stock in the stock market, thereby reducing the number of shares outstanding.[4] Therefore, only those shareholders who *choose* to sell some of their shares will receive cash. Let us assume that when cash is distributed through a share repurchase, *all else the same,* the share price remains unchanged.

For example, Cashrich Corporation has total assets with a market value of $12 million: $2 million in cash, and $10 million in other assets. The market value of its debt is $2 million and of its equity $10 million. There are 500,000 shares of Cashrich common stock outstanding, each with a market price of $20.

Table 4 illustrates the different effects of Cashrich Corporation's paying out cash to its shareholders through a cash dividend and a share repurchase. If Cashrich distributes a cash

---

[4]The corporation keeps the shares that it has repurchased as treasury stock and can decide to resell them to raise cash at a future date.

TABLE 4 Cash Dividends and Share Repurchase for Cashrich, Inc.

a. Original Balance Sheet

Assets		Liabilities and Shareholders' Equity	
Cash	$2 million	Debt	$2 million
Other assets	$10 million	Equity	$10 million
Total	$12 million	Total	$12 million

Number of shares outstanding = 500,000.
Price per share = $20.

b. Balance Sheet after Payment of Cash Dividend

Assets		Liabilities and Shareholders' Equity	
Cash	$1 million	Debt	$2 million
Other assets	$10 million	Equity	$9 million
Total	$11 million	Total	$11 million

Number of shares outstanding = 500,000.
Price per share = $18.

c. Balance Sheet after Share Repurchase

Assets		Liabilities and Shareholders' Equity	
Cash	$1 million	Debt	$2 million
Other assets	$10 million	Equity	$9 million
Total	$11 million	Total	$11 million

Number of shares outstanding = 450,000.
Price per share = $20.

dividend of $2 per share, the market value of its assets declines by $1 million, and its equity declines by $1 million to $9 million.

Because there are still 500,000 shares outstanding, the market price of each share declines by $2. If, instead, Cashrich repurchases shares worth $1 million, it will retire 50,000 shares, leaving 450,000 shares with a price per share of $20.

Under the assumptions used in constructing Table 4, the wealth of shareholders is unaffected by the choice of method Cashrich uses to pay out the $1 million. In the case of a cash dividend of $2 per share, all shareholders receive cash in proportion to the number of shares they own, and the market value of their shares declines by $2 per share, ex-dividend. In the case of a share repurchase, only those shareholders who choose to sell shares receive cash, and the others experience no change in the market value of their shares.

> **Quick Check 3**
>
> Compare the effects of Cashrich's paying $1.5 million in cash dividends versus repurchasing shares for $1.5 million.

5.2 Stock Dividends

Corporations sometimes declare *stock splits* and distribute *stock dividends*. These activities do not distribute cash to shareholders; they increase the number of shares of stock outstanding.

For example, suppose that Cashrich's management declares a two-for-one stock split. This means that each old share will now be counted as two shares. The total number of Cashrich shares outstanding will increase from 500,000 to 1 million. Under the assumption that shareholder wealth is unaffected by this management action, the market price of a share will immediately drop from $20 to $10.

In the case of a stock dividend, the corporation distributes additional shares of stock to each stockholder. Payment of a stock dividend can be seen as distributing a cash dividend to existing shareholders, and then requiring them to immediately use the cash to buy additional shares of the company's stock. The company does not pay out any cash to shareholders, and there are no tax effects.

Let us return to the example of Cashrich Corporation to clarify the different effects of paying a cash dividend and a stock dividend. Suppose that Cashrich normally would pay out a cash dividend of $2 per share, but management thinks the company has extraordinary investment opportunities and decides to keep the $1 million in cash that it would otherwise pay out in cash dividends. Instead of the cash dividend, management, therefore, decides to pay a 10% stock dividend. This means that shareholders will receive one new share for every 10 old shares they own, and the company keeps the $1 million in cash that would have been paid in cash dividends.

Table 5 illustrates and compares the effects of the payment of cash dividends and stock dividends on the assumption that shareholder wealth is unaffected by either. First compare

TABLE 5 Cash Dividends versus Stock Dividends for Cashrich, Inc.

a. Original Balance Sheet

Assets		Liabilities and Shareholders' Equity	
Cash	$2 million	Debt	$2 million
Other assets	$10 million	Equity	$10 million
Total	$12 million	Total	$12 million

Number of shares outstanding = 500,000.
Price per share = $20.

b. Balance Sheet after Payment of Cash Dividend

Assets		Liabilities and Shareholders' Equity	
Cash	$1 million	Debt	$2 million
Other assets	$10 million	Equity	$9 million
Total	$11 million	Total	$11 million

Number of shares outstanding = 500,000.
Price per share = $18.

c. Balance Sheet after Stock Dividend

Assets		Liabilities and Shareholders' Equity	
Cash	$2 million	Debt	$2 million
Other assets	$10 million	Equity	$10 million
Total	$12 million	Total	$12 million

Number of shares outstanding = 550,000.
Price per share = $18.18.

Panel A with Panel C. Panel C of Table 5 shows Cashrich's market value balance sheet after the stock dividend is paid. The totals for assets, liabilities, and shareholders' equity are identical to Panel A, which shows Cashrich's market value balance sheet before the stock dividend is paid. The only difference between the two is that in Panel C, the number of shares has increased to 550,000 and, therefore, the price per share drops to $18.18.

> **Quick Check 4**
>
> What would be the effect of Cashrich's paying a 20% stock dividend?

5.3 Dividend Policy in a Frictionless Environment

We have assumed that the payment of cash to shareholders by means of a cash dividend or a share repurchase has no effect on the wealth of shareholders. Is this a valid assumption? Or is there possibly a way for a corporation to use dividend policy to increase shareholder wealth?

In 1961, Modigliani and Miller (M&M) presented an argument to prove that in a "frictionless" financial environment, in which there are no taxes and no costs of issuing new shares of stock or repurchasing existing shares, a firm's dividend policy can have no effect on the wealth of its current shareholders.[5] The essence of the M&M argument is that shareholders can achieve the effect of any corporate dividend policy by costlessly reinvesting dividends or selling shares of stock on their own.

Let us illustrate the M&M argument for the case of Cashrich Corporation. First, suppose that Cashrich's managers decide *not* to pay out the $2 million in cash, but rather to invest it in a project that leaves the total market value of the firm unchanged. Suppose a shareholder who owns 100 shares of Cashrich stock would have preferred a cash dividend of $2 per share. The shareholder can simply sell 10 shares of stock at the current market price of $20. He winds up with Cashrich stock worth $1,800 and cash of $200—exactly the same result as if the company had paid a dividend of $2 per share.

But the reverse situation is also possible. Suppose Cashrich pays out a cash dividend of $2 per share, and a shareholder who owns 100 shares of Cashrich stock does not want the cash. After the payment of the dividend, she has $200 in cash and $1,800 in stock. She can easily reestablish her original position by using the $200 in cash she received to buy more shares of the stock at the new price of $18 per share.

What about the case in which the firm has to raise cash to finance a new investment project that has a positive *NPV*? Surely in that case one might think that the firm's managers can increase shareholder wealth by cutting the cash dividend and reinvesting the money in the firm. But M&M argue that in a frictionless financial environment, the price of the stock will reflect the *NPV* of the project. Therefore, it will not make any difference to the wealth of the firm's existing shareholders whether the firm finances the new investment project by cutting dividends (internal equity financing) or by issuing new stock (external equity financing).

To understand the M&M argument, let us consider a specific example. Consider Cashpoor Corporation, which currently has assets consisting of cash of $0.5 million, plant and equipment worth $1 million, and debt with a market value of $1 million. Suppose that Cashpoor has an investment opportunity requiring an immediate outlay of $0.5 million on additional plant and equipment, and the project's *NPV* is $1.5 million. There are 1 million shares of Cashpoor common stock outstanding. The market price per share is $2, and it reflects the information that Cashpoor has an investment opportunity with an *NPV* of $1.5 million. Table 6 shows Cashpoor's market value balance sheet before making the investment.

---

[5]Franco Modigliani and Merton Miller, "Dividend Policy, Growth and the Valuation of Shares," *Journal of Business* (October 1961), pp. 411–33.

TABLE 6 Cashpoor Corporation Market Value Balance Sheet

Assets		Liabilities and Shareholders' Equity	
Cash	$0.5 million	Debt	$1 million
Plant and equipment	$1.0 million		
NPV of new investment project	$1.5 million	Equity	$2 million
Total	$3.0 million	Total	$3 million

Number of shares outstanding = 1 million.
Price per share = $2.

Cashpoor could use its $0.5 million in cash to finance the new project internally, or it could pay out the $0.5 million as a cash dividend to shareholders and finance the new investment by issuing new shares. In a frictionless financial environment, the same information is costlessly available to all investors, and the cost of issuing new shares is negligible. Therefore, in such an idealized world, the wealth of existing shareholders will be unaffected by the dividend policy decision.

If Cashpoor uses its $0.5 million in cash to finance the investment, then the balance sheet will reflect this by a $0.5 million reduction in the firm's cash account and an increase of $0.5 million in plant and equipment. There will be 1 million shares outstanding, each with a price of $2.

What happens if Cashpoor pays the $0.5 million in cash to shareholders as a cash dividend ($0.50 per share) and issues new stock to finance the purchase of plant and equipment? According to M&M, the price of a share will decline by the amount of the cash dividend paid (i.e., from $2 to $1.50 per share). The wealth of old shareholders is still $2 million—the $0.5 million they receive in cash dividends and the $1.5 million in the market value of their shares. Cashpoor will have to issue 333,333 new shares ($500,000/$1.50 per share = 333,333 shares) to raise the $0.5 million needed for the new plant and equipment.

> **Quick Check 5**
>
> What would happen under the M&M assumptions if a cash dividend of $0.25 million is paid to Cashpoor's current shareholders, and the remaining $0.25 million for the new investment is raised by issuing new stock?

5.4 Dividend Policy in the Real World

We have seen that in a hypothetical, frictionless financial environment, dividend policy does not matter from a shareholder-wealth perspective. In the real world, however, there are a number of frictions that can cause dividend policy to have an effect on the wealth of shareholders. In this section we consider the most important ones: taxes, regulations, the costs of external finance, and the informational content of dividends.

In the United States and many other countries, the tax authorities require shareholders to pay personal income taxes on cash dividends. Thus, if a corporation distributes cash by paying dividends, it forces all of its shareholders to pay taxes. If instead the firm distributes the cash by repurchasing shares, it does not create a tax liability for all of its shareholders. From a shareholder tax perspective it is, therefore, always better for the corporation to pay out cash by repurchasing shares.

However, in the United States, there are laws that prevent corporations from using share repurchase as an alternative to dividends as a regular mechanism for paying cash to

| Box 1 | Dividend Policy and Investment Decisions |

Dividend Policy and Investment Decisions

Box 1

The proportion of U.S. companies paying cash dividends to shareholders rises and falls based on a number of factors. First, as the number of small companies listed on public markets increases, ceteris paribus, the proportion of companies paying dividends decreases. Small companies typically have little or no earnings and strong growth prospects, so they have incentives to reinvest cash instead of paying it out to shareholders. Second, if dividends are taxed at a higher rate than capital gains, then shareholders prefer growth to dividends, so, ceteris paribus, the proportion of companies paying dividends will fall. Third, the use of stock options as executive compensation encourages executives to bolster stock prices by reinvesting rather than paying out cash. Finally, if dividend-paying stocks are considered less risky, then investors will prefer dividend-paying stocks in bull markets.

Traditionally, an increase in a company's dividend payout signals that management is optimistic about future performance. After all, a company must have extra cash to afford cash dividend payments. However, increased transparency and improved corporate governance has reduced the role of dividends as a signaling device. While it might be unclear exactly why dividends wax and wane in popularity, changes in the number of small businesses entering the market, tax policy, market trends, and corporate governance all play a role in dividend policy and investors' decisions.

Source: Adapted from "Why Cash Has Become King Once Again," *Financial Times,* February 13, 2005.

---

shareholders. The authorities take the view that taxes ought to be paid on these distributions of cash. Indeed, there are also laws that prevent corporations from retaining cash in the business that is not needed to run the business. The tax authorities view such retentions as ways of avoiding the payment of personal taxes on dividends.

Another factor favoring the nonpayment of cash to shareholders, either in the form of dividends or repurchase of shares, is the cost of raising funds externally. The investment bankers who intermediate the sale of new shares to outside investors have to be paid, and it is the firm's current shareholders who bear that cost.

Another cost arises from differences in information that is available to the firm's management (insiders) and the potential buyers of new stock issued by the firm (outsiders). The outsiders may be skeptical about the reasons for issuing new stock and worry that the insiders know something negative about the firm. They will, therefore, have to be offered a bargain price to induce them to buy new shares. Thus, internal equity financing is likely to be more wealth enhancing for the firm's existing shareholders than issuing new shares to outsiders.

Another potentially important real-world factor influencing a firm's dividend policy is the informational content of dividends. Outside investors may interpret an increase in a corporation's cash dividend as a positive sign and, therefore, a dividend increase might cause a rise in the stock's price. Conversely, a decrease in the cash dividend might be interpreted as a bad sign and cause a decline in the stock price. Because of this informational impact, corporate management is cautious about making changes in dividend payouts and usually offers an explanation to the investing public whenever such changes are made.

Quick Check 6

Why do tax considerations and the cost of issuing new stock favor the nonpayment of cash dividends?

Summary

The discounted cash flow (*DCF*) method of valuing assets consists of discounting expected future cash flows at a risk-adjusted discount rate.

The discounted dividend model (*DDM*) for valuing shares of stock starts from the observation that an investor in common stock expects a rate of return (consisting of cash dividends and price appreciation) that is equal to the market capitalization rate. The resulting formula shows that the current price of a share is the present value of all expected future dividends.

In the constant growth rate *DDM,* the growth rate of dividends is also the expected rate of price appreciation.

Growth per se does not add value to a share's current price. What adds value is the opportunity to invest in projects that yield a rate of return in excess of the market capitalization rate.

In a frictionless financial environment, in which there are no taxes and no transaction costs, the wealth of shareholders is the same no matter what dividend policy the firm adopts.

In the real world there are a number of frictions that can cause dividend policy to have an effect on the wealth of shareholders. These include taxes, regulations, the costs of external finance, and the informational content of dividends.

Summary of Formulas

The price of a share of stock is the present value of all expected future dividends discounted at the market capitalization rate:

$$P_0 = \frac{D_1}{(1+k)} + \frac{D_2}{(1+k)^2} + \cdots = \sum_{t=1}^{\infty} \frac{D_t}{(1+k)^t}$$

The price of a share of stock in terms of earnings and investments is:

$$P_0 = \sum_{t=1}^{\infty} \frac{D_t}{(1+k)^t} = \sum_{t=1}^{\infty} \frac{E_t}{(1+k)^t} - \sum_{t=1}^{\infty} \frac{I_t}{(1+k)^t}$$

where E_t is earnings in year t and I_t is net investment in year t.

The present value of a perpetual stream of dividends growing at a constant rate, $g,$ is:

$$P_0 = \frac{D_1}{k - g}$$

The formula for the growth rate of dividends and earnings per share is:

$$g = \text{Earnings Retention Rate} \times \text{Rate of Return on New Investments} = r \cdot r_i$$

We can express the value of a share of stock as:

$$P_0 = E_1/k + NPV \text{ of Future Investments}$$

Key Terms

- dividend yield
- price/earnings ratio
- discounted dividend model
- risk-adjusted discount rate
- market capitalization rate
- growth stocks

- dividend policy
- cash dividend
- share repurchase

Internet Reference Materials

Bloomberg.com: Market Data—Stocks
    http://www.bloomberg.com/markets/stocks/movers_index_dow.html
Financial Times: Market Data—Equities http://markets.ft.com/ft/markets/worldEquities.asp
MarketWatch.com: Research—Stocks http://www.marketwatch.com/tools/stockresearch/

Answers to Quick Check Questions

Quick Check 1   XYZ stock is expected to pay a dividend of $2 per share a year from now, and its dividends are expected to grow by 6% per year thereafter. If its price is now $20 per share, what must be the market capitalization rate?

Answer: Use the constant growth formula $P_0 = D_1/(k - g)$ to solve for k.

$$k = D_1/P_0 + g = 2/20 + 0.06 = 0.16 \text{ or } 16\%$$

Quick Check 2   An analyst uses the constant-growth DDM to evaluate QRS stock. She assumes expected earnings of $10 per share, an earnings retention rate of 75%, an expected rate of return on future investments of 18% per year, and a market capitalization rate of 15% per year. What is her estimate of QRS's price? What is the implied net present value of future investments?

Answer: Use the constant-growth formula $P_0 = D_1/(k - g)$.

$$P_0 = \$2.50/(0.15 - 0.135) = \$166.67$$

Next apply the formula $P_0 = E_1/k = \$10/0.15 = \$66.67$.
    The *NPV* of future investments is the difference between the two values:

$$\$166.67 - \$66.67 = \$100.00$$

Quick Check 3   Compare the effects of Cashrich's paying $1.5 million in cash dividends versus repurchasing shares for $1.5 million.

Answer: In the case of a cash dividend the share price will decline by the amount of the $3 dividend per share—from $20 to $17. In the case of the share repurchase, the price of a share will remain $20 but the number of shares outstanding will fall by 75,000 to 425,000.

Quick Check 4   What would be the effect of Cashrich's paying a 20% stock dividend?

Answer: The number of shares outstanding would increase to 600,000, and the price per share would fall to $16.67.

Quick Check 5   What would happen under the M&M assumptions if a cash dividend of $0.25 million is paid to Cashpoor's current shareholders, and the remaining $0.25 million for the new investment is raised by issuing new stock?

Answer: The stock price will fall by $0.25 per share to $1.75, and the number of new shares issued would be 142,857 ($250,000/$1.75 per share). The wealth of current shareholders is not affected.

Quick Check 6   Why do tax considerations and the cost of issuing new stock favor the nonpayment of cash dividends?

Answer: Payment of cash dividends may cause some shareholders to have to pay income taxes that they could avoid if cash dividends are not paid. Raising cash by issuing new stock is more costly to the corporation than raising cash by forgoing the payment of dividends. Existing shareholders bear these costs.

Questions and Problems

Reading Stock Listings

1. Consider the following NYSE listing from May 6, 2002:

Stock	Div	PE	Vol 100s	Hi	Lo	Close	Net Chg
Boeing	0.68	16	20,969	45.19	43.33	43.38	−1.25

Calculate the dividend yield and estimate the sum of the earnings per share over the most recent four quarters. What was the closing price of Boeing on the previous day?

The Discounted Dividend Model

2. Under the discounted dividend model, what is the value per share of a company expected to pay a $3.75 end-of-year dividend and have an ex-dividend price of $27.50 if the market capitalization rate is 7.5%? Suppose a bad news report about the company drops the expected end-of-year ex-dividend price by 10%. Will the current stock price decrease by more or less than 10%?

3. Under the constant-growth-rate discounted dividend model assume we hold the expected dividend one period ahead constant. What will happen to the price per share of a stock that sees both its growth rate and the market capitalization rate rise by the same proportion, for example, a 25% increase in both variables?

4. The constant-growth-rate discounted dividend model formula is given by: $P_0 = \frac{D_1}{k-g}$. This can be rewritten as: $k = g + \left(\frac{D_1}{P_0}\right)$.
   How would you interpret this equation?

5. The Rusty Clipper Fishing Corporation is expected to pay a cash dividend of $5 per share this year. You estimate that the market capitalization rate for this stock should be 10% per year. If its current price is $25 per share, what can you infer about its expected growth rate of dividends?

6. The DDM Corporation has just paid a cash dividend (D_0) of $2 per share. It has consistently increased its cash dividends in the past by 5% per year, and you expect it to continue to do so. You estimate that the market capitalization rate for this stock should be 13% per year.
   a. What is your estimate of the intrinsic value of a share (derived using the DDM model)?
   b. Suppose that the actual price of a share is $20. By how much would you have to adjust each of the following model parameters to "justify" this observed price: (i) the growth rate of dividends and (ii) the market capitalization rate.

7. The Amazing.com Corporation currently pays no cash dividends, and it is not expected to for the next 5 years. Its sales have been growing at 25% per year.
   a. Can you apply the constant growth rate DDM to estimate its intrinsic value? Explain.

b. It is expected to pay its first cash dividend of $1 per share 5 years from now. If its market capitalization rate is 20% and its dividends are expected to grow by 10% per year, what would you estimate its intrinsic value to be?

c. If its current market price is $100 per share, what would you infer the expected growth rate of its future dividends to be?

8. From the previous problem calculate the price and dividend streams per share for each of the coming ten years along with the current dividend yield. Diagram the price and dividend streams with two alternative scales: a normal scale and a log scale. The log scale has the property that variables with constant rates of growth plot linearly.

9. Suppose a company has a constant market capitalization rate of 10% and a current dividend growth rate of 2%. Assume further that the current dividend level is $5 per share. What is the current price per share of the company. Now suppose there will be a one-time upward shift in the growth rate. If dividend growth is expected to rise to and remain at 2.5% after five years, what is the current price per share of the company?

10. *Challenge Problem:* The 2Stage Co. just paid a dividend of $1 per share. The dividend is expected to grow at a rate of 25% per year for the next 3 years and then to level off to 5% per year forever. You think the appropriate market capitalization rate is 20% per year.

a. What is your estimate of the intrinsic value of a share of the stock?

b. If the market price of a share is equal to this intrinsic value, what is the expected dividend yield?

c. What do you expect its price to be one year from now? Is the implied capital gain consistent with your estimate of the dividend yield and the market capitalization rate?

Earnings and Investment Opportunities

11. Maastricht Barge Builders (MBB) has expected next period earnings of €5.00 per share, retains 50% of its earnings, has a market capitalization rate of 8%, and expects to earn 12% on its new investments. What is your estimate of the current share price of MBB? What is the estimated net present value of MBB's future investments?

12. Comment on the validity of the following statement:

Since a firm's growth rate is determined by its return on new investments and its retention rate, a firm can increase its growth rate and therefore the price per share by retaining a larger portion of earnings.

13. Tabled below are the relevant statistics for three competing firms.

	Winkin	Blinkin	Nod
Capitalization rate (k)	15%	16%	18%
Return on new investment	12%	14%	20%
Retention rate	40%	50%	60%
Expected dividend (D_1)	$3.00	$1.00	$2.50

Under the constant-growth-rate discounted dividend model what should be the current price per share for each company's stock? Of the three firms one could be best described as a growth firm. Which firm is it and what is its growth rate?

14. The constant Growth Corporation (CGC) has expected earnings per share (E_1) of $5. It has a history of paying cash dividends equal to 20% of earnings. The market

capitalization rate for CGC's stock is 15% per year, and the expected ROE on the firm's future investments is 17% per year. Using the constant-growth-rate discounted dividend model,

  a. What is the expected growth rate of dividends?
  b. What is the model's estimate of the present value of the stock?
  c. If the model is right, what is the expected price of a share a year from now?
  d. Suppose that the current price of a share is $50. By how much would you have to adjust each of the following model parameters to "justify" this observed price: (i) the expected ROE on the firm's future investments, (ii) the market capitalization rate, and (iii) the dividend payout ratio.

15. As a stock analyst for CNBC you have been arguing with your sister, who holds a similar position at MSNBC. You both have been using a growth-based dividend discount model to value the future prospects of the expanding Phrivolis satellite radio network. The company has been paying a token 50¢ dividend per share for the past several years. You both agree that the new planned expansion of the network will allow the company to grow via an internally financed route and the expected return on equity or retained earnings will rise to 15%. The problem is that the low dividend payout rate of 10% cannot be changed much to provide additional retained earnings to finance the expansion. You expect the company to cut its payout rate to 5% starting two years from now to provide the opportunity for additional growth. With a 15% discount rate, what is your estimate of the correct current share price for Phrivolis? Your sister thinks the company will not be able to bring the project on-line as soon or be able to cut the payout rate by as much. She thinks the payout rate will only fall to 8% starting four years from now. With an identical 15% discount rate, what is her estimate of the correct current share price for Phrivolis? How much of your and your sister's predicted values are due to the future growth opportunity for the company?

16. The stock of Slogro Corporation is currently selling for $10 per share. Earnings per share in the coming year are expected to be $2 per share. The company has a policy of paying out 60% of its earnings each year in dividends. The rest is retained and invested in projects that earn a 20% rate of return per year. This situation is expected to continue forever.

  a. Assuming the current market price of the stock reflects its intrinsic value as computed using the constant growth rate DDM, what rate of return do Slogro's investors require?
  b. By how much does its value exceed what it would be if all earnings were paid as dividends and nothing were reinvested?
  c. If Slogro were to cut its dividend payout ratio to 25%, what would happen to its stock price? What if Slogro eliminated the dividend altogether?
  d. Suppose that Slogro wishes to maintain its current 60% dividend payout policy but that it also wishes to invest an amount each year equal to that year's total earnings. All the money would be invested in projects earning 20% per year. One way that Slogro could do so would be to issue an amount of new stock each year equal to one-half that year's earnings. What do you think would be the effect of this policy on the current stock price?

17. The Digital Growth Corp. pays no cash dividends currently and is not expected to for the next 5 years. Its latest EPS was $10, all of which was reinvested in the company. The firm's expected r_i for the next 5 years is 20% per year, and during this time it is expected to continue to reinvest all of its earnings. Starting 6 years from now, the firm's r_i on new investments is expected to fall to 15%, and the company is expected to start paying out 40% of its earnings in cash dividends, which it will continue to do forever after. DG's market capitalization rate is 15% per year.

a. What is your estimate of DG's intrinsic value per share?

b. Assuming its current market price is equal to its intrinsic value, what do you expect to happen to its price over the next year? The year after?

c. What effect would it have on your estimate of DG's intrinsic value if you expected DG to pay out only 20% of earnings starting in year 6?

18. The Bearded Ladies' Stock guide offers the following method for selecting stocks:

Compute the stock's PEG ratio by dividing its P/E multiple by its growth rate of earnings. Select only those stocks whose PEG ratio is in the lowest quartile.

If the stock is fairly priced according to the constant-growth-rate DDM, what should be its PEG ratio as a function of the following three variables: the stock's market capitalization rate (k), the expected profitability of its future investments (r_i), and its retention ratio (r)? Assume the PE ratio used in computing PEG is the ratio of the stock's current price to its expected earnings per share, $\frac{P_0}{E_1}$. Compute the PEG ratios for three firms differing only by their r_is, assuming the payout rates are all 50% and each firm has a market capitalization rate of 10%. Firm 1 has a r_i of 10%, Firm 2 has a r_i of 12.5%, and Firm 3 has a r_i of 15%. What do you think of this investment ranking scheme?

19. Working with the constant-growth-rate discounted dividend model consider a company with a constant retention rate (r) and constant rate of return on new investments (r_i). Let E_0 represent the current earnings per share and k be the market capitalization rate. Explain concisely the determinants of the growth over time in net new investment per share for the firm.

A Reconsideration of the Price/Earnings Multiple Approach

20. Suppose a normal firm has a market capitalization rate equal to its return on new investments at 7.5%. If the firm's payout rate is 30%, what is the firm's growth rate and what value with the equilibrium expected PE ratio take?

Does Dividend Policy Affect Shareholder Wealth?

21. Suppose that a company has had an extraordinarily profitable year, and it announces that it will use most of its net cash inflow to buy back shares of its stock in the market. Would you expect the price of its stock to rise or fall when the announcement is made? Explain.

22. Consider the current balance sheet of the Ostende Oar Company, which has 2,000,000 shares outstanding at a price per share of €20.

Derive the new balance sheet after the payment of a 25% stock dividend and compute the new share price.

Assets		Liabilities and Equity	
Cash	€10,000,000	Debt	€20,000,000
Other assets	€50,000,000	Equity	€40,000,000
Total	€60,000,000	Total	€60,000,000

23. Divido Corporation is an all-equity financed firm with a total market value of $100 million. The company holds $10 million in cash-equivalents and has $90 million in other assets. There are 1,000,000 shares of Divido common stock outstanding, each with a market price of $100. What would be the impact on Divido's stock price and on

the wealth of its shareholders of the payment of a cash dividend of $10 per share? The company's repurchases 100,000 shares.

24. Continuing the previous problem, analyze the impact on Divido's stock price and on the wealth of its shareholders of the company paying a 10% stock dividend. The company making a 2-for-1 stock split. The company investing $10 million in an expansion that has an expected rate of return on investment equal to the firm's rate of market capitalization.

Integrative Problem

25. Use the Bloomberg.com Web site to research Home Depot, one of the 30 stocks included in the Dow Jones Industrial Average. Use one of the stock valuation models discussed in this chapter together with information that you can find by searching the Internet to compute the intrinsic value for the stock. A good place to start is at http://www.bloomberg.com. Simply enter the company symbol *HD* in the box at the upper left of the page. You may choose to make use of the *Earnings* information. Compare your estimate of intrinsic value with the stock's actual price. Would you be willing to make an investment decision on the basis of your research? Why or why not?

Suggested Readings

Bodie, Z., A. Kane, and A. Marcus. *Investments.* 7th Ed. Boston: Irwin/McGraw-Hill, 2008.

Cornell, B., "Dividends, Stock Repurchases, and Valuation." *Journal of Applied Finance* 15, Fall/Winter 2005.

Foerster, S., and S. Sapp. "The Dividend Discount Model in the Long-Run: A Clinical Study." *Journal of Applied Finance* 15, Fall/Winter 2005.

Graham, J., and A. Kumar. "Do Dividend Clienteles Exist? Evidence on Dividend Preferences of Retail Investors." *Journal of Finance* 61, June 2006.

Miller, M., and F. Modigliani. "Dividend Policy, Growth, and the Valuation of Shares." *Journal of Business* 34, October 1961.

——— and M. S. Scholes. "Dividends and Taxes." *Journal of Financial Economics* 6, December 1978.

Principles of Risk
Management

OBJECTIVES

- To explore how risk affects financial decision making.
- To provide a conceptual framework for the management of risk.
- To explain how the financial system facilitates the efficient allocation of risk bearing.

CONTENTS

From Chapter 10 of *Financial Economics*, 2/e. Zvi Bodie, Robert C. Merton, David L. Cleeton.

At the outset, we said that there are three analytical "pillars" to finance as an intellectual discipline—the time value of money, valuation, and risk management. Now we will focus on the third pillar, risk management.

We have already discussed some aspects of risk management, showed that the redistribution of risks is a fundamental function of the financial system, and described some of the institutional mechanisms that have developed for facilitating the redistribution of risk and reaping the benefits of diversification.

Here we begin a more detailed treatment of these topics. This chapter offers an overview of the basic principles of risk management. Section 1 clarifies the meaning of risk and risk aversion. Section 2 examines the ways in which risk influences the financial decisions of each of the major types of economic organizations—households, firms, and government. Section 3 explores the steps in the risk-management process: identifying and assessing risks, selecting techniques to manage risk, and implementing and revising risk-management decisions. Section 4 analyzes the methods available to transfer risk: *hedging, insuring,* and *diversifying.* Section 5 explores how the facility to transfer risks among people permits effective risk bearing and the efficient allocation of resources to risky projects. Section 6 considers the scope of institutional arrangements for the efficient management of risk and the factors that limit it. Section 7 discusses portfolio theory, which is the quantitative analysis of the optimal trade-off between the costs and benefits of risk management, and section 8 explains probability distributions of rates of return.

1 What Is Risk?

We begin by distinguishing between uncertainty and risk. *Uncertainty* exists whenever one does not know for sure what will occur in the future. *Risk* is uncertainty that "matters" because it affects people's welfare. Thus, uncertainty is a necessary but not a sufficient condition for risk. Every risky situation is uncertain, but there can be uncertainty without risk.

To illustrate, suppose that you plan to have a party, and you invite a dozen of your friends. Your best guess is that 10 of the 12 invitees will come, but there is uncertainty—all 12 might show up, or only 8. There is, however, risk only if the uncertainty affects your plans for the party. Would having a perfect forecast of the number of guests change your actions? If not, then there is uncertainty but no risk.

For example, in providing for your guests, you have to decide how much food to prepare. If you knew for sure that 10 people will show up, then you would prepare exactly enough for 10—no more and no less. If 12 actually show up, there will not be enough food, and you will be displeased with that outcome because some guests will be hungry and dissatisfied. If 8 actually show up, there will be too much food, and you will be displeased with that too because you will have wasted some of your limited resources on surplus food. Thus, the uncertainty matters and, therefore, there is risk in this situation.

On the other hand, suppose that you have told your guests that there will be a potluck dinner, and that each guest is to bring enough food for one person. Then it might not matter to you in planning the party whether more or fewer than 10 people come. In that case, there is uncertainty but no risk.[1]

---

[1] A subtle point: If you chose to have a potluck dinner because of uncertainty about the number of guests, then there is risk. Having a potluck dinner is the action you took to manage that risk.

In many risky situations, the possible outcomes can be classified either as losses or gains in a simple and direct way. For example, suppose that you invest in the stock market. If the value of your stock portfolio goes down, it is a loss, and if it goes up, it is a gain. People normally consider the "downside" possibility of losses to be the risk, not the "upside" potential for a gain.

But there are situations in which there is no obvious downside or upside. Indeed, your planned party is an example. The uncertainty regarding the number of people who will attend your party creates risk whether more or fewer than the expected number of guests show up. Thus, in some situations, deviations from the expected value can be undesirable or costly no matter in which direction.

Risk aversion is a characteristic of an individual's preferences in risk-taking situations. It is a measure of willingness to pay to reduce one's exposure to risk. In evaluating trade-offs between the costs and benefits of reducing risk, risk-averse people prefer the lower-risk alternatives for the same cost. For example, if you are generally willing to accept a lower expected rate of return on an investment because it offers a more predictable rate of return, you are risk averse. When choosing among investment alternatives with the *same* expected rate of return, a risk-averse individual chooses the alternative with the lowest risk.

1.1 Risk Management

Let us assume that your party cannot possibly be a potluck affair and, therefore, the uncertainty does matter. Moreover, you prefer that there is just enough food for those guests who show up. There are several alternative courses of action open to you, each with a certain cost.

For instance, you could order enough for 12 together with an option to return any surplus to the caterer for a refund. Instead, you could order enough for only 8 together with an option to order more at the last minute if needed. You almost surely will have to pay extra for these options.

Thus, there is a trade-off between the benefit of eliminating the risk of having the wrong amount of food and the cost of that risk reduction. The process of formulating the benefit-cost trade-offs of risk reduction and deciding on the course of action to take (including the decision to take no action at all) is called **risk management.**

People at times express regret at having taken costly measures to reduce risk when the bad outcomes they feared do not subsequently materialize. If you sell a risky stock just before it triples in price, you will surely regret that decision. It is, however, important to remember that all decisions made with respect to uncertainty must be made *before* that uncertainty is resolved. What matters is that your decision is the best one you could make based on the information available to you at the time you made it. Everyone has "20/20 hindsight"; no one, however, has perfect foresight.

It is difficult in practice to distinguish between the skill and the luck of a decision maker. By definition, risk-management decisions are made under conditions of uncertainty and, therefore, multiple outcomes are possible. After the fact, only one of these outcomes will occur. Neither recriminations nor congratulations for a decision seem warranted when such are based on information not available at the time the decision was made. *The appropriateness of a risk-management decision should be judged in the light of the information available at the time the decision is made.*

For example, if you carry an umbrella with you to work because you think it might rain, and it does not, then you should not recriminate yourself for having made the wrong decision. On the other hand, suppose all the weather forecasters say rain is very likely, and you do not take your umbrella. If it does not rain, you should not congratulate yourself on your wisdom. You were just lucky.

> **Quick Check 1**
>
> To eliminate the risk of a decline in house prices over the next three months, Joe agrees to sell his house three months from now at a price of $100,000. After three months, by the time of the transfer of ownership and the conclusion of the sale, housing prices have gone up and it turns out that Joe could have gotten $150,000 for his house. Should Joe chastise himself for his decision to eliminate his price risk?

1.2 Risk Exposure

If you face a particular type of risk because of your job, the nature of your business, or your pattern of consumption, you are said to have a particular **risk exposure.** For example, if you are a temporary office worker, your exposure to the risk of a layoff is relatively high. If you are a tenured professor at a major university, your exposure to the risk of a layoff is relatively low. If you are a farmer, you are exposed both to the risk of a crop failure and to the risk of a decline in the price at which you can sell your crops. If your business significantly involves imports or exports of goods, you are exposed to the risk of an adverse change in currency exchange rates. If you own a house, you are exposed to the risks of fire, theft, storm damage, earthquake damage, as well as the risk of a decline in its market value.

Thus, *the riskiness of an asset or a transaction cannot be assessed in isolation or in the abstract.* In one context, the purchase or sale of a particular asset may add to your risk exposure; in another, the same transaction may be risk reducing. Thus, if I buy a one-year insurance policy on my life, it is risk reducing to my family because the benefit paid offsets their loss in income in the event that I die. If people unrelated to me buy the policy on my life they are not reducing risk; they are betting that I will die during the year. Or if a farmer with wheat ready to be harvested enters a contract to sell wheat at a fixed price in the future, the contract is risk reducing. But for someone who has no wheat to sell, entering into that same contract is to speculate that wheat prices will fall because they profit only if the market price at the contract delivery date is below the contractually fixed price.

Speculators are defined as investors who take positions that increase their exposure to certain risks in the hope of increasing their wealth. In contrast, **hedgers** take positions to reduce their exposures. The same person can be a speculator on some exposures and a hedger on others.

2 Risk and Economic Decisions

Some financial decisions, such as how much insurance to buy against various risk exposures, relate exclusively to the management of risk. But many general resource allocation decisions, such as saving, investment, and financing decisions, are also significantly influenced by the presence of risk and, therefore, are partly risk-management decisions.

For example, some household saving is motivated by the desire for the increased security that comes from owning assets that can cover unanticipated expenses in the future. Economists call this **precautionary saving.** We showed how households can use time value of money concepts to make optimal saving decisions over the life cycle. In that analysis, however, we ignored risk and precautionary saving. In the real world, households should not and do not ignore it.

In the sections to follow, we discuss the influence of risk on some of the major financial decisions of households, firms, and government. But first let us recall why we begin with households (i.e., people). The ultimate function of the financial system is to help implement optimal consumption and resource allocation of households. Economic organizations such as firms and governments exist primarily to facilitate the achievement of that ultimate function and, therefore, we cannot properly understand the optimal functioning of those organizations without first understanding the financial-economic behavior of people, including their response to risk.

2.1 Risks Facing Households

Although many possible risk classification schemes are possible, we distinguish among five major categories of risk exposures for households:

- *Sickness, disability, and death:* Unexpected sickness or accidental injuries can impose large costs on people because of the need for treatment and care and because of the loss of income caused by the inability to work.
- *Unemployment risk:* This is the risk of losing one's job.
- *Consumer-durable asset risk:* This is the risk of loss arising from ownership of a house, car, or other consumer-durable asset. Losses can occur due to hazards such as fire or theft, or due to obsolescence arising from technological change or changes in consumer tastes.
- *Liability risk:* This is the risk that others will have a financial claim against you because they suffer a loss for which you can be held responsible. For example, you cause a car accident through reckless driving and are required to cover the cost to others of personal injury and property damage.
- *Financial-asset risk:* This is the risk arising from holding different kinds of financial assets such as equities or fixed-income securities denominated in one or more currencies. The underlying sources of financial-asset risk are the uncertainties faced by the firms, governments, or other economic organizations that have issued these securities.

The risks faced by households influence virtually all of their economic decisions. Consider, for example, an individual's decision to invest in a graduate education. Elsewhere we analyzed this decision using time value of money techniques and ignored risk. However, an important reason to invest in more education is to increase the *flexibility* of one's human capital. A person with a broader education is generally better equipped to deal with the risk of unemployment.

Quick Check 2

Think of an insurance policy that you or someone you know has recently purchased or canceled. List the steps that led to the decision.

2.2 Risks Facing Firms

Firms are organizations whose primary economic function is to produce goods and services. Virtually every activity of the firm entails exposures to risks. Taking risks is an essential and inseparable part of business enterprise.

Business risks of the firm are borne by its stakeholders: shareholders, creditors, customers, suppliers, employees, and government. The financial system can be used to transfer risks faced by firms to other parties. Specialized financial firms, such as insurance companies, perform the service of pooling and transferring risks. Ultimately, however, all risks faced by firms are borne by people.

Consider, for example, the risks associated with producing baked goods. Bakeries are the firms that carry on this activity. Bakeries, like firms in other industries, face several categories of risks:

- *Production risk:* This is the risk that machines (e.g., ovens, delivery trucks) will break down, that deliveries of raw materials (e.g., flour, eggs) will not arrive on time, that workers will not show up for work, or that a new technology will make the firm's existing equipment obsolete.
- *Price risk of outputs:* This is the risk that the demand for the baked goods produced by the bakery will unpredictably change because of an unanticipated shift in consumer preferences (e.g., celery becomes a popular substitute for bread at restaurants) and, therefore, the market price of baked goods might fall. Or competition can become more intense, and the bakery might be forced to lower its prices.
- *Price risk of inputs:* This is the risk that the prices of some of the inputs of the bakery will change unpredictably. Flour can become more expensive, or wage rates rise. If the bakery borrows money to finance its operations at a floating interest rate, it is exposed to the risk that interest rates might rise.

The bakery's owners are not the only people who bear the risks of the business. Its managers (if they are different from the owners) and its other employees bear some of them, too. If profitability is low or if the production technology changes, some of them may be forced to take a cut in pay or even lose their jobs altogether.

Expertise in managing risks is part of the skill recipe for effective management of a bakery. The firm's management team can manage these risks using several techniques: It can keep extra flour in inventory to protect itself against delays in delivery; it can maintain spare parts for its machinery; and it can subscribe to services that forecast trends in the demand for its products. It can also buy insurance against some risks, such as accidental injury to its employees or theft of its equipment. It can also reduce some price risks by either engaging in fixed-price contracting with customers and suppliers directly or by transacting in the forward, futures, and options markets for commodities, foreign exchange, and interest rates. Making trade-offs among the costs and benefits of these risk-reducing measures is an essential part of managing a bakery.

The size and organizational form of the firm itself can also be affected by risk. Bakeries come in many different types and sizes. At one extreme are small production and retail operations owned and operated by a single individual or family. At the other extreme are large corporations such as Continental Baking Company, with a workforce of thousands of people and an even larger number of shareholder owners. One purpose (and usually not the only one) of organizing as a large corporation is to better manage the production, demand, or price risks of the business.

Quick Check 3

Think of a fast-food restaurant. What risks is such a business exposed to, and who bears them?

2.3 The Role of Government in Risk Management

Governments at all levels play an important role in managing risks either by preventing them or redistributing them. People often rely on government to provide protection and financial relief from natural disasters and various human-caused hazards, including war and pollution of the environment. An argument in favor of an activist role for government in economic development is that government can readily spread the risk of an investment in infrastructure among all of the taxpayers within its jurisdiction. Government managers often use the markets and other channels of the financial system to implement their own risk-management policies in much the same way that managers of firms and other non-governmental economic organizations do.

As is the case with these other organizations, however, all risks are ultimately borne by the people. Whether government offers insurance against the risk of natural disasters or insurance against default on bank deposits, it is not free. The government either charges the insured parties a price sufficient to cover the costs of these insurance services, or taxpayers pay the claims.

> **Quick Check 4**
>
> If the government mandates that all automobile owners must buy accident insurance, who bears the risk of auto accidents?

3 The Risk-Management Process

The **risk-management process** is a systematic attempt to analyze and deal with risk. The process can be broken down into five steps:

- *Risk identification*
- *Risk assessment*
- *Selection of risk-management techniques*
- *Implementation*
- *Review*

3.1 Risk Identification

Risk identification consists of figuring out what the most important risk exposures are for the unit of analysis, be it a household, a firm, or some other entity. Households or firms are sometimes not aware of all of the risks to which they are exposed. For example, a person who has never missed a day of work because of illness or injury may give little thought to the risk of disability. Buying insurance against disability risk might make sense, but may not even be considered.

On the other hand, there may be some risks for which a person buys insurance coverage, but does not have an exposure. For example, many single people who have no dependents buy retirement saving instruments with survivors' benefits. Should they die before retirement, their designated beneficiaries receive the accumulated value in the account. But if they have no dependents, they do not need this protection (see Box 1).

Effective risk identification requires that one take the perspective of the entity as a whole and consider the totality of uncertainties affecting it. For example, consider a household's exposure to stock market risk. If you work as a stockbroker, then your future earnings depend critically on how well stocks perform. Your human capital is, therefore, exposed to the performance of the stock market, and you probably should not invest your other non–human-capital wealth in stocks as well. On the other hand, your friend, who is your age but works as a government administrator earning a salary equal to yours, may be well advised to invest a large fraction of her investment portfolio in stocks because her human capital is not as exposed to the risk of the stock market.

The principle that one should take the perspective of the entity as a whole when identifying risks applies to firms, too. For example, consider the impact of foreign-exchange uncertainty on a firm that sells products and buys inputs abroad in prices that are fixed in foreign currencies. It makes little sense for the firm's managers to consider the effect of

---

Box 1
Who Needs Life Insurance?

1. *You're single with no dependents.* Forget life insurance. Buy disability coverage, and add to your investments instead.

2. *You're single with dependents.* What happens to those dependents if you die? If you're divorced and the other spouse can afford to take care of the kids, then you don't need life insurance.

3. *You're a DINK—a double-income couple with no kids.* If each spouse is self-supporting, you don't need life insurance.

4. *You're an OINK—a one-income couple with no kids.* The working spouse probably needs life insurance,

if you want to preserve the standard of living of the other spouse.

5. *You're married with young children.* You need a lot of life insurance. Those kids have to be raised and educated, and it's not cheap. But you probably need the coverage only until they're on their own.

Source: Adapted with permission of Simon & Schuster, Inc., from *Making the Most of Your Money* by Jane Bryant Quinn. Copyright © 1991 by Berrybrook Publishing Inc.

---

exchange-rate uncertainty *only* on the firm's revenues or on its costs. What matters to all of the firm's stakeholders is the net effect of exchange-rate uncertainty on the firm's revenues less its costs. Even though its revenues and its costs might each be greatly affected by fluctuations in exchange rates, the firm's net exposure to exchange-rate uncertainty might be zero.

Or consider farmers whose revenues are subject to both price and quantity uncertainty. Suppose crop failures always cause prices to rise so that farm revenue (equal to price × quantity) is constant. Although at first it might appear that the farmer is exposed to *both* price risk *and* quantity risk (the risk of crop failure), there may be no risk at the level of analysis of total farm revenue. Taking steps to reduce the farmer's exposure to the volatility of farm prices might have the "perverse" effect of increasing the uncertainty of the farmer's total revenue.

To help in identifying risk exposures, it is a good idea to have a checklist that enumerates all of the entity's potential exposures and the relations among them. In the case of a firm, this may require a good deal of detailed knowledge about the economics of the industry in which the firm competes, the technology of the firm, and its sources of supply.

3.2 Risk Assessment

Risk assessment is the quantification of the costs associated with the risks that have been identified in the first step of risk management. For example, consider a single woman who has just graduated from college and started a job. When she was in college, she was covered by her parents' health insurance policy, but now she has no health insurance coverage. She, therefore, identifies illness as a major risk exposure. To assess her exposure, information is needed. How likely is it that someone of her age and health status will get sick? What is the cost of treatment?

Clearly, she needs information, and information may be costly to gather. One of the main functions of insurance companies is to provide this kind of information. They employ **actuaries,** who are professionals specially trained in mathematics and statistics, to gather and analyze data and estimate the probabilities of illness, accidents, and other such risks.

In the realm of financial-asset risks, households and firms often need expert advice in assessing their exposures and in quantifying the trade-offs between the risks and rewards of investing in various categories of assets, such as stocks and bonds. They typically turn to professional investment advisors, mutual funds, or other financial intermediaries and service firms that help them make those assessments.

3.3 Selection of Risk-Management Techniques

There are four basic techniques available for reducing risk:

- *Risk avoidance*
- *Loss prevention and control*
- *Risk retention*
- *Risk transfer*

Let us briefly explain each technique.

- *Risk avoidance:* A conscious decision not to be exposed to a particular risk. People may decide to avoid the risks of going into certain professions and firms may avoid certain lines of business because they are considered too risky. But it is not always feasible to avoid risks. For example, all people are inevitably exposed to the risk of illness by virtue of being human. They cannot avoid it.
- *Loss prevention and control:* Actions taken to reduce the likelihood or the severity of losses. Such actions can be taken prior to, concurrent with, or after a loss occurs. For example, you can reduce your exposure to the risk of illness by eating well, getting plenty of sleep, not smoking, and keeping your distance from people known to have fresh colds. If you catch a cold, you can stay in bed and reduce the possibility of having it turn into pneumonia.
- *Risk retention:* Absorbing the risk and covering losses out of one's own resources. This sometimes happens by default, as for example, when one is unaware that there was any risk or one chooses to ignore it. But one may make a conscious decision to absorb certain risks. For example, some people may decide to absorb the costs of treating illnesses from their own accumulated wealth and do not buy health insurance. Household precautionary saving is to facilitate risk retention.
- *Risk transfer:* Transferring the risk to others. Selling a risky asset to someone else and buying insurance are examples of this technique of risk management. Taking no action to reduce risk and relying on others to cover your losses is another example.

There are three basic methods of accomplishing the transfer of risk: hedging, insuring, and diversifying. They are explained in Section 4 of this chapter.

3.4 Implementation

Following a decision about how to handle the risks identified, one must implement the techniques selected. The underlying principle in this step of the risk-management process is to minimize the costs of implementation. Thus, if you decide to buy health insurance of a certain kind, you should shop around for the lowest-cost provider. If you have decided to invest in the stock market, you should compare the costs of doing so through mutual funds or buying stocks through a broker.

3.5 Review

Risk management is a dynamic feedback process in which decisions are periodically reviewed and revised. As time passes and circumstances change, new exposures may arise, information about the likelihood and severity of risks may become more readily available, and techniques for managing them may become less costly. Thus, you will probably decide not to purchase life insurance if you are single, but reverse that decision if you get married and have children. Or you may decide to change the proportion of your asset portfolio invested in stocks.

Quick Check 5

Identify a major risk in your life and describe the steps you take to manage it.

---

4 The Three Dimensions of Risk Transfer

Among the four techniques of risk management listed in Section 3.3, transferring some or all of the risk to others is where the financial system plays the greatest role. The most basic method of transferring risk is to simply sell the asset that is the source of the risk. For example, an owner of a house is subject to at least three risk exposures: fire, storm damage, and the risk that the market value of the house will decline. By selling the house, the owner gets rid of all three of those exposures.

However, suppose that one either cannot or does not choose to sell the asset that is the source of the risk. It is nevertheless possible to manage some of the risks of ownership in other ways. For example, one can buy insurance against fire and storm damage, and thereby retain only the market-value risk of the house.

We distinguish among three methods for transferring risks, called the three dimensions of risk transfer: **hedging, insuring,** and **diversifying.** We explain and illustrate each method in the sections to follow.

4.1 Hedging

One is said to *hedge* a risk when the action taken to reduce one's exposure to a loss also causes one to give up of the possibility of a gain. For example, farmers who sell their future crops before the harvest at a fixed price to eliminate the risk of a low price at harvest time also give up the possibility of profiting from high prices at harvest time. They are hedging their exposure to the price risk of their crops. If you subscribe to a magazine for three years instead of subscribing one year at a time, you are hedging against the risk of a rise in the price of the magazine. You eliminate the potential loss due to an increase in the price of a subscription, but you give up the gain from a potential drop in subscription prices.

4.2 Insuring

Insuring means paying a *premium* (the price paid for the insurance) to avoid losses. By buying insurance, you substitute a sure loss (the premium you pay for the policy) for the possibility of a larger loss if you do not insure. For example, if you own a car, you almost surely have bought some insurance against the risks of damage, theft, and injury to yourself and others. The premium may be $1,000 today to insure your car for the next year against the potential losses stemming from these contingencies. The sure loss of $1,000 is substituted for the possibility of losses that can run to hundreds of thousands of dollars.

There is a fundamental difference between insuring and hedging. When you hedge, you eliminate the risk of loss by giving up the potential for gain. When you insure, you pay a premium to eliminate the risk of loss and *retain* the potential for gain.

For example, suppose you live in the United States and own an import/export business. A month from now you know that you will receive €100,000. The dollar price of a euro is $1.30 per euro now, but you do not know what it will be a month from now. You are, therefore, exposed to exchange-rate risk.

You can manage this risk either by hedging or by insuring. Hedging involves entering into a contract now to sell your €100,000 at the end of the month at a fixed dollar price of, say, $1.30 per euro. The contract that protects you against a decline in the dollar price of the euro costs you nothing, but by hedging you have also given up the potential gain from a rise in the dollar price of the euro over the next month.

Alternatively, you could insure against a decline in the dollar price of the euro by paying a premium now for a put option that gives you the right (but not the obligation) to sell your €100,000 a month from now at a price of $1.30 per euro.[2] If the dollar price of the euro falls below $1.30, you are protected because you can exercise your option a month from now and sell your euros at $1.30 per euro. But, if the dollar price of the euro rises, you get the benefit of the increased dollar value of your €100,000.

Quick Check 6

Suppose you are a U.S. citizen studying in Germany. A month from now you know that you will receive $10,000 from the United States as a scholarship grant. How can you hedge your foreign-exchange risk? How can you insure against it?

4.3 Diversifying

Diversifying means holding similar amounts of many risky assets instead of concentrating all of your investment in only one. Diversification thereby limits your exposure to the risk of any single asset.

For example, consider the diversification of business risks. Suppose that you are thinking about investing $100,000 in the biotechnology business because you believe that the discovery of new genetically engineered drugs offers great profit potential over the next several years. You could invest all $100,000 in a single firm that is developing a single new drug. In that case, your biotech investment would be concentrated, not diversified.

Diversification can be carried out by the individual investor directly in the market, or by the firm, or by a financial intermediary. Thus, you can diversify your investment in the biotechnology business by:

- Investing in several firms, each of which is developing a new drug.
- Investing in a single firm that is developing many drugs.
- Investing in a mutual fund that holds shares in many firms that are developing new drugs.

To illustrate how diversification reduces your exposure to risk, compare your situation if you have all $100,000 invested in the development of a single new drug with the situation if you have $50,000 invested in each of two different drugs. Suppose that for each drug, success means that you will quadruple your investment, but failure means a loss of your entire investment. Thus, if you invest $100,000 in a single drug, either you wind up with $400,000 or nothing.

If you diversify by investing $50,000 in each of two drugs, there is still a chance of winding up with either $400,000 (if both drugs succeed) or nothing (if both drugs fail). However, there is also the intermediate possibility that one drug succeeds and the other fails. In that event, you will wind up with $200,000 (four times your investment of $50,000 in the drug that succeeds and zero from the drug that fails).

Diversification does not reduce your risk exposure if the individual drugs you invest in always either succeed or fail together. That is, in the two-drug example, if there is *no* chance that one drug succeeds and the other fails, it would make no difference to your risk whether you invested all $100,000 in a single drug or split your investment among the two.

---

[2] A put option is a security that gives its holder the right to sell some asset at a specified price, called the *exercise* or *strike price,* on or before some specified expiration date.

Either way, there are only two possible outcomes—either you wind up with $400,000 (from success on all drugs) or you lose your entire investment (from the failure of all drugs). In such a case, the risks of commercial success for each separate drug are said to be *perfectly correlated* with each other. In order for diversification to reduce your risk exposure, the risks must be less than perfectly correlated with each other.[3]

Diversification can improve households' welfare by reducing the exposure to any particular risky venture borne by each household. However, diversification by itself does not reduce uncertainty in the aggregate. Thus, if 1,000 new drugs are discovered each year, the aggregate uncertainty about the number that will be commercially successful does not depend on how widely the uncertainty is spread among investors in drug company stocks. However, the adverse impact of that uncertainty on households' welfare is reduced through diversification.

When comparing the ex post performance of diversified investors with those who do not diversify, the more spectacular winners are most likely to come from among undiversified investors. But this is also the group that produces the more spectacular losers. By diversifying your portfolio, you reduce your chances of ending up at either extreme.

To underscore this point, let us return to the previous example of investing in the development of new drugs. For each drug that succeeds you quadruple your investment, but for each that fails, you lose your entire investment. Thus, if you concentrate your investment of $100,000 in a single drug, either you wind up with $400,000 or nothing.

Consider two investors, each of whom invests $100,000 in a single new drug. Investor 1 invests in drug A, and investor 2 invests in drug B. Now add a third investor. Investor 3 invests half his money in drug A and the other half in drug B.

Suppose drug A succeeds and B fails. Then investor 1 makes $400,000. She may find herself labeled an investment "genius" for quadrupling her money. Investor 2, however, is correspondingly labeled a "dunce" for the colossal failure of losing his entire investment. Suppose, however, that drug A fails and B succeeds. Then the labels attached to investors 1 and 2 are reversed. The diversified investor, investor 3, makes "only" $200,000 in either scenario and, thus, is the "middle" or "average" performer.

Of course, one always prefers to be a big winner and called a genius. But if that can only be accomplished by a decision ex ante that results in either being a big winner or a big loser ex post, then perhaps it is preferable to choose an alternative that leaves you in the middle.

As obvious as this point may seem, people often lose sight of it. Good luck is often interpreted as skill. Thus, it is not uncommon to find press reports about the spectacular successes of particular stock market investors who do not diversify their portfolios at all but concentrate instead in a single stock. Although such investors may indeed be investment geniuses, it is more likely that they are simply lucky.

It is also not uncommon to find stories about big losers who are portrayed as "sinful" or stupid for not choosing the stocks that had big payoffs. A more valid criticism might be that they were undiversified.

> **Quick Check 7**
>
> How might farmers reduce their exposure to risks of crop failure through diversification?

5 Risk Transfer and Economic Efficiency

Institutional arrangements for the transfer of risk contribute to economic efficiency in two fundamental ways—they reallocate existing risks to those most willing to bear them, and they cause a reallocation of resources to production and consumption in accordance with

---

[3]A precise statistical definition of *correlation* is given.

the new distribution of risk bearing. By allowing people to reduce their exposure to the risk of undertaking certain business ventures, they may encourage entrepreneurial behavior that can have a benefit to society. We now explore each of these in greater detail.

5.1 Efficient Bearing of Existing Risks

We first investigate how the facility to reallocate risks among people can make everyone better off. Consider the hypothetical case of two investors in very different economic circumstances. The first is a retired widow who has an accumulated "nest egg" of $100,000, which is her sole source of income. The second is a college student who has $100,000 and who anticipates a good stream of earnings in the future after graduating from college.

Typically, the widow is assumed to be a more conservative investor and the student more aggressive. That is, we would expect the widow to be concerned primarily with the safety of her stream of investment income, whereas we might expect the student to be willing to bear more risk in exchange for a higher expected return.

Suppose the widow currently holds all of her wealth in the form of a portfolio of stocks left to her by her recently deceased husband, and suppose the college student has all of her wealth in a bank certificate of deposit (CD) that her parents started for her years before. Both would be better off if they could somehow swap their assets so that the widow winds up holding the CD and the student the stock portfolio.

One of the most important functions of the financial system is to facilitate such transfers of risk. One way for this transfer of risk to take place is for the widow to simply sell her stocks and for the student to buy them. Typically, several financial intermediaries would be involved in the process. For example, the widow might have her stocks in an account at a brokerage firm. She gives the broker an order to sell them and to invest the proceeds of the sale in a bank CD. The student, on the other hand, cashes in her CD at the bank and buys the stocks through her broker.

In this set of transactions no immediate change occurs in the wealth of either party except that each must pay the cost of carrying out the transactions (i.e., broker fees and bank charges). The student and the widow each had $100,000 of assets before, and immediately afterwards they each have $100,000 (less the broker fees and bank charges). The sole purpose and result of the transactions is to allow each party to hold the portfolio of assets offering them the combination of risk and expected return most attractive for their circumstances.

5.2 Risk and Resource Allocation

Now let us consider how the ability to reallocate risks facilitates the undertaking of valuable projects that might not otherwise be undertaken because they are too risky. The ability to pool and share risks can lead to an increase in inventive activity and the development of new products.

For example, consider the case of creating new pharmaceuticals. The research and development effort that goes into the discovery, testing, and production of new drugs requires enormous amounts of investment extended over a considerable period of time. The return on that investment is highly uncertain. Even if an individual investor had the wealth necessary to finance the development of a new drug, risk aversion might deter him from doing so on his own.

To be more specific, suppose that a scientist discovers a new drug designed to treat the common cold. She requires $1 million to develop, test, and produce it. At this stage, the drug has a small probability of commercial success. Even if the scientist has $1 million in her bank account, she might not be willing to risk it all on the drug. She might instead set up a firm to develop the drug, and bring in other investors to share both the risks and the potential rewards of her discovery.

In addition to risk pooling and sharing, *specialization* in the bearing of risks can also facilitate undertaking risky investments. Potential investors may be willing to accept some of the exposures associated with a business enterprise, but not others.

For example, suppose a real estate developer is planning to construct a new shopping mall in a downtown location. A consortium of banks and other lending institutions agrees to finance the project but only on the condition that it is insured against fire. That is, the lenders accept the risk that the mall might not be a commercial success, but they do not accept the exposure of their investment to the risk of a fire. The existence of specialized insurance companies that accept the risk of fire makes possible the financing of the new shopping mall.

> ### Quick Check 8
>
> Give an example of an investment project or a new business that would not be feasible if the risks associated with it could not be shared or transferred through the financial system.

6 Institutions for Risk Management

Imagine a hypothetical world in which there exists such a wide range of institutional mechanisms (such as securities markets and insurance contracts) that people can pick and choose exactly those risks they wish to bear and those they want to shed. In such a hypothetical world, we would all be able (for a price) to shed the risks associated with job loss or a decline in the market value of our house. This world would represent the theoretical limiting case of what the financial system can provide in the way of efficient risk allocation for society (see Box 2).

Over the centuries, various economic organizations and contractual arrangements have evolved to facilitate a more efficient allocation of risk bearing both by expanding the scope of diversification and by permitting greater specialization in the management of risk. Insurance companies and futures markets are examples of institutions whose primary economic function is to further these ends.

The allocation of risks is also an important consideration in the design of securities. Debt and equity securities issued by firms are intentionally designed to differ in the risks of the

Box 2 — Arrow on Complete Markets for Risk

Suppose that we could introduce into the economic system any institutions we wish for shifting risks instead of being confined to those developed historically. . . . It is not hard to see what an ideal arrangement would consist of. We would want to find a market in which we can insure freely against any economically relevant event. That is, an individual should be able to bet, at fixed odds, any amount he wishes on the occurrence of any event that will affect his welfare in any way. The odds, or, in a different and more respectable language, the premium on the insurance, should be determined, as any other price, so that supply and demand are equal.

Under such a system, productive activity and risk bearing can be divorced, each being carried out by the one or ones best qualified.

Source: Adapted from Kenneth Arrow, *Aspects of the Theory of Risk Bearing* (Helsinki: Yejö Johannsonin Säätio, 1965).

business that they carry. By choosing to invest in either the debt or the equity securities of a firm or some combination of them, people can thus select the kinds of risk they wish to bear.

In the last few decades, the rate of introduction of innovations that facilitate risk management has greatly accelerated because of changes on both the supply side and the demand side of the markets for risk bearing. New discoveries in telecommunications, information processing, and finance theory have significantly lowered the costs of achieving greater global diversification and specialization in the bearing of risks. At the same time, increased volatility of exchange rates, interest rates, and commodity prices has increased the demand for ways to manage risk. Thus, the rapid and widespread development of futures, options, and swap contracts starting in the 1970s and 1980s can largely be explained as market responses to these cost and demand factors.

But the theoretical ideal of complete markets for allocating risks can never be fully achieved because in the real world there are a number of limiting factors that can never be overcome entirely. Two key categories of factors limiting the efficient allocation of risks are *transactions costs* and *incentive problems.*

Transactions costs include the costs of establishing and running institutions such as insurance companies or securities exchanges and the costs of writing and enforcing contracts. These institutions will not come into existence unless the pecuniary benefits from their creation exceed the costs.

The primary incentive problems standing in the way of the development of institutions for efficient risk sharing are moral hazard and adverse selection. The **moral hazard** problem exists when having insurance against some risk causes the insured party to take greater risk or to take less care in preventing the event that gives rise to the loss. Moral hazard can lead to unwillingness on the part of insurance companies to insure against certain types of risk.

For example, if a warehouse owner buys fire insurance, the existence of the insurance reduces his incentive to spend money to prevent a fire. Failure to take the same precautions makes a warehouse fire a more likely occurrence. In an extreme case, the owner may be tempted to actually start a fire in order to collect the insurance money if the coverage exceeds the market value of the warehouse. Because of this potential moral hazard, insurance companies may limit the amount they will insure or simply refuse to sell fire insurance under certain circumstances.

Another class of incentive problems is **adverse selection**—those who purchase insurance against risk are more likely than the general population to be at risk. For example, consider **life annuities,** which are contracts that pay a fixed amount of money each month for as long as the purchaser lives. A firm selling such annuities cannot assume that the people who buy them will have the same expected length of life as the general population.

For example, suppose that a firm sells life annuities to people retiring at age 65. There are equal numbers of three types of people in the general population: type A live for 10 years, type B for 15 years, and type C for 20 years. On average, people aged 65 live for 15 years. If the firm charges a price that reflects a 15-year life expectancy, however, it will find that the people who buy the annuities are disproportionately of types B and C. Type A people will think that your annuities are not a good deal for them, and will not purchase them.

If the annuity firm knew the type of each potential customer—A, B, or C—and could charge a price that reflected the true life expectancy for that type, then there would be no adverse selection problem. But the annuity firm cannot get enough information about each potential customer to know as much about their true life expectancies as they themselves do. Unless the insurer can charge a price that accurately reflects each person's true life expectancy, a disproportionately large number of the annuities sold will be bought by healthy people who expect to live a long time. In our example, the average life expectancy of buyers of annuities might be 17.5 years, which is $2\frac{1}{2}$ years longer than in the general population.

Therefore, if annuity firms used life expectancies of the general population to price their annuities without adding more to adjust for the adverse selection problem, they would all lose money. As a result, firms in this market charge a price for annuities that is relatively unattractive to people with an average life expectancy, and the market is much smaller than it would be if there were no problem of adverse selection.

To examine the real-world limitations to efficient risk allocation and to illustrate how they are addressed, let us consider the risk of ownership of consumer-durable assets such as automobiles. People reduce some of the risks of car ownership by buying insurance. Insurance contracts against theft and accidental damage are generally available. But insurance against the risk of technological obsolescence is rarely available as a direct contractual arrangement.

Instead, institutional arrangements for dealing with the risk of obsolescence include *renting* or *leasing*. Rental contracts run for periods up to a year. Lease contracts are rental contracts for periods exceeding a year. Rental and leasing firms allow people to have the use of a car without exposure to the risk of obsolescence.

There is a cost to providing the facilities for car rentals and, therefore, they are not available everywhere. Specially equipped garages have to be built, and the cars must be serviced. Rentals are more readily available in tourist and vacation areas, where the demand for short-term rentals is relatively high.

There is a problem of adverse selection in the auto rental and leasing businesses. People who drive a lot and who do not want to service their cars will tend to rent rather than buy. Rental companies have few ways to detect in advance what kind of a driver a customer is. When firms set rental and lease rates, they therefore must presume that their customers will have a tendency to drive more than the average automobile owner.

There is also a moral hazard problem in the auto-rental business. People who rent rather than buy have a reduced incentive to maintain the cars in good condition and they are, therefore, more likely to abuse rented cars than their own.

To deal with problems of adverse selection and moral hazard, rental companies often charge extra for extra miles over a specified limit and for excessive wear and tear to the rented vehicle. But in the absence of a low-cost way to screen out the more costly customers, rental companies will have to charge higher prices for all renters. For people who take good care of cars, it will in general pay to own rather than rent.

7 Portfolio Theory: Quantitative Analysis for Optimal Risk Management

Portfolio theory is defined as quantitative analysis for optimal risk management. Whether the unit of analysis is a household, a firm, or some other economic organization, applying portfolio theory consists of formulating and evaluating the trade-offs between the benefits and costs of risk reduction in order to find an optimal course of action.

For households, consumption and risk preferences are taken as given. Preferences do change over time, but the mechanisms and reasons for those changes are not addressed by the theory. Instead, portfolio theory addresses the problem of how to choose among financial alternatives so as to maximize their given preferences. In general, the optimal choice involves evaluating the trade-off between receiving a higher expected return and taking greater risk.

However, not every decision to reduce one's risk exposure involves incurring a cost of either lower expected return or greater risk. There are circumstances in which both parties to a risk-transfer contract can reduce their risks at no cost other than the expense of drawing up the contract. For example, a buyer and a seller of a house can contractually settle on a transaction price for the house now even though the transfer of ownership will not take place until three months from now. Such an agreement is an example of a *forward contract.* By agreeing to enter into this forward contract, both parties eliminate the uncertainty associated with price volatility in the housing market during the next three months.

Thus, when different parties perceive the same event from opposite risk perspectives, both can be made better off with a contractual transfer of risks without either party incurring significant costs.

Quick Check 9

Describe an uncertain event that two parties perceive from opposite risk perspectives. How might they achieve a mutual reduction in risk?

Risk-management decisions in which there are no costs borne by either party are the exception rather than the norm. In general, there is a trade-off between the costs and benefits of risk reduction. This trade-off is perhaps most apparent in household decisions about how to allocate their wealth among asset categories, such as equities, fixed-income securities, and residential real estate.

The early formal models in portfolio theory were developed to deal with this class of risk-management decision.[4] These models use **probability distributions** to quantify the trade-off between risk and expected return. An asset portfolio's expected return is identified with the **mean** of the distribution, and its risk with the **standard deviation.**

These concepts are developed more fully in the next section.

8 Probability Distributions of Returns

Consider the case of Genco stock. Suppose you buy shares of Genco Corporation at a price of $100 per share and intend to hold it for a year. The *total* rate of return can be decomposed into the sum of a dividend-income component and a price-change component:

$$r = \frac{\text{Cash Dividend}}{\text{Beginning Price}} + \frac{\text{Ending Price of a Share} - \text{Beginning Price}}{\text{Beginning Price}}$$

$$r = \text{Dividend-Income Component} + \text{Price-Change Component}$$

In Genco's case, suppose that you expect the dividend component to be 3%, and the price-change component to be 7% so that the *expected* rate of return is 10%:

$$r = 3\% + 7\% = 10\%$$

A commonly used measure of the riskiness of an asset such as Genco stock is **volatility.**[5] Volatility is related to the range of possible rates of return from holding the stock and to their likelihood of occurring. *A stock's volatility is larger, the wider the range of possible outcomes and the larger the probabilities of those returns at the extremes of the range.*

---

[4]This model is associated with the name of the man who pioneered it, Harry Markowitz. Markowitz's seminal article, "Portfolio Selection," appeared in the *Journal of Finance* in 1952.
[5]The cost of insuring against a risk depends directly on volatility. So using volatility as a measure of risk is similar to using the cost of insuring against it.

TABLE 1 **Probability Distribution of Rate of Return on Genco**

State of the Economy	Rate of Return on Genco	Probability
Strong	30%	0.20
Normal	10%	0.60
Weak	−10%	0.20

For example, if asked to give a best "point estimate" of next year's rate of return on Genco stock, your answer would be 10%. You would not be surprised, however, if the actual return turned out to be different from 10%. It might turn out to be as low as −50% or as high as +80%. The wider the range of possible outcomes, the greater is the volatility.

To derive a further understanding of volatility, let us consider the entire probability distribution of rates of return on Genco stock. All possible returns are assigned probabilities ranging from zero (no possibility of occurring) to one (absolutely certain to occur).

Perfect certainty is the "degenerate" case of a probability distribution. Suppose it is absolutely certain that the return will be 10% over the next year. In that case there is only one possible rate of return, and its probability of occurrence is 1.0.

Now suppose that several different rates of return on Genco are possible, depending on the state of the economy. If the economy is strong over the coming year, Genco's sales and profits will tend to be high, and the rate of return on its stock will be 30%. If the economy is weak, the rate of return will be −10%, a loss. If the economy is just normal, the realized return will be 10%. The estimated probabilities for each of these states in this hypothetical example are shown in Table 1 and illustrated in Figure 1.

The probability distribution in Table 1 implies that if you invest in Genco stock, 10% is the most likely return that you will receive. It is three times more likely than either of the other two possible returns, −10% or 30%.

The **expected rate of return** (the mean) is defined as the sum over all possible outcomes of each possible rate of return multiplied by the respective probability of its happening:

$$E(r) = P_1 r_1 + P_2 r_2 + \cdots + P_n r_n$$

$$E(r) = \sum_{i=1}^{n} P_i r_i \tag{1}$$

FIGURE 1

Probability Distribution of Returns for Genco

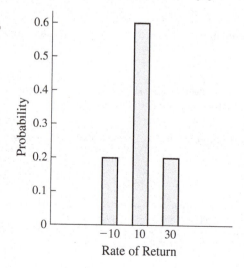

TABLE 2 Probability Distributions of Rate of Return on Risco and Genco

State of the Economy	Rate of Return on Risco	Rate of Return on Genco	Probability
Strong	50%	30%	0.20
Normal	10%	10%	0.60
Weak	−30%	−10%	0.20

Applying this formula to the case at hand, we find that the expected rate of return on Genco is:

$$E(r) = 0.2 \times 30\% + 0.6 \times 10\% + 0.2 \times -10\% = 10\%$$

You are obviously more uncertain about the rate of return in this case than in the special case of complete certainty. But now consider another stock, Risco, that has a wider range of possible rates of return than Genco. The probability distribution of Risco is compared to that of Genco in Table 2 and in Figure 2.

Note that the event probabilities are the same for both stocks, but Risco has a wider range of possible returns. If the economy is strong, Risco will produce a return of 50% compared to Genco's 30%. But if the economy is weak, Risco will produce a return of −30% compared to Genco's −10%. Risco is, therefore, more volatile.

9 Standard Deviation as a Measure of Risk

The volatility of a stock's return was shown to depend on the range of possible outcomes and on the probabilities of extreme values occurring. The statistic that is used most widely in finance to quantify and measure the volatility of a stock's probability distribution of returns is *standard deviation*, which is computed as follows:

$$\sigma = \sqrt{\sum_{i=1}^{n} P_i (r_i - E(r))^2} \tag{2}$$

FIGURE 2

Probability Distribution of Returns for Genco and Risco

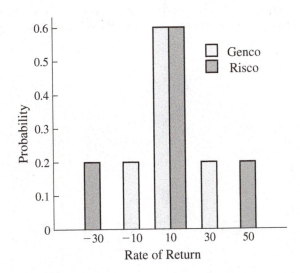

The larger is the standard deviation, the greater is the volatility of the stock. The standard deviation for the riskless investment that pays 10% with certainty would be zero:

$$\sigma = \sqrt{1.0(10\% - 10\%)^2} = 1.0(0.0) = 0$$

The standard deviation for Genco stock is

$$\sigma = \sqrt{[(0.2)(30\% - 10\%)^2 + (0.6)(10\% - 10\%)^2 + (0.2)(-10\% - 10\%)^2]}$$

$$\sigma = 12.65\%$$

The standard deviation for Risco stock is

$$\sigma = \sqrt{[(0.2)(50\% - 10\%)^2 + (0.6)(10\% - 10\%)^2 + (0.2)(-30\% - 10\%)^2]}$$

$$\sigma = 25.30\%$$

Risco's standard deviation is twice that of Genco because the possible deviations from its expected value are twice those of Genco.

Quick Check 10

Suppose that XYZ stock's rate of return can take three possible values: −50%, 50%, and 100%, each with equal probability. What is XYZ's expected rate of return and its standard deviation?

In the real world, the range of stock returns is not limited to a few numerical values as in our previous examples. Instead, the rate of return can be virtually any number. We, therefore, say that the distribution of stock returns is a **continuous probability distribution.** The most widely used distribution of that sort is the **normal distribution** with its familiar bell-shaped curve, shown in Figure 3.

For the normal distribution and other symmetric distributions similar to it, standard deviation is a natural measure of volatility. (Its symbol, σ, is pronounced "sigma.") The terms *volatility* and *sigma* are often used interchangeably.

The normal distribution encompasses an unbounded range of rates of return, from minus infinity to plus infinity. To interpret different values of the standard deviation, one usually employs **confidence intervals**—a certain range of values ("an interval") within which the actual return on the stock in the next period will fall with a specified probability. Thus, with a normal distribution, a return on the stock that falls within a confidence interval

FIGURE 3

Normal Distribution of Stock Returns

Note: The expected return is 10% and the standard deviation is 20%.

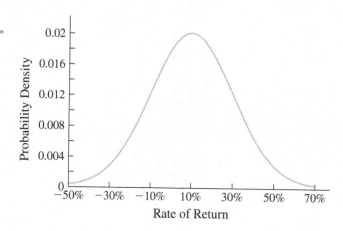

that encompasses all rates of return that are within one standard deviation on either side of the mean has a probability of about 0.68. A corresponding two-standard-deviation confidence interval has a probability of about 0.95, and a three-standard-deviation confidence interval encompasses a probability of about 0.99.

For example, consider a stock with an expected return of 10% and a standard deviation of 20%. If it is normally distributed, then there is a probability of about 0.95 that the actual return will turn out to fall in the interval between the expected return plus two standard deviations ($10\% + 2 \times 20\% = 50\%$) and the expected return minus two standard deviations ($10\% - 2 \times 20\% = -30\%$). The range of rates of return that is bounded on the low end by -30% and on the upper end by 50% is a 0.95 confidence interval for this stock's rate of return.

Quick Check 11

What are the bounds of a 0.99 confidence interval for this stock's rate of return?

Summary

Risk is defined as uncertainty that matters to people. *Risk management* is the process of formulating the benefit-cost trade-offs of risk reduction and deciding on a course of action to take. *Portfolio theory* is the quantitative analysis of those trade-offs to find an optimal course of action.

All risks are ultimately borne by people in their capacity as consumers, stakeholders of firms and other economic organizations, or taxpayers.

The riskiness of an asset or a transaction cannot be assessed in isolation or in the abstract; it depends on the specific frame of reference. In one context, the purchase or sale of a particular asset may add to one's risk exposure; in another, the same transaction may be risk reducing.

Speculators are investors who take positions that increase their exposure to certain risks in the hope of increasing their wealth. In contrast, hedgers take positions to reduce their exposures. The same person can be a speculator on some exposures and a hedger on others.

Many resource allocation decisions, such as saving, investment, and financing decisions, are significantly influenced by the presence of risk and, therefore, are partly risk-management decisions.

We distinguish among five major categories of risk exposures for households: sickness, disability, and death; job loss; consumer-durable asset risk; liability risk; and financial asset risk.

Firms face several categories of risks: production risk, price risk of outputs, and price risk of inputs.

There are five steps in the risk-management process:

- Risk identification
- Risk assessment
- Selection of risk-management techniques
- Implementation
- Review

There are four techniques of risk management:

- Risk avoidance
- Loss prevention and control

- Risk retention
- Risk transfer

There are three dimensions of risk transfer: hedging, insuring, and diversifying.

Diversification improves welfare by spreading risks among many people, so that the existing uncertainty matters less.

From society's perspective, risk-management institutions contribute to economic efficiency in two important ways. First, they shift risk away from those who are least willing or able to bear it to those who are most willing to bear it. Second, they cause a reallocation of resources to production and consumption in accordance with the new distribution of risk bearing. By allowing people to reduce their exposure to the risk of undertaking certain business ventures, they may encourage entrepreneurial behavior that can have a benefit to society.

Over the centuries, various economic organizations and contractual arrangements have evolved to facilitate a more efficient allocation of risk bearing by expanding the scope of diversification and the types of risk that are shifted.

Among the factors limiting the efficient allocation of risks are transactions costs and problems of adverse selection and moral hazard.

Key Terms

- risk aversion
- risk management
- risk exposure
- speculators
- hedgers
- precautionary saving
- risk-management process
- actuaries
- hedging
- insuring
- diversifying
- moral hazard

- adverse selection
- life annuities
- portfolio theory
- probability distributions
- mean
- standard deviation
- volatility
- expected rate of return
- continuous probability distribution
- normal distribution
- confidence intervals

Answers to Quick Check Questions

Quick Check 1   To eliminate the risk of a decline in house prices over the next three months, Joe agrees to sell his house three months from now at a price of $100,000. After three months, by the time of the transfer of ownership and the conclusion of the sale, housing prices have gone up and it turns out that Joe could have gotten $150,000 for his house. Should Joe chastise himself for his decision to eliminate his price risk?

Answer: No. Based on the information Joe had at the time and his preference to eliminate risk, Joe made the right decision.

Quick Check 2   Think of an insurance policy that you or someone you know has recently purchased or canceled. List the steps that led to the decision.

Answer: Answers will vary with each student's specific situation.

Quick Check 3   Think of a fast-food restaurant. What risks is such a business exposed to, and who bears them?

Answer: *Major Risks*
- Risk that ovens will break down.
- Risk that raw materials will not arrive on time.
- Risk that employees will be late or absent.
- Risk of new competition in the area.
- Risk that raw material prices will increase unpredictably.

Who Bears the Risk

Shareholders in the business bear the bulk of the risks as they impact the value of the business.

Quick Check 4   If the government mandates that all automobile owners must buy accident insurance, who bears the risk of auto accidents?

Answer: If all automobile owners are required to purchase accident insurance, then all automobile owners ultimately are the ones who bear the risk of auto accidents through the payment of higher insurance premiums.

Quick Check 5   Identify a major risk in your life and describe the steps you take to manage it.

Answer: Sample Answer:

Major Risks

Sickness (hospitalization)
Unemployment (difficulty finding a job)
Liability risk (car accident)

Typical Management Techniques

Purchase health insurance.
Invest in higher education to increase likelihood of getting a job.
Purchase liability insurance (usually with auto insurance policy).

Quick Check 6   Suppose you are a U.S. citizen studying in Germany. A month from now you know that you will receive $10,000 from the United States as a scholarship grant. How can you hedge your foreign-exchange risk? How can you insure against it?

Answer: In order to hedge your risk, you would enter into a contract now to sell your $10,000 at a fixed price per euro. If you wanted to insure against a decline in the euro price of the dollar, you could pay a premium now for a put option that would give you the right to sell your $10,000 a month from now at a fixed euro price per dollar.

Quick Check 7   How might farmers reduce their exposure to risks of crop failure through diversification?

Answer: Farmers could plant several different types of plants instead of just one. In addition, they could own plots of land in several locations rather than own the same amount of land in just one location.

Quick Check 8   Give an example of an investment project or a new business that would not be feasible if the risks associated with it could not be shared or transferred through the financial system.

Answer: Examples:
Chemical company
Child safety products company
Airline

Bank
Hospital
Environmental consulting
Hazardous waste disposal

Quick Check 9 Describe an uncertain event that two parties perceive from opposite risk perspectives. How might they achieve a mutual reduction in risk?

Answer: Suppose a college with large heating oil bills is concerned about rising oil prices. A reseller of heating oil is concerned about falling prices. These two parties could contractually agree on a price per gallon that would eliminate price risk for both parties.

Quick Check 10 Suppose that XYZ stock's rate of return can take three possible values: -50%, 50%, and 100%, each with equal probability. What is XYZ's expected rate of return and its standard deviation?

Answer:

$$E(r) = \frac{1}{3} \cdot -50\% + \frac{1}{3} \cdot 50\% + \frac{1}{3} \cdot 100\% = 0.333 = 33.33\%$$

$$\sigma = \sqrt{\frac{1}{3} \cdot (-50\% - E(r))^2 + \frac{1}{3} \cdot (50\% - E(r))^2 + \frac{1}{3} \cdot (100\% - E(r))^2}$$

$$= 0.6236$$

$$= 62.36\%$$

Quick Check 11 What are the bounds of a 0.99 confidence interval for this stock's rate of return?

Answer: The bounds are three standard deviations on either side of the expected return.

Questions and Problems

What Is Risk?

1. Suppose you are aware of the following investment opportunity: You could open a coffee shop around the corner from your home for $25,000. If business is strong, you could net $15,000 in after-tax cash flows each year over the next 5 years.
   a. If you knew for certain the business would be a success, would this be a risky investment?
   b. Now assume this is a risky venture and that there is a 50% chance it is a success and a 50% chance you go bankrupt within 2 years. You decide to go ahead and invest. If the business subsequently goes bankrupt, did you make the wrong decision based on the information you had at the time? Why or why not?

2. Suppose your new business venture will last only one year. For $110,000 you plan to purchase 20 acres of farmland next to a site that may be developed into a retail shopping mall. You will sell the land in a year and, based on the outcome of the zoning hearing, there is an equal chance that it will be worth either $100,000, or $125,000, or $145,000 next year. The bank is willing to make you a riskless loan to finance the purchase of the property at an interest rate of 10%. The loan balance in total will be paid in one year when you sell the property. What is the most the bank will be willing to lend?

Risk and Economic Decisions

3. Suppose you are a pension fund manager and you know today that you need to make a $100,000 payment in 3 months.
   a. What would be a risk-free investment for you?
   b. If you had to make that payment in 20 years instead, what would be a risk-free investment?
   c. What do you conclude from your answers to parts a and b of this question?
4. Suppose you are a Japanese banker: Is it riskier to make a loan denominated in dollars or in yen? What if you are an English banker?
5. You are the CEO of a Mexican company that took out a dollar-denominated loan from an American bank one year ago when the peso–dollar exchange rate was 10 pesos per dollar. You borrowed $100,000 at 8% interest and promised to repay the entire balance and interest in one payment at the end of the year. The current exchange rate is 9.5 pesos per dollar. What effective pesos-denominated rate of interest did you pay for the loan?

The Risk-Management Process

6. Which risk management technique has been chosen in each of the following situations?
   • Installing a smoke detector in your home
   • Investing savings in T-bills rather than in stocks
   • Deciding not to purchase collision insurance on your car
   • Purchasing a life insurance policy for yourself
7. You are considering a choice between investing $1,000 in a conventional one-year T-Bill offering an interest rate of 8% and a one-year Index-Linked Inflation Plus T‐Bill offering 3% plus the rate of inflation.
   a. Which is the safer investment?
   b. Which offers the higher expected return?
   c. What is the real return on the Index-Linked Bond?
8. Suppose you are a fanatical follower of a particular major league baseball team (e.g., the Cubs) about to start playing in the World Series. You know that if your team loses again this time you will need serious psychological help and expect you will probably have to spend thousands of dollars on counseling services. Is there a way to insure against this risk? Would gambling on the World Series be categorized as *speculation*?

The Three Dimensions of Risk Transfer

9. What dimension of risk transfer are you engaged in if you make a restaurant reservation for your party of six? Why do some restaurants refuse to take reservations?
10. Suppose you are interested in financing your new home purchase. You have your choice of a myriad financing options. You could enter into any one of the following agreements: 8% fixed rate for 7 years, 8.5% fixed rate for 15 years, 9% fixed for 30 years. In addition, you could finance with a 30-year variable rate that begins at 5% and increases and decreases with the prime rate, or you could finance with a 30-year variable rate that begins at 6% with ceilings of 2% per year to a maximum of 12% and no minimum.
    a. Suppose you believe that interest rates are on the rise. If you want to completely eliminate your risk of rising interest rates for the longest period of time, which option should you choose?

    b. Would you consider that hedging or insuring? Why?

    c. What does your risk-management decision "cost" you in terms of quoted interest rates during the first year?

11. Referring to the information in the previous problem (problem 10), answer the following:

    a. Suppose you believe interest rates are going to fall; which option should you choose?

    b. What risk do you face in that transaction?

    c. How might you insure against that risk? What does that cost you (in terms of quoted interest rates)?

12. Suppose you are thinking of investing in real estate. How might you achieve a diversified real estate investment?

13. Suppose you are planning to invest in the human capital embodied in your teenage daughter. In the context of the choice of a college and a major, discuss the risk-management strategy of diversification.

Risk Transfer and Economic Efficiency

14. *Challenge Problem:* Suppose you have been hired to manage an encyclopedia sales team. Discuss the efficiency issues involved in the compensation scheme for the salesmen. Should they be paid a fixed wage based only on the hours they work? Why not? If they are paid on a commission basis their earnings will be riskier. Is it efficient to have them bear this risk?

Institutions for Risk Management

15. Many insurance policies ranging from automobile, to homeowner's, to health insurance contain deductible provisions. A deductible is a fixed amount per claim, or over a given period of time, which is not reimbursed under the policy. What efficiency role do deductibles play in insurance markets?

16. Recently when I checked into a hotel in Strasbourg, France, I inquired about parking alternatives. The clerk remarked that there was a free parking lot behind the hotel but that it was not "safe." Knowing that Strasbourg has a bad reputation for youth crime, including burning cars on the street, I was not surprised at the clerk's remarks. Undeterred I promptly parked the car I was driving in the hotel parking lot where I left it for most of the three days I stayed at the hotel. Do you draw any inferences about the ownership of the new vehicle I was driving? Is this an example of moral hazard or adverse selection?

Portfolio Theory: Quantitative Analysis for Optimal Risk Management

17. Suppose you are to receive a 3,000 Turkish lira check from your publishing agent in three months. You have the opportunity to enter the forward currency market and sign a contract to purchase dollars in three months at a price of 1.4 TL per dollar.

    a. What will be your dollar proceeds in three months if you hedge your exchange rate risk?

    b. How many dollars will you gain or lose by hedging versus risk retention if the price of a dollar three months hence is 1.35 TL?

18. Given the information in the previous question, suppose rather than using a forward contract to hedge your risk you had used an option contract to insure. Suppose a zero-cost option contract allows you to purchase dollars in three months at a price 1.42 TL per dollar.

    a. How will your dollar proceeds be determined in three months?

b. How many dollars will you gain or lose by insuring versus hedging if the price of a dollar three months hence is 1.35 TL?

Probability Distributions of Returns

19. Suppose we have the following information on prices and dividends for a share of Taltavull Transfer Corporation stock.

Year	1 Jan Price	31 Dec Price	Cash Dividend
20×0		$65.00	
20×1	$65.00	$72.00	$5.00
20×2	$72.00	$77.00	$5.00
20×3	$77.00	$80.00	$5.00
20×4	$80.00	$79.00	$7.50
20×5	$79.00	$85.00	$7.50

Calculate the annual total rates of return on an investment in TTC. Using each year as an observation, what is the expected annual total rate of return?

Standard Deviation as a Measure of Risk

20. Find the expected return and variability of the returns measured as the standard deviation from the following return distribution:

Probability	Return
15%	50%
25%	40%
25%	25%
25%	10%
10%	−30%

21. Suppose the following represents the historical returns for Microsoft and Lotus Development Corporation:

	Historical Returns	
Year	MSFT	LOTS
1	10%	9%
2	15%	12%
3	−12%	−7%
4	20%	18%
5	7%	5%

a. What is the mean return for Microsoft? For Lotus?

b. What is the standard deviation of returns for Microsoft? For Lotus?

22. Continuing the previous problem (problem 21), suppose the returns for Microsoft and Lotus have normally distributed returns with means and standard deviations calculated above. For each stock, determine the range of returns within one expected standard deviation of the mean and within two standard deviations of the mean.

23. Suppose you invest in a security having a normal distribution of returns with an expected return of 12% and a standard deviation of 3%. If you realize a rate of return of 18%, how lucky should you consider yourself?

24. *Challenge Problem:* Refer to the data in the previous problems (problems 21 and 22). Suppose over the past five years you had undertaken the following portfolio strategy. At the beginning of each year you divided your money, say $1,000, equally between investments in Microsoft and Lotus. At the end of the year you collected your returns and restarted the process of dividing your investment between the two stocks. What would have been the return each year on your total investment? What is the mean return and standard deviation of returns for this portfolio? How are the mean and standard deviation related to the means and standard deviations calculated in the previous problem?

APPENDIX

Leasing, A Cost-Benefit Analysis of Eliminating the Risk of Obsolescence

Leases were analyzed, in which the concept of present value is used to evaluate whether it costs less to buy or lease an asset. The analysis concluded that you would lease the asset if the present value of the after-tax lease payments is less than the present value of the after-tax cash outflows associated with buying it. That analysis considered only the role of interest rates and taxes and ignored the effect of uncertainty about the asset's future price. However, price uncertainty is an important consideration in the analysis of leasing.

For example, suppose that you are in the habit of buying a new car every three years. Your present car is almost three years old, and you are considering whether to buy a new one or lease it. The new model has a purchase price of $20,000. You can either buy the car or you can lease it from the dealer for 36 months at a rate of $402.84 per month. If you buy it, the dealer can arrange for you to borrow the full purchase price of $20,000 at an interest rate of 8% per year (*APR*), so that you make monthly payments on the car loan that will match the $402.84 per month lease payments.[6] The loan is fully amortized over a five-year period, so the balance of the loan at the end of 36 months will be $8,907.06. The maintenance expenses, taxes, and insurance will be the same whether you lease or buy.

Under these conditions, what is the difference between leasing the car and buying it on credit? Table A.1 summarizes the cash flows.

Under both arrangements, you have the use of the car for 36 months in return for a monthly payment of $402.84. The difference is that if you purchase the car now, then three years from now you will sell it at an uncertain market price and pay off the $8,907.06 balance of your loan. Your net cash flow will be the difference between the price of the car on the used-car market three years in the future and $8,907.06.

If you lease the car, however, at the end of three years you neither own it nor owe any money on it. In effect, it is as if you had sold the car in advance for $8,907.06—the balance of your loan. Thus, under the lease arrangement, the dealer effectively agrees in advance to

---

[6]*APR* stands for *annual percentage rate*. When payments are monthly, an *APR* of 8% is equivalent to a monthly interest rate of $\frac{2}{3}$%.

TABLE A.1 Comparison of Leasing a Car or Buying It on Credit

Alternative	Monthly Payment	Final Cash Flow
Lease for three years	$402.84	0
Buy on credit and sell at end of three years	$402.84	Resale price minus $8,907.06
Difference	0	Resale price minus $8,907.06

repurchase the car from you three years from now at a price equal to the remaining balance of the loan.[7]

If you were absolutely sure that the car's residual value after three years was going to be $11,000, then clearly it would pay to purchase the car now rather than lease it. This is because you could resell it in three years, pay off the $8,907 balance of the loan, and pocket the $2,093 difference.

But you do not know the resale value with certainty. Even if you take very good care of it, the resale value of the car three years from now will be determined by a variety of factors (such as consumer tastes, cost of gasoline, level of economic activity) that can only be estimated now.

Appendix: Leasing to Eliminate the Risk of Obsolescence

25. Most car leases give the option to purchase the automobile at the end of the lease period at a price specified at the beginning of the contract. Thus the lease has an imbedded call option on the car exercisable at the end of the lease. According to the classifications of the three dimensions of risk transfer, explain how the lease with the call option is different from the lease without the option.

Suggested Readings

Arrow, K. J. "The Role of Securities in the Optimal Allocation of Risk Bearing." *Review of Economic Studies* 31, April 1964. Trans. of 1953 article in French.

Crouhy, M., D. Galai, and R. Mark. *The Essentials of Risk Management.* New York: McGraw-Hill Irwin, 2006.

Doherty, N. *Integrated Risk Management: Techniques and Strategies for Managing Corporate Risk.* New York: McGraw-Hill Irwin, 2000.

Merton, R. C., and Z. Bodie. "On the Management of Financial Guarantees." *Financial Management* 21, Winter 1992.

Smithson, C., and B. Simkins. "Does Risk Management Add Value? A Survey of the Evidence." *Journal of Applied Corporate Finance* 17, Summer 2005.

---

[7]Real-world leases contain certain provisions designed to deter customers who wear cars out quickly and to discourage abuse of the car. Thus, customers who exceed a certain mileage limitation must pay extra and must pay for any damage done to the car. Many leases also give you the right, but not the obligation, to purchase the car at a prespecified price at the lease's end. This right has value and is similar to a call option.

Hedging, Insuring, and Diversifying

From Chapter 11 of *Financial Economics*, 2/e. Zvi Bodie, Robert C. Merton, David L. Cleeton.

Hedging, Insuring, and Diversifying

OBJECTIVES

- To explain the various methods and institutional mechanisms for the transfer of risk through the financial system by hedging, insuring, and diversifying.
- To explain how diversification can reduce the cost of insurance.

CONTENTS

Previously we said that there are three ways of transferring risk to others: hedging, insuring, and diversifying. The purpose of this chapter is to give you a more detailed and concrete understanding of all three methods and how they are used in practice.

One is said to hedge a risk when reducing one's exposure to a loss entails giving up the possibility of a gain. Thus, farmers who sell their future crops at a fixed price in order to eliminate the risk of a low price at harvest time give up the possibility of profiting from higher prices at harvest time. Financial markets offer a variety of mechanisms for hedging against the risks of uncertain commodity prices, stock prices, interest rates, and exchange rates. In this chapter we explore the use of derivatives and the matching of assets to liabilities in order to hedge market risks.

Insuring means paying a *premium* (the price paid for the insurance) to avoid losses. By buying insurance, you substitute a *sure* loss (the premium you pay for the policy) for the *possibility* of a larger loss if you do not insure.

In addition to insurance policies, there are other types of contracts and securities not usually called insurance that serve the same economic function of providing compensation for losses. A common example is a *credit guarantee*, which insures creditors against losses stemming from a debtor's failure to make promised payments. *Option contracts* are another means for insuring against losses. This chapter explores these different contractual mechanisms for insuring against risk.

Finally, diversifying is the pooling and sharing of risks. Diversifying your portfolio of stocks means splitting your investment among several stocks rather than concentrating it all in just a single stock. The volatility of a diversified portfolio is generally less than the volatilities of each of its individual components. In this chapter we will explore the way diversification works to reduce volatility and the cost of insurance.

1 Using Forward and Futures Contracts to Hedge Risk

Any time two parties agree to exchange some item in the future at a prearranged price they are entering into a **forward contract.** Often people enter into forward contracts without knowing that is what they are called.

For example, you may be planning a trip from Boston to Tokyo a year from now. You make your flight reservations now, and the airline reservation clerk tells you that you can either lock in a price of $1,000 now or you can pay whatever the price may be on the day of your flight. In either case payment will not take place until the day of your flight. If you decide to lock in the $1,000 price, you have entered into a forward contract with the airline.

In entering the forward contract you eliminate the risk of the cost of your airfare going above $1,000. If the price of a ticket turns out to be $1,500 a year from now, you will be happy that you had the good sense to lock in a forward price of $1,000. On the other hand, if the price turns out to be $500 on the day of your flight, you will still have to pay the $1,000 forward price to which you agreed. In that case, you will regret your decision.

The main features of forward contracts and the terms used to describe them are as follows:

- Two parties agree to exchange some item in the future at a price specified now—the **forward price.**[1]
- The price for *immediate* delivery of the item is called the **spot price.**

---

[1]More precisely, the *forward price* is that delivery price that makes the value of the forward contract equal to zero at the time the contract is made.

- No money is paid in the present by either party to the other.
- The **face value** of the contract is the quantity of the item specified in the contract times the forward price.
- The party who agrees to *buy* the specified item is said to take a **long position,** and the party who agrees to *sell* the item is said to take a **short position.**

A **futures contract** is essentially a *standardized* forward contract that is traded on some organized exchange. The exchange interposes itself between the buyer and the seller, so that each has a separate contract with the exchange. Standardization means that the terms of the futures contract (e.g., quantity and quality of the item to be delivered, etc.) are the same for all contracts.

A forward contract can often reduce the risks faced by both the buyer and the seller. Let us illustrate how with a detailed example.

Suppose a farmer has planted her fields with wheat. It is now a month before harvest time, and the size of the farmer's crop is reasonably certain. Because a large fraction of the farmer's wealth is tied up in her wheat crop, she may want to eliminate the risk associated with uncertainty about its future price by selling it now at a fixed price for future delivery.

Let's also suppose that there is a baker who knows that he will need wheat a month from now to produce bread. The baker has a large fraction of his wealth tied up in his bakery business. Like the farmer, the baker is also faced with uncertainty about the future price of wheat, but the way for him to reduce the price risk is to *buy* wheat now for future delivery. Thus, the baker is a natural match for the farmer, who would like to reduce her risk by selling wheat now for future delivery.

The farmer and the baker, therefore, agree to a certain *forward* price that the baker will pay the farmer at the time of delivery.

The forward contract stipulates that the farmer will deliver a specified quantity of wheat to the baker at the forward price *regardless of what the spot price turns out to be at the delivery date.*

Let's put some actual quantities and prices into our example to see how forward contracts work. Suppose that the size of the farmer's wheat crop is 100,000 bushels and that the forward price for delivery a month from now is $2 per bushel. The farmer agrees to sell her entire crop to the baker with delivery a month from now at $2 per bushel. At that time, the farmer will deliver 100,000 bushels of wheat to the baker and receive $200,000 in return. With an agreement such as this, both parties eliminate the risk associated with the uncertainty about the spot price of wheat at the delivery date. They are both hedging their exposures.

Now let us consider why it is convenient to have standardized *futures* contracts for wheat that are traded on exchanges instead of forward contracts. The forward contract in our example calls for the farmer to deliver wheat to the baker on the contract delivery date. However, it can be difficult for a farmer to find a baker who wants to buy wheat at the time and place that are most convenient to the farmer. Similarly, it may be difficult for the baker to find a farmer who wants to sell wheat at the time and place that are most convenient to the baker.

For example, suppose that the farmer and the baker are separated by a great distance, for example, the farmer might be located in Kansas and the baker in New York. The baker usually buys wheat from a local supplier in New York and the farmer usually sells her wheat to a local distributor in Kansas. By using wheat futures contracts, the farmer and the baker can retain the risk-reducing benefits of the forward contract (and save paying costs to transport wheat) without having to change their usual supplier and distributor relationships.

The futures exchange operates as an intermediary matching buyers and sellers. Indeed, the buyer of a wheat futures contract never knows the identity of the seller because the contract is officially between the buyer and the futures exchange. Similarly, the seller never knows the identity of the buyer. Only a small fraction of the wheat futures contracts traded on the exchange result in actual delivery of wheat. Most of them are settled in cash.

Let us illustrate how this works in the case of the farmer and the baker. Instead of entering a forward contract calling for the farmer in Kansas to deliver her wheat to the baker in New York at a delivery price of $2 per bushel, there are two separate transactions. The farmer and baker each enter a wheat futures contract with the futures exchange at a futures price of $2 per bushel. The farmer takes a short position; the baker takes a long position, and the exchange matches them. In a month's time, the farmer sells her wheat to her normal distributor in Kansas, and the baker buys his wheat from his normal supplier in New York at the spot price. They settle their futures contract by paying to (or receiving from) the futures exchange the *difference* between the $2 per bushel futures price and the spot price multiplied by the quantity specified in the contract (100,000 bushels). The futures exchange transfers the payment from one party to the other.[2]

Let us further illustrate how this all works step by step with the help of Table 1. Consider first the farmer, whose situation is shown in the top panel. To hedge her exposure to the price risk, she takes a short position in a one-month wheat futures contract for 100,000 bushels at a futures price of $2 per bushel.

Table 1 illustrates what happens at three different spot prices on the delivery date: $1.50, $2.00, and $2.50 per bushel. If the spot price of wheat turns out to be $1.50 per bushel a month from now (column 1), the farmer's proceeds from the sale of wheat to the distributor in Kansas are $150,000. However, she gains $50,000 from her futures contract. Thus, her total receipts are $200,000.

If the spot price turns out to be $2.00 per bushel (column 2), the farmer's proceeds from the sale of her wheat to the distributor in Kansas are $200,000, and there is no gain or loss on the futures contract. If the spot price turns out to be $2.50 per bushel, the farmer

TABLE 1 Hedging Price Risk with Futures Contracts

Farmer's Transaction	Spot Price of Wheat on Delivery Date		
	$1.50 per bu. (1)	$2.00 per bu. (2)	$2.50 per bu. (3)
Proceeds from sale of wheat to distributor	$150,000	$200,000	$250,000
Cash flow from the futures contract	$50,000 paid to farmer	0	$50,000 paid by farmer
Total receipts	$200,000	$200,000	$200,000

Baker's Transaction	Spot Price of Wheat on Delivery Date		
	$1.50 per bu. (1)	$2.00 per bu. (2)	$2.50 per bu. (3)
Cost of wheat bought from supplier	$150,000	$200,000	$250,000
Cash flow from the futures contract	$50,000 paid by baker	0	$50,000 paid to baker
Total outlays	$200,000	$200,000	$200,000

The futures price is $2.00 per bushel, and the quantity is 100,000 bushels.

---

[2]Rather than wait until the contract maturity date, the cash value of futures contracts are usually settled on a daily basis; this reduces the risk to the exchange of either party defaulting on their contracts.

receives $250,000 from the sale of her wheat to the distributor in Kansas but loses $50,000 on the futures contract. Her total receipts are then $200,000.

Thus, no matter what the spot price of wheat turns out to be, the farmer winds up with total receipts of $200,000 from the combination of selling her wheat to the distributor in Kansas and her short position in the wheat futures contract.

The bottom panel of Table 1 shows the situation of the baker. A month from now the baker buys wheat from his supplier in New York at the spot price. If the spot price is $1.50 per bushel (column 1), the baker pays only $150,000 to the supplier for the wheat but also loses $50,000 on his wheat futures contract. His total outlay is, therefore, $200,000. If the spot price is $2.00 per bushel (column 2), the baker pays the supplier $200,000, and there is no gain or loss on the futures contract. If the spot price is $2.50 per bushel (column 3), the baker pays the supplier $250,000 for wheat but gains $50,000 on his futures contract, thus making his total outlay $200,000.

To better understand Table 1 consider what would happen *without* the futures contract. If the spot price of wheat turns out to be $1.50 per bushel, then the farmer receives and the baker pays $150,000. If the spot price turns out to be $2.50, then the farmer receives and the baker pays $250,000. But *with* the futures contract, no matter what the spot price turns out to be, the farmer receives and the baker pays a *total* of $200,000. Because both parties know for certain what they will get and what they will pay out, the futures contract has eliminated the risk posed by price uncertainty.

Figure 1 displays the same information that is contained in the top panel of Table 1. It shows the *total* cash flows to the farmer from selling her wheat *and* the futures contract combined for *any* spot price on the delivery date.

Figure 1 illustrates that no matter what the spot price of wheat turns out to be on the delivery date, the farmer will wind up with $200,000.

To summarize, the farmer is able to eliminate the price risk she faces from owning the wheat by taking a *short* position in a futures contract, effectively *selling* the wheat for future delivery at the futures price. The baker too is able to eliminate the price risk he faces by taking a *long* position in the futures market for wheat, effectively *buying* wheat for future delivery at a fixed price. Futures contracts make it possible for both the farmer and

FIGURE 1

Farmer's Total Cash Flows from Hedging with Futures

Notes: The farmer's wheat crop is 100,000 bushels, and the futures price of wheat that she has agreed to in her futures contract is $2 per bushel. Gains or losses on the futures contract serve to keep her total receipts at $200,000 regardless of the spot price of wheat on the delivery date.

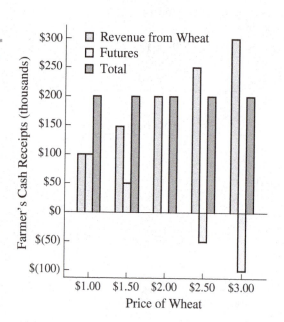

the baker to hedge their exposure to price risk while continuing their normal relationships with distributors and suppliers.

Quick Check 1

Show what happens to the farmer and the baker if the spot price on the delivery date is:
a. $1.00 per bushel.
b. $3.00 per bushel.

The example of the farmer and the baker illustrates three important points about risk and risk transfer:

- *Whether a transaction is risk reducing or risk increasing depends on the particular context in which it is undertaken.*

Transactions in futures markets are sometimes characterized as being very risky. But for the farmer, whose wealth is tied up in the business of growing wheat, taking a short position in a wheat futures contract is risk reducing. For the baker, whose wealth is tied up in the business of baking bread, taking a long position in a wheat futures contract is risk reducing.

Of course, for someone who is not in the business of either growing wheat or producing products that require wheat as an input, taking a position in wheat futures might be risky.[3] Thus, the transaction of buying or selling wheat futures should not be characterized as risky in the abstract. It may be risk reducing or risk increasing depending on the context.

- *Both parties to a risk-reducing transaction can benefit by it even though in retrospect it may seem as if one of the parties has gained at the expense of the other.*

When entering the futures contract, neither the farmer nor the baker knows whether the price of wheat will turn out to be greater or less than $2.00 per bushel. By entering the futures contract, they *both* achieve a reduction in risk and are thereby *both* made better off. In a month's time, if the spot price of wheat is different from $2.00, one of them will gain and the other will lose on the futures contract. But that does not alter the fact that they were both made better off by entering the contract when they did.

- *Even with no change in total output or total risk, redistributing the way the risk is borne can improve the welfare of the individuals involved.*

This last point is related to the second. From a social perspective, the total quantity of wheat produced in the economy may not be directly affected by the existence of the futures contract between the farmer and the baker. It might, therefore, appear as though there is no gain in social welfare from the existence of futures contracts. However, as we have seen, by allowing both the farmer and the baker to lower their exposure to price risk, the futures contract improves their welfare.

Using futures contracts to hedge commodity price risk has a long history. The earliest known futures markets came into existence in the Middle Ages to meet the needs of farmers and merchants. Today many organized futures exchanges exist around the world not only for commodities (such as grains, oilseeds, livestock, meat, metals, and petroleum products) but also for a variety of financial instruments (such as currencies, bonds, and stock market

---

[3] Such parties are known as *speculators.*

indexes). The futures contracts traded on these exchanges allow businesses to hedge against commodity-price risk, foreign-exchange risk, stock market risk, and interest-rate risk and the list is constantly expanding to include other sources of risk.

2 Hedging Foreign-Exchange Risk with Swap Contracts

A swap is another type of contract that facilitates the hedging of risks. A **swap contract** consists of two parties exchanging (or "swapping") a series of cash flows at specified intervals over a specified period of time. The swap payments are based on an agreed principal amount (the *notional* amount). There is no immediate payment of money and, hence, the swap agreement itself provides no new funds to either party.

In principle, a swap contract could call for the exchange of anything. In current practice, however, most swap contracts involve the exchange of returns on commodities, currencies, or securities.

Let's look at how a currency swap works and how it can be used to hedge risk. Suppose that you have a computer software business in the United States, and a German company wants to acquire the right to produce and market your software in Germany. The German company agrees to pay you 100,000 euros (€100,000) each year for the next 10 years for these rights.

If you want to hedge the risk of fluctuations in the dollar value of your expected stream of revenues (due to fluctuations in the dollar/euro exchange rate), you can enter a currency swap now to exchange your future stream of euros for a future stream of dollars at a set of forward exchange rates specified now.

The swap contract is, therefore, equivalent to a series of forward contracts. The notional amount in the swap contract corresponds to the face value of the implied forward contracts.

To illustrate with numbers, suppose the dollar/euro exchange rate is currently $1.30 per euro and that that exchange rate also applies to all forward contracts covering the next 10 years. The notional amount in your swap contract is €100,000 per year. By entering the swap contract, you lock in a dollar revenue of $130,000 per year (€100,000 × $1.30 per euro). Each year on the settlement date you will receive (or pay) an amount of cash equal to €100,000 times the difference between the forward rate and the actual spot rate at that time.

Thus, suppose that one year from now on the settlement date, the spot rate of exchange is $1.20 per euro. The party on the other side of your swap contract, called the **counterparty** (perhaps a European company in our example), is obliged to pay you €100,000 times the difference between the $1.30 per euro forward rate and the $1.20 per euro spot rate (i.e., $10,000).

Without the swap contract, your cash revenues from the software license agreement would be $120,000 (€100,000 times the spot rate of $1.20 per euro). But with the swap contract, your total revenues will be $130,000: You receive €100,000 from the German company, which you sell to get $120,000, and you receive another $10,000 from the counterparty to your swap contract.

Now suppose that in the second year on the settlement date, the spot rate of exchange is $1.40 per euro. You will be obliged to pay the counterparty to your swap agreement €100,000 times the difference between the $1.40 per euro spot rate and the $1.30 per euro forward rate (i.e., $10,000). Without the swap contract your cash revenues from the software license agreement would be $140,000 (€100,000 times the spot rate of $1.40 per euro). But with the swap contract, your total revenues will be $130,000. Thus, in the second year, you will probably wish that you did not have the swap contract. But the possibility of giving up potential gains in order to eliminate potential losses is the essence of hedging.

Quick Check 2

Suppose that in the third year, on the settlement date the spot rate of exchange is $1.30 per euro. How much money is transferred between the counterparties to the swap contract?

The international swap market began in the early 1980s and has grown rapidly. In addition to currency and interest-rate swaps, many other items can be and are exchanged through swap agreements, for example, returns on different stock indexes, and even bushels of wheat for barrels of oil.

3 Hedging Shortfall Risk by Matching Assets to Liabilities

Insurance companies and other financial intermediaries that sell insured savings plans and other insurance contracts need to assure their customers that the product they are buying is free of default risk. One way to assure customers about the risk of contract default is for insurance companies to hedge their liabilities in the financial markets by investing in assets that match the characteristics of their liabilities.

For example, suppose that an insurance company sells a customer a guaranteed investment contract that promises to pay $1,000 five years from now for a one-time premium today of $783.53. (This implies that the customer is earning an interest rate of 5% per year.) The insurance company can *hedge* this customer liability by buying a default-free zero-coupon bond with a face value of $1,000 issued by the government.

The insurance company is *matching assets to liabilities*. In order to earn a profit on this set of transactions, the insurance company has to be able to buy the five-year government bond for less than $783.53. (In other words, the interest rate on the five-year government bond must be greater than 5% per year.) If instead of hedging its liability by buying a bond, the insurance company invests the premium in a portfolio of stocks, then there will be a risk of a shortfall—the value of the stocks in five years may turn out to be less than the $1,000 promised to the customer.

Many financial intermediaries pursue hedging strategies that involve matching their assets to their liabilities. In each case, the objective is to reduce the risk of a shortfall. The nature of the hedging instrument varies with the type of customer liability.

Thus, if a savings bank has customer liabilities that are short-term deposits earning an interest rate that floats, the appropriate hedging instrument is a floating-rate bond, or a strategy of "rolling over" short-term bonds. Another way the bank might hedge its floating-rate deposit liabilities is to invest in long-term fixed-rate bonds and enter into a swap contract to swap the fixed rate it receives on its bonds for a floating rate.

4 Minimizing the Cost of Hedging

As just noted, there is often more than one mechanism for hedging risk available to a decision maker. When there is more than one way to hedge risk, a rational manager will choose the one that costs the least.

For example, suppose that you live in Boston and are planning to move to Tokyo a year from now for an extended visit. You have found a wonderful apartment there and have agreed to buy it for 10.3 million yen, which you will pay to the apartment's current owner at the time you move in. You have just sold your condominium in Boston for $100,000, and plan to use that money to pay for the apartment in Tokyo. You have invested the money in one-year U.S. Treasury bills at an interest rate of 3%, so you know that you will have $103,000 a year from now.

The dollar/yen exchange rate is currently $0.01 per yen (or 100 yen per dollar). If it remains unchanged for a year, you will have exactly the 10.3 million yen you need to pay for the Tokyo apartment a year from now. But you discover that in the past year the dollar/yen exchange rate has fluctuated quite a bit. It was as low as $0.008 per yen and as high as $0.011. You are, therefore, concerned that, one year from now, your $103,000 may not buy enough yen to pay for the Tokyo apartment.

If the exchange rate is $0.008 per yen in a year, you will receive 12.875 million yen for your $103,000 ($103,000/$0.008 per yen)—enough to buy the apartment and some nice furnishings. If, however, the exchange rate is $0.012 per yen a year from now, then you will get only 8.583 million yen ($103,000/$0.012 per yen), and you will be 1.717 million yen short of the purchase price you agreed to a year earlier.

Suppose that there are two ways you can eliminate your exposure to the risk of a rise in the dollar price of the yen. One way is to get the owner of the Tokyo apartment to sell it to you for a price fixed in U.S. dollars. The other way is by entering a forward contract for yen with a bank.

Let us compare the costs to you of the two methods of hedging the foreign-exchange risk. Suppose that in our example the bank's forward price is $0.01 per yen. By entering into a forward contract with the bank to exchange your $103,000 in a year at $0.01 per yen, you can completely eliminate your risk. No matter what happens to the dollar/yen exchange rate over the next year, you will have the 10.3 million yen you need to buy your apartment in Tokyo one year from now.

Now consider the other alternative of negotiating a fixed price in U.S. dollars with the owner of the apartment. If the owner of the Tokyo apartment is willing to sell you the apartment for a dollar price less than $103,000, then that is a better deal than entering into a forward contract with the bank.

On the other hand, if the owner of the Tokyo apartment demands a dollar price higher than $103,000, then you are better off setting the price in yen (10.3 million yen) and entering into a forward contract with the bank to exchange the yen for dollars at the forward price of $0.01 per yen. You also have to consider the transaction costs (broker fees, the amount of time and effort involved, etc.) associated with each method of hedging the risk.

The important point to recognize in this example is that *the mechanism chosen to implement the hedge should be the one that minimizes the cost of achieving the desired reduction of risk.*

5 Insuring versus Hedging

There is a fundamental difference between insuring and hedging. When you hedge, you eliminate the risk of loss by giving up the potential for gain. When you insure, you pay a premium to eliminate the risk of loss and *retain* the potential for gain.

Let us return to an earlier example to clarify the difference between insuring and hedging. You are planning a trip from Boston to Tokyo a year from now. You make your flight reservations now, and the airline reservation clerk tells you that you can either lock in a price of $1,000 now, or you can pay whatever the price turns out be on the day of your flight. If you decide to lock in the $1,000 price, you have *hedged* against the risk of loss.

It costs you nothing to do so, but you have given up the possibility of paying less than $1,000 for your flight a year from now.

Alternatively, the airline may offer you the possibility of paying $20 now for the *right* to purchase your ticket a year from now at a price of $1,000. By buying this right you have insured that you will pay no more than $1,000 to fly to Tokyo. If the price should turn out to be more than $1,000 a year from now, you will exercise this right; otherwise you will let it expire. By paying $20 you have purchased insurance against the risk that you will have to pay more than $1,000 for the ticket and, thus, you have insured that the total cost to you will not exceed $1,020 ($1,000 for the ticket plus $20 for the insurance).

Earlier we discussed a farmer who has wheat to sell in another month. The size of the farmer's wheat crop is 100,000 bushels, and the forward price for delivery a month from now is $2 per bushel. If the farmer hedges with a short position in a forward contract for 100,000 bushels, she will receive $200,000 a month from now regardless of what the price of wheat turns out to be on the delivery date.

Instead of taking a short position in the forward market, however, she can buy insurance that guarantees a *minimum* price of $2 per bushel.[4] Say the insurance costs $20,000. Then, should the price of wheat turn out to be higher than $2.00 per bushel, the farmer will simply not need to use the insurance, and the policy will expire. If, however, the price should turn out to be less than $2.00 per bushel, the farmer will collect on her insurance and wind up with $200,000 less the cost of the insurance, or $180,000.

Figure 2 illustrates the difference between the farmer's revenues a month from now under three different alternative courses of action: (1) taking no measures to reduce her exposure to price risk, (2) hedging with a forward contract, and (3) insuring.

The horizontal axis measures the price of wheat a month from now, and the vertical axis measures the farmer's revenue. In the case of insuring (alternative 3), the revenue is net of the premium paid for the insurance.

Note that by insuring, the farmer retains much of the economic benefit of an increase in the price of wheat while eliminating the downside risk. This benefit comes at the cost of paying a premium for the insurance.

FIGURE 2

Hedging versus Insuring against Price Risk: The Farmer

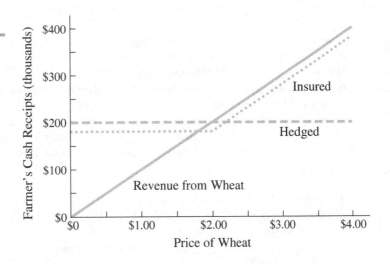

---

[4]As we will see later in this chapter, this is done by buying a put option.

Note that none of the three alternatives depicted in Figure 2 is superior to the others under *all* circumstances. Of course, it would never pay to buy the insurance if the future price were known with certainty.

Thus, if the farmer knew for sure that the price was going to be higher than $2.00 per bushel, she would choose not to reduce her risk exposure at all (alternative 1). If she knew the price was going to be lower than $2.00 per bushel, she would *sell forward* at $2.00 (alternative 2). But the essence of the farmer's risk-management problem is that she does *not* know in advance what the price will be.

Quick Check 3

Look at this question from the point of view of a baker, who is concerned about the price of wheat *rising* rather than falling. How can the baker insure against his risk exposure?

---

6 Basic Features of Insurance Contracts

In discussing insurance contracts and understanding how to use them to manage risk, it is important to understand some basic terms and features. Four of the most important features of insurance contracts are **exclusions, caps, deductibles,** and **copayments.** Let us briefly explain each.

6.1 Exclusions and Caps

Exclusions are losses that might *seem* to meet the conditions for coverage under the insurance contract but are specifically excluded. For example, life insurance policies pay benefits if the insured party dies, but such policies typically exclude payment of death benefits if the insured person takes his own life. Health insurance policies may exclude from coverage certain illnesses the insured party had *before* the policy was purchased. Thus, a health insurance policy may state that it excludes coverage for preexisting medical conditions.

Caps are limits placed on compensation for particular losses covered under an insurance contract. Thus, if a health insurance policy is capped at $1 million, it means the insurance company will pay no more than this amount for the treatment of an illness.

6.2 Deductibles

A *deductible* is an amount of money that the insured party must pay out of his or her own resources before receiving any compensation from the insurer. Thus, if your automobile insurance policy has a $1,000 deductible for damage due to accidents, you must pay the first $1,000 in repair costs and the insurer will only pay for the amount in excess of $1,000.

Deductibles create incentives for insured parties to control their losses. People with automobile insurance who have to pay the first $500 of repair costs out of their own pockets tend to drive more carefully than drivers with no deductibles. However, this incentive to control losses disappears once the loss exceeds the deductible amount.

6.3 Copayments

A *copayment* feature means that the insured party must cover a fraction of the loss. For example, an insurance policy might stipulate that the copayment is 20% of any loss, and the insurance company pays the other 80%.

Copayments are similar to deductibles in that the insured party winds up paying part of the losses. The difference is in the way the partial payment is computed and in the incentives created for the insured party to control losses.

Take the case of a health insurance policy that covers visits to the physician. With a copayment feature, the patient must pay part of the fee for each visit. If the policy had a $1,000 deductible instead of a copayment feature, the patient would pay the entire cost of all visits until the $1,000 deductible was met and then nothing for additional visits. Thus, the deductible feature does not create any incentive for patients to forgo additional visits once the $1,000 deductible is met; a copayment feature does. Insurance policies can contain both deductibles and copayments.

7 Financial Guarantees

Financial guarantees are insurance against **credit risk,** which is the risk that the other party to a contract into which you have entered will default. A *loan guarantee* is a contract that obliges the guarantor to make the promised payment on a loan if the borrower fails to do so. Loan guarantees are pervasive in the economy, playing a critical role in facilitating trade.

For example, consider credit cards, which in today's world have become a principal means of payment by consumers. Banks and other issuers of credit cards guarantee to merchants that they will stand behind all customer purchases made with their credit cards. Credit card issuers thus provide merchants with insurance against credit risk.

Banks, insurance companies, and on occasion, governments offer guarantees on a broad spectrum of financial instruments ranging from credit cards to interest-rate and currency swaps. Parent corporations routinely guarantee the debt obligations of their subsidiaries. Governments guarantee residential mortgages, farm and student loans, loans to small and large business firms, and loans to other governments. Governments sometimes serve as the guarantor of last resort, guaranteeing the promises made by guarantors in the private sector such as banks and pension funds. However, in cases in which the credit standing of a governmental organization is in doubt, private sector organizations have been called upon to guarantee the government's debts.

8 Caps and Floors on Interest Rates

Interest-rate risk depends on one's perspective—whether you are a borrower or a lender. For example, suppose you have $5,000 on deposit in a bank money market account in which the interest rate you earn is adjusted on a daily basis to reflect current market conditions. From your perspective as a depositor (i.e., a lender), interest-rate risk is the risk that the interest rate will *fall*. An interest-rate insurance policy for you would take the form of an **interest-rate floor,** which means a guarantee of a *minimum* interest rate.

But suppose that you are a borrower. For example, suppose that you just bought a house and took a $100,000 adjustable-rate mortgage loan from a bank. Suppose the mortgage interest rate you pay is tied to the one-year U.S. Treasury bill rate. Then from your perspective, interest-rate risk is the risk that the interest rate will *rise*. An interest-rate insurance policy for you would take the form of an **interest-rate cap,** which means a guarantee of a *maximum* interest rate.

Most adjustable-rate mortgage loans (ARMs) made in the United States during the 1980s and 1990s contain interest-rate caps. Often the cap takes the form of a maximum amount that the mortgage interest rate can rise in any one-year period and then there may also be a *global* cap on the interest rate for the life of the mortgage loan.

9 Options as Insurance

Options are another ubiquitous form of insurance contract. An **option** is the right to either purchase or sell something at a fixed price in the future. As we saw before in the case of the

317

airline ticket, the purchase of an option to reduce risk is *insuring* against loss. An option contract is to be distinguished from a forward contract, which is the *obligation* to buy or sell something at a fixed price in the future.

Any contract that gives one of the contracting parties the right to buy or sell something at a prespecified exercise price is an option. There are as many different kinds of option contracts as there are items to buy or sell: commodity options, stock options, interest rate options, foreign-exchange options, and so on. Some kinds of option contracts have standardized terms and are traded on organized exchanges such as the Chicago Board Options Exchange in the United States or the Osaka Options and Futures Exchange in Japan.

There is a special set of terms associated with option contracts:

- An option to *buy* the specified item at a fixed price is a **call;** an option to *sell* is a **put.**
- The fixed price specified in an option contract is called the option's **strike price** or **exercise price.**
- The date after which an option can no longer be exercised is called its **expiration date** or *maturity* date.

If an option can be exercised on the expiration date only, it is called a *European-type* option. If it can be exercised at any time up to and including the expiration date it is called an *American-type* option.

9.1 Put Options on Stocks

Put options on stocks protect against losses from a decline in stock prices. For example, consider Lucy, a manager working for XYZ Corporation. Suppose that she has received shares of XYZ stock as compensation in the past and now owns 1,000 shares. The current market price of XYZ is $100 per share. Let us consider how she can insure against the risk associated with her shares of XYZ stock by buying XYZ put options.

An XYZ put option gives her the right to sell a share of XYZ stock at a fixed exercise price, thus insuring her that she will receive at least the exercise price at the option's expiration date. For example, she can buy XYZ puts at an exercise price of $100 per share expiring in 1 year. Say the current price of a one-year European-style put on a single share of XYZ with a $100 exercise price is $10. Then the premium she must pay to insure her 1,000 shares of XYZ (currently worth $100,000) for the year is $10,000.

Buying put options on a stock portfolio is similar in many respects to buying term insurance on an asset such as a house or a car. For example, suppose that in addition to her shares of XYZ, Lucy owns an apartment in a condominium complex. The apartment's market value is $100,000. Although she cannot buy a put option on her apartment to protect her against a decline in its market value, she can buy insurance against losses of certain types. Suppose she buys a one-year fire insurance policy with a $100,000 cap for $500.

Table 2 summarizes the analogy between a put option and a term insurance policy. The insurance policy provides Lucy with protection against losses in the value of her

TABLE 2   Similarity between a Term Insurance Policy and a Put Option

	Insurance Policy	Put Option
Asset insured	Condominium	1,000 shares of XYZ stock
Asset's current value	$100,000	$100,000
Term of policy	1 year	1 year
Insurance premium	$500	$10,000

Box 1 — Credit Default Swaps

When thinking about the risk associated with an investment, it is important to consider how well one might be able to recover from a poor investment. In the credit default swap (CDS) market, investors can buy insurance over a large series of investment types. Specifically, investors may be able to obtain a payoff if a borrower defaults on a debt to a lender. The larger issue, however, is the risk associated with how much value remains in the defaulting firm. Recovery risk is most simply explained as analogous to the proportion of value an individual would have remaining in say a car after it crashed—the proportion of what the wrecked car is worth to the original precrash value.

Many trades in the CDS market assume a particular rate of recovery is associated with a firm that will go bankrupt. That is, a lender might expect to usually receive 40 cents for every dollar owed to them from the bankrupt firm. Though this rate of return is the market average, it may not apply to individual firms whose bonds are traded on the market at a lower price when they go bankrupt because these bonds will be bought back at the lower market price.

The idea is that individual firms might have their own recovery risks, just like wrecked cars might sell at different prices, (e.g., cars may have been worth different amounts initially but sustained the same amounts of damage). This fact has led to the development of recovery locks. Recovery locks guarantee a particular amount of recovery on certain investment. Basically, an investor can buy a bond knowing that if the firm goes bankrupt, the firm will buy back the bond at a prearranged amount, regardless of the price that the bonds are traded at on the market. In effect, the recovery rate is built into the default swap contract.

The fact that the International Swaps and Derivatives Association has released a standard business contract for recovery locks suggests that the way that investors think about recovery risk will change dramatically in the short term.

Source: Adapted from "Why Retrieving Value is Not Always the Same after a Crash," *Financial Times,* June 8, 2006.

apartment that stem from fire for a period of one year. The put option provides her with protection against losses in the value of her XYZ stocks that stem from a decline in their market price for a period of one year.

Lucy can lower the cost of her fire insurance by having a deductible. For example, if Lucy's fire insurance policy has a deductible of $5,000, then she has to pay the first $5,000 of any losses, and the insurance company compensates her only for losses in excess of $5,000. Analogously, Lucy can lower the cost of the insurance on her XYZ stock by choosing puts with a lower exercise price. If the current stock price is $100, and Lucy buys puts with an exercise price of $95, then she must absorb the first $5 per share of any loss resulting from a stock price decline. By choosing a put with a lower exercise price, she increases the deductible and lowers the cost of the insurance.

Quick Check 4

Suppose Lucy wanted market value insurance on her 1,000 shares of XYZ stock with a deductible of $10 per share and a copayment of 20%. How could she achieve this with XYZ put options?

9.2 Put Options on Bonds

Even when bonds are free of default risk, their prices can fluctuate substantially as a result of changes in interest rates. When bonds are subject to default risk, then their prices can change either because of changes in the level of risk-free interest rates or changes in the possible losses to bondholders from default. A put option on a bond, therefore, provides insurance against losses stemming from *either* source of risk.

For example, consider hypothetical 20-year zero-coupon bonds issued by Risky Realty Corporation. The bonds are secured by the fictitious firm's assets, which consist of apartment houses in various cities in the northeastern part of the United States. The firm has no other debt. The face value of the bonds is $10 million and the value of the firm's real estate holdings is currently $15 million.

The market price of the bonds reflects both the current level of risk-free interest rates, say 6% per year, and the market value of the real estate securing the bonds. Suppose that the yield to maturity on the bonds is 15% per year. Then the current market price of the bonds is $611,003.[5]

Suppose that you buy a one-year put option on the bonds with an exercise price of $600,000. If the bond's price then falls, either because the level of risk-free interest rates rises during the year (say from 6% per year to 8% per year) or because the value of the apartment houses securing the bonds falls (say from $15 million to $8 million), you are guaranteed a minimum price of $600,000 for the bonds.

10 The Diversification Principle

Diversifying means splitting an investment among many risky assets instead of concentrating it all in only one. Its meaning is captured by the familiar saying: "Don't put all your eggs in one basket." The **diversification principle** states that by diversifying across risky assets people can sometimes achieve a reduction in their overall risk exposure with no reduction in their expected return.

10.1 Diversification with Uncorrelated Risks

To clarify how portfolio diversification can reduce your total risk exposure, let us consider an example in which risks were uncorrelated with each other.[6] You are thinking about investing $100,000 in the biotechnology business because you believe that the discovery of new genetically engineered drugs offers great profit potential over the next several years. For each drug you invest in, success means that you will quadruple your investment, but failure means a loss of your entire investment. Thus, if you invest $100,000 in a single drug, either you wind up with $400,000 or nothing.

Assume there is a 0.5 probability of success for each drug and a 0.5 probability of failure. Table 3 shows the probability distribution of final payoffs and rates of return on an investment in a single drug.

If you diversify by investing $50,000 in each of two drugs, there is still a chance of winding up with either $400,000 (if both drugs succeed) or nothing (if both drugs fail).

TABLE 3 **Probability Distribution for Investment in a Single Drug**

Outcome	Probability (P_j)	Payoff (X_j)	Rate of Return (r_j)
Drug does not succeed	0.5	0	−100%
Drug succeeds	0.5	$400,000	300%

Note: The cost of developing a drug is $100,000. The rate of return is the payoff minus the cost divided by the cost.

---

[5]$10 million/$1.15^{20}$ = $611,003.
[6]The precise statistical meaning and measurement of correlation is discussed in the appendix to this chapter.

However, there is also the intermediate possibility that one drug succeeds and the other fails. In that event, you will wind up with $200,000 (four times your investment of $50,000 in the drug that succeeds and zero from the drug that fails).

Thus, there are now four possible outcomes and three possible payoffs:

1. Both drugs succeed, and you receive $400,000.
2. Drug 1 succeeds and drug 2 doesn't, so you receive $200,000.
3. Drug 2 succeeds and drug 1 doesn't, so you receive $200,000.
4. Both drugs fail, and you receive nothing.

Thus, by diversifying and holding a portfolio of two drugs you reduce the probability of losing your entire investment to only one-half of what it would be without diversification. On the other hand, the probability of winding up with $400,000 has fallen from 0.5 to 0.25. The other two possible outcomes result in your receiving $200,000. The probability of this happening is 0.5 (computed as $2 \times 0.5 \times 0.5$). Table 4 summarizes the probability distribution of payoffs facing you if you split your investment between two drugs.

Now let us look at this probability distribution of payoffs in terms of expected payoffs and standard deviations. The formula for the expected payoff is:

$$E(X) = \sum_{i=1}^{n} P_i X_i$$

Applying the formula for the expected payoff to the case of a single drug, we find:

$$E(X) = 0.5(0) + 0.5(400,000) = \$200,000$$

The formula for the standard deviation is:

$$\sigma = \sqrt{0.5(0 - 200,000)^2 + 0.5(400,000 - 200,000)^2} = \$200,000$$

For the case of a portfolio of two uncorrelated drugs, we find:

$$E(X) = 0.25(0) + 0.5(200,000) + 0.25(400,000) = \$200,000$$

$$\sigma = \sqrt{0.25(0 - 200,000)^2 + 0.5(200,000 - 200,000)^2 + 0.25(400,000 - 200,000)^2}$$
$$= \frac{200,000}{\sqrt{2}}$$
$$= \$141,421$$

Thus, when we diversify between two uncorrelated drugs the expected payoff remains $200,000, but the standard deviation falls by a factor of $1/\sqrt{2}$ from $200,000 to $141,421. The standard deviation of the rate of return falls from 200% to 141.4%.

TABLE 4 Diversification with Two Drugs

Outcome	Probability (P_i)	Payoff (X_i)	Rate of Return (r_i)
No drugs succeed	0.25	0	−100%
One drug succeeds	0.50	$200,000	100%
Both drugs succeed	0.25	$400,000	300%

Now consider what happens to the expected payoff and the standard deviation as the number of drugs in the portfolio increases even further (under the assumption that the success of each drug is uncorrelated with the success of the others).[7] The expected payoff stays the same, but the standard deviation declines in proportion to the square root of the number of drugs:

$$\sigma_{\text{portfolio}} = \$200,000/\sqrt{N}$$

Quick Check 5

How many uncorrelated drugs have to be in the portfolio for the standard deviation to be $100?

10.2 Nondiversifiable Risk

In our example of diversification in the previous section, we assumed that the risks were uncorrelated with each other. In practice, many important risks are positively correlated with each other.[8] This is because they are affected by common underlying economic factors.

For example, the returns to investors who buy shares in stocks are all related to the health of the economy. An economic downturn will tend to have an adverse impact on the profits of almost all firms, resulting in poor stockholder returns for almost all stocks. Consequently, one's ability to reduce one's exposure to stock market risk by buying many different stocks is limited.

Suppose that you invest in a randomly selected portfolio of stocks traded on the NYSE, the AMEX, or the NASDAQ. The excess standard deviation of a portfolio is defined as the difference between the standard deviation of the portfolio's returns and the standard deviation produced from an equally weighted index.

Figure 3 shows the effect of increasing the number of stocks selected. On the vertical axis we plot the annualized excess standard deviation over the sample periods: 1963–73 (solid line), 1974–85 (lower dashed line), and 1986–97 (upper dashed line). The diagram shows that, two to four decades ago, investing in a single randomly selected stock could be expected to produce a standard deviation 35 percentage points higher than having invested in an equally weighted index of all available domestic equities. By the time the randomly selected portfolio included 20 stocks this excess risk had been reduced to a very modest level of around 5 percentage points. More recently, however, the level of excess returns has shifted upward and a single randomly chosen stock would have been expected to produce a standard deviation over 60 percentage points higher than having invested in an equally weighted equity index. Furthermore, it would have taken much more diversification, on the order of 50 randomly chosen stocks, to bring the excess risk down to the 5% level.

The part of the portfolio volatility that *can* be eliminated by adding more stocks is the **diversifiable risk**, and the part that remains no matter how many stocks are added is the **nondiversifiable risk**.

What accounts for nondiversifiable risk?

Stock prices fluctuate for many reasons, some of which are common to many stocks and some of which are relevant to a single firm or at most a small group of firms. Stock

---

[7]The probability distribution of the portfolio rate of return in the case of one drug is the *binomial distribution*. As the number of drugs in the portfolio becomes large, the distribution can be closely approximated by a *normal distribution*.

[8]The precise statistical meaning of correlation is discussed in the appendix to this chapter.

FIGURE 3

Excess Standard Deviation by Time and Number of Stocks

Source: "Have Individual Stocks Become More Volatile? An Empirical Exploration of Idiosyncratic Risk," John Y. Campbell, Martin Lettau, Burton G. Malkiel, and Yexiao Xu, *Journal of Finance*, Vol. 56, No. 1, February 2001. Used by permission (Blackwell Publishing).

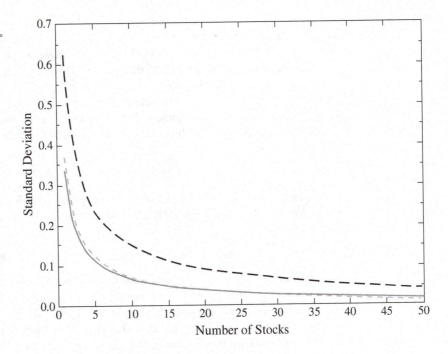

prices respond to random events that affect the current and expected future profits of firms. If an event occurs that affects many firms, such as an unanticipated downturn in general economic conditions, then many stocks will be affected. The risk of loss stemming from such events is sometimes called *market risk*.

On the other hand, random events that affect the prospects of only one firm, such as a lawsuit, a strike, or a new-product failure, give rise to random losses that are uncorrelated across stocks and can, therefore, be diversified away. The risk of loss stemming from this kind of event is called *firm-specific risk*.

These concepts of diversifiable and nondiversifiable risk apply to international diversification. By combining stocks of firms located in different countries it is possible to reduce the risk of one's stock portfolio, but there is a limit to this risk reduction. There are still common factors that affect nearly all firms no matter where in the world they are located. Thus, although international diversification can improve the prospects for risk reduction for people around the world, a significant amount of risk remains for even the best-diversified global stock portfolio.

Quick Check 6

Suppose you invest in a firm that produces software for personal computers. What would be some firm-specific risks affecting the rate of return on this investment?

11 Diversification and the Cost of Insurance

The cost of insuring a diversified portfolio of risks against a loss is almost always less than the cost of insuring against each risk separately. To see why, let us return to the biotechnology example of Section 10.1. You are investing $100,000 in drug stocks. The success or failure of each drug is independent of the others.

Let us assume that you have decided to invest $50,000 in each of two drug stocks and, therefore, face the probability distribution in Table 4. For each separate drug stock there is a probability of 0.5 that you will lose 100% of your investment in that drug. But for the portfolio as a whole there is a probability of 0.25 that you will lose 100% of your $100,000 investment.

If you insure *each* $50,000 stock investment against a loss, it will cost more than insuring the $100,000 portfolio of *both* stocks against a loss. To see this, suppose that the cost of insurance equals the expected amount that the insurance company will pay you. Then the cost of an insurance policy on the total portfolio would be the probability of a loss times the magnitude of the loss:

$$0.25 \times \$100,000 = \$25,000$$

The cost of insuring each of the two separate investments would be the probability of both stocks losing (0.25) times $100,000 plus the probability of only one losing (0.5) times $50,000:

$$0.25 \times \$100,000 + 0.5 \times \$50,000 = \$50,000$$

So insuring each stock separately would cost *twice* as much as insuring the portfolio of two stocks. To protect against loss of wealth, you do not need separate insurance on each stock. If only one of the two drugs fails, then the profit from the successful drug will more than offset the loss from the failed one, so that your total wealth will be $200,000. You only need insurance against the risk that *both* drugs will fail (see Box 2). This example suggests the following general proposition:

The more diversified are the risks in a portfolio of a given size, the less it will cost to insure the portfolio's total value against a loss.

Quick Check 7

How much should it cost to insure a portfolio of stocks, if it consists of $25,000 invested in each of four drug stocks whose chances of success are each 0.5 and are independent of each other?

Box 2 | The Advantages of Integrated Risk Management

Big changes are occurring in the way both the insurance industry and its corporate clients are approaching the management of risk. The new trend is called *integrated risk management*, and its goal is to lower the costs of managing the whole collection of risks faced by a firm.

In the past, corporations tended to compartmentalize the management of risks: currency, interest-rate, and credit risk exposures were handled by treasury, safety issues by human resources, environmental liability and asset protection by engineering, and property/casualty exposures by risk management. Now some firms are integrating these separate exposures and purchasing insurance against aggregate losses in excess of some level deemed to be acceptable.

A steel manufacturing company, for example, bought a combined workers' compensation and nonoccupational disability policy from an insurance company and estimates that the policy was about a third cheaper than what it previously paid for two separate policies. As another example, AIG has sold Honeywell a multirisk policy that includes foreign-exchange protection along with property and liability coverage. Honeywell retains a deductible of slightly more than its expected aggregate combined losses.

Summary

- Market mechanisms for *hedging* risk exposures are forward and futures contracts, swaps, and matching assets to liabilities.
- A forward contract is the obligation to deliver a specified asset at a specified future delivery date at a specified price. Futures contracts are standardized forward contracts that are traded on exchanges.
- A swap contract consists of two parties exchanging a series of payments at specified intervals over a specified period of time. A swap contract could call for the exchange of almost anything. In current practice, however, most swap contracts involve the exchange of commodities, currencies, or securities.
- Financial intermediaries such as insurance companies often hedge their customer liabilities by matching their assets to their liabilities. This is done to reduce the risk of a shortfall.
- When there is more than one way to hedge a given risk exposure, the mechanism chosen should be the one that minimizes the cost of achieving the desired reduction of risk.
- There is a fundamental difference between insuring and hedging. When you hedge, you eliminate the risk of loss by giving up the potential for gain. When you insure, you pay a premium to eliminate the risk of loss and *retain* the potential for gain.
- Put options on stocks protect against losses from a decline in stock prices.
- Financial guarantees act as insurance against credit risk. Interest-rate floors and caps offer insurance against interest-rate risk to lenders and borrowers, respectively. A put option on a bond offers the bondholder insurance against *both* default risk and interest-rate risk.
- The more diversified are the risks in a portfolio of a given size, the less it will cost to insure the portfolio against a loss.

Key Terms

- forward contract
- forward price
- spot price
- face value
- long position
- short position
- futures contract
- swap contract
- counterparty
- exclusions
- caps
- deductibles
- copayments
- financial guarantees

- credit risk
- interest-rate floor
- interest-rate cap
- option
- call
- put
- strike price
- exercise price
- expiration date
- diversification principle
- diversifiable risk
- nondiversifiable risk
- correlation

Answers to Quick Check Questions

Quick Check 1   Show what happens to the farmer and the baker if the spot price on the delivery date is:

    a. $1.00 per bushel.

    b. $3.00 per bushel.

Answer:

Farmer's Transaction	$1.00/Bushel	$3.00/Bushel
Proceeds from sale of wheat	$100,000	$300,000
Cash flow from futures contract	$100,000 paid to farmer	$100,000 paid by farmer
Total receipts	$200,000	$200,000

Baker's Transaction	$1.00/Bushel	$3.00/Bushel
Cost of wheat from supplier	$100,000	$300,000
Cash flow from futures contract	$100,000 paid by baker	$100,000 paid to baker
Total outlays	$200,000	$200,000

Quick Check 2   Suppose that in the third year on the settlement date, the spot rate of exchange is $1.30 per euro. How much money is transferred between the counterparties to the swap contract?

Answer: Because the spot price is the same as the forward price on the settlement date, no money changes hands.

Quick Check 3   Look at this question from the point of view of the baker, who is concerned about the price of wheat rising rather than falling. How can the baker insure against his risk exposure?

Answer: The baker needs to buy 100,000 bushels of wheat in another month. The baker is concerned about rising wheat prices. The baker could take a long position in the forward market, committing to buy 100,000 bushels of wheat at $2.00 per bushel. However, the baker is locked in at that price and will not benefit at all if prices fall. By purchasing an option to purchase wheat at $2.00 a bushel; the baker now knows he will pay a maximum of $2.00 a bushel; but if prices fall, he will not exercise the option and buy wheat at the market or spot price. This option will cost him something, however. Assume that it will cost $20,000 as the illustrated put option did.

Quick Check 4   Suppose Lucy wanted market value insurance on her 1,000 shares of XYZ stock with a deductible of $10 per share and a copayment of 20%. How could she achieve this with XYZ put options?

Answer: A deductible of $10 means the strike price must be $90 ($100 − $10). A copayment of 20% means that she will only buy puts on 800 shares rather than the full 1,000.

Quick Check 5   How many uncorrelated drugs have to be in a portfolio for the standard deviation to be $100?

Answer: Solve the equation for the number of drugs (N): $\sigma = \$100 = \frac{\$200,000}{\sqrt{N}}$. This gives: $\sqrt{N} = 2,000$ or $N = 2,000^2 = 4,000,000$ uncorrelated drugs.

Quick Check 6   Suppose you invest in a firm that produces software for personal computers. What would be some firm-specific risks affecting the rate of return on this investment?

Answer: The risks would be failure of the personal computing software because of defects in the programming, or other technical difficulties; competition from other software manufacturers; pending lawsuit on the firm's practices; loss of the major software developers to other companies, and so on.

Quick Check 7 How much should it cost to insure a portfolio of stocks, if it consists of $25,000 invested in each of four drug stocks whose chances of success are each 0.5 and are independent of each other?

Answer: There is now a different probability distribution of loss on the portfolio. The only possibility of a loss is if all four drugs fail. (If three drugs fail and the fourth succeeds, then the portfolio will be worth $4 \times \$25,000 = \$100,000$.) The probability of this happening is $0.5^4 = 0.0625$. Therefore, the cost of the insurance will be the expected value of the payout or $0.0625 \times \$100,000 = \$6,250$.

Questions and Problems

Using Forward and Futures Contracts to Hedge Risk

1. Suppose you own a grove of orange trees. The harvest is still two months away but you are concerned about price risk. You want to guarantee that you will receive $1.00 per pound in two months regardless of what the spot price is at that time. You are selling 250,000 pounds.
    a. Show the economics of a short transaction in the forward market if the spot price on delivery date is $0.75 per pound, $1.00 per pound, or $1.25 per pound.
    b. What would have happened to you if you had not entered the hedge and each scenario is equally likely?
    c. What is the variability of your receipts after the hedge is in place?
2. Suppose in six months' time the cost of a litre of heating oil will either be $0.90 or $1.10. The current price is $1.00 per litre.
    a. What are the risks faced by a reseller of heating oil that has a large inventory on hand? What are the risks faced by a large user of heating oil with a very small inventory?
    b. How can these two parties use the heating oil futures market to reduce their risks and lock in a price of $1.00 per litre? Assume each contract is for 50,000 litres and they each need to hedge 100,000 litres.
    c. Can you say that each party has been made better off? Why or why not?
3. Suppose you are treasurer of a large municipality in Michigan and you are investing in cattle futures. You purchase futures contracts worth 400,000 pounds of cattle with an exercise price of $0.60 per pound and an expiration date in one month.
    a. Show the economics of a futures transaction if the price of cattle at delivery date is $0.40 per pound, $0.60 per pound, or $0.80 per pound.
    b. Is this a risk-reducing transaction?
    c. Would your answer to "b" be different if the treasurer were investing in oil futures? What about interest rate futures?
4. Your cousin is a hog farmer and he invests in pork belly futures and options contracts. He has told you that he believes pork belly prices are on the rise. You decide to purchase a call option on pork bellies with a strike price of $0.50 per pound. That way, if pork belly prices go up, you can exercise the call, buy the pork bellies, and sell them for the higher spot price. Assume the price of an option on 40,000 pounds is $1,000 and you purchase five options for $5,000 on 200,000 pounds.
    a. Would this be a risk-reducing or speculative transaction for you?
    b. What is your downside risk in dollars and percentage terms?
    c. If the price per pound increases to $0.55 per pound, how much would you net after paying for the options?

5. Suppose you are expecting your fourth child in six months and you need a bigger car. You have your eye on a used three-year-old minivan that currently costs approximately $10,000. You are concerned about the pricing and availability of this specific car in six months' time, but you won't have enough money to purchase the car until six months from today.

   a. How could you advertise in the newspaper for a forward contract with a counterparty that would eliminate your risk?

   b. Who would be willing to take the short position on your forward contract? (Who is the likely counterparty?)

6. Suppose that Yankee Savings Bank pays its depositors an interest rate on six-month CDs that is 25 basis points (0.25%) higher than the six-month Treasury bill rate. Because its assets are long-term fixed-rate mortgages, Yankee would prefer to be borrowing at a ten-year, fixed interest rate. If it borrowed on its own, Yankee would have to pay 12% per year. On the other hand, suppose Global Products, Inc. has good access to fixed-rate borrowing overseas. It can borrow for 10 years at a fixed rate of 11%. However, it would prefer to borrow on floating-rate terms. If it did so, it would have to pay 50 basis points over the six-month Treasury bill. Show how both companies could improve their situations through an interest-rate swap.

Hedging Foreign-Exchange Risk with Swap Contracts

7. Suppose you are treasurer of Photo Processing, Inc. Approximately 50% of your sales are in the United States (headquarters) whereas 40% are in Japan and 10% are in the rest of the world. You are concerned about the dollar value of your Japanese sales over the next five years. Japanese sales are expected to be 2,700,000,000 yen each year over the next five years. The current dollar/yen exchange rate is 90 yen to the U.S. dollar and you would be happy if this would remain so during all five years.

   a. How could you use swap contracts to eliminate the risk that the dollar depreciates against the yen?

   b. What is the notional amount of your swap contract per year?

   c. Who might take the opposite side of this swap contract (who is a logical counterparty)?

8. Suppose you are a consultant living in the United States and have been engaged by a French company to perform a market study, which should take 18 months to complete. They are planning to pay you 20,000 euros monthly. The current exchange rate is $0.92 per euro. You are concerned that the euro will strengthen versus the dollar and that you will receive fewer U.S. dollars each month. The French company does not want to have to come up with dollars to pay you each month and is not willing to agree to a fixed exchange rate of $0.92 per euro.

   a. How could you use swap contracts and a financial intermediary to eliminate your risk?

   b. Suppose that in the sixth month, the spot price of the euro is $0.90. Without the swap contract, what would be your cash revenues in dollars? With the swap contract what will they be?

   c. Suppose that in the tenth month, the spot price of the euro is $0.95. Without the swap contract, what would be your cash revenues in dollars? With the swap contract what will they be?

9. You are a bright new hire in the risk-management division at SoftCola, a multinational cola company, and have recently been put in charge of managing the euro/dollar exchange-rate risks that SoftCola faces. Consider SoftCola's operations in France and the United States.

a. Suppose monthly revenues in France average 20 million euros and monthly production and distribution costs average 15 million euros. If the resulting profits are repatriated to the production unit in the United States monthly, what risk does this production unit face? How might it hedge this risk?

b. SoftCola's worldwide retirement benefits unit is located in the United States and has an obligation to pay its retired French employees 5 million euros monthly. What risk does this unit face and how could it hedge the risk?

c. Given the transactions of the production and retirement units as given previously, what do you conclude are the exchange-rate risks faced by SoftCola as a whole in France? Does SoftCola need to enter into forward contracts?

Hedging Shortfall-Risk by Matching Assets to Liabilities

10. At Montgomery Bank and Trust most of its liabilities are customer deposits, which earn a variable interest rate tied to the three-month Treasury bill rate. On the other hand, most of its assets are fixed-rate loans and mortgages. Montgomery Bank and Trust does not want to stop selling fixed-rate loans and mortgages, but it is worried about rising interest rates, which would cut into their profits. How could Montgomery Bank and Trust develop a hedge against interest rate risk without selling the loans? Assume that its exposure is $100 million at an average fixed rate of 9% while paying out T-bills + 75 basis points.

11. Federal deposit insurance originated in 1933 in part to protect the small investor and in part to safeguard the financial system. By insuring the savings of hundreds of thousands of individuals, the government has increased public confidence in the banking system and has reduced the number of speculative runs on banks and savings institutions. Banks and savings and loan (S&L) associates covered by this insurance pay the FDIC a premium. You work at the Federal Deposit Insurance Corporation (FDIC) and it is your job to evaluate the portfolios of the institutions that the agency covers. Consider the assets and liabilities of one S&L, Mismatch Ltd. It has liabilities of $100 million in checking, money-market, and short-term deposits for which it pays current market interest rates. Its assets are in the form of long-term consumer mortgages and other business loans made at fixed rates.

a. What do you conclude are the risks faced by Mismatch?

b. What steps could you recommend that Mismatch take in order to reduce or eliminate its risks? You are asked by your employers to think next about banks: The insured liabilities are predominantly in the form of liquid checking and savings accounts, whereas the assets tend to be more opaque and illiquid loans to firms and businesses. One risk involved in banking is that of default by borrowers. Banks as intermediaries can diversify this risk by making loans to several different borrowers. However, they cannot get rid of the risk entirely and in the absence of deposit insurance, this risk would have to be borne by the customers of the bank, the depositors.

c. What risk-free and liquid assets could banks hold to cover their liabilities? If banks in fact held these assets, would we continue to require deposit insurance?

d. How might banks obtain funds to make loans? Who would bear the risks of default in this case? Would government insurance be required to protect them?

Insuring versus Hedging

12. Note whether the following are ways to avoid losses through hedging or insuring:
   • Lock in a $979.00 fare home for the holidays.
   • Purchase a put option on a stock you do own.
   • Agree to purchase a house in one year for a fixed price of $200,000.

- Lease a car with an option to purchase it in three years.
- Enter into a swap contract to exchange fixed interest payments for floating-rate payments because you have floating-rate assets.
- As a wheat grower, enter into a forward contract to sell your wheat in two months at a fixed price set today.
- Pay a premium for catastrophic health care coverage.
- Pay for a credit guarantee on a loan you are worried about collecting.

Financial Guarantees

13. Suppose you are a local dry cleaner. Historically you have accepted cash and checks as payments for services rendered. However, over the years you realize you have lost a lot of money on "bad check." How could you obtain insurance against credit risk without moving to a policy of "cash only"? How would you pay for this insurance?

14. Suppose the midwestern part of the country is flooded and many farmers lose all their crops. If the government sets up a flood relief plan that reimburses those farmers who did not have private insurance, is that an insurance plan? Who pays for this "insurance" program?

Caps and Floors on Interest Rates

15. Suppose you just signed a purchase and sale agreement on a new home and you have six weeks to obtain a mortgage. Interest rates have been falling, so fixed-rate loans are now very attractive. You could lock in a fixed rate of 7% (annual percentage rate) for 30 years. On the other hand, rates are falling, so you are thinking about a 30-year variable-rate loan, which is currently at 4.5% and is tied to the six-month Treasury bill rate. A final mortgage option is a variable-rate loan that begins at 5% and cannot fall below 3% but that can increase by only as much as 2% per year up to a maximum of 11%.
    a. If you wanted to hedge all risk of interest rate exposure, which financing plan would you choose?
    b. What would be your monthly payment on a $100,000, 30-year, fixed-rate mortgage?
    c. If you took out a fixed-rate mortgage, what would happen to your monthly payment if interest rates increased to 10%?

16. Refer to the information from the previous problem (problem 15).
    a. If you wanted to take advantage of a possible fall in rates but not assume the risk that rates would increase dramatically, which financing plan would you choose?
    b. What is the interest rate cap in this example?
    c. What is the interest rate floor in this example?
    d. How is an interest rate cap like buying insurance? How are you paying for this insurance?

Options as Insurance

17. Suppose you own a grove of orange trees. The harvest is still two months away but you are concerned about price risk. You want to guarantee that you will receive $1.00 per pound in two months regardless of what the spot price is at that time. You are selling 250,000 pounds. Now suppose instead of taking a short position in the futures market, you purchase insurance (in the form of a put option on 250,000 pounds) that guarantees you a minimum price of $1.00 per pound. Assume the option cost you $25,000.

    a. Show the economics of this transaction if the spot price on the delivery date is $0.75, $1.00, or $1.25 per pound. Under what circumstances would you exercise your option?

    b. How does your potential for gain differ between the hedge transaction and the insurance transaction?

18. Suppose you own a small company in the import/export business. You have ordered some doll clothing, which is being sewn in China. The company in China has asked for the money up front to do this work because it is nervous about your company as a credit risk. If you are unwilling to live by these terms, how might you go about purchasing insurance that would make the company in China satisfied that it will receive the money owed? Would you be able to obtain this insurance for free? How might you pay for it?

19. Suppose you are interested in taking a safari to Kenya, Africa, next summer but are worried about the price of the trip, which has ranged from $2,500 to $3,500 over the past five years. The current price is $3,000. Suppose you wanted to maintain the possibility of a lower price.

    a. How could you eliminate the risk of rising prices but still maintain the possible gain from lower prices?

    b. How might you pay for this option?

20. Suppose you own a stock that is currently trading for $65. You purchased it for $60. You would like to wait a while before you sell it because you think there is a good chance the stock will increase further.

    a. How can you structure a transaction that will insure that you can sell the stock for $65, even if it falls below that price, say, to $60 or $55.

    b. If that option costs you $5 and the stock reaches $75, at which time you sell it, what was your dollar profit? Did you exercise the option? Why or why not? Was buying the option a "waste of money"?

    c. If the price of the stock falls to $57, what is your dollar profit or loss?

21. *Challenge Problem:* In the drug example in Section 10.1, it was illustrated that diversifying investment from a single drug company to two drug companies lowered the probability of ending up with nothing from 0.5 to 0.25. Suppose that there are four medical supply companies all racing to develop products and gain FDA approval for their products. Market forecasts suggest that large profits will be enjoyed by any company that gains FDA approval and takes its product to market. Investors in such a company stand to gain $100,000 on a $20,000 investment. Assume that the probability for success for each company is 0.5; that is, a company will either gain FDA approval, or not, and that the FDA's decision for a company is independent of its decision on the other companies.

    a. If you invest 25% of your money in each company, what are all of the possible outcomes, along with their probabilities?

    b. What is the net payoff of each outcome?

    c. What is the expected net return of the strategy?

    d. What is the probability of ending up with nothing? How does this compare to the results in section 10.1?

    e. What is the probability of earning more than the $20,000 original investment?

    f. Your strategy of investing 25% of your money in each of the four companies is an attempt to reduce what type of risk?

    g. For each company, what is that specific risk in this example?

22. *Challenge Problem:* Suppose you are Swedish and are considering graduate study in the United States. It is April and you have been admitted into a two-year masters program at a good school. Your tuition per semester will be $5,000 and living expenses will amount to $1,000 per month. (You, therefore, estimate needing a total of $22,000 per year.) You are assured by the college that you will be able to find on-campus work to pay for your living expenses. You, therefore, need only worry about paying tuition. It is now July. You applied for and just received a tuition scholarship from the Swedish government for the amount of SKr100,000 per annum for two years. The current exchange rate between the dollar and the krone is 10SKr/$. You are obviously ecstatic about having won the award. You are told that you will get the money for the first year in September.

a. What risks do you face? Upon inquiry at your bank, you find that the forward price for a September contract to buy dollars is 10SKr per dollar. How might you hedge your exchange-rate risk for the first year?

b. If in September the market rate for the dollar turns out to be 9.5SKr/$, would you gain or lose on the forward contract? Does this mean that because you are worse off you shouldn't have entered the contract in the first place?

It is still July. The representative at the Swedish government award office is offering you a set of choices for how you can be paid your award: You could get SKr100,000 krone this coming September and the same amount the following September. Or, you could avoid the exchange-rate risk this coming year by being paid $5,000 per semester for the coming year (get paid in September and February) and then you would have the option to decide next July how you wish to be paid for the following year.

In addition, you know the following: The forward price of the dollar for a September contract is 10SKr/$ and the U.S. risk-free interest rate is 5% per annum.

c. Which payment option would you choose and why?

23. Using the information from the previous problem (problem 22):

a. If instead of hedging you chose to insure yourself against a rise in the price of the dollar, how might you do this? What is the difference between hedging and insuring in this case?

b. Suppose that instead of promising you SKr100,000 krone for your second year in college, the Swedish government made the second-year grant conditional on your grades and progress in your first year. What is the Swedish government hoping to achieve by doing this?

c. It is now July after your first year Tuition at your college is unchanged. You worked hard in your first year and your funding has been approved for another year. You have to decide, as you did last year, how you wish to get the funds for your coming year of schooling. This year the forward price of the dollar for a September contract is 10.2SKr/$ and the dollar risk-free rate has gone up to 7% per annum. Would you choose to get Skr100,000 krone in September or $5,000 per semester?

APPENDIX

Correlation and Regression

When mixing two risky assets, the **correlation** between the two rates of return plays an important part in determining the standard deviation of the resulting portfolio. Intuitively, correlation means the degree to which the rates of return on the assets tend to "move together."

The significance of the degree of correlation between the returns on two different risky assets and its implication for risk reduction through diversification are best illustrated with an example involving two stocks. Our first stock is Genco, which has the probability distribution

TABLE A.1 Rate of Return Assumptions for Genco and Negacorr

State of the Economy (1)	Probability (2)	Rate of Return on Genco (3)	Rate of Return on Negacorr (4)
Strong	1/3	0.385	0.225
Normal	1/3	0.140	0.020
Weak	1/3	0.105	0.265i

shown in column 3 of Table A.1. Genco's stock returns are *procyclical*, that is, the stock does well when the economy is strong and does poorly when the economy is weak. The second stock is Negacorr, which is *countercyclical:* It performs poorly when the economy is strong and performs well when the economy is weak. The fourth column of Table A.1 shows the probability distribution of rates of return on Negacorr stock.

Table A.2 shows the calculation of the expected rate of return and the standard deviation for the two stocks. Because each state of the economy is equally likely and because the probability distributions are symmetric, the computation is fairly simple. The expected rate of return on Genco is equal to its rate of return in a normal state of the economy: 0.14 per year. Similarly, the expected rate of return on Negacorr is equal to its rate of return in a normal state of the economy: 0.02 per year. The standard deviation (the square root of the variance) is the same for both stocks: 0.20.

Now consider an equally weighted portfolio consisting of 50% Genco stock and 50% Negacorr stock. What is its expected return and standard deviation?

Table A.3 shows us. It assumes a total investment of $100,000, with $50,000 invested in each of the two stocks.

First, look at the row corresponding to the strong state of the economy. The $50,000 invested in Genco will grow to $69,250 ($50,000 × 1.385), and the $50,000 invested in Negacorr stock will decline to $38,750. The portfolio will have a total value of $69,250 + $38,750 = $108,000. The rate of return in the strong state of the economy is therefore 0.08.

Now consider what happens if the state of the economy turns out to be weak. The $50,000 invested in Genco will decline to $44,750 ($50,000 × 0.895), and the $50,000 invested in

TABLE A.2 Computation of Expected Rate of Return and Volatility

State of the Economy	Genco			Negacorr		
	Rate of Return (r)	Deviation from Expected Return	Squared Deviation	Rate of Return (r)	Deviation from Expected Return	Squared Deviation
Strong	0.385	0.245	0.0600	−0.225	−0.245	0.0600
Normal	0.140	0.000	0.0000	0.020	0.000	0.0000
Weak	−0.105	−0.245	0.0600	0.265	0.245	0.0600
Expected return (E(r))	1/3 (0.385 + 0.14 − 0.105) = 0.14			1/3 (−0.225 + 0.02 + 0.265) = 0.02		
Variance (σ²)	1/3 (0.0600 + 0 + 0.0600) = 0.04			1/3 (0.0600 + 0 + 0.0600) = 0.04		
Standard deviation (σ)	0.20			0.20		

TABLE A.3 Rates of Return on a Portfolio of Perfectly Negatively Correlated Stocks

State of the Economy (1)	Rate of Return on Genco (2)	Rate of Return on Negacorr (3)	Dollar Payoff from $50,000 Investment in Genco (4)	Dollar Payoff from $50,000 Investment in Negacorr (5)	Total Dollar Payoff from $100,000 Portfolio (6)=(4)+(5)
Strong	0.385	−0.225	1.385 × $50,000 = $69,250	0.775 × $50,000 = $38,750	$69,250 + $38,750 = $108,000
Normal	0.140	0.020	1.14 × $50,000 = $57,000	1.02 × $50,000 = $51,000	$57,000 + $51,000 = $108,000
Weak	−0.105	0.265	0.895 × $50,000 = $44,750	1.265 × $50,000 = $63,250	$44,750 + $63,250 = $108,000
Expected return ($E(r)$)	0.140	0.020			
Standard deviation (σ)	0.200	0.200			

Negacorr stock will grow to $63,250. Again, you will have a portfolio with a total value of $108,000. The portfolio rate of return in the weak state of the economy is therefore also 0.08.

The second row of Table A.3 reveals that the same 0.08 rate of return occurs in the normal state of the economy. Regardless of the state of the economy the portfolio's rate of return is 0.08. Therefore, the volatility of the portfolio's rate of return is zero. *All* of the risk is eliminated.

The reason all of the risk could be eliminated in this example is because the two stocks are *perfectly negatively correlated*, which means that they vary in opposite directions with respect to each other. The statistic used to measure the degree of covariation between two rates of return is the *correlation coefficient*. To understand the correlation coefficient, however, we first define *covariance*.

Table A.4 shows how to calculate the covariance between the rates of return on Genco and Negacorr. For each state of the economy, we compute the deviation of each stock's rate of return from its expected value and multiply them together to find the product of the deviations. The products of the deviations are negative in our case because the rates of return move in opposite directions with the state of the economy. If they tended to move in the same direction, the products would tend to be positive.

The covariance is the average (the probability weighted sum) of these products of deviations over all states of the economy. It, therefore, gives us a measure of the average

TABLE A.4 Covariance and Correlation Coefficient

State of the Economy	Genco		Negacorr		Product of Deviations
	Rate of Return	Deviation from Expected Return	Rate of Return	Deviation from Expected Return	
Strong	0.385	0.245	−0.225	−0.245	−0.0600
Normal	0.140	0.000	0.020	0.000	0.0000
Weak	−0.105	−0.245	0.265	0.245	−0.0600

$\sigma_{1,2}$ = Covariance = 1/3(−0.0600 + 0 − 0.0600) = −0.04.
$\rho_{1,2}$ = Correlation Coefficient = −0.04/0.04 = −1.

tendency of the returns to *vary* in the same (positive) direction or in opposite directions (negative), hence, the term *covariance*. The mathematical formula for the covariance between the rates of return on two risky assets is:

$$\sigma_{1,2} = \sum_{i=1}^{n} P_i[r_{1i} - E(r_1)][r_{2i} - E(r_2)]$$

To standardize the covariance measure so that it is easier to interpret, we divide it by the product of the standard deviations of each stock. The resulting ratio is called the *correlation coefficient*. It is denoted by the Greek letter ρ (pronounced "rho"). Its formula is:

$$\rho_{1,2} = \sigma_{1,2}/\sigma_1\sigma_2$$

Correlation coefficients can range from values of $+1$ (perfect positive correlation) to -1 (perfect negative correlation). If $\rho = 0$, the two stocks are said to be uncorrelated. Correlation measures the degree of linear relationship between the returns. If the paired return combinations all lie exactly along a straight line the correlation coefficient will be either $+1$ or -1, depending on whether the line slopes upward or downward. In our example:

$$\rho_{1,2} = \text{Covariance/(Product of Standard Deviations)}$$
$$= -0.04/0.04$$
$$= -1$$

Quick Check 8

You are given the following assumptions for the rate of return on Posicorr stock:

State of the Economy (1)	Probability (2)	Rate of Return on Posicorr (3)
Strong	1/3	0.46
Normal	1/3	0.16
Weak	1/3	−0.14

Compute the correlation coefficient between the rate of return on Posicorr and on Genco stocks.

Table A.5 takes a postwar sample beginning in 1947 and restates the annual returns on the five major asset classes in the form of excess returns. The excess returns are the amount by which the asset class returns exceed the return on U.S. T-bills, or the T-bill level of return each year is subtracted from the returns of the other asset classes. Summary statistics are given at the bottom of the table. For example, if the sample was used to derive a point estimate of the expected annual excess return for World Equity, an estimate using the calculated mean or arithmetic average would be 7.87%. This point estimate, however would be centered in a rather wide confidence interval given the large standard deviation of 16.92%.

TABLE A.5   Excess Rates of Return 1947–2003 (over the year)

	World Portfolio		U.S. Market		
Year	Equity Return in U.S. Dollars	Bond Return in U.S. Dollars	Small Stocks	Large Stocks	Long-Term T-Bonds
1947	−1.55	−8.72	−2.57	4.42	−1.65
1948	2.08	4.18	−7.29	4.31	2.09
1949	16.24	1.08	20.10	17.13	4.92
1950	23.23	1.25	45.60	31.47	−2.17
1951	27.21	−0.94	5.02	21.99	−3.43
1952	12.57	3.18	3.19	17.27	0.29
1953	3.59	1.86	−7.41	−3.52	2.05
1954	47.34	6.94	62.76	51.69	4.02
1955	21.38	−1.33	22.51	29.88	−2.90
1956	6.20	−6.73	2.73	4.03	−7.54
1957	−9.99	−0.10	−17.56	−14.27	6.33
1958	35.36	−1.87	63.92	42.36	−5.13
1959	22.14	−2.38	18.44	10.13	−6.37
1960	5.13	7.91	−7.67	−2.39	11.20
1961	17.70	−0.18	26.80	25.47	−1.97
1962	−9.92	6.90	−14.00	−11.51	4.09
1963	11.20	−0.39	14.97	19.48	−3.64
1964	7.53	−0.33	15.74	13.15	0.99
1965	6.52	−1.12	35.14	8.53	−4.24
1966	−11.18	0.66	−11.64	−14.96	−1.01
1967	19.60	−7.47	99.17	19.96	−11.56
1968	14.63	−3.19	44.98	5.71	−6.49
1969	−12.80	−8.92	−37.87	−14.92	−13.11
1970	−9.32	3.41	−23.79	−2.28	6.31
1971	14.90	10.70	13.58	9.85	13.15
1972	21.34	4.01	−3.67	15.25	1.66
1973	−21.42	−2.76	−45.14	−21.81	−5.66
1974	−32.09	−3.01	−35.25	−34.48	−2.55
1975	26.02	1.68	53.00	31.44	2.68
1976	11.60	6.07	43.56	16.82	5.91
1977	1.28	11.02	22.29	−12.41	−4.25
1978	13.83	6.26	17.24	−0.81	−11.47
1979	7.33	−10.25	30.16	8.08	−1.67
1980	18.91	−8.68	28.56	20.96	1.65
1981	−19.04	−18.55	−16.37	−19.84	−11.25
1982	0.60	11.50	17.19	11.43	−4.14
1983	15.01	−7.15	25.27	13.52	−9.38
1984	−6.61	−2.42	−20.17	−3.50	5.33
1985	32.69	26.53	21.39	24.32	25.00

TABLE A.5 **(Continued)**

| | World Portfolio | | U.S. Market | | |
| | Equity Return in U.S. Dollars | Bond Return in U.S. Dollars | Small Stocks | Large Stocks | Long-Term T-Bonds |
Year					
1986	32.52	24.60	−2.18	12.34	17.90
1987	10.81	13.37	−19.32	−0.04	−8.03
1988	15.53	−1.17	12.29	10.54	2.08
1989	10.73	−1.80	0.83	23.12	11.27
1990	−25.34	4.30	−34.89	−10.88	−0.55
1991	13.42	13.10	43.25	25.15	12.88
1992	−9.66	1.31	17.70	4.31	4.39
1993	17.61	17.32	16.18	6.97	12.58
1994	2.79	−5.56	−9.24	−2.59	−11.06
1995	14.98	21.03	28.16	32.13	26.09
1996	7.06	−1.48	11.47	17.93	−5.95
1997	10.89	1.79	18.78	28.09	10.00
1998	15.77	12.54	−12.02	23.80	8.74
1999	22.54	−10.16	35.59	16.48	−13.30
2000	−18.89	2.51	−11.62	−14.89	14.48
2001	−19.54	−4.08	25.13	−15.61	0.49
2002	−18.68	20.98	−13.27	−23.76	15.13
2003	36.75	10.42	73.56	27.68	1.37

Excess Return statistics

Average	7.87	2.42	11.99	8.50	1.31
Standard deviation	16.92	8.97	28.78	17.77	8.96
Minimum	−32.09	−18.55	−45.14	−34.48	−13.30
Maximum	47.34	26.53	99.17	51.69	26.08

Sources:
Inflation data: Bureau of Labor Statistics
Security return data for 1926–1995: Center for Research in Security Prices
Security return data since 1996. Returns on appropriate index portfolios,
Large stocks: S&P 500
Small stocks: Fama & French 1st quantile
LT Government bonds: Lehman Bros LT Treasury index
ST Government bonds: Lehman Bros. Intermediate-term Treasury index
T-bills: Salomon Smith Barney 3-month U.S. T-bill index

Figure A.1 shows the comovement over time of these excess return series for the two asset classes of World Equity and U.S. large stocks. The striking similarity of the time series patterns of these annual excess returns are indicative of a high degree of correlation in the returns. Figure A.2 plots the same data where each point represents a pair of yearly excess returns for the same two asset classes. This scatter plot once again demonstrates a strong positive relationship between the excess returns of these two asset classes. Using the sample data the calculated correlation coefficient is +0.8837 as shown in Table A.6.

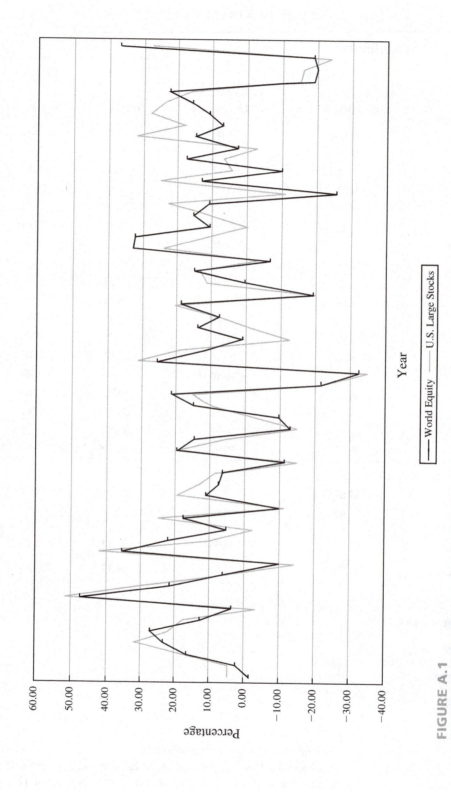

FIGURE A.1

Annual Excess Rates of Returns 1947–2003

Year

Percentage

— World Equity ——— U.S. Large Stocks

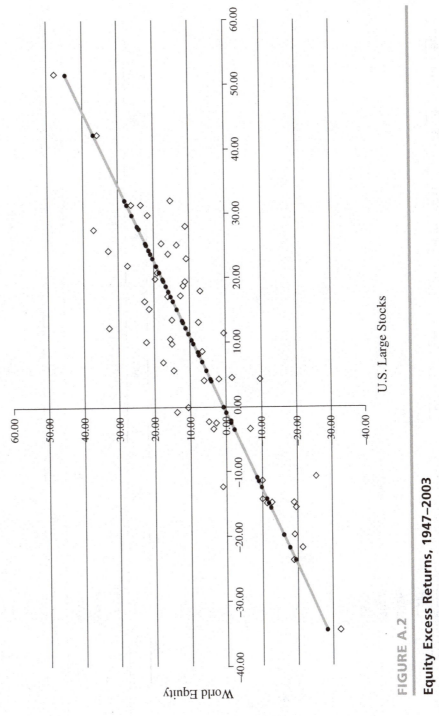

FIGURE A.2

Equity Excess Returns, 1947–2003
Y = 0.711 + 0.842X

TABLE A.6

CORR (excess returns)	World Equity	World Bonds	U.S. Small Stocks	U.S. Large Stocks	U.S. Long-Term T-Bonds
World Equity	1.0000				
World Bonds	0.2426	1.0000			
U.S. Small Stocks	0.7012	0.0093	1.0000		
U.S. Large Stocks	0.8837	0.1540	0.7167	1.0000	
U.S. Long-Term T-Bonds	0.0974	0.7216	−0.0509	0.1619	1

SUMMARY OUTPUT

Regression Statistics

Multiple R	0.8837
R Square	0.7808
Adjusted R Square	0.7769
Standard Error	7.9945
Observations	57.0000

ANOVA

	df	SS	MS	F	Significance F
Regression	1.0000	12524.4621	12524.4621	195.9653	0.0000
Residual	55.0000	3515.1390	63.9116		
Total	56.0000	16039.6011			

	Coefficients	Standard Error	t Stat	P-value
Intercept	0.7109	1.1759	0.6046	0.5479
Slope	0.8417	0.0601	13.9988	0.0000

Note that this is the highest degree of correlation for any pairing of the five asset classes. The lowest correlation of -0.0509 is between the excess returns of U.S. small stocks and U.S. long-term T-bonds.

The tool of regression analysis allows us to estimate the best-fitting linear relationship. If we consider the two asset classes of World Equity and U.S. large stocks we might imagine wanting to improve our estimate of the excess return for World Equity conditioned on knowing the excess return on U.S. large stocks. Given the high degree of correlation between the paired returns we would simply be using this knowledge of how the returns move together to raise and lower in a systematic fashion our estimate of World Equity return based on knowing whether U.S. large stocks are returning above or below their average.

The estimates of the intercept (α) and slope (β) of the best-fitting line[*] $Y = \alpha + \beta X$ are given by:

$$\beta = \frac{COV_{xy}}{\sigma_{x^2}} \qquad\qquad \alpha = E(y) - \beta.E(x)$$

In this example we would use U.S. large stocks as the independent x variable and World Equity as the dependent y variable. The slope (β) of the line is calculated as the ratio of the covariance between the excess returns to the variance of the independent variable, here the variance of the excess returns of U.S. large stocks. The intercept (α) is simply the mean or expected value of the y variable less β times the mean or expected value of the x variable.

Table A.6 shows the results of the regression analysis using Excel. At the bottom of the table the regression coefficients for the intercept, 0.7109, and the slope, 0.8417, are given. These coefficients were used to plot the estimated regression line in Figure A.2.

Quick Check 8   Compute the correlation coefficient between the rate of return on Posicorr and on Genco stocks.

Answer: Expected return on Posicorr stock is 0.16 and the standard deviation is 0.245 whereas for Genco it is 0.14 and 0.2, respectively. The covariance between the two stocks is 0.049 and the correlation coefficient = $(0.049)/(0.245 \times 0.2) = 1$. The two are perfectly positively correlated.

Appendix: Correlation
The Diversification Principle

24. Consider an opportunity to invest in two Canadian stocks or an equally weighted portfolio with return distributions as follow.

State of Economy	Probabilities	Return on Maple	Return on Walrus	50/50 Portfolio
Boom	1/3	25%	20%	22.5%
Stagnant	1/3	15%	12.5%	13.75%
Bust	1/3	0%	1.25%	0.625%

[*]The best-fitting line would be the line where the sum of the squared deviations of the y variable's actual values from the line's estimated y values is minimized. Each observation will have an actual and a fitted value. The difference between these values, or the vertical distance between the line and the data point, is the error in the estimate or the deviation of the estimate from the actual value. Thus the regression technique fits the line that produces the minimal sum of these squared errors.

Calculate the expected returns and standard deviations of the returns for the two stocks and the portfolio. Calculate the covariance of the returns on the two stocks.

25. Using the information from the previous problem (problem 24) calculate the correlation coefficient for Maple and Walrus. Does this explain the relationship among the standard deviations for Maple, Walrus, and the portfolio?

Suggested Reading

Bodie, Z., A. Kane, and A. Marcus. *Investments.* 7th Ed. Boston: Irwin/McGraw-Hill, 2008.

Portfolio Opportunities and Choice

OBJECTIVES

- To understand the process of personal portfolio selection in theory and in practice.
- To build a quantitative model of the trade-off between risk and reward.

CONTENTS

From Chapter 12 of *Financial Economics*, 2/e. Zvi Bodie, Robert C. Merton, David L. Cleeton.
Copyright © 2008 by Pearson Prentice Hall. All rights reserved.

This chapter is about how people should invest their wealth, a process called *portfolio selection*. A person's wealth portfolio includes all of his or her assets (stocks, bonds, shares in unincorporated businesses, houses or apartments, pension benefits, insurance policies, etc.) and all of his or her liabilities (student loans, auto loans, home mortgages, etc.).

There is no single portfolio selection strategy that is best for all people. There are, however, some general principles, such as the principle of diversification, that apply to all *risk-averse* people. Earlier, we discussed diversification as a method of managing risk. This chapter extends that discussion and analyzes the quantitative trade-off between risk and expected return.

Section 1 examines the role of portfolio selection in the context of a person's life-cycle financial planning process and shows why there is no single strategy that is best for all people. It also examines how the investor's time horizon and risk tolerance affect portfolio selection. Section 2 analyzes the choice between a single risky asset and a riskless asset, and Section 3 examines optimal portfolio selection with many risky assets.

1 The Process of Personal Portfolio Selection

Portfolio selection is the study of how people should invest their wealth. It is a process of trading off risk and expected return to find the best portfolio of assets and liabilities. A narrow definition of portfolio selection includes only decisions about how much to invest in stocks, bonds, and other securities. A broader definition includes decisions about whether to buy or rent one's house, what types and amounts of insurance to purchase, and how to manage one's liabilities. An even broader definition includes decisions about how much to invest in one's human capital (e.g., by furthering one's professional education). The common element in all of these decisions is the trade-off between risk and expected return.

This chapter is devoted to exploring the concepts and techniques you need to know to evaluate risk-reward trade-offs and to manage your wealth portfolio efficiently. A major theme is that although there are some general rules for portfolio selection that apply to virtually everyone, there is no single portfolio or portfolio strategy that is best for everyone. We begin by explaining why.

1.1 The Life Cycle

In portfolio selection the best strategy depends on an individual's personal circumstances (age, family status, occupation, income, wealth, etc.). For some people holding a particular asset may add to their total risk exposure, but for others the same asset may be risk reducing. An asset that is risk reducing at an early stage in the life cycle may not be at a later stage.

For a young couple starting a family it may be optimal to buy a house and take out a mortgage loan. For an older couple about to retire it may be optimal to sell their house and invest the proceeds in some asset that will provide a steady stream of income for as long as they live.

Consider the purchase of life insurance. The optimal insurance policy for Miriam, a parent with dependent children, will differ from the policy appropriate for Sanjiv, a single person with no dependents, even if the two people are the same in all other respects (age, income, occupation, wealth, etc.). Miriam would be concerned about protecting her family in the event of her death and would, therefore, want a policy that provides cash benefits payable to her children upon her death. Sanjiv, on the other hand, would not be concerned about benefits payable if he dies; therefore, the purchase of life insurance would not be risk reducing for him. At a later stage in her life, Miriam too may find that her children can provide for themselves and no longer need the protection afforded by life insurance.

Now consider the situation of Miriam and Sanjiv after they reach retirement age. Miriam has children and is happy to have them inherit any assets that are left after she dies. If she should live an extraordinarily long time and exhaust her own wealth, she is confident her children will provide financial support for her.

Sanjiv is a loner with no one to whom he cares to leave a bequest. He would like to consume all of his wealth during his own lifetime but is concerned that if he increases his spending he will exhaust his wealth if he happens to live an extraordinarily long time. For Sanjiv buying an insurance policy that guarantees him an income for as long as he lives would be risk reducing; for Miriam it would not be. Such an insurance policy is called a **life annuity.**

As these examples make clear, even people of the same age, with the same income and wealth, may have different perspectives on buying a house or buying insurance. The same is true of investing in stocks, bonds, and other securities. There is no single portfolio that is best for all people.

To see this, consider two different individuals of the same age and family status. Chang is 30 years old and works as a security analyst on Wall Street. His current and future earnings are very sensitive to the performance of the stock market. Obi is also 30 years old and teaches English in the public school system. Her current and future earnings are not very sensitive to the stock market. For Chang, investing a significant proportion of his investment portfolio in stocks would be more risky than it would be for Obi.

Quick Check 1

How would the investment portfolio that is best for a young person with a secure job differ from the one that is best for a retired person whose only source of income is an investment portfolio?

1.2 Time Horizons

In formulating a plan for portfolio selection you begin by determining your goals and time horizons. The *planning horizon* is the total length of time for which one plans.

The longest time horizon would typically correspond to the retirement goal and would be the balance of one's lifetime.[1] Thus, for a 25-year-old who expects to live to age 85, the planning horizon would be 60 years. As one ages, the planning horizon typically gets shorter and shorter (see Box 1).

There are also shorter planning horizons that correspond to specific financial goals, such as paying for a child's education. For example, if you have a child who is three years old and plan to pay for her college education when she reaches age 18, the planning horizon for this goal is 15 years.

The *decision horizon* is the length of time between decisions to revise the portfolio. The length of the decision horizon is controlled by the individual within certain limits.

Some people review their portfolios at regular intervals, for example, once a month (when they pay their bills), or once a year (when they file income tax forms). People of modest means with most of their wealth invested in bank accounts might review their portfolios very infrequently and at irregular intervals determined by some triggering event such as getting married or divorced, having a child, or receiving a bequest. A sudden rise or fall in the price of an asset a person owns might also trigger a review of the portfolio.

---

[1]Some people plan not only for their own lifetimes but also for those of future generations. For them the planning horizon might be very long, perhaps infinite.

Box 1 — Computing Life Expectancy

Your life expectancy is the number of years that you are expected to live. It is computed using statistics on mortality (i.e., death) rates collected and analyzed by actuaries, who are professional that specialize in the mathematical techniques relevant to computing insurance premiums.

To estimate the probability of death at a given age, actuaries use *mortality tables* such as the one that follows, which is for U.S. residents. For each age from 60 to 95 the table states the mortality rate in terms of deaths per 1,000 and the expectation of life (expected value of the number of years remaining before death). There are separate statistics given for males and females and broken down by smokers and non-smokers.

The second column of the table shows that a 60-year old male as a 0.0099 probability of dying before reaching the age of 61 (9.9/1,000), a 0.0109 probability of dying before reaching the age of 62, and so on. The third column shows the life expectancy for a male at each age, computed using the death rates in the second column. Thus, a 60-year-old male has a life expectancy of an additional 20.6 years, a 61-year-old make has a life expectancy of another 19.8 years, and so on. A 95-year-old male faces a probability of 0.2692 of dying before reaching the age of 96 and has a life expectancy of another 2.8 years. Columns 4 and 5 show the comparable statistics for females.

Mortality Table, Ages 60–95

Age	Males		Females	
	Deaths per 1,000	Life Expectancy (years)	Deaths per 1,000	Life Expectancy (years)
60	9.9	20.6	8.0	24.1
61	10.9	19.8	8.7	23.3
65	16.9	16.8	11.9	20.1
70	25.8	13.3	17.8	16.4
75	41.9	10.2	27.9	13.0
80	70.1	7.5	43.9	9.9
85	116.6	5.4	74.5	7.3
90	187.7	3.8	121.9	5.3
95	269.2	2.8	193.7	3.8

Source: Commissioners Standard Ordinary (CSO) 2001 Mortality Table.
For an interesting on-line graphical presentation see the Wolfram demonstration project at:
http://demonstrations.wolfram.com/The2001CSOMortalityTables/

People with substantial investments in stocks and bonds might review their portfolios every day or even more frequently. The shortest possible decision horizon is the *trading horizon,* defined as the *minimum* time interval over which investors can revise their portfolios.

The length of the trading horizon is not under the control of the individual. Whether the trading horizon is a week, a day, an hour, or a minute is determined by the structure of the markets in the economy (e.g., when the securities exchanges are open or whether organized off-exchange markets exist).

In today's global financial environment trading in many securities can be carried on somewhere on the globe around the clock. For these securities at least the trading horizon is very short.

Portfolio decisions you make today are influenced by what you think might happen tomorrow. A plan that takes account of *future* decisions in making *current* decisions is called a **strategy.**

How frequently investors can revise their portfolios by buying or selling securities is an important consideration in formulating investment strategies. If you know that you can adjust the composition of your portfolio frequently, you may invest differently than if you cannot adjust it.

For example, a person may adopt a strategy of investing "extra" wealth in stocks, meaning wealth in excess of the amount needed to insure a certain threshold standard of living. If the stock market goes up over time, a person will increase the proportion of his or her portfolio invested in stocks. However, if the stock market goes down, a person will reduce the proportion invested in stocks. If the stock market falls to the point at which the person's threshold standard of living is threatened, he or she will get out of stocks altogether. An investor pursuing this particular strategy is more likely to have a higher threshold if stocks can only be traded infrequently.

Quick Check 2

Do you have a decision horizon of fixed length? How long is it?

1.3 Risk Tolerance

A person's *tolerance* for bearing risk is a major determinant of portfolio choices.[2] We expect risk tolerance to be influenced by such characteristics as age, family status, job status, wealth, and other attributes that affect people's ability to maintain their standard of living in the face of adverse movements in the market value of their investment portfolio. One's attitude toward risk also plays a role in determining a person's tolerance for bearing risk. Even among people with the same apparent personal, family, and job characteristics, some may have a greater willingness to take risk than others.

When we refer to a person's risk tolerance in our analysis of optimal portfolio selection, we do not distinguish between capacity to bear risk and attitude toward risk. Thus, whether a person has a relatively high tolerance for risk because he is young or rich, because he handles stress well, or because he was brought up to believe that taking chances is the morally right path, all that matters in the analysis to follow is that he is more willing than the average person to take on additional risk to achieve a higher expected return.

Quick Check 3

Do you think that risk tolerance increases with a person's wealth? Why?

1.4 The Role of Professional Asset Managers

Most people have neither the knowledge nor the time to carry out portfolio optimization. Therefore they hire an investment advisor to do it for them or they buy a "finished product" from a financial intermediary. Such finished products include various investment accounts and mutual funds offered by banks, securities firms, investment companies, and insurance companies.

---

[2]Previously, we used the term *risk aversion* instead of *risk tolerance.* One is the mirror image of the other. The more risk tolerant the person is, the less risk averse.

When financial intermediaries decide what asset choices to offer to households, they are in a position analogous to a restaurant deciding on its menu. There are many ingredients available (the basic stocks, bonds, and other securities issued by firms and governments) and an infinite number of possible ways to combine them, but only a limited number of items will be offered to customers. The portfolio theory developed in the rest of this chapter offers some guidance in finding the least number of items to offer that still cover the full array of customer demands.

2 The Trade-Off between Expected Return and Risk

The next two sections present the analytical framework used by professional portfolio managers for examining the quantitative trade-off between risk and expected return. The objective is to find the portfolio that offers investors the highest expected rate of return for any degree of risk they are willing to tolerate. Throughout the analysis we will refer to *risky* assets without specifically identifying them as bonds, stocks, options, insurance policies, and so on. This is because, as explained in the preceding sections of this chapter, the riskiness of a particular asset depends critically on the specific circumstances of the investor.

Portfolio optimization is often done as a two-step process: (1) Find the optimal combination of risky assets, and (2) mix this optimal risky-asset portfolio with the riskless asset. For simplicity, we start with the second step: mixing a single risky-asset portfolio and a riskless asset. (We discuss the identity of the riskless asset in the next section.) The single risky-asset portfolio is composed of many risky assets chosen in an optimal way. In Section 3.4 we investigate how the optimal composition of this risky-asset portfolio is found.

2.1 What Is the Riskless Asset?

Prviously we discussed interest rates and showed that there is a different riskless asset that corresponds to each possible unit of account (dollars, yen, etc.) and to each possible maturity. Thus, a 10-year, dollar-denominated, zero-coupon bond that offers a default-free yield-to-maturity of 6% per year is riskless only in terms of dollars and only if held to maturity. The dollar rate of return on that same bond is uncertain if it is sold before maturity because the price to be received is uncertain. And even if held to maturity, the bond's rate of return denominated in yen or in terms of consumer purchasing power is uncertain because future exchange rates and consumer prices are uncertain.

In the theory of portfolio selection the riskless asset is defined as a security that offers a perfectly predictable rate of return in terms of the unit of account selected for the analysis and the length of the investor's *decision horizon*. When no specific investor is identified, the riskless asset refers to an asset that offers a predictable rate of return over the *trading horizon* (i.e., the shortest possible decision horizon).

Thus, if the U.S. dollar is taken as the unit of account and the trading horizon is a day, the riskless rate is the interest rate on U.S. Treasury bills maturing the next day.

> **Quick Check 4**
>
> What is the riskless asset if the unit of account is the Swiss franc and the length of the decision horizon is a week?

2.2 Combining the Riskless Asset and a Single Risky Asset

Suppose that you have $100,000 to invest. You are choosing between a riskless asset with an interest rate of 0.06 per year and a risky asset with an expected rate of return of 0.14 per year and standard deviation of 0.20.[3] How much of your $100,000 should you invest in the risky asset?

We examine all of the risk-return combinations open to you with the aid of Table 1 and Figure 1. Start with the case in which you invest all of your money in the riskless asset. This corresponds to the point labeled F in Figure 1 and the first row in Table 1. Column 2 in Table 1 gives the proportion of the portfolio invested in the risky asset (0) and column 3 the proportion invested in the riskless asset (100%). The proportions always add to 100%. Columns 4 and 5 of Table 1 give the expected return and standard deviation that correspond to portfolio F:$E(r)$ of 0.06 per year and σ of 0.00.

The case in which you invest all of your money in the risky asset corresponds to the point labeled S in Figure 1 and the last row in Table 1. Its expected return is 0.14 and its standard deviation 0.20.

In Figure 1 the portfolio expected rate of return, $E(r)$, is measured along the vertical axis and the standard deviation, σ, along the horizontal axis. The portfolio proportions are not explicitly shown in Figure 1; however, we know what they are from Table 1.

Figure 1 graphically illustrates the trade-off between risk and reward. The line connecting points F, G, H, J, and S in Figure 1 represents the set of alternatives open to you by choosing different combinations (portfolios) of the risky asset and riskless asset. Each point on the line corresponds to the mix of these two assets given in columns 2 and 3 of Table 1.

At point F, which is on the vertical axis in Figure 1, with $E(r)$ of 0.06 per year and σ of zero, all of your money is invested in the riskless asset. You face no risk, and your expected return is 0.06 per year. As you shift money out of the riskless asset and into the risky asset, you move to the right along the trade-off line and face both a higher expected rate of return and a greater risk. If you invest all of your money in the risky asset, you would be at point S, with expected return, $E(r)$, of 0.14 and standard deviation, σ, of 0.20.

Portfolio H (corresponding to the third row of Table 1) is half invested in the riskless asset and half in the risky asset. With $50,000 invested in the risky asset and $50,000

TABLE 1   Portfolio Expected Rate of Return and Standard Deviation as a Function of the Proportion Invested in the Risky Asset

Portfolio (1)	Proportion Invested in the Risky Asset (2)	Proportion Invested in Riskless Asset (3)	Expected Rate of Return $E(r)$ (4)	Standard Deviation σ (5)
F	0	100%	0.06	0.00
G	25%	75%	0.08	0.05
H	50%	50%	0.10	0.10
J	75%	25%	0.12	0.15
S	100%	0	0.14	0.20

[3]The definitions and formulas for the expected rate of return and its standard deviation are presented in sections 10.8 and 10.9. Note that in this chapter we write rates of return as decimal fractions rather than percentages.

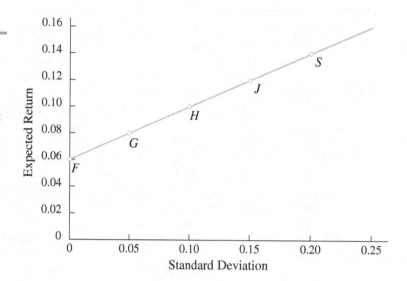

FIGURE 1

The Risk–Reward Trade-Off Line

Notes: At point *F*, the portfolio is 100% invested in riskless securities offering a rate of 0.06 per year. At point *S*, it is 100% invested in the risky asset, with an expected rate of return of 0.14 per year and σ of 0.20. At point *H*, the portfolio is half in the risky asset and half in the riskless asset.

invested in the riskless asset, you would have an expected rate of return that is halfway between the expected return on the all-stock portfolio (0.14) and the riskless rate of interest (0.06). The expected rate of return of 0.10 is shown in column 4 and the standard deviation of 0.10 in column 5.

Quick Check 5

Locate the point corresponding to portfolio *J* in Figure 1. Consult Table 1 for the portfolio's composition, its expected rate of return, and standard deviation. How much of your $100,000 would be invested in the risky asset if you chose portfolio *J*?

Now let us show how we can find the portfolio composition for *any* point lying on the trade-off line in Figure 1, not only the points listed in Table 1. For example, suppose we want to identify the portfolio that has an expected rate of return of 0.09. We can tell from Figure 1 that the point corresponding to such a portfolio lies on the trade-off line between points *G* and *H*. But what is the portfolio's composition and what is its standard deviation? In answering this question we shall also derive the formula for the trade-off line connecting all of the points in Figure 1.

Step 1: Relate the portfolio's expected return to the proportion invested in the risky asset.

Let *w* denote the proportion of the $100,000 investment to be allocated to the risky asset. The remaining proportion, $1-w$, is to be invested in the riskless asset. The expected rate of return on any portfolio, $E(r)$, is given by:

$$E(r) = wE(r_s) + (1 - w)r_f$$
$$= r_f + w[E(r_s) - r_f] \tag{1}$$

where $E(r_s)$ denotes the expected rate of return on the risky asset and r_f is the riskless rate. Substituting 0.06 for r_f and 0.14 for $E(r_s)$ we get:

$$E(r) = 0.06 + w(0.14 - 0.06)$$
$$= 0.06 + 0.08w$$

Equation 1 is interpreted as follows. The base rate of return for any portfolio is the riskless rate (0.06 in our example). In addition, the portfolio is expected to earn a risk premium which depends on (1) the risk premium on the risky asset, $E(r_s) - r_f$ (0.08 in our example) and (2) the proportion of the portfolio invested in the risky asset, denoted by w.

To find the portfolio composition corresponding to an expected rate of return of 0.09, we substitute in equation 1 and solve for w:

$$0.09 = 0.06 + 0.08w$$
$$w = \frac{0.09 - 0.06}{0.08} = 0.375$$

Thus, the portfolio mix is 37.5% risky asset and 62.5% riskless asset.

Step 2: Relate the portfolio standard deviation to the proportion invested in the risky asset.

When we combine a risky and a riskless asset in a portfolio, the standard deviation of that portfolio is the standard deviation of the risky asset times the weight of that asset in the portfolio. Denoting the standard deviation of the risky asset σ_s, we have an expression for the portfolio's standard deviation:

$$\sigma = \sigma_s w = 0.2w \tag{2}$$

To find the standard deviation corresponding to an expected rate of return of 0.09, we substitute 0.375 for w in equation 2 and solve for σ:

$$\sigma = \sigma_s w = 0.2 \times 0.375 = 0.075$$

Thus, the portfolio standard deviation is 0.075.

Finally, we can eliminate w to derive the formula directly relating the expected rate of return to standard deviation along the trade-off line.

Step 3: Relate the portfolio expected rate of return to its standard deviation.

To derive the exact equation for the trade-off line in Figure 1, we rearrange equation 2 to find that $w = \sigma/\sigma_s$. By substituting for w in equation 1, we have that:

$$E(r) = r_f + \frac{E(r_s) - r_f}{\sigma_s}\sigma = 0.06 + 0.40\sigma \tag{3}$$

In words, the portfolio's expected rate of return expressed as a function of its standard deviation is a straight line, with an intercept $r_f = 0.06$ and a slope:

$$\frac{E(r_s) - r_f}{\sigma_s} = \frac{0.08}{0.2} = 0.40$$

The slope of the trade-off line measures the extra expected return the market offers for each unit of extra risk an investor is willing to bear.

2.3 Achieving a Target Expected Return: 1

Find the portfolio corresponding to an expected rate of return of 0.11 per year. What is its standard deviation?

SOLUTION:

To find the portfolio composition corresponding to an expected rate of return of 0.11, we substitute in equation 1 and solve for *w*:

$$0.11 = 0.06 + 0.08w$$

$$w = \frac{0.11 - 0.06}{0.08} = 0.625$$

Thus, the portfolio mix is 62.5% risky asset and 37.5% riskless asset.

To find the standard deviation corresponding to an expected rate of return of 0.11, we substitute 0.625 for *w* in equation 2 and solve for σ.

$$\sigma = 0.2w = 0.2 \times 0.625 = 0.125$$

Thus, the portfolio standard deviation is 0.125.

Quick Check 6

What happens to the intercept and the slope of the trade-off line in Figure 1 if the risk-free rate changes to 0.03 per year and the expected rate of return on the risky asset to 0.10 per year?

2.4 Portfolio Efficiency

An **efficient portfolio** is defined as the portfolio that offers the investor the highest possible expected rate of return at a specified level of risk.

The significance of the concept of portfolio efficiency and how to achieve it are illustrated by adding a second risky asset to our previous example. Risky Asset 2 has an expected rate of return of 0.08 per year and a standard deviation of 0.15 and is represented by point *R* in Figure 2.

FIGURE 2

Portfolio Efficiency

Notes: At point *R*, the portfolio is 100% invested in Risky Asset 2 offering an expected return of 0.08 and a σ of 0.15. The investor can have both a higher expected rate of return and a lower standard deviation at any point on the line connecting points *G* and *J*.

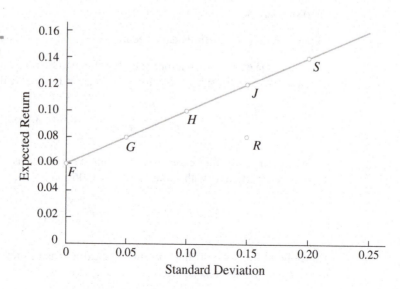

An investor requiring an expected rate of return of 0.08 per year could achieve this by investing all of his or her money in Risky Asset 2 and, thus, would be at point *R*. But point *R* is *inefficient* because the investor can get the *same* expected rate of return of 0.08 per year *and* a lower standard deviation at point *G*.

From Table 1 we know that at point *G* the standard deviation is only 0.05 and that this is achieved by holding 25% of the portfolio in Risky Asset 1 and 75% in the riskless asset. Indeed, we can see that a risk-averse investor would be better off at any point along the trade-off line connecting points *G* and *S* than at point *R*. All of these points are feasible and are achieved by mixing Risky Asset 1 with the riskless asset. For example, portfolio *J* has a standard deviation equal to that of Risky Asset 2 ($\sigma = 0.15$), but its expected return is 0.12 per year rather than 0.08. From Table 1 we know that its composition is 75% Risky Asset 1 and 25% riskless asset.

We can use equations 1 and 2 to find the composition of other efficient portfolios that lie between points *G* and *J* and, therefore, have both a higher expected rate of return and a lower standard deviation than Risky Asset 2. For example, consider a portfolio that consists of 62.5% Risky Asset 1 and 37.5% riskless asset. Its expected rate of return is 0.11 per year and its standard deviation is 0.125.

> ### Quick Check 7
>
> How can an investor achieve an expected rate of return of 0.105 per year with Risky Asset 1 and the riskless asset? What is the standard deviation of this portfolio? Compare it to the standard deviation of Risky Asset 2?

3 Efficient Diversification with Many Risky Assets

Although holding Risky Asset 2 by itself is inefficient, what about holding portfolios that mix the two risky assets? Or portfolios that mix the two risky assets with the riskless asset?

We will explore the ways to efficiently combine the three assets in two steps. The first step is to consider the risk and return combinations attainable by mixing only Risky Assets 1 and 2, and then in the second step we add the riskless asset.

3.1 Portfolios of Two Risky Assets

Combining two risky assets in a portfolio is similar to combining a risky asset with a riskless asset discussed in section 2. (Take a moment to review Table 1, Figure 1, and equations 1 and 2.) When one of the two assets is riskless, the standard deviation of its rate of return and its correlation with the other asset are zero. When both assets are risky, the analysis of the risk and return trade-off is somewhat more involved.

The formula for the mean rate of return of any portfolio consisting of a proportion *w* in Risky Asset 1 and a proportion $(1-w)$ in Risky Asset 2 is:

$$E(r) = wE(r_1) + (1 - w)E(r_2) \tag{4}$$

and the formula for variance is:

$$\sigma^2 = w^2\sigma_1^2 + (1 - w)^2\sigma_2^2 + 2w(1 - w)\rho_{1,2}\sigma_1\sigma_2 \tag{5}$$

These two equations should be compared to equations 1 and 2. Equation 4 is essentially the same as equation 1 with the expected return on Risky Asset 2, $E(r_2)$, substituted for the interest rate on the riskless asset, r_f. Equation 5 is a more general form of equation 2. When asset 2 is riskless, then $\sigma_2 = 0$, and equation 5 simplifies to equation 2.

TABLE 2 **Distribution of Rates of Return on Risky Assets**

	Risky Asset 1	Risky Asset 2
Mean [$E(r)$]	0.14	0.08
Standard deviation (σ)	0.20	0.15

Table 2 summarizes our assessments of the probability distribution of the rates of return on Risky Assets 1 and 2. We will make alternative assumptions concerning the correlation coefficient for the pairs of asset returns.

Table 3 and Figure 3 show the combinations of mean and standard deviation of returns attainable by combining Risky Asset 1 and Risky Asset 2, conditional on alternative assumptions about the correlation coefficient. The top and bottom rows of Table 3 correspond to the end points of the curves in Figure 3 and correspond to portfolios comprised of investing either only in Risky Asset 1 (bottom row of Table 3 or upper right endpoint, S,

TABLE 3 **The Risk–Reward Trade-Off for Portfolios of Two Risky Assets**

Correlation ($\rho_{1,2}$)	Proportion Invested in Risky Asset 1 (w)	Proportion Invested in Risky Asset 2 ($1-w$)	Expected Rate of Return $E(r)$	Standard Deviation (σ)
			Risky Asset 2	Risky Asset 2
1.00	0.00%	100.00%	8.00%	*15.00%
	25.00%	75.00%	9.50%	16.25%
	50.00%	50.00%	11.00%	17.50%
	75.00%	25.00%	12.50%	18.75%
0.50	23.08%	76.92%	9.38%	*14.41%
	25.00%	75.00%	9.50%	14.42%
	50.00%	50.00%	11.00%	15.21%
	75.00%	25.00%	12.50%	17.18%
0.00	25.00%	75.00%	9.50%	12.31%
	36.00%	64.00%	10.16%	*12.00%
	50.00%	50.00%	11.00%	12.50%
	75.00%	25.00%	12.50%	15.46%
−0.50	25.00%	75.00%	9.50%	9.76%
	40.54%	59.46%	10.43%	*8.54%
	50.00%	50.00%	11.00%	9.01%
	75.00%	25.00%	12.50%	13.52%
−1.00	25.00%	75.00%	9.50%	6.25%
	42.86%	57.14%	10.57%	*0.00%
	50.00%	50.00%	11.00%	2.50%
	75.00%	25.00%	12.50%	11.25%
	100.00%	0.00%	14.00%	20.00%

*Portfolio with minimum standard deviation, given the correlation coefficient. The formula for the proportion of Risky Asset 1 that minimizes the variance, and standard deviation, of the portfolio is given by: $w_{min} = \dfrac{\sigma_2^2 - \rho_{1,2}\sigma_1\sigma_2}{\sigma_1^2 + \sigma_2^2 - 2\rho_{1,2}\sigma_1\sigma_2}$.

FIGURE 3

The Risk–Reward Trade-Off Curve: Risky Assets Only

Note: Two-Asset portfolios constructed from Risky Assets given in Table 3 with correlations over the range (+1, +0.5, 0, −0.5, −1).

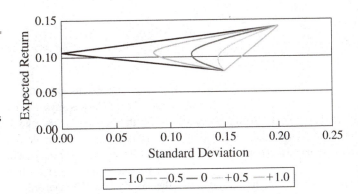

in Figure 3) with an expected return of 14% paired with a standard deviation of 20% or only in Risky Asset 2 (top row of Table 3 or lower left endpoint, *R*, in Figure 3) with an expected return of 8% combined with a standard deviation of 15%.

Equations 4 and 5 were used to produce the expected rates of return and standard deviations in Table 3. Using the alternative values for the portfolio weights given in the second and third columns of Table 3, along with the data on expected returns in Table 2 for the two risky assets, we use equation 4 to calculate the expected rate of return on the portfolios. These results are given in the fourth column of Table 3. For a given set of portfolio weights the expected returns of the portfolio are independent of the assumption about the correlation coefficient. *The expected return on any portfolio of risky assets is a simple weighted average of the expected returns of the assets in the portfolio, where the weights are the proportions invested in the assets.* For example, a 50–50 mix between the two risky assets produces a portfolio with an expected return of 11% = 50%(14%) + 50%(8%). This result is independent of the correlation between the pair of assets returns.

The standard deviation, the square root of the variance, of the portfolios are calculated using equation 5. When the risky assets have a perfect positive correlation ($\rho_{1,2} = +1.0$) the portfolio risk–return relationship is linear and there is always a trade-off between higher variability and higher return. In the case of less than perfect positive correlation, the risk–return trade-off becomes nonlinear and in fact over certain ranges the investor faces no trade-off as variability can be reduced while expected return increases. This can be illustrated in Table 3 when the correlation coefficient is zero ($\rho_{1,2} = +0.0$).

Starting with a portfolio fully invested in Risky Asset 2, as money is initially shifted toward Risky Asset 1 the expected return of the portfolio increases whereas the standard deviation decreases. With all the funds invested in Risky Asset 2, the expected return is 8% and the standard deviation is 15%, but with 25% in Risky Asset 1 and 75% in Risky Asset 2, the expected return rises to 9.5% whereas the standard deviation declines to 12.31. This favorable effect of diversification continues until the portfolio with a minimum standard deviation of 12% is reached. This requires investment proportions of 36% in Risky Asset 1 and 64% in Risky Asset 2 and has a corresponding expected return of 10.16%. This point is the **minimum-variance portfolio** of Risky Asset 1 and Risky Asset 2. In Figure 3 this is represented as the furthest left point along the middle portfolio trade-off curve. Increasing the proportion invested in Risky Asset 1 beyond 36% creates a trade-off as the expected return of the portfolio continues to increase but the standard deviation increases at an increasing rate.

Quick Check 8

What are the mean and standard deviation of a portfolio that is 60% Risky Asset 1 and 40% Risky Asset 2, if the correlation coefficient is 0.1?

Box 2	Low-Priced Art Beats the Masters in the Long Run

3 Nov 2003

Financial Times

Art investors who snap up lower-priced works at auction consistently achieve better returns than those who buy multimillion dollar masterpieces, according to new research.

Of 4,000 paintings and sculptures purchased and resold at sales between 1950 and 2002, those priced in the bottom third generated annualized returns of about 13%. This compares with 10.5% for the most expensive third and 11.2% for the middle tier. It also beats the Standard & Poor's 500 U.S. equity index, which recorded growth of 11.1% per year.

Michael Moses and Jianping Mei, the New York University professors who authored the study, say their findings refute a common art market myth. Dealers and auctioneers have long advised clients to "buy the best they can afford"—pitching costly Rembrandts, Monets, and Picassos as low-risk, high-reward investments.

But "our results show the market to be quite democratic," Prof. Moses says. "Even low-priced works were hit by the bursting of the late 1980s art market bubble; annualised returns for bottom-tier auction pieces have slipped below 6% over the past decade."

But masterpieces saw about half that appreciation and the stock market has yielded negative annualised returns since 1997.

The S&P 500 does have a lower standard deviation, signifying lower risk, but prices for the least expensive third of auction art seem to be less volatile than more expensive works.

None of the art indices had strong correlation to the S&P 500. "Art is an excellent long-term store of wealth" and "useful in portfolio diversification," the authors concluded in previous studies.

Source: Adapted from "Low-Priced Art Beats the Masters in the Long Run," *Financial Times,* November 3, 2003.

3.2 The Optimal Combination of Risky Assets

Now let us consider the risk-reward combinations we can obtain by combining the riskless asset with Risky Asset 1 and Risky Asset 2. Figure 4 presents a graphical description of all possible risk-reward combinations and also illustrates how one locates the optimal combination of risky assets to mix with the riskless asset.

First consider the straight line connecting point F with point S. This should be familiar to you as the risk–reward trade-off line we looked at in Figure 1. It represents the risk-reward combinations that can be obtained by mixing the riskless asset with Risky Asset 1.

A straight line connecting point F to *any* point along the curve connecting points R and S represents a risk–reward trade-off line involving a particular mix of Risky Assets 1 and 2 and the riskless asset. The highest trade-off line we can get to is the one connecting points F and T. Point T is the *point of tangency* between a straight line from point F drawn to the curve connecting points R and S. We call this particular risky portfolio, which corresponds to the tangency point T in Figure 4, the **optimal combination of risky assets.** It is the portfolio of risky assets that is then mixed with the riskless asset to achieve the most efficient portfolios. The formula for finding the portfolio proportions at point T is:

$$w_1 = \frac{[E(r_1) - r_f]\sigma_2^2 - [E(r_2) - r_f]\rho_{1,2}\sigma_1\sigma_2}{[E(r_1) - r_f]\sigma_2^2 + [E(r_2) - r_f]\sigma_1^2 - [E(r_1) - r_f + E(r_2) - r_f]\rho_{1,2}\sigma_1\sigma_2}$$

$$w_2 = 1 - w_1 \tag{6}$$

FIGURE 4

The Optimal Combination of Risky Assets

Note: Assumptions are from Table 2 with zero correlation.

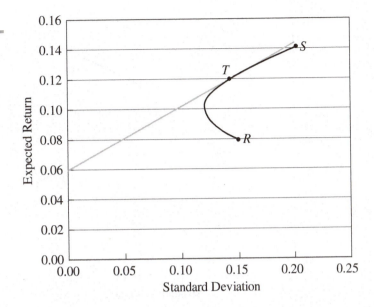

Substituting into equation 6, we find that the optimal combination of risky assets (the tangency portfolio) is composed of 69.23% Risky Asset 1 and 30.77% Risky Asset 2. Its mean rate of return, $E(r_T)$, and standard deviation, σ_T, are:

$$E(r_T) = 0.122$$
$$\sigma_T = 0.146$$

Thus, the new efficient trade-off line is given by the formula:

$$E(r) = r_f + w[E(r_T) - r_f]$$
$$= r_f + \frac{[E(r_T) - r_f]}{\sigma_T}\sigma$$
$$= 0.06 + \frac{0.122 - 0.06}{0.146}\sigma$$
$$= 0.06 + 0.42\sigma$$

where the slope, the reward-to-risk ratio, is 0.42.

Compare this to the formula for the old trade-off line connecting points *F* and *S:*

$$E(r) = 0.06 + 0.40\sigma$$

where the slope is 0.40. Clearly the investor is better off now because he or she can achieve a higher expected rate of return for any level of risk he or she is willing to tolerate.

3.3 Selecting the Preferred Portfolio

To complete the analysis, let us now consider the investor's choice of his or her preferred portfolio along the efficient trade-off line. Recall from our discussion in section 1 that a person's preferred portfolio will depend on his or her stage in the life cycle, planning horizon, and risk tolerance. Thus, an investor might choose to be at a point that is halfway between points *F* and *T*. Figure 5 shows this as point *E*. The portfolio that corresponds to point *E* consists of 50% invested in the tangency portfolio and 50% invested in the riskless asset. By transforming equations 1 and 2 to reflect the fact that the tangency portfolio is

FIGURE 5

Selection of the Preferred Portfolio

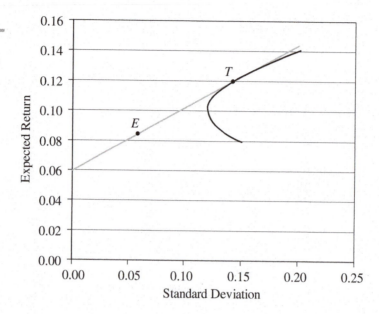

now the single risky asset to combine with the riskless asset, we find that the expected return and standard deviation of portfolio E are:

$$E(r_E) = r_f + 0.5 \times [E(r_T) - r_f]$$
$$= 0.06 + 0.5(0.122 - 0.06) = 0.091$$
$$\sigma_E = 0.5 \times \sigma_T$$
$$= 0.5 \times 0.146 = 0.073$$

Noting that the tangency portfolio is itself composed of 69.2% Risky Asset 1 and 30.8% Risky Asset 2, the composition of portfolio E is found as follows:

Weight in riskless asset	50.0%
Weight in Risky Asset 1	$0.5 \times 69.2\% = 34.6\%$
Weight in Risky Asset 2	$0.5 \times 30.8\% = 15.4\%$
Total	100.0%

Thus, if you were investing $100,000 in portfolio E, you would invest $50,000 in the riskless asset, $34,600 in Risky Asset 1, and $15,400 in Risky Asset 2.

Let us now summarize what we have learned about creating efficient portfolios when the raw materials are two risky assets and a riskless asset. There is a single portfolio of the two risky assets that it is best to combine with the riskless asset. We call this particular risky portfolio, which corresponds to the tangency point T in Figure 4, the *optimal combination of risky assets*. The preferred portfolio is always some combination of this tangency portfolio and the riskless asset.

3.4 Achieving a Target Expected Return: 2

Suppose you have $100,000 to invest and want an expected rate of return of 0.10 per year. Compare the standard deviation you would have to tolerate under the old risk–reward trade-off line (connecting points F and S) with the standard deviation under the new trade-off line (connecting points F and T). What is the composition of each of the two portfolios you are comparing?

SOLUTION:

First, let us write down the formula relating the expected return on the portfolio to the proportion invested in risky assets and solve it to find the proportion to invest in risky assets. For the new trade-off line using the optimal combination of two risky assets it is:

$$E(r) = E(r_T)w + r_f(1 - w)$$
$$E(r) = 0.122w + 0.06(1 - w)$$

Setting the expected rate of return on the portfolio equal to 0.10 and solving for w we find:

$$E(r) = 0.06 + 0.062w = 0.10$$
$$w = \frac{0.10 - 0.06}{0.062} = 0.65$$

Thus, 65% of the $100,000 must be invested in the optimal combination of risky assets and 35% in the riskless asset.

The standard deviation of this portfolio is given by:

$$\sigma = w\sigma_T$$
$$= 0.65 \times 0.146 = 0.095$$

Because the optimal combination of risky assets is itself composed of 69.2% Risky Asset 1 and 30.8% Risky Asset 2, the composition of the final desired portfolio with expected return of 0.10 per year is found as follows:

Weight in riskless asset	35%
Weight in Risky Asset 1	$0.65 \times 69.2\% = 45\%$
Weight in Risky Asset 2	$0.65 \times 30.8\% = 20\%$
Total	100%

For the old trade-off line with a single risky asset the formula relating the expected return and w was:

$$E(r) = E(r_s)w + r_f(1 - w)$$
$$E(r) = 0.14w + 0.06(1 - w)$$

Setting the expected rate of return on the portfolio equal to 0.10 and solving for w we find:

$$E(r) = 0.06 + 0.08w = 0.10$$
$$w = \frac{0.10 - 0.06}{0.08} = 0.50$$

Thus, 50% of the $100,000 must be invested in Risky Asset 1 and 50% in the riskless asset.

The standard deviation of this portfolio is given by:

$$\sigma = w\sigma_s$$
$$= 0.5 \times 0.2 = 0.10$$

Quick Check 9

Suppose an investor chooses a portfolio that is three-fourths of the way between points F and T in Figure 5. In other words, it has 75% invested in the tangency portfolio and 25% in the riskless asset. What is the expected rate of return and standard deviation of this portfolio? If the investor has $100,000, how much will he invest in each of the three assets?

It is important to note that in finding the *optimal combination of risky assets* we do *not* need to know anything about investor wealth or preferences. The composition of this portfolio depends only on the expected rate of returns and standard deviations of Risky Asset 1 and Risky Asset 2 and on the correlation between them. This implies that *all investors who agree on the probability distributions for rates of return will want to hold this same tangency portfolio in combination with the riskless asset.*

This is a general result that carries over to the case in which there are many risky assets in addition to Risky Asset 1 and Risky Asset 2:

There is always a particular optimal portfolio of risky assets that all risk-averse investors who share the same forecasts of rates of return will combine with the riskless asset to reach their most preferred portfolio.

3.5 Portfolios of Many Risky Assets

When there are many risky assets we use a two-step method of portfolio construction similar to the one used in the previous section. In the first step, we consider portfolios constructed from the risky assets only, and in the second step we find the *tangency* portfolio of risky assets to combine with the riskless asset. Because the computation involves a lot of number crunching, it is best done using computers.

The **efficient portfolio frontier** is defined as the set of *portfolios* of risky assets offering the highest possible expected rate of return for any given standard deviation.

The reason the individual basic assets lie *inside* the efficient frontier is that there is usually some combination of two or more basic securities that has a higher expected rate of return than the basic security for the same standard deviation.

The optimal combination of risky assets is then found as the point of tangency between a straight line from the point representing the riskless asset (on the vertical axis) and the efficient frontier of risky assets. The straight line connecting the riskless asset and the tangency point representing the *optimal combination of risky assets* is the best risk–reward trade-off line achievable.

We now return to the issue raised in Section 1. How can a financial intermediary, such as a firm offering mutual funds to the investing public, decide on the menu of asset choices to offer to its customers? We just showed that the composition of the optimal combination of risky assets depends only on the expected returns and standard deviations of the basic risky assets and on the correlations among them. It does *not* depend on investor preferences. Therefore, one does not need to know anything about investor preferences in order to create this portfolio.

The value of foundations' endowments may fluctuate as their investments rise and fall in value, and as they spend endowment funds on grants or program costs and attract new funding from various donors. Foundations' endowments are usually invested in a combination of stocks and alternative investments such as hedge funds and private equity.

The endowments of 247 major American foundations were worth a total of approximately $349 billion after attaining a median return of 9.6% during their 2005 fiscal years. This relatively strong performance reflects the strong performance of stocks and alternative investments in 2005. The best improved performance was recorded by the $1.9 billion endowment of the Memorial Sloan-Kettering Cancer Center in New York. In 2004 it posted a 6% return compared to the 15.7% garnered in 2005.

The largest endowments in 2005 were the $29.1 billion Bill & Melinda Gates Foundation fund, followed by Harvard's $25.8 billion and Yale's $15.2 billion. The Cleveland Foundation topped the list of community foundations with $1.7 billion of assets.

Source: Adapted from "How Endowments of 247 Major Nonprofit Organizations Performed," *Chronicle of Higher Education*, June 2, 2006.

If customers delegate the task of forecasting expected asset returns, standard deviations, and correlations to a financial intermediary that specializes in doing it and they delegate the task of combining the basic assets in the optimal proportions, then the only choice the customers need to make is the proportion to invest in the optimal risky portfolio.

The static mean-variance model thus leads to an elementary theory of mutual fund financial intermediation. Since the late 1960s, academic research on optimal portfolio selection has gone beyond that model to dynamic versions that integrate intertemporal optimization of the life-cycle consumption–saving decisions with the allocation of those savings among alternative investments. In these models, the demands for individual assets depend on more than just optimal diversification as presented here; they also come from the desire to *hedge* various risks not included in the original model. Some of the risks identified as creating these hedging demands in portfolio decisions are mortality risk and stochastic changes in interest rates and in the trade-off between expected return and risk, in returns to human capital, and in relative consumption goods prices. These models provide a richer theory for the role of securities and financial intermediation than the static mean-variance model.[4]

The basic mean-variance approach to quantitative investment management is still the dominant one used in the practice of asset management. However, this is changing. The more complete models of portfolio selection provide design guidance for investment firms to offer a wider "family" of mutual funds beyond just the optimal combination of risky assets and the riskless asset. Those additional funds represent optimal hedging portfolios more tailored to the needs of different clienteles. The investment firm can create integrated products from its funds by putting various combinations of its member funds together in proportions that reflect the right mix for customers in various stages of their life cycle.

Summary

- There is no single portfolio selection strategy that is best for all people.
- Stage in the life cycle is an important determinant of the composition of a person's optimal portfolio of assets and liabilities.

[4]See R. C. Merton, *Continuous-Time Finance*, Blackwell, 1992.

- Time horizons are important in portfolio selection. We distinguish among three time horizons: the planning horizon, the decision horizon, and the trading horizon.
- In making portfolio selection decisions, people can in general achieve a higher expected rate of return only by exposing themselves to greater risk.
- One can sometimes reduce risk without lowering expected return by diversifying more completely either within a given asset class or across asset classes.
- The power of diversification to reduce the riskiness of an investor's portfolio depends on the *correlations* among the assets that make up the portfolio. In practice, the vast majority of assets are *positively correlated* with each other because they are all affected by common economic factors. Consequently, one's ability to reduce risk through diversification among risky assets without lowering expected return is limited.
- Although in principle people have thousands of assets to choose from, in practice they make their choices from a menu of a few final products offered by financial intermediaries such as bank accounts, stock and bond mutual funds, and real estate. In designing and producing the menu of assets to offer to their customers, these intermediaries make use of the latest advances in financial technology.

Key Terms

- portfolio selection
- life annuity
- strategy
- efficient portfolio
- minimum-variance portfolio
- optimal combination of risky assets
- efficient portfolio frontier

Answers to Quick Check Questions

Quick Check 1   How would the investment portfolio that is best for a young person with a secure job differ from the one that is best for a retired person whose only source of income is his investment portfolio?

Answer: The young person with a secure job can look forward to a long period of earning a salary that will probably increase with the rate of inflation. For her, investment in stocks would not be as risky as for the older person who needs to ensure a steady source of income for the rest of his life. The young person is somewhat protected against inflation but the older person is not and may have to try to find insurance against price increases.

Quick Check 2   Do you have a decision horizon of fixed length? How long is it?

Answer: Answer will vary by student.

Quick Check 3   Do you think that risk tolerance increases with a person's wealth? Why?

Answer: A wealthier individual may be willing to take more risks (than a poorer person) because his capacity to take bigger gambles and lose is higher. That is, he may still be quite wealthy after his losses.

Quick Check 4   What is the riskless asset if the unit of account is the Swiss franc and the length of the decision horizon is a week?

Answer: A Swiss-franc-denominated, one-week, zero-coupon bond.

Quick Check 5 Locate the point corresponding to portfolio J in Figure 1. Consult Table 1 for the portfolio's composition, its expected rate of return and standard deviation. How much of your $100,000 would be invested in the risky asset if you chose portfolio J?

Answer: $75,000 would be invested in the risky asset and $25,000 in the risk-free asset.

Quick Check 6 What happens to the intercept and the slope of the trade-off line in Figure 1 if the risk-free rate changes to 0.03 per year and the expected rate of return on the risky asset to 0.10 per year?

Answer: The y intercept falls to 0.03 and the slope of the line falls from 0.4 to 0.35.

Quick Check 7 How can an investor achieve an expected rate of return of 0.105 per year with Risky Asset 1 and the riskless asset? What is the standard deviation of this port-folio? Compare it to the standard deviation of Risky Asset 2.

Answer: Hold 56.25% in the risky asset and the rest in the risk-free asset to achieve an expected rate of return of 0.105. The standard deviation of the portfolio is 0.1125 compared to Risky Asset 2's standard deviation of 0.15.

Quick Check 8 What are the mean and standard deviation of a portfolio that is 60% Risky Asset 1 and 40% Risky Asset 2, if the correlation coefficient is 0.1?

Answer:

$$E(r) = 0.6 \times 0.14 + 0.4 \times 0.08 = 0.116$$

$$\sigma^2 = (0.6)^2 \times (0.2)^2 + (0.4)^2 \times (0.15)^2 + 2(0.6)(0.4)(0.1)(0.2)(0.15) = 0.01944$$

$$\sigma^2 = 0.1394$$

Quick Check 9 Suppose an investor chooses a portfolio that is three-fourths of the way between points F and T in Figure 5. In other words it has 75% invested in the tangency portfolio and 25% in the riskless asset. What is the expected return and standard deviation of this portfolio? If the investor has $100,000, how much will he invest in each of the three assets?

Answer:

$$E(r) = 0.12154 \times 0.75 + 0.06 \times 0.25 = 0.1602$$

$$= 0.75 \times 0.1495 = 0.105$$

Invest 25% in the riskless asset, 51.9% (0.75 × 69.2) in Risky Asset 1, and 23.1% (0.75 × 30.8) in Risky Asset 2.

Questions and Problems

The Process of Personal Portfolio Selection

1. Analyze the expert's answers to the following questions:
   a. *Question:* I have approximately one-third of my investments in stocks, and the rest in a money market. What do you suggest as a somewhat "safer" place to invest another one-third? I like to keep one-third accessible for emergencies.
   Expert's answer: Well, you could try 1- or 2-year Treasury bonds. You'd get a little bit more yield with no risk.
   b. *Question:* Where would you invest if you were to start today? *Expert's answer:* That depends on your age and short-term goals. If you are very young—say, under 40—and don't need the money you're investing for a home or college tuition or such, you would put it in a stock fund. Even if the market tanks, you have time to

recoup. And, so far, nothing has beaten stocks over a period of 10 years or more. But if you are going to need money fairly soon, for a home or for your retirement, you need to play it safer.

2. Suppose that your 58-year-old father works for the Ruffy Stuffed Toy Company and has contributed regularly to his company-matched savings plan for the past 15 years. Ruffy contributes $0.50 for every $1.00 your father puts into the savings plan, up to the first 6% of his salary. Participants in the savings plan can allocate their contributions among four different investment choices: a fixed-income bond fund; a "blend" option that invests in large companies, small companies, and the fixed-income bond fund; a growth-income mutual fund whose investments do not include other toy companies; and a fund whose sole investment is stock in the Ruffy Stuffed Toy Company. Over Thanksgiving vacation, Dad realizes that you have been majoring in finance and decides to reap some early returns on that tuition money he's been investing in your education. He shows you the most recent quarterly statement for his savings plan, and you see that 98% of its current value is in the fourth investment option, that of the Ruffy Company stock.

   a. Assume that your Dad is a typical risk-averse person who is considering retirement in five years. When you ask him why he has made the allocation in this way, he responds that the company stock has continually performed quite well, except for a few declines that were caused by problems in a division that the company has long since sold off. In addition, he says, many of his friends at work have done the same. What advice would you give your dad about adjustments to his plan allocations? Why?

   b. If you consider the fact that your dad works for Ruffy in addition to his 98% allocation to the Ruffy stock fund, does this make his situation more risky, less risky, or does it make no difference? Why?

The Trade-Off between Expected Return and Risk

3. Suppose we define a data set from the outcomes of football games between Ohio State and Michigan over the past hundred years. Each game represents an observation and the winner of the game is given a value of one with the loser given a zero value. Assuming no ties, how do you interpret the expected values calculated from the data series? What will the correlation be between the two series?

4. Determine the correlation between price movements of stocks A and B using the forecasts of their rate of return and the assessments of the possible states of the world in the following table. Before doing the calculation, form an expectation of whether that correlation will be closer to 1 or -1 by merely inspecting the numbers.

State of the Economy	Probability	Stock A: Rate of Return	Stock B: Rate of Return
Moderate recession	0.05	-0.02	-0.20
Slight recession	0.15	-0.01	-0.10
2% growth	0.60	0.15	0.15
3% growth	0.20	0.15	0.30

5. Given the information below about the risks and returns of five alternative portfolios, plot the risks and returns. Which do not represent efficient portfolios?

Portfolio	Expected Return	Risk
I	0.05	0.00
II	0.075	0.12
III	0.075	0.05
IV	0.075	0.04
V	0.05	0.05

6. If the risk–reward trade-off line for a riskless asset and a risky asset results in a negative slope, what does that imply about the risky asset vis-a-vis the riskless asset?
7. Consider two assets with expected returns and risk given in the table below.

	Blau	Zwartz
Expected Return	0.15	0.12
Standard Deviation	0.10	0.08

If these asset returns have a correlation coefficient of +0.5, what is the risk and return of a portfolio equally divided between the two securities? What mix of the two securities produces the portfolio having the lowest risk? What level of risk is this?

8. Repeat the previous problem when the two assets are uncorrelated.
9. *Challenge Problem:* Suppose we have two risky assets with uncorrelated returns $[\rho = 0]$. Suppose the first asset has levels of expected return and risk equal to twice the level of the expected return and risk of the second asset or in other words it offers twice the level of expected return for bearing twice the level of risk $[E(r_1) = 2 \cdot E(r_2)$ and $\sigma_1 = 2 \cdot \sigma_2]$. In particular assume $E(r_2) = 0.06$ and $\sigma_2 = 0.02$. Suppose you wish to bear the same level of risk as that offered by the second asset. Can you construct a portfolio comprised of both assets with the same return as the second asset but a higher expected rate of return? What is the composition of this portfolio? How much of an expected return premium does this portfolio offer over that of the second asset?
10. Consider two uncorrelated assets with expected returns and risk given in the table below.

	Blanc	Rouge
Expected Return	0.075	0.125
Standard Deviation	0.05	0.075

Among the portfolios made up of positive investments in both assets, which are inefficient?

Efficient Diversification with Many Risky Assets

11. When the riskless rate is 0.04, assume the optimal combination of risky assets produces a portfolio with an expected rate of return equal to 0.13 and a standard deviation of 0.10. Along the efficient trade-off line, the reward-to-risk ratio with have what value? Suppose you wish to tolerate only 3/4 of the risk present in the optimal risky portfolio. How must you divide you investment between the risk-free asset and the optimal risky portfolio? What expected rate of return do you achieve?
12. Referring to the previous question, suppose your mother prefers to tolerate a good deal of risk. In fact she wishes to bear twice the risk as offered by the optimal risky

portfolio. How can she build a portfolio from the risk-free asset and the optimal risky portfolio with the risk level she desires? When she satisfies her appetite for risk what will be the level of expected return on her portfolio?

13. Refer to Table 1 in the text.

   a. Perform the calculations to verify that the expected returns of each of the portfolios (F, G, H, J, S) in the table (column 4) are correct.

   b. Do the same for the standard deviations in column 5 of the table.

14. Referring to the previous problem, assume that you have $1 million to invest. Allocate the money as indicated in the Table 1 for each of the five portfolios and calculate the expected dollar return of each of the portfolios. Which of the portfolios would someone who is extremely risk tolerant be most likely to select?

   Use the following information to answer questions 15–19. Suppose that you have the opportunity to buy stock in AT&T and Microsoft.

	AT&T	Microsoft
Expected Return	0.10	0.21
Standard Deviation	0.15	0.25

15. What is the minimum-risk (standard deviation) portfolio of AT&T and Microsoft if the correlation between the two stocks is 0? 0.5? 1? −1? What do you notice about the change in the allocations between AT&T and Microsoft as the correlation coefficient moves from −1 to 0? to 0.5? to +1? Why might this be? What is the standard deviation of each of these minimum-risk portfolios?

16. What is the optimal combination of these two securities in a portfolio for each of the four given values of the correlation coefficient, assuming the existence of a money market fund that currently pays a risk-free 0.045? Do you notice any relation between these weights and the weights for the minimum-variance portfolios? What is the standard deviation of each of the optimal portfolios? What is the expected return of each of the optimal portfolios?

17. Derive the risk–reward trade-off line for the optimal portfolio when the correlation is 0.5. How much extra expected return can you anticipate if you take on an extra unit of risk?

18. Using the optimal portfolio of AT&T and Microsoft stock when the corre- lation of their price movements is 0.5, along with the results of problem 17, determine:

   a. the expected return and standard deviation of a portfolio that invests 100% in a money market fund returning a current rate of 0.045. Where is this point on the risk-reward trade-off line?

   b. the expected return and standard deviation of a portfolio that invests 90% in the money market fund and 10% in the portfolio of AT&T and Microsoft stock.

   c. the expected return and standard deviation of a portfolio that invests 25% in the money market fund and 75% in the portfolio of AT&T and Microsoft stock.

   d. the expected return and standard deviation of a portfolio that invests 0% in the money market fund and 100% in the portfolio of AT&T and Microsoft stock. What point is this?

19. Again using the optimal portfolio of AT&T and Microsoft stock when the correlation of their price movements is 0.5, take $10,000 and determine the allocations among the riskless asset, AT&T stock, and Microsoft stock for:

   a. a portfolio that invests 75% in a money market fund and 25% in the portfolio of AT&T and Microsoft stock. What is this portfolio's expected return?

   b. a portfolio that invests 25% in a money market fund and 75% in the portfolio of AT&T and Microsoft stock. What is this portfolio's expected return?

c. a portfolio that invests nothing in a money market fund and 100% in the portfolio of AT&T and Microsoft stock. What is this portfolio's expected return?

20. A mutual fund company offers a safe money market fund whose current rate is 0.05. The same company also offers an equity fund with an aggressive growth objective that historically has exhibited an expected return of 0.20 and a standard deviation of 0.25.
   a. Derive the equation for the risk–reward trade-off line.
   b. How much extra expected return would be available to an investor for each unit of extra risk that she bears?
   c. What allocation should be placed in the money market fund if an investor desires an expected return of 0.15? What risk will he bear with this investment?

21. In a portfolio comprised of two risky assets (A and B) it is possible to obtain a riskless portfolio if the assets have a correlation coefficient of -1.0. If w is the proportion invested in Asset A, how should w be set so as to obtain a riskless portfolio?

22. What strategy is implied by moving further out to the right on a risk–reward trade-off line beyond the tangency point between the line and the risky asset risk-reward curve? What type of an investor would be most likely to embark on this strategy? Why?

23. Suppose the most efficient risky portfolio to combine with a risk-free asset paying 0.05 is a portfolio with an expected return of 0.12 and a standard deviation of 0.10. What is the expected return and risk of a leveraged investment where for each $100 of your own funds you borrow $50 at the risk-free rate and invest the entire $150 in the optimal risky portfolio? Here the market price of risk, the increase in expected return per unit of risk borne, takes on what value?

24. Suppose the mix of risky assets and risky portfolios is unchanged but the risk-free rate increases. Explain what will happen to the reward-to-risk ratio and the optimal risky portfolio in terms of its expected return and risk characteristics.

25. *Challenge Problem:* Suppose we consider a simple portfolio investment strategy involving similar assets all have identical expected returns and risks. Assume further that all pairs of the assets are uncorrelated. Let n be the number of these similar assets in the portfolio and follow the simple rule of equal proportional investment in all the assets. So if we have 5 assets we put one-fifth of our money in each, with 10 assets one-tenth in each, and so on. Derive the expression for the risk (standard deviation) of the overall portfolio as a function of n, the number of assets in the portfolio. Start with the general formula for the risk of a portfolio of multiple assets given by:

$$\sigma_p^2 = \sum\sum w_i w_j \sigma_{ij}$$
$$= \sum\sum w_i w_j \rho_{ij} \sigma_i \sigma_j$$

Summary of Formulas

The expected rate of return on any portfolio, $E(r)$, is given by:

$$E(r) = wE(r_s) + (1 - w)r_f$$
$$= r_f + w[E(r_s) - r_f]$$

where w is the fraction of the portfolio invested in the risky asset, $E(r_s)$ is the expected rate of return on the risky asset, and r_f is the riskless rate. The standard deviation of the portfolio is given by:

$$\sigma = \sigma_s w$$

where σ_s is the standard deviation on the risky asset.

The formula for the trade-off line between risk and expected return is:

$$E(r) = r_f + w[E(r_s) - r_f]$$

$$= r_f + \frac{[E(r_s) - r_f]}{\sigma_s}\sigma$$

The formula for the standard deviation of a portfolio of two risky assets is:

$$\sigma = \sqrt{w^2\sigma_1^2 + (1-w)^2\sigma_2^2 + 2w(1-w)\rho_{1,2}\sigma_1\sigma_2}$$

APPENDIX

The Fallacy of Time Diversification

There is a widespread—but mistaken—belief that stocks are less risky in the long run than in the short run. Based on this belief, it is generally inferred that you should invest more of your money in stocks the longer your planned holding period.

Two propositions have been used to persuade skeptics that this so-called time diversification effect is valid:

- The longer the investor's holding period, the smaller the standard deviation of the annualized rate of return on stocks.
- The longer the investor's holding period, the lower the probability that stocks will earn a rate of return less than the corresponding risk-free interest rate on bonds.

Although they are true, these propositions do not support the validity of the claim that stocks are less risky in the long run than in the short run or that you should invest more in stocks because you have a longer planned holding period. Let us explain why.

First, the fact that the standard deviation of the *annualized* rate of return on an investment in stocks declines as the length of the holding period increases is merely an artifact of expressing investment performance in terms of the annualized rate of return. There is no genuine diversification in this situation. You care about the amount of wealth that you will have at the end of the holding period, and there is no decline in its standard deviation. For example, compare the results of investing all of your money in stocks versus risk-free bonds for one year and for 25 years. Even though the standard deviation of your annualized rate of return for the 25-year period is approximately one-fifth of the one-year result, the standard deviation of your ending wealth for the 25-year holding period is five times *greater* than the one-year standard deviation.

Second, it is true that the longer the holding period, the lower the probability of a *shortfall*—defined as the stock portfolio's earning less than the risk-free interest rate over that same period. However, the risk of a shortfall depends on its *severity* when it happens as well as its probability of happening. If we consider measures of risk that take account of *both* the severity and the probability of a shortfall, there is no decline in risk as the holding period lengthens. For example, consider as a measure of risk the price of insuring a stock portfolio against a shortfall. It actually *increases* with the length of the holding period.[5]

---

[5]Such an insurance policy is equivalent to a put option on the ending value of the stock portfolio. Later on, we demonstrate that the price of this put must increase as the holding period lengthens.

Suggested Readings

Bodie, Z. "On the Risk of Stocks in the Long Run." *Financial Analysts Journal,* May–June 1995.
———, R. C. Merton, and W. Samuelson. "Labor Supply Flexibility and Portfolio Choice in a Life-Cycle Model." *Journal of Economic Dynamics and Control* 15, 1992.

Markowitz, H. "Portfolio Selection." *Journal of Finance* 7, March 1952.
——— *Portfolio Selection: Efficient Diversification of Investments.* New York: John Wiley & Sons, 1959.

McDonald, R. *Derivatives Markets,* 2nd ed. Boston, MA: Pearson Addison Wesley, 2006.

Merton, R. C. "An Analytical Derivation of the Efficient Portfolio Frontier." *Journal of Financial and Quantitative Analysis* 10, September 1972.
——— *Continuous-Time Finance.* Rev. ed. London: Basil Blackwell, 1992.

Tobin, J. "Liquidity Preference as Behavior Towards Risk." *Review of Economic Studies* 25, February 1958.

Capital Market Equilibrium

OBJECTIVES

- Explain the theory behind the capital asset pricing model (CAPM).
- Explain how to use the CAPM to establish benchmarks for measuring the performance of investment portfolios.
- Explain how to infer from the CAPM the correct risk-adjusted discount rate to use in discounted cash flow valuation models.
- Explain how the CAPM has been modified and supplemented by other theories to add greater realism.

CONTENTS

From Chapter 13 of *Financial Economics*, 2/e. Zvi Bodie, Robert C. Merton, David L. Cleeton.
Copyright © 2008 by Pearson Prentice Hall. All rights reserved.

The capital asset pricing model (CAPM) is a theory about equilibrium prices in the markets for risky assets. It builds on the theory of portfolio selection developed earlier and derives the quantitative relations that must exist among expected rates of return on risky assets on the assumption that asset prices adjust to equate supply and demand.

The CAPM is important for two reasons. First, it provides a theoretical justification for the widespread practice of passive investing known as *indexing.* Indexing means holding a diversified portfolio in which securities are held in the same relative proportions as in a broad market index such as the Standard & Poor's 500 or the Morgan Stanley index of international stocks. Today many billions of dollars invested worldwide by pension funds, mutual funds, and other institutions are managed passively by indexing, and indexing provides a simple feasible benchmark against which the performance of active investment strategies are measured.

Second, the CAPM provides a way of estimating expected rates of return for use in a variety of financial applications. For example, risk-adjusted expected rates of return are needed as inputs to discounted-cash-flow valuation models for stocks. Corporate managers also use these models in making capital-budgeting decisions. The CAPM is also used to establish "fair" rates of return on invested capital in regulated firms or in firms that do business on a cost-plus basis.

1 The Capital Asset Pricing Model in Brief

The **capital asset pricing model** is an equilibrium theory that is based on the theory of portfolio selection presented. The CAPM was developed in the early 1960s.[1] It was derived by posing the question: What would risk premiums on securities be in equilibrium if people had the same set of forecasts of expected returns and risks and all chose their portfolios optimally according to the principles of efficient diversification?

The fundamental idea behind the CAPM is that in equilibrium the market rewards people for bearing risk. Because people generally exhibit risk-averse behavior, the risk premium for the aggregate of all risky assets must be positive to induce people to willingly hold all of the risky assets that exist in the economy.

But the market does not reward people for holding inefficient portfolios—that is, for exposing themselves to risks that could be eliminated by optimal diversification behavior. The risk premium on any individual security is, therefore, not related to the security's "stand-alone" risk, but rather to its contribution to the risk of an efficiently diversified portfolio.

Every efficient portfolio can be constructed by mixing just two particular assets: the riskless asset and the optimal combination of risky assets (i.e., the tangency portfolio). To derive the CAPM, we need two assumptions:

- *Assumption 1:* Investors agree in their forecasts of expected rates of return, standard deviations, and correlations of the risky securities, and they, therefore, optimally hold risky assets in the same relative proportions.
- *Assumption 2:* Investors generally behave optimally. In equilibrium, the prices of securities adjust so that when investors are holding their optimal portfolios, the aggregate demand for each security is equal to its supply.

From these two assumptions, because every investor's relative holdings of risky assets is the same, the only way the asset market can clear is if those optimal relative proportions are the proportions in which they are valued in the marketplace. A portfolio that holds all assets in proportion to their observed market values is called the **market portfolio.**

---

[1]William F. Sharpe received the 1990 Nobel Prize in economics for his work on the CAPM published in 1964. Others who independently developed the CAPM at about the same time were John Lintner and Jan Mossin.

The composition of the market portfolio reflects the supplies of existing assets evaluated at their current market prices.

Let us clarify what is meant by the market portfolio. In the market portfolio, the fraction allocated to security *i* equals the ratio of the market value of the *i*th security outstanding to the market value of all assets outstanding. Thus, for simplicity suppose that there are only three assets: GM stock, Toyota stock, and the risk-free asset. The total market values of each at current prices are $66 billion of GM, $22 billion of Toyota, and $12 billion of the risk-free asset. The total market value of all assets is $100 billion. The composition of the market portfolio is, therefore, 66% GM stock, 22% Toyota stock, and 12% risk-free asset.

The CAPM says that *in equilibrium any investor's relative holdings of risky assets will be the same as in the market portfolio.* Depending on their risk aversion, investors hold different mixes of risk-free and risky assets, but the relative holdings of risky assets are the same for all investors. Thus, in our simple example, all investors will hold GM and Toyota stock in the proportions of 3 to 1 (i.e., 66/22). Another way to state this is to say that the composition of the risky part of any investor's portfolio will be 75% GM stock and 25% Toyota stock.

Consider two investors, each with $100,000 to invest. Investor 1 has risk aversion equal to the average for all investors and, therefore, holds each asset in the same proportions as the market portfolio—$66,000 in GM, $22,000 in Toyota stock, and $12,000 in the risk-free asset. Investor 2 is more risk averse than the average and, therefore, chooses to invest $24,000 (twice as much as Investor 1) in the risk-free asset and $76,000 in risky assets. Investor 2's investment in GM stock will be 0.75 × $76,000 or $57,000, and the investment in Toyota stock will be 0.25 × $76,000 or $19,000. Thus, both investors will hold three times as much in GM stock as in Toyota stock.

Quick Check 1

Investor 3 has a $100,000 portfolio with nothing invested in the risk-free asset. How much is invested in GM and how much in Toyota?

This basic idea of the CAPM can also be explained with the help of Figure 1, which depicts the risk–reward trade-off line facing each investor. Because the tangency portfolio or optimal combination of risky assets has the same relative holdings of risky assets as the market portfolio, the market portfolio is located somewhere on the risk–return trade-off line. In the CAPM, the trade-off line is called the **capital market line** (CML). In Figure 1, point *M* represents the market portfolio, point *F* is the risk-free asset, and the CML is the straight line connecting these two points.

The CAPM says that in equilibrium, the CML represents the best risk-reward combinations available to all investors. Although everyone will strive to achieve points that are above the CML, the forces of competition will move asset prices so that everyone expects to achieve points that are on the line.

The CML's formula is

$$E(r) = r_f + \frac{E(r_M) - r_f}{\sigma_M} \sigma \tag{1}$$

The slope of the CML is, thus, the risk premium on the market portfolio divided by its standard deviation:

$$\text{Slope of CML} = \frac{E(r_M) - r_f}{\sigma_M}$$

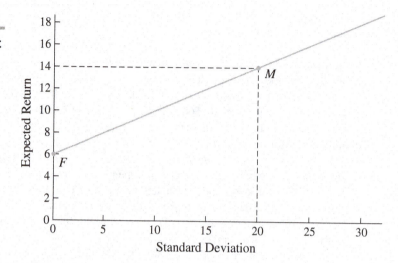

FIGURE 1

The Capital Market Line

Note: The CML is given by the formula:

$$E(r) = r_f + \frac{E(r_M) - r_f}{\sigma_M}\sigma$$
$$= 0.06 + 0.40\sigma$$

The CAPM implies that most investors would do just as well to passively combine the risk-free asset with an index fund holding risky assets in the same proportions as in the market portfolio as they would by actively researching securities and trying to "beat" the market. Especially diligent and competent investors do tend to earn rewards for their efforts, but over time the competition among them reduces those rewards to the minimum necessary to induce them to perform their work. The rest of us can then benefit from their work by investing passively.

Another implication of the CAPM is that the risk premium on any individual security is proportional only to its contribution to the risk of the market portfolio. The risk premium does not depend on the security's stand-alone risk. Thus, according to the CAPM, in equilibrium, investors get rewarded with a higher expected return only for bearing market risk. This is an *irreducible* or necessary risk that they must take to get their desired expected return.

The logic here is that because all efficient risk-reward combinations can be achieved simply by mixing the market portfolio and the risk-free asset, the only risk an investor need bear to achieve an efficient portfolio is market risk. Therefore, the market does not reward investors for bearing any nonmarket risk.

The market does not reward investors for choosing inefficient portfolios.

Sometimes this implication of the CAPM is emphasized by saying that only the market-related risk of a security "matters."

> **Quick Check 2**
>
> According to the CAPM, what is a simple way for investors to form their optimal portfolios?

2 Determinants of the Risk Premium on the Market Portfolio

According to the CAPM, the size of the risk premium of the market portfolio is determined by the aggregate risk aversion of investors and the volatility of the market return. To be induced to accept the risk of the market portfolio, investors must be offered an expected

Box 1	Passive vs. Active Investing

Passive investing guarantees returns that match those of a stock market index, but at the cost of the chance to benefit from market inefficiencies. The relative market capitalization alone of a particular stock determines the proportion that a passive investor holds of that stock. Active investors, on the other hand, try to beat an index. Still, active investors don't necessarily achieve higher returns than passive investors; in fact, just over half of actively managed mutual funds beat the S&P 500 in 2005.

Research has shown that passive investing accounted for most of the trading volume on U.S. stock markets during the early 2000s. At the same time, the amount invested in passive funds in 2005 was less than one-fifth of the amount invested in active funds. This contradiction indicates that even actively managed funds may take a passive approach, preferring mediocre returns to the risk of trying to beat the market. As passive investing grows in popularity, prices may reflect less of the information relevant to their pricing, creating more opportunity for active investors to profit from market inefficiencies.

Source: Adapted from "Passive Aggression," *The Economist,* January 26, 2006.

rate of return that exceeds the risk-free rate of interest. The greater the average degree of risk aversion of the population, the higher the risk premium required.

In the CAPM, the equilibrium risk premium on the market portfolio is equal to the variance of the market portfolio times a weighted average of the degree of risk aversion of the holders of wealth (A):

$$E(r_M) - r_f = A\sigma_M^2 \tag{2}$$

A should be thought of as an *index* of the degree of risk aversion in the economy.

Suppose that the standard deviation of the market portfolio is 0.20, and the average degree of risk aversion is 2. Then the risk premium on the market portfolio is 0.08:

$$E(r_M) - r_f = 2(0.2)^2 = 2(0.04) = 0.08$$

Thus, according to the CAPM, the market risk premium can change over time either because the variance of the market changes, because the degree of risk aversion changes, or both.

Note that the CAPM explains the *difference* between the riskless interest rate and the expected rate of return on the market portfolio, but not their *absolute* levels. As discussed in previously, the absolute level of the equilibrium expected rate of return on the market portfolio is determined by factors such as the expected productivity of the capital stock and household intertemporal preferences for consumption.

Given a particular level for the expected return on the market, the CAPM can be used to determine the riskless rate of interest. In our numerical example, if the expected return on the market portfolio is 0.14 per year, then the CAPM implies that the risk-free rate must be 0.06 per year.

Substituting these values into equation 1, the CML is given by the following formula:

$$E(r) = r_f + \frac{E(r_M) - r_f}{\sigma_M}\sigma$$
$$= 0.06 + 0.40\sigma$$

where the slope, the market *reward-to-risk ratio,* is 0.40.

3 Beta and Risk Premiums on Individual Securities

By definition, equilibrium asset prices and expected returns are such that knowledgeable investors willingly hold the assets they have in their optimal portfolios. With the idea that investors must be compensated in terms of expected return for bearing risk, we define the *risk of a security* by the size of its equilibrium expected return. Thus, the risk of security A is larger than the risk of security B if in equilibrium the expected return on A exceeds the expected return on B. By inspection of the CML in Figure 1, among optimal (*efficient*) portfolios, the larger the standard deviation of its return, the larger the equilibrium expected return $E(r)$, and, therefore, the larger the risk. Hence, the *risk of an efficient portfolio* is measured by σ. However, standard deviation of return *does not* measure generally the risk of securities in the CAPM. Instead, the general measure of a security's risk is its **beta** (the Greek letter β). Technically, beta describes the marginal contribution of that security's return to the standard deviation of the market portfolio's return. The formula for the beta of security j is given by

$$\beta_j = \frac{\sigma_{jM}}{\sigma_M^2}$$

where σ_{jM} denotes the covariance between the return on security j and the return on the market portfolio.[2]

According to the CAPM, in equilibrium, the risk premium on any asset is equal to its beta times the risk premium on the market portfolio. The equation expressing this relation is

$$E(r_j) - r_f = \beta_j[E(r_M) - r_f] \tag{3}$$

This is called the **security market line** (SML) relation, and it is depicted in Figure 2. Note that in Figure 2, we plot the security's beta on the horizontal axis and its expected excess return on the vertical. The slope of the SML is the risk premium on the market portfolio. In our example, because the market risk premium is 0.08 or 8% per year, the SML relation is

$$E(r_j) - r_f = 0.08\beta_j$$

Beta also provides a proportional measure of the sensitivity of a security's realized return to the realized return on the market portfolio. Thus, if the realized return on the market portfolio is $N\%$ greater (less) than was expected, then the realized return on security j will tend to be $\beta_j \times N\%$ greater (less) than was expected. Thus, securities with high betas (greater than 1) are called "aggressive" because their returns tend to accentuate those of the overall market portfolio, going up more in up markets and down more in down markets. Similarly, securities with low betas (less than 1) are called "defensive." The market portfolio, by definition, has a beta of 1, and securities with a beta of 1 are said to have "average risk."

---

[2]Beta corresponds to the *regression coefficient* estimator of the slope from the linear regression model outlined earlier. In the regression the independent variable (X) is the return from the market portfolio and the return on the individual security is the dependent variable (Y).

FIGURE 2

The Security Market Line

Note: All securities (not just efficient portfolios) plot on the SML, if they are correctly priced according to the CAPM.

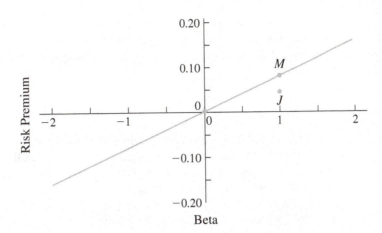

If any security had an expected return and beta combination that was not on the SML, it would be a contradiction of the CAPM. In particular, imagine a security with an expected return/beta combination represented by point J in Figure 2. Because it lies below the SML, its expected return is "too low" to support equilibrium. (Equivalently, we can say that its market price is too high.)

The existence of such a situation contradicts the CAPM because it implies either that the market is not in equilibrium or that investors do not agree on the distribution of returns or that investors are not behaving as mean-variance optimizers. Under the assumptions of the CAPM, investors could improve their portfolios by investing less in security J and more in the other securities. Therefore, there is excess supply of security J and excess demand for the other securities.

Any portfolio that lies on the CML (i.e., any portfolio formed by mixing the market portfolio and the riskless asset) has a beta equal to the fraction of the portfolio invested in the market portfolio. For example, the beta of a portfolio that is 0.75 invested in the market portfolio and 0.25 invested in the risk-free asset is 0.75.

Quick Check 4

Suppose you are examining a stock that has a beta of 0.5. According to the CAPM, what should be its expected rate of return? Where should the stock be located in relation to the CML and the SML?

The CAPM can be used to decompose the total risk (σ_j^2) of an individual security's return into diversifiable and undiversifiable components. As was noted earlier, the risk premium of a security doesn't depend on the security's total risk but rather on its market-related risk. Because in equilibrium every investor holds risky assets in proportion to the market weights in the aggregate market portfolio, it is the undiversifiable component of an individual security's risk that the investor bears whereas the diversifiable component of the security's risk is eliminated.

For any risky security, its undiversifiable risk is given by $\beta_j^2 \cdot \sigma_M^2$ whereas the diversifiable risk can be found as the residual by subtracting the undiversifiable risk from the total risk: $\sigma_j^2 \cdot -\left(\beta_j^2 \cdot \beta_M^2\right)$. For example a security with a beta of $+1$ would have undiversifiable risk equal to that of the market portfolio. Because in equilibrium, in the CAPM the risk premium is dependent only on the undiversifiable risk, such a security would offer an expected risk premium equal to that of the market portfolio. When held as part of the market portfolio its diversifiable risk would have been eliminated and therefore be of no concern. If, on the other hand, an investor were unwise and held the security by itself, she would be subjected to both the diversifiable and undiversifiable risk components while only being rewarded for the latter source of risk.

4 Using the CAPM in Portfolio Selection

As we saw in section 3, the CAPM implies that the market portfolio of risky assets is an efficient portfolio. This means that an investor will do as well by simply following a passive portfolio selection strategy of combining a market index fund and the risk-free asset as by following an active strategy of trying to beat the market.

Whether or not the CAPM applies to real-world asset prices, it nevertheless provides a rationale for a simple passive portfolio strategy:

- Diversify your holdings of risky assets in the proportions of the market portfolio, and
- Mix this portfolio with the risk-free asset to achieve a desired risk-reward combination.

The same passive strategy can serve as a risk-adjusted benchmark for measuring the performance of active portfolio selection strategies.

Let us illustrate. Suppose that you have $1 million to invest. You are deciding how to allocate it among two risky asset classes: stocks and bonds and the risk-free asset. You know that in the economy as a whole, the net relative supplies of these three asset classes are 60% in stocks, 40% in bonds, and 0% in the risk-free asset. This, therefore, is the composition of the market portfolio.

If you have an average degree of risk aversion, then you will invest $600,000 in stocks, $400,000 in bonds, and nothing in the risk-free asset. If you are more risk averse than average, you will invest some of your $1 million in the risk-free asset and the rest in stocks and bonds. Whatever amount you invest in stocks and bonds will be allocated in the proportions 60% in stocks and 40% in bonds.

In assessing the performance of portfolio managers on a risk-adjusted basis, the CAPM suggests a simple benchmark based on the CML. It consists of comparing the rate of return earned on the managed portfolio to the rate of return attainable by simply mixing the market portfolio and risk-free asset in proportions that would have produced the same volatility.

The method requires one to compute the volatility of the managed portfolio over the relevant period in the past—for instance, the last 10 years—and then to figure out what the average rate of return would have been on a strategy of mixing the market portfolio and risk-free asset to produce a portfolio with that same volatility. Then compare the managed portfolio's average rate of return to this simple benchmark portfolio's average rate of return.[3]

In practice, the market portfolio actually used in measuring the performance of portfolio managers is a well-diversified portfolio of stocks rather than the true market portfolio of all risky assets. It turns out that the simple benchmark strategy has been a difficult one to beat. Studies of the performance of managed equity mutual funds consistently find that the simple strategy outperforms around two-thirds of the funds. As a result, more households and pension funds have been adopting the passive investment strategy used as the performance benchmark. This type of strategy has come to be known as **indexing**, because the portfolio used as a proxy for the market portfolio often has the same weights as well-known stock market indexes such as the Standard & Poor's 500.

---

[3]For details on alternative measures of risk adjusted return see: Franco and Leah Modigliani, "Risk-Adjusted Performance: How to Measure It and Why," *Journal of Portfolio Management* (Winter 1997), pp. 45–54.

Whether or not the CAPM is a valid theory, indexing is an attractive investment strategy for at least two reasons. First, as an empirical matter, it has historically performed better than most actively managed portfolios. Second, it costs less to implement than an active portfolio strategy, because one does not incur the costs of research to look for mispriced securities, and the cost of transactions is typically much less.

As we have seen, the CML provides a convenient and challenging benchmark for measuring the performance of an investor's entire portfolio of assets. However, households and pension funds often use several different portfolio managers, each of whom manages only a part of the whole portfolio. For measuring performance of such managers, the CAPM suggests a different benchmark—the SML.

As we saw in section 3, the CAPM holds that every security has a risk premium equal to its beta times the risk premium on the market portfolio. The difference between the average rate of return on a security or a portfolio of securities and its SML relation is called **alpha** (the Greek letter α).

If a portfolio manager can consistently produce a positive alpha, then her performance is judged to be superior, even if the managed portfolio does not outperform the CML as a stand-alone investment.

To understand this puzzle, consider how a fund with a positive alpha can be used by an investor in combination with the market portfolio and the risk-free asset to create a total portfolio that outperforms the CML. Let us illustrate with an example.

Assume that the risk-free rate is 6% per year, the risk premium on the market portfolio is 8% per year, and the standard deviation on the market portfolio is 20% per year. Suppose the Alpha Fund is a managed mutual fund with a beta of 0.5, an alpha of 1% per year, and a standard deviation of 15%.

Figures 3 and 4 show the relation of Alpha Fund to the SML and the CML. In both figures, point *Alpha* represents the Alpha Fund. In Figure 3, *Alpha* lies above the SML. Alpha Fund's α is measured as the vertical distance between *Alpha* and the SML.

In Figure 4, *Alpha* lies below the CML and, therefore, is not efficient. Alpha Fund would never be held by any investor as a total portfolio because investors could achieve lower risk and/or a higher expected return by mixing the market portfolio and the risk-free asset. However, by combining Alpha Fund with the market portfolio in certain optimal proportions, investors can achieve points that lie above the CML.

Point Q in Figure 4 corresponds to the optimal combination of Alpha Fund and the market portfolio. By mixing this portfolio with the risk-free asset, investors can achieve risk-return combinations anywhere along the line connecting points F and Q, the dashed line that lies above the CML. Thus, *if you can find a portfolio manager with a positive α, you can beat the market (indexing investment strategy).*

FIGURE 3

Alpha Fund and the Security Market Line

Note: The SML has a slope of 8% per year. Alpha Fund is a managed mutual fund with a β of 0.5 and an α of 1% per year.

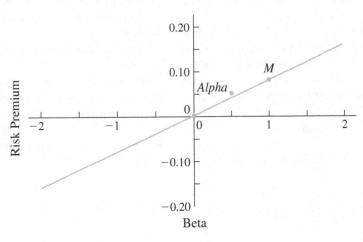

FIGURE 4

Alpha Fund and the Capital Market Line

Note: The risk-free rate is 6% per year, the risk-premium on the market portfolio is 8% per year, and the standard deviation on the market portfolio is 20% per year. The CML has a slope of 0.4. Alpha Fund is a managed mutual fund with an expected rate of return of 11% per year and a σ of 15%.

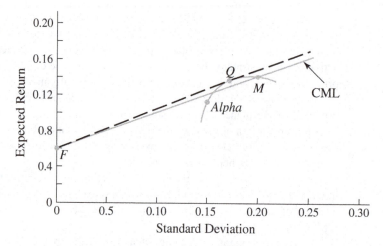

Quick Check 5

If the CAPM were empirically accurate, then what should be the alpha of all portfolios?

5 Valuation and Regulating Rates of Return

In addition to their use in portfolio selection, risk premiums derived from the CAPM are employed in discounted cash flow (DCF) valuation models and in capital-budgeting decisions of firms. They are also used to establish "fair" rates of return on invested capital in regulated firms or in firms that do business on a cost-plus basis. In this section, we offer brief examples of each of these applications.

Box 2	The Exchange-Traded Fund Fad

Exchange-traded funds (ETFs) were first introduced in the United States in 1993, and have since become a popular alternative to other types of investments. Like mutual funds, ETFs offer investors shares in a fund that owns securities; however, ETFs are traded continuously on an exchange, like stocks. They also offer investors the low trading costs and tax efficiency associated with index investing. Continuous trading allows for short-term speculation and protects ETFs from late trading and market timing, malpractices associated with some American mutual funds.

The popularity of ETFs among various types of investors, from hedge funds to small traders, led to the creation of new ETFs in the United States, Europe, and Japan during the late 1990s and early 2000s. However, many ETFs were forced to close down because demand was insufficient to cover costs, especially with high fees charged by index providers.

ETFs are also performing well in some emerging markets. Since Mexico started to permit ETFs to be held in its retirement system, Barclays' iShares Funds now have a 15% share of all stock market trading. While there might not be room for much more than one of each type of index-linked ETF, new types of ETFs entering the market may give investors even more options.

Source: Adapted from "Entirely Too Frenetic?" *The Economist*, July 29, 2004.

5.1 Discounted Cash Flow Valuation Models

Some widely used methods of valuing a firm's stock view the price of a share as the present value of all expected future dividends discounted at the market capitalization rate.

$$P_0 = \frac{D_1}{(1+k)} + \frac{D_2}{(1+k)^2} + \cdots = \sum_{t=1}^{\infty} \frac{D_t}{(1+k)^t}$$

where D_t is the expected dividend per share in period t and k is the risk-adjusted discount rate, which is the expected rate of return that investors require to invest in the stock. In applying this formula, analysts often employ the CAPM to compute k.

For example, Steadygrowth Corporation's dividends per share are expected to grow at a constant rate of 10% per year. The expected stream of future dividends is

D_1	D_2	D_3	etc.
$5	$5.50	$6.05	etc.

The present value of a perpetual stream of dividends growing at a constant rate, g, is

$$P_0 = \frac{D_1}{k-g}$$

With Steadygrowth's data, this implies that the price of the stock is

$$P_0 = \frac{5}{k-0.10}$$

One way to find k is to estimate Steadygrowth's beta and infer Steadygrowth's risk premium from the SML relation:

$$k_{steady} = r_f + \beta_{steady}[E(r_M) - r_f]$$

Thus, suppose that the risk-free rate is 0.03, $\beta_{steady} = 1.5$, and the risk premium on the market portfolio is 0.08. Then $k = 0.15$ per year. Substituting this value into the constant growth rate DDM, the estimated value of Steadygrowth stock is

$$P_0 = \frac{5}{k-0.10} = \frac{5}{0.15-0.10} = 100$$

> **Quick Check 6**
>
> What would be the estimated value of Steadygrowth stock if its beta were 2 instead of 1.5?

5.2 Cost of Capital

Corporate financial managers need to know their firm's cost of capital to make investment (capital-budgeting) decisions. The firm's cost of capital is a weighted average of its cost of equity capital and debt. Practitioners often use a CAPM-based method similar to the one we just demonstrated for Steadygrowth Corporation to estimate the cost of equity capital.

For example, suppose that you are the financial manager of ABC Corporation and you want to compute your firm's cost of equity capital. You compute the beta of ABC stock and find it to be 1.1. The current risk-free rate is 0.06 per year, and you assume that the market risk premium is 0.08 per year. Then according to the SML, the equilibrium expected rate of return on ABC stock is

$$E(r_{ABC}) = r_f + \beta_{ABC}[E(r_M) - r_f]$$
$$= 0.06 + 1.1(0.08) = 0.148$$

Thus, 14.8% per year is ABC's cost of equity capital.

5.3 Regulation and Cost-Plus Pricing

Regulators may use the CAPM to establish a "fair" rate of return on invested capital for public utilities and other firms subject to price regulation. For example, a commission regulating an electric power company may have to establish a price that the company is allowed to charge its customers for electricity. The commission will do so by computing the cost of producing the electricity, including an allowance for the cost of capital.

Similarly, in situations in which a price is negotiated by two parties based on production cost, there is often a need to decide on a fair allowance for the cost of capital. An example would be a noncompetitive (secret) contract to develop or produce military equipment for a government.

In computing the cost of capital, a regulatory commission must compensate the providers of capital for the risk they bear by investing in the electric utility. Because the investors are able to diversify their investment portfolios, the only risk the regulators need to compensate them for is market risk, as measured by beta.

6 Modifications and Alternatives to the CAPM

As early as the 1970s, researchers testing the empirical validity of the Security Market Line using the historical returns of common stocks in the United States found that it did not seem to fit the data well enough to explain fully the structure of expected returns on assets. Subsequent and currently ongoing research formulated and tested a variety of enriched CAPM and alternative models using data from a variety of asset markets around the world. A consensus has emerged that the original simple version of the CAPM needs to be modified.[4]

Potential explanations for the apparent deviations from the CAPM fall into three categories. One such is that the CAPM actually does hold, but the "market" portfolios used in the testing were incomplete and inadequate representations of the true market portfolio. Another focuses on market imperfections not contemplated in the CAPM, such as borrowing costs and constraints, shortsale restrictions and costs, different tax treatments for various assets, and the nontradability of some important assets such as human capital. These elements are likely to change over time with changes in technology, institutional structures, and regulations. A third approach has been to add greater realism to the modeling assumptions, while maintaining the CAPM's basic methodology. This means retaining the fundamental assumption of the CAPM that investors (or their agents) follow the principles

---

[4]See F. Black, M. Jensen, and M. Scholes, "The Capital Asset Pricing Model: Some Empirical Tests," in M. Jensen, ed., *Studies in the Theory of Capital Markets,* New York: Praeger, 1972; E. Fama and J. MacBeth, "Risk, Return and Equilibrium: Some Empirical Tests," *Journal of Political Economy,* 8, 1973; E. Fama and K. French, "Multifactor Explanations of Asset Pricing Anomalies," *Journal of Finance,* 51, 1996.

of optimal portfolio selection, and deriving the equilibrium implications of such optimizing behavior in the presence of additional complicating factors. One such model is the multifactor Intertemporal Capital Asset Pricing Model (ICAPM), in which equilibrium risk premiums on securities in this dynamic model come from several dimensions of risks, reflected not only by their return sensitivities or beta on the market portfolio but also by their sensitivity to other systematic risks such as changes in interest rates and expected returns on assets and changes in consumption good prices. In this world, securities have a richer set of hedging roles in addition to their place in the market portfolio.

Another line of research has been to develop alternative theories. The most prominent is the Arbitrage Pricing Theory (APT). According to the APT a relation similar to the Security Market Line can exist even if investors are not mean-variance optimizers. If there are enough different securities to "diversify away" all but market risk, the APT shows that an expected-return-to-beta relation will exist as a consequence of there not being any arbitrage opportunities. Although the specific structure of asset risks in these models differs from the CAPM, the basic insights of the CAPM—that the risk premiums are related to broad systematic risk factors that matter to large segments of the population—still hold.

Summary

The CAPM has three main implications:

- In equilibrium, everyone's relative holdings of risky assets are the same as in the market portfolio.
- The size of the risk premium of the market portfolio is determined by the risk aversion of investors and the volatility of the return.
- The risk premium on any asset is equal to its beta times the risk premium on the market portfolio.

Whether or not the CAPM is strictly true, it provides a rationale for a very simple passive portfolio strategy:

- Diversify your holdings of risky assets according to the proportions of the market portfolio, and
- Mix this portfolio with the risk-free asset to achieve a desired risk-reward combination.

The CAPM is used in portfolio management primarily in two ways:

- to establish a logical and convenient starting point in asset allocation and security selection, and
- to establish a benchmark for evaluating portfolio-management ability on a risk-adjusted basis.

In corporate finance, the CAPM is used to determine the appropriate risk-adjusted discount rate in valuation models of the firm and in capital-budgeting decisions. The CAPM is also used to establish a "fair" rate of return on invested capital for regulated firms and in cost-plus pricing.

Today few financial scholars consider the CAPM in its simplest form to be an accurate model for fully explaining or predicting risk premiums on risky assets. However, modified versions of the model are still a central feature of the theory and practice of finance.

The APT gives a rationale for the expected return—beta relation that relies on the condition that there be no arbitrage profit opportunities; the CAPM requires that investors be mean-variance portfolio optimizers. The APT and CAPM are not incompatible; rather, they complement each other.

Key Terms

- capital asset pricing model
- market portfolio
- capital market line
- beta
- security market line
- indexing
- alpha

Answers to Quick Check Questions

Quick Check 1 Investor 3 has a $100,000 portfolio with nothing invested in the risk-free asset. How much is invested in GM and how much in Toyota?

Answer: $75,000 is invested in GM stock and $25,000 in Toyota stock.

Quick Check 2 According to the CAPM, what is a simple way for investors to form their optimal portfolios?

Answer: According to the CAPM, a simple way for investors to form their optimal portfolios is to combine the market portfolio with the risk-free asset.

Quick Check 3 What would the slope of the CML be if the average degree of risk aversion increased from 2 to 3?

Answer: If risk aversion increased from 2 to 3, the risk premium on the market portfolio would increase from 0.08 to 0.12, and the slope of the CML would increase from 0.4 to 0.6.

Quick Check 4 Suppose you are examining a stock that has a beta of 0.5. According to the CAPM, what should be its expected rate of return? Where should the stock be located in relation to the CML and the SML?

Answer: A stock with a beta of 0.5 should have an expected risk premium equal to half the risk premium on the market portfolio. If the market risk premium is 0.08, then the stock's expected rate of return should be the risk-free rate plus 0.04. The stock would be located on the SML at a point halfway between the vertical axis and point M. It would be located on or below the CML at a latitude corresponding to its expected rate of return of $r_f + 0.04$.

Quick Check 5 If the CAPM were empirically accurate, then what should be the alpha of all portfolios?

Answer: According to the CAPM, all portfolios should have an alpha of zero.

Quick Check 6 What would be the estimated value of Steadygrowth stock if its beta was 2 instead of 1.5?

Answer: If Steadygrowth's beta is 2, then $k = 0.19$, and $P_0 = 5/(0.19 - 0.10) = \$55.56$ per share.

Questions and Problems

The Capital Asset Pricing Model in Brief

1. Suppose there are only three risky assets, IAM stock, IBM stock, and ICM stock. The total market equity values of these companies at current prices are $150 million for IAM, $300 million for IBM, and $1,500 million for ICM. In addition there is $50 million of riskless bonds in the market. The proportion of the riskless asset held in the aggregate market portfolio would be?

2. Capital markets in Flatland exhibit trade in four securities, the stocks X, Y, and Z, and a riskless government security. Evaluated at current prices in U.S. dollars, the total market values of these assets are, respectively, $24 billion, $36 billion, $24 billion, and $16 billion.

   a. Determine the relative proportions of each asset in the market portfolio.

   b. If an investor holds risky assets in proportion to their market values and divides their aggregate portfolio of $100,000 with $30,000 invested in the riskless asset, how much is invested in securities X, Y, and Z?

3. With a riskless rate of 0.06, an equity market premium of 0.05, and a Capital Market Line of slope 0.75, we can infer what about the risk of the market portfolio?

4. If the Treasury bill rate is currently 0.04 and the expected return to the market portfolio over the same period is 0.12, determine the risk premium on the market. If the standard deviation of the return on the market is 0.20, what is the equation of the Capital Market Line?

5. The riskless rate of interest is 0.06 per year, and the expected rate of return on the market portfolio is 0.15 per year.

   a. According to the CAPM, what is the efficient way for an investor to achieve an expected rate of return of 0.10 per year?

   b. If the standard deviation of the rate of return on the market portfolio is 0.20, what is the standard deviation on the above portfolio?

   c. Plot the CML and locate the foregoing portfolio on the same graph.

   d. Plot the SML and locate the fore- going portfolio on the same graph.

6. Given the information from the previous problem (problem 2). Estimate the value of a stock with an expected dividend per share of $5 this coming year, an expected dividend growth rate of 0.04 per year forever, and a beta of 0.8. If its market price is less than the value you have estimated (i.e., if it is under-priced), what is true of its expected rate of return?

7. If the CAPM is valid, which of the following situations is possible? Explain. Consider each situation independently.

   a.

Portfolio	Expected Return	Beta
A	0.20	1.4
B	0.25	1.2

   b.

Portfolio	Expected Return	Standard Deviation
A	0.30	35%
B	0.40	25%

   c.

Portfolio	Expected Return	Standard Deviation
Risk free	0.10	0
Market	0.18	24%
A	0.16	12%

d.

Portfolio	Expected Return	Standard Deviation
Risk free	0.10	0
Market	0.18	24%
A	0.20	22%

Determinants of the Risk Premium on the Market Portfolio

8. Suppose the risk-free rate is 0.10 and a security with a beta of $+1$ has an equilibrium expected rate of return of 0.15. What is the equity market premium?

9. Suppose the equity market premium is 4% and a security with a beta of $+1.25$ has an equilibrium expected rate of return of 0.10. If the government wishes to issue risk-free zero-coupon bonds with a term to maturity of one period and a face value per bond of $100,000, how much can the government expect to receive per bond?

10. Consider a portfolio exhibiting an expected return of 0.20 in an economy in which the riskless interest rate is 0.08, the expected return to the market portfolio is 0.13, and the standard deviation of the return to the market portfolio is 0.25. Assuming this portfolio is efficient, determine:
   a. its beta.
   b. the standard deviation of its return.
   c. its correlation with the market return.

Beta and Risk Premiums on Individual Securities

11. Suppose the realized rate of return on the market portfolio is one percentage point greater than its expected return. Then a security with a beta of $+2$ would have a realized rate of return that compares how with its expected return?

12. Security i's beta can be written as: $\beta_i = \frac{\sigma_{im}}{\sigma_m^2}$ where σ_{im} is the covariance between the return on security i and the return on the market portfolio, m. In turn the covariance is the product of the correlation and the standard deviations or: $\sigma_{im} = \rho_{im}\sigma_i\sigma_m$. What risk characteristics do securities with betas equal to $+1$ possess? Those with betas equal to zero?

13. If the return on the market portfolio is 0.12 and the riskless rate is 0.07, use the CAPM to determine if the following stocks are mispriced:

Stock	Expected Return	Beta
M	0.115	0.8
M&M	0.135	1.2

14. The Suzuki Motor Company is contemplating issuing stock to finance investment in producing a new sports-utility vehicle, the *Seppuku*. Financial analysts within Suzuki forecast that this investment will have precisely the same risk as the market portfolio, where the annual return to the market portfolio is expected to be 0.15 and the current risk-free interest rate is 0.05. The analysts further believe that the expected return to the *Seppuku* project will be 0.20 annually. Derive the maximal beta value that would induce Suzuki to issue the stock.

15. St. Petersburg Associates, a firm of financial analysts specializing in Russian financial markets, forecasts that the stock of the Siberian Drilling Company will be worth 1,000 rubles per share one year from today. If the riskless interest rate on Russian government securities is 0.10 and the expected return to the market portfolio is 0.18, determine how much you would pay for a share of Siberian Drilling stock today if:
    a. the beta of Siberian Drilling is 3.
    b. the beta of Siberian Drilling is 0.5.

Using the CAPM in Portfolio Selection

16. Suppose that the stock of the new cologne manufacturer, Eau de Rodman, Inc., has been forecast to have a return with standard deviation 0.30 and a correlation with the market portfolio of 0.9. If the standard deviation of the yield on the market is 0.20, determine the relative holdings of the market portfolio and Eau de Rodman stock to form a portfolio with a beta of 1.8.

17. The current price of a share of stock in the Down Under Clothing Company of Australia is A\$50 and its expected yield over the year is 0.14. The market risk premium in Australia is 0.08 and the riskless interest rate 0.06. What would happen to the stock's current price if its expected future payout remains constant while the covariance of its rate of return with the market portfolio falls by 50 percent?

18. Suppose that you believe that the price of a share of IBM stock a year from today will be equal to the sum of the price of a share of General Motors stock plus the price of a share of Exxon-Mobil, and further you believe that the price of a share of IBM stock in one year will be \$100 whereas the price of a share of General Motors today is \$30. If the annualized yield on 91-day T-bills (the riskless rate you use) is 0.05, the expected yield on the market is 0.15, the variance of the market portfolio is 1, and the beta of IBM is 2, what price would you be willing to pay for one share of Exxon-Mobil stock today?

19. *Challenge Problem:* During the most recent 5-year period, the Pizzaro mutual fund earned an average annualized rate of return of 0.15 and had an annualized standard deviation of 0.30. The average risk-free rate was 0.05 per year. The average rate of return in the market index over that same period was 0.10 per year and the standard deviation was 0.20. How well did Pizzaro perform on a risk-adjusted basis? Adjust the risk to be equal to that of the market portfolio by building a portfolio of Pizzaro and the riskless asset with the same level of risk as the market portfolio.

20. There are only two risky assets in the economy: stocks and real estate. Their relative supplies are 50% stocks and 50% real estate, thus, the market portfolio will be half stocks and half real estate. The standard deviations are 0.20 for stocks, 0.20 for real estate, and the correlation between them is zero. The market portfolio's expected return is 0.14. The riskless rate is 0.08 per year.
    a. According to the CAPM what must be the equilibrium risk premium on the market portfolio, on stocks, and on real estate?
    b. Draw the Capital Market Line. What is its slope? Draw the SML. What is its formula?

21. *Challenge Problem:* Consider a market with only the following three risky assets:

	Expected Return % per month	Risk % σ_i	Covariance with market σ_{im}
Asset 1	2.03	2	1.12
Asset 2	1.79	1	0.90
Asset 3	1.49	1	0.62
Market Portfolio		0.92	

Consider the market portfolio comprised of 4% invested in Asset 1, 76% invested in Asset 2, and 20% invested in Asset 3. What is the expected return of this portfolio? What are the betas of the three risky assets? Suppose the riskless rate of interest is 0.8% (8/10ths of one percent per month). Are these three securities priced correctly? What is the beta of the market portfolio calculated as a weighted average of the betas of its components?

Valuation and Regulating Rates of Return

22. Suppose a company's current dividend of $1.50 per share is expected to grow at a constant 0.05 rate into the indefinite future. In capital markets the market risk premium is 0.08 and the risk-free rate is 0.02. If the stable beta of the company's stock is 0.8, what is the estimated current stock price?

23. Consider the results of the previous problem (problem 22). What will a 25 percent increase in the covariance between the returns on the company's stock and the market portfolio do to the equity market capitalization rate for the company? By how much will the current stock price change?

24. The Clotted Blood Corporation, a home health supply company serving hemophiliacs, is considering purchasing a new delivery van that will increase the radius of its service area. For an initial outlay of $21,250 the van is estimated to produce the following incremental net after-tax cash flows:

Time period	ACF
1	$5,000
2	$6,000
3	$7,000
4	$6,000
5	$5,000

In capital markets the market risk premium is 0.10 and the risk-free rate is 0.04. If the stable beta of the company's stock is 1.25, what is the net present value of the investment using the estimated market capitalization rate?

25. Consider the results of the previous problem (problem 24). How will a ½ of one percentage point increase in the expected return on the market portfolio impact the net present value of the investment?

Suggested Readings

Bodie, Z., A. Kane, and A. Marcus. *Investments.* 7th Ed. Boston: Irwin/McGraw-Hill, 2008.

Lintner, J. "The Valuation of Risk Assets and the Selection of Risky Investments in Stock Portfolios and Capital Budgets." *Review of Economics and Statistics* 47, February 1965.

Merton, R. C. "An Intertemporal Capital Asset Pricing Model." *Econometrica* 41, September 1973.

——— "A Reexamination of the Capital Asset Pricing Model." *Studies in Risk and Return.* Eds. J. Bicksler and I. Friend. Cambridge: Ballinger, 1977.

Mossin, J. "Equilibrium in a Capital Asset Market." *Econometrica* 35, October 1966.

Ross, S. A. "Arbitrage Theory of Capital Asset Pricing." *Journal of Economic Theory* 13, December 1976.

Sharpe, W. "Capital Asset Prices: A Theory of Market Equilibrium." *Journal of Finance* 19, September 1964.

Forward and Futures Markets

OBJECTIVES

- To learn how to use forward and futures contracts for hedging, speculating, and arbitrage.
- To understand the relations among spot, forward, and futures prices of commodities, currencies, and securities.
- To learn what kinds of useful information can be inferred from the relations among spot and forward prices.

CONTENTS

From Chapter 14 of *Financial Economics*, 2/e. Zvi Bodie, Robert C. Merton, David L. Cleeton.

Earlier, we introduced forward and futures contracts and showed how they are used to hedge against risks. In this chapter, we explain how their prices are determined and how to extract information from them.

We begin with commodities such as wheat and show how forward and futures prices guide decisions about how much wheat to store from one growing season to the next. Next, we examine the relation between the spot and forward prices of gold and show how one can infer from them the implicit cost of carrying gold from one period to another. We then turn to the prices of **financial futures**, that is, stocks, bonds, and foreign currencies for future delivery.

1 Distinctions between Forward and Futures Contracts

Any agreement between two parties that calls for delivery of an item on a specified future date for an agreed-upon price that is paid in the future is called a **forward contract**. We can summarize the main features of a forward contract as follows:

- Two parties agree to exchange some item in the future at a delivery price specified now.
- The *forward price* is defined as the delivery price that makes the current market value of the contract zero.
- No money is paid in the present by either party to the other.
- The *face value* of the contract is the quantity of the item specified in the contract times the forward price.
- The party who agrees to buy the specified item is said to take a *long* position, and the party who agrees to sell the item is said to take a *short* position.

A simple way to remember who pays what to whom is the following rule:

If the spot price on the contract maturity date is higher than the forward price, the party who is long makes money. But if the spot price on the contract maturity date is lower than the forward price, the party who is short makes money.

Futures contracts serve many of the same purposes as forward contracts, but they differ in several respects.

Forward contracts are negotiated between two parties (usually business firms) and, therefore, can have unique specifications that depend on the demands of those parties. This "customization" is a disadvantage if one of the parties wants to terminate the contract before the delivery date because it makes the contract illiquid.

By contrast, futures contracts are standardized contracts that are traded on exchanges. The exchange specifies the exact commodity, the contract size, and where and when delivery will be made. It is, therefore, easy for parties to a futures contract to "close out"—that is, to terminate—their positions before the specified delivery date. Indeed, the vast majority of futures contracts are terminated before the final contract delivery date.

To illustrate, the wheat futures contract traded on the Chicago Board of Trade (CBT) specifies a quantity of 5,000 bushels of a specific grade of wheat. Table 1 shows a listing of CBT wheat futures contracts and prices from the CBT as reported by the *Financial Times* Web site (http://www.ft.com/marketdata/commodities).

The futures contracts in Table 1 differ from each other in their delivery months given in the first column. The second and third columns show the settlement price, which is usually

TABLE 1 Wheat Futures Contracts and Prices

		Chicago Board of Trade, June 23, 2006				
	Settlement Price	Day's Change	High	Low	Vol 000s	Interest
Jul	363.25	−2.25	369.00	362.00	9.22	39.7
Sep	381.50	−0.75	387.50	380.00	21.40	216.8
Dec	400.25	−1.50	405.00	398.00	10.60	106.1
Mar	417.00	−1.50	420.00	416.00	1.01	28.8
Jul	432.50	−1.25	436.00	432.00	3.08	54.2
Total					**47.40**	**470.5**

5,000 bu min; cents/60 lb bushel
Source: Financial Times
http://www.ft.com/marketdata/commodities

an average of the prices of the last few trades of the day and the change from the previous day's settlement price. These listings are followed by the day's high and low prices. The final two columns show the volume of trade in the contracts during the day and the outstanding number of contracts at the end of the day, called the open interest. These final two columns are aggregated to give the total daily contract volume and total outstanding interest.

The parties who are long and short on these wheat futures have contracts with the CBT rather than with each other, although the exchange is careful to exactly match the number of long and short positions outstanding. Orders are carried out through brokers who have seats on the exchange.

To make sure that the parties to a futures contract do not default, the exchange requires that there be enough collateral (called the *margin requirement*) posted in each account to cover any losses. All accounts are marked to market at the end of each trading day based on that day's settlement price.

Let us illustrate how futures contracts work using the prices in Table 1. You place an order to take a long position in a July wheat futures contract on June 22, 2006. The broker requires you to deposit money in your account—say, $1,500—to serve as collateral.[1]

On June 23, the futures price closes 2¼ cents per bushel lower. Thus, you have lost 2¼ cents × 5,000 bushels or $112.50 that day, and the broker takes that amount out of your account even though you may not have made any trades. The money is transferred to the futures exchange, which transfers it to one of the parties who was on the short side of the contract.

If the collateral in your account falls below a prespecified level, you will receive a **margin call** from the broker asking you to add money. If you do not respond immediately, then the broker liquidates your position at the prevailing market price and returns any leftover collateral.

This process of daily *realization* of gains and losses minimizes the possibility of contract default. Another consequence of daily marking to market of futures contracts is that no matter how great their face value, their market value is always zero at the beginning of each day.

Because of their careful procedures to protect against the risk of contract default by requiring the posting of margin, futures markets are used by individuals and firms whose credit ratings may be costly to check. Forward contracts, on the other hand, tend to be used when the credit rating of the contracting parties is high and easy to verify. Thus, forward

---

[1]The collateral can be in the form of interest-bearing government securities, and you receive the interest earned.

contracts are common in the foreign currency market when the contracting parties are two banks or a bank and one of its corporate customers.

The pricing relations to be discussed later in this chapter that apply to forward prices apply with minor modification to futures prices. They may differ because of the daily marking-to-market feature of futures contracts. In practice, however, for most assets the futures and forward prices hardly differ at all.[2]

Quick Check 1

What would happen in your futures trading account if you take a long position in wheat futures and instead of going down by 7¼ cents per bushel, the futures price went up by that amount?

2 The Economic Function of Futures Markets

The most obvious function of commodity futures markets is to facilitate the reallocation of exposure to commodity price risk among market participants. However, commodity futures prices also play an important informational role for producers, distributors, and consumers of commodities who must decide how much wheat to sell (or consume) now and how much to store for the future. *By providing a means to hedge the price risk associated with storing a commodity, futures contracts make it possible to separate the decision of whether to physically store a commodity from the decision to have financial exposure to its price changes.*

For example, suppose that it is one month before the next harvest and a wheat distributor has a ton of wheat in storage from the last harvest. The spot price of wheat is $2 per bushel, and the futures price for delivery a month from now (after the new crop has been harvested) is F. The distributor can hedge its exposure to price changes by either (1) selling the wheat in the spot market for $2 per bushel and delivering it immediately, or (2) selling short a futures contract at a price of F and delivering the wheat a month from now. In either case, he has complete certainty about the price he will receive for his wheat.

Suppose that a distributor's cost of physically storing the wheat—the "cost of carry," which includes interest, warehousing, and spoilage costs—is 10 cents per bushel per month. This distributor will choose alternative (2) and carry the ton of wheat for another month (i.e., past the next harvest) only if F is greater than $2.10. For example, if the futures price is $2.12 per bushel, then the distributor will choose to carry the wheat in storage for another month.

Now suppose that there is another distributor whose cost of carry is 15 cents per bushel per month. At $2.12, this "high-storage-cost" distributor will choose alternative (1) and sell his wheat immediately in the spot market rather than carry it and hedge by taking a short futures position. Thus, a distributor will choose to carry the wheat for another month only if his cost of carrying it is less than the difference between the futures and spot prices of wheat.

Letting S be the spot price of wheat and C_j be the cost of carry for distributor j, we can generalize from our example to say that distributor j will choose to carry the wheat in storage for another month only if $C_j < F - S$. Thus, the difference between the futures and the spot price, called the **spread,** governs how much wheat will be stored in aggregate and by whom:

The futures and forward markets contribute to economic efficiency by creating a structure in which the least-cost distributors will do the necessary physical storage.

---

[2]See Bradford Cornell and Marc R. Reinganum, "Forward and Futures Prices: Evidence from the Foreign Exchange Markets," *Journal of Finance* 36 (December 1981).

Suppose that the next wheat harvest is expected to be an especially bountiful one, and, therefore, it would be socially desirable to consume all of the wheat currently available in storage. The forward market makes it possible to hedge the price risk without physically storing the wheat. The forward price carries the message not to store to all producers and distributors of wheat by trading below the current spot price, so that it would not pay for anyone to store wheat from now until after the harvest, even if it were costless to do so (i.e., $C = 0$).[3]

> **Quick Check 2**
>
> Suppose you are a distributor of corn and you observe that the spot price is $3 per bushel and the futures price for delivery a month from now is $3.10. If your cost of carrying corn is $0.15 per bushel per month, what should you do?

3 The Role of Speculators

Producers, distributors, and consumers of wheat may be in the best position to forecast future wheat prices (perhaps because they have low costs of gathering the relevant information), but others are not banned from the market. Anyone using a futures contract to reduce risk is called a **hedger.** But much of the trading of futures contracts is carried on by **speculators,** who take positions in the market based on their forecasts of the future spot price.

Because speculators are not trying to reduce their risk exposure, their motivation for participating in the futures market is to make a profit on their futures trades. Speculators typically gather information to help them forecast prices, and then buy or sell futures contracts based on those forecasts.

The same party can be both a hedger and a speculator. Indeed, one might say that if a farmer, baker, and a distributor choose *not* to hedge their price risk in the futures market, then they are speculating on the price of wheat. Competition among active forecasters in the futures markets will encourage those who have comparative advantage in forecasting wheat prices to specialize in it.

For example, suppose you are a wheat speculator. You gather information on all the supply and demand factors that determine the price of wheat, such as total acreage planted, rainfall, production plans of major baked goods producers, and so on, and come up with a forecast of next month's spot price of wheat. Say it is $2 per bushel. If the current futures price for delivery a month from now is less than $2 per bushel, you buy the futures contract (take a long position) because you expect to make a profit from it.

To see this, suppose the current futures price for wheat to be delivered a month from now is $1.50 per bushel. By taking a long position in this futures contract, you lock in a buying price of $1.50 per bushel for wheat to be delivered a month from now. Because you expect the spot price to be $2 at that time, your expected gain is $0.50 per bushel.

On the other hand, suppose that the current futures price for delivery a month from now is greater than $2 per bushel (your forecast); say it is $2.50 per bushel. Then to earn an expected profit, you sell the futures contract (take a short position). By taking a short position in this futures contract, you lock in a selling price of $2.50 per bushel for wheat to be delivered a month from now. You expect to be able to buy wheat at a spot price of $2 per bushel at that time. You, therefore, expect a gain of $0.50 per bushel.

---

[3]Furthermore, this price structure would induce arbitrageurs to find any holders of physical wheat who might plan to store and try to borrow their wheat, sell it in the spot market, and hedge their "short" exposure by going long a forward contract. Thus, in seeking arbitrage profits, the arbitrageurs increase the quantity of wheat that is delivered for current consumption.

Energy Traders and the Corn Market

Energy traders flooded the corn futures market as demand for corn-based ethanol increased during 2006, raising open interest in the Chicago Board of Trade's corn futures contracts by more than 60%. During the period of September 2006 through January 2007, the spot price of a bushel of corn jumped by 70% to reach a decade-old high. Mexico's new president, Felipe Calderón, responded by capping the price of corn tortillas in January. America's fast-growing ethanol industry is clearly behind this price trend.

Agricultural interests, food processors, and other traditional players in the corn futures market may be mostly focused on the intermediate term over the next crop or two, but energy traders showed interest in these as well as crops to be produced longer term. Energy traders were using the futures market to hedge positions in anticipation of rapid increases in the percentage of U.S. corn used to make ethanol over the next few years.

Source: Adapted from "Corn Futures Trading Volumes Reach Record," *Financial Times,* June 20, 2006.

As a speculator, you take whatever position gives you an expected profit. Of course, because you do not know for sure what the spot price will be a month from now, you could lose money on your futures contract. But you accept that risk in pursuit of what you believe to be expected profit.

Speculative activity in futures markets is sometimes perceived by critics as having no social value. Indeed, it is often portrayed as being the economic equivalent of gambling. However, there are at least two economic purposes served by the activity of speculators that differentiate it from gambling in sports or at the casino.

First, commodity speculators who consistently succeed do so by correctly forecasting spot prices. Their activity, therefore, makes futures prices better predictors of the direction of change of spot prices. Second, speculators take the opposite side of a hedger's trade when other hedgers cannot readily be found to do so. Thus, the activity of speculators makes futures markets more *liquid* than they would otherwise be. Indeed, if only hedgers bought and sold futures contracts, there might not be enough trading to support an organized futures exchange. Thus, the presence of speculators may be a necessary condition for the very existence of some futures markets.

4 Relation between Commodity Spot and Futures Prices

As we saw in Section 2, distributors can completely hedge their inventory exposure to wheat price changes by either (1) selling wheat in the spot market for $2 per bushel and delivering it immediately, or (2) selling short a futures contract at a price of F, storing the wheat, and delivering it a month from now.

By buying wheat now and following (2), arbitrageurs could lock in a sure arbitrage profit if the futures price were too far above the spot price. This consideration establishes an upper bound on the spread between the spot and futures prices:

The futures price cannot exceed the spot price by more than the cost of carry:

$$F - S \leq C \tag{1}$$

Because the cost of carry can vary both over time and across market participants, the upper bound on the spread is not constant.

5 Extracting Information from Commodity Futures Prices

It is sometimes said that futures prices can provide information about investor expectations of spot prices in the future. The reasoning is that the futures price reflects what investors expect the spot price to be at the contract delivery date and, therefore, one should be able to retrieve that expected future spot price.

What information can one extract from the forward price of wheat?

We must distinguish between two conditions: (1) no wheat is in storage, and (2) wheat is in storage.

1. If there is no wheat in storage—a condition called a *stock out*—then equation 1 holds as a strict inequality, and the spot and forward prices are not linked precisely through an arbitrage-pricing relation. In this case, the forward price will provide information about the expected future spot price that is not extractable from the current spot price.[4]

2. If wheat is being stored, then no further inference about the future expected spot price is possible beyond that extractable from the current spot price. The reason is that, because by the force of arbitrage, equation 1 must hold as an equality. Hence, the forward price is completely specified by knowing the spot price and the cost of carry, independently of what the assessments are about the future expected spot price. Therefore, if we observe that a commodity, an asset, or a security is being stored, then the forward price provides no additional information about the expected future spot price. However, the forward price, when combined with the current spot price, can be used to extract an estimate of the cost of carry.[5]

> ## Quick Check 3
>
> When does the forward price provide no additional information about expected future spot prices than can be extracted from the current spot price?

6 Forward-Spot Price Parity for Gold

Just as the force of arbitrage establishes the spread between the futures and spot prices of wheat when it is being stored, so it establishes the spread in the case of gold. The resulting relation between the futures and spot prices is called the **forward-spot price-parity relation.**

Suppose you are contemplating investing in an ounce of gold for the next year. There are two ways for you to do it. The first is to buy gold at the current spot price, S, put it into storage, and at the end of the year sell it at a price of S_1. Let s be the cost of storing the gold for the year as a fraction of the spot price. Your rate of return is, therefore,

$$r_{gold} = \frac{S_1 - S}{S} - s \tag{2}$$

---

[4]But even in this case when it does provide information, it is not necessarily an unbiased forecast of the future spot price. We discuss this issue in greater detail in Section 9.

[5]If storage occurs and the forward and spot prices imply a negative cost of carry, then almost surely there are benefits to holding the physical commodity, asset, or security that are not being taken into account in the analysis. The magnitude of these implied benefits is called the *convenience yield* (for owning the physical).

For example, if the spot price of gold is $300 and storage costs are 2% per year, your rate of return is

$$r_{\text{gold}} = \frac{S_1 - 300}{300} - 0.02$$

Another way to invest in gold for the year is to take the same $300 and instead of investing it in gold, invest it in *synthetic* gold. You create synthetic gold by investing $300 (i.e., the spot price) in the risk-free asset and at the same time taking a long position in a gold forward contract with a delivery date a year from now and a forward price of F. The rate of return on this investment in synthetic gold will be

$$\hat{r}_{\text{gold}} = \frac{S_1 - F}{S} + r \tag{3}$$

For example, if the risk-free rate is 8%, your rate of return on synthetic gold will be

$$\hat{r}_{\text{gold}} = \frac{S_1 - F}{300} + 0.08$$

By the Law of One Price, these two equivalent investments must offer the same return, so by equating 2 and 3 we get

$$\frac{S_1 - F}{S} + r = \frac{S_1 - S}{S} - s$$

Rearranging terms we get the forward-spot price-parity relation for gold:

$$F = (1 + r + s)S \tag{4}$$

In our example, the forward price for delivery of gold in one year should be $330 per ounce:

$$F = (1 + r + s)S = 1.10 \times 300 = 330$$

If, in violation of equation 4, the forward price exceeds $330 per ounce, it would pay an arbitrageur to buy gold at the spot price and simultaneously sell it for future delivery at the forward price. If on the other hand, the forward price were less than $330 per ounce, an arbitrageur would sell gold short in the spot market (i.e., borrow it and sell it immediately), invest the proceeds of the short sale in the risk-free asset, and go long the forward contract.

In practice, the parties who maintain the forward-spot price-parity relation are gold dealers. This is because they typically have the lowest storage and transaction costs.

Table 2 shows the arbitrage opportunity that would be available if the forward price were $340 per ounce instead of $330. A dealer would borrow, use the funds to buy gold for

TABLE 2 Arbitrage Opportunity When Forward Price of Gold Is Too High

Arbitrage Position	Immediate Cash Flow	Cash Flow 1 Year From Now
Sell a forward contract	0	$340 - S_1$
Borrow $300	$300	-$324
Buy an ounce of gold	-$300	S_1
Pay storage costs		-$6
Net cash flows	0	$340 - $330 = $10

TABLE 3 Arbitrage Opportunity When Forward Price of Gold Is Too Low

Arbitrage Position	Immediate Cash Flow	Cash Flow 1 Year From Now
Sell short an ounce of gold	$300	$-S_1$
Buy a forward contract	0	$S_1 - \$320$
Invest $300 in 1-year pure discount bonds	$-\$300$	$324
Receive storage costs		$6
Net cash flows	0	$\$330 - \$320 = \$10$

$300 per ounce, and simultaneously sell gold forward at $340 per ounce. After paying off the loan and the storage costs a year from now, there would be $10 left over *regardless of what the spot price turns out to be at that time.*

Now consider the situation if the forward price of gold were only $320 per ounce. Table 3 shows the arbitrage opportunity that would be available to a gold dealer if the forward price were $320 per ounce instead of $330. The dealer would sell gold short on the spot market at $330 per ounce, invest the funds in the risk-free asset, and simultaneously buy gold forward at $320 per ounce. After paying off the loan and collecting the storage costs a year from now, there would be $10 left over *regardless of what the spot price turns out to be at that time.*[6]

The forward-spot price-parity relation does not carry any causal implications. It does not say that the forward price is determined by the spot price and the cost of carry. Rather, the forward and spot prices are jointly determined in the market. If we know one of them, then by the Law of One Price we know what the other must be.

> **Quick Check 4**
>
> Suppose that $r = 0.06$, $S = \$400$, and $s = 0.02$. What must the forward price of gold be? Show how, if it is not, there would be an arbitrage opportunity.

6.1 The "Implied" Cost of Carry

A consequence of the forward-spot price-parity relation for gold is that one cannot extract any additional information about the expected future spot price from the forward price than can be gotten from the spot. In the case of wheat discussed in section 4, we saw that when there is no storage, the forward price contains information about the expected future spot price that is not embodied in the current spot price. Because gold is stored, no such information about expected future prices can be extracted from the forward price.

The only information one can infer from the observed spot and forward prices of gold is the *implied cost of carry,* defined as the spread between the futures and the spot price:

$$\text{Implied Cost of Carry} = F - S$$

It represents the implied marginal carrying cost for an investor who is at the point of indifference between investing in physical gold or in synthetic gold.

---

[6]When a gold dealer sells short gold in the spot market, he in effect borrows it from a customer for whom he is storing it in inventory. In principle, any stored commodity can be sold short in a similar fashion.

From the forward-spot price-parity relation in equation 4, we know that the carrying cost as a fraction of the spot price is the sum of the risk-free interest rate and storage costs:

$$F = S(1 + r + s)$$

$$\frac{F - S}{S} = r + s$$

Thus, by subtracting the observed risk-free interest rate from the implied cost of carry, one can infer the implied cost of storing gold:

$$s = \frac{F - S}{S} - r$$

For example, suppose we observe that the spot price of gold is $300 per ounce, the one-year forward price is $330, and the risk-free interest rate is 8%. What are the implied cost of carry and the implied storage cost?

Implied Cost of Carry $= F - S = \$330 - \$300 = \$30$ per ounce

Implied Storage Cost $= (F - S)/S - r = 0.10 - 0.08 = 0.02$ or 2% per year

Quick Check 5

Suppose the spot price of gold is $300 per ounce and the one-year forward price is $324. What is the implied cost of carrying gold? If the risk-free interest rate is 7% per year, what is the implied storage cost for gold?

7 Financial Futures

We now focus on the prices of *financial futures*—that is, stocks, bonds, and foreign currencies for future delivery. Unlike commodities such as wheat or gold, financial securities have no intrinsic value. They are not consumed, used as inputs to physical production, or held for their own sake. Rather, they represent claims to streams of income in the future.

Securities can be produced and stored at very low cost, and this is reflected in the relation between their spot and futures prices. Indeed, to a first approximation, we can ignore those costs completely in deriving parity relations between spot and forward prices.

Consider a hypothetical stock called S&P, which is a share in a mutual fund that invests in a broadly diversified portfolio of stocks. It reinvests all dividends received and pays no dividends. A forward contract on a share of S&P is the promise to deliver a share at some specified delivery date at a specified delivery price. Let us denote this forward price by F. The party who is long the forward contract agrees to pay F dollars at the delivery date to the party who is short. We denote the stock price on the delivery date by S_1.

Rather than actually delivering the stock, the contract is usually settled in cash. This means that no delivery of stock takes place; only the *difference* between F and S_1 is paid at the contract maturity date. For example, suppose the forward price is $108 per share. Then if the stock price at the delivery date turns out to be $109, the party who is long receives $1 from the party who is short. However, if the spot price turns out to be $107, the party who is long must pay $1 to the party who is short.

Now let us consider the relation between the forward and spot prices of S&P stock. Assume that the spot price of S&P is $100, that the risk-free interest rate is 8% per year, and that the delivery date is one year from now. What must the forward price be?

Note that we can replicate the share of S&P by buying a pure discount bond with face value F and simultaneously taking a long position in a forward contract for a share of S&P.

TABLE 4 Replication of Non-Dividend-Paying Stock Using a Pure Discount Bond and a Stock Forward Contract

Position	Immediate Cash Flow	Cash Flow 1 Year From Now
Buy a share of stock	$-\$100$	S_1
Replicating Portfolio (Synthetic Stock):		
Go long a forward contract on stock	0	$S_1 - F$
Buy a pure discount bond with face value of F	$-F/1.08$	F
Total replicating portfolio	$-F/1.08$	S_1

At the maturity date of the forward contract, we cash in the bond at its face value of F and use the money to buy a share of S&P at the forward price.

Thus, the forward contract plus the pure discount bond constitute a synthetic share of S&P with exactly the same probability distribution of payoffs as S&P stock itself. By the Law of One Price, the two equivalent securities must have the same price.

Table 4 shows the transactions and payoffs involved in replicating the stock with a pure discount bond and a forward contract. Note that the S&P stock and its replicating portfolio have the same payoff a year from now, namely S_1.

Setting the cost of the synthetic stock equal to the cost of the actual stock, we get:

$$S = \frac{F}{1+r} \qquad (5)$$

which says that the spot price equals the present value of the forward price discounted at the risk-free interest rate.

Rearranging equation 5, we find the formula for the forward price, F, in terms of the current spot price, S, and the risk-free interest rate, r:

$$F = S(1+r) = \$100 \times 1.08 = \$108$$

More generally, when the maturity of the forward contract and the pure discount bond are equal to T years, we get the following forward-spot price-parity relation:

$$F = S(1+r)^T \qquad (6)$$

which says that the forward price equals the future value of the spot price compounded at the risk-free interest rate for T years.

This relation is maintained by the force of arbitrage. Let us illustrate by imagining that it is violated. First, suppose that given the risk-free rate and the spot price, the forward price is too high. For example, suppose that $r = 0.08$, $S = \$100$, and the forward price, F, is $109 instead of $108. Thus, the forward price is $1 higher than the parity relation implies.

Provided that there is a competitive market for S&P stock and S&P forward contracts, then there is an arbitrage opportunity. To exploit it, an arbitrageur would buy the stock in the spot market and simultaneously sell it forward. Thus, the arbitrageur would buy S&P stock, finance that purchase by borrowing 100% on margin, and simultaneously hedge it by going short an S&P forward contract. The result of this would be a zero net cash flow at the beginning of the year and a positive net cash inflow of $1 per share at the end of the year. If the quantity of shares involved were 1 million, then the arbitrage profit would be $1 million.

Table 5 summarizes the transactions involved in carrying out this arbitrage. Arbitrageurs would attempt to carry out these transactions in very large amounts. Their buying

TABLE 5 Arbitrage in Stock Futures

Arbitrage Position	Immediate Cash Flow	Cash Flow 1 Year From Now
Sell a forward contract	0	$109 - S_1$
Borrow $100	$100	-108
Buy a share of stock	$-$100	S_1
Net cash flows	-0	$1

and selling activities in the spot and forward markets will cause the forward price to fall and/or the spot price to rise until the equality in equation 6 is restored.

As we saw with gold, the forward-spot price-parity relation does not imply any causal implications. It does not say that the forward price is determined by the spot price and the riskless interest rate. Instead, all three of the variables—F, S, and r—are jointly determined in the market. If we know any two of them, then by the Law of One Price, we know what the third must be.

8 The "Implied" Riskless Rate

Just as one can replicate the stock using the riskless asset and a forward contract, one can replicate a pure discount bond by buying a share of stock and simultaneously taking a short position in a forward contract. We assume that F is $108, S is $100, and T is one year. We can replicate a one-year pure discount bond with a face value of $108 by buying a share of stock for $100 and simultaneously taking a short forward position in a share for delivery in one year at the forward price of $108.

The initial outlay is $100, and the payoff a year from now will be $108 no matter what the spot price of the stock (S_1) turns out to be. Therefore, if you can buy a synthetic one-year pure discount bond with a face value of $108 for a total cost of $100, the implied risk-free interest rate is 8%. Table 6 summarizes the transactions involved.

More generally, the implied risk-free interest rate obtainable by buying the stock and going short the forward contract is

$$\hat{r} = \frac{F - S}{S} \tag{7}$$

TABLE 6 Replication of a Pure Discount Bond Using a Stock and a Forward Contract

Position	Immediate Cash Flow	Cash Flow 1 Year From Now
Buy a T-bill with face value of $108	$-$108/(1 + r)$	$108
Replicating Portfolio (Synthetic T-Bill):		
Buy a share of stock	$-$100	S_1
Go short a forward contract	0	$108 - S_1$
Total replicating portfolio	$-$100	$108

9 The Forward Price Is Not a Forecast of the Future Spot Price

In the case of a stock that pays no dividend and offers a positive risk premium to investors, it is straightforward to show that the forward price is *not* a forecast of the expected future spot price. To see this, assume that the risk premium on S&P stock is 7% per year and the riskless interest rate is 8%. The expected rate of return on S&P is, therefore, 15% per year.

If the current spot price is $100 per share, then the expected spot price one year from now is $115. This is because to earn an expected rate of return of 15% on S&P in the absence of any dividends, the ending spot price must be 15% higher than the beginning spot price:

$$\text{Expected Rate of Return on S\&P} = \frac{\text{Ending Price} - \text{Beginning Price}}{\text{Beginning Price}}$$

$$\bar{r}_{SP} - \frac{\bar{S}_1 - S}{S} = 0.15$$

$$\bar{S}_1 = 1.15S = 1.15 \times 100 = 115$$

But the forward-spot price-parity relation tells us that the forward price of the S&P for delivery in one year must be $108. An investor who buys the synthetic stock (a pure discount

Box 2

Exposing Expectations on Exchanges

During the 2006 World Cup, shares of national teams were traded on on-line exchanges, revealing traders' expectations for the outcome of the World Cup. These shares were denominated in various imaginary and real currencies, depending on the exchange. The higher the perceived probability of a team advancing to the next round, the higher that team's share price. In some cases, shares were redeemed for a preset price or prize determined by the team's performance; in others, the payout depended on how much players put at risk.

Some exchanges skewed prices by offering interim prizes or dividends, and some required traders to engage in active trading and arbitrage to win. Still, most of these markets demonstrated that they were efficient, quickly incorporating news into share prices. Some researchers believe that traded markets reveal participants' expectations and responses to information better than other tools. Unlike opinion polls, these exchanges force people to back their forecasts with investment funds.

Source: Adapted from "Trading World Cup Volatility," *The Economist,* June 6, 2006.

bond plus a long forward position) is expected to earn the same 7% per year risk premium as one who buys the stock itself.

10 Forward-Spot Price-Parity Relation with Cash Payouts

In the previous section, we derived the forward-spot price-parity relation on the assumption that the stock would not pay any cash dividends during the term of the forward contract. Let us consider how the existence of cash dividends causes us to modify the forward-spot price-parity relation for stocks in equation 6.

Suppose that everyone expects the stock to pay a cash dividend of D per share at the end of the year. It is not possible to replicate the payoff from the stock with certainty because the dividend is not known with certainty. But it is possible to determine a forward-spot relation in terms of the expected dividend. The replicating portfolio will now involve buying a pure discount bond with a face value of $F + D$ and going long a forward contract, as shown in Table 7.

Setting the price of the stock equal to the cost of the replicating portfolio, we get:

$$S = \frac{D + F}{(1 + r)}$$
$$F = S(1 + r) - D \tag{8}$$
$$F = S + rS - D$$

The forward price will be greater than the spot price if and only if D is less than rS, or equivalently, if the stock's dividend yield (D/S) is less than the riskless interest rate. Because D is not known with complete certainty, the full force of arbitrage cannot be relied on to maintain the forward-spot price-parity relation. In such cases, we say that there is a *quasi-arbitrage* situation.

> **Quick Check 8**
>
> Compare the forward-spot price-parity relation for gold to the one for stocks. What is the cost of carry for stocks?

TABLE 7 Replication of a Dividend-Paying Stock Using a Pure Discount Bond and a Stock Futures Contract

Position	Immediate Cash Flow	Cash Flow 1 Year From Now
Buy stock	$-S$	$D + S_1$
Replicating Portfolio (Synthetic Stock):		
Go long a futures contract on a share of stock	0	$S_1 - F$
Buy a pure discount bond with face value of $D + F$	$-\dfrac{(D + F)}{(1 + r)}$	$D + F$
Total replicating portfolio	$-\dfrac{(D + F)}{(1 + r)}$	$D + S_1$

11 "Implied" Dividends

We saw in section 8 that for a stock that pays no dividends, one can infer an implied risk-free rate from the spot and forward prices. In the case of a stock that does pay dividends, we can infer an **implied dividend**. By rearranging equation 8 we find that:

$$\bar{D} = S(1 + r) - F$$

Thus, if we know that $S = \$100$, $r = 0.08$, and $F = \$103$, then the implied value for the expected dividend is $5:

$$\bar{D} = 100 \times 1.08 - 103 = 5$$

12 The Foreign-Exchange Parity Relation

Now let us consider the relation between the forward price of a foreign currency and its spot price. Let us take U.S. dollars and yen as the two currencies and express the forward and spot prices in dollars per yen.

The forward-spot price-parity relation involves two riskless interest rates:

$$\frac{F}{(1 + r_\$)} = \frac{S}{(1 + r_¥)} \qquad (9)$$

where F is the forward price of the yen, S is the current spot price, $r_¥$ is the yen interest rate, and $r_\$$ is the dollar interest rate. The maturity of the forward contract and the interest rates is one year.

For example, suppose we know three of the four variables: $S = \$0.01$ per yen, $r_\$ = 0.08$ per year, and $r_¥ = 0.05$ per year. By the Law of One Price, the fourth variable, F, must be $0.0102857 per yen:

$$F = 0.01 \times \frac{1.08}{1.05} = 0.0102857$$

This is because one can replicate a yen-bond using dollar-bonds and a yen-forward contract. This is done by entering a forward contract for ¥1 at a forward price of F and simultaneously buying a dollar bond with a face value of F. The dollar cost today of this synthetic yen-bond is $F/(1 + r_\$)$. Both the yen-bond and the replicating portfolio have a sure payoff of ¥1 a year from now, which will be worth exactly S_1 dollars. Table 8 summarizes this information.

Because they are equivalent securities, by the Law of One Price the current dollar price of the yen-bond must be equal to the current dollar cost of the synthetic yen-bond. We, therefore, have the forward-spot price-parity relation for dollars and yen:

$$\frac{F}{(1 + r_\$)} = \frac{S}{(1 + r_¥)} \qquad (10)$$

The expression on the right side of equation 10 is the current dollar price of a yen-bond (that pays ¥1 with certainty at maturity), and the expression on the left side is the current dollar cost of replicating the yen-bond's payoff with dollar-bonds and yen-forward contracts.

Like the forward-spot price-parity relations for stocks and for bonds, the foreign-exchange parity relation does not carry any causal implications. It simply implies that given any three of the four variables, the fourth is determined by the Law of One Price.

TABLE 8 **Replication of a Yen-Bond Using Dollar-Bonds and a Yen-Forward Contract**

Position	Immediate Cash Flow in \$	Cash Flow 1 Year From Now in \$
Buy a yen-bond	$-S/(1 + r_¥)$	S_1
Replicating Portfolio (Synthetic Yen-Bond):		
A long position in a forward contract on ¥1	0	$S_1 - F$
Buy a dollar bond with face value of F	$-F/(1 + r_\$)$	F
Total replicating portfolio	$-F/(1 + r_\$)$	S_1

Quick Check 9

Suppose that $r_\$ = 0.06$, $r_¥ = 0.03$, and $S = \$0.01$. What must the forward price of a yen be? Show how, if it is not, there would be an arbitrage opportunity.

13 The Role of Expectations in Determining Exchange Rates

A popular theory of the determination of exchange rates is the **expectations hypothesis,** which holds that the forward price of a currency is equal to its expected future spot price.

Applied in the example of the preceding section, if S_1 denotes the spot dollar price of the pound one year from now and $E(S_1)$ is the expected future spot price, then the expectations hypothesis can be expressed as

$$F = E(S_1) \tag{11}$$

To illustrate, Table 9 shows the *Financial Times* listing of spot and forward prices of the British pound at the close of the day's trading in London on June 23, 2006. If the expectations hypothesis is correct, then from the fact that the forward prices increase as the contract maturity lengthens, we can infer that the dollar price of the pound was expected to rise in the future. For example, from the ratio of the 1-year forward price to the current spot price of the pound, $1.8332/1.8193 = 1.00764$, we can infer that the dollar price of the pound was expected to increase over the year by 0.764%.

If equation 11 is valid, then the foreign-exchange parity relation equation (10) tells us that the same information is reflected in the other three variables:

$$F = S(1 + r_\$)/(1 + r_£) = E(S_1) \tag{12}$$

If the expected future price of the pound rises, that causes both the forward price (on the left side of equation 11), and the expression on the left side of equation 12 to rise. In other words, if the expectations hypothesis is true, there are two equally valid ways of using market information to derive an estimate of the future spot price: (1) Look at the forward price, or (2) look at the expression on the left side of equation 12.

Empirical studies of the currency markets do not seem to provide much support for the expectations hypothesis. Furthermore, the theory has the unfortunate feature that if it applies in one currency, it cannot in another, and this follows as a matter of

TABLE 9 Selected Exchange Rates (Closing on June 23, 2006)

Country	Price in U.S.$
United Kingdom (£)	1.8193
1-month forward	1.8204
3-months forward	1.8232
1-year forward	1.8332

Notes: These are London foreign-exchange rates that apply to trading among banks in amounts of $1 million and more, as of the close of the day.
Source: Financial Times Web site, http://www.ft.com/marketdata/spotdollar

mathematics.[7] That is, if equation 11 applies for the dollar price of the pound, then it *cannot* apply for the pound price of the pound. Hence, if it held empirically for dollar-pound, then it *must* fail empirically for pound-dollar. Despite its lack of theoretical robustness across currencies and the lack of empirical support, the expectations hypothesis continues to be cited as a model for determining exchange rate expectations.

Summary

Futures contracts make it possible to separate the decision of whether to physically store a commodity from the decision to have financial exposure to its price changes.

Speculators in futures markets improve the informational content of futures prices and they make futures markets more liquid than they would otherwise be.

The futures price of wheat cannot exceed the spot price by more than the cost of carry:

$$F - S \leq C$$

The forward-spot price-parity relation for gold is that the forward price equals the spot price times one plus the cost of carry:

$$F = (1 + r + s)S$$

where F is the forward price, S is the spot price, r is the riskless interest rate, and s are storage costs. This relation is maintained by the force of arbitrage.

One can infer the implied cost of carry and the implied storage costs from the observed spot and forward prices and the riskless interest rate.

The forward-spot price-parity relation for stocks is that the forward price equals the spot price times 1 plus the riskless rate less the expected cash dividend:

$$F = S(1 + r) - D$$

This relation can, therefore, be used to infer the implied dividend from the observed spot and forward prices and the riskless interest rate.

The forward-spot price-parity relation for the dollar/yen exchange rate involves two riskless interest rates:

$$\frac{F}{(1 + r_\$)} = \frac{S}{(1 + r_¥)}$$

[7]To see this, note that $1/S$ is the spot pound price of the dollar one year from now, and $1/F$ is the forward price of the dollar in terms of pound. If equation 11 applies to pound-dollar as well, then $1/F = E(1/S_1)$. For this and $F = E(S_1)$ to both apply, it must be that $E(1/S_1) = 1/E(S_1)$. But, by a mathematical theorem called Jensen's inequality, this is false because $E(1/S_1) > 1/E(S_1)$.

where F is the forward price of the yen, S is the current spot price, $r_{¥}$ is the yen interest rate, and $r_{\$}$ is the dollar interest rate.

Key Terms

- financial futures
- forward contract
- margin call
- spread
- hedger

- speculators
- forward-spot price-parity relation
- implied dividend
- expectations hypothesis

Answers to Quick Check Questions

Quick Check 1   What would happen in your futures trading account if you take a long position in wheat futures and instead of going down by 7¼ cents per bushel, the futures price went up by that amount?

Answer: You gain 7¼ cents × 5,000 bushels or $362.50 that day, and the broker adds that amount to your account even though you may not have made any trades. The money is transferred from one of the parties who was on the short side of the contract.

Quick Check 2   Suppose you are a distributor of corn and you observe that the spot price is $3 per bushel and the futures price for delivery a month from now is $3.10. If your cost of carrying corn is $0.15 per bushel per month, what should you do?

Answer: You should sell any corn you are storing for delivery a month from now and enter into a long futures contract to take delivery a month from now.

Quick Check 3   When does the forward price provide no additional information about expected future spot prices than can be extracted from the current spot price?

Answer: When there is storage of the commodity, asset, or security and equation 1 holds as an equality.

Quick Check 4   Suppose that $r = 0.06$, $S = \$400$, and $s = 0.02$. What must the forward price of gold be? Show how, if it is not, there would be an arbitrage opportunity.

Answer: The forward price for delivery of gold in one year should be $432 per ounce:

$$F = (1 + r + s)S = 1.08 \times 400 = \$432$$

If the forward price exceeds $432 per ounce, it would pay an arbitrageur to buy gold at the spot price and simultaneously sell it for future delivery at the forward price. If, on the other hand, the forward price was less than $432 per ounce, an arbitrageur would sell gold short in the spot market (i.e., borrow it and sell it immediately), invest the proceeds of the short sale in the riskless asset, and go long the forward contract.

Quick Check 5   Suppose the spot price of gold is $300 per ounce and the one-year forward price is $324. What is the implied cost of carrying gold? If the riskless interest rate is 7% per year, what is the implied storage cost for gold?

Answer:

Implied Cost of Carry $= F - S = \$324 - \$300 = \$24$ per ounce
Implied Storage Cost $= (F - S)/S - r = 0.08 - 0.07 = 0.01$ or 1% per year

Quick Check 6 Suppose the spot price of S&P is $100 and the one-year forward price is $107. What is the implied risk-free rate? Show that if the actual riskless rate were 8% per year, there would be an arbitrage opportunity.

Answer: The implied riskless interest rate obtainable by buying the stock and going short the forward contract is

$$\hat{r} = \frac{F - S}{S} = \frac{107 - 100}{100} = 0.07$$

If the actual riskless rate is 8%, arbitrage profits can be made by selling short the stock at $100, investing the proceeds at the riskless rate of 8%, and taking a long position in the forward contract at a forward price of $107. The riskless arbitrage profit is $1 per share to be received a year from now.

Quick Check 7 Suppose the risk premium on S&P stock is 6% per year instead of 7%. Assuming the riskless rate is still 8% per year, how does this affect the expected future spot price? How does it affect the forward price?

Answer: The expected rate of return on S&P is 14% per year. If the current spot price is $100 per share, then the expected spot price one year from now must be $1 This is because in order to earn an expected rate of return of 14% on S&P in the absence of any dividends, the ending spot price must be 14% higher than the beginning spot price. But the forward-spot price-parity relation tells us that the forward price of the S&P for delivery in one year must still be $108.

Quick Check 8 Compare the forward-spot price-parity relation for gold to the one for stocks. What is the cost of carry for stocks?

Answer: The cost of carry for stocks is the negative of the dividend because the holder of the stock receives the dividend paid during the carrying period.

Quick Check 9 Suppose that $r_\$ = 0.06$, $r_¥ = 0.03$, and $S = \$0.01$. What must the forward price of a yen be? Show how, if it is not, there would be an arbitrage opportunity.

Answer: The forward price must be 0.0102913 yen per dollar:

$$F = 0.01 \times \frac{1.06}{1.03} = 0.0102913$$

If the forward price is too high, then arbitrage profits can be made by borrowing in dollars at 6%, lending in yen at 3%, and hedging the exchange risk at the delivery date by selling the yen for future delivery at the current forward price. If the forward price is too low, then arbitrage profits can be made by borrowing in yen at 3%, lending in dollars at 6%, and hedging the exchange risk at the delivery date by buying yen for future delivery at the current forward price. In either case the arbitrage profit will be the absolute value of the difference between the expressions on the two sides of equation 10.

$$\frac{F}{(1 + r_\$)} = \frac{S}{(1 + r_¥)} \tag{10}$$

The expression on the right of equation 10 is the current dollar price of a yen-bond (that pays ¥1 with certainty at maturity), and the expression on the left is the current dollar cost of replacing the yen-bond's payoff with dollar-bonds and yen-forward contracts.

Questions and Problems

Distinctions Between Forward and Futures Contracts

1. Explain why an investor might take an illiquid position in a forward contract rather than using an exchange-traded futures contract?
2. Explain in detail what is meant by a "speculator taking a short position in Australian dollar futures."

The Economic Function of Futures Markets

3. Suppose you are the manager of a municipal electric company that buys electricity on the wholesale market and distributes it to residential customers and charges by passing on the price of the electricity plus operating costs. Without a fixed-price supply contract, what futures market position could you undertake to hedge the resident's exposure to higher cooling bills this summer if an electricity shortage were to develop?

Relation Between Commodity Spot and Futures Prices

4. Suppose you are a distributor of canola seed and you observe the spot price of canola to be $7.45 per bushel while the futures price for delivery one month from today is $7.60. Assuming a $0.10 per bushel carrying cost, what would you do to hedge your price uncertainty?
5. As a speculator observing the futures price for hogs to be delivered in six months you see a price of $14 per hundred weight while you believe the spot price for hogs will be $15 in six months. Explain what position you should take and how much profit you expect to make. What are the expected cash flows from this position?

Extracting Information from Commodity Futures Prices

6. You are a dealer in kryptonite and are contemplating a trade in a forward contract. You observe that the current spot price per ounce of kryptonite is $180.00, the forward price for delivery of one ounce of kryptonite in one year is $205.20, and annual carrying costs of the metal are 4% of the current spot price.
   a. Can you infer the annual return on a riskless zero-coupon security implied by the Law of One Price?
   b. Can you describe a trading strategy that would generate arbitrage profits for you if the annual return on the riskless security is only 5%? What would your arbitrage profit be, per ounce of kryptonite?

Spot-Futures Price Parity for Gold

7. Infer the spot price of an ounce of gold if you observe the price of one ounce of gold for forward delivery in three months is $435.00, the interest rate on a 91-day Treasury bill is 1%, and the quarterly carrying cost as a percentage of the spot price is 0.2%.
8. Calculate the implicit cost of carrying an ounce of gold and the implied storage cost per ounce of gold if the current spot price of gold per ounce is $425.00, the forward price of an ounce of gold for delivery in 273 days is $460.00, the yield over 91 days on a zero-coupon Treasury bill is 2%, and the term structure of interest rates is flat.

Financial Futures

9. The forward price for a share of stock to be delivered in 182 days is $410.00, whereas the current yield on a 91-day T-bill is 2%. If the term structure of interest rates is flat, what spot price for the stock is implied by the Law of One Price?

10. On your first day of trading in Vietnamese forward contracts, you observe that the share price of Giap Industries is currently 54,000 dong whereas the one-year forward price is 60,000 dong. If the yield on a one-year riskless security is 15%, are arbitrage profits possible in this market? If not, explain why not. If so, devise an appropriate trading strategy.

11. Suppose the current spot price of a riskless zero-coupon bond with one year to maturity is $94.34 per $100 of face value. If a non-dividend-paying stock is currently selling for $37.50 per share, what is implied about its forward price for delivery in one year? Use the forward-spot price-parity relationship.

12. Referring to the information from the previous problem (problem 11) suppose the actual forward price of the stock for delivery in one year is $40. What arbitrage opportunity exists? Demonstrate the cash flows from the strategy.

13. You observe that the one-year forward price of a share of stock in Kramer, Inc., a New York tour-bus company and purveyor of fine clothing, is $45.00 whereas the spot price of a share is $41.00. If the riskless yield on a one-year zero-coupon government bond is 5%:
    a. What is the forward price implied by the Law of One Price?
    b. Can you devise a trading strategy to generate arbitrage profits? How much would you earn per share?

14. The share price of Schleifer and Associates, a financial consultancy in Moscow, is currently 10,000 rubles whereas the forward price for delivery of a share in 182 days is 11,000 rubles. If the yield on a riskless zero-coupon security with term to maturity of 182 days is 15%, infer the expected dividend to be paid by Schleifer and Associates over the next six months.

The Implied Risk-Free Rate

15. Infer the yield on a 273-day, zero-coupon Japanese government security if the spot price of a share of non-dividend-paying stock in Mifune and Associates is 4,750 yen whereas the forward price for delivery of a share in 273 days is 5,000 yen.

The Forward Price Is Not a Forecast of the Spot Price

16. Suppose a risky non-dividend-paying stock is currently priced at $45 per share. If the stock's risk premium is 5% and the riskless rate is 5%, what is the expected spot price of the share one year hence? What does the forward-spot price-parity relation imply about the forward price of the share for delivery one year hence?

Forward-Spot Parity with Cash Payouts

17. Refer to problems 11 and 12. How would your answers change if the stock is expected to pay a $1 dividend at the end of the coming year?

18. Suppose that the Treasury yield curve is flat at an interest rate of 7% per year (compounded semiannually).
    a. What is the spot price of a 30-year Treasury bond with an 8% coupon rate assuming coupons are paid semiannually?
    b. What is the forward price of the bond for delivery six months from now?

19. Continuing the previous problem (problem 18) show that if the forward price is $1 less than the answer found in problem 18, part b, then there is an arbitrage opportunity. Detail the procedure by which you would produce an arbitrage profit and calculate the magnitude of the profit.

Implied Dividends

20. A stock has a spot price of $100; the riskless interest rate is 7% per year (compounded annually), and the expected dividend on the stock is $3, to be received a year from now.

a. What should be the one-year futures price?

b. If the futures price is $ (1 higher than your answer to part a), what might that imply about the expected dividend?

The Foreign-Exchange Parity Relation

21. The spot rate of exchange of yen for Canadian dollars is currently 113 yen per dollar but the one-year forward rate is 110 yen per dollar. Determine the yield on a one-year zero-coupon Canadian government security if the corresponding yield on a Japanese government security is 2.21%.

22. Assume the current spot price of the South African rand is $0.0995 and the one-year forward price is $0.0997. If the riskless annual dollar interest rate is 5%, what is the implied riskless annual rand interest rate?

23. *Challenge Problem:* Suppose that you are planning a trip to England. The trip is a year from now, and you have reserved a hotel room in London at a price of £50 per day. You do not have to pay for the room in advance. The exchange rate is currently $1.50 to the pound sterling.

a. Explain several possible ways that you could completely hedge the exchange rate risk in this situation.

b. Suppose that $r_£ = 0.12$ and $r_\$ = 0.08$. Because S = $1.50, what must the forward price of the pound be?

c. Show that if F is $0.10 higher than in your answer part b, there would be an arbitrage opportunity.

The Role of Expectations in Determining Exchange Rates

24. *Challenge Problem:* Suppose the one-year forward price of the dollar is K49.5 (Slovakian koruna) whereas the spot exchange rate is K46.95. The riskless annual dollar rate of interest is 2.75%. If the expectations hypothesis holds, what is the dollar/koruna spot exchange rate expected to be one year hence?

APPENDIX

Pricing of Swap Contracts

A swap contract consists of two parties exchanging (or "swapping") a series of cash flows at specified intervals over a specified period of time. The swap payments are based on an agreed principal amount (the notional amount). There is no immediate payment of money and, hence, the swap agreement itself provides no new funds to either party.

The pricing of swap contracts is an extension of the principles for pricing forward contracts already covered in this chapter. This is because a swap can always be decomposed into a series of forward contracts.

For example, consider a yen-dollar currency swap. Suppose it is a contract extending over two years, with a notional principal of ¥100 million. At the end of each of the next two years, one of the two counterparties will have to pay the other the difference between the prespecified rate of exchange between dollars and yen and the actual spot rate of exchange at that time multiplied by ¥100 million.

The one- and two-year forward rates of exchange between dollars and yen are observable in the forward market. For example, suppose that the one-year forward price of the yen is $0.01 and the two-year forward price is $0.0104. If instead of a swap the two counterparties entered a series of two forward contracts for delivery of ¥100 million each, we can compute the dollar amounts that would have to be paid in each year in exchange for ¥100 million. In the first year it is $1 million, and in the second it is $1.04 million.

But a currency swap calls for a single swap exchange rate to apply in both years. How can the swap rate be determined?

Assume that the riskless dollar interest rate is 8% per year, and is the same for one- and two-year maturities. Let F be the swap rate in dollars per yen. The swap contract can be seen as the obligation for one of the counterparties to pay $100,000,000F$ dollars this year and next year in return for a prespecified quantity of yen in each of those years.

As we just saw, if the quantities to be paid were set in accordance with the separate one- and two-year forward prices of $0.01 per yen and $0.0104, then the amounts would be $1 million in the first year and $1.04 million in the second year. By the Law of One Price, the present value of those payments discounted at the risk-free rate has to be the same as the present value of the payments under the actual swap agreement calling for a single swap rate of F. Thus, F is found by solving

$$\text{\$1 million}/1.08 + \text{\$1.04 million}/1.08^2 = 100,000,000F(1/1.08 + 1/1.08^2)$$

$$F = \frac{\text{\$1 million}/1.08 + \text{\$1.04 million}/1.08^2}{100,000,000(1/1.08 + 1/1.08^2)}$$

$$F = \$0.010192307 \text{ per yen}$$

Pricing of Swap Contracts

25. In the forward market the one-year and two-year forward prices of the euro are $0.901 and $0.903 respectively. A two-year swap with a notional principle of 1 million euros is priced when the dollar riskless rate is 5% per annum. What is the agreed swap rate?

Suggested Readings

Brown, K. C., and D. J. Smith. *Interest Rate and Currency Swaps: A Tutorial.* Charlottesville, Va.: Institute of Chartered Financial Analysts, 1995.

Hull, J. C. *Options, Futures, and Other Derivatives.* 6th Ed. Upper Saddle River, N.J.: Pearson Prentice-Hall, 2005.

McDonald, R. *Derivatives Markets,* 2nd ed. Boston, MA: Pearson Addison Wesley, 2006.

Pritamani, M., D. Shome, and V. Singal. "Exchange Rate Exposure of Exporting and Importing Firms." *Journal of Applied Corporate Finance* 17, Summer 2005.

Markets for Options and Contingent Claims

From Chapter 15 of *Financial Economics*, 2/e. Zvi Bodie, Robert C. Merton, David L. Cleeton.

Markets for Options and Contingent Claims

OBJECTIVES

- How to use options to modify one's exposure to investment risk.
- To understand the pricing relationships that exist among calls, puts, stocks, and bonds.
- To explain the binomial and Black-Scholes option-pricing models and apply them to the valuation of corporate bonds and other contingent claims.
- To explore the range of financial decisions that can be fruitfully analyzed in terms of options.

CONTENTS

Any contract that gives one of the contracting parties the right to buy or sell something at a prespecified exercise price is an option. There are as many different kinds of option contracts as there are items to buy or sell. Stock options, interest-rate options, foreign-exchange options, and commodity options are traded both on and off organized exchanges all around the world. This chapter explains how these options are used to manage risks and how they are priced.

Options are an example of a broader class of assets called contingent claims. A **contingent claim** is any asset whose future payoff is contingent on (i.e., depends on) the outcome of some uncertain event. For example, corporate bonds are contingent claims because if the issuing corporation goes bankrupt, the bondholders will receive less than the full interest and principal promised by the issuer. This chapter shows how the same methods developed to value options can be applied to the valuation of corporate bonds and other contingent claims.

The most familiar model for the pricing of options is the Black-Scholes model, discovered in the early 1970s. The Chicago Board Options Exchange (CBOE), the first public options exchange, began its operations in April 1973, and by 1975, traders on the CBOE were using the Black-Scholes formula to both price and hedge their option positions. Such a rapid transition from theory to practice on such a large scale was unprecedented in the history of finance.

Since then, option-pricing technology has been applied to the pricing of other contingent claims, and it has played a fundamental role in supporting the creation of new financial products and markets around the globe. A knowledge of option-pricing principles has become essential for the serious student of finance.

We begin this chapter by explaining how options work and how they can be used to create a variety of payoff patterns from an underlying risky asset. We then apply the Law of One Price to derive parity relations among the prices of calls, puts, stocks, and bonds, and we explain the binomial and Black-Scholes option-pricing models. Then we show how corporate debt and equity securities may be described in terms analogous to options and priced accordingly. We conclude the chapter by discussing the range of applications to which contingent-claims pricing technology has been applied.

1 How Options Work

An option is a contract that gives its owner the *right* to buy or to sell some asset at a prespecified price. It differs from a forward contract, which *obliges* the long holder to buy and the short holder to sell.

There is a special terminology associated with options:

- An option to *buy* the specified item at a fixed price is a **call;** an option to *sell* is a **put.**
- The fixed price specified in an option contract is called the option's **strike price** or **exercise price.**
- The date after which an option can no longer be exercised is called its **expiration date** or *maturity date.*
- An **American-type option** can be exercised at any time up to and including the expiration date. A **European-type option** can only be exercised on the expiration date.

Exchange-traded options have standard terms defined by the options exchange. The exchange matches buyers and sellers of options and guarantees payment in the event of default by either party. Options not traded on an exchange are called **over-the-counter options.**

In addition to its type (call or put) and the name of the underlying security, an option is identified by its strike price and its expiration date. For exchange-traded options, these are

TABLE 1 **Listing of Home Depot Option Prices**

Calls				Puts			
Strike	Expiration	Last Sale	Open Interest	Strike	Expiration	Last Sale	Open Interest
32.50	July	4.30	313	32.50	July	0.15	722
35.00		2.40	4635	35.00		0.25	4278
37.50		0.45	8953	37.50		1.45	7136
40.00		0.05	6727	40.00		3.40	842
32.50	Aug	4.60	310	32.50	Aug	0.25	1861
35.00		2.65	8476	35.00		0.65	8462
37.50		1.40	16612	37.50		1.65	17212
40.00		0.30	16364	40.00		3.60	30992

Source: Chicago Board Options Exchange Web site: http://www.cboe.com/DelayedQuote/
Closing Prices Monday, June 26, 2006.
Home Depot (HD).
Underlying Stock Price: 36.64.

determined by the rules of the exchange. Thus, on the Chicago Board Options Exchange (CBOE), a single call-option contract gives its owner the right to buy 100 shares of the underlying stock and is of the American type. Original maturities of CBOE options vary from three months to three years, and they all expire on the third Friday of the month in which they mature.[1] Table 1 shows a list of the prices of Home Depot (HD) stock options traded on the CBOE.

Table 1 lists the closing price of HD stock on Monday, June 26, 2006, at 36.64 per share. In the table itself, the first data row lists a strike price of 32.5 and the expiration month of July. On June 26, the July HD call options had just a bit less than a month left to go before expiration. The entry in the column labeled "Last Sale" gives the price at which the July HD call traded was 4.3, which means $430 per contract. The next column, which is labeled "Open Interest," is the total number of CBOE contracts of that type in existence on June 26. The final two columns give the closing price and open interest for the July 32.5 put option.

The hypothetical value of an option *if it were expiring immediately* is called its **intrinsic value** (or **tangible value**). If the July HD 32.5 call were expiring immediately, how much would it be worth? Because the price of HD stock was 36.64 per share and the option's exercise price is 32.5, the value of the call if exercised immediately would be 4.14 per share of stock. The option's price of 4.3, therefore, exceeds its intrinsic value by 0.16. This difference between an option's price and its intrinsic value is called the option's **time value.**

An American option's time value is greater the longer it has to go before expiration. For example, in Table 1 look at the prices of HD 35 calls that were expiring in July and August. Both had the same intrinsic value of 1.64, but prices of the calls options were 2.40 and 2.65, respectively. Similar patterns hold for HD 35.0 put options.

When an option's intrinsic value is zero, it is said to be **out of the money.** For example, the HD 32.5 put options were out of the money. The HD 32.5 calls, on the other hand, are said to have been **in the money.** Whenever a call is in the money, then the corresponding put is out of the money, and vice versa. An option whose exercise price is equal to the price of the underlying stock is said to be **at the money.**

---

[1]CBOE options with maturities of one year and longer are called LEAPS®, an acronym that stands for longterm equity anticipation securities.

There is an inverse relation between the price of a call and its strike price. For puts, this relationship is reversed. To see this, look at the options in Table 1 that expire in July. As the strike price goes from 32.5 to 40, the prices of the calls go from 4.3 to 0.05, and the prices of the puts go from 0.15 to 3.4.

Quick Check 1

Using Table 1, compute the intrinsic value and the time value of the August HD 37.50 call. Do the same for the put.

1.1 Index Options

In addition to options on individual securities such as HD stock, there are also **index options.** For example, the CBOE offers trading in calls and puts on the S&P 500 stock index under the symbol SPX. SPX options are effectively calls or puts on a hypothetical index fund that invests in a portfolio composed of the stocks that make up the S&P 500 index, each of the 500 companies in proportion to the total value of its shares outstanding.

Table 2 shows a listing of the prices and trading activity for these options on Tuesday, June 26, 2006. SPX options are of the European type and can, therefore, only be exercised at expiration.[2] In addition to the open interest column, the table shows the trading volume during the day.

The SPX contract specifies that if the call option is exercised, the owner of the option will receive a cash payment of $100 times the difference between the index value and the strike price. For example, assume that when the July 1260 call option listed in Table 2 expired on July 24, 2006, the value of the index was 1,275. Upon expiration its owner would have received $1,500, which is:

$$100 \cdot (1,275 - 1,260) = 1,500$$

TABLE 2 Listing of S&P 500 Index Option Prices

		Calls					Puts		
Strike	Expiration	Last Sale	Vol.	Open Interest	Strike	Expiration	Last Sale	Vol.	Open Interest
1245	June	7.00	429	205	1245	June	8.10	127	558
1260		1.90	765	369	1260		16.00	56	7
1275		0.60	2068	840	1275		29.90	0	16
1245	July	19.00	530	3745	1245	July	17.00	153	14001
1260		10.80	1535	20206	1260		24.00	117	19838
1275		5.40	1322	76551	1275		33.60	52	63534
1245	Aug	29.00	3	33	1245	Aug	24.10	50	59
1260		20.00	30	1613	1260		30.00	1	2025
1275		13.00	411	22403	1275		37.00	1	5178

Source: Chicago Board Options Exchange Web site: http://www.cboe.com/DelayedQuote/
1:45 P.M. Tuesday, June 26, 2006.
Underlying Index Value 1244.56.

---

[2]Information about the contract specifications is available at the CBOE's Internet site, http://www.cboe.com/Products/

This process of **cash settlement** differs from what happens in the case of CBOE options on individual stocks. For example, assume Home Depot's stock price is $35, and an owner of an HD call option with a strike price of $32.5 exercises her option. She pays $3,250 and receives 100 shares of HD stock worth $3,500. If the HD call option were settled in cash as in the case of index options, the seller would pay the owner of the call option $250 (i.e., $3,500–$3,250) instead of delivering the shares of HD stock and receiving $3,250 in cash.

> ### Quick Check 2
>
> Suppose you bought an SPX July 1260 call option on June 26, 2006, for the price listed in Table 2. If the value of the index at expiration on July 24, 2006, turned out to be 1,300, what would be your rate of return?

2 Investing with Options

Options make it possible for investors to modify their risk exposure to the underlying assets. The kind of modifications possible can be described using **payoff diagrams** that depict the

---

Box 1 — Derivatives and Risk

Firms generally use the class of financial instruments known as derivatives to hedge against risk, though some traders take a purely speculative interest in derivatives. The most "exotic" forms of these financial assets have come under fire for undermining market stability. But what makes such complex derivatives so dangerous? To answer this question we must begin with the basics.

In general terms, a derivative is any financial asset whose value is based on the value of some other, underlying asset. Some commonly used derivatives are options, futures, and swaps, which are discussed in this chapter. In practice, the possibilities for new forms of derivatives are endless: Think of all the ways to combine futures contracts, options, and payment swaps on various stocks or commodities.

So-called exotic derivatives can be exceedingly complex. Some such instruments require teams of mathematicians and computers simply to discern whether the instrument has gained or lost value after price changes in the underlying asset pool. Critics worry that these derivatives encourage treasurers of public firms to gamble with the property of their shareholders. Such assets are simply too risky to hold, the argument goes. This complaint is ironic: In practice, the power of complex derivatives is that—when used correctly—they allow firms to hedge against increasingly specific types of risk.

One specific subset of these assets is comprised by credit derivatives. A credit derivative is a contract that promises its owner a payoff when a given firm defaults on its debt. In this way, credit derivatives can act as insurance policies. If, for example, a certain trader holds bonds issued by Firm Z, then holding a credit derivative for Firm Z protects the trader should Firm Z find itself unable to pay off debt. This class of derivatives has exploded over the past several years, and credit derivatives are substantially unregulated in the United States.

This has sparked concern among policy makers, who wonder whether such instruments could destabilize markets if, for some reason, there were a string of defaults. Others have noted the degree to which complex derivatives can be used by clever investors to evade taxes: Derivatives can sometimes mask capital gains as short-term losses or other forms of income subject to lower tax rates. The most complex derivatives can, like many financial instruments, be used fraudulently. But it appears that cases of this are rare, and most nonfirm traders of derivatives simply speculate on these financial instruments. Indeed, derivatives are used chiefly by firms to hedge against real economic risk—and they can be useful tools well-suited to this purpose.

Source: Adapted from "Financial WMD?" *The Economist*, January 22, 2004.

FIGURE 1

Call Option Payoff Diagram

Note: The exercise price is 100 for the call.

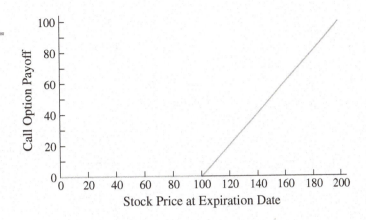

relation between the value of an option (measured on the vertical axis) and the price of the underlying asset (on the horizontal axis). Figure 1 shows the payoffs on the expiration date for a call option on a stock whose current value is 100. The strike price is 100.

At expiration the payoff from the call is max $(S_T - 100, 0)$, where S_T is the stock price on the expiration date of the option. In Figure 1, the value of the call increases one for one with the stock price to the right of 100. But to the left of 100, the call is worthless.

Now consider the payoffs from the put, which is max $(100 - S_T, 0)$. The put payoff diagram is shown in Figure 2. If the stock price at expiration is less than the exercise price, then the value of the put *increases* one for one (to a maximum of 100) as the price takes on lower values. If, on the other hand, the stock price exceeds the exercise price, then the put expires worthless.

In addition to using options to modify risk exposure as just described, buying or selling options is an alternative way for a person who does not own the underlying asset to take a position. Let's see how this works. Because the price of a call option is only a fraction of the price of the underlying stock, investing the same amount of money in calls as in the stock provides leverage. For example, suppose that you are bullish on stocks and have $100,000 to invest. Assume that the riskless interest rate is 5% per year and that the stock pays no dividends. Compare your portfolio's rate of return for three alternative investment strategies over a one-year holding period:

1. Invest all $100,000 in the stock.
2. Invest all $100,000 in calls.
3. Invest $10,000 in calls and the rest in the risk-free asset.

FIGURE 2

Put Option Payoff Diagram

Note: The exercise price is 100 for the put.

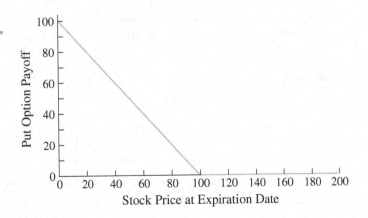

FIGURE 3

Payoff Diagrams for Alternative Bullish Stock Strategies

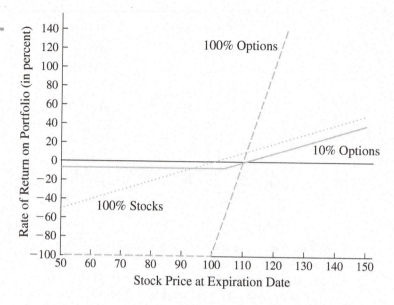

Assume that the price of a share of stock is 100, and the price of a call is 10. This means that under strategy 1 you buy 1,000 shares of stock, and under strategy 2 you buy calls on 10,000 shares. Now consider your payoffs, which are depicted in Figure 3.

Figure 3 plots the stock price along the horizontal axis and your portfolio's rate of return along the vertical axis. For strategy 1—the dotted line in Figure 3—the payoff graph is a straight line with a break-even price of 100. At that index value, your rate of return will be zero. If the price turns out to be higher than 100, your rate of return will increase by 1% for every one-point increase. If the price is lower than 100, your rate of return will fall by 1% for every one-point decrease in stock price.

Under strategy 2—the dashed line in Figure 3—the break-even price is 110. To the right of the kink point, its slope is 10 times the slope of strategy 1. This is because a call provides the same dollar upside potential as a share of stock, and under strategy 2 you have 10 times as many calls as stocks under strategy 1. If, however, the stock price is less than 100, the solid line shows that you lose your entire investment under strategy 2, and your rate of return is –100%.

Your payoff graph for strategy 3 is the kinked solid line in Figure 3. To the right of the strike price of 100 it has the same slope as the 100% stock strategy (the dotted line), but to the left of the stock price it is flat at –5.5%. This is because if the stock price falls, the worst that can happen is that you will lose your $10,000 investment in calls. The $90,000 that you invested in the riskless asset will grow to $94,500 and, therefore, your minimum portfolio rate of return will be –5.5%.[3] Strategy 3, thus, provides an example of how options are used to provide minimum-return-guarantee products.[4]

---

[3]Under strategy 3, the formula for the total rate of return on your portfolio is:

$$\text{Portfolio Rate of Return} = \frac{\text{Value at End of Year} - \text{Value at Beginning of Year}}{\text{Value at Beginning of Year}}$$

$$= \frac{\$90,000(1.05) + 1,000 \max(S_T - 100, 0) - \$100,000}{\$100,000}$$

$$= -0.055 + 0.01 \max(S_T - 100, 0)$$

[4]In an early real-world application, Merton and Scholes developed the first options-strategy mutual fund in the United States, Money Market/Options Investments, Inc., in February 1976. The strategy invested 90% of its assets in money market instruments and 10% in a diversified portfolio of stock call options.

TABLE 3 **Probability Distribution of Returns for Bullish Strategies**

State of Economy	Probability	Riskless	Rate of Return on Portfolio		
			Strategy 1 100% Stocks	Strategy 2 100% Calls	Strategy 3 10% Calls
Boom	0.2	5%	50%	400%	44.5%
Normal	0.6	5%	10%	0	4.5%
Recession	0.2	5%	−30%	−100%	−5.5%

All three of the strategies under consideration are bullish in that you would only choose them if you believe that the stock price is likely to rise. But to determine which of the three is best for you, you must define more precisely your expectations about the stock price and your tolerance for risk.

For example, suppose that you have scenario forecasts for three possible states of the economy as shown in Table 3. You believe there is a probability of 0.2 that there will be a boom and the stock price will rise by 50% during the year, a probability of 0.6 that the economy will be normal and the market will rise by 10%, and a probability of 0.2 that there will be a recession and the stock will fall by 30%.

Table 3 shows the rate of return for each strategy in each scenario. Look at the row corresponding to a boom. Under strategy 1 (100% stocks), your rate of return would be 50%. Under strategy 2 (100% call options), your options will be worth $500,000 at expiration, and your rate of return will be 400%. Under strategy 3 (10% call options), your options would be worth $50,000 and your bonds $94,500, so your rate of return would be:

$$\frac{\$50,000 + \$94,500 - \$100,000}{\$100,000} = 0.445 \text{ or } 44.5\%$$

Let us compare the probability distributions for the three strategies across all three scenarios. Notice that none of the strategies outperforms the others in all three scenarios. Strategy 2 (100% call options) performs best in a boom and worst in the other scenarios. Scenario 3 performs best in a recession and worst in the other scenarios. Scenario 1 performs best in a normal scenario, but comes in second in the other two scenarios.

Thus, none of the strategies dominates the others. Depending on an investor's tolerance for risk, he or she might choose any one of them. Indeed, a very risk-averse investor might rationally prefer the strategy of investing all $100,000 in the risk-free asset to earn 5% for sure.

Quick Check 3

Strategy 4 is to invest $96,000 in the riskless asset and $4,000 in options. What is the minimum guaranteed rate of return? What is the slope of the payoff graph to the right of the exercise price?

---

3 The Put-Call Parity Relation

In the previous section, we saw that a strategy of investing some of your money in the riskless asset and some in a call option can provide a portfolio with a guaranteed minimum value and an upside slope equal to that of investing in the underlying stock. There is another way of creating that same pattern of payoffs: Buy a share of stock and a put option.

Box 2	Short Selling . . . Naked

Short selling is a legal and commonly used tool for investors, but the practice can prove to be disruptive when short sellers are unprepared to deliver on their promises. To sell short, as we have seen, is essentially to bet that a stock will fall: A short seller borrows a share and sells it at the current price, aiming to buy that share back later at a lower price, thus turning a profit. Sometimes, though, investors sell short without first borrowing the shares in question, or without making sure that those shares can, in fact, be borrowed. This practice has been dubbed "naked short selling," and it can create problems in financial markets.

Imagine an investor sells a stock short without first securing the shares she needs. When the contract calls for the investor to deliver the shares she has sold, suppose she is unable to find a source for those shares. That is, it turns out that she has no place from which to borrow: This investor is unable to make good on her promises. Such a situation, popularly called a "fail-to-deliver," can be the source of lawsuits and market instability.

In the United States, regulators have taken an interest in this. The code of the state of Utah now contains a law intended to make naked short selling very unattractive. At the national level, too, the Securities and Exchange Commission has entered the fray. In January 2005 that body created a set of regulations that require investors to track down a source of shares before they can sell short. This was not, however, the end of the story. In the summer of 2006, the Senate Judiciary Committee held hearings to inspect the practice of short selling, and more legislation may appear in the future.

Critics of naked short selling complain that the practice is unfair to the firms whose shares are being sold. The stock prices of those firms, some say, are driven down by excessive short selling. Others object for different reasons. When a trader takes a naked short position and is unable to deliver on her promises, one argument goes, market efficiency is obstructed. Lawsuits clog up the legal system and investors may lose confidence in the market, for fear of being on the losing end of a "fail-to-deliver."

But some naked short selling is actually welcomed by investors. For example, intermediaries in trading environments sometimes take naked short positions to ensure liquidity when demand for a given stock exceeds the supply of shares. In general, short selling is considered a perfectly reasonable tool for stock traders. When such traders sell short without first verifying that they will be able to deliver on their promises, however, obstacles to smoothly running markets—and an onslaught of lawsuits—can result.

Source: Adapted from "Betting on Losers." *The Economist,* June 22, 2006.

Table 4a and Figure 4a describe the payoffs from the two separate components of this "protective put" strategy and show how they add up to an insured position in the stock. The minimum value of this portfolio is the exercise price of 100. Table 4b and Figure 4b describe the payoffs from the two separate components of the bond plus call strategy and show how they add up to an insured position in the stock. Thus, a portfolio consisting of a

TABLE 4a Payoff Structure for Protective Put Strategy

	Value of Position at Maturity Date	
Position	If $S_T < \$100$	If $S_T > \$100$
Stock	S_T	S_T
Put	$\$100 - S_T$	0
Stock plus put	$\$100$	S_T

FIGURE 4a

Payoff Diagram for
Protective Put
Strategy

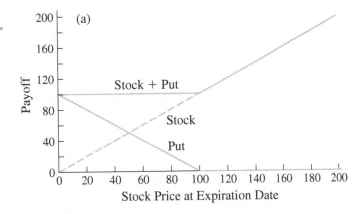

stock plus a European put option (with exercise price E) is equivalent to a pure discount default-free bond (with face value E) plus a European call option (with exercise price E).[5] By the Law of One Price, they must have the same price.

Equation 1 expresses this price relation:

$$S + P = \frac{E}{(1+r)^T} + C \qquad (1)$$

where S is the stock price, E represents the exercise price, P the price of the put, r the riskless interest rate, T the maturity of the option, and C the price of the call.[6]

Equation 1 is known as the **put-call parity relation.** In addition to its use in determining the price of any one of the four securities from the values of the other three, equation 1 can be used as a "recipe" for *synthesizing* any one of the four from the other three. For example, by rearranging equation 1, we find that a call is equivalent to holding a share of the

TABLE 4b **Payoff Structure for a Pure Discount Bond Plus a Call**

Position	Value of Position at Maturity Date	
	If $S_T < \$100$	If $S_T > \$100$
Pure discount bond with face value of $100	$100	$100
Call	0	$S_T - \$100$
Pure discount bond plus call	$100	S_T

[5]This equivalence must be modified for American-type options, which can be exercised prior to the expiration date.

[6]To this point in the discussion, we have assumed that no dividends are paid on the stock during the life of the option. In general, the possibility of dividends complicates the put-call parity relation. However, one case in which adjusting the parity relation is straightforward is if the dividend yield paid per year, d, is known for certain and constant. Then the relation is:

$$S(1-d)^T + P = \frac{E}{(1+r)^T} + C$$

FIGURE 4b

Payoff Diagram for Pure Discount Bond Plus Call

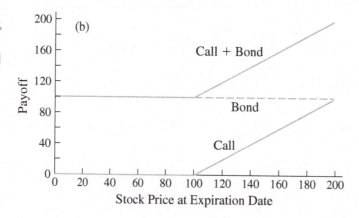

stock, borrowing the present value of the exercise price (i.e., selling short a pure discount default-free bond with face value E), and buying a put:

$$C = S - \frac{E}{(1+r)^T} + P \qquad (2)$$

Equation 2 gives us some insight into the nature of a call option. In effect, it says that the characteristics of a call option can be broken into three components:

1. Buying the stock.
2. Borrowing part of the money to do so (leverage).
3. Buying insurance against downside risk (the put).

Equation 2 can also be regarded as a formula for *converting* a put into a call and vice versa. For example, suppose that the values on the right side of equation 2 are:

$$S = \$100, \ E = \$100, \ T = 1 \ \text{year}, r = 0.08, \ \text{and} \ P = \$10$$

Then the price of the call, C, would have to be $17.41, computed as:

$$C = 100 - 100/1.08 + 10 = 17.41$$

To see why, suppose that C is $18 and that there are no barriers to arbitrage. Then the call's price is too high. It will pay an arbitrageur to sell calls and buy the equivalent of the calls by using a replicating strategy. In other words, sell dear and buy cheap. The outlay on the stock is $100 less $92.59 borrowed. The net outlay on the levered position in the stock is, thus, $7.41. The insurance against downside risk (the put) costs $10, so the total cost of the synthetic call is $17.41. The arbitrageur would sell calls at a price of $18 and pocket the $0.59 difference between the price of the call and the $17.41 cost of synthesizing it. Table 5 shows the transactions involved.

We can gain some additional insight into the nature of the relation among puts, calls, stocks, and bonds by rearranging the terms in equation 2 as follows:

$$C - P = S - \frac{E}{(1+r)^T}$$

In this form, the put-call parity relation implies that:

- If the stock price *equals* the present value of the option's exercise price, then the price of the call equals the price of the put.

TABLE 5   Put-Call Arbitrage

Position	Immediate Cash Flow	Cash Flow at Maturity Date	
		If $S_T < \$100$	If $S_T > \$100$
Sell a call	$18.00	0	$-(S_T - \$100)$
Buy Replicating Portfolio (Synthetic Call)			
Buy a stock	−$100.00	S_T	S_T
Borrow the present value of $100	$92.59	−$100	−$100
Buy a put	−$10.00	$\$100 - S_T$	0
Net cash flows	$0.59	0	0

- If the stock price *exceeds* the present value of the option's exercise price, then the price of the call exceeds the price of the put.
- If the stock price *is less than* the present value of the option's exercise price, then the price of the put exceeds the price of the call.

> **Quick Check 4**
>
> Show how one can synthesize a share of the stock using a put, a call, and a pure discount bond with a face value of E.

4 Volatility and Option Prices

The higher the volatility of a stock's price, the higher the prices of *both* puts *and* calls on that stock. To see why, consider the case in which the stock price can take only one of two values a year from now—either $120 or $80—each with a probability of 0.5.

Low-Volatility Scenario

Now	In 1 Year	
Stock Price	Stock Price	Call Option Payoff
$100	$120	$20
	$80	0
Expected Value:	$100	$10

The expected value of the end-of-year stock price is, therefore, $0.5 \times \$120 + 0.5 \times \$80 = \$100$.

Now consider a call option on the stock with an exercise price of $100 expiring in one year. At expiration, the call will pay either $20 if the stock price is $120, or it will pay nothing if the stock price is $80. The expected payoff on the call is, therefore, $0.5 \times \$20 + 0.5 \times 0 = \$10$.

Suppose the stock becomes more volatile with no change in its expected end-of-year price. For example, suppose the two possible values for the end-of-year stock price are now $200 and 0, each with probability 0.5.

High-Volatility Scenario

Now	In 1 Year	
Stock Price	Stock Price	Call Option Payoff
	$200	$100
$100		
	$0	0
Expected Value:	$100	$50

The expected value of the end-of-year stock price is still $100 (0.5 × $200 + 0.5 × 0), but the volatility is much greater. The expected value of the payoff on the call option, however, is now $50 (0.5 × $100 + 0.5 × 0), higher by $40. Clearly, the price of the call option will increase. Thus, we see that an increase in volatility (holding constant the current price of the stock) causes the expected value of the payoffs on a call option on the stock to increase and, therefore, raises its current price. The same is true with a put.

The same reasoning applies in the more general case of a continuous probability distribution for the underlying stock price. The payoff from an option at expiration cannot be negative. At worst, the option will be worthless and not be exercised. Therefore, the probability distribution for the option's payoff is truncated at zero. This truncation makes the expected payoff on the option an increasing function of the underlying stock's price volatility, holding fixed the expected payoff on the stock.

In summary, an increase in a stock's volatility, holding constant the current price and expected rate of return on the stock, will cause the expected returns on puts and calls on that stock to rise. Consequently, the prices of puts and calls increase with the volatility of the stock. Moreover, the put-call parity relation implies that an increase in stock-price volatility will result in the exact *same* increase in the price of both the call and the corresponding put (i.e., the put with the same maturity and exercise price as the call).

Quick Check 5

Suppose that at a given stock-price volatility, $S = \$100$, $E = \$100$, $T = 1$ year, $r = 0.08$, $C = \$17.41$, and $P = \$10$. Now volatility goes up and the price of the call rises to $20. What must be the new price of the put if S, E, T, and r remain unchanged?

---

5 Two-State (Binomial) Option Pricing

As we saw in equation 2, the put-call parity relation allows us to express the price of a call in terms of the price of the underlying stock, the riskless rate of interest, and the price of the corresponding put. But we would like to have a way of computing the price of a call without knowing the price of the put. To do so, we have to make some assumptions about the probability distribution of future stock prices.

In this section we assume that the stock price can take only one of two possible values at the expiration date of the option. Although this assumption is unrealistic, the *two-state model* forms the basis for a more realistic option-pricing model known as the *binomial model,* which is widely used in practice. The intuitive understanding one can derive from the two-state model also carries over to the Black-Scholes model.

The method is similar to the one we used to derive the put-call parity relation. We construct a synthetic call using only stocks and riskless borrowing. Then by the Law of One Price, we know that the price of the call must equal the cost of the synthetic call that we have constructed.

Consider a one-year call with an exercise price of $100. We assume that the underlying stock price is now $100 and it can either rise or fall by 20% during the year. Thus, at the option expiration date one year from now, the stock price can be either $120 or $80. The riskless interest rate is 5% per year.

The payoffs to the stock and to the call can be described by the following "tree":

Now	In 1 Year	
Stock Price	Stock Price	Call Option Payoff
	$120	$20
$100		
	$80	0

Now compare the call option payoffs to the payoffs on a portfolio consisting of a share of the stock, financed in part by riskless borrowing. Because the collateral for the loan will be the stock itself, the most that the investor can borrow at the riskless rate is the present value of the stock's minimum price a year from now. The minimum price is $80, so the amount borrowed today is $80/1.05 = $76.19. The payoffs on this portfolio depend on the stock price a year from now as follows:

Position	Immediate Cash Flow	Cash Flow at Maturity Date	
		If $S_1 = \$120$	If $S_1 = \$80$
Buy 1 share of stock	−$100.00	$120	$80
Borrow $76.19	+$76.19	−$80	−$80
Total portfolio	−$23.81	$40	0

Now	In 1 Year	
Cost of Portfolio	Stock Price	Portfolio Payoff
	$120	$40
$23.81		
	$80	0

Next, we need to find what fraction of a share of stock is needed to replicate the payoffs from the call option. This fraction of a share of stock is called the option's **hedge ratio**. More generally, an option's hedge ratio in the two-state model is the difference between the

TABLE 6 Creating a Synthetic Call through Replication

Position	Immediate Cash Flow	Cash Flow at Maturity Date	
		If $S_1 = \$120$	If $S_1 = \$80$
Call option		$20	0
	Synthetic Call		
Buy ½ share of stock	−$50.000	$60	$40
Borrow $38.095	$38.095	−$40	−$40
Total portfolio	−$11.905	$20	0

two possible payoffs of the option divided by the difference in the two possible terminal prices of the underlying stock. In our case this is:

$$\text{Hedge Ratio} = \frac{\text{Range of Option Values}}{\text{Range of Stock Values}}$$

$$= \frac{\$20 - 0}{\$120 - \$80} = 0.5$$

Thus, if we were to buy ½ a share of the stock and borrow only $38.095, we would have a synthetic call. The amount to borrow is the maximum amount that can be paid back with interest at the expiration date with complete certainty. Because in our example the worst possible outcome for the half share of stock is a value of $40, the amount to borrow is the present value of $40 discounted at the riskless rate of 5%, which is $38.095.

Table 6 summarizes the payoffs from the call itself and the synthetic call created by this replicating portfolio.

By the Law of One Price, the call and its replicating portfolio (the synthetic call) must have the same price, so the call's price must be:

$$C = 0.5S - \$38.095$$

$$= \$50 - \$38.095$$

$$= \$11.905$$

> **Quick Check 6**
>
> Suppose that the underlying stock is more volatile than in the previous example. It can rise or fall by 30% during the year. Use the two-state model to derive the price of the option.

6 Dynamic Replication and the Binomial Model

The assumption that there are only two possible prices that the stock can have a year from now is clearly unrealistic. To move in the direction of greater realism, therefore, we subdivide the one-year period into two sixth-month periods and assume that the stock price can either go up or down by $10 over each subperiod. Thus, the maximum amount the price can change during the year is $20 up or down. There will now be three possible stock prices at the end of the year ($120, $100, or $80) and the corresponding payoffs for the call option are $20, 0, and 0.

FIGURE 5

Decision Tree for Dynamic Replication of Call Option

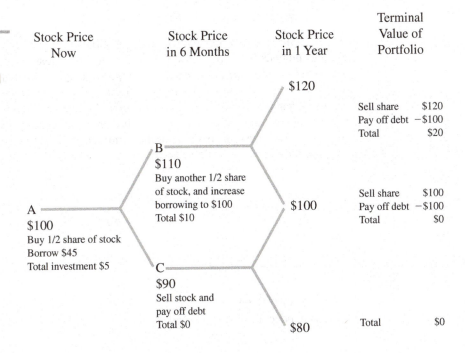

The method now consists of finding a **self-financing investment strategy,** that replicates the call option payoff structure. The strategy is a *dynamic* one that calls for adjusting the number of shares of stock and the amount of borrowing after six months according to the stock price that materializes at that time. Subsequent to the original cash outlay, no additional funds are added or withdrawn by the investor.

At each point in time, the replication strategy boils down to the one we already considered in the two-state model of the previous section. Figure 5 shows what is involved in the form of a **decision tree.**

The stock price starts out at $100 (point *A*). Initially, you buy 1/2 share of stock for $50, borrowing $45. Your net cash outlay is, therefore, $5. At the end of the first sixth-month subperiod, the stock price is either $110 (point *B*) or $90 (point *C*). If you find yourself at point *B*, you borrow $55 more to buy another half share of stock. If, however, you are at point *C*, you sell your half share of stock and pay off your debt of $45 with the proceeds. This strategy produces exactly the same payoffs at the end of the year as does the option.

The strategy is completely self-financing subsequent to the original cash outlay. That is, no additional funds are added or withdrawn prior to the option expiration date by the investor. The conclusion is that because the initial cost of the dynamic self-financing portfolio strategy that replicates the payoffs from the call is $5, by the Law of One Price, $5 must be the call price.

The option-pricing model we have just derived improves on the two-state model. It is called a **binomial option-pricing model.**[7] Greater realism and accuracy can be achieved with this binomial model by subdividing the one-year period into shorter and shorter time intervals. Binomial option-pricing models are widely used in practice. The number of time intervals used depends on the degree of accuracy required in any particular application.

---

[7]For a development of the binomial model, see Cox, Ross, and Rubinstein, "Option Pricing: A Simplified Approach," *Journal of Financial Economics,* 7 (1979), 229–263.

7 The Black-Scholes Model

A more realistic model frequently used by practitioners to price stock options is the **Black-Scholes model.**[8] Its derivation follows a similar line of reasoning to the one we just presented but assumes that one *continuously* adjusts the replicating portfolio over time.

The original Black-Scholes formula for the price of a European call option on stock has five parameters, four of which are directly observable: S, the price of the stock; E, the exercise price; r, the riskless interest rate (the annualized continuously compounded rate on a safe asset with the same maturity as the option); and T, the time to maturity of the option.

The formula is:

$$C = N(d_1)S - N(d_2)Ee^{-rT}$$
$$d_1 = \frac{\ln(S/E) + (r + \sigma^2/2)T}{\sigma\sqrt{T}}$$
$$d_2 = d_1 - \sigma\sqrt{T}$$

$$(4)$$

where:[9]

C = price of the call

S = price of the stock

E = exercise price

r = riskless interest rate (the annualized continuously compounded rate on a safe asset with the same maturity as the option)

T = time to maturity of the option in years

σ = standard deviation of the annualized continuously compounded rate of return on the stock

ln = natural logarithm

e = the base of the natural log function (approximately 2.71828)

$N(d)$ = the probability that a random draw from a standard normal distribution will be less than d

We can derive the formula for the value of a put by substituting for C in the put-call parity condition that $P = C - S + Ee^{-rT}$. The resulting formula for the value of the put is:

$$P = (N(d_1) - 1)S + (1 - N(d_2))Ee^{-rT}$$

In deriving their formula, Black and Scholes assumed that no dividends are paid during the life of the option. The model was generalized by Merton to allow for a constant continuous dividend yield, d.[10] That dividend-adjusted option-pricing formula is:

$$C = N(d_1)Se^{-dT} - N(d_2)Ee^{-rT}$$
$$d_1 = \frac{\ln(S/E) + (r - d + \sigma^2/2)T}{\sigma\sqrt{T}}$$
$$d_2 = d_1 - \sigma\sqrt{T}$$

$$(5)$$

---

[8]Fischer Black, and Myron Scholes, "The Pricing of Options and Other Corporate Liabilities," *Journal of Political Economy,* 81 (May/June 1973).
[9]The continuously compounded rate of return is equal to the natural logarithm of (1 + the rate of return).
[10]Robert C. Merton, "Theory of Rational Option Pricing," *Bell Journal of Management Science,* 4 (Spring 1973).

TABLE 7   Option Price Calculation Table

S	E	r	T	d	σ	Result	
100	100	0.08	0.5	0.03	0.2	C = $6.79	P = $4.35

Note that the expected return on the stock does not explicitly appear in the option-pricing formula. Its effect comes through the stock price: Any change in expectations about the future stock price or in the expected return required on the stock will cause the stock price to change and thereby change the price of the call. But at any *given* stock price, the option price can be derived without knowing the expected return on the stock. Analysts who disagree about the expected return on the stock will nevertheless agree about the right price for the option, *given* the current observed price of the stock.

In the real world, neither volatility (σ) nor the dividend yield (d) are known with certainty, and empirical evidence suggests that both vary stochastically over time. Models that incorporate these stochastic variations have been developed and are used in practice. The dividend-adjusted option pricing formula in Equation 5 is easily computed using an electronic spreadsheet. We have included one in the supplements to this text.

For convenience we organize the information in a tabular form. For example, suppose that we want to compute the price of a six-month call option with a strike price of $100 whose underlying stock price is $100, dividend yield 3% per year, and volatility 0.20. The riskless rate is 8% per year. The inputs and outputs of the option-pricing program are presented in Table 7.

Table 8 summarizes the effects of the six input parameters on the prices of calls and puts as reflected in equation 5.

The table should be interpreted as follows:

- An increase in the price of the underlying stock results in an increase in the price of the call and a decrease in the price of the put.
- An increase in the strike price results in a decrease in the price of the call and an increase in the price of the put.
- An increase in volatility results in an increase in the prices of both the call and the put.
- An increase in the time to expiration results in an increase in the price of the call and an increase in the price of the put.[11]
- An increase in the interest rate results in an increase in the price of the call and a decrease in the price of the put.
- An increase in the dividend yield results in a decrease in the price of the call and an increase in the price of the put.

TABLE 8   Determinants of Option Prices

Increase in	Call	Put
Stock Price, S	Increase	Decrease
Strike Price, E	Decrease	Increase
Volatility, σ	Increase	Increase
Time to Expiration, T	Increase	Increase
Interest Rate, r	Increase	Decrease
Cash Dividends, d	Decrease	Increase

---

[11]This applies only for American-type options.

For the special case in which the price of the underlying stock equals the present value of the strike price (i.e., $S = Ee^{-rT}$), there is a convenient approximation that one can use to calculate option prices:

$$\frac{C}{S} \approx 0.4\sigma\sqrt{T}$$

This approximation is also valid for the price of the put. Thus, if the stock price is $100, the strike price is $108.33, the maturity is one year, the riskless interest rate is 8%, dividend yield zero, and volatility 0.20, then the approximate price of the call and of the put is 0.08 of the stock price or $8.[12]

If we use the exact formula (equation 5) to calculate these option prices, we find that the approximation is not bad:

S	E	r	T	d	σ	Result	
100	108.33	0.08	1	0	0.2	C = $7.97	P = $7.97

Quick Check 7

Suppose that the volatility of the underlying stock is 0.3 instead of 0.2 in the previous example. What is the approximate price of the call?

8 Implied Volatility

Implied volatility is defined as the value of σ that makes the observed market price of the option equal to the value computed using the option-pricing formula. Thus, in the previous example, suppose that we observe the values on the left side of the table (including a price of $7.97 for the call).

S	E	r	T	d	C	σ
100	108.33	0.08	1	0	7.97	?

If we substitute these values into equation 5 and solve for σ, we have found the volatility implied by this option's price. In this case the implied volatility is 0.2.

The CBOE has constructed an implied volatility index for the S&P 100 stock price index to be used as the basis for creating new futures and options contracts on implied volatility itself.[13] This implied volatility index July 2005 has been designed to minimize statistical bias while using information from the prices of eight S&P 100 index options with a maturity of approximately 30 days.

Figure 6 shows the value of the implied volatility index over the period from July 2005 through June 2006. It is evident that the implied volatility of the stock price index has

---

[12]Note that the interest rate does not appear in the approximation formula.
[13]For a detailed description of the construction of the CBOE's VIX index, see R. E. Whaley, "Derivatives on Market Volatility: Hedging Tools Long Overdue," *Journal of Derivatives* (Fall 1993), pp. 80–82. Information on the implied volatility indices and other volatility tools can be found on the CBOE Web site at: http://www.cboe.com/TradTool/

FIGURE 6

Implied Volatility SPX (July 2005–June 2006)

Source: Chicago Board Options Exchange Web site: http://www.cboe.com/ TradTool/

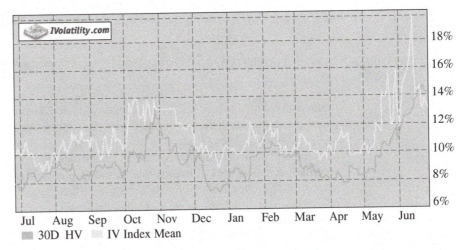

Spx: DAILY 1-YEAR VOLATILITY CHART IV INDEX Mean

30D HV   IV Index Mean

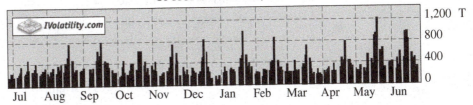

OPTIONS VOLUME, CONTRACTS

Box 3 — The Option for Scandal

An option—the right to buy or sell a financial asset at a given price—can gain or lose value very quickly with changes in the price of that underlying asset. An option to buy a share of stock, for instance, has no *intrinsic value* when such a share has a price below the option's strike price. If, however, the stock in question quickly rises so that the price of a share exceeds the strike price of the option, then the option immediately begins to gain value.

It is clear that options can be lucrative. This is one reason why stock options, in particular, have become one of the most common forms of extrasalary compensation for executives in recent years. These instruments, though, are also easily manipulated: In 2006, a number of American firms were accused of improper conduct with respect to stock options granted to their executives.

Firms embroiled in the ensuing scandal were charged with "backdating" the options they awarded as compensation to their executives. Whenever such a firm noticed a sharp rise in its stock, the charges held, managers would record that the options had been issued just before the stock's sudden increase, with firms setting the strike price below the actual current price of a share. The backdated options held good value from the moment of their actual issuance.

This scandal first came to light after a handful of economists, chief among them Erik Lie of the University of Iowa, noticed a trend in their research on stock options. It was apparent that a preponderance of options had official issue dates that immediately preceded significant rises in the underlying stock. Backdating seemed the most likely explanation. After these findings were published, the authorities took an interest. At least 20 firms were immediately suspected of wrongdoing, among them Mercury Interactive, UnitedHealth Group, and McAfee.

Recall that it only takes as long for the value of an option to change as it does for the value of the underlying asset to change—and we know that stocks, for example, can rise or fall in price dramatically in very short periods of time. This is what can make options so profitable and, evidently, so tempting to manipulate.

Source: Adapted from "Nuclear Options," *The Economist,* June 1, 2006.

fluctuated in an upward direction with a range of nearly 100% from the initial low point in July 2005 to the crest in early June 2006. The lower chart in Figure 6 tracks the corresponding volume of option contracts traded over the same time interval.

9 Contingent Claims Analysis of Corporate Debt and Equity

Contingent claims analysis (CCA) is the application of the replication methodology used in option pricing to the valuation of other securities. In this section we will show how it is used to value the debt and equity of a firm, given information about the firm's total value.

Our hypothetical firm, Debtco, is in the real estate business. It has issued two types of securities: common stock (1 million shares) and zero-coupon bonds with an aggregate face value of $80 million (80,000 bonds each with a face value of $1,000). Debtco's bonds mature one year from now. If we know that the total market value of Debtco is $100 million, what are the separate market values of its stocks and bonds?

Let:

V be the current market value of Debtco's assets ($100 million)

E be the current market value of Debtco's equity

D be the current market value of Debtco's debt

We know that the combined market value of the firm's debt and equity is $100 million:

$$V = D + E = \$100 \text{ million}$$

We want to find the values of each separately: E and D.

Consider the possible payoffs to the holders of Debtco's securities when the bonds mature a year from now. The payoff diagrams are shown in Figures 7 and 8. If the value of the firm's assets exceeds the face value of its debt (i.e., if $V_1 > \$80$ million), the stockholders receive the difference between the two (i.e., $V_1 - \$80$ million). However, if the value of the assets falls short of $80 million, then the company will default on the debt, and the stockholders will get nothing. The bondholders will receive all of the firm's assets.[14]

Figure 7 shows that for values of the firm less than $80 million, the bondholders receive the value of all the assets, and for values greater than $80 million, the bondholders receive $80 million. Figure 8 shows that for values of the firm less than $80 million, the

FIGURE 7

Payoff Diagram for Debtco's Bonds

Note: For values of the firm less than $80 million, the bondholders receive all the firm's assets, and for values greater than $80 million, the bondholders receive $80 million.

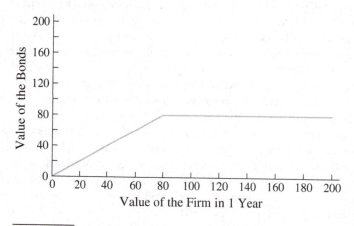

FIGURE 8

Payoff Diagram for Debtco's Stock

Note: For values of the firm less than $80 million, the stockholders receive nothing, and for values greater than $80 million, they receive the value of the firm less $80 million.

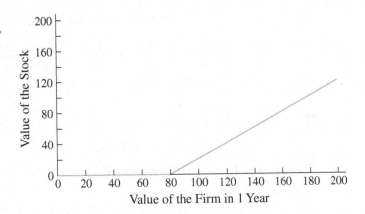

stockholders receive nothing, and for values greater than $80 million, they receive the value of the firm minus $80 million.

Note that the payoff diagram for Debtco's equity is identical to that of a call option in which the underlying asset is the firm itself, and the exercise price is the face value of its debt. We can, therefore, apply formula 5 with a change of symbols. The resulting formula for the value of the firm's equity is:

$$E = N(d_1)V - N(d_2)Be^{-rT}$$
$$d_1 = \frac{\ln(V/B) + (r + \sigma^2/2)T}{\sigma\sqrt{T}}$$
$$d_2 = d_1 - \sigma\sqrt{T}$$

(6)

where

V = value of the firm

E = value of the equity in the firm

B = face value of the pure discount debt

r = riskless interest rate

T = time to maturity of the debt in years

σ = standard deviation of the annualized continuously compounded rate of return on the firm's assets

$\ln$ = natural logarithm

e = the base of the natural log function (approximately 2.71828)

$N(d)$ = the probability that a random draw from a standard normal distribution will be less than d

The value of the debt, D, is by definition equal to $V - E$. The continuously compounded *promised* rate of interest on the debt, R, is therefore equal to:

$$R = \frac{\ln(B/D)}{T}$$

In implementing equation 6, we can use the same programs as we did in pricing options according to equation 5. We simply have to change the interpretation of the inputs and the output. Let the riskless interest rate be 8% per year, and the volatility of the firm's asset value be 0.3. Then Table 7 becomes 7a.

TABLE 7a   Corporate Equity Calculation Table

V	B	r	T	σ	Result
100	80	0.08	1	0.3	E = $28.24

The value of the debt is equal to $V - E$:

$$D = \$100 \text{ million} - \$28.24 \text{ million} = \$71.76 \text{ million}$$

The continuously compounded *promised* rate of interest on the debt, R, is therefore equal to:

$$R = \ln(80/71.76) = 0.1087 \text{ or } 10.87\% \text{ per year}$$

So we find that Debtco's bonds must offer a promised yield to maturity of 10.87% when the riskless interest rate is 8% per year.

Now consider the special case in which the value of the firm's assets equals the present value of the face value of the debt evaluated using the riskless interest rate; that is,

$$PV = 80e^{-0.08}$$

The approximate value of the corporation's equity in this case is:

$$\frac{E}{V} \approx 0.4\sigma\sqrt{T}$$

Let $V = 100$, $B = 108.33$, $\sigma = 0.3$, $T = 1$, and apply the approximation to get:

$$E = \$12 \text{ million}$$

If we apply the exact formula, we find:

V	B	r	T	σ	Result
100	108.33	0.08	1	0.3	E = $11.92

Quick Check 8

What would be the yield to maturity on Debtco's debt in the special case just examined?

10 Credit Guarantees

Guarantees against credit risk pervade the financial system and play an important role in corporate and public finance. Parent corporations routinely guarantee the debt obligations of their subsidiaries. Commercial banks and insurance companies offer guarantees in return for fees on a broad spectrum of financial instruments ranging from traditional letters of credit to interest rate and currency swaps.

The largest providers of financial guarantees are almost surely governments and governmental agencies. Even in the United States, where the prevailing philosophy is one of limited government involvement in the private sector, the federal and local governments provide a wide range of financial guarantees. The most important of these, both economically and politically, is deposit insurance. However, guarantees are also used extensively elsewhere. In the corporate sector, the government has guaranteed the debt of small businesses and on occasion it has done so for very large businesses. The Pension Benefit Guarantee Corporation (PBGC) provides limited insurance of corporate pension plan benefits. Residential mortgages and farm and student loans are examples of noncorporate obligations that the government has guaranteed. The U.S. government has also given guarantees of other sovereigns' debt as a form of foreign aid.

But guarantees are even more pervasive than this list of *explicit* guarantees would suggest. Anytime a loan is made, an *implicit* guarantee of that loan is involved. To see this, consider the fundamental identity, which holds in both a functional and a valuation sense:

$$\text{Risky Loan} + \text{Loan Guarantee} = \text{Default-Free Loan}$$

$$\text{Risky Loan} = \text{Default-Free Loan} - \text{Loan Guarantee}$$

Thus, whenever lenders make dollar-denominated loans to anyone other than the U.S. government, they are implicitly also selling loan guarantees. The lending activity, therefore, consists of two functionally distinct activities: pure default-free lending and the bearing of default risk by the lender.

To see this point more clearly, it will perhaps be helpful to think of the lending activity taking place in two steps: (1) the purchase of a guarantee and (2) the taking of a loan. Suppose that the guarantor and the lender are two distinct entities. In the first step, the borrower buys a guarantee from the guarantor for $10. In the second step, the borrower takes this guarantee to the lender and borrows $100 at a default-free interest rate of 10% per year. The borrower winds up receiving a net amount of ($100 – $10 =) $90 in return for a promise to pay back $110 in a year.

Of course, often the lender and the guarantor are the same entity—for example, a commercial bank—and the borrower simply receives the net $90 from the bank in return for a promise to repay $110 in a year. The promised interest rate on the loan is then stated as 22.22%, that is, ($110 – $90)/$90. This promised rate reflects both the riskless interest rate and the charge for the guarantee. To see that the two are separable activities, note that the holder of the risky debt could buy a third-party guarantee for $10. The holder would then be making a total investment of $90 + $10 = $100 and would receive a sure payment of $110.

The purchase of any real-world loan is, thus, functionally equivalent to the purchase of a pure default-free loan and the simultaneous issue of a guarantee of that loan. In effect, the creditor simultaneously pays for the default-free loan and receives a "rebate" for the guarantee of that loan. The magnitude of the value of the guarantee relative to the value of the default-free loan component varies considerably. A high-grade bond (rated AAA) is almost an all default-free loan with a very small guarantee component. A below-investment-grade or "junk" bond, on the other hand, typically has a large guarantee component.

Guarantees are also involved in other financial contracts besides loans. In swap contracts, for example, guarantees of performance by both parties to the swap agreement are often provided by a third-party financial intermediary. If such a guarantee is not purchased, then each of the parties is providing de facto a guarantee of its counterparty's performance. As nonfinancial firms increasingly use such contracts, their managers need to better understand how to efficiently manage the explicit and implicit guarantees associated with them.

Options theory can be used to analyze the efficient management of such guarantees. Guarantees are like put options. The guarantor must make the promised payment on a financial contract if the issuer fails to do so. The loss to the guarantor is equal to the difference between the promised payment on the guaranteed contract and the price received from the sale of the assets that are available from the issuer as collateral for this obligation.[15] This difference is called the *shortfall*. It is generally assumed that the issuer will only default if the shortfall is nonnegative.

For example, consider the profit from the sale of a single guarantee. If the value of collateral assets, V, exceeds the promised payments, E, the guarantor keeps the premium and pays nothing. But if the value of assets is less than the promised payments, the guarantor must pay the difference, $E - V$. The guarantor's maximum profit is equal to the premium plus interest earned from investing the premium prior to payment of losses or expiration of the guarantee. This maximum profit is diminished by the shortfall or loss experience from issuer defaults. The maximum loss exposure is the promised payment. The guarantor's profit function is, thus, given by $P - \max[0, E - V]$, where P is the premium plus the interest earned from investing it.

10.1 A Hypothetical Example

We return to the example of Debtco Corporation introduced in the previous section. Suppose that a bank, insurance company, or the government undertakes to guarantee the debt of Debtco against default. What is the fair market value of this guarantee? One way to compute its value is to take the difference between the present value of riskless bonds promising the same cash flows as Debtco bonds and the value of Debtco bonds without the guarantee.

Because the riskless interest rate is 0.08 per year continuously compounded, and the debt promises $80 million at maturity a year from now, its value as risk-free debt is

$$PV = 80e^{-0.08} \text{ million} = \$73.849 \text{ million}$$

Because its value without the guarantee is $71.759 million, the value of the guarantee must be the difference:

$$\text{Value of guarantee} = \text{Value with guarantee} - \text{Value without guarantee}$$
$$= \$73.849 \text{ million} - \$71.759 \text{ million}$$
$$= \$2.09 \text{ million}$$

But there is another way to compute the value of the guarantee. The credit guarantee is equivalent to writing a put option on Debtco's assets with a strike price equal to the face value of the debt. The guarantee's value can, therefore, be computed using the adjusted put-option-pricing formula:

$$G = (N(d_1) - 1)V + (1 - N(d_2))Be^{-rT}$$
$$d_1 = \frac{\ln(V/B) + (r + \sigma^2/2)T}{\sigma\sqrt{T}}$$
$$d_2 = d_1 - \sigma\sqrt{T}$$

V	B	r	T	σ	Result
100	80	0.08	1	0.3	$G = \$2.09$

---

[15]We use the term *collateral* to refer to all assets of the liability issuer that the guarantor has recourse to seize, even if they are not formally pledged and segregated.

11 Other Applications of Option-Pricing Methodology

Many financial contracts contain embedded options.[16] Examples from household finance are the prepayment right that gives the homeowner the right to renegotiate the interest rate paid to the lender if rates fall; a car lease that gives the customer the right, but not the obligation, to purchase the car at a prespecified price at the end of the lease.

Many option-pricing applications do not involve financial instruments. The family of such applications is called *real options*. The most developed area for real-option application is investment decisions by firms. However, real-options analysis has also been applied to real estate investment and development decisions. The common element for using option-pricing here is the same as in the preceding examples: The future is uncertain (if it were not, there would be no need to create options because we know now what we will do later), and in an uncertain environment, having the flexibility to decide what to do after some of that uncertainty is resolved definitely has value. Option-pricing theory provides the means for assessing that value.

The major categories of options within project-investment valuations are the option to initiate or expand, the option to abandon or contract, and the option to wait, slow down, or speed up development. There are growth options, which involve creating excess capacity as an option to expand, and research and development as creating the opportunity to produce new products and even new businesses, but not the obligation to do so if they are not economically viable.

An example of an application of the real options technology is in the generation of electric power, the power. A power plant can be constructed to use a single fuel such as oil or natural gas or it can be built to operate on either. The value of that option is the ability to use the least-cost fuel available at each point in time and the cost of that option is manifest in both the higher cost of construction and less efficient energy conversion than with the corresponding specialized equipment.

Another example comes from the entertainment industry and involves the decision about making a sequel to a movie. The choices are either to produce both the original movie and its sequel at the same time, or wait and produce the sequel after the success or failure of the original is known. One does not have to be a movie production expert to guess that the incremental cost of producing the sequel is going to be less if the first path is followed. Although this is done, more typically the latter is chosen, especially with higher-budget films. The economic reason is that the second approach provides the option not to make the sequel (if, e.g., the original is not a success). If the producer knew (almost certainly) that the sequel will be produced, then the option value of waiting for more information is small and the cost of doing the sequel separately is likely to exceed the benefit. Hence, once again, we see that the amount of uncertainty is critical to the decision, and the option-pricing model provides the means for quantifying the cost-benefit trade-off.

The individual's decision as to how much vocational education to acquire can be formulated as an option-valuation problem in which the optimal exercise conditions reflect when to stop training and start working. In the classic labor–leisure trade-off, one whose job provides the flexibility to increase or decrease the number of hours worked and, hence, his or her total compensation, on relatively short notice, has a valuable option relative to those whose available work hours are fixed. Wage, welfare, and pension plan floors that provide for minimum compensation have an optionlike structure.

Health care insurance contains varying degrees of flexibility, a major one being whether the consumer agrees in advance to use only a prespecified set of doctors and hospitals (HMO

---

[16]For extensive references, see R. C. Merton, "Applications of Option-Pricing Theory: Twenty-Five Years Later," *American Economic Review* (June 1998), pp. 323–349, from which this section was drawn.

plan) or retain the right to choose an out-of-plan doctor or hospital. In making the decision on which to take the consumer solves an option-pricing problem as to the value of that flexibility. Much the same structure of valuation occurs in choosing between pay-per-view and flat-fee payment for cable television services.

Option value can be a significant proportion of the total value of government-granted offshore drilling rights and pollution rights. Option-pricing analysis quantifies the government's economic decision whether to build roads in less populated areas depending on whether it has the policy option to abandon rural roads if they are not used enough.

Various legal and tax issues involving policy and behavior have been addressed using the option model. Among them is the valuation of plaintiffs' litigation options, bankruptcy laws including limited-liability provisions, tax delinquency on real estate and other property as an option to abandon or recover the property by paying the arrears, tax evasion, and valuing the tax timing option for the capital-gains tax in a circumstance when only realization of losses and gains on investments triggers a taxable event.

Option theory has proven to be a fruitful framework for the analysis of strategic decisions. Early strategic applications are in energy- and power-generation industries that need long-term planning horizons and have major fixed-cost components on a large scale with considerable uncertainty. Because energy and power generation are fundamental in every economy, this use for derivatives offers mainline applications in both developed and developing countries. Eventually, option models may become standard tools for implementing strategic objectives.

Summary

- Options can be used to modify an investor's exposure to investment risk. By combining the risk-free asset and stock-index call options, an investor can achieve a guaranteed minimum rate of return plus substantial upside participation in the stock market.

- A portfolio consisting of a stock plus a European put option is equivalent to a riskless bond with a face value equal to the option's exercise price plus a European call option. Therefore, by the Law of One Price, we get the *put-call parity relation:*

$$S + P = \frac{E}{(1 + r)^T} + C \tag{1}$$

where S is the stock price, P the price of the put, r the riskless interest rate, T the maturity of the option, and C the price of the call.

- One can create a *synthetic option* from the underlying stock and the riskless asset through a dynamic replication strategy that is self-financing after the initial investment. By the Law of One Price, the option's price is given by the formula:

$$C = N(d_1)Se^{-dT} - N(d_2)Ee^{-rT}$$
$$d_1 = \frac{\ln(S/E) + (r - d + \sigma^2/2)T}{\sigma\sqrt{T}} \tag{5}$$
$$d_2 = d_1 - \sigma\sqrt{T}$$

where:

C = price of the call

S = price of the stock

E = exercise price

r = riskless interest rate (the annualized continuously compounded rate on a safe asset with the same maturity as the option)

T = time to maturity of the option in years

σ = standard deviation of the annualized continuously compounded rate of return on the stock

d = continuous dividend yield on the stock

ln = natural logarithm

e = the base of the natural log function (approximately 2.71828)

$N(d)$ = the probability that a random draw from a standard normal distribution will be less than d

- The same methodology used to price options can be used to value many other contingent claims, including corporate stocks and bonds, loan guarantees, and the real options embedded in investments in research and development and flexible manufacturing technology.

Key Terms

- contingent claim
- call
- put
- strike price
- exercise price
- expiration date
- American-type option
- European-type option
- exchange-traded option
- over-the-counter option
- intrinsic value
- tangible value
- time value
- out of the money

- in the money
- at the money
- index option
- cash settlement
- payoff diagram
- put-call parity relation
- hedge ratio
- self-financing investment strategy
- decision tree
- binomial option-pricing model
- Black-Scholes model
- implied volatility

Answers to Quick Check Questions

Quick Check 1 Using Table 1, compute the intrinsic value and the time value of the August HD 37.50 call. Do the same for the put.

Answer: Because the HD 37.50 August call is currently out of the money, its intrinsic value is zero, and its time value equals its price of 1.40. The August HD 37.50 put has an intrinsic value of $37.50 - 36.64 = 0.86$. Since its price is 1.65, its time value is $1.65 - 0.86 = 0.79$.

Quick Check 2 Suppose you bought an SPX July 1260 call option on June 26, 2006, for the price listed in Table 2. If the value of the index at expiration on July 24, 2006, turned out to be 1,300, what would be your rate of return?

Answer: The rate of return on the investment in the call option is given by:

$$\frac{1,300 - 1,260}{10.80} = 3.704 = 370.4\%$$

Quick Check 3 Strategy 4 is to invest $96,000 in the riskless asset and $4,000 in options. What is the minimum guaranteed rate of return? What is the slope of the payoff graph to the right of the exercise price?

Answer: By investing the $4,000 in one-year call options at a price of $10, you can buy 400 options. Your payoff from the options will be $400 \max(S_T - 100, 0)$. If the options expire worthless, you will have $100,800 from your investment in the riskless asset. This is a rate of return of 0.8% on your $100,000. The slope of the upward-sloping part of the payoff graph is 0.004. The formula for the total rate of return on your portfolio is:

$$\text{Portfolio Rate of Return} = \frac{\text{Value at End of Year} - \text{Value at Beginning of Year}}{\text{Value at Beginning of Year}}$$

$$= \frac{\$96,000(1.05) + 400\max(S_T - 100,0) - \$100,000}{\$100,000}$$

$$= 0.008 + 0.004\max(S_T - 100,0)$$

Payoff Diagram for Stock Market Strategies

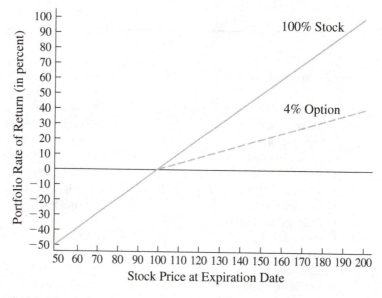

Quick Check 4 Show how one can synthesize a share of the stock using a put, a call, and a pure discount bond with a face value of E.

Answer: By rearranging equation 1 so that the stock price is on the left we get:

$$S = \frac{E}{(l + r)^T} + C - P$$

This implies that one can create a synthetic share of stock by purchasing a pure discount bond with a face value of E, purchasing a call, and selling a put.

Payoff Structure for a Pure Discount Bond Plus a Call Minus a Put

Position	Value of Position at Maturity Date	
	If $S_T < E$	If $S_T > E$
Pure discount bond with face value of E	E	E
Long a call	0	$S_T - E$
Short a put	$S_T - E$	0
Pure discount bond plus call minus put	S_T	S_T

Quick Check 5   Suppose that at a given volatility, $S = \$100$, $E = \$100$, $T = 1$ year, $r = 0.08$, $C = \$17.41$, and $P = \$10$. Now volatility goes up and the price of the call rises to \$20. What must be the new price of the put if S, E, T, and r remain unchanged?

Answer: The price of the put has to increase by exactly the same amount as the price of the call, which in this case is \$2.59. So the put price will be \$12.59.

Quick Check 6   Suppose that the underlying stock is more volatile than in the previous example. It can rise or fall by 30% during the year. Use the two-state model to derive the price of the option.

Answer:

$$\text{Hedge Ratio} = \frac{\text{Range of Option Values}}{\text{Range of Stock Values}} = \frac{\$30 - 0}{\$130 - \$70} = 0.5$$

The amount to borrow is the maximum amount that can be paid back with interest at the expiration date with complete certainty. Because in our example the worst possible outcome for the half share of stock is a value of \$35, the amount to borrow is the present value of \$35 discounted at the riskless rate of 5%, which is \$33.33.

The price of the call equals the cost of the replicating portfolio, which is equal to the hedge ratio times the current stock price minus the amount borrowed. By the Law of One Price this is the price of the call option:

$$\begin{aligned}
C &= 0.5S - \$33.33 \\
&= \$50 - \$33.33 \\
&= \$16.67
\end{aligned}$$

Quick Check 7   Suppose that the volatility of the underlying stock is 0.3 instead of 0.2 in the previous example. What is the approximate price of the call?

Answer: $C = 0.4 \times 0.3 \times \$100 = \$12$

Quick Check 8   What would be the yield to maturity on the corporation's debt in this special case?

Answer: Using the approximate value of \$12 million for the value of the equity,

$$D = \$100 \text{ million} - \$12 \text{ million} = \$88 \text{ million}$$

The continuously compounded promised rate of interest on the debt, R, is therefore equal to:

$$R = \ln(108.33/88) = 0.2078 \text{ of } 20.78\% \text{ per year}$$

Questions and Problems

How Options Work

1. Which has unlimited downside risk, a long or short position in a call option? What about a long or short position in a put option? Explain your answers.
2. Describe the key defining characteristics of a put or call option on any asset.
3. Graph the payoff for a European put option selling for a premium of \$5 with exercise price (E) of \$50, written on a stock with value S, when:
   a. You hold a long position (i.e., you buy the put)
   b. You hold a short position (i.e., you sell the put)

4. Graph the payoff to a portfolio of one European call option and one European put option, each with the same expiration date and each with exercise price (E) of $25, when both options are on a stock with value S. What is the portfolio payoff if the stock price is $40 at expiration? What if the price is $20?

Investing with Options

5. If an investor paid a $4.75 premium to obtain a long position in a put option with an exercise price of $47, the underlying asset break-even point corresponds to what price? Diagram the position.

6. The risk-free one-year rate of interest is 4%, and the Globalex stock index is at 100. The price of one-year European call options on the Globalex stock index with an exercise price of 104 is 8% of the current price of the index. Assume that the expected dividend yield on the stocks in the Globalex index is zero. You have $1 million to invest for the next year. You plan to invest enough of your money in one-year T-bills to ensure that you will at least get back your original $1 million, and you will use the rest of your money to buy Globalex call options. If you think that there is a probability of 0.5 that the Globalex index a year from now will be up 12%, a probability of 0.25 that it will be up 40%, and a probability of 0.25 that it will be down 20%, what is the probability distribution of your portfolio rate of return?

The Put-Call Parity Relation

7. Given the following variables: $S = \$55$, $E = \$75$, $T = 1$ year, $r = 5\%$, and $P = \$20$; if the call option is selling for $10 ($C = \$10$), what arbitrage opportunity exists? Outline the strategy and the profit to be realized.

8. Using the put-call parity relation:
   a. Show how one can replicate a one-year pure discount bond with a face value of $100 using a share of stock, a put and a call.
   b. Suppose that $E = \$100$, $S = \$100$, $P = \$10$, and $C = \$15$. What must be the one-year interest rate?
   c. Show that if the one-year risk-free interest rate is lower than in your answer to part b, there would be an arbitrage opportunity.

9. A 90-day European call option on a share of the stock of Wimendo is currently trading at 20 euros whereas the current price of the share itself is 24 euros. Ninety-day zero-coupon securities issued by the government of France are selling for 98.55 euros per 100 euros of face value. Infer the price of a 90-day European put option on this stock if both the call and put have a common exercise price of 20 euros.

10. Gordon Gekko has assembled a portfolio consisting of ten 90-day U.S. Treasury bills, each having a face value of $1,000 and a current price of $990.10, and 200 90-day European call options, each written on a share of Paramount stock and having an exercise price of $50. Gekko is offering to trade you this portfolio for 300 shares of Paramount stock, which is currently valued at $215 a share. If 90-day European put options on Paramount stock with a $50 exercise price are currently valued at $25,
    a. Infer the value of the calls in Gekko's portfolio.
    b. Determine whether you should accept Gekko's offer.

11. The stock of Kakkonen, Ltd., a hot tuna distributor, currently lists for $50 a share, whereas one-year European call options on this stock, with an exercise price of $20, sell for $40 and European put options with a similar expiration date and exercise price sell for $8.457.
    a. Infer the yield on a one-year, zero-coupon U.S. government bond sold today.
    b. If this yield is actually at 9%, construct a profitable trade to exploit the potential for arbitrage.

Volatility and Option Prices

12. Which has more value, (1) a portfolio composed of call options on ten different stocks or (2) a single call option on a portfolio composed of the same ten stocks? Assume the exercise price of (2) is equal to the sum of the exercise prices of the call options in (1) and all option expiration dates are identical. Explain you answer.

Two-State (Binomial) Option Pricing

13. The share value of Drummond, Griffin and McNabb, a New Orleans publishing house, is currently trading at $100 but is expected, 90 days from today, to rise to $150 or to decline to $50, depending on critical reviews of its new biography of Ezra Pound. Assuming the risk-free interest rate over the coming 90-day period is 1%, can you value a European call option written on a share of DGM stock if the option carries an exercise price of $85? What is the hedge ratio?

14. *Challenge Problem:* Let *s* be the fixed percentage change by which the stock price rises or falls over a given period. Derive the formula for the price of a put option using a one-period two-state model. Referring to the previous problem (problem 13), use the model to price a put option on DGM with the same maturity and exercise price as the call option. Use the call-put parity to verify the answers for the values of the call and the put.

Dynamic Replication and the Binomial Model

15. Using the binomial call option model to find the current value of a call option with a $40 exercise price on a stock currently priced at $50. Assume the option expires at the end of two periods, the riskless interest rate is 5% per period and the share price will rise or fall by 10% per period. What are the hedge ratios?

16. *Challenge Problem:* In the particular case in the previous problem (problem 15) the option is so deep in the money relative to the limited price movement possible over the remaining time to maturity that we are sure the option will be exercised at expiration. In this case the current value of the call option has a simple expression in terms of three variables: the current underlying stock price (S), the exercise price (E), and the riskless rate of interest (r). Please formulate the expression, explain it and use it to verify the call option price found in the previous problem.

The Black-Scholes Model

17. Using the Black-Scholes model, find the premium on a call option with an exercise price of $35 on a share currently priced at $40. Assume the riskless rate of 10% per annum and the option has six months to expiration. The risk of the stock is measured by a value of 0.25. Decompose the premium into intrinsic value and time value.

18. Use the Black-Scholes formula to find the price of a 3-month European call option on a non-dividend-paying stock with a current price of $50. Assume the exercise price is $51, the continuously compounded risk-free interest rate is 8% per year, and is 0.4.
    a. What is the composition of the initial replicating portfolio for this call option?
    b. Use the put-call parity relation to find the Black-Scholes formula for the price of the corresponding put option.

19. As a financial analyst at Yew and Associates, a Singaporean investment house, you are asked by a client if she should purchase European call options on Rattan, Ltd. stock, which are currently selling in U.S. dollars for $30. These options have an exercise price of $50. Rattan stock currently exhibits a share price of $55, and the estimated rate of return variance of the stock is 0.04. If these options expire in 25 days and the risk-free interest rate over that period is 5% per year, what do you advise your client to do?

Implied Volatility

20. Use the Black-Scholes model to infer the volatility of the returns on the underlying share of stock paying no cash dividend. Assume the following parameters: $S = 90$, $E = 100$, $r = 10\%$, $T = \frac{1}{2}$. What is σ? If the call option premium is 3.05? What if the premium is 5.52?

Contingent Claims Analysis of Corporate Debt and Equity

21. *Challenge Problem:* Five years ago you purchased at face value a newly issued Zurich Insurance Corporation fixed-rate bond with a 5% annual coupon and a six-year maturity. The bond was structured with a put feature that allows you to exercise the option at a strike price of 98 one year before maturity, that is, you have the option to sell the bond back to ZIC at the strike price. Currently the one-year yields on short-term bonds with similar credit risks are 8% and if you exercised the option you could take the proceeds and invest in the short-term bonds. Explain whether you should exercise the option (i.e., sell the bond back to the company at 98 and invest the money for a year at 8%), as opposed to keeping the bond until maturity. Given your decision, how would you calculate the effective annual rate of return you have earned on your six-year investment? How would you calculate the effective annual cost of funds paid by ZIC to finance its borrowings over the six-year period? A cash-flow diagram for ZIC's borrowings and option dealings would be in order.

22. Suppose Notaboek Tablets Company has a current market value balance sheet with $250 million. Suppose the highly leveraged company has its entire debt financed with a single issue of zero-coupon bonds with aggregate face value of $240 million. These bonds mature in one year. Use the Black-Scholes model to calculate the aggregate market value of the firm's equity if the riskless interest rate is 8% and the standard deviation of the rate of return on the firm's assets is 10%.

23. Referring to the previous problem (problem 22), suppose the company is stunned to learn that the government has just canceled a major supply contract. This immediately decreases the market value of Notaboek's assets whereas also increasing the standard deviation of the rate of return on the firm's assets. How do you expect this to impact on the equity value of the firm?

24. Suppose Wally's World is a small real estate developer with a total market value of assets equal to $100,000. The assets are financed with a commercial paper issue (short-term zero-coupon bonds) paying a face value of $50,000 at maturity in 90 days. An appraisal of Wally's real estate portfolio estimates the assets will be worth $170,000 if real estate zoning changes are granted in 90 days or only $45,000 if the changes are not approved. In effect Wally's shareholders possess a 90-day European call option on the firm's assets with an exercise price equal to the face value of the debt. Assume the riskless 90-day interest rate is 2.5%. Using the two-state option pricing model value the firm's equity.

Credit Guarantees

25. Given the information from the previous problem (problem 24), what is the market price of a payment guarantee to the Wally's World commercial paper holders?

Suggested Readings

Black, F., and M. S. Scholes. "The Pricing of Options and Corporate Liabilities." *Journal of Political Economy* 81, May–June 1973.

Finnerty, J. "Extending the Black-Scholes-Merton Model to Value Employee Stock Options." *Journal of Applied Finance* 15, Fall/Winter 2005.

Merton, R. C. "Theory of Rational Option Pricing." *Bell Journal of Economics and Management Science* 4, Spring 1973.

———— "An Analytic Derivation of the Cost of Loan Guarantees and Deposit Insurance: An Application of Modern Option Pricing Theory." *Journal of Banking and Finance* 1, June 1977.

———— "On the Pricing of Contingent Claims and the Modigliani-Miller Theorem." *Journal of Financial Economics* 5, November 1977.

———— "Applications of Option-Pricing Theory: Twenty-Five Years Later." *Les Prix Nobel 1997.* Stockholm: Nobel Foundation. Rpt. in *American Economic Review,* June 1998.

Scholes, M. S. "Derivatives in a Dynamic Environment." *Les Prix Nobel 1997.* Stockholm: Nobel Foundation. Rpt. in *American Economic Review,* June 1998.

Financial Structure
of the Firm

OBJECTIVES

- To understand how a firm can create value through its financing decisions.
- To show how to take account of a firm's financing mix in evaluating investment decisions.

CONTENTS

From Chapter 16 of *Financial Economics*, 2/e. Zvi Bodie, Robert C. Merton, David L. Cleeton.
Copyright © 2008 by Pearson Prentice Hall. All rights reserved.

This chapter deals with decisions regarding a firm's capital structure, that is, its mix of debt, equity, and other financing instruments. The central question is how to determine an *optimal* capital structure for the firm assuming that the objective is to maximize the wealth of its existing shareholders. In capital structure decisions the unit of analysis is the firm *as a whole*.

The starting point for analyzing corporate capital structure is a frictionless financial environment, defined as one in which there are no taxes or transaction costs, and contracts are costless to make and enforce. In such an environment the value of the firm is not affected by its financing mix and, therefore, the wealth of existing shareholders cannot be increased by policies that change only the firm's capital structure, such as borrowing to repurchase stock or issuing new stock to retire debt.

In the real world, however, there are many different frictions that make capital structure matter very much. Because contract law, taxes, and regulations differ from place to place and change over time, we will find that there is no single optimal financing mix that applies to all firms. Rather, finding the optimal capital structure for a corporation involves making trade-offs that depend on the particular legal and tax environment in which the corporation finds itself.

The chapter begins with an overview of the major types of financing available to firms. It then presents the reasons why in a frictionless economic environment the total value of a firm is determined only by the earning power of its assets and is not affected by its capital structure. Then the chapter considers the most important frictions that exist in the real world of finance and how they influence a firm's capital structure. Finally, we show how to take account of a firm's capital structure in evaluating investment decisions, such as whether to expand the size of the business.

1 Internal versus External Financing

In analyzing capital structure decisions, it is important to distinguish between *internal* and *external* sources of funds. **Internal financing** arises from the operations of the firm. It includes sources such as retained earnings, accrued wages, or accounts payable. For example, if a firm earns profits and reinvests them in new plant and equipment, this is internal financing. **External financing** occurs whenever the corporation's managers must raise funds from outside lenders or investors. If a corporation issues bonds or stocks to finance the purchase of new plant and equipment, it is external financing.

The decision processes that take place within a corporation are usually different for internal and external financings. For a corporation that is well established and not undertaking any major expansions that would require extraordinarily large amounts of funds, financing decisions are routine and almost automatic. Financing policy consists of deciding on a dividend policy (e.g., to regularly pay out one-third of its earnings as cash dividends to shareholders) and maintaining a line of credit with a bank. The amount of managerial time and effort required to make these internal financing decisions and the degree of scrutiny of planned expenditures are usually less than for external financing.

If a corporation raises funds from external sources, as it might if it needs to finance a major expansion, the process is more complicated and time consuming. In general, outside providers of funds are likely to want to see detailed plans for the use of the funds and will want to be convinced that the investment project will produce sufficient future cash to justify the expenditure. They will scrutinize the plans and are likely to be more skeptical about the prospects for success than the corporation's own managers. External financing, therefore, subjects the corporation's plans more directly to the discipline of the capital market than internal financing does.

2 Equity Financing

The defining feature of equity financing is that equity is a claim to the residual that is left over after all debts have been paid. There are three major types of equity claims: *common stock, stock options,* and *preferred stock.* Common stocks are also called *shares,* so when we refer to the corporation's shareholders, we mean the holders of its common stock. Common stock confers on its holder the **residual claim** to the corporation's assets. In other words, after all other parties with a claim on the corporation have been paid, whatever is left goes to the holders of the common stock. Each share of stock is entitled to a *pro rata* share of the residual assets.

The managers of the corporation owe their primary allegiance to the shareholders. Indeed, in many legal jurisdictions, managers and boards of directors can be held liable for failure to fulfill their fiduciary responsibilities to the shareholders.

Often there is more than one class of common stock. Classes of common stock can differ in terms of their voting rights and the ability of the holder to sell them to other parties. For example, some corporations issue Class A common stock that has voting rights and Class B common stock that does not. Restricted stock is often issued to the founders of a corporation, and it usually constrains them not to sell their shares for a certain number of years. Stock options give their holders the right to buy common stock at a fixed exercise price in the future. Thus, suppose a firm with assets worth $100 million has only two types of claims outstanding—10 million shares of common stock, and 10 million stock options expiring a year from now with an exercise price of $10 per share. Because the holders of the options can convert them into common stock by paying $10 per share, they share ownership of the firm with the holders of the common stock. Often managers and other employees of a corporation will receive part of their compensation in the form of stock options. This is especially true in the United States in the start-up phase of a business.

Preferred stocks differ from common stock in that they carry a specified dividend that must be paid before the firm can pay any dividends to the holders of the common stock. It is in this sense that they are *preferred* over common stocks. However, preferred stocks receive only their promised dividends and do not get to share in the residual value of the firm's assets with the holders of the common stock. Failure to pay preferred dividends does not trigger a default.

3 Debt Financing

Corporate debt is a contractual obligation on the part of the corporation to make promised future payments in return for the resources provided to it. Debt financing in its broadest sense includes loans and debt securities, such as bonds and mortgages, as well as other promises of future payment by the corporation, such as accounts payable, leases, and pensions. For many corporations, long-term lease and pension liabilities may be much larger than the amount of debt in the form of loans, bonds, and mortgages.

Box 1	Leveraged Finance

Highly leveraged deals used to come with highly scrutinized restrictions and covenants from bank lenders; nowadays they are so commonplace that no one even raises an eyebrow. Lenders not only want rates that are proportionate to the risk but also the ability to monitor the company and control the risks. Protective covenants usually came in two forms. In one, a company was limited to weakening its balance sheet voluntarily, through dividends or acquisitions. In the other, the company was carefully monitored and the switch could be pulled at any time by the lenders when a collapse looked likely.

It seems that nowadays, with the increased flow of leverage buy-outs, covenants are becoming much less common instead of more so. This is likely due to the changes in loan and debt structures rather than a change in risk aversion: As bank loans became traded in the secondary markets like bonds, the risks are constantly being shuffled, bought up, and redistributed so that the lenders share much less of the risk burden. The presence of collateralized debt obligations and other structured finance products enable the spreading out of the risk from lenders to other buyers in the market. As a result, lenders are much less interested in allocating their attention to meticulously crafted covenants and careful monitoring than when the debt was on their own books.

Source: Adapted from "Going Naked," *The Economist,* April 20, 2006.

In the next three sections we describe three important forms of corporate debt not discussed previously: secured debt, long-term leases, and pension liabilities.

3.1 Secured Debt

When a corporation borrows money, it promises to make a series of payments in the future. In some cases, the corporation pledges a particular asset as security for that promise. The asset pledged as security is called **collateral** and the debt is called *secured.*

Collateralized borrowing by corporations is similar to an individual taking a mortgage loan to buy a house. The house serves as collateral for the loan. If the homeowner defaults, the lender is paid from the proceeds of the sale of the house. If there is any money left over, it reverts to the homeowner. However, if the proceeds from the sale of the house are not sufficient to pay off the balance of the mortgage loan, the lender can try to recoup the rest from the homeowner's other assets.

When a borrowing corporation secures a loan by designating specific assets as collateral, the secured lender gets first priority on those assets in the event of nonpayment. For example, an airline might borrow money to finance the purchase of airplanes and pledge the airplanes as collateral for the loan. If the airline subsequently goes bankrupt before the secured loan is completely paid off, the secured lenders are paid out of the proceeds from the sale of the airplanes. Lenders who made unsecured loans to the airline may not get paid anything.

Quick Check 3

Would you expect the interest rate on a secured loan to be higher or lower than the rate on an otherwise identical unsecured loan? Why?

3.2 Long-Term Leases

Leasing an asset for a period of time that covers much of the asset's useful life is similar to buying the asset and financing the purchase with debt secured by the leased asset.

TABLE 1   Market-Value Balance Sheets of Airbond and Airlease Corporations

a. Airbond Corporation

Assets		Liabilities and Shareholders' Equity	
Fleet of airplanes	$750 million	30-year bonds	$750 million
Other assets	$250 million	Equity	$250 million
Total	$1 billion	Total	$1 billion

b. Airlease Corporation

Assets		Liabilities and Shareholders' Equity	
Fleet of airplanes	$750 million	30-year lease	$750 million
Other assets	$250 million	Equity	$250 million
Total	$1 billion	Total	$1 billion

For example, suppose an airline signs a contract to lease an airplane for 30 years. The airline gets the exclusive use of the plane in return for the promise to make fixed lease payments each year. Alternatively, the airline might buy the plane and issue 30-year bonds secured by the airplanes to raise the money needed to make the purchase.

Table 1 compares the market-value balance sheets for two hypothetical airlines: Airbond and Airlease. In both cases the main corporate asset is a fleet of airplanes with a market value of $750 million. Both companies have equity with a market value of $250 million and debt of $750 million. The difference between the companies is that for Airbond Corporation the debt takes the form of 30-year secured bonds and for Airlease it takes the form of a 30-year lease.

The main difference between the secured bonds and the lease as a form of debt financing is in who bears the risk associated with the residual market value of the leased asset at the end of the term of the lease.[1] Because Airbond Corporation has bought its planes, it bears this risk. In Airlease's case, however, it is the *lessor*—the firm that has leased the plane to Airlease Corporation—that bears this residual-value risk.

Quick Check 4

Should a long-term lease be considered debt financing or equity financing?

3.3 Pension Liabilities

Pension plans are classified into two types: defined contribution and defined benefit. In a *defined-contribution* pension plan, each employee has an account into which the employer and usually the employee too make regular contributions. At retirement, the employee receives a benefit whose size depends on the accumulated value of the funds in the retirement account.

---

[1]There are possibly tax and accounting differences, depending on the type of lease and its term.

In a *defined-benefit* pension plan, the employee's pension benefit is determined by a formula that takes into account years of service for the employer and, in most cases, wages or salary. A typical benefit formula would be 1% of average preretirement salary for each year of service. For corporations with defined-benefit pension plans, promises to pay future pension benefits to employees are a significant part of the firm's total long-term liabilities, and differences across countries in corporate pension-funding practices produce different patterns of corporate capital structure. For example, in the United States and the United Kingdom the law requires firms to establish a separate pension trust with a pool of assets sufficient to pay those promised benefits. This is called funding the pension plan. The pension liabilities are, therefore, a form of corporate debt secured by the pension assets as collateral.

However, in many countries pension liabilities are not funded in this way. In Germany, for example, corporations do not set aside a separate pool of assets to serve as collateral for their pension liabilities. The obligation to pay pension benefits is, therefore, an *unsecured debt* of the corporation.[2]

To clarify, consider Table 2, which contrasts the economic balance sheets of AmeriPens Corporation and DeutschePens Corporation.

AmeriPens has a fully funded pension plan, which means that the market value of the pension assets ($400 million) equals the present value of its pension liability. The pension assets consist of securities (stocks, bonds, mortgages, etc.) issued by other entities such as businesses, governments, and individuals. AmeriPens has also issued bonds with a market value of $400 million. Its shareholders' equity is worth $600 million.

Like AmeriPens, DeutschePens Corporation has operating assets worth $1 billion, a pension liability of $400 million, and shareholders' equity worth $600 million.

TABLE 2 Balance Sheets of AmeriPens and DeutschePens Corporations

a. AmeriPens Balance Sheet

Assets		Liabilities and Shareholders' Equity	
Operating assets: plant, equipment, etc.	$1 billion	Bonds	$400 million
		Pension liability	
Pension assets: stocks, bonds, etc.	$400 billion	Shareholders' equity	$400 million
Total	$1.4 billion	Total	$1.4 billion
	$600 million		

b. DeutschePens Balance Sheet

Assets		Liabilities and Shareholders' Equity	
Operating assets: plant, equipment, etc.	$1 billion	Pension liability	$400 million
		Shareholders' equity	$600 million
Total	$1 billion	Total	$1 billion

[2]Corporate accounting rules in Germany do require the corporation to show the present value of its pension obligations on its balance sheet as a form of corporate indebtedness.

DeutschePens, however, has no separate pool of securities serving as collateral securing its pension liability. Its pension plan is, therefore, said to be *unfunded*.

Quick Check 5

Suppose AmeriPens Corporation's pension assets were worth only $300 million. If its pension liability still had a present value of $400 million, what would be its shareholders' equity?

4 The Irrelevance of Capital Structure in a Frictionless Environment

We have seen that there is a wide array of possible corporate capital structures. We now turn our attention to the factors that determine why a firm chooses one rather than another.

To understand how a firm's management can enhance shareholder wealth through its capital structure decisions, a good way to start is by clarifying what does *not* matter. Modigliani and Miller (M&M) showed that in an economist's idealized world of frictionless markets the total market value of all the securities issued by a firm would be governed by the earning power and risk of its underlying real assets and would be independent of how the mix of securities issued to finance it was divided.[3]

Merton Miller has explained the M&M capital-structure proposition in terms of a pie: "Think of the firm as a gigantic pizza, divided into quarters. If now, you cut each quarter in half into eighths, the M&M proposition says that you will have more pieces, but not more pizza."

M&M's frictionless environment assumes the following conditions:

1. No income taxes.
2. No transactions costs of issuing debt or equity securities.
3. Investors can borrow on the same terms as the firm.
4. The various stakeholders of the firm are able to costlessly resolve any conflicts of interest among themselves.

In this frictionless environment, the total market value of the firm is independent of its capital structure. To see why, let us compare the values of two firms with identical assets differing only in their capital structures: Nodett Corporation, which issues only stock, and Somdett Corporation, which issues bonds and stock.

Nodett Corporation currently has total earnings of $10 million per year, which we will refer to as *EBIT* (earnings before interest and taxes). Nodett pays out all $10 million per year of its *EBIT* as dividends to the holders of its 1 million shares of common stock.

Let us assume that the market capitalization rate on Nodett's expected dividends is 10% per year. Then the firm's total value would be the present value of the $10 million perpetuity or

$$\frac{\$10 \text{ million}}{0.1} = \$100 \text{ million}$$

and its price per share would be $100.

Somdett is identical to Nodett in its investment and operating policies. Therefore, its *EBIT* has the same expected value and risk characteristics as Nodett's. Somdett differs from

---

[3]Prior to their path-breaking work, finance theorists and practitioners just assumed that capital structure did matter, but for the wrong reasons. See Franco Modigliani and Merton Miller, "The Cost of Capital, Corporation Finance, and the Theory of Investment," *American Economic Review* (June 1958), pp. 261–297.

Nodett only in its capital structure, in that it is partially debt financed. Somdett has issued bonds that have a face value of $40 million at an interest rate of 8% per year. Thus, the bonds promise to pay a coupon of $3.2 million per year ($0.08 \times$ $40 million). We assume the bonds are in perpetuity.[4]

Let us assume that Somdett's bonds are default free and that the riskless rate of interest is 8% per year. The interest payments will be the same $3.2 million per year regardless of the realized value of *EBIT*. The formula for the earnings available to Somdett's shareholders after the payment of interest on the bonds is:

$$\text{Somdett's Net Earnings} = EBIT - \$3.2 \text{ million}$$

The total cash payments made to Somdett's bondholders and stockholders *combined* is:

$$\text{Somdett's Total Payments} = \text{Somdett's Net Earnings} + \text{Interest Payments}$$

$$\text{Somdett's Total Payments} = EBIT - \$3.2 \text{ million} + \$3.2 \text{ million} = EBIT$$

The intuition behind the M&M capital structure irrelevance proposition is that because Somdett offers exactly the same future cash flows as Nodett, the market value of Somdett should be $100 million, which is the same as Nodett's. Because the interest payments on Somdett's bonds are assumed to be riskless, the bonds will have a market value equal to their $40 million face value. Thus, the market value of Somdett's equity should be $60 million ($100 million total firm value less $40 million of debt). Assuming that the number of shares of Somdett stock is 600,000 (60% of the number of Nodett shares), the price of a share should be $100. We can prove it by means of an arbitrage argument.

Suppose that the price of Somdett stock was less than the price of Nodett stock. For example, suppose that Somdett's price was $90 per share instead of $100. This would violate the Law of One Price. To see this, note that one can replicate or "synthesize" Nodett stock by buying proportional amounts of the stock and bonds of Somdett. For example, holding 1% of the shares of Nodett stock (10,000 shares) has exactly the same future cash flows as holding 1% of the shares of Somdett (6,000 shares) and 1% of the bonds of Somdett. An arbitrageur could therefore make an immediate $60,000 in arbitrage profits with no outlay of his own money by selling short 1% of the total amount of Nodett stock for $1 million and simultaneously buying 1% of the stock and bonds of Somdett for $940,000. Table 3a summarizes the relevant cash flows.

Now suppose that the price of Somdett stock was greater than the price of Nodett stock. For example, suppose that Somdett's price was $110 per share rather than $100. This

TABLE 3a Arbitrage When Somdett Sells for $90 per Share

Position	Immediate Cash Flow	Cash Flow in the Future
Sell short 1% of the shares of Nodett stock at $100 per share	$1,000,000	−1% of *EBIT*
Buy Replicating Portfolio (Synthetic Nodett):		
Buy 1% of the shares of Somdett at $90 per share	−$540,000	1% of (*EBIT* −$3.2 million per year)
Buy 1% of the bonds of Somdett	−$400,000	1% of $3.2 million per year
Total replicating portfolio	−$940,000	1% of *EBIT*
Net cash flows	$60,000	0

---

[4]Alternatively, we assume that the bonds are simply "rolled over," that is, replaced with new bonds, as they mature.

TABLE 3b   Arbitrage When Somdett Sells for $110 per Share

Position	Immediate Cash Flow	Cash Flow in the Future
Sell short 1% of the shares of Somdett stock at $110 per share	$660,000	−1% of (EBIT − $3.2 million per year)
Buy Replicating Portfolio (Synthetic Somdett):		
Buy 1% of the shares of Nodett at $100 per share	−$1,000,000	1% of EBIT
Borrowing $400,000 in perpetuity	$400,000	−$32,000 per year
Total replicating portfolio	−$600,000	1% of (EBIT − $3.2 million per year)
Net cash flows	$60,000	0

too would violate the Law of One Price. To see this, note that one can replicate Somdett stock by buying a certain proportion of the stock of Nodett and borrowing to finance its purchase using the same personal debt-to-equity mix as Somdett. For example, buying 1% of the shares of Nodett stock (10,000 shares for $1,000,000) financed by borrowing 40% of the purchase price ($400,000), produces exactly the same future cash flows as holding 1% of the shares of Somdett (6,000 shares for $660,000). Table 3b summarizes the relevant cash flows.

Although a share of stock in each of the companies has the same price, the expected returns to shareholders and the risks of the stock investments differ. Let us flesh out the numerical example a bit in order to highlight these differences. Suppose the probability distribution of future EBIT is as shown in Table 4.

The columns labeled EPS show the earnings per share (and, therefore, dividends per share because we assume no reinvestment of earnings) corresponding to each value of EBIT. The formula for Nodett's EPS is:

$$EPS_{\text{Nodett}} = \frac{EBIT}{1,000,000 \text{ shares}}$$

TABLE 4   Probability Distribution of EBIT and EPS for Somdett and Nodett

State of the Economy	EBIT	Nodett EPS (1 million shares)	Somdett Net Earnings	Somdett EPS (600,000 shares)
Bad business	$5 million	$5	$1.8 million	$3.00
Normal business	10	10	6.8	11.33
Good business	15	15	11.8	19.67
Mean	10	10	6.8	11.33
Standard deviation		4.08		6.80
Beta	1.0	1.0		1.67

Note: Each state of the economy is equally likely.

457

The interest payments will be the same $3.2 million per year (0.08 × $40 million) regardless of the realized value of *EBIT*. Somdett's *EPS* is, therefore:

$$EPS_{Somdett} = \frac{\text{Net Earnings}}{600,000 \text{ shares}} = \frac{EBIT - \$3.2 \text{ million}}{600,000 \text{ shares}}$$

Comparing the *EPS* of Nodett with Somdett in Table 4, it is clear that the effect of increased financial leverage (changing only the financing mix and not the assets) is to increase both the mean *EPS* and the risk of *EPS*. Somdett's *EPS* is higher in the good state when *EBIT* = $15 million and lower in the bad state when *EBIT* = $5 million.

In the case of Nodett, the total risk of uncertain *EBIT* is spread among 1 million shares. In Somdett's case the same total risk exposure is spread among only 600,000 shares because the debtholders have a riskless claim. Somdett's stock, therefore, has a higher expected return and higher risk than Nodett's stock, yet the total values of the two *firms* are equal.

The implication of the M&M analysis in a frictionless environment is that capital structure does not matter. The wealth of existing shareholders will not be affected by either reducing or increasing the firm's debt ratio.

If Nodett Corporation (with 1 million shares of stock outstanding) were to announce an issue of $40 million of debt to be used to repurchase and retire common stock, what would be the effect on the share price? After the stock repurchase how many shares of stock would be outstanding?

The answer is that the price of the common stock would remain unchanged at $100 per share. The $40 million debt issue would be used to repurchase and retire 400,000 shares of stock, thus leaving 600,000 shares outstanding with a total market value of $60 million.

Quick Check 6

Mordett is a firm with assets identical to Nodett and Somdett, but with $50 million of risk-free debt outstanding (interest rate of 8% per year) and 500,000 shares of stock. What is Mordett's probability distribution of *EPS*? What is the price of a share? If Nodett Corporation (with 1 million shares of stock outstanding) were to announce an issue of $50 million of debt to be used to repurchase and retire common stock, what would be the effect on its share price? After the stock repurchase, how many shares of stock would be outstanding?

5 Creating Value through Financing Decisions

We have established that in a frictionless economic environment capital structure does *not* affect the value of the firm. In the real world there are frictions of many sorts. For both investors and firms, the tax treatment of interest income and expense from debt and equity securities may be different from payments on equity securities. And it is costly to make and enforce contracts specifying the allocation of the firm's cash flows to the holders of different classes of securities under all possible circumstances. Moreover, laws and regulations differ from place to place and change over time. Finding the optimal capital structure for a corporation involves making trade-offs that depend on the particular legal and tax environment the corporation finds itself in.

In view of the frictions that exist in the real world of corporate financing, let us now consider the ways that management might be able to add value through its capital structure-decisions. They fall into three categories:

- By its choice of capital structure the firm can reduce its costs or circumvent burdensome regulations. Examples of such costs are taxes and bankruptcy costs.
- By its choice of capital structure the firm may be able to reduce potentially costly conflicts of interest among various stakeholders in the firm: for example, conflicts between managers and shareholders or between shareholders and creditors.
- By its choice of capital structure the firm may be able to provide stakeholders with financial assets not otherwise available to them. The firm, therefore, expands the opportunity set of financial instruments available and earns a premium for doing so. To the extent that the firm engages in this activity, it is performing the functions of a financial intermediary.

6 Reducing Costs

By its choice of capital structure the firm can reduce its costs. Examples are taxes, subsidies, and the costs of financial distress. Let us consider each separately.

6.1 Taxes and Subsidies

In addition to shareholders and creditors, there is an additional claimant to the *EBIT* generated by a firm, namely, the government tax authority. Some taxes are paid at the corporate level (the corporate income tax) and some at the level of the individual shareholder (personal income taxes on cash dividends and realized capital gains).

A firm's capital structure matters in the presence of corporate income taxes in the United States because interest expense is deductible in computing a firm's taxable income whereas dividends are not. Therefore, by using debt financing the firm can reduce the amount of its cash flow that must be paid to the government tax authority.

For example, consider the two firms of Section 4, Nodett and Somdett corporations. In the case of Somdett Corporation the *EBIT* flow will be divided among three classes of claimants in order of priority:

- creditors (interest payments)
- government (taxes)
- shareholders (residual)

To illustrate this tax effect, let us consider the case in which there is a corporate tax rate of 34% and *no* personal taxes. The formula for Somdett's total after-tax cash flow to shareholders and creditors combined is:

$$
\begin{aligned}
CF_{\text{Somdett}} &= \text{Net Earnings} + \text{Interest} \\
&= 0.66\,(EBIT - \text{Interest}) + \text{Interest} \\
&= 0.66EBIT + 0.34\,\text{Interest} \\
&= CF_{\text{Nodett}} + 0.34\,\text{Interest}
\end{aligned}
$$

Somdett's total market value is maximized by having as much debt as possible. To see why, look at the after-tax cash flows to shareholders and creditors of the firm presented in Table 5. It shows that in every possible scenario the after-tax cash flow from Somdett exceeds that from Nodett by $1.088 million.

TABLE 5 Probability Distribution of After-Tax Cash Flow for Nodett and Somdett

Possible Levels of *EBIT* ($ million)	Nodett	Somdett	
	After-Tax Cash Flow ($ million)	Net Earnings ($ million)	After-Tax Cash Flow ($ million)
$5	$3.3	$1.188	$4.388
10	6.6	4.488	7.688
15	9.9	7.788	10.988

The market value of Somdett should, therefore, *exceed* the value of Nodett by the present value of the tax savings created by the interest payments on the debt:

Market Value of Somdett = Market Value of Nodett + *PV* of Interest Tax Shield

Under the assumption that Somdett's debt is free of default risk, the present value of the tax shield is equal to the tax rate of 34% times the value of the debt:

PV of Somdett's Interest Tax Shield = $0.34 \times \$40$ million = $13.6 million

Comparing Somdett to Nodett illustrates the effect of debt financing on the distribution of the firm's value between the shareholders and bondholders on the one hand and the government tax authority on the other. Table 6 shows the breakdown.

For both Somdett and Nodett, the total value of *all* claims (including the government's) is $100 million. In the case of Nodett, the value of the equity is $66 million and the value of the government's tax claim is $34 million. In the case of Somdett, the value of the equity is $39.6 million, the value of the debt is $40 million, and the value of the government's tax claim is only $20.4 million.

If Nodett Corporation (with 1 million shares of stock outstanding) were to announce an issue of $40 million of debt to be used to repurchase and retire common stock, what would be the effect on its share price? After the stock repurchase how many shares of stock would be outstanding?

With all-equity financing the price of a share of Nodett common stock would be $66. If management announced that it was issuing $40 million worth of bonds to retire stock, the stock price would rise to reflect the $13.6 million present value of the interest tax shield. The value of the 1 million shares would rise to $79.6 million or $79.6 per share. The number of shares repurchased and retired would be 502,513 shares ($40 million/$79.6 per share), thus leaving 497,487 shares outstanding. The original owners of the 1 million shares, thus, experience a gain of $13.60 per share. Those who sell shares take the gain in cash; those who keep their shares have an unrealized capital gain. Under these assumptions, management would want to maximize the proportion of debt in the firm's capital structure.

TABLE 6 Breakdown of Values of Claims for Nodett and Somdett

Claimant	Nodett	Somdett
Creditors	0	$40 million
Shareholders	$66 million	$39.6 million
Government Tax Authority	$34 million	$20.4 million
Total	$100 million	$100 million

Irrelevance Theorems and Capital Structure

After many years of head-scratching, economist have finally come to the conclusion that the much revered "Irrelevance Theorems" may actually be irrelevant to the study of capital structure. The main theory of capital structure was initially developed by Nobel Prize winners, Franco Modigliani and Merton Miller, and it stated that fine-tuning capital structure, mainly the composition of a company's debt and equity structure, does little in increasing overall shareholder value.

One of the main assumptions behind the theory is that the goal of the firm is to maximize shareholder value and that the "size of the pie" has already been made as large as possible; therefore, altering the capital structure only serves to distribute the firm's value differently. However, this assumption is too strong for the theory to hold up except for very rare circumstances.

Are companies really making the pie as large as possible? The main source of the problem appears to lie in agency costs. Many times the discretion of corporate insiders can lead them astray from the goal of maximizing shareholder value. Some of these tactics may include: insufficient effort, extravagant investments, entrenchment and poison-pill techniques, and self-dealing. Though some of these may be harder to prove than others, all of them are costly to the shareholders.

One way to decrease these agency costs may be to increase debt, as the firms would have an obligation to pay returns to debtholders, a market-based enforcement mechanism that may be lacking for shareholders. Of course, if we view things from this angle we would have to again consider the tax shield from debt and the cost of debt versus equity, but this time taking into account agency cost and performance tradeoffs. Other ways to reduce agency costs are to attempt to align incentives of management with that of shareholders through stock options or to better monitor the management for productive behavior. All in all, since the executives running firms are but human, there will always be agency costs that will disturb the equilibrium of the "Irrelevance Theorems" and make financial structure a potentially viable way to add more value to the pie.

Source: Adapted from "Beyond Irrelevance," *The Economist,* February 9, 2006.

Quick Check 7

Mordett is a firm with assets identical to Nodett and Somdett, but with $50 million of risk-free debt outstanding. Assuming a corporate tax rate of 34%, what is Mordett's total value and how is it divided among the equity, the debt, and the government's tax claim? If Nodett Corporation (with 1 million shares of stock outstanding) were to announce an issue of $50 million of debt to be used to repurchase and retire common stock, what would be the effect on the share price? After the stock repurchase, how many shares of stock would be outstanding?

SUBSIDIES

Sometimes *subsidies* are available for a particular form of financing, thus making it advantageous for firms to tilt their capital structure in that direction. An example would be when a governmental body offers to guarantee the debt of a firm that invests in an economically depressed area. For instance, suppose that if Hitek Corporation invests $100 million in Eldesealand, the World Bank will guarantee the debt at no cost to Hitek. Because the guarantee is only available if Hitek uses debt to finance its investment, the wealth of Hitek's shareholders is enhanced by choosing to finance with debt. One would, therefore, expect Hitek to choose debt rather than equity financing.

Quick Check 8

Besides a free government guarantee, what other forms might a subsidy to debt financing take?

6.2 Costs of Financial Distress

As the proportion of debt in a firm's capital structure increases, so too does the likelihood that it might default on that debt should future cash flow be less than expected. Firms that are in imminent danger of defaulting on their debt obligations are said to be in *financial distress.* In such circumstances firms usually incur significant costs that reduce the firm's total value below what it would be if there were no debt. These costs include the time and effort of the firm's managers in avoiding bankruptcy and fees paid to lawyers specializing in bankruptcy proceedings. Most important, business can be lost because customers, suppliers, and employees become greatly concerned by the threat of bankruptcy followed by the possibility of a liquidation of the firm.

Taking the costs of financial distress into consideration as well as the tax savings associated with higher levels of debt financing produces a trade-off. To illustrate this trade-off, consider Nodett Corporation again.

We showed in section 3.1 that the tax saving associated with issuing debt would lead Nodett's management to want to issue debt to retire shares. If the firm issued $40 million in debt, the stock price would rise from $66 to $79.60; and if it issued $50 million in debt, the stock price would rise to $83 per share. Now suppose that for higher levels of debt, there is a substantial probability that the firm could go bankrupt and incur substantial bankruptcy costs. In that case, if it announced that it was going to issue $60 million in debt to repurchase shares of its common stock, the stock price would fall rather than rise.

Figure 1 illustrates the possible effect of higher and higher debt ratios on the price of the firm's stock. The optimal debt ratio is at the point at which the stock price is maximized.

One could imagine a corporation announcing various levels of debt that it intends to issue to repurchase shares, observing the effect of its announcements on the firm's stock price, and then choosing the amount of debt that maximizes the share price. This rarely (if ever) happens in practice. In practice it is very difficult to find the precise mix of debt and equity financing that maximizes the firm's value. Nonetheless, the direction of improvement might be clear for a firm that has far too little or far too much debt.

Quick Check 9

How would a decrease in the costs of financial distress affect corporate capital structure?

FIGURE 1

Effect of the Debt Ratio on Stock Price

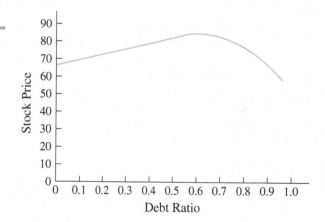

Box 3	Bankruptcy

In America today, bankruptcy serves as a way for many companies to reduce the burdens of pension promises and union contracts. Indeed, America's flawed bankruptcy system often seems to coddle firms in troubled times.

The effects of this can be quite drastic, a lesson learned painfully in Japan. During Japan's "lost decade," loans to the nation's weakest firms were subsidized and were at much lower rates than the risk warranted in comparative competitive markets. These companies became known as "zombies." Sectors with the most zombies tended to end up losing the fewest jobs in the 1990s because they were able to receive credit more easily than more productive and stronger borrowers. Productivity fell in these sectors as unproductive firms lingered and productive firms did not emerge. Even healthy companies in these sectors suffered because the zombies were wasting resources and congesting the market.

Though America does not have such a skewed lending system, the bankruptcy system may have a similar effect on some sectors of the economy. An example of this is the airline industry. Southwest Airlines, a healthy and profitable carrier, would have captured market share much more quickly if the industry was not overrun with zombie flyers. Though the system does seem to be improving, bankruptcy still serves as a way for companies to escape restructuring and to disturb market forces. In dynamic economies innovation relies on creative destruction, so mitigating destruction will in turn reduce the incentives for innovation.

Source: Adapted from "Don't Feed the Zombies," *The Economist*, April 6, 2006.

7 Dealing with Conflicts of Interest

A second path by which capital structure decisions can create wealth for shareholders is by reducing potentially costly conflicts of interest among various stakeholders in the firm: for example, conflicts between managers and shareholders or between shareholders and creditors. These costs are generally referred to as **agency costs**. Let us consider each separately.

7.1 Incentive Problems: Free Cash Flow

Earlier, we discussed the problem of conflicts of interest between the managers and shareholders of corporations. When managers have a lot of discretion about how to allocate a firm's cash flows, there is a temptation to use the cash to invest in projects that do not increase the wealth of shareholders. Examples include investments with negative *NPV* that increase the power, prestige, or perks of the managers. In order to mitigate this incentive problem created by free cash flow, a certain amount of debt may be a good thing.

Debt forces management to distribute cash to the firm's debtholders in the form of prescheduled payments of interest and principle. Issuing debt to repurchase shares can, therefore, be a way of creating value for the shareholders by reducing the amount of free cash flow available to managers.

Quick Check 10
What incentive problem is created by free cash flow and how does issuing debt help deal with the problem?

7.2 Conflicts between Shareholders and Creditors

We have already discussed the costs of financial distress and showed how they limit the optimal amount of debt in a firm's capital structure. But there is also a problem of incentive alignment between shareholders (and managers acting in the interest of shareholders) and creditors in firms with significant amounts of debt. The incentive problem arises because shareholders have little incentive to limit the firm's losses in the event of a bankruptcy. Managers acting in the best interests of shareholders will, therefore, choose to undertake more volatile investments that have the effect of increasing the wealth of shareholders at the expense of the debtholders.

For example, suppose the firm's current assets are worth $100 million. The firm has debt with a face value of $104 million maturing a year from now. Management has the choice of investing all $100 million in riskless T-bills maturing in one year that pay an interest rate of 4%, or investing in a venture that will either be worth $200 million or nothing a year from now.

Even if the probability of the new venture's succeeding is quite small, management (acting in the best interests of shareholders) will choose to undertake the risky venture. The reason is that if management invests in T-bills, then the value of the firm's shares will fall to zero. If the firm has some chance, no matter how small, of being worth more than $104 million a year from now, then the shares will have some value now. The creditors in this example bear all the downside risk of the risky venture, and the shareholders get all of the incremental upside potential for gain.

Thus, creditors face a potential moral hazard problem when they lend to certain firms. In firms with large amounts of debt, *managers might have an incentive to redeploy the firm's assets in a way that actually reduces the firm's total value (the size of the whole pie) in order to increase share price* (the size of the equity piece). Because creditors are aware that under certain adverse circumstances managers might be tempted to do them in, they will limit their lending in the first place.

Box 4 — Stock Buybacks

In 2005, share buybacks were increasing at record levels. As profits and earnings outgrew investment in 2004, many S&P 500 companies were left with more cash than they knew what to do with, so many of them simply bought back their own stocks. But should shareholders thank them for this? In a word, yes!

A company buying back its own equity can mean three things: It thinks the stock is undervalued; it wants to have enough shares to allow employees to exercise stock options or purchases shares; or it simply does not see any current profitable investment opportunities and wants to give shareholders the opportunity to add value externally to the firm. Because a buyback decreases the total number of shares outstanding in the market, it increases the earnings spread for the remaining shareholders. As earnings per share increases, this would increase the price of the stock as a result. The stock price can also rise because buybacks are a way of signaling: If a company buys back its own stock, it is telling the shareholders that the company knows something they don't—after all, who would know more about the company than itself? Typically, a company announcing that it is purchasing shares because it thinks its stock is undervalued tends to increase the share price more than by simply announcing that the buyback is motivated to decrease dilution and increase earnings per share.

Because buybacks are often associated with higher share prices, it may offer a cheaper way for the company to raise capital in the future, in essence, buying back equity now and selling it subsequently at a higher price. Hence the benefit is twofold. When a company is faced with unused cash, a share buyback many times creates the best value-added course of action.

Source: Adapted from "A Valuable Alternative to Empire Building," *The Economist,* April 19, 2005.

8 Creating New Opportunities for Stakeholders

The third path by which capital structure decisions can create value is by creating opportunities for some of the firm's stakeholders that otherwise would be available to them at greater cost or not at all. The idea is that by altering the claims it issues to stakeholders, the firm can create value without any change in the size or composition of its operating assets.

An example of creating opportunities for stakeholders is the use of pension promises as a form of corporate financing. This may create value for the employees of the firms sponsoring the pension plans by providing a type of retirement benefit not otherwise available to them. By sponsoring a pension plan, the firm's shareholders might gain by obtaining labor services at a lower total present-value cost than otherwise possible. However, the creation of new financial instruments for investors is generally more efficiently done by specialized financial-service firms instead of the typical nonfinancial firm.

9 Financing Decisions in Practice

Financing decisions always involve trade-offs that depend on the specific circumstances of the firm. For example, a firm that pays no corporate income tax because it has been losing money will evaluate the trade-off between tax benefits and costs of financial distress quite differently from a firm that does have to pay taxes. Having considered some of the main ways that financing decisions can generally matter to the owners and to the managers of a firm, let us now consider some specific cases.

Next we describe five different company situations and five different financing methods. We ask the reader to suggest the financing method that seems most appropriate for each situation. Our answers are summarized in Table 7.

9.1 The Five Companies

ORR OIL COMPANY

Orr Oil Company needs $10 million to finance the test drilling of some land it owns in New Guinea. If the tests are favorable, the company will need an additional $10 million to develop the site. Orr Oil common stock is currently selling at $10 per share, and earnings are $2 per share. Other firms in the oil industry sell at from 10 to 12 times earnings. Orr Oil's debt ratio is 25% compared to an industry average of 40%. Total assets at the last balance sheet date were $105 million.

GORMEH FOODS, INC.

This company operates a chain of gourmet food stores in the southeastern United States. It is owned by the five Gormeh sisters, each of whom holds one-fifth of the outstanding stock. The company is profitable, but rapid growth has put it under severe financial strain. The real estate is all heavily mortgaged, the inventory is being used to secure a bank line of credit,

TABLE 7   Match of Financing Methods to Company Circumstances

Company	Financing Method	Reasons
Orr Oil Company	Debt with warrants	If oil is found, then the price of Orr stock will rise and new equity financing will be forthcoming to finance the additional investment needed.
Gormeh Foods, Inc.	Leasing arrangement	No more debt capacity. Leasing provides debt financing secured by the leased equipment.
Bombay Textile Company	Factoring	Rather than having to carry and finance receivables that might be costly to monitor and collect, it is more efficient to sell them to an institution that specializes in collecting receivables.
Holey's Burger Queen	Loans from friends or relatives	Cannot borrow from any institutional lender unless he has more capital of his own. Only those who know him and trust him would provide the capital to him.
Lee Productions	Common stock	Agency costs of debt financing would be very high.

and the accounts receivable are being factored. With total assets of $15 million, the company now needs an additional $2 million to purchase equipment for the shipping department.

BOMBAY TEXTILE COMPANY

Bombay Textile Company manufactures cotton cloth in India and exports about half of it to small clothing companies operating in Singapore. The company's plant and equipment have been financed in part by a loan from the government, and this is its only long-term debt. It pays cash for its inputs, and offers 60 days' credit to its customers in Singapore. Recent growth in its export sales to $5 million per year has created the need for an additional $500,000 in financing.

HOLEY'S BURGER QUEEN

Jarvis Holey has been driving a cab in Philadelphia for five years, and has saved up $50,000 toward the purchase of a Burger Queen franchise. Burger Queen Corporation (BQC) requires that each of its franchisees invest at least $100,000 of equity capital, and then BQC arranges debt financing for the remainder. Holey has just learned that the owner of an existing Burger Queen franchise in his neighborhood wants to sell out for $250,000, and Holey wants to buy the business from him.

LEE PRODUCTIONS

Lee Productions is a small independent movie production company that has recently attracted attention because of the unexpected success of its film, *Red Tide Rising*. There are currently 10 owners, and they want to double the number of new movies the company produces. The company recently incorporated and now wants to raise $10 million from outside investors.

9.2 The Five Financing Methods

LOANS FROM FRIENDS OR RELATIVES

This "family" institutional form of financing is appropriate when a business is starting out as a small enterprise, and its future prospects are very uncertain. The success of the business will depend largely on the determination and character of the entrepreneur(s).

Only people who know the owners of the firm personally and trust them will lend them money.

LEASING ARRANGEMENT

In a leasing arrangement, the lessor provides some real asset—an office, a warehouse, equipment—to the lessee in return for contractually fixed payments over a set period of time. Functionally, leasing is essentially no-recourse debt financing secured by the leased asset. (Check the discussion in Section 3.2.)

COMMON STOCK

Issuing common stock is a method of financing that is used when the firm is organized as a corporation. It is typically used either when the firm goes public for the first time or when it wants to undertake a major expansion.

DEBT WITH WARRANTS

Warrants are call options giving their owners the right to buy shares of the issuing company's stock at a fixed price. Warrants are attached to a debt issue when the company envisions a need for raising new equity capital some time before the debt has to be repaid. The debt bears a lower interest rate than it would if it had no warrants attached.

FACTORING RECEIVABLES

When a company factors its receivables, it sells its accounts receivable (at a discount) to a **factor**, which is a firm that specializes in investing in receivables. Factoring is raising cash by selling a company asset rather than by borrowing or issuing new equity.

10 How to Evaluate Levered Investments

Earlier, we studied how to use discounted cash flow concepts to analyze investment decisions such as whether to enter a new line of business or to automate production. We concluded that a firm should accept any project that has a positive net present value. In this section we extend that analysis to show how to take into account a company's capital structure in evaluating investment projects.

We will examine three alternative methods used in practice:

- adjusted present value (*APV*)
- flows to equity (*FTE*)
- weighted average cost of capital (*WACC*)

In principle, all three methods should result in the same estimate of the *NPV* of an investment project. In the following example we will illustrate how this is possible.

10.1 Three Valuation Methods Compared

To explain the three methods, let us look at a specific project. The Global Connections Corporation (GCC), which provides satellite communications services to customers around the world, is considering investing in a new satellite to increase its capacity. The current market capitalization of GCC (debt plus equity) is $1 billion. The new investment requires an initial outlay of $100 million, and it is expected to result in increased revenue of $20 million per year. Annual maintenance expense on the new satellite is estimated to be $5 million, and it is expected to last indefinitely. The effective tax rate on GCC's profits is 30%. Its capital structure is 20% debt and 80% equity, based on the market value of the firm. GCC expects to maintain these proportions if the new project is done. The GCC debt is riskless with an interest rate of 8% per year. If the required rate of return on unlevered investments in the satellite communications business is 10% per year, what is the project's *NPV*?

The point of departure is to compute the project's *NPV* if it were financed with 100% equity. Then we will compare how each of the three valuation methods accounts for the impact of the debt financing.

The project's expected after-tax incremental cash flow is the expected revenue of $20 million less maintenance of $5 million multiplied by 1 minus the tax rate:

$$\text{Unlevered Expected Cash Flow} = (1 - 0.3) \times (\$20 \text{ million} - \$5 \text{ million})$$
$$= 0.7 \times \$15 \text{ million} = \$10.5 \text{ million}$$

Using 10% as the market discount rate, we find that the present value of the project is:

$$PV \text{ of Unlevered Investment} = \frac{\$10.5 \text{ million}}{0.1} = \$105 \text{ million}$$

Subtracting the initial outlay of $100 million, we find that the *NPV* of the project is:

$$NPV \text{ without Leverage} = \$105 \text{ million} - \$100 \text{ million} = \$5 \text{ million}$$

Now let us consider the three different methods of adjusting for the effect of debt financing.

THE ADJUSTED PRESENT VALUE (*APV*) METHOD

The **adjusted present value** (*APV*) method is based directly on the tax-shield valuation method we used in section 6.1. The *APV* of the project is equal to the project's unlevered *PV* plus the present value of the interest tax shields from additional debt financing created by taking the project. By the assumed financing policy for GCC, the amount of new debt created by taking the project is 20% of the increase in the market value of the firm, or $0.20 \times APV$ of the project. Because the new debt is perpetual, the present value of the additional tax shield created equals the tax rate times the amount of new debt, or $0.30 \times 0.20 \times APV = 0.06 \times APV$. So the project's *APV* is:

$$APV = \text{Unlevered } PV + PV \text{ of Incremental Tax Shield}$$
$$= \$105 \text{ million} + (0.06 \times APV)$$
$$= \$105 \text{ million}/0.94 = \$111.70 \text{ million}$$

Multiplying 0.06 times *APV*, we have that the *PV* of the incremental interest tax shield is $6.70 million. The increase in value to GCC shareholders given by the adjusted net present value (*ANPV*) of the project is:[5]

$$ANPV = \text{Unlevered } NPV + PV \text{ of Incremental Tax Shield}$$
$$= \$5.00 \text{ million} + \$6.70 \text{ million} = \$11.70 \text{ million}$$

---

[5]In situations where the dollar amount of new debt to be issued as a result of doing the project is specified, one can compute the *PV* of the incremental tax shield, and thus *ANPV*, directly without computing *APV* first as done here. It is common terminology to shorten *ANPV* as used here to *APV*, but the context should make the meaning unambiguous.

THE FLOWS TO EQUITY (*FTE*) METHOD

In the *FTE* method we calculate the incremental expected after-tax cash flows to the firm's shareholders and then compute *NPV* by discounting using the cost of *equity* capital, k_e, which can be computed using the formula:[6]

$$k_e = k + (1 - t)(k - r)d \tag{1}$$

where

k = the cost of capital with no leverage

t = the tax rate

r = the rate of interest on the debt, which is assumed to be default free

d = market debt-to-equity ratio

Since GCC maintains a capital structure with a debt-to-equity ratio, $d = 0.20/0.80 = 0.25$, we have by substitution into equation 1 that the cost of equity capital in our case is:

$$k_e = 0.10 + (1 - 0.30) \times (0.10 - 0.08) \times 0.25 = 0.1035$$

The expected incremental after-tax cash flow to GCC's *shareholders* from the satellite project, *CFS*, is:

$$CFS = \text{Unlevered Expected Cash Flow} - \text{After-tax Interest Expense}$$
$$= \$10.5 \text{ million} - (1 - t) \times r \times D = \$10.5 \text{ million} - 0.70 \times 0.08 \times D$$
$$= \$10.5 \text{ million} - 0.056D$$

where D denotes the increase in GCC debt outstanding after the project is undertaken. We find that the increase in the present value of equity outstanding, E, is:

$$E = CFS/k_e = \$101.45 \text{ million} - 0.5411D$$
$$= \$101.45 \text{ million} - (0.5411 \times 0.25 \times E) = \$101.45 \text{ million} - 0.1353E$$
$$= \$101.45 \text{ million}/1.1353 = \$89.36 \text{ million}$$

and $D = \$22.34$ million because GCC financing policy has $D = 0.25E$. The amount of new equity to be issued to finance the project is 100.0 million $-$ 22.34 million $=$ 77.66 million. Therefore, the *NPV* to the shareholders from undertaking the project is 89.36 million $-$ 77.66 million $=$ 11.70 million, the same amount derived in the adjusted present value method.

THE WEIGHTED AVERAGE COST OF CAPITAL (*WACC*) METHOD

With this method, we estimate the project's *PV* by discounting the expected *unlevered* after-tax cash flow using a **weighted average cost of capital** (*WACC*), and then we subtract the full $100 million investment outlay.

The formula for *WACC* is:

$$WACC = k_e \frac{1}{1 + d} + (1 - t)r \frac{d}{1 + d} \tag{2}$$

---

[6]This formula applies only if the debt of the firm is riskless in terms of default. It is not correct to extend it to risky debt by simply applying the formula using either the *promised* or the *expected* debt rate as a substitute for the riskless rate. The correct valuation of the tax shield when the debt has default risk is complex and beyond the level of this book.

In words, the *WACC* is a weighted average of the cost of equity capital and the after-tax cost of debt. The weights are the market values of equity and debt as a fraction of the present value of the project. Thus, in the satellite project, the *WACC* is:

$$WACC = 0.1035 \times 0.80 + 0.7 \times 0.08 \times 0.20 = 0.094$$

The *NPV* of the project is computed as the expected unlevered after-tax annual cash flow discounted at the *WACC* less the $100 million initial investment outlay:

$$NPV = \frac{\$10.5}{0.094} - \$100 = \$111.7 - \$100.0 = \$11.7 \text{ million}$$

> ### Quick Check 13
>
> Assume that GCC has a market debt-to-firm-value ratio of 30% instead of 20%, and that this is the ratio for the satellite project to be financed. Assuming all else is the same as in the text, use the *APV* method to find the satellite project's *NPV*. Then use the *FTE* and *WACC* methods to verify that you get the same estimate of *NPV* as when you use the *APV* method.

Summary

- External financing subjects a corporation's investment plans more directly to the discipline of the capital market than internal financing does.
- Debt financing in its broadest sense includes loans and debt securities, such as bonds and mortgages, as well as other promises of future payment by the corporation, such as accounts payable, leases, and pensions.
- In a frictionless financial environment in which there are no taxes or transaction costs, and contracts are costless to make and enforce, the wealth of shareholders is the same no matter what capital structure the firm adopts.
- In the real world there are a number of frictions that can cause capital structure policy to have an effect on the wealth of shareholders. These include taxes, regulations, and conflicts of interest between the stakeholders of the firm. A firm's management might, therefore, be able to create shareholder value through its capital structure decisions in one of three ways: (1) by reducing tax costs or the costs of burdensome regulations, (2) by reducing potential conflicts of interest among various stakeholders in the firm, and (3) by providing stakeholders with financial assets not otherwise available to them.
- There are three alternative methods used in estimating the net present value of an investment project to take account of financial leverage: the adjusted present value method, the flows to equity method, and the weighted average cost of capital method.

Key Terms

- internal financing
- external financing
- residual claim
- collateral
- agency costs

- factor
- adjusted present value
- weighted average cost of capital

Answers to Quick Check Questions

Quick Check 1   How does the need for external financing impose market discipline on a corporation?

Answer: Outside providers of funds are likely to want to see detailed plans for the use of the funds and will want to be convinced that proposed investments will produce sufficient future cash to justify the expenditure.

Quick Check 2   In what way is preferred stock like debt, and in what way is it like equity?

Answer: Preferred stock is like debt in that there is a contractually specified fixed payment that must be made before the holders of common stock can be paid anything. It is like equity in that failure to pay the promised dividends on preferred stock does not trigger a default.

Quick Check 3   Would you expect the interest rate on a secured loan to be higher or lower than the rate on an otherwise identical unsecured loan? Why?

Answer: Lower. The risk of loss to the lender in the event of default is lower.

Quick Check 4   Should a long-term lease be considered debt financing or equity financing?

Answer: It has elements of both. The fixed payments are like debt. But because the residual value of the asset stays with the lessor, a lease might also be considered a form of equity financing.

Quick Check 5   Suppose AmeriPens Corporation's pension assets were worth only $300 million. If its pension liability still had a present value of $400 million, what would be its shareholders' equity?

Answer: Shareholders' equity would be only $500 million. Total assets would be $1.3 billion and total liabilities $800 million.

Quick Check 6   Mordett is a firm with assets identical to Nodett and Somdett, but with $50 million of risk-free debt outstanding (interest rate of 8% per year) and 500,000 shares of stock. What is Mordett's probability distribution of *EPS*? What is the price of a share? If Nodett Corporation (with 1 million shares of stock outstanding) were to announce an issue of $50 million of debt to be used to repurchase and retire common stock, what would be the effect on the share price? After the stock repurchase, how many shares of stock would be outstanding?

Answer: The expected *EPS* of Mordett is $12, its standard deviation $8.165, and its beta 2. The price of a share of Mordett will be $100. Although its expected *EPS* is higher than Somdett's and Nodett's, its risk is higher too. The increase in riskiness exactly offsets the increase in expected *EPS*. If Nodett issued $50 million of debt to repurchase shares, it would have no effect on the stock price. It would use the $50 million to repurchase 500,000 shares, thus leaving 500,000 shares outstanding.

Quick Check 7   Mordett is a firm with assets identical to Nodett and Somdett, but with $50 million of risk-free debt outstanding. Assuming a corporate tax rate of 34%, what is Mordett's total value and how is it divided among the equity, the debt, and the government's tax claim? If Nodett Corporation (with 1 million shares of stock outstanding) were to announce an issue of $50 million of debt to be used to repurchase and retire common stock, what would be the effect on the share price? After the stock repurchase, how many shares of stock would be outstanding?

Probability Distribution of *EBIT* and *EPS* for Mordett

State of the Economy	EBIT	Nodett EPS (1 million shares)	Mordett Net Earnings	Mordett EPS (500,000 shares)
Bad business	$5 million	$5	$1 million	$2.00
Normal business	10	10	6	12.00
Good business	15	15	11	22.00
Mean	10	10	6	12.00
Standard deviation		4		8.165
Beta	1.0	1.0		2.0

Answer: Mordett's $50 million debt creates an interest tax shield with a present value of $17 million. The total market value of Mordett's debt plus equity will, therefore, be $83 million ($66 million + $17 million). Mordett's debt will have a value of $50 million, its equity $33 million, and the government's tax claim $17 million. By issuing $50 million in debt, Nodett's management could increase the wealth of shareholders by $17 million. The price of a share would increase from $66 to $83. The number of shares repurchased would be 602,410 ($50 million/$83 per share), leaving 397,590 shares of stock outstanding.

Quick Check 8 Besides a free government guarantee, what other forms might a subsidy to debt financing take?

Answer: Government might offer to pay part of the interest on the debt or to forgo part of the repayment of principal.

Quick Check 9 How would a decrease in the costs of financial distress affect corporate capital structure?

Answer: Corporations would make greater use of debt financing.

Quick Check 10 What incentive problem is created by free cash flow and how does issuing debt help deal with the problem?

Answer: When managers have a lot of discretion about how to allocate a firm's cash flows, they may be tempted to use the cash to invest in projects that do not increase the wealth of shareholders. Debt forces management to distribute cash to the firm's debtholders in the form of prescheduled payments of interest and principle.

Quick Check 11 What kind of investments might increase the wealth of a firm's shareholders at the expense of the firm's creditors?

Answer: Risky investment projects. The creditors bear much of the downside risk of such projects, whereas most of the upside potential goes to the shareholders.

Quick Check 12 How might offering a pension plan to its employees increase the wealth of a firm's shareholders?

Answer: By fulfilling a need of the employees, it might lower the present value of the firm's labor costs.

Quick Check 13 Suppose that GCC had a market debt-to-firm-value ratio of 30% instead of 20%, and that this is the ratio for the satellite project to be financed. Assuming all else is the same, use the *APV* method to find the satellite project's *NPV*. Then use the *FTE* and *WACC* methods to verify that you get the same estimate of *NPV*.

Answer: Using the *APV* method, we add to the project's unlevered *NPV* the value that is created through the debt financing. Because 30% of the *APV* of the project will be new debt, there will be an additional tax shield created with a value equal to the amount of new debt times the tax rate of 0.3, or 0.09 *APV*. So the project's *APV* and *ANPV* are

$$APV = \$105 \text{ million}/0.91 = \$115.4 \text{ million}$$
$$ANPV = \text{Unlevered } NPV + PV \text{ of Incremental Tax Shield}$$
$$= \$5.0 \text{ million} + \$10.4 \text{ million} = \$15.4 \text{ million}$$

In the *FTE* method with $d = 0.30/0.70 = 0.429$, we calculate $k_e = 0.1060$.

$$CFS = (\text{Unlevered Expected Cash Flow} - \text{After-tax Interest Expense})$$
$$= \$10.5 \text{ million} - 0.056D$$

The increase in the *PV* of equity is computed by discounting the expected cash flow to shareholders using the cost of equity capital:

$$EC = FS/k_e = \$99.06 \text{ million} - 0.5283D$$
$$= \$99.06 \text{ million} - 0.5283 \times 0.429E$$
$$= \$99.06 \text{ million} - 0.2264E$$
$$= \$80.77 \text{ million}$$

and $D = 0.429E = \$34.63$ million.

When we subtract the additional \$65.37 million of equity capital to be invested in the new project by shareholders, we find that the *NPV* is the same \$15.4 million that we estimated using the *APV* method. To use the *WACC* method, we first compute:

$$WACC = 0.106 \times 0.70 + 0.7 \times 0.08 \times 0.30 = 0.0910$$

The *NPV* of the project is computed as the expected unlevered after-tax annual cash flow discounted at the *WACC* less the \$100 million initial investment outlay:

$$NPV = \frac{\$10.5}{0.0910} - \$100 = \$115.4 - \$100 = \$15.4 \text{ million}$$

Questions and Problems

Internal versus External Financing

1. Considering your family as the limiting boundary, what are examples of both internal and external financing options available to pay for you summer school tuition to make up the elementary corporate finance course you failed last semester?

Debt Financing

2. Plentilease and Nolease are virtually identical corporations. The only difference between them is that Plentilease leases most of its plant and equipment whereas Nolease buys its plant and equipment and finances it by borrowing. Compare and contrast their market-value balance sheets.

3. Hanna-Charles Company needs to add a new fleet of vehicles for their sales force. The purchasing manager has been working with a local car dealership to get the best value for the company dollar. After some negotiations, a local dealer has offered Hanna-Charles two options: (1) a three-year lease on the fleet of cars or (2) 15% off

the top to purchase outright. Option 1 would cost Hanna-Charles company an estimated 5% less as an all-in cost over the three years.

a. What are the advantages and disadvantages of leasing?

b. Which option should the purchasing manager at Hanna-Charles pursue and why?

4. Europens and Asiapens are virtually identical corporations. The only difference between them is that Europens has a completely unfunded pension plan, and Asiapens has a fully funded pension plan. Compare and contrast their market-value balance sheets. What difference does the funding status of the pension plan make to the stakeholders of these two corporations?

The Irrelevance of Capital Structure in a Frictionless Environment

5. Divido Corporation is an all-equity financed firm with a total market value of $100 million. The company holds $10 million in cash-equivalents and has $90 million in other assets. There are 1,000,000 shares of Divido common stock outstanding, each with a market price of $100. Divido Corporation has decided to issue $20 million of bonds and to repurchase $20 million worth of its stock.

a. What will be the impact on the price of its shares and on the wealth of its shareholders? Why?

b. Assume that Divido's *EBIT* has an equal probability of being $20 million, or $12 million, or $4 million. Show the impact of the financial restructuring on the probability distribution of earnings per share in the absence of taxes. Why does the fact that the equity becomes riskier not necessarily affect shareholder wealth?

Creating Value through Financing Decisions

6. Recently, legislation has been proposed that would limit the deductibility of interest paid on so-called junk bonds when the bonds were issued to pay for the takeover of a corporation by another group (such bonds generally have relatively high coupon rates reflecting the relatively high risks). What do you think is the reasoning behind the proposal? Which corporate stakeholders would gain and/or lose from such legislation?

Reducing Costs

7. The Tiberius Company expects an *EBIT* of $100,000 every year forever. Tiberius can borrow at 10%. Tiberius currently has no debt, and its cost of equity is 14%. If the corporate tax rate is 34%, what is the value of the firm? What will the value be if Tiberius borrows $200,000 and uses the proceeds to buy up stock? Explain your answers and state concisely any assumption you make.

8. Comfort Shoe Company of England has decided to spin off its Tango Dance Shoe Division as a separate corporation in the United States. The assets of the Tango Dance Shoe Division have the same operating risk characteristics as those of Comfort. The capital structure of Comfort has been 40% debt and 60% equity in terms of marketing values, and is considered by management to be optimal. The required return on Comfort's assets (if unlevered) is 16% per year, and the interest rate that the firm (and the division) must currently pay on their debt is 10% per year. Sales revenue for the Tango Shoe Division is expected to remain indefinitely at last year's level of $10 million. Variable costs are 55% of sales. Annual depreciation is $1 million, which is exactly matched each year by new investments. The corporate tax rate is 40%.

a. How much is the Tango Shoe Division worth in unlevered form?

b. If the Tango Shoe Division is spun off with $5 million in debt, how much would it be worth?

c. What rate of return will the shareholders of the Tango Shoe Division require?

   d. Show that the market value of the equity of the new firm would be justified by the earnings to the shareholders.

9. Based on the above problem, suppose that Foxtrot Dance Shoes makes custom designed dance shoes and is a competitor of Tango Dance Shoes. Foxtrot has similar risks and characteristics as Tango except that it is completely unlevered. Fearful that Tango Dance Shoes may try to take over Foxtrot in order to control their niche in the market, Foxtrot decides to lever the firm to buy back stock.

   a. If there are currently 500,000 shares outstanding, what is the value of Foxtrot's stock?

   b. How many shares can Foxtrot buy back and at what value if it is willing to borrow 30% of the value of the firm?

10. Recalculate the answers to part (b) of the previous problem (problem 9) if the management is willing to borrow 40% of the value of the firm. Should Foxtrot borrow more?

11. Havem and Needem companies are exactly the same, differing only in their capital structures. Havem is an unlevered firm issuing only stocks whereas Needem issues stocks and bonds. Neither firm pays corporate taxes. Havem pays out all of its yearly earnings in the form of dividends and has 1 million shares outstanding. Its market capitalization rate is 11% and the firm is currently valued at $180 million. Needem is identical except that 40% of its value is in bonds and has 500,000 shares outstanding. Needem's bonds are risk free and pay a coupon of 9% per year and are rolled over every year.

   a. What is the value of Needem's shares?

   b. As an investor forecasting the upcoming year, you examine Havem and Needem using three possible states of the economy that are all equally likely: normal, bad, and exceptional. Assuming the earnings will be the same, one-half, and one and a half respectively, produce a table that shows the earnings and the earnings per share for both Havem and Needem in all three scenarios.

12. Using the foregoing problem (problem 11), let us now assume that Havem and Needem must pay taxes at the rate of 40% annually. Given the same distribution of possible outcomes as previously:

   a. What are the possible after-tax cash flows for Havem and Needem?

   b. What are the values of the shares?

   c. If one was not risk averse, which company would that person invest in?

13. Rambo Corporation has no debt outstanding and a total market value of $10,000. *EBIT* is projected to be $1,000 if economic conditions are normal. If there is a strong expansion in the economy, then *EBIT* will be 20% higher. If there is a another downturn in the economy, then *EBIT* will be 40% lower. Rambo is considering a $5,000 debt issue with a 9% interest rate. The proceeds will be used to buy up stock. There are currently 100 shares outstanding. The corporate tax rate is 50%.

   a. Calculate earnings per share (*EPS*) under each of the three economic scenarios before any debt is issued. Also, calculate the percentage changes in *EPS* when the economy expands or enters a recession.

   b. Repeat part (a) assuming that Rambo goes through with the recapitalization.

Dealing with Conflicts of Interest

14. The Griffey-Lang Food Company faces a difficult problem. In management's effort to grow the business, they accrued a debt of $150 million while the value of the company is only $125 million. Management must come up with a plan to alleviate the situation in one year or face certain bankruptcy. Also upcoming are labor relations meetings with the union to discuss employee benefits and pension funds. Griffey-Lang at this time has

three choices they can pursue: (1) Launch a new, relatively untested product that if successful (probability of 0.12) will allow G-L to increase the value of the company to $200 million, (2) sell off two food production plants in an effort to reduce some of the debt and the value of the company, thus making it even less likely to avoid bankruptcy (0.45 probability of success), or (3) do nothing (probability of failure = 1.0).

a. As a creditor, what would you like Griffey-Lang to do, and why?

b. As an investor?

c. As an employee?

Creating New Financing Opportunities for Stakeholders

15. The DL Corporation (DLC) has recently developed a dividend reinvestment plan. The plan allows investors to reinvest cash dividends automatically in DLC in exchange for new shares of stock. Over time, investors in DLC will be able to build their holding by reinvesting dividends to purchase additional shares of the company.

Many thousands of companies offer dividend reinvestment plans. Most companies with dividend reinvestment plans charge no brokerage or service fees. In fact, shares of DLC will be purchased at a 10% *discount* from the market price. A consultant for DLC estimates that about 75% of DLC's shareholders will take part in this plan. This is slightly higher than the average.

Evaluate DLC's dividend reinvestment plan. Will it increase shareholder wealth? Give both pros and cons.

16. *Challenge Problem:* The Obieland Corporation has a zero-coupon bond issue, the only outstanding debt, with a face value of $1,000 that is coming due in one year. The value of Obieland's assets is currently $1,200. Nancy Stern, the CEO, believes that the assets in the firm will be worth $800 or $1,600 in a year, with equal probabilities. The going rate on one-year T-bills is 6%.

a. What is the value of the firm's equity? The value of the debt?

b. Suppose that Obieland can reconfigure its existing assets such that the value in a year will be $400 or $2,000. If the current value of the assets is unchanged, would the stockholders favor such a move? Why?

Financing Decisions in Practice

17. The following article was taken from the December 19, 2000, issue of the *Financial Times.*

Bouygues seeks $5.3bn for 3G

By Raphael Minder in Paris

Bouygues, the French construction and communications group, is looking to borrow €6bn ($5.33bn) to help finance a third-generation wireless network for its mobile phone subsidiary, Bouygues Telecom.

Bouygues said it was in talks with a number of banks but would not say whether the quest for additional financing was linked to the breakdown of its talks with Telecom Italia, which had hoped to lift its 10.8 per cent stake in Bouygues Telecom.

The move comes before a January 31 deadline to apply for the French auction of 3G mobile phone licences. Telecom Italia's mobile phone unit, Telecom Italia Mobile, had hoped to raise its holding before that date and have more influence over the management of Bouygues Telecom.

Bouygues said two weeks ago that it was "no longer" negotiating with Telecom Italia, without specifying why talks had been called off. The French company said it was already talking to a "restricted number" of companies that might want a stake in Bouygues Telecom alongside Telecom Italia.

Still, Bouygues has made clear it wants to keep majority control of the mobile phone unit. It said it was looking for a long-term loan of between 8 to 10 years. About €2.3bn of the €6bn will be to refinance an existing loan. The company said investors in Bouygues Telecom had already invested €5.1bn which can be used to develop the new network.

Earlier this year, Bouygues discussed a possible collaboration with NTT DoCoMo, the Japanese telecoms company. Deutsche Telekom has also shown interest in the French auction and has indicated it would not want to make a bid on its own.

Explain how the proposed method of financing Bouygues 3G mobile network will affect the capital structure of the firm?

18. The following report is from the December 18, 2000, edition of the *Financial Times*.

Icahn bids to block Reliance

By Adrian Michaels in New York

Carl Icahn, the US financier, is increasing the pressure he is exerting on Reliance, the insurance company controlled by Saul Steinberg, another corporate raider and financial icon.

High River, one of Mr Icahn's corporate affiliates, said on Monday that it and other Icahn vehicles planned to buy about $61m of bonds issued by Reliance with a view to blocking any further plans for the troubled insurer that it does not like.

Reliance, which has been in trouble for some time and is now trying to find someone to look after outstanding policies while it shuts down, was this month delisted from the New York Stock Exchange in another blow to the pride of the once-mighty Mr Steinberg.

High River said it planned to buy the 9 per cent senior bonds at 17 cents on the dollar, above the 6–8 cents on the dollar at which it said the bonds have been trading in December.

Mr Icahn, who would rather see state regulators run Reliance than accede to the management's plan, is worried that if the company files for bankruptcy protection, bondholders would receive nothing.

High River said: "We believe that the plan now under consideration . . . would provide a very low or no possibility of a successful recovery for the bonds from the assets of the Reliance Insurance Company and will leave the bondholders without influence."

Mr Icahn already has a stake in Reliance's debt which it bought in November. Mr Steinberg, who once struck fear into the heart of Walt Disney and Chemical Bank with daring raids, has already liquidated much of his personal fortune during Reliance's demise.

Reliance, which has already sold 75 per cent of its business, is seeking to wind up operations.

Explain why someone with an interest in a distressed firm wish to increase their position? Why purchase the debt of the distressed firm rather than the equity?

19. Below is an article from the April 20, 2006, edition of *The Economist*.

Credit Derivatives: The Tender Age

Unexpected twists in the booming market for credit-default swaps

THE past few months have been trying for buyers of credit derivatives. They include banks and hedge funds that have acquired credit-default swaps (CDSs), the cornerstone of the market. This still young area of the financial world now consists of contracts worth $17 trillion, more than all the world's outstanding corporate debt. A credit derivative provides insurance if a borrower goes bus—or a means to bet that it will do so. Lately, a few of those bets have gone spectacularly wrong.

First, hardly any companies went under in the first quarter. Rating agencies say that the number of defaults is the lowest for almost a decade. Though good news for companies, it is bad for owners of swaps. Meanwhile, analysts report a sharp rise in the number of CDS contracts being written. All this has lowered the premium, or spread, on credit derivatives (see chart). Those who own protection have lost money (although sellers have benefited).

But the issue that has most hurt credit-derivatives buyers, analysts say, is an arcane and technical one. A few companies have unexpectedly tendered for their own bonds. Because buy-backs eliminate the risk of default, the consequences for the price of CDS contracts written on these bonds have been uniformly brutal.

The companies include J. Sainsbury, a British supermarket chain, which last month bought back all £1.7 billion ($3.0 billion) of its outstanding bonds in order to cut its financing costs. That meant no "deliverable" debt was left to be insured—it was replaced by mortgage-backed securities in two new entities, named after Britain's Longstone and Eddystone lighthouses. CDS investors have ended up on the rocks. Last year, when Sainsbury was struggling, some of these swaps were priced at 150 basis points per unit of debt insured. Now they fetch around 20.

Something similar happened at TDC, a Danish telecoms company acquired last year in Europe's largest leveraged buy-out so far. CDS premiums written on its bonds, which had been expected to soar, plunged when TDC declared that it would redeem its bonds at par as part of the deal.

In America panic among CDS buyers has been rarer. But a restructuring at Cendant, a diversified travel, leisure and property group, created deep confusion and a sharp drop in CDS premiums last month. It is expected to tender for its bonds as it breaks itself up into four units.

In each case, holders of CDS contracts suddenly found themselves committed to paying for protection on bonds on the verge of extinction—rather like paying for insurance on a car heading for the scrapyard. According to Jon Jonsson, European credit-derivatives strategist at Merrill Lynch, they were particularly caught by differences between European and American corporate law.

As a result, the International Swaps and Derivatives Association is investigating whether standard CDS documents may need changing to incorporate the risks from reorganisations or leveraged buy-outs. "There are a host of these we can see in the pipeline," says Kimberly Summe, ISDA's general counsel.

Of course, what's bad for buyers is good for sellers. But such technical disruptions undermine confidence for everyone. As the IMF pointed out recently, the credit-derivatives market helps to steady the financial system. It enables banks to offload credit risk, provides transparency on lending conditions and may even smooth the ups and downs of the credit cycle.

The secondary market, however, is prone to worries about liquidity and bouts of panic. Panic is an understandable reaction for buyers who suddenly find that their insurance contracts are worthless. Now they have at least been warned.

When examining a firm's optimal capital structure, the key elements of the analysis come from the Modigliani and Miller model, the effects of corporate and personal taxes, and the issues surrounding bankruptcy costs. How would the existence of a market for credit-default swaps enter and/or alter this analysis? The article states: "A credit derivative provides insurance if a borrower goes bust. ..." Does the existence of an instrument to hedge bankruptcy costs mean that more debt in the capital structure is optimal? Is the availability of such instruments therefore likely to affect the firm's cost of capital? Derivative instruments such as put options also exist and can be used to limit the downside loss of equity investments: Would the existence of such instruments change the optimal capital structure and cost of capital as well?

How to Evaluate Levered Investments

20. Suppose Fitzroy's Flamethrowers Inc. (FFI) has a market value of debt equal to twice the market value of equity. FFI has a cost of equity capital of 12% ($k_e = 12\%$) and an interest rate on debt of 8% ($r = 8\%$). If the company faces a corporate tax rate of 40% what is its weighted average cost of capital ($WACC$)? How would a one-percentage point increase in its interest rate on debt affect the $WACC$? A one-percentage point increase in its cost of equity capital? A one-percentage point increase in both?

21. Financial Technology Corporation (FTC) has a current market value of $2 billion divided equally between riskless debt, paying 8%, and equity. In the financial technology business, the required rate of return on equity-financed investments is 10% and the effective corporate tax rate is 40%. FTC has the opportunity to invest in an expanded data transmission network forecasted to produce an incremental before-tax net revenue of $24 million per year in perpetuity for an initial upfront cost of $150 million. What is the NPV of the project if it is financed entirely with equity? What is its $ANPV$ (adjusted net present value) if it is financed to maintain to the current capital structure?

22. From the previous problem (problem 21) calculate FTC's cost of equity capital when the investment is funded maintaining the original capital structure of a 50–50 debt-equity mix. What is the $WACC$?

23. For $1 million (this a net figure equal to the cash outlay less the present value of the depreciation tax shield provided by the project), an investment project yields a distribution one period later of:

$$\overline{EBIT} = \begin{cases} 2,960,000 & \frac{1}{2} \\ 2,740,000 & \frac{1}{2} \end{cases}$$

That is, it is equally likely that the project will have an $EBIT$ of $2,960,000 or $2,740,000. Suppose that a tax rate of 50% applies to all these earnings except bond interest, which may be deducted from taxable income. Suppose the project is entirely financed by one-period bonds yielding 10% and all investors are risk neutral, meaning they look only at expected values. What is the increase in the current market value of the equity position of the firm if the project is undertaken?

24. *Challenge Problem:* Suppose all investors, debt and equity holders, in Gargantua Ltd. are risk neutral and require an expected rate of return equal to 10%. The stockholders, optimists, believe that one period from now Gargantua's assets follow the distribution:

$$\overline{V} = \begin{cases} 24,000,000 & \frac{1}{3} \\ 22,000,000 & \frac{1}{3} \\ 20,000,000 & \frac{1}{3} \end{cases}$$

Or it is equally likely that the market value of the assets will be either $24000,000 or $22,000,000 or $20,000,000. Gargantua's president, E. G. Pantagruel, likes to borrow as much as he possibly can, since he thinks this minimizes problems with the stockholders. The lenders, however, think that Gargantua's prospects are better described by

$$\bar{W} = \begin{Bmatrix} 19,800,000 & \frac{1}{2} \\ 17,600,000 & \frac{1}{2} \end{Bmatrix}$$

Assume the firm will be liquidated after one period and bond interest is not taxable. What debt-equity ratio should Pantagruel aim for if the corporate tax rate is 40%? *Hint:* What debt-equity ratio would minimize the weighted average cost of capital?

25. *Challenge Problem:* The Foreseeable Future Company (FFC) operates in a world of certainty where corporate tax rates are 40%. The current owners of the company have only one asset. It is the knowledge of a new technological process for extracting wine from water, which can generate $450 of *EBIT,* once and only once, one period from now for an upfront investment of $150. FFC can borrow up to $100 using debt; the rest must be equity. This new equity can be in the form of preferred stock, which would be risk-free just like the debt. Thus both the debt and preferred stock would carry a risk-free interest rate of 10%. The interest payments on the debt would be tax deductible but the dividend on the preferred stock would not be tax deductible. (*Hint:* Fill in the table below using the left column for the case where $100 of bonds and $50 of preferred stock are issued. Remember these figures are one period ahead.) Determine the present value of the existing owner's equity, and the weighted average cost of capital (*WACC*), that is, what is the after-tax weighted average cost of financing the $150 investment by issuing the $100 of debt and $50 of preferred stock? If the company could increase its debt-equity ratio, say by issuing $150 of debt to finance the project (see the right column of the table below), would anyone benefit? If so, who, by how much, and why?

$450	*EBIT*	$450
−$10	Interest	−$15
$440	*EBT*	$435
−$	Taxes (40%)	−$
$	Earnings after tax	$
−$100	Repayment of bond face	−$150
$	Residual for equity	$
−$55	Payment to preferred stock	$0
$	Payment to common stock	$

Suggested Readings

Barclay, M., and C. Smith. "The Capital Structure Puzzle: The Evidence Revisited." *Journal of Applied Corporate Finance* 17, Winter 2005.

Berk, J. and P. DeMarzo. *Corporate Finance. Boston,* MA: Pearson Addison Wesley, 2007.

Brealey, R., S. Myers, and F. *Allen. Principles of Corporate Finance,* 8th ed. New York: McGraw-Hill Irwin, 2006.

Harris, M., and A. Raviv. "The Theory of Capital Structure." *Journal of Finance* 46, March 1991.

Merton, R. C. "On the Pricing of Corporate Debt: The Risk Structure of Interest Rates." *Journal of Finance* 29, May 1974.

Miles, J., and R. Ezzel. "The Weighted Average Cost of Capital, Perfect Capital Markets and Project Life: A Clarification." *Journal of Financial and Quantitative Analysis* 15, September 1980.

Modigliani, F., and M. Miller. "The Cost of Capital, Corporation Finance, and the Theory of Investment." *American Economic Review* 48, June 1958.

Myers, S. C. "Interactions of Corporate Finance and Investment Decisions: Implications for Capital Budgeting." *Journal of Finance* 29, March 1974.

Ross, S. "Capital Structure and the Cost of Capital." *Journal of Applied Finance* 15, Spring/Summer 2005.

Ross, S., R. Westerfield, and J. Jaffe, *Corporate Finance,* 8th ed. New York: McGraw-Hill Irwin, 2008.

Real Options

OBJECTIVE

- To demonstrate how to use models from capital budgeting analysis and financial option pricing to analyze complex strategic decisions involving the timing, scale, and sequences of real investment opportunities.

CONTENTS

From Chapter 17 of *Financial Economics*, 2/e. Zvi Bodie, Robert C. Merton, David L. Cleeton.

This chapter shows how to apply financial economic theory to strategic decision making within firms. Both in theory and in practice, the criterion for the managers of a firm in evaluating strategic decisions should be the maximization of the wealth of the company's owners. Earlier, we showed how to apply discounted cash flow analysis to estimate an investment's contribution to the wealth of a firm's owners. In this chapter we extend that analysis to examine basic aspects of corporate strategy. We analyze how option theory can be applied to evaluate management's ability to time the start of an investment project, to expand it, or to abandon it after it has begun.

1 Investing in Real Options

To this point we have ignored an extremely important aspect of many (if not most) corporate investment opportunities—the ability of managers to delay the start of a project, or once started, to expand it or to abandon it. Failure to take account of these *real* options (as contrasted with financial options) will cause an analyst evaluating the project to underestimate its *NPV*.

The movie industry provides a good example of the importance of real-option values in evaluating investment projects. Often a movie studio will buy the rights to a movie script and then wait to decide if and when to actually produce it. Thus, the studio has the option to wait. Once production starts, and at every subsequent step in the process, the studio has the option to discontinue the project in response to information about cost overruns or changing tastes of the moviegoing public.

Another very important managerial option in the movie business is the option of the film studio to make sequels. If the original movie turns out to be a success, then the studio has the exclusive right to make additional movies with the same title and characters. The option to make sequels can be a significant part of a movie project's total value.

There is a fundamental similarity between the options in investment projects and call options on stocks: In both cases the decision maker has the *right* but not the *obligation* to buy something of value at a future date.

Recognizing the similarity between call options and managerial options is important for three reasons:

- It helps in structuring the analysis of the investment project as a sequence of managerial decisions over time.
- It clarifies the role of uncertainty in evaluating projects.
- It gives us a method for estimating the option value of projects by applying the quantitative models developed for valuing call options on stocks.

1.1 Types of Real Options

Real options can be categorized into a number of generic types in terms of the flexibility offered in altering the terms of a real investment opportunity. And by analogy they can be valued similarly to types of financial options to which we have already been introduced. The option to postpone the beginning of an investment project is a **deferral option** and can be mapped nicely into an American call option. Here the exercise price of the option is the project's required initial investment and the maturity date of the option corresponds to the final decision point beyond which the decision cannot be postponed.

An **option to abandon** a project corresponds to an American put option. The exercise price for the option would be the amount that must be paid to terminate the project. This could be a contracted amount or simply the market value of the project if it is liquidated. On both sides of a deferral option and an option to abandon may lie possibilities to exercise an

option to rescale the project where the project can be expanded or contracted for some fixed price.

More complex real options would include *switching options*, which *requires* the payment of a fixed amount to change operating or production modes. An example would be an electric generating plant that could switch between using alternative sources of fuel (perhaps coal and natural gas). The option to close down and restart a production line, or exit and then reenter a market are also examples of switching options that can be modeled as portfolios of American put and call options.

Complex investment projects, which are typically organized into a set of alternative stages with critical decision at the end of each stage, can be analyzed as *compound options* in which options on options exist. For example, a major drug company's product cycles consist of a research stage in which alternative compounds are tested, a product development stage in which clinical trials are conducted, and a marketing stage in which the final product is brought to market. Each stage involves new investments that are conditional on exercise of the option to proceed with the previous stage.

1.2 An Example

An example may help to clarify how the analogy between call options and managerial options can help in analyzing an investment project. Consider a film studio's decision about whether to purchase the movie rights to a book currently being written by a best-selling author.

Assume the author charges $1 million for the exclusive right to make a movie out of her novel that is scheduled for publication a year from now. If the novel is a success as a book, then the film studio will make a movie out of it, but if the book is a commercial failure the studio will not exercise its right to make it into a movie. Figure 1 shows this investment project as a *decision tree*.

Box 1 — Measuring Intangible Investments

For years, the national-account statistics have demonstrated America's macroeconomic weaknesses, but the question lies in whether the picture gets brighter when we accurately take into account the sizable amount of intangible investments in the economy. Just as a company can invest in a factory or a piece of machinery, it also can invest in intangible assets, such as a brand name. Current methods to measure national income account for the former type of investment only and overlook intangible investments altogether.

The pace of intangible investments has grown much faster than investment in capital in general. Though America's investment rate has been relatively constant over the last few years, if we added the trend for intangible investments the overall rate would have been steadily increasing. But does that change the perspective on our economic status? Higher investment due to intangibles would push up productivity, though it would not be able to explain the trend of acceleration in productivity after 1995. If overall investment has been driven up by intangible investments, then so has overall savings. This would not solve the nation's external current account deficit, which is defined as being the difference between total savings and investment.

Some optimists would say that proper accounting for the role of intangible investments would affect us directly as the record would show a large volume of intangible assets being exported, such as technical knowledge and managerial know-how. Others would argue that our borrowing is not to support consumption spending but rather investment into developing intangible assets via spending on research and developing human capital. On the bottom line, both arguments are thin and the magnitude of intangible investments is insufficient to mitigate the much larger problem of our aggregate macroeconomic deficit.

Source: Adapted from "Getting a Grip on Prosperity," *The Economist,* March 2, 2006.

FIGURE 1

Decision Tree for Movie Project

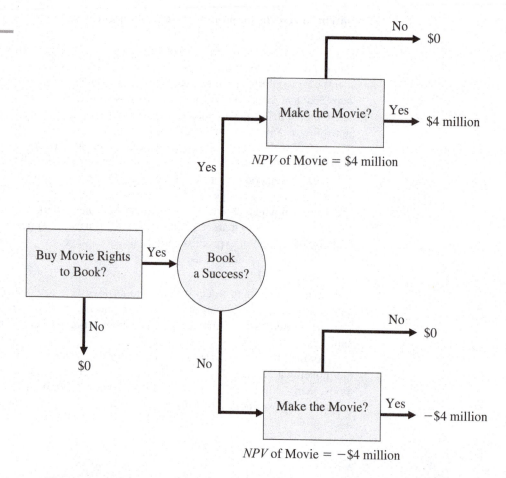

The studio's current decision is whether to pay the $1 million price the author demands. This is represented by a decision box at the left of the tree. The right branch coming out of the first decision box corresponds to a decision to pay the $1 million for the movie rights and the lower branch to a decision not to pay the $1 million.

The circle attached to the horizontal decision branch represents an event not under the control of management: whether the book is a commercial success. There are two branches coming out of this event circle: The upper branch corresponds to the possibility that the novel is a success, and the lower branch to the possibility that the novel is a failure. Each has a probability of 0.5. Analysts at the studio estimate that if the book is a success, then the *NPV* of the movie a year from now will be $4 million. If, however, the book is a failure then the *NPV* of the movie a year from now will be −$4 million.

Note that attached to the right side of each branch extending from the event circle is another decision box representing the decision management must make about whether to actually produce the movie. If the project were analyzed without taking account of management's ability to abandon it a year from now, then the project would be rejected. This is because the project's expected present value today would be zero at *any* cost of capital no matter how low. Management would surely not spend $1 million to buy the rights to make a movie that has an expected present value of zero.

But this is a misspecification of the investment opportunity. Because management has the *right* and not the *obligation* to make the movie, the possible payoffs a year from now are an *NPV* of $4 million if the book turns out to be a success and an *NPV* of 0 if the novel is a failure. This payoff distribution has an expected value of $2 million. As long as the cost of capital used to discount this $2 million expected *NPV* to the present is less than 100% per year, the project's expected present value will exceed the $1 million cost of the movie rights to the book. Thus, we see that it is extremely important in structuring the analysis of the project to take account of management's ability to change course in the future.

We also learn something about the impact of uncertainty on the project's *NPV* from thinking about it in terms of options. For example, suppose the range of possible future *NPV*s doubled whereas the expected value remained 0: $8 million if the book is a success and −$8 million if it is a failure. Because management will not make the movie if the book is a failure, the worst possible outcome is still only 0 and not −$8 million. Because management will choose to abandon the project if the book turns out to be a failure, the expected *NPV* a year from now increases from $2 million to $4 million. Thus, the project's expected *NPV* doubles as a result of the doubling in the range of possible future outcomes. In this sense, an increase in the uncertainty about the project's future payoffs increases its value.

How important is the value of managerial options as a component of an investment project's total value? The answer depends on the type of project, but it is difficult to think of any investment project where management has *no* discretion to alter its plans once the project has begun. It is especially important to take option value into account when considering investments in research and development. The use of the financial theory of options in capital budgeting has been adopted by at least one large pharmaceutical company. In general, the greater the uncertainty about future outcomes of the project, the greater the need to account explicitly for any options.

2 A Deferral Option: The Case of Uncertainty and Irreversibility

We shall illustrate and examine in some detail the analysis of real options by presenting an example of a deferral option under conditions of uncertainty. Dixit and Pindyck provide an example where the investment decision is irreversible.[1] The deferral option is to undertake the investment immediately or to postpone the decision for a period in order to obtain information about pricing relevant to the investment's future payoffs.

Consider the situation of a company contemplating whether to invest in a factory. The investment is completely irreversible, meaning that the custom-buildt facility can be used to produce no alternative product nor can it be modified to do so except at a prohibitive cost. Hence after the initial investment the factory immediately has no value in an alternative use. This is for practical purposes equivalent to assuming the salvage value is zero. Once the investment is undertaken the costs are sunk and cannot be recovered. We assume the factory can be built instantly, at a cost I and will produce one aggregated unit of output per period indefinitely into the future under conditions of a zero operating or marginal cost. The current price of the factory's output is P_0 per unit. Price uncertainty is reflected in a single one-time discrete movement in this price to a new level, P_1, at the start of the next period. Thus next period the price will either increase by u, with probability q, or decrease by d, with probability $(1-q)$. The price will then continue at this level into the future.

$$P_1 = \begin{pmatrix} (1+u)P_0 & \text{with probability } q \\ (1-d)P_0 & \text{with probability } (1-q) \end{pmatrix} = P_2 = P_3 = \cdots = P_\infty$$

[1]A. K. Dixit and R. S. Pindyck, *Investment under Uncertainty,* "Developing the Concepts Through Simple Examples," (Princeton, N.J: Princeton University Press, 1994).

Letting r be the interest rate per period, the NPV of the project on an expected value basis if investment occurs now is given by:

$$NPV_0(I, P_0, q, u, d, r) = -I + P_0 + q \cdot \left[\sum_{t=1}^{\infty} \frac{(1+u) \cdot P_0}{(1+r)^t} \right] + (1-q) \cdot \left[\sum_{t=1}^{\infty} \frac{(1-d) \cdot P_0}{(1+r)^t} \right]$$

Recognizing the bracketed terms are expressions for the present value of perpetuities we can simplify the project's NPV as:

$$NPV_0(I, P_0, q, u, d, r) = -I + P_0 + P_0 \cdot \left[\frac{q \cdot (1+u)}{r} + \frac{(1-q) \cdot (1-d)}{r} \right]$$

If, for example, the interest rate was 10% per period, the factory's cost was $1,600, the initial output price was $200, and there was a 50% chance the price would either rise or fall by 50%, the NPV of deciding to invest immediately would be $600. In this case, the price uncertainty will be resolved next period: The price will either rise to $300 or fall to $100, with equal probabilities for the two outcomes, but the expected price remains at its current level of $200. Next period, if the price decreases, the perpetuity stream at the lower price will have an expected present value of $500 = $\frac{1}{2} \frac{\$100}{10\%}$ whereas if the price increases, the present value of the perpetuity stream will be $1,500 = $\frac{1}{2} \frac{\$300}{10\%}$. Adding the net cash flow from the

current period we obtain the NPV of investing today of $NPV_0 = \$2,000 + \$200 - \$1,600 = \$600$.

If the investment decision is postponed until the price uncertainty is resolved in the next period we can calculate the NPV of deferring the decision in a straightforward fashion, first by calculating the NPV at the time the decision is made and then by discounting it back one period to obtain the current NPV_1.

If the price increases, the NPV at the time the decision is made is given by:

$$V_u(I, u, r, P_0) = \max\left(0, \left(1 + \frac{1}{r}\right)(1+u)P_0 - I \right)$$

Here we clearly see the option to make the investment after the price level uncertainty is resolved has value. If the project's NPV at that point in time is negative, the project is not undertaken. In principle, the calculation is symmetric because if the price decreases:

$$V_d(I, d, r, P_0) = \max\left(0, \left(1 + \frac{1}{r}\right)(1-d)P_0 - I \right)$$

The value of being able to defer the decision has an expected NPV in the present given by:

$$NPV_1(I, P_0, q, u, d, r) = \frac{1}{1+r} \cdot \left[q \cdot V_u(I, u, r, P_0) + (1-q) \cdot V_d(I, d, r, P_0) \right]$$

Using the same parameters as before we see that if the price drops, the deferred option to invest is not taken up, as it would not make sense to invest the required $1,600 to be able to collect an immediate perpetuity stream of $100 per period:

$$\left(1 + \frac{1}{r}\right)(1-d)P_0 - I = \$100 + \frac{\$100}{10\%} - \$1,600 = \$1,100 - \$1,600 = -\$500$$

But if the price rises, the option is executed:

$$\left(1 + \frac{1}{r}\right)(1+u)P_0 - I = \$300 + \frac{\$300}{10\%} - \$1,600 = \$3,300 - \$1,600 = \$1,700$$

This produces an expected *NPV* today of:

$$NPV_1 = \frac{1}{1.1}[0.5(\$1{,}700) + 0.5(\$0)] = \$772.73$$

This example illustrates that the option to defer the investment decision is valuable even if the expected price in the future is equal to the current price, or a mean-preserving spread in the price occurs.

2.1 Sensitivity Analysis

The *NPV* profiles of the immediate investment versus the deferred option to invest are plotted in Figure 2.

As the variability in the future price increases, holding the expected value at the current price, the value of the deferral option increases. For example, if the price were equally likely to rise or fall by 75%, the *NPV*s would take on the following values:

$$NPV_0 = \frac{1}{2}\frac{\$50}{10\%} + \frac{1}{2}\frac{\$350}{10\%} + \$200 - \$1{,}600 = \$2{,}000 - \$1{,}400 = \$600$$

$$NPV_1 = \frac{1}{1.1}[0.5(\$2{,}250) + 0.5(\$0)] = \$1{,}022.73$$

We can proceed to test the sensitivities of the *NPV*s to mean-preserving spreads around alternative values of the initial price. At alternative initial prices (P_0) we keep equal chances of seeing a 50% increase or decrease in the price. The *NPV*s are plotted in Figure 3 on the following page.

The results of this analysis allow us to summarize an optimal investment strategy by saying if the initial price is less than $96.97, never invest in the factory. If the initial price is between $96.97 and $249.35, defer the decision to invest and do so only if the price increases. If the initial price exceeds $249.35, invest now rather than deferring the decision.

$$I = \$1{,}600 \quad P_0 = 200 \quad q = 50\% \quad u = q \quad d = u$$

FIGURE 2

***NPV* Profiles for Current and Deferred Decisions**

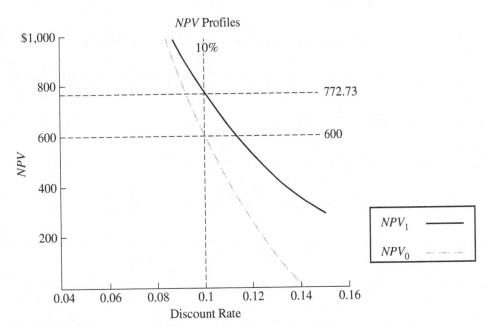

$$I = \$1,600 \quad q = 50\% \quad u = q \quad d = u \quad r = 10\%$$

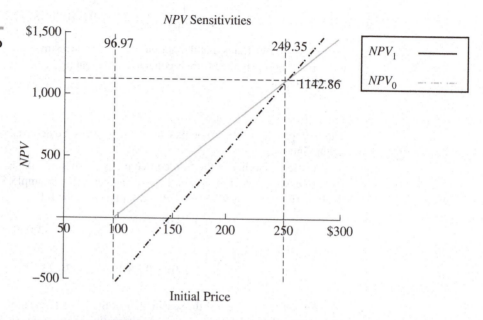

FIGURE 3

NPV Sensitivities to Initial Price Parameter (P_0)

NPV Sensitivities

Quick Check 1

Calculate NPV_0 and NPV_1 if the initial price is $150 rather than $200. Continue to assume the price uncertainty will be modeled by assuming a symmetric 50% increase or decrease in the price over the coming period.

Returning to the base case of an initial price P_0 of $200 with an equal chance of a 50% increase or decrease in the price, a set of *NPV* sensitivities can be performed with respect to alternative levels for the initial investment cost *I*. On the following page in Figure 4 is a plot of the *NPV* profiles.

If the cost of the investment falls below $1,288.33, it would be best to invest immediately rather than to defer the investment option and wait for the realization of the future price. At an investment cost between $1,288.33 and $3,300 it is best to exercise the deferral option and wait until the price uncertainty is resolved to decide whether to invest. Finally, if the investment cost were above $3,300, investing in the factory will never be profitable even with the option to defer the investment.

2.2 Valuing the Deferral Option Using the Binomial Option Pricing Model

If we assume there exists a futures market for the product produced by the factory, then we can imagine how to build a risk-free investment portfolio consisting of the investment project with the underlying price risk fully hedged. Consider the deferral option as a call option on a stream of factory output at the maturity of the option one period from now. The exercise price of the option is the investment cost of the factory, $E = I$. At maturity the value of the option is given by:

$$C_1(P_1) = \begin{pmatrix} P_1 + \dfrac{P_1}{r} - I & \text{if } P_1 + \dfrac{P_1}{r} > I \\ 0 & \text{otherwise} \end{pmatrix}$$

$$P_0 = \$200 \quad q = 50\% \quad u = q \quad d = u \quad r = 10\%$$

FIGURE 4

NPV Sensitivities to Initial Investment Cost (I)

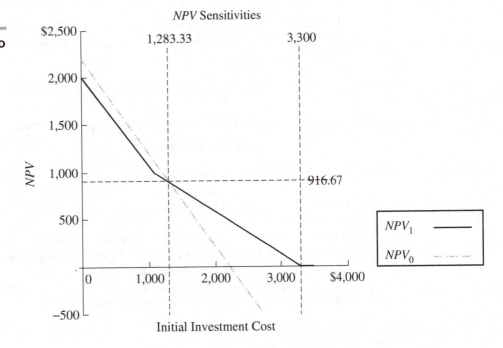

We have already calculated these contingent values under the original set of parameters and found the following: $C_1(\$100) = 0$ and $C_1(\$300) = \$1,700$. This simply says that at the lower realization for the price, investment will not be undertaken, and therefore the value of the payoff from the option is zero, whereas at the higher price the investment will be made and produce at that point in time a positive NPV of $1,700.

In order to build a hedged portfolio we can calculate the hedge ratio h as follows:

$$\frac{\Delta C_1(P_1)}{\Delta P_1} = h = \frac{C_1(\$300) - C_1(\$100)}{\$300 - \$100} = \frac{\$1,700 - 0}{\$200} = 8.5$$

The hedged portfolio would consist of selling the call option and using the futures market to take a long position in h units of the factory's output. The cash flows from the long position are that you pay out hP_0 now and receive one period ahead the amount $hP_1 + rhP_0$. The first term is the normal capital gain or loss on the long position whereas the second term is similar to taking a position in a dividend-paying stock. If the price of the underlying commodity next period has an expected value equal to the current price, as is the case here, no investor would hold a long position unless they were compensated with a fair rate of return on their investment. Thus the cash flows associated with the hedged portfolio now and one period ahead are:

$$CF_0 = C_0 - 8.5(\$200) \quad CF_1 = 8.5P_1 + (0.10)8.5(\$200) - C_1(P_1)$$

We can check that this is a hedged portfolio by seeing that the payoff next period is identical—regardless of how the commodity price evolves. If the price falls, the payoff is given by:

$$8.5(\$100) + \$170 - C_1(\$100) = \$850 + \$170 - 0 = \$1,020$$

491

and if the price rises the payoff is:

$$8.5(\$300) + \$170 - C_1(\$300) = \$2,550 + \$170 - \$1,700 = \$1,020$$

Thus the hedged portfolio requires an initial outlay of CF_0 to lock in a payoff of $1,020 one period later. Using the 10% discount rate we can discount the future cash flow and equate it to the initial outflow:

$$CF_0 = -C_0 + 8.5(\$200) = \frac{\$1,020}{1 + 10\%} = \$927.27$$

Solving for the current value of the deferral option we obtain:

$$C_0 = 8.5(\$200) - \$927.27 = \$1,700 - 927.27 = \$772.73$$

The value of deferring the option to invest until next period is currently worth $772.73 and we can see why it is not optimal to currently exercise the option to invest. The net cash payout from currently exercising the option is $NPV_0 = \$600 = \$2,200 - \$1,600$ but in addition to this we would have the opportunity cost of forgoing deferral of the option. When we consider the total cost of investing today, the required investment in the factory and the loss of the value of deferring the option, it amounts to $1,600 + $772.73 = $2,372.73, which is more than the present value of the expected future cash flows from the factory's output, $2,200. The option to invest should not be exercised today but kept alive for one period until the price uncertainty is resolved.

Quick Check 2

Recognizing the similarity between call options and managerial options is important for three reasons. What are they?

---

3 Applying the Black-Scholes Formula to Value Real Options

Now that we have recognized the importance of taking account of the option value in investment opportunities, how do we quantify that value? One way is to apply the Black-Scholes formula.

For example, suppose that a firm, Rader Inc., is considering acquiring another firm, Target Inc. Let us assume they are both 100% equity-financed firms, that is, neither firm has

---

Box 2 — Option Analysis at Merck

In an interview with the editors of the *Harvard Business Review* some years ago, Judy Lewent, the CFO of the pharmaceutical firm Merck, described her company's extensive use of option analysis in capital budgeting. As just one example, Merck frequently enters into business relationships with universities in order to gain access to early-stage research projects. The contractual agreements are often structured so that Merck will make an initial payment to the university followed by a series of progress payments that are contingent on the outcome of the research. Merck analyzes these contracts using the tools of option-pricing theory.

any debt outstanding. Each firm has 1 million shares of common stock outstanding that can be freely bought and sold in a competitive market. The current market value of Target's assets is $100 million and the standard deviation of the proportional change in its value is 0.20. Suppose that Target's management offers Rader an option to acquire 100% of Target's shares a year from now for $106 million. The riskless interest rate is 6% per year.

If the option costs $6 million, is the investment worthwhile?

From Rader's perspective this is a capital budgeting decision. The initial outlay is the $6 million cost of the option to acquire Target's assets a year from now. To determine the value of this option we can use the same valuation models developed to price a European call option on a stock. Applying the Black-Scholes formula:[2]

$$C = N(d_1)S - N(d_2)Ee^{-rT}$$
$$d_1 = \frac{\ln(S/E) + (r + \sigma^2/2)T}{\sigma\sqrt{T}}$$
$$d_2 = d_1 - \sigma\sqrt{T}$$

where

C = price of the option

S = price of the stock

E = exercise price

T = time to maturity of the option in years

σ = standard deviation of the annualized continuously compounded rate of return on the stock

Option Price Calculation Table

S	E	r	T	σ	Result
100	106	0.06	1	0.2	C = $8 million

The value of the option is approximately $8 million. The *NPV* of the investment opportunity is $2 million—the option's value to Rader less its $6 million cost—so it is worthwhile.

Now let us consider how option theory can help to evaluate an investment opportunity that does not involve the *explicit* purchase of an option but does contain a managerial option. Suppose Electro Utility has the opportunity to invest in a project to build a power-generating plant. In the first phase an initial outlay of $6 million is required to build the facility to house the equipment. In the second phase, one year from now, equipment costing $106 million must be purchased. Suppose that viewed from today's perspective the value of the completed plant a year from now is a random variable with a mean of $112 million and a proportional standard deviation of 0.2.

Suppose that we do a conventional DCF analysis of this investment opportunity. At a discount rate of k, the present value of the completed plant is $112 million/$(1 + k)$. Because

---

[2]Because in this case the exercise price of the option equals the future value of the underlying firm compounded at the riskless interest rate, we can use the linear approximation to the Black-Scholes formula:

$$\frac{C}{S} \approx 0.4\sigma\sqrt{T}.$$

the $106 million investment outlay for power-generating equipment is known for certain, its present value is computed by discounting at the riskless rate. If that rate is 6%, then the present value of the outlay is $100 million. In addition, the initial outlay to build the facility is $6 million. Thus, the project's NPV is given by

$$NPV = \$112 \text{ million}/(1 + k) - \$100 \text{ million} - \$6 \text{ million}$$
$$= \$112 \text{ million}/(1 + k) - \$106 \text{ million}$$

The NPV of the project so computed will be negative for any k greater than 5.66%, which is even less than the riskless rate of interest. For example, if the k is 12%, then the present value of the completed plant is $100 million, and the project's computed NPV is $-$6.0 million.

But to do this is to ignore the important fact that management has the right to abandon the project a year from now. In other words, management will invest an additional $106 million in the second stage of the project *only if* the value of the plant turns out to be more than $106 million.[3]

How can we evaluate this investment taking management's flexibility into account? The answer is that we can apply the same method we just applied in evaluating Rader Inc.'s option to buy Target Inc. Although the circumstances are somewhat different, the two situations have the same structure and even the same payoffs.

To see this, note that by undertaking the first phase of the project, Electro Utility would in effect be paying $6 million to "buy an option" that will mature in one year. The option is to undertake phase two of the project, and its "exercise price" is $106 million. The present value of the completed project is $100 million.

The Black-Scholes formula says that this option is worth approximately $8 million. The project, therefore, has a positive NPV of $2 million instead of the negative NPV computed when we ignored management's option to discontinue the project after the first year.

Our conclusion is that taking management's flexibility explicitly into account increases a project's NPV. Moreover, from the theory of option pricing, we know that the value of flexibility increases with the volatility of the project.

Again, consider the example of Electro Utility. Suppose that the value of the power-generating plant is actually more volatile than was at first thought. Instead of the standard deviation being 0.20, suppose it is 0.40. This makes the investment project *more* attractive. Applying the Black-Scholes formula, we find that the option value is now $16 million. The project's NPV is, therefore, $10 million, rather than the $2 million computed earlier.

Virtually *all* future investment opportunities can be viewed as call options because firms can almost always wait before making their initial outlay and can decide *not* to proceed with it. The amount of time the firm can wait is analogous to the option's time to expiration; the initial outlay is analogous to the exercise price; and the present value of the project's expected future cash flows is analogous to the price of the underlying stock. The project's conventionally computed NPV is, thus, analogous to the option's intrinsic value, that is, what it would be worth if it were expiring immediately. Conventional NPV understates the value of the project because it ignores the option's time value.

Quick Check 3

What is the option value of the Electro Utility investment project if the volatility of the power-generating plant is 0.3 instead of 0.2?

---

[3]We assume for simplicity that the $6 million initial outlay is lost completely if the plant is not completed. That is, the salvage value is zero.

Summary

- An extremely important feature of investment projects is the ability of managers to delay the start of a project, or once started, to expand it or to abandon it. Failure to take account of these management options will cause an analyst evaluating the project to underestimate its *NPV*.
- Recognizing the similarity between financial options and real managerial options is important for three reasons: (1) It helps in structuring the analysis of the investment project as a sequence of managerial decisions over time, (2) it clarifies the role of uncertainty in evaluating projects, and, (3) it gives us a method for estimating the option value of projects by applying the quantitative models developed for valuing call options on stocks.

Key Terms

- deferral option
- option to abandon
- option to rescale
- irreversibility

Answers to Quick Check Questions

Quick Check 1   Recognizing the similarity between call options and managerial options is important for three reasons. What are they?

Answer:
- It helps in structuring the analysis of the investment project as a sequence of managerial decisions over time.
- It clarifies the role of uncertainty in evaluating projects.
- It gives us a method for estimating the option value of projects by applying the quantitative models developed for valuing call options on stocks.

Quick Check 2   Calculate NPV_0 and NPV_1 if the initial price is $150 rather than $200. Continue to assume the price uncertainty will be modeled by assuming a symmetric 50% increase or decrease in the price over the coming period.

Answer: With an intial price of $150 we also have an expected future price of $150. So the expected *NPV* of investing today is: $NPV_0 = \$150 + \frac{\$150}{0.10} - \$1{,}600 = \$50$. The *NPV* of postponing the investment until the price uncertainty is resolved is given by:

$$NPV_1 = \frac{1}{2}[0] + \frac{\frac{1}{2}\left[\$225 + \frac{\$225}{0.1} - \$1{,}600\right]}{1 + 0.10} = \frac{\frac{1}{2}[\$2{,}475 - \$1{,}600]}{1.1} = \frac{\frac{1}{2}\$875}{1.1} = \$397.73$$

Quick Check 3   What would happen to the net present value of the investment project if the standard deviation of the value of the power-generating plant is 0.3 instead of 0.2?

Answer:

$$\frac{C}{S} \approx 0.4\sigma\sqrt{T}$$

The inputs to the model are:

$$S = \$100 \text{ million}, T = 1 \text{ year}, \sigma = 0.3$$

The value of the option is, therefore, approximately $12 million. The *NPV* of the investment is $6 million (the option's value to Rader less its $6 million cost), and it is worthwhile.

Questions and Problems

1. Tony knows that, at any point in time over the next five years, he can close down half of his production facilities and liquidate the property, building, and equipment for a sum of $10 million. However, the value of the remaining operations would be adversely impacted and the decline in value would be 40%. Describe the option involved in terms of the underlying risky asset, the exercise price, the time to maturity, and the volatility.

2. During many periods of past history and in many jurisdictions there have been statutes outlawing usury, the charging of excessive interest. Consider the following scheme to bypass such prohibitions. Suppose you were a merchant and found it necessary to finance your warehouse but loans at a positive rate of interest are illegal. From the investor you accept cash, and in exchange present the deed to the warehouse. You promise to repurchase the property at a specified price ($P) in two years and the investor also promises to sell the warehouse to you for $P on the same date. If you initially needed $500,000 to acquire the warehouse, and the investor requires a 20% per year return on investment, at what value should $P have been set? What options are involved in this plan and what risk would the investor bear?

3. Commercial banks make a significant share of their fee-based income from establishing precommitted lines of credit. In exchange for a fee assessed against the limit on the borrowing line, they guarantee to lend at a predetermined fixed or floating rate. From the borrower's point of view, what option position do they have, what is the underlying uncertainty, and what is the exercise price?

4. With one out in the top of the ninth and a runner on third, a baseball team trailing by one run considers the strategy of executing a squeeze play. From the manager's perspective, is the squeeze play a risky bet or an option? Does it matter if we are talking about a safety squeeze or a suicide squeeze? (*Wikipedia* may help you answer the question if you are less than a truly dedicated baseball fan.)

5. Refer to the Electro Utility example in Section 3 of the text. What is the break-even riskless interest rate for the project? What is the break-even risk level for the plant?

6. A film studio, Nadir Productions, has to decide whether to make a movie out of the book "Planetary Wars," which it has acquired the rights to. The studio's experts estimate that the production costs for the film will be $30 million and the subsequent cash flows net of distribution costs and taxes to be received a year later are expected to be $60 million with a probability of 0.5 and $10 million with a probability of 0.5. The studio uses a discount rate of 20% in deciding whether to accept such projects.

    a. What is the *NPV* of the project? Should the project be accepted? At this point a new MBA on the CFO's staff suggests that they have not taken account of the option to produce a sequel to the movie. If the movie succeeds at the box office, then surely they will want to make "Planetary Wars II" the following year.

    b. Draw a decision tree for the project.

    c. Assuming that the cost estimates and the distribution of future cash flows for the sequel are the same as for the original movie, how does taking account of the option to make a sequel affect the desirability of the project?

    d. Suppose that Nadir's executives believe that a successful film of this genre can have as many as three sequels. What is the *NPV* of the project taking account of this?

7. Caribou Construction Company owns land in the great white north of Canada, but is not certain whether there is oil to be found on the property. The land has absolutely no other commercial value. An exploratory well can be drilled today at a cost of C$10 million. Company geologists estimate an 80% chance an exploratory well will come empty of oil. If the exploratory well is a dry hole, there remains some chance that there is oil to be found on the property. Whether the exploratory well is successful or not, productive capacity can be installed over the next year for C$100 million. The discount rate for both phases of the project is estimated to be 10%. Once productive capacity is installed, the same amount of after-tax cash flow is expected to be generated in perpetuity. This amount will not be known until after the productive capacity is installed. The probability distributions of annual cash flows are conditional on the outcome of the exploratory well and are given in the table below. Note that these cash flows start two years from now.

Exploratory	Well Successful	Exploratory	Well Unsuccessful
Cash Flow	Probability	Cash Flow	Probability
C$10 million	25%	C$0 million	60%
C$30 million	50%	C$15 million	30%
C$50 million	25%	C$30 million	10%

   Diagram the decision tree for the investment project. Should the firm invest in the exploratory well? What should it do based on the outcome of the exploratory well?

8. Continuing the previous problem (problem 7), suppose the land in question could be sold as a hunting preserve for C$5 million at the end of year 1 after the exploratory well is completed. How would your analysis change? What is the current value of the option to sell rather than develop the land?

9. Suppose Microstuff Corporation has the opportunity to invest in a new computer technology that would use television sets to connect to the Internet. In the first phase an initial outlay of $100 million is required for a pilot project to determine the feasibility of the technology. In the second phase, one year from now, an additional investment of $1 billion would be required. Suppose that viewed from today's perspective the value of the project a year from now is a random variable with a mean of $1.1 billion. The required rate of return on the project is 10% per year. The standard deviation of the continuously compounded rate of return on this project is 0.2. The continuously compounded riskless interest rate is 5%. Use the Black-Scholes options pricing model to help determine whether this is a worthwhile investment.

10. Referring to the previous problem (problem 9), what is the break-even value for the riskless interest rate? What is the break-even value for the risk of the project?

11. Referring back to the example in the chapter on valuing deferral options, use a one-period binomial option pricing model to evaluate the current value of the option to defer investment in the factory. Assume the investment cost I is $2,000, the initial price of the factory output (P_0) is $250, and this price will increase or decrease by 50% next period and then remain constant into the indefinite future. Assume the relevant discount rate is 10%. Given the value of the option to defer investment for a period, does it make sense to invest today?

12. Referring to the previous problem (problem 11), how would your answers change if the discount rate decreased to 5%?

Suggested Readings

Amram, M., F. Li, and C. Perkins. "How Kimberly-Clark Uses Real Options." *Journal of Applied Corporate Finance* 18, Spring 2006.

Borison, A. "Real Options Analysis: Where Are the Emperor's Clothes?" *Journal of Applied Corporate Finance* 17, Spring 2005.

Coase, R. H. "The Nature of the Firm." *Economica* 4, 1937.

———— *The Firm, the Market, and the Law.* Chicago: University of Chicago Press, 1988.

Copeland, T., and V. Antikarov. *Real Options: A Practitioner's Guide.* Thomson/TEXERE, 2003.

————. "Real Options: Meeting the Georgetown Challenge." *Journal of Applied Corporate Finance* 17, Spring 2005.

Copeland, T., and P. Tufano. " A Real-World Way to Manage Real Options." *Harvard Business Review,* March 2004.

Dixit, A., and R. Pindyck. *Investment under Uncertainty.* Princeton: Princeton University Press, 1994.

Jensen, M. "Agency Costs of Free Cash Flow, Corporate Finance and Takeovers." *American Economic Review* 76, May 1986.

———— and W. H. Meckling. "Theory of the Firm: Managerial Behavior, Agency Costs, and Ownership Structure." *Journal of Financial Economics* 3, October 1976.

McDonald, R. "The Role of Real Options in Capital Budgeting: Theory and Practice." *Journal of Applied Corporate Finance* 18, Spring 2006.

Merton, R. C., and S. C. Mason. "The Role of Contingent Claims Analysis in Corporate Finance." *Recent Advances in Corporate Finance.* Ed. E. I. Altman and M. G. Subrahmanyam. Homewood, Ill.: Richard D. Irwin, 1985.

Glossary

acquisition The acquiring by one firm of a controlling interest in another.

actuaries Professionals trained in mathematics and statistics who gather and analyze data and estimate the probabilities of illness, accidents, and other such risks.

adjusted present value A method of calculating a project's net present value that takes into account the value that is created by the project's debt financing.

adverse selection A type of incentive problem in which those who purchase insurance against risk are more likely to be at risk than the general population.

after-tax interest rate The interest rate earned after paying income taxes.

alpha The difference between the average rate of return on a security or portfolio of securities and the rate predicted by the Capital Asset Pricing Model.

amortization The process of paying off a loan's principal gradually over time.

amortization schedule A table that shows the portions of loan payments that go toward principal and interest over the period of the loan.

annual percentage rate The annualized rate of interest on loans and savings accounts, with a certain frequency of compounding (contrast with effective annual rate).

annualized capital cost The annual cash payment that has a present value equal to the initial outlay.

arbitrage The purchase and immediate sale of equivalent assets in order to earn a sure profit from a difference in their prices.

asset Anything that has economic value.

asset allocation Choosing how much to invest in major asset classes such as stocks, bonds, and cash.

at-the-money The state of an option whose exercise price is equal to the current price of the underlying security.

before-tax interest rate The interest rate earned without taking into account income taxes.

beta A measure of a security's market-related risk, showing how much a security's rate of return tends to change when the return on the market portfolio changes; risk as measured in the CAPM.

binomial option pricing model A widely used model for pricing options that assumes that in each period the underlying security can take only one of two possible values.

Black-Scholes formula The most widely used option pricing model, named for its developers, Fischer Black and Myron Scholes. It assumes a lognormal distribution and continuous adjustment of the replicating portfolio.

book value The value of an asset as listed on its company's officially recognized balance sheet.

break-even point The sales volume at which either net profit or the net present value of a project is zero.

call option An instrument that gives its holder the right to buy some asset at a specified price on or before some specified expiration date. Sometimes shortened to *call*.

capital asset pricing model An equilibrium theory based on the mean-variance theory of portfolio selection.

capital gain The gain in the market price of an asset over the period it is held.

capital loss The loss in the market price of an asset over the period it is held.

CAPM The capital asset pricing model.

capital market The market for long-term debt and equity securities.

capital market line In the capital asset pricing model, the risk–return trade-off line between standard deviation and expected return which represents the best risk–reward combinations available to all investors.

caps Upper limits placed on compensation under an insurance contract.

cash budget A short-term plan to forecast cash outflows and inflows.

cash cycle time The number of days between the date a firm must start to pay cash to its suppliers and the date it begins to receive cash from its customers.

cash dividend A distribution of cash to the shareholders of a corporation.

cash settlement The settlement of a forward or option contract in cash rather than by delivery of the underlying commodity or security.

collateral The asset pledged as security for a debt.

collateralization Giving the lender the right to seize specific business assets in the event of default. It is widely used to reduce the incentive problems associated with lending.

commercial banks Financial intermediaries that perform two functions: taking deposits and making loans.

commercial loan rate The rate charged by banks on loans made to businesses.

compound interest Interest paid on interest earned in previous periods.

compounding The process of going from present value to future value.

confidence interval A certain range of values for a random variable with a specified probability of occurrence.

continuous probability distribution A random variable has such a distribution when it can take any numerical value within its range.

copayments A fraction of a loss that an insured party must cover from his or her own resources.

corporation A firm that is a legal entity distinct from its owners.

correlation A statistical measure of the degree to which two random variables tend to move together.

cost of capital The capitalization rate used to discount a project's cash flows in computing its net present value.

counterparty Also called *counterpart*. The party on the other side of a contract.

coupon bond A bond that obligates the issuer to make periodic payments of interest (called *coupon payments*) to the bondholder for the life of the bond.

credit risk The risk that the counterparty to a contract will default.

current yield A bond's annual coupon divided by its price.

decision tree A graphic representation of the sequence of decisions and possible consequences involved in making a strategic decision.

deductible An amount of money that the insured party must pay out of his or her own resources before receiving any compensation from the insurer.

default risk The possibility that some portion of the interest or the principal on a fixed-income instrument will not be paid in full.

defined-benefit pension plan A type of pension plan in which the employee's pension benefit is determined by a formula that takes into account years of service and, in most cases, wages or salary.

defined-contribution pension plan A type of pension plan in which the employer and usually the employee too make regular contributions and the beneficiary receives the value of the assets plus the accumulated earnings.

derivatives Financial instruments whose payoffs are defined in terms of the prices of other assets.

discounted cash flow analysis Making decisions based on the calculation of net present value of future cash flows.

discounted dividend model Any model that computes the value of a share of stock as the present value of its expected future cash dividends.

diversifiable risk The part of a security's risk that can be eliminated by combining it with other risky assets.

diversification principle The theory that by diversifying across risky assets investors can sometimes achieve a reduction in their overall risk exposure with no reduction in their expected return.

diversifying A method of reducing risk by holding small amounts of many risky assets instead of concentrating in only one or a few risky assets.

dividend policy A corporation's policy regarding paying out cash to its shareholders.

dividend yield A stock's annualized dollar dividend divided by its price, expressed as a percentage.

effective annual rate An equivalent interest rate on a loan or savings account if interest were compounded only once per year (contrast with APR).

efficient markets hypothesis The proposition that an asset's current price fully reflects all publicly available information about future economic fundamentals affecting the asset's value.

efficient portfolio   A portfolio that offers the investor the highest possible expected rate of return at a specified level of risk.

efficient portfolio frontier   A graph showing the best combinations of portfolio risk and return than an investor can attain by diversifying. See also *capital market line.*

exchange rate   The price of one currency in terms of another.

exclusions   Losses that might seem to meet the conditions for coverage under the insurance contract but are specifically excluded.

exercise price   The price that must be paid for the underlying asset in an option contract. Also called *strike price.*

expectations hypothesis   The theory that the forward price of an asset equals its expected future spot price.

expected rate of return   The sum over all possible outcomes of each possible rate of return multiplied by its probability.

expiration date   The last date by which an option can be exercised.

external financing   Funding that originates from outside a firm, usually from lenders or investors.

face value   The promised cash payment on a bond's maturity date.

feasible consumption plan   A life-cycle spending plan that has a present value less than or equal to the present value of the household's lifetime resources.

finance   The study of how people allocate resources over time in an uncertain environment.

financial futures   Futures contracts in which the underlying asset is a stock, bond, or other financial asset.

financial guarantees   Insurance against credit risk.

financial system   The set of markets and other institutions used for financial contracting and the exchange of assets and risks.

fixed-income instruments   Also called *debt instruments.* They promise to pay fixed sums of cash in the future.

flow of funds   The flows of saving, investment, and external financing among different economic sectors over a period of time.

forward contract   An agreement between two parties to exchange some item in the future at a prearranged price.

forward price   The delivery price of an item specified at the time a forward contract is entered into that makes the value of the contract equal to zero.

fundamental value   The price well-informed investors would pay for an asset in a free and competitive market.

future value   The amount of money an investment will grow to at some date in the future by earning interest at a compound rate.

futures contract   A standardized forward contract that is traded on some organized exchange.

growth annuity   An annuity in which the cash flows from an investment grow at a constant rate.

growth stocks   Stocks that have relatively high price/earnings ratios because their future investments are expected to earn rates of return in excess of the market capitalization rate.

hedge ratio   The fraction of one unit of an asset needed in a portfolio designed to replicate the payoffs from a derivative security (such as a call option) on that asset.

hedgers   Parties who reduce their exposure to risk by giving up part of the potential for gain.

hedging   A method of transferring risk in which an action taken to reduce one's exposure to loss also causes one to give up possible gains.

human capital   The present value of one's future labor income.

immediate annuity   A periodic cash flow that starts immediately, as in a savings plan or a lease.

implied dividend   A dividend that can be inferred from the futures price of a stock index.

implied volatility   The value of volatility that makes the observed market price of the option equal to the value computed using the option pricing formula.

index options   Calls and puts on a stock index or any other economic index.

indexing   An investment strategy of matching the performance of some index.

index-linked bonds   Bonds whose interest and principal are denominated in terms of the basket of goods and services used to compute the cost of living in a particular country.

insuring   Paying some amount for sure to avoid the possibility of incurring larger losses.

intangible assets   Assets whose physical embodiment is irrelevant to their value.

interest-rate arbitrage Borrowing at a lower rate and lending at a higher rate when default risk is held constant.

interest-rate cap An interest-rate insurance policy in which the maximum interest rate is guaranteed.

interest-rate floor A guarantee of a minimum interest rate on a loan.

internal financing Funding that originates within a firm, including retained earnings, accrued wages, and accounts payable.

intertemporal budget constraint The restriction that the present value of one's lifetime consumption spending cannot exceed present value of one's lifetime resources.

in-the-money The state of an option that would have positive value if the current time were its expiration date.

intrinsic value Also called *tangible value*. The hypothetical value of an option if it were exercised immediately.

investment banks Firms whose primary function is to help businesses, governments, and other entities raise funds to finance their activities.

Law of One Price The idea that, in a competitive market, if two assets are equivalent, they will have the same market price.

liability Any claim on the assets of an entity other than owner's equity.

life annuities Contracts that promise periodic payments for as long as the purchaser lives.

limited liability A feature of common stock whereby if a firm is liquidated and the proceeds from the sale are insufficient to pay off all the firm's debts, the creditors cannot assess the common stockholders for more money to meet this shortfall.

liquidity The relative ease and speed with which an asset can be converted into cash.

long position In a financial contract, the term used to describe the position of the buyer.

margin call A demand from a broker or a counterparty for an investor to add more collateral.

market capitalization rate Also called *risk-adjusted discount rate*. The expected rate of return that anonymous investors require in order to be willing to invest in the specified risky asset.

market portfolio A portfolio that holds all assets in proportion to their outstanding total market values.

market-weighted stock indexes A type of index that represents the price performance of a portfolio that holds each stock in proportion to its total market value.

maturity For fixed-income instruments, the length of time until the repayment of the entire amount borrowed.

mean In probability distribution, the sum over all possible outcomes of each possible rate of return multiplied by its probability.

merger The joining of two firms into a single firm.

minimum-variance portfolio The portfolio of risky assets with the lowest possible variance.

money market The market for short-term debt (less than one year).

moral hazard A situation in which having insurance against some risk causes the insured party to take greater risk or to take less care in preventing the event that gives rise to the loss.

mortgage rate The interest rate that home buyers pay on the loans they take to finance their homes.

mutual fund A portfolio of stocks, bonds, or other assets purchased in the name of a group of investors and managed by a professional investment company or other financial institution.

net present value The amount by which a project is expected to increase the wealth of a firm's current shareholders.

net worth The value of an entity's assets minus liabilities.

nominal future value The future value of a sum not adjusted for inflation.

nominal interest rate An interest rate not adjusted for inflation (contrast with real interest rate).

nominal prices Prices in terms of some currency not adjusted for inflation.

nondiversifiable risk The portion of a portfolio's risk that cannot be eliminated by diversification.

normal distribution The most widely used continuous probability distribution, typified by its bell-shaped curve.

opportunity cost of capital The rate that could be earned on capital if it were invested elsewhere in assets of the same risk.

optimal combination of risky assets The portfolio of risky assets that is mixed with a riskless asset to achieve the most efficient portfolio.

option The right to purchase or sell something at a fixed price in the future.

ordinary annuity An annuity in which the cash flows start at the end of the current period rather than immediately.

out-of-the-money The state of an option that would be worthless if the current time were its expiration date.

over-the-counter markets Also called *off-exchange markets*. Networks for trading assets that have no central location.

par bonds Coupon bonds with a market price equal to their face value.

partnership An unincorporated firm with two or more owners who share the equity in the business.

payoff diagram A chart that shows the relation between the value of a derivative at expiration and the price of its underlying asset.

percent-of-sales method A planning forecast that assumes that most of the items on a company's income statement and balance sheet will maintain the same ratio to sales in the next year as in the previous year.

permanent income The constant level of consumption spending that has a present value equal to one's human capital.

perpetuity A stream of cash flows that lasts forever.

portfolio selection The process of making choices about how to invest one's wealth.

portfolio theory Quantitative analysis for risk management.

precautionary saving Saving that is motivated by the desire to have enough wealth to cover unanticipated expenses in the future.

premium bond A bond whose market price is higher than its face value.

present value The sum in hand today that would be equivalent in value to some specified future payments.

price/earnings multiple The ratio of a firm's stock price to its earnings per share.

principal-agent problem A situation arising when agents do not make the same decisions that the principals would have made if the principals knew what the agents knew and were making the decisions themselves.

probability distributions The statistical term for a random variable's set of possible values and associated probabilities.

purchasing-power parity The theory that exchange rates adjust so as to maintain the same inflation-adjusted price of a representative basket of goods and services in different currency areas.

pure discount bonds Also called *zero-coupon bonds*. Bonds that promise a single payment of cash at some date in the future, called the maturity date.

put The option to sell a specified item at a fixed price.

put option An instrument that gives its holder the right to sell some asset at a specified price on or before some specified expiration date.

put-call parity relation The price relation among the price of the put, the price of the call, the price of the underlying security, and the present value of the exercise price.

rate of return on capital Capital's productivity expressed as a percentage per year.

real future value The future value adjusted for inflation.

real interest rate The interest rate corrected for inflation.

real interest-rate parity The theory that the expected real interest rate on riskless loans is the same all over the world.

real prices Prices corrected for inflation.

reinvestment rate The interest rate at which funds invested for more than a single period can be reinvested.

residual claim The type of claim represented by common stock, in which the owners of common stock are entitled to any assets of the firm left over after meeting all the firm's other financial obligations.

risk aversion A measure of one's willingness to pay to reduce one's exposure to risks.

risk exposure The degree to which an entity's welfare is affected by a source of risk.

risk management The process of formulating the benefit-cost trade-offs of risk reduction and deciding on the course of action to take.

risk-adjusted discount rate Also called *market capitalization rate*. The expected rate of return that investors require in order to be willing to invest in a project.

risk-management process A systematic attempt to analyze and deal with risk.

security market line In the capital asset pricing model, the relation showing that the risk premium on any asset is equal to its beta multiplied by the risk premium on the market portfolio.

self-financing investment strategy An investment strategy that requires only an initial cash outlay with no subsequent cash infusions.

sensitivity analysis A method of testing a project's worthiness even if some of the underlying variables turn out to be different from what was originally assumed.

share repurchase A method of cash distribution by a corporation to its shareholders in which the corporation pays cash to buy shares of its stock in the stock market, thereby reducing the number of shares outstanding.

short position In a financial contract, the term used to describe the position of the seller.

simple interest The interest rate times the original principal, not including interest on interest.

sole proprietorship A firm in which the assets and liabilities of the firm are the personal assets and liabilities of the proprietor.

speculators Investors who take positions that increase their exposure to risks in the hope of increasing their wealth.

spot price The price specified for immediate delivery of an item in a forward contract.

spot-futures price-parity relation The relation among the futures price, the spot price, and the riskless interest rate.

spread The difference between two asset prices or rates of return.

standard deviation The statistic that is most widely used to measure the volatility of a stock's probability distribution of returns. The larger the standard deviation, the greater the volatility of the stock.

strategy A plan that takes into account future decisions in making current decisions.

strike price The fixed price specified in an option contract. See also *exercise price*.

sustainable growth rate The rate of growth in a firm's owners' equity. A firm cannot grow any faster than its sustainable growth rate.

swap contract An agreement between two parties to exchange a series of cash flows at specified intervals over a specified period of time.

synergy The combination of two companies that results in the value of the operating assets of the combined firm exceeding those of the two companies taken separately.

time line A diagram used for analyzing the timing of cash flows.

time value (of an option) The difference between an option's price and its value if the current time were its expiration date.

time value of money The concept that a given amount of money in hand today is worth more than the claim to the same amount to be received in the future.

transaction costs Costs that accompany a sale, including the costs of shipping, handling, insuring, and broker fees.

triangular arbitrage An arbitrage transaction that involves three currencies.

unit of account The medium in which payments are denominated, usually a currency (e.g., dollars, francs, and yen), sometimes a commodity such as gold or silver or some standard basket of goods and services.

volatility A commonly used measure of an asset's riskiness, related to the range of possible rates of return and to their likelihood of occurring. In options trading, used synonymously with standard deviation, as in *implied volatility*.

weighted average cost of capital A method of calculating a project's net present value using a weighted average of the cost of equity capital and the after-tax cost of debt. The weights are the market values of equity and debt as a fraction of the present value of the investment.

working capital The difference between a firm's current assets and current liabilities.

yield curve A curve depicting the relation between the promised interest rates (yields) on fixed-income instruments of a given risk and the maturity of the instrument.

yield spread The difference in yields between two instruments.

yield-to-maturity The discount rate that makes the present value of a bond's stream of promised cash payments equal to its price; the internal rate of return of a bond.

Index

Page references followed by "f" indicate illustrated figures or photographs; followed by "t" indicates a table.